Lecture Notes of the Institute for Computer Sciences, Social Informatics and Telecommunications Engineering 684

The LNICST series publishes ICST's conferences, symposia and workshops.

LNICST reports state-of-the-art results in areas related to the scope of the Institute.

The type of material published includes

- Proceedings (published in time for the respective event)
- Other edited monographs (such as project reports or invited volumes)

LNICST topics span the following areas:

- General Computer Science
- E-Economy
- E-Medicine
- Knowledge Management
- Multimedia
- Operations, Management and Policy
- Social Informatics
- Systems

Lei Zhang · Kim-Kwang Raymond Choo
Editors

Mobile and Ubiquitous Systems

Computing, Networking and Services

22nd EAI International Conference, MobiQuitous 2025
Shanghai, China, November 7–9, 2025
Proceedings, Part II

Editors
Lei Zhang
East China Normal University
Shanghai, China

Kim-Kwang Raymond Choo
University of Texas at San Antonio
San Antonio, TX, USA

ISSN 1867-8211 ISSN 1867-822X (electronic)
Lecture Notes of the Institute for Computer Sciences, Social Informatics and Telecommunications Engineering
ISBN 978-3-032-22502-3 ISBN 978-3-032-22503-0 (eBook)
https://doi.org/10.1007/978-3-032-22503-0

This Springer imprint is published by the registered company Springer Nature Switzerland AG
The registered company address is: Gewerbestrasse 11, 6330 Cham, Switzerland

Preface

We are delighted to present the proceedings of the 22nd European Alliance for Innovation (EAI) International Conference on Mobile and Ubiquitous Systems (MobiQuitous 2025). Hosted by East China Normal University, China, the conference was held from November 7–9, 2025. The conference brought together researchers, developers, and practitioners from around the world who advance research and development in security, efficiency, architectures, and algorithms within intelligent systems and information technologies. The theme of MobiQuitous 2025 was "Mobile and Ubiquitous Systems: Computing, Networking and Services."

The technical program of MobiQuitous 2025 featured 50 full papers and 1 poster paper. The conference tracks were organized into four sessions: Session 1 – Federated Learning and Large Language Models; Session 2 – Secure, Reliable, and Efficient Intelligent Systems; Session 3 – Architectures and Algorithms for IoT; and Session 4 – Cryptographic Schemes. These papers were selected from 144 submissions through a rigorous double-blind review process, with each paper receiving at least three reviews. In addition to high-quality technical paper presentations, the program included two keynote speeches, which were delivered by Dusit Niyato from Nanyang Technological University and Jungong Han from Tsinghua University.

The success of this conference would not have been possible without the coordination and support of the steering committee chairs—Tao Gu, Takahiro Hara, and Max Mühlhäuser. We sincerely appreciate their continuous guidance and encouragement. It has also been a great pleasure to work with an outstanding organizing committee whose dedicated efforts were instrumental in planning and supporting the conference. Special thanks go to the General Chairs, Weizhi Meng and Josep Domingo-Ferrer, who successfully guided the conference organization. Our appreciation also goes to Workshop Chairs: Wenjuan Li and Wei-Yang Chiu; Publicity Chairs: Ningjing Wan, Rishikesh Sahay, and Meikang Qiu; Publication Chair: Liantao Wu; and Web Chair: Xinyu Meng. Also thanks to all Program Committee Members, who helped the peer-review process and contributed to a high-quality technical program. We are also grateful to conference manager Natasha Onofrei for her valuable support, as well as to all authors who submitted their work to MobiQuitous 2025.

We firmly believe that the MobiQuitous conference provides an excellent forum for researchers, developers, and practitioners to discuss all aspects of science and technology related to security, efficiency, architectures, and algorithms in intelligent systems and information technologies. We also look forward to future editions of MobiQuitous being as successful and inspiring as the contributions collected in this volume.

Lei Zhang
Kim-Kwang Raymond Choo

Organization

Steering Committee

Tao Gu	Macquarie University, Australia
Takahiro Hara	Osaka University, Japan
Max Mühlhäuser	Technical University of Darmstadt, Germany

Organizing Committee

General Chair

Weizhi Meng	Lancaster University, UK

General Co-chair

Josep Domingo-Ferrer	University of Rovira i Virgili, Spain

TPC Chairs and Co-chairs

Lei Zhang	East China Normal University, China
Kim-Kwang Raymond Choo	University of Texas at San Antonio, USA

Sponsorship and Exhibit Chair

Xiang Zhou	East China Normal University, China

Local Chair

Dehui Du	East China Normal University, China

Workshops Chairs

Wei-Yang Chiu	Technical University of Denmark, Denmark
Wenjuan Li	Education University of Hong Kong, China

Publicity and Social Media Chairs

Ningjing Wan	East China Normal University, China
Rishikesh Sahay	University of Illinois Springfield, USA
Meikang Qiu	Augusta University, USA

Publications Chair

Liantao Wu	East China Normal University, China

Web Chair

Xinyu Meng	Shanghai Maritime University, China

Technical Program Committee

Abhishek Kumar	University of Oulu, Finland
Akif Quddus Khan	OsloMet, Norway
Arda Goknil	SINTEF, Norway
Bo Qin	Renmin University of China, China
Branislav Kusy	CSIRO Data61, Australia
Brent Lagesse	University of Washington at Bothell, USA
Chao Qian	University of Duisburg-Essen, Germany
Chunhua Su	University of Aizu, Japan
Cornelia Győrödi	University of Oradea, Romania
Cristian Borcea	New Jersey Institute of Technology, USA
Dimitris Kavallieros	Informatics and Telematics Institute, Greece
Fusang Zhang	Institute of Software, Chinese Academy of Sciences, China
Gyu Myoung Lee	Liverpool John Moores University, UK
Hao Wang	Shandong Normal University, China
Hu Xiong	University of Electronic Science and Technology of China, China
Hua Deng	Changsha University of Science & Technology, China
Huaqun Wang	Nanjing University of Posts and Telecommunications, China
Huber Flores	University of Tartu, Estonia
Ivan Miguel Pires	Instituto de Telecomunicações/University of Aveiro, Portugal
Jianchang Lai	Southeast University, China

Jingao Xu	University of Hong Kong, China
Jinguang Han	Southeast University, China
Josep Domingo-Ferrer	Universitat Rovira i Virgili, Spain
Jun Shao	East China University of Science and Technology, China
Kai Zhang	Shanghai University of Electric Power, China
Kim-Kwang Raymond Choo	University of Texas at San Antonio, USA
Kun He	Wuhan University, China
Lei Yang	Hong Kong Polytechnic University, China
Lei Zhang	East China Normal University, China
Liantao Wu	East China Normal University, China
Lifei Wei	Shanghai Maritime University, China
Nan Jiang	Harbin Institute of Technology (Shenzhen), China
Nuno Garcia	Universidade da Beira Interior, Portugal
Oladayo Bello	New Mexico State University, USA
Peter Zdankin	University of Duisburg-Essen, Germany
Qiong Huang	South China Agricultural University, China
Rongmao Chen	National University of Defense Technology, China
Rui Zhang	Southwestern University of Finance and Economics, China
Sanjay Madria	Missouri University of Science and Technology, USA
Shihang Lu	Southern University of Science and Technology, China
Shuangyang Li	Technische Universität Berlin, Germany
Tao Chen	University of Pittsburgh, USA
Weizhi Meng	Lancaster University, UK
Xinyu Li	Southeast University, China
Xiujin Shi	Donghua University, China
Ye Dong	National University of Singapore, Singapore

Contents

Architectures and Algorithms for IoT

Architectures and Algorithms for IoT

Unmanned Aerial Vehicle Identity Authentication Method for Open-Set of RF Signal and Cross-Domain Scenario

Xin Cao[1], Weijie Tan[2,3](✉), Qiangqiang Gao[1], and Chunguo Li[4]

[1] The College of Computer Science and Technology, Guizhou University, Guiyang 550025, China
{gs.xcao23,gs.qqgao23}@gzu.edu.cn

[2] State Key Laboratory of Public Big Data, College of Computer Science and Technology, Guizhou University, Guiyang 550025, China

[3] The Advanced Cryptography and System Security Key Laboratory of Sichuan Province, Chengdu 610025, China
wjtan@gzu.edu.cn

[4] School of Information Science and Engineering, Southeast University, Nanjing 210096, China
chunguoli@seu.edu.cn

Abstract. Reliable identity verification of unmanned aerial vehicle (UAV) is crucial for airspace security. Radio frequency fingerprint identification (RFFI) is an effective approach, and deep learning (DL) is widely applied in this field due to its advantages in feature extraction and classification. However, in practice, the UAV radio frequency fingerprint identification (UAV-RFFI) based on DL faces the problems of low model recognition accuracy in cross-domain environments and insufficient generalization ability of open-set scenes, making it difficult to accurately identify UAV devices and detect rogue devices. Therefore, we propose a robust UAV-RFFI method based on cross-domain attention mechanism and metric adversarial learning (CDAM-MAL). Specifically, the signal quality is optimized through Hamming window preprocessing, and the time-frequency features are extracted by short-time Fourier transform. By leveraging triple metric adversarial learning to enhance feature discriminability and focusing on key features through cross-domain attention mechanisms, the reliability of open-set scene identification and cross-domain generalization ability are improved, thus forming a robust identity verification scheme for UAV-RFFI. Experiments on open-source real-world UAV datasets show that this method significantly improves the recognition performance of UAVs in open-set and cross-domain scenarios. The recognition rate of unknown UAV devices in the open-set scenario reached 98.77%, and the recognition accuracies on two different cross-domain datasets are 99.25% and 96.41% respectively.

Supported by the National Natural Science Foundation of China (No. 62361010, 62462012), the Open Fund of Advanced Cryptography and System Security Key Laboratory of Sichuan Province (No. SKLACSS-202414), and the Major Scientific and Technological Special Project of Guizhou Province (No. [2024]014).

L. Zhang and K.-K. R. Choo (Eds.): MobiQuitous 2025, LNICST 684, pp. 3–18, 2026.
https://doi.org/10.1007/978-3-032-22503-0_1

Keywords: Cross-domain authentication · Cross-domain attention mechanism · Metric adversarial learning · Open-set authentication · Radio frequency fingerprint identification · Unmanned aerial vehicles

1 Introduction

With the rapid advancement of unmanned aerial vehicle (UAV) technology, UAVs have been widely deployed across civilian, industrial, and military sectors, including aerial mapping, logistics transportation, and environmental monitoring, thereby bringing significant convenience to social production and daily life [1–3]. However, the popularity of UAV has also raised serious airspace security issues, including unauthorized entry into no-fly zones, privacy leaks, and even potential threats to public and national security [4–6]. Therefore, reliable UAV identity verification has become a key link in airspace management and security defense, and there is an urgent need to develop efficient and robust drone identification technology.

Radio frequency fingerprint identification (RFFI) provides a highly potential solution for the identity verification of UAV. It takes advantage of the unique hardware characteristics of radio frequency (RF) circuits that are unintentionally embedded into the transmitted signals during the manufacturing and operation of the equipment [7,8]. These inherent radio frequency fingerprints are difficult to forge or imitate, and non-intrusive and highly secure device identification can be achieved without relying on encryption or protocol layer information [9,10].

In recent years, deep learning (DL) has achieved remarkable results in the field of RFFI with its powerful ability to automatically extract complex features from high-dimensional data [11–13]. Cai et al. [14] proposed an efficient and low-complexity radio frequency fingerprint identification method for UAV (UAV-RFFI) in view of the high requirements for computing and storage in DL-based methods. Zhou et al. [15] combined convolutional neural networks and Transformers and proposed an innovative hybrid model for UAV-RFFI. Wang et al. [16] proposed a universal radio frequency signal enhancement framework to address the interference of noise on UAV-RFFI.

However, the above-mentioned methods face two major problems in practical applications: Firstly, under different environmental conditions, the distribution of radio frequency fingerprint features varies significantly, resulting in a sudden drop in the performance of the model when deployed in new domains. Secondly, the system may encounter unknown UAV devices not covered by the training set, and the existing closed set recognition models lack the ability to distinguish between known and unknown devices, making it difficult to effectively detect rogue intruders. Therefore, to address the above issues, meet the requirements of UAV identity authentication in open-set scenarios, and enhance the adaptability of the model in cross-domain environments, we proposes a robust UAV-RFFI method based on cross-domain attention mechanism and metric adversarial learning (CDAM-MAL). Through the synergistic effect of signal preprocessing, feature optimization and attention mechanism, the discriminability and stability of radio frequency fingerprint (RFF) features are enhanced. The main contributions of this paper are as follows:

- We propose a feature extraction scheme based on Hamming window preprocessing and short-time Fourier transform, which reduces the signal boundary effect and constructs high-quality time-frequency features to alleviate the interference of different channels on RF signal recognition.
- We present the CDAM-MAL feature optimization model. By integrating triplet metric adversarial learning and cross-domain attention mechanism, it enhances feature discriminability and focuses on key features, effectively improving the reliability of open-set scene recognition and cross-domain generalization ability.
- We conducted experiments on the open-source UAV dataset to evaluate the effectiveness of the proposed method. The performance verification on open-set scenarios and cross-domain datasets indicates that this method significantly improves the recognition performance of UAVs in open-set and cross-domain scenarios.

2 System Model and Problem Description

2.1 System Model

The UAV-RFFI system model based on CDAM-MAL consists of three parts: data preprocessing, model training and classification detection, as shown in Fig. 1. In the data preprocessing stage, the original signal is processed with Hamming windows to reduce spectral leakage and optimize quality. Then, it is transformed into a two-dimensional time-frequency matrix through short-time Fourier transform (STFT) to comprehensively capture the inherent fingerprint of the equipment. During the model training phase, triplet metric adversarial learning is introduced. The feature aggregation and discrimination are strengthened through the "anchor point - positive example - negative example" pattern. At the same time, a cross-domain attention mechanism is integrated to focus on key features, suppress redundancy, and enhance cross-domain adaptability. In the classification detection stage, based on the extracted features, the K-NN algorithm is used to complete the open-set, cross-domain device classification and rogue device detection.

2.2 Problem Description

RFFI Problem: Suppose the dataset of UAV is $\mathbf{D} = \{d_1, d_2, \ldots, d_k\}$, and the original sequence of its radio frequency signal in the time domain is represented as $\mathrm{s}_i(t) \in \mathbb{R}^{\mathrm{T}}$ (T is the number of sampling points). Due to environmental interference and hardware differences, the actual received signal is:

$$\mathbf{r}_i(t) = h(\mathrm{s}_i(t); \theta) + n(t) \tag{1}$$

where $h(\cdot; \theta)$ is the channel distortion function and $n(t) \sim \mathcal{N}(0, \sigma^2)$ is additive Gaussian white noise. The objective of RFFI is to construct a mapping function $f : \mathbf{r}_i(t) \rightarrow d_k$ to achieve precise identification of device identity d_k.

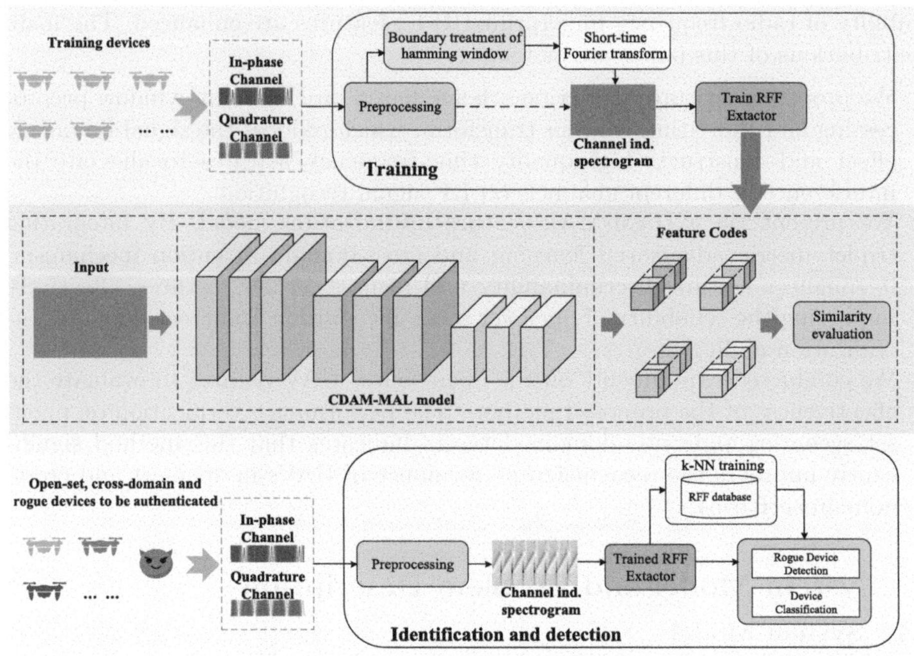

Fig. 1. CDAM-MAL model framework.

RFFI Problem of Open-Set: Define the known category dataset $\mathbf{D}_{know} \in \mathbf{D}$ and the unknown rogue device dataset $\mathbf{D}_{unknow}$. The classifier needs to meet:

$$f(\mathbf{r}_i(t)) = \begin{cases} d_k & \text{if } d_k \in \mathbf{D}_{know} \\ \text{unknown} & \text{otherwise} \end{cases} \tag{2}$$

where the optimization objective is to maximize the detection rate of unknown devices, $\max \mathbb{P}(f(\mathbf{r}_i)) = \text{unknown} | d_i \in \mathbf{D}_{unknow}$.

RFFI Problem of Cross-Domain: Suppose the distribution of the training data domain $S_{tr} = \{\mathbf{r}_i^{tr}(t)\}$ and the test data domain $S_{te} = \{\mathbf{r}_j^{te}(t)\}$ satisfies $\mathcal{P}_{tr} \neq \mathcal{P}_{te}$, and learn the domain invariant feature $\phi(\mathbf{r}(t))$ such that:

$$\min_{\phi} \mathcal{D}_{KL}(\mathcal{P}_{tr}(\phi) || \mathcal{P}_{te}(\phi)) \tag{3}$$

where $\mathcal{D}_{KL}$ is the Kullback-Leibler divergence, which measures the difference between feature distributions.

3 The Proposed CDAM-MAL Model Framework

We propose a UAV-RFFI framework based on CDAM-MAL as shown in Fig. 1, and its specific implementation process is as follows.

3.1 Hamming Window Preprocessing

In the UAV-RFFI task, the truncation of radio frequency signals often leads to discontinuities at the signal boundaries, causing spectral leakage phenomena, which will reduce the accuracy of subsequent feature extraction. To reduce the influence of boundary effects on time-frequency analysis, we use the Hamming window to window the original signal for preprocessing. By smoothing both ends of the signal and suppressing the pseudo-spectral components introduced by truncation, the Hamming window function is defined as:

$$\omega(n) = 0.54 - 0.46\cos\left(\frac{2\pi n}{N-1}\right), \quad 0 \leq n \leq N-1 \tag{4}$$

where N represents the window length, which is set 256, and n represents the sample index. The signal expression after windowing is:

$$x_w(n) = x(n) \cdot \omega(n) \tag{5}$$

3.2 Short-Time Fourier Transform

The radio frequency signal of UAV is non-stationary and vulnerable to nonlinear distortion and environmental noise, forming specific patterns in the frequency domain. Therefore, STFT is used to analyze windowed signals. The frequency variation over time is observed by sliding the time window to enhance feature discrimination and robustness and reduce the impact of channel conditions on recognition performance. The process is as follows:

$$\text{STFT}\{x(t)\}(m, \omega) = \int_{-\infty}^{\infty} x(\tau) \cdot \omega(\tau - m) \cdot e^{-j\omega\tau} d\tau \tag{6}$$

where $x(\tau)$ represents the windowed signal, $\omega(\tau - m)$ is the sliding window function, m is the window center moment, and ω is the angular frequency.

3.3 Metric Adversarial Learning

In the UAV-RFFI task, there are inherent intra-class variations and inter-class similarities among signal samples. Especially in the open-set recognition scenario, the discrimination ability of the model for unknown devices urgently needs to be improved. Relying solely on conventional classification losses (such as cross-entropy) is difficult to ensure an excellent distribution of the feature space structure. To this end, we introduce a triplet metric adversarial learning mechanism, explicitly constraining the aggregation and discreteness of feature representations, and enhancing the discriminability and generalization ability of the feature space.

The triplet loss function is based on the anchor sample x^a, the positive sample x^p and the negative sample x^n. The optimization objective is that the distance between the anchor and the positive sample is less than at least one threshold α of the distance between the anchor and the negative sample. Described as:

$$\mathcal{L}_{triplet} = \frac{1}{N}\sum_{i=1}^{N}\left[\|f(x_i^a) - f(x_i^p)\|_2^2 - \|f(x_i^a) - f(x_i^n)\|_2^2 + \alpha\right]_+ \tag{7}$$

where N represents the number of triplet samples, $f(\cdot)$ is the feature map, and $[\cdot]_+$ indicates values greater than zero. In addition, to enhance the stability and convergence speed of training, a hard sample mining strategy is introduced, where the farthest positive sample and the nearest negative sample are selected for each anchor sample:

$$x_i^p = \arg\max_{x^p} \|f(x_i^a) - f(x^p)\|_2^2 \tag{8a}$$

$$x_i^n = \arg\max_{x^n} \|f(x_i^a) - f(x^n)\|_2^2 \tag{8b}$$

To enhance the robustness and generalization ability of the model, we introduce an adversarial training mechanism. Adding a small perturbation δ to the model input and generate the most perturbed adversarial sample through VAT. The adversarial perturbation δ is generated by the following formula:

$$\delta = \arg\max_{\|\delta\|_2 \leq \varepsilon} \mathcal{D}(p(y|\mathbf{x};\theta), p(y|\mathbf{x}+\delta;\theta)) \tag{9}$$

where $\mathcal{D}(\cdot,\cdot)$ represents the Kullback-Leibler (KL) divergence between the two probability distributions, ε is the magnitude of the perturbation, which is set to 1.0. The KL divergence can be defined as:

$$\mathcal{D}(p(y|\mathbf{x}), p(y|\mathbf{x}+\delta)) = \sum_{c=1}^{C} p(y=c|\mathbf{x}) \log \frac{p(y=c|\mathbf{x})}{p(y=c|\mathbf{x}+\delta)} \tag{10}$$

After calculating δ by the approximation method, the loss of the adversarial sample is added to the total loss function. The specific measurement of adversarial training loss is:

$$\mathcal{L}_{ad} = \frac{1}{N}\sum_{i=1}^{N}\left[\|f(x_i^a+\delta) - f(x_i^p+\delta)\|_2^2 - \|f(x_i^a+\delta) - f(x_i^n+\delta)\|_2^2 + \alpha\right]_+ \tag{11}$$

Through the above-mentioned multi-level metric adversarial learning mechanism, the model can obtain more robust and discriminative feature representations. Enhance the model's discrimination ability for unknown devices in open-set recognition scenarios.

3.4 Cross-Domain Attention Mechanism

Radio frequency signals show significant inter-domain distribution differences in different geographical locations and channel environments, which directly affect the consistency of features and the generalization performance of the model. To alleviate the problem of distribution drift, we designs a cross-domain attention mechanism, enabling the model to adaptively focus on regional features strongly related to device identity and suppress redundant features caused by geographical or channel differences, thereby achieving cross-domain robust recognition.

Suppose the input time-frequency characteristic tensor is $\mathbf{F} \in \mathbb{R}^{C\times T\times F}$, where C, T, and F represent the channel, time, and frequency dimensions respectively. First, through the global pooling layer dimension reduction, perform global average pooling on $\mathbf{F}$ in the channel dimension to obtain the time-frequency description vector:

$$\mathbf{z} = \frac{1}{C}\sum_{c=1}^{C}\mathbf{F}_{c,:,:} \in \mathbb{R}^{T\times F} \tag{12}$$

Secondly, time-frequency attention weights are generated through two layers of fully connected networks and activation functions:

$$\mathbf{A} = \sigma(\mathbf{W}_2 \cdot \delta(\mathbf{W}_1 \cdot \mathrm{Flatten}(\mathbf{z}))) \tag{13}$$

where $\mathbf{W}_1 \in \mathbb{R}^{d\times TF}$, $\mathbf{W}_2 \in \mathbb{R}^{TF\times d}$, $\delta(\cdot)$ is relu activation, $\sigma(\cdot)$ is sigmoid activation, $\mathrm{Flatten}(\cdot)$ flattens the tensor into a vector, $\mathbf{A} \in \mathbb{R}^{TF}$. Then, through weight reshaping and weighted feature fusion, $\mathbf{A}$ is reshaped back to $T \times F$ and multiplied element-by-element with the original feature:

$$\mathbf{F}'_{c,:,:} = \mathbf{F}_{c,:,:} \odot \mathbf{A} \tag{14}$$

Finally, the attention consistency loss is introduced to constrain the similarity of attention distributions in different source domains and target domains:

$$\mathcal{L}_{cdam} = \|\mathbf{A}_S - \mathbf{A}_T\|_2^2 \tag{15}$$

where $\mathbf{A}_S$ and $\mathbf{A}_T$ are the attention weights of the source domain and the target domain respectively. The final loss function is expressed as:

$$\mathcal{L}_{CDAM-MAL} = \mathcal{L}_{ad} + \lambda_{cdam}\mathcal{L}_{cdam} \tag{16}$$

where λ_{cdam} is a hyperparameter, weighing the contribution of the cross-domain attention mechanism to the training. Figure 2 depicts the framework of the RFF extractor, and Algorithm 1 describes the complete process mentioned above.

3.5 Classification and Detection

We implement UAV classification and rogue detection based on K-NN algorithm.

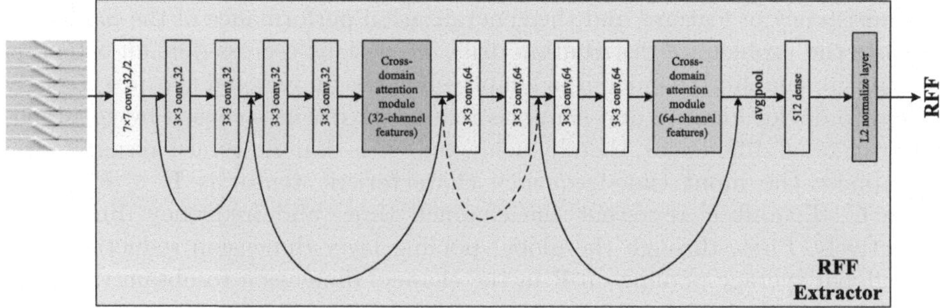

Fig. 2. The framework of the RFF extractor.

Rogue UAV Detection: Rogue UAV detection is achieved through the K-NN algorithm. The RFF of the received signal is extracted, and the average distance between it and the K nearest neighbors in the database is calculated as the detection score to determine whether it is a legitimate device:

$$D_{\text{arg}} = \frac{1}{K}\sum_{i=1}^{K} D_i \tag{17}$$

where D_i is the euclidean distance to the i-th adjacent point. Then make a judgment by a threshold λ. When the detection score D_{arg} is higher than the threshold λ, it is determined to be an illegal device and the authentication fails. When it is below the threshold λ, it is regarded as a registered device and will be further classified.

Device Classification: The device classification adopts the majority voting K-NN algorithm. Calculate the euclidean distance between the device to be classified and all devices in the training set, take the K nearest neighbors, determine the label of the device to be classified by majority voting based on their labels, and then evaluate the model effect with accuracy.

4 Analysis of Experimental Results

4.1 Experimental Environment and Parameter Settings

The proposed CDAM-MAL was experimented on open-source real-world unmanned aerial vehicle datasets. The detailed process of signal acquisition can be found in paper [17]. This dataset contains downlink I/Q signal samples from seven DJI M100 drones of the same model in an anechoic chamber, collected by an Ettus USRP X310 receiver with UBX 160 sub-board at four distances of 6/9/12/15 ft. Each sample averages approximately 92,000 I/Q data points, ultimately containing about 13,000 independent examples, covering communication features of multiple drones and distances. During the model training process, training, validation, and test data are distributed in an 8:1:1 ratio. The

Algorithm 1. The proposed CDAM-MAL algorithm

Input:

- The original radio frequency signal dataset of UAV $\mathbf{D} = \{(x_i, y_i)\}_{i=1}^{N}$;
- θ, λ_{cdam}: Model parameters and Model hyperparameters;
- T, B: Number of iterations, number of iteration batches

Output:

Optimized parameter θ; $\mathcal{L}_{CDAM-MAL} \leftarrow$ Cross-domain metric adversarial loss;

Training process:

1: **for** $i = 1$ to N **do**
2: Hamming window $\omega(n)$ is used for preprocessing to obtain the windowed signal:
$\omega(n) = 0.54 - 0.46\cos\left(\frac{2\pi n}{N-1}\right), \quad 0 \leq n \leq N-1$;
$x'_i(n) = x_i(n) \cdot \omega(n)$;
3: Perform STFT on the windowed signal x'_i:
$\text{STFT}\{x_i(t)\}(m, \omega) = \int_{-\infty}^{\infty} x_i(\tau) \cdot \omega(\tau - m) \cdot e^{-j\omega\tau} d\tau$
4: **end for**
5: **for** $t = 1$ to T **do**
6: **for** $b = 1$ to B **do**
7: Triplet sampling, triplet construction and optimization objective:
$\mathcal{L}_{triplet} = \frac{1}{N}\sum_{i=1}^{N}\left[\|f(x_i^a) - f(x_i^p)\|_2^2 - \|f(x_i^a) - f(x_i^n)\|_2^2 + \alpha\right]_+$;
8: Calculate the metric adversarial loss:
$\mathcal{L}_{ad} = \frac{1}{N}\sum_{i=1}^{N}\left[\|f(x_i^a + \delta) - f(x_i^p + \delta)\|_2^2 - \|f(x_i^a + \delta) - f(x_i^n + \delta)\|_2^2 + \alpha\right]_+$;
9: Global pooling dimension reduction to obtain time-frequency description features:
$\mathbf{z} = \frac{1}{C}\sum_{c=1}^{C} \mathbf{F}_{c,:,:} \in \mathbb{R}^{T\times F}$;
10: Attention weight generation and weighted fusion:
$\mathbf{A} = \sigma(\mathbf{W}_2 \cdot \delta(\mathbf{W}_1 \cdot \text{Flatten}(\mathbf{z})))$;
$\mathbf{F}'_{c,:,:} = \mathbf{F}_{c,:,:} \odot \mathbf{A}$
11: Introduce attention consistency loss:
$\mathcal{L}_{cdam} = \|\mathbf{A}_S - \mathbf{A}_T\|_2^2$;
12: Final loss calculation:
$\mathcal{L}_{CDAM-MAL} = \mathcal{L}_{ad} + \lambda_{cdam}\mathcal{L}_{cdam}$;
13: Model parameter update: $\theta \leftarrow \theta - \nabla_\theta \mathcal{L}_{CDAM-MAL}$;
14: **end for**
15: **end for**
16: **return** $\mathcal{L}_{CDAM-MAL}$ **and** θ

experimental parameters are shown in Table 1. To evaluate the detection effect of rogue devices, the F1 score for unknown drone recognition is introduced: the harmonic mean of the proportion of actually unknown samples predicted as unknown (*Precision*) and the proportion of actually unknown samples predicted as unknown to all unknown samples in the total sample (*Recall*), that is:

$$\text{F1} = 2 \times (\textit{Precision} \times \textit{Recall})/(\textit{Precision} + \textit{Recall}) \tag{18}$$

Table 1. Experimental parameter settings

Parameter	Parameter value
Deep learning framework	Tensorflow 1.2.1
Hardware accelerator	GTX 1080Ti
Model	CVCNN [18] and K-NN classifier
dataset	UAV [17]
Optimizer	RMSprop
Learning rate	0.0001
Batch size	32
Epoch	100
Adversarial perturbation δ	$[0, 2.5 \times 10^{-2}]$
Cross-domain attention mechanism weight λ_{CDAM}	0.45

4.2 Classification of UAV in Same Domain

In the classification of UAV in the same domain, 8,000 RF signals collected by the receiver at three transmission distances of 6, 9, and 12 ft are fused as the model input data, and another 1,872 signals at the same distance are fused as the evaluation data. Since the classification model K-NN has a registration stage, we take the training data as the registration data and the evaluation data as the data to be classified, the classification results were plotted into a confusion matrix as shown in Fig. 3. The results show that the correct classification rate of unmanned aerial vehicle models is: $(262+281+230+240+299+283+263)/1872 \times 100\% = 99.25\%$.

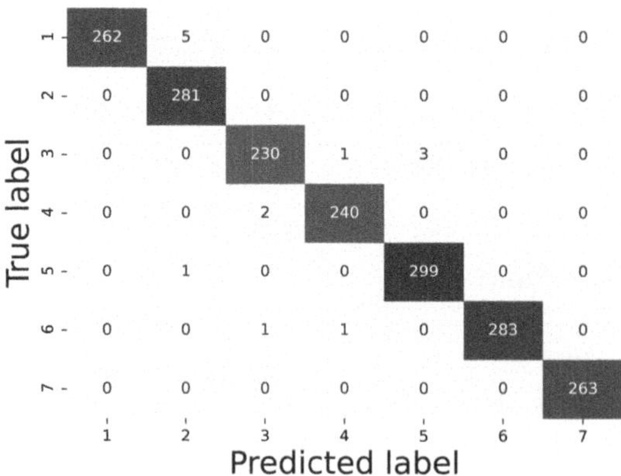

Fig. 3. Confusion matrix for classification of UAV in the same domain.

To compare the semantic feature extraction ability of CDAM-MAL, the t-SNE nonlinear dimensionality reduction technique [19] was adopted to reduce

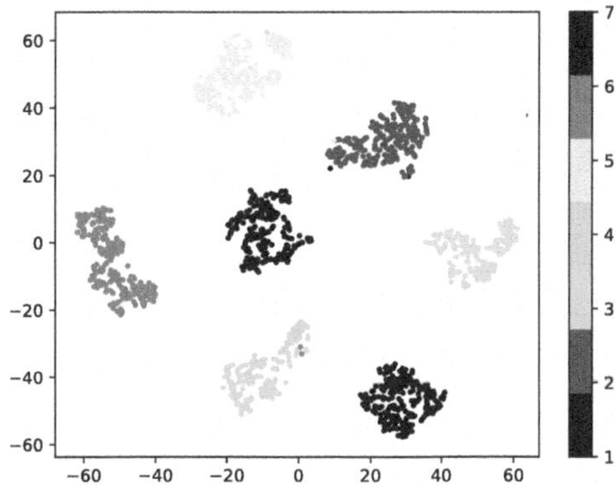

Fig. 4. Semantic visualization analysis of sympatric UAV.

the high-dimensional semantic features extracted by the deep learning model to two-dimensional visualization, as shown in Fig. 4. Its contour coefficient is 0.6291, indicating excellent clustering effect and strong result separation.

4.3 Classification of UAV in Different Domain

In the classification of cross-domain UAV, 8,000 RF signals of 6, 9, and 12 ft are fused as model input, and 2,284 signals of 15 ft are evaluated. Since the classification model K-NN has a registration stage, we take 15 pieces of data within 15 ft as the registration data and the rest as the data to be classified. The classification results are plotted as a confusion matrix as shown in Fig. 5. Since only one piece of data was collected from device 7 15 ft below, we only classified devices 1 to 6. The correct classification rate of their models is: $(301+385+299+340+372+468)/2284 \times 100\% = 94.79\%$

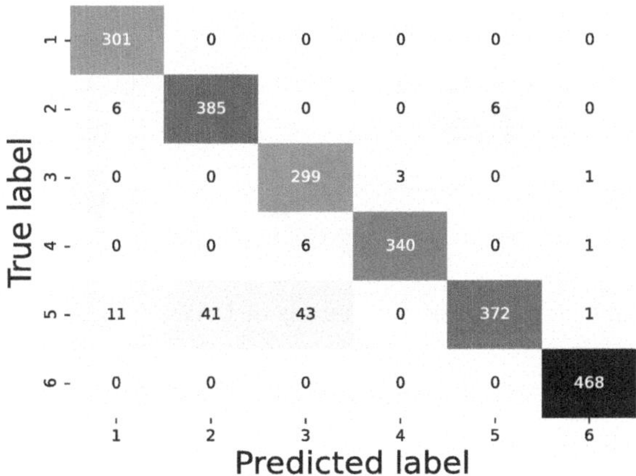

Fig. 5. Confusion matrix for classification of UAV in the different domain.

Meanwhile, in order to further study the impact of the number of registered UAV devices on the recognition performance of UAV devices, we conducted experiments with 8, 10, 12, 15, 17, and 20 registered samples respectively. The results are shown in Fig. 6. Specifically, the results are as follows: 91.24%, 92.03%, 94.40%, 94.79%, 95.27%, and 96.41% respectively.

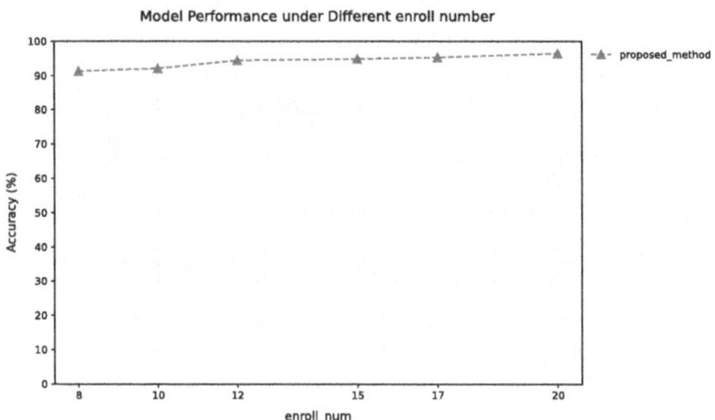

Fig. 6. The recognition accuracy under different numbers of registered devices.

As above, based on t-SNE, the high-dimensional semantic features extracted from the UAV dataset by the model were reduced to two dimensions for visual analysis, as shown in Fig. 7. Its contour coefficient is 0.4987. It indicates that the clustering effect is good and the model has strong separability.

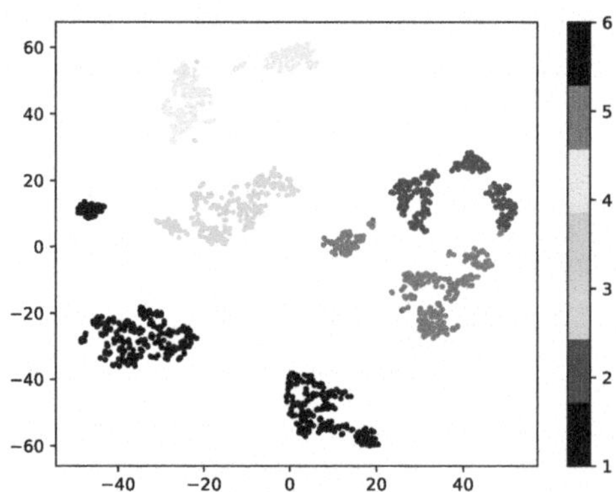

Fig. 7. Semantic visualization analysis of UAVs in different domains.

4.4 Classification of Open-Set UAV

In the classification of open-set UAV, the model input is the fusion data of 5,691 RF signals from devices 1 to 5 at 6, 9, and 12 ft respectively, and the evaluation data is 1,872 signals from devices 1 to 7 at the same distance. Taking the training data as the K-NN registration data and the rest as the data to be classified, the confusion matrix of the classification results is shown in Fig. 8. The results show that the overall recognition accuracy of the model is 98.77%, that of device 6 is 97.19%, that of device 7 is 100%, and the comprehensive accuracy is 98.35%, indicating its excellent classification generalization ability.

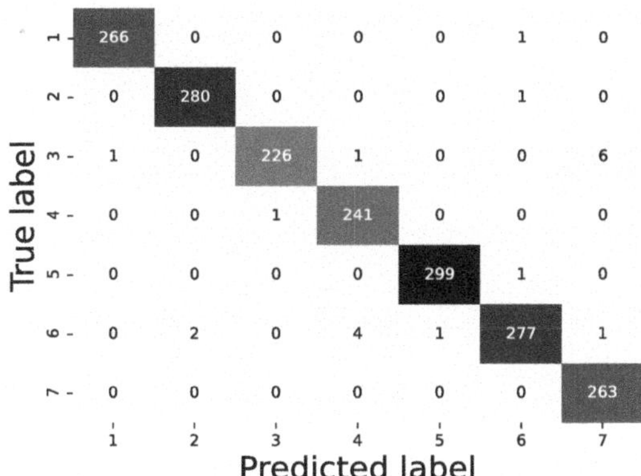

Fig. 8. Confusion matrix for open-set UAV device classification.

4.5 Rogue UAV Detection

Detection of Rogue UAV in Same Domain: Rogue UAV refer to devices outside of model training. In the worst-case scenario, rogue devices have similar characteristics to legitimate ones. Therefore, we specially selected the three types of UAV RF signals with transmission distances of 6, 9, and 12 ft collected by the receiver for fusion, making devices 1–4 legal and devices 5–7 illegal. The ROC curve is shown in Fig. 9, which is obtained by plotting the true positive rate (TPR) and the false positive rate (TPR). We can obtain that the Precision metric is 99.88%, the Recall metric is 99.88%, and the corresponding F1 score is 0.9988. Meanwhile, the classification accuracy rate for legal devices is 99.61%.

Detection of Rogue UAV in Different Domain: Similarly, the simulation was conducted by fusing the radio frequency signals of 6, 9, and 12-foot UAV. Devices 1–4 at 15 ft were set as legal devices, and devices 5–7 were set as illegal devices. The ROC curve is shown in Fig. 10. The results show that the Precision is 87.68%, the Recall is 92.50%, the F1 score is 0.9002, and the accuracy rate of legal device classification reaches 90.12%.

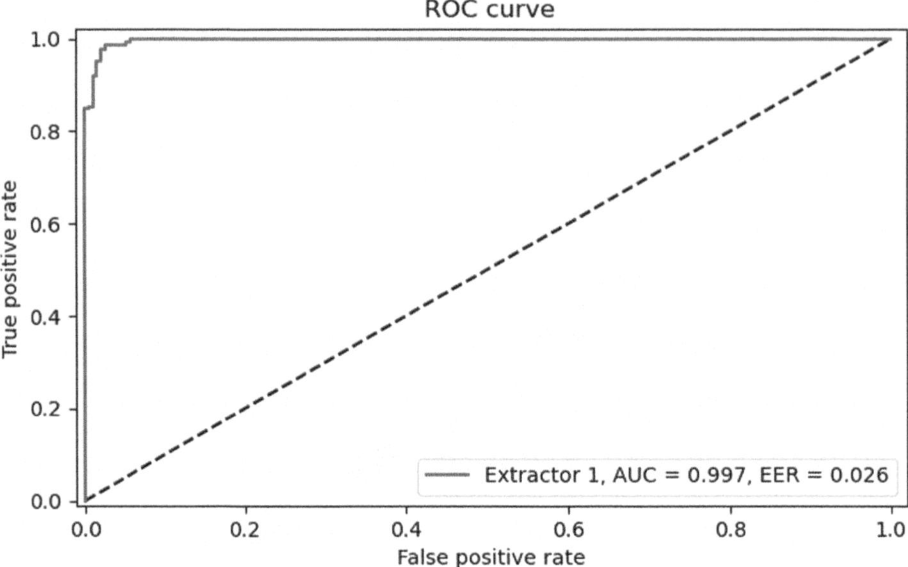

Fig. 9. ROC curve for detecting rogue UAV in same domain.

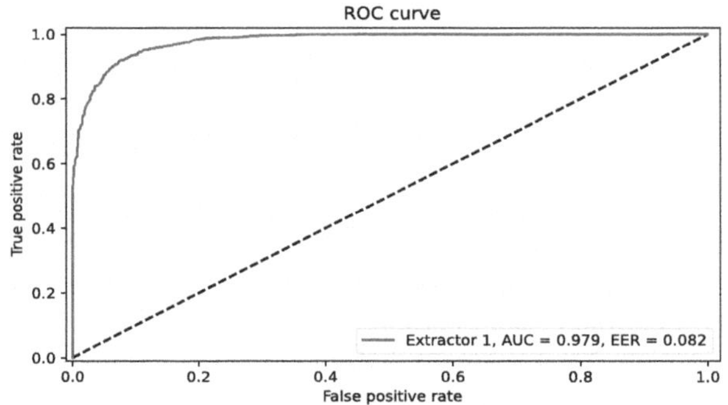

Fig. 10. ROC curve for detecting rogue UAV in different domain.

4.6 Complexity Analysis

We evaluate the complexity complexity of the model as shown in Table 2. From the perspectives of floating-point operation volume, parameter scale, storage occupation, and iteration time, the model demonstrates low computational complexity and compact resource occupation. This lightweight feature lays the foundation for its deployment and application in edge scenarios and other areas, and also enables it to better adapt to resource-constrained operating environments.

Table 2. Complexity of Model

Method	Flops	Params(MB)	Storage(MB)	Iter_time/s
CDAM-MAL	1.68×10^8	2.76	7.13	0.75

5 Conclusion

In this paper, we propose a robust UAV-RFFI method based on CDAM-MAL, which solves the problems of low model recognition accuracy in cross-domain, insufficient generalization ability of open-set scenarios, and difficulty in accurately identifying UAV devices and effectively detecting rogue devices. Specifically, the signal quality is optimized through Hamming window preprocessing to reduce boundary effects. The time-frequency features are extracted with the help of STFT. The feature discriminability is strengthened by using triplet metric adversarial learning. Then, the key features are focused through the cross-domain attention mechanism to collaboratively improve the reliability of open-set scene recognition, enhance cross-domain generalization ability and achieve precise detection of rogue devices. Finally, Classify and detect UAV using the K-NN classifier. The simulation results show that the recognition rate of unknown UAV in the open-set scenario reaches 98.77%, and the corresponding F1 score is 0.9988. The recognition accuracies on two different cross-domain datasets are 99.25% and 96.41% respectively, significantly enhancing the recognition performance and rogue device detection capability in open-set and cross-domain scenarios.

References

1. Javed, S., et al.: State-of-the-art and future research challenges in UAV swarms. IEEE Internet Things J. **11**(11), 19023–19045 (2024). https://doi.org/10.1109/JIOT.2024.3364230
2. Kumar, N., Chaudhary, A.: Surveying cybersecurity vulnerabilities and countermeasures for enhancing UAV security. Comput. Netw. **252**, 110695–110718 (2024). https://doi.org/10.1016/j.comnet.2024.110695
3. Tlili, F., Ayed, S., Chaari Fourati, L.: Advancing UAV security with artificial intelligence: a comprehensive survey of techniques and future directions. Internet Things **27**, 101281–101307 (2024). https://doi.org/10.1016/j.iot.2024.101281
4. Sarıkaya, B.S.: Şerif Bahtiyar: a survey on security of UAV and deep reinforcement learning. Ad Hoc Netw. **164**, 103642–103664 (2024). https://doi.org/10.1016/j.adhoc.2024.103642
5. Wang, X., et al.: A survey on security of UAV swarm networks: Attacks Countermeasures **57**(3), 1–37 (2024). https://doi.org/10.1145/3703625
6. Pandey, G.K., Gurjar, D.S., Yadav, S., Jiang, Y., Yuen, C.: UAV-assisted communications with rf energy harvesting: a comprehensive survey. IEEE Commun. Surv. Tutor. **27**(2), 782–838 (2025). https://doi.org/10.1109/COMST.2024.3425597
7. Cao, X., Tan, W., Gao, Q., Hu, Z., Li, C.: IntML-KNN: a few-shot radio frequency fingerprint identification scheme for lora devices. IEEE Signal Process. Lett. **32**, 2259–2263 (2025). https://doi.org/10.1109/LSP.2025.3569211

8. Peng, Y., et al.: Supervised contrastive learning for RFF identification with limited samples. IEEE Internet Things J. **10**(19), 17293–17306 (2023). https://doi.org/10.1109/JIOT.2023.3272628
9. Yin, P., et al.: Multi-channel CNN-based open-set rf fingerprint identification for LTE devices. IEEE Trans. Cogn. Commun. Network. **10**(5), 1788–1800 (2024). https://doi.org/10.1109/TCCN.2024.3391293
10. Fu, X., et al.: Semi-supervised specific emitter identification via dual consistency regularization. IEEE Internet Things J. **10**(21), 19257–19269 (2023). https://doi.org/10.1109/JIOT.2023.3281668
11. Podder, P., Zawodniok, M., Madria, S.: Deep learning for UAV detection and classification via radio frequency signal analysis. In: 2024 25th IEEE International Conference on Mobile Data Management (MDM), pp. 165–174 (2024). https://doi.org/10.1109/MDM61037.2024.00040
12. Cai, Z., Lu, G., Wang, Y., Gui, G., Sha, J.: Robust cross-domain UAV RFFI method using domain-invariant adversarial learning and manifold regularization. IEEE Trans. Cogn. Commun. Network. **12**, 443–453 (2025). https://doi.org/10.1109/TCCN.2025.3561305
13. Lin, D., Wu, W.: Optimization of a secure UAV-based Iot: RF-fingerprint authentication and resource allocation. IEEE Internet Things J. **10**(21), 19208–19217 (2023). https://doi.org/10.1109/JIOT.2023.3281344
14. Cai, Z., Wang, Y., Jiang, Q., Gui, G., Sha, J.: Toward intelligent lightweight and efficient UAV identification with rf fingerprinting. IEEE Internet Things J. **11**(15), 26329–26339 (2024). https://doi.org/10.1109/JIOT.2024.3395466
15. Zhou, K., Li, Q., Cao, P., Cai, Z., Shi, X., Wang, F.: Lightweight and efficient hybrid network for UAV identification using radio frequency fingerprinting. IEEE Internet Things J. **12**(20), 42728–42740 (2025). https://doi.org/10.1109/JIOT.2025.3594571
16. Wang, Z., Cao, Z., Xie, J., Zhang, W., He, Z.: Rf-based drone detection enhancement via a generalized denoising and interference-removal framework. IEEE Signal Process. Lett. **31**, 929–933 (2024). https://doi.org/10.1109/LSP.2024.3379006
17. Soltani, N., Reus-Muns, G., Salehi, B., Dy, J., Ioannidis, S., Chowdhury, K.: Rf fingerprinting unmanned aerial vehicles with non-standard transmitter waveforms. IEEE Trans. Veh. Technol. **69**(12), 15518–15531 (2020). https://doi.org/10.1109/TVT.2020.3042128
18. He, K., Zhang, X., Ren, S., Sun, J.: Deep residual learning for image recognition. In: Proceedings of the IEEE Conference on Computer Vision and Pattern Recognition, pp. 770–778 (2016)
19. Maaten, L.v.d., Hinton, G.: Visualizing data using t-SNE. J. Mach. Learn. Res. **9**(Nov), 2579–2605 (2008)

DASFO: Dependency-Aware Scalable Function Offloading Framework for Intelligent Connected Vehicles

Jiayin Zhang(✉), Shuo Li, Yifan Du, and Nan Li

Corporate Research, Robert Bosch GmbH, Shanghai, China
{jiayin.zhang,shuo.li1,yifan.du,nan.li3}@cn.bosch.com

Abstract. Advances in edge and cloud computing have increased the accessibility of bandwidth and computational resources, allowing Intelligent Connected Vehicles (ICV) to offload perception functions to the cloud, reducing dependence on high-power onboard units. However, these perception applications often consist of interdependent tasks and must operate under dynamic network conditions, making it difficult to balance real-time performance with energy and cost constraints. To address these challenges, this paper proposes DASFO, a multi-stage framework that jointly optimizes offloading decisions, bandwidth allocation, and scalable resource management. DASFO aims to maintain long-term queue stability while respecting energy and cost budgets, explicitly accounting for function dependencies. At its core, we employ a Deep Reinforcement Learning (DRL) agent enhanced with Graph Convolutional Network (GCN) embeddings to model inter-function dependencies, with a near-optimal strategy for bandwidth allocation and resource scaling. Experimental results demonstrate that DASFO effectively balances processing latency, energy consumption, and cost, while incurring minimal decision-making overhead.

Keywords: Intelligent Connected Vehicles · Function Offloading · Resource Allocation · Lyapunov Optimization · Reinforcement Learning

1 Introduction

In recent years, intelligent transportation systems have advanced significantly through the integration of edge and cloud computing, enabled by improvements in network bandwidth and computational power. Meanwhile, in the domain of Intelligent Connected Vehicles (ICVs), the growing complexity of applications—driven by advances in autonomous driving and the adoption of large-scale models—has significantly increased computational demands, leading to higher hardware costs and energy consumption. To address these challenges, recent studies have explored offloading computation to cloud and edge resources, leveraging improvements in network bandwidth and distributed infrastructure

L. Zhang and K.-K. R. Choo (Eds.): MobiQuitous 2025, LNICST 684, pp. 19–38, 2026.
https://doi.org/10.1007/978-3-032-22503-0_2

to reduce reliance on high-performance onboard units [12]. However, offloading introduces new trade-offs between latency, energy consumption, and operational cost. As a result, it becomes essential to balance the distribution of computation across cloud and vehicle-side resources to ensure both system efficiency and resource sustainability.

As a motivation example, we conduct an experiment on a perception application, which includes pre-processing tasks like resizing, encoding, and inference. For inference, We deploy an open-source vision language model [8] in a Horizon RDK Ultra (setup shown in Fig. 1). Processing a single frame with a raw size of 4692 KB takes approximately 3000ms. This phenomenon motivates us to conduct an in-depth study of VLM deployment. Then, we offload the same model to a GPU-powered cloud. As a result, the end-to-end latency drops significantly to around 536 ms, even when the uplink network bandwidth is limited to 10 Mbps. In this case, the breakdown of time across stages is as follows: 83ms for pre-processing, 250 ms for the uplink transmission, 183ms for cloud-based inference, and 20 ms for downlink transmission. The performance boost is phenomenal, however, constraints in processing power, energy consumption, and cost management make it crucial to optimize the offloading strategy to balance on-device execution with the cloud effectively.

Perception workloads in ICV are particularly challenging due to complex sensor processing and machine learning pipelines with tightly coupled stages and inter-task dependencies, where delays in one task can propagate and degrade overall performance. For example, in a driver assistance system (Fig. 1), limited processing resources can delay object detection, disrupt tracking, and force decisions based on outdated information, compromising control accuracy. While cloud offloading can relieve onboard computational pressure, it introduces additional variability, as network fluctuations caused by congestion or mobility [1] may lead to transmission bottlenecks, reducing responsiveness in latency-sensitive applications. Addressing such dynamic, non-linear offloading problems requires balancing decision quality with timeliness. Although evolutionary algorithms [18] offer flexibility for dependency-aware offloading, their iterative nature incurs substantial overhead, limiting real-time applicability. Deep Reinforcement Learning (DRL) [3], on the other hand, provides faster, policy-based decisions via offline training and has shown promise in this domain. However, existing methods rarely offer a unified framework that jointly considers function dependencies, queuing behavior, and coordinated management of computational and network resources.

To address these gaps, we propose DASFO, a DRL-based framework for dependency-aware function offloading and joint resource orchestration across multiple vehicles (or user equipment, UE), considering both processing efficiency and long-term constraints such as device energy and cost. The main contributions of this paper are listed as follows:

1. We address dependency-aware function offloading in ICV applications under real-time demands and limited resources. To this end, we propose DASFO, a multi-stage framework integrating offloading, bandwidth allocation, and

scalable resource management to maintain long-term workload stability under energy and cost budgets.
2. Offloading decisions are made via Lyapunov Optimization, decomposing long-term objectives into tractable per-slot subproblems. A DRL agent with GCN embeddings exploits queue states and application topologies to generate budget-aware offloading actions that ensure queue stability.
3. DASFO further introduces coordinated resource control tools: a signal-aware bandwidth allocation scheme for offloaded traffic, and a queuing-query-driven resource scaler that minimizes queueing delay while balancing energy and cost via optimal instance provisioning.

The remainder of this paper is organized as follows: Sect. 2 reviews recent literature in related research fields. Section 3 introduces the mathematic system model and formulates the abstracted function offloading problem. Section 4 presents the detailed design of DASFO and the corresponding training process. Evaluation results are then illustrated and discussed in Sect. 5. Finally, we conclude this paper in Sect. 6.

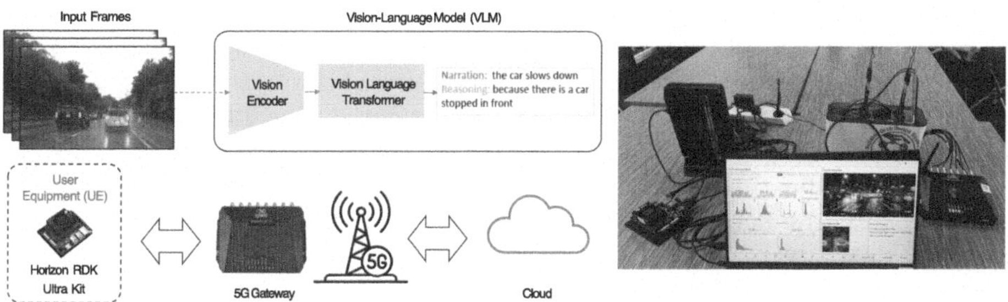

Fig. 1. A testbed for E2E latency measurements of a VLM application.

2 Related Works

Function offloading has emerged in recent years as a critical area of research on device-cloud collaboration [12], addressing the on-device computational limitations and energy consumption budget by leveraging the cloud for resource-intensive tasks. Additionally, the dynamic nature of ICV application workloads, such as handling various number of detected objects or fluctuating network conditions, complicates decision-making. A common practice is to formulate a multi-objective optimization problem that seeks the balance of on-device energy consumption, execution latency, etc. [19], and then treat each arrived task as an independent object of offloading decision-making [4]. However, such modeling can neglect function dependencies, limiting usability in multi-modal perception applications with interdependent functions (e.g. Object detection pipeline [10], VLM workflow [21], etc.).

As for the offloading decision-making, a growing number of investigations can be seen targeting interdependent functions, such as approaches based on convex optimization [22], evolutionary algorithm [18], and Deep Reinforcement Learning [3]. While convex optimization can provide precise and problem-specific solutions, evolutionary algorithms are known for more adaptive, generalized search strategies [18], making them better suited for exploring the complex and dynamic nature of offloading problems. However, meta-heuristics-based approaches can still suffer from increased computational overhead due to the evolution process [20]. Such trade-off between adaptability and computational efficiency poses challenges in scenarios where timely decision-making is crucial, highlighting the need for more efficient approaches to balance thorough exploration with rapid decision-making. Recent advances in Deep Reinforcement Learning (DRL) with specially designed embedding networks and offline training have significantly improved function offloading strategies, allowing systems to dynamically adjust offloading decisions based on the latest environment status with efficient decision-making [3]. However, ignoring queue latency can degrade the comprehensiveness of the performance analysis [14], hence limiting the adaptability of these approaches to latency-critical scenarios, like perception applications.

After the offloading decision is made, it's essential to strategically allocate network and computation resource to balance the workload-processing performance with the time-average energy consumption and the cost. Moreover, despite network resource allocation being widely investigated, like TDMA-based bandwidth allocation [1], transmission energy management [11], etc., little effort has been put into adjusting the computation resource in correspondence to the bottlenecks caused by network congestion, like reduced bandwidth capacity.

3 System Model and Problem Formulation

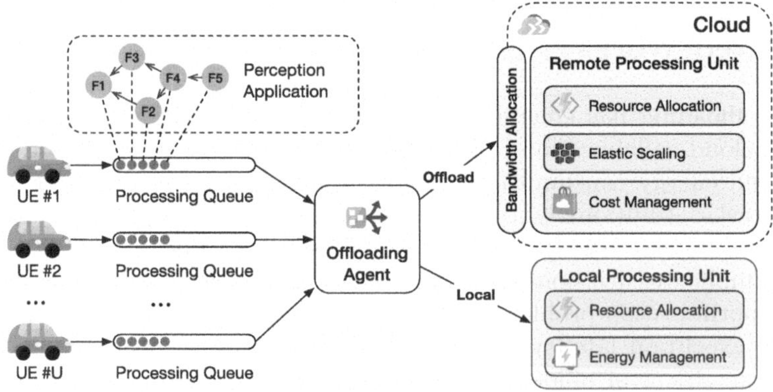

Fig. 2. Proposed DASFO framework.

We model the system as a discrete time-segmented system with equal duration $\Delta\mathcal{T}$, where a centralized offloading agent serves as the access point for function offloading, serving U UEs (indexed with i). As illustrated in Fig. 2, the framework's main role is to make respective decisions at each time step for each UE regarding:

1. Offloading decision: to offload the requested workloads to the cloud or process them on-device.
2. Network bandwidth allocation: determining the network bandwidth allocated for each UE that offloads its workload to the cloud.
3. Scalable computation resource allocation: determining the number of homogeneous runtime instances and per-instance resource allocation.

The logical sequence of an application can be formulated as a direct acyclic graph (DAG). Let $\mathcal{G} = (\mathcal{V}, \mathcal{VL})$ denote an application DAG with N nodes (functions), where $\mathcal{V} = \{v_j\}_{j=1}^{N}$ and $\mathcal{VL} = \{l_{j,k} | \forall v_j, v_k \in \mathcal{V}\}$ are sets of function nodes and their inter-links, respectively. The runtime of each function in the application is assumed to be pre-deployed on both the UEs and the cloud, and the DAG stays static, thus the startup latency is ignored. The workload (measured in GFLOPs) required for each function $v_j \in \mathcal{V}$ to execute is denoted with $|v_j|$. $\mathcal{A} = \mathcal{V} \times \mathcal{V}$ denotes the adjacency matrix of $\mathcal{G}$, reflecting the dependency between each function, where $l_{j,k} = 1$ indicates that the v_j is a direct predecessor of v_k, i.e. for the same set of input data, the execution of function v_k requires the completion of v_j.

At each time step $t = 1, 2, \ldots, \mathcal{T}$, UE $i \in 1, 2, \cdots, U$ triggers the application with an arrival rate λ_i^t, which follows an exponential distribution with a mean $\mathbb{E}(\lambda_i^t) = \bar{\lambda}_i$. Further, since we focus on a static pre-deployed application, the workload arrival of each UE is assumed to follow a general i.i.d distribution with a bounded second moment. Then, the actual workload required to execute the function provided by $v_j \in \mathcal{V}$ at t can be calculated as:

$$a_i^j(t) = |v_j| \lambda_i^t \tag{1}$$

Then, to express the dependency between functions on workload processing, we introduce a binary indicator $I_i^j(t)$ for the processing availability of each function (i.e. whether all workloads at time step t on predecessors of the function are completed):

$$I_i^j(t) = \begin{cases} 1, & \text{all predecessors of } a_i^j(t) \text{ are completed,} \\ 0, & \text{otherwise.} \end{cases} \tag{2}$$

The workloads can be executed by functions deployed on the cloud or on-device at each time step. Here, we adopt the widely used binary offloading rule [1], where the binary variable $\chi_i^t = 0$ and 1 indicate processing the workloads on-device and offloading to the cloud at each time step, respectively. Then, We model the workload processing with Erlang's formula for M/M/c queue. The decision variables consist of the per-instance resource configuration and instance number allocated on-device or in the cloud, denoted with μ_i^t and c_i^t, respectively. Their available range depends on the offloading decision, where μ_i^t lies in $[\mu_{i,\chi_i^t}^{\min}, \mu_{i,\chi_i^t}^{\max}]$, and c_i^t lies in $[1, c_{i,\chi_i^t}^{\max}]$.

When processing on-device ($\chi_i^t = 0$), we disable the horizontal scaling due to its constrained computation resource, thus μ_i^t stays as an adjustable variable, while c_i^t is fixed at 1. Let ϵ^{idle} and ϵ^{full} denote the UE computing unit's idle and full-load energy consumption, respectively, we formulate the energy consumption throughout the time step with an approximate linear model:

$$e_i^t = (1 - \chi_i^t)(\epsilon^{idle} + \frac{\mu_i^t}{\mu_{i,\chi_i^t}^{\max}}(\epsilon^{full} - \epsilon^{idle}))\Delta T \tag{3}$$

Otherwise, when processing over the cloud ($\chi_i^t = 1$), technologies like MPS [13] enable the application runtime to scale horizontally and vertically, where the primary concern of the UEs becomes the rental cost of accessing the cloud computing services. Here we adopt the widely-used pay-as-you-go pricing model, where the rental cost increases linearly with the allocated resource at each time step:

$$p_i^t = \chi_i^t \delta \mu_i^t c_i^t \Delta T \tag{4}$$

where δ is the per-time-step rental price for 1 GFLOPS.

Then, we model the departure of the workload processing queue (denoted with D_i^t) and the time-average departure rate of each time step (denoted with d_i^t) as:

$$D_i^t = \sum_{j=1}^{\mathcal{V}} I_i^j(t)\mu_i^t c_i^t \Delta T,\ d_i^t = \frac{D_i^t}{\Delta T} \tag{5}$$

With the centralized offloading agent design, assumed to leverage a dedicated network slice, we model all UEs connecting to this agent sharing the bandwidth capacity in an OFDMA manner [16]. Note that we ignore the transmission energy consumption as it can be considered minimal compared to the computation energy consumption. Let w_i^t denote bandwidth proportion allocated to each UE and W for the bandwidth capacity, based on the Shannon-Hartley theorem, the maximum amount of data that can be transmitted over the network is:

$$d_{net,i}^t = w_i^t \log_2(1 + \frac{Ph_i^t}{w_i^t W N_0}) \tag{6}$$

where P denotes the transmission power, which we assume to be a constant without loss of generality, and h_i^t is the channel gain, which stays constant within each time step while changing independently across various time steps, and N_0 is the noise power. As a result, from the perspective of the cloud, the bandwidth can be a bottleneck that limits the workload arrival A_i^t, which is defined as:

$$A_i^t = \left\{\chi_i^t \min(\sum_{j=1}^{N} a_i^j(t), d_{net,i}^t) + (1-\chi_i^t)\sum_{j=1}^{N} a_i^j(t)\right\}_{i=1}^{U} \tag{7}$$

Let Q_i^t denote the processing queue status of each UE, respectively, we can define the processing queue dynamics as:

$$Q_i^{t+1} = \max\{Q_i^t - D_i^t + A_i^t, 0\} \tag{8}$$

where $\mathbb{E}[A_i^t] = \bar{\lambda}_i \sum_{j=1}^{N} |v_j|$. The queuing system utilization rate can be defined as:

$$\rho_i^t = \frac{\sum_{j=1}^{N} a_i^j(t)}{d_i^t} \tag{9}$$

where we consider the queue to have infinity capacity (i.e. the workloads never get dropped until being processed), without loss of generality. Besides, workloads inside the processing queue are handled FIFO with no ranking manipulation.

Our primary optimization goal is to maximize the long-term workload-processing throughput with constraints on energy consumption, and cloud rental budget. Let the time step duration $\Delta\mathcal{T} = 1$ hereinafter for the sake of clearness, We formulate the long-term online optimization problem as a two-stage mixed integer nonlinear programming (MINLP) problem (**P1**):

$$\mathbf{P1}: \max_{\chi_i^t, \mu_i^t, c_i^t, w_i^t} \lim_{\mathcal{T}\to\infty} \frac{1}{\mathcal{T}} \sum_{t=1}^{\mathcal{T}} \sum_{i=1}^{U} d_i^t \tag{10}$$

$$s.t.\ \chi_i^t \in \{0,1\}, \forall t, i \tag{10a}$$

$$\lim_{\mathcal{T}\to\infty} \frac{1}{\mathcal{T}} \sum_{t=1}^{\mathcal{T}} \mathbb{E}[e_i^t] \le \hat{E}_i, \lim_{\mathcal{T}\to\infty} \frac{1}{\mathcal{T}} \sum_{t=1}^{\mathcal{T}} \mathbb{E}[p_i^t] \le \hat{P}_i, \forall i \tag{10b}$$

$$\mu_i^t \in [\mu_{i,\chi_i^t}^{\min}, \mu_{i,\chi_i^t}^{\max}], \mu_i^t \in \mathbb{Z}, c_i^t \in [1, c_{i,\chi_i^t}^{\max}], c_i^t \in \mathbb{Z}, \forall t, i \tag{10c}$$

$$\rho_i^t < 1, \forall t, i \tag{10d}$$

$$D_i^t \le Q_i^t, \forall t, i \tag{10e}$$

$$\sum_{i}^{U} w_i^t = 1 \text{ if } \sum_{i}^{U} \chi_i^t \ge 1, \forall t, i \tag{10f}$$

where (10a) indicates the binary nature of offloading decisions. (10b) is the time-average budgets of energy consumption $\hat{E}_i$ and cost $\hat{P}_i$, respectively. (10c) indicates the available range of per-instance resource allocation and instance number, respectively, depending on the offloading decision. (10d) constrains the maximum queuing system utilization. (10e) indicates the data causality. (10f) limits the total bandwidth allocation, which only applies when there exist UEs that offload their workload to the cloud.

However, achieving an optimal solution for a long-term optimization problem with time-average constraints typically necessitates knowledge of future task loads, which is hard to obtain due to the dynamic nature of UEs. To address this issue, we leverage Lyapunov Optimization to transform the long-term optimization challenge into a queue stability problem, which can be handled within each time step. We first define two virtual queues E_i^t and P_i^t for the long-term energy consumption and cost, respectively.

$$E_i^{t+1} = \max\{E_i^t + \alpha^e(e_i^t - \hat{E}_i), 0\},\ P_i^{t+1} = \max\{P_i^t + \alpha^p(p_i^t - \hat{P}_i), 0\} \tag{11}$$

where α^e and α^p are positive scaling factors of the penalty for violating their respective budgets. Intuitively, when the energy consumption or cost exceeds the preset budget, the respective virtual queue would be populated, otherwise, the queue would be consumed. Thus the time-average value would not exceed its budget only if the corresponding virtual queue is stabilized. Let $\mathbf{\Theta}^t = \{\mathbf{Q}^t, \mathbf{E}^t, \mathbf{P}^t\}$, where $\mathbf{Q}^t = \{Q_i^t\}_{i=1}^U$, $\mathbf{E}^t = \{E_i^t\}_{i=1}^U$, and $\mathbf{P}^t = \{P_i^t\}_{i=1}^U$, the long-term energy consumption and cloud service cost optimization process are combined and transformed into a joint queue stabilization problem. Then, we define the quadratic Lyapunov function and Lyapunov drift as:

$$L(\mathbf{Q}^t) \triangleq \frac{1}{2}\sum_{i=1}^{U}(Q_i^t)^2,\ L(\mathbf{E}^t) \triangleq \frac{1}{2}\sum_{i=1}^{U}(E_i^t)^2,\ L(\mathbf{P}^t) \triangleq \frac{1}{2}\sum_{i=1}^{U}(P_i^t)^2 \tag{12}$$

$$L(\mathbf{\Theta}^t) \triangleq L(\mathbf{Q}^t) + L(\mathbf{E}^t) + L(\mathbf{P}^t),\ \Delta L(\mathbf{\Theta}^t) \triangleq \mathbb{E}[L(\mathbf{\Theta}^{t+1}) - L(\mathbf{\Theta}^t)|\mathbf{\Theta}^t] \tag{13}$$

where we seek to minimize the drift in the long term, thereby stabilizing the combined queue $\mathbf{\Theta}(t)$. Then, we construct the upper-bounded Lyapunov drift-minus-utility function with Lemma 1:

Lemma 1. *The Lyapunov drift-minus-utility function satisfies the upper bound:*

$$\begin{aligned}\Delta L(\mathbf{\Theta}^t) - V\sum_{i=1}^{U}\mathbb{E}[d_i^t|\mathbf{\Theta}^t] \leq \Upsilon + \sum_{i=1}^{U}\{&Q_i^t\mathbb{E}[A_i^t - D_i^t|\mathbf{\Theta}^t] \\ &+E_i^t\mathbb{E}[e_i^t - \hat{E}_i|\mathbf{\Theta}^t] + P_i^t\mathbb{E}[p_i^t - \hat{P}_i|\mathbf{\Theta}^t] - V\mathbb{E}[d_i^t|\mathbf{\Theta}^t]\}\end{aligned} \tag{14}$$

where $\Upsilon = \frac{1}{2}\sum_{i=1}^U[(\bar{\lambda}_i\sum_{j=1}^N|v_j|)^2 + (\mu_{i,1}^{\max}c_{i,1}^{\max})^2] + \frac{\alpha^e}{2}\sum_{i=1}^U[(\hat{E}_i)^2 + (\epsilon^{full})^2] + \frac{\alpha^p}{2}\sum_{i=1}^U[(\hat{P}_i)^2 + (\delta\mu_{i,1}^{\max}c_{i,1}^{\max})^2]$ *and stays constant.* V *is the Lyapunov penalty weight, where* $V = 0$ *indicates minimizing the drift only, and* $V > 0$ *indicates a joint optimization of the drift and the processing queue backlog.*

Proof. Let $\Delta L(\mathbf{Q}^t) \triangleq \mathbb{E}[L(\mathbf{Q}^{t+1}) - L(\mathbf{Q}^t)|\mathbf{\Theta}^t]$, we have:

$$\begin{aligned}\Delta L(\mathbf{Q}^t) &= \mathbb{E}[\frac{1}{2}\sum_{i=1}^{U}(Q_i^{t+1})^2 - \frac{1}{2}\sum_{i=1}^{U}(Q_i^t)^2|\mathbf{\Theta}^t] \\ &\leq \sum_{i=1}^{U}Q_i^t\mathbb{E}[(A_i^t - D_i^t)|\mathbf{\Theta}^t] + \frac{1}{2}\sum_{i=1}^{U}[(\bar{\lambda}_i\sum_{j=1}^{N}|v_j|)^2 + (\mu_{i,1}^{\max}c_{i,1}^{\max})^2] \\ &\triangleq \sum_{i=1}^{U}[(\bar{\lambda}_i\sum_{j=1}^{N}|v_j|)^2 + \Upsilon^Q\end{aligned} \tag{15}$$

Similarly, let $\Delta L(\mathbf{E}^t) \triangleq \mathbb{E}[L(\mathbf{E}^{t+1}) - L(\mathbf{E}^t)|\boldsymbol{\Theta}^t]$ and $\Delta L(\mathbf{P}^t) \triangleq \mathbb{E}[L(\mathbf{P}^{t+1}) - L(\mathbf{P}^t)|\boldsymbol{\Theta}^t]$, we have:

$$\begin{aligned}
\Delta L(\mathbf{E}^t) &= \mathbb{E}[\frac{1}{2}\sum_{i=1}^{U}(E_i^{t+1})^2 - \frac{1}{2}\sum_{i=1}^{U}(E_i^t)^2|\boldsymbol{\Theta}^t] \\
\leq & \alpha^e \sum_{i=1}^{U} E_i^t \mathbb{E}[e_i^t - \hat{E}_i|\boldsymbol{\Theta}^t] + \frac{\alpha^e}{2}\sum_{i=1}^{U}[(\epsilon^{full})^2 + (\hat{E}_i)^2] \\
\triangleq & \alpha^e \sum_{i=1}^{U} E_i^t \mathbb{E}[e_i^t - \hat{E}_i|\boldsymbol{\Theta}^t] + \Upsilon^E
\end{aligned} \tag{16}$$

$$\begin{aligned}
\Delta L(\mathbf{P}^t) &= \mathbb{E}[\frac{1}{2}\sum_{i=1}^{U}(P_i^{t+1})^2 - \frac{1}{2}\sum_{i=1}^{U}(P_i^t)^2|\boldsymbol{\Theta}^t] \\
\leq & \alpha^p \sum_{i=1}^{U} P_i^t \mathbb{E}[p_i^t - \hat{P}_i|\boldsymbol{\Theta}^t] + \frac{\alpha^p}{2}\sum_{i=1}^{U}[(\delta\mu_{i,1}^{\max} c_{i,1}^{\max})^2 + (\hat{P}_i)^2] \\
\triangleq & \alpha^p \sum_{i=1}^{U} P_i^t \mathbb{E}[p_i^t - \hat{P}_i|\boldsymbol{\Theta}^t] + \Upsilon^P
\end{aligned} \tag{17}$$

Let $\Upsilon = \Upsilon^Q + \Upsilon^E + \Upsilon^P$, then summing (15), (16), and (17) leads to the proof.

With such formulations, the long-term constrained optimization problem **P1** is converted to a series of per-time-step sub-problems, where we seek to greedily minimize the upper bound of the drift-minus-utility function at each time step. With all constants and uncontrolled variables omitted, we can formulate the per-time-step sub-problem (**P2**) as:

$$\begin{aligned}
\mathbf{P2}: \max_{\chi_i^t, \mu_i^t, c_i^t, w_i^t} & \sum_{i=1}^{U}\{\alpha^Q(Q_i^t + V)d_i^t - E_i^t e_i^t - P_i^t p_i^t\} \\
& s.t.\ (10a), (10c), (10d), (10e)
\end{aligned} \tag{18}$$

where α^Q is an adjustable factor for magnitude control.

Theorem 1. ***P1*** *and* ***P2*** *are NP-hard problems.*

Proof. Consider a degraded version of **P2**, where the objective is restricted to minimizing the queue length at each time step, disregarding the energy and cost objectives. This simplified problem is equivalent to the constrained sum partition problem, where the task is to partition a set of integers into two subsets with constraints on the sums of the subsets, which is known to be NP-hard. Since **P2** represents a simplified form of **P1**, **P1** is also NP-hard.

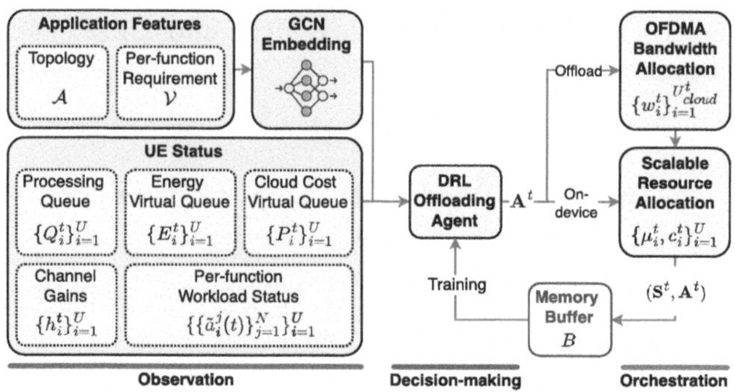

Fig. 3. DASFO architecture overview.

4 Design of DASFO

As illustrated in Fig. 3, DASFO continuously gathers information from the environment and feed into the DRL agent, which decides whether offloading workloads to the cloud. For UEs opting to offload, network bandwidth is allocated based on their signal strength and queuing status. Finally, computation resources are elastically allocated on-demand.

4.1 DRL Offloading Agent

State Observation: Let $\tilde{a}_i^j(t)$ denote the observed workloads on function j, we can categorize the state observation as:

1. UE status $\{Q_i^t, E_i^t, P_i^t, h_i^t\}_{i=1}^U$: Length of the workload processing queue, energy consumption and cost virtual queue, and channel gains.
2. Per-function workload status $\{\{\tilde{a}_i^j(t)\}_{j=1}^N\}_{i=1}^U$: The observed remaining workloads on each function.

Action: As the initial output of the neural network within the DRL agent is naturally a continuous variable $\tilde{\chi}_i^t \in [0, 1]$, we leverage order-preserving quantization (OPQ) [7] to discretize the output, and generate up to $U - 1$ candidate actions in addition, while preserving the orignal order.

Reward: As P2 can be solved within each time step, we directly utilize its objective as the reward.

The policy network is a neural network that approximates the policy, defining the DRL agent's strategy for selecting actions given the current state of the environment. In this case, as functions often exhibit dependencies that directly affect execution order and performance [17], utilizing the topology information of the application is beneficial for making more strategic offloading decisions. We adopt Graph Convolutional Network (GCN) for the application DAG embedding, which is widely known to be able to effectively capture the structural dependencies [23] and provide a foundational understanding of the DAG topology and per-function features. Then, the topology embedding, together with the state observation $\mathbf{S}^t \leftarrow \{Q_i^t, E_i^t, P_i^t, h_i^t, \{\tilde{a}_i^j(t)\}_{j=1}^N\}_{i=1}^U$, are fed into a two-layer Multi-Layer Perceptron, ending with a Sigmoid layer, outputting the continuous action $\tilde{\chi}_i^t \in [0,1]$.

4.2 OFDMA Bandwidth Allocation

In this phase, we seek to find a near-optimal network bandwidth allocation for each UE that offloads its workloads to the cloud. The primary focus here is maximizing the overall utility (i.e. the network throughput) by strategically distributing the bandwidth capacity, where a higher allocation is expected when a UE has a longer processing queue backlog or higher channel gain. Let $\mathcal{U}_{cloud}^t$ denote the set of UEs that offload their workloads to the cloud and $\mathbf{w^t} = \{w_i\}_{i=1}^{\mathcal{U}_{cloud}^t}$, we formulate the bandwidth allocation sub-problem:

$$\begin{aligned} \mathbf{P3}: \max_{\mathbf{w^t}} \sum_{i=1}^{\mathcal{U}_{cloud}^t} \{\alpha^Q(Q_i^t + V)d_{net,i}^t\} \\ s.t.\ (10e), (10f) \end{aligned} \tag{19}$$

Despite the objective being a monotonic function over the allocated bandwidth, it's challenging to obtain a closed-form solution that maximizes the overall utility for all UEs. Here we leverage the Lagrange primal-dual method to simplify and solve **P3** sub-optimally. Let $\Psi(\mathbf{w}^t) \triangleq \sum_{i=1}^{\mathcal{U}_{cloud}^t}\{\alpha^Q(Q_i^t + V)d_{net,i}^t\}$, we formulate the Lagrangian function as:

$$\mathcal{L}(\mathbf{w}^t, \phi) = \sum_{i=1}^{\mathcal{U}_{cloud}^t} \Psi(w_i^t) - \phi\left(\sum_{i=1}^{\mathcal{U}_{cloud}^t} w_i^t - 1\right) \tag{20}$$

where ϕ is the dual variable, and $\left(\sum_{i=1}^{\mathcal{U}_{cloud}^t} w_i^t - 1\right)$ indicates the violation of the bandwidth constraint. Then, we define the dual function:

$$\mathcal{D}(\phi) = \max_{\mathbf{w}^t} \mathcal{L}(\mathbf{w}^t, \phi) \tag{21}$$

where the objective is now minimizing the dual function $\mathcal{D}(\phi)$ with respect to ϕ, which can be solved per UE. We first set the derivative of $\mathcal{L}(w_i^t, \phi)$ to zero:

$$\Psi^{'}(w_i^t) = \alpha^Q(Q_i^t + V)\{\log_2(\frac{Ph_i^t}{N_0 W w_i^t} + 1) - \frac{Ph_i^t}{\ln(2)N_0 W w_i^t\left(\frac{Ph_i^t}{N_0 W w_i^t} + 1\right)}\} \tag{22}$$

$$\frac{\mathrm{d}\mathcal{L}(w_i^t, \phi)}{\mathrm{d}w_i^t} = \Psi^{'}(w_i^t) - \phi = 0 \tag{23}$$

where the term $\frac{Ph_i^t}{\ln(2)N_0 W w_i^t\left(\frac{Ph_i^t}{N_0 W w_i^t}+1\right)}$ is approximately a constant, especially under a higher signal-to-noise ratio (SNR, calculated with $\frac{Ph_i^t}{N_0 W w_i^t}$). Merge this term into ϕ and obtain an approximated solution for (23) for a fixed ϕ:

$$w_i^t = \frac{Ph_i^t}{N_0 W(2^{\frac{\phi}{\alpha Q(Q_i^t+V)}} - 1)} \tag{24}$$

where ϕ must be positive due to the monotonically increasing nature of $\Psi(\mathbf{w}^t)$. Finally, we can leverage gradient descent ($\Delta\phi \leftarrow \sum_{i=1}^{|\mathcal{U}_{cloud}^t|} w_i^t - 1$) to iteratively optimize ϕ. Suppose the algorithm takes I_ϕ iterations to converge, the computation complexity is $O(I_\phi \cdot |\mathcal{U}_{cloud}^t|)$.

4.3 Scalable Computation Resource Allocation

Here the primary focus shifts to allocating the computation resource at each time step based on the offloading decision. We set the goal of this phase to minimize the estimated steady-state queue length, and seek a balance with energy consumption or cost, depending on the current offloading decision.

Based on Erlang's formula for M/M/c queue, we can obtain the steady-state length of the processing queue as:

$$\lim_{t\to\infty} Q_i^t = \lambda_i^t(\frac{\mathcal{P}_i^t}{p_i^t - \lambda_i^t} + \frac{1}{\mu_i^t}) \tag{25}$$

$$\mathcal{P}_i^t \triangleq [\sum_{i=0}^{k-1} \frac{k!(1-\rho_i^t)}{i!(k\rho_i^t)^{k-i}} + 1]^{-1} \tag{26}$$

where $\mathcal{P}_i^t \triangleq [\sum_{i=0}^{k-1} \frac{k!(1-\rho_i^t)}{i!(k\rho_i^t)^{k-i}} + 1]^{-1}$ represents the probability that an arriving workload is forced to join the queue (i.e. all instances are occupied). Then, we can formulate the resource allocation sub-problem (P4):

$$\begin{aligned} \mathbf{P4}: \min_{\mu_i^t, c_i^t} & \sum_{i=1}^{U} \lim_{t\to\infty} Q_i^t + \sum_{i=1}^{U}\{E_i^t e_i^t\} + \sum_{i=1}^{U}\{P_i^t p_i^t\} \\ s.t.\ & (10d), (10e), (10f) \end{aligned} \tag{27}$$

where the first term is the estimated steady-state processing queue length, which has already been proven to be convex over the per-instance resource and the number of instances [20]. The latter two terms are both proportional to the allocated resource, as formulated in (3) and (4), respectively. As a result, **P4** is a multi-convex optimization problem [15] that can be solved per UE.

Since obtaining a closed-form solution for **P4** is challenging due to its complexity and non-linearity, we adopt a bi-section-based approach to obtain the sub-optimal allocation at each time step. Intuitively, within each iteration, the algorithm seeks the zero point of the first derivative of the objective function over per-instance resource and the number of instances. We treat the per-instance resource as a continuous variable during the optimization and round it before outputting. Suppose the inner and outer loops take I_μ and I_c iterations to converge, respectively, the computation complexity is $O(I_\mu \cdot I_c)$.

4.4 Execution and Training

The DRL agent of DASFO leverages an actor-critic-like architecture. First, the policy network π_θ is initialized with random parameters, and a static embedding of the application topology is generated using the GCN-based embedding network. The main process operates over time $t = 1, 2, \ldots, \mathcal{T}$, where at each time step, the current state of the system $\mathbf{S}^t$ is observed, which includes information about the queues and remaining workloads for all UEs. Using the policy network π_θ, a continuous action is generated based on the current state and the static DAG embedding, representing potential offloading decisions. These continuous actions are then quantized into a set of discrete candidate actions with OPQ. Unlike typical model-free critics (DDPG [9], SAC [5], etc.) built with DNN to estimate the value of each action, the critic in this algorithm solves the computation resource allocation problem analytically. After that, each candidate action is evaluated by calculating its reward based on the objective function of **P2**, where the action with the highest reward is selected for execution in the actual environment. The selected state-action pair is then stored in the memory buffer B, serving as guidance for future training.

At regular intervals determined by Δt, if the size of the memory B grows beyond a fixed threshold $\hat{B}$, the offline training process is triggered. A batch of historical data is sampled from the memory to train the DRL agent by minimizing the loss function, progressively refining the decision-making process and adapting to the changing environments. Here we leverage Adam algorithm with Mean Squared Error (MSE) as the loss function.

5 Evaluation and Discussion

5.1 Simulation Setup

The workload arrival across all UEs follows an exponential distribution with an equal mean rate. Without loss of generality, we set up a homogeneous computing architecture on both the UE and the cloud. Thus the available per-instance computing resource lies in a unified range $[128, 1536]$. For workloads processed on-device ($\chi_i^t = 0$), we let $\max(c_{i,0}^{\max})$ stay fixed at 1, indicating the limited performance. On the contrary, the cloud has a wider set of choices, where the available number of instances ranges from $[1, 3]$, allowing multiple scalable instances in parallel. Table 1 presents other environment setup parameters, which unify across all UEs and stay fixed unless specifically stated.

The GCN embedding network is equipped with 2 hidden layers with 64 neurons and a dropout rate of 0.2. The policy network is a single linear layer with 64 neurons, and the output is a Sigmoid function. The agent is trained every 10 time step with an initial learning rate set to $1e-3$, along with a scheduler that runs at every 10 training step with a decay rate of $1e-2$. The memory buffer size is set to $B = 1000$, and the batch size is set to 100. For the output quantization, the initial number of candidate actions is set to $Z^t = U$ and updated with:

$$Z^t = 1 + \max\{argmax\{\hat{\mathbf{A}}_z^{t-j}\}_{z=1}^{Z^{t-j}}\}_{j=1}^{\Delta T^{OPQ}} \tag{28}$$

Table 1. Simulation environment parameters setup

Average arrival rate $\bar{\lambda}_i = 1$	Function number $N = 5$
Time step $\Delta T = 1$	Cloud rental price $\delta = 1e-3$
Idle energy consumption $\epsilon^{idle} = 3.5$	Full-load energy consumption $\epsilon^{full} = 50$
Cost budget $\hat{P}_i = 2.5$	Energy budget $\hat{E}_i = 10$
Energy penalty scaling factor $\alpha^e = 1$	Cost penalty scaling factor $\alpha^p = 1e-3$
Lyapunov penalty weight $V = 1e6$	Queue magnitude control $\alpha^Q = 1e-7$

where ΔT^{OPQ} is the update interval respective to the training steps. Intuitively, as training progresses, a smaller index of the selected candidate action indicates a more strategic set of offloading decisions, as actions closer to the initial output become more likely to be chosen.

For comparison, we employ the following baseline approaches:

1. LOCAL: All workloads are processed on-device, thus the cost stays at 0.
2. CLOUD: All workloads are offloaded to the cloud, thus the energy consumption stays at 0.
3. RANDOM: Workloads are randomly processed on-device or over the cloud.
4. CD: A near-optimal solution for **P2** based on [2] that iteratively updates the binary offloading decision variable through one-dimensional searches, while at the cost of higher decision-making duration.
5. ETHC [20]: A DRL-based approach modified to use the same environment formulation, action space, and reward design as DASFO, but without dependency awareness and relying only on an MLP-based policy network.

5.2 Performance Results

Impact of time-average budget configuration: Budget configuration directly influences the dynamics of the energy and cost virtual queues. Tighter budgets tend to cause longer virtual queues, increasing the risk of budget violations. Since virtual queue length determines the corresponding weight in solving **P4**, this also impacts the resource allocation phase. Figure 4 compares various budget settings using time-averaged metrics after ETHC and DASFO converge. LOCAL and RANDOM consistently violate the energy budget and are excluded from the queue length graph due to instability. Similarly, CLOUD is excluded from the cost graph for exceeding the cost budget under the lowest setting and from the energy graph due to zero energy consumption. CD is omitted due to its performance being similar to DASFO. As shown in Figs. 4aand 4b, increasing the cost or energy budget enables more offloading, which slightly reduces average energy consumption and cost, respectively. Higher budgets reduce the risk of virtual queue accumulation, lowering their impact on resource allocation and ultimately shortening the processing queue. Both ETHC and DASFO

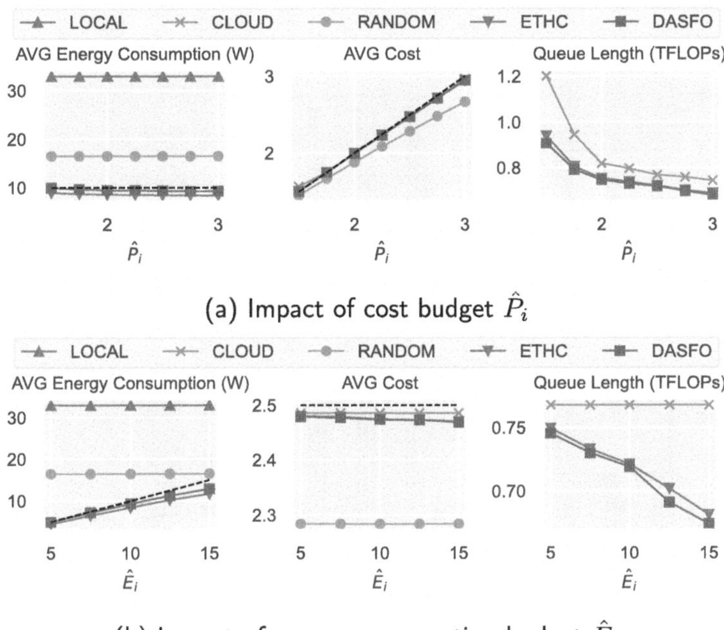

(a) Impact of cost budget $\hat{P}_i$

(b) Impact of energy consumption budget $\hat{E}_i$

Fig. 4. Impact of average budget configuration.

strategically offload to the cloud while adhering to energy constraints, achieving shorter processing queues than even the fully offloaded CLOUD baseline. In contrast, CLOUD frequently exceeds its cost budget, leading to a growing cost virtual queue that shifts the optimization focus toward cost minimization at the expense of processing latency, particularly under load surges. Across all scenarios, DASFO maintains both energy and cost within budget and consistently outperforms ETHC in minimizing processing queue length, especially under stricter cloud rental budgets.

Impact of Penalty Coefficient: The penalty coefficient determines how rapidly a virtual queue grows when the time-average budget is violated. A higher coefficient accelerates accumulation, shifting resource allocation priorities toward budget enforcement at the expense of processing queue minimization, potentially reducing throughput. As shown in Fig. 5a, increasing the cost penalty reduces average cost across all approaches but raises energy consumption. ETHC is particularly sensitive to penalty changes, struggling to stabilize the processing queue and meet energy constraints under high cost penalties. In contrast, DASFO closely matches CD's near-optimal performance, maintaining energy compliance and queue stability through more effective offloading, despite using fewer cloud resources. A similar pattern is observed for the energy penalty in Fig. 5b. Notably, at $\alpha^e = 0.01$, DASFO's energy consumption is lower than at $\alpha^e = 0.1$ because the agent retains more workloads locally under weaker penal-

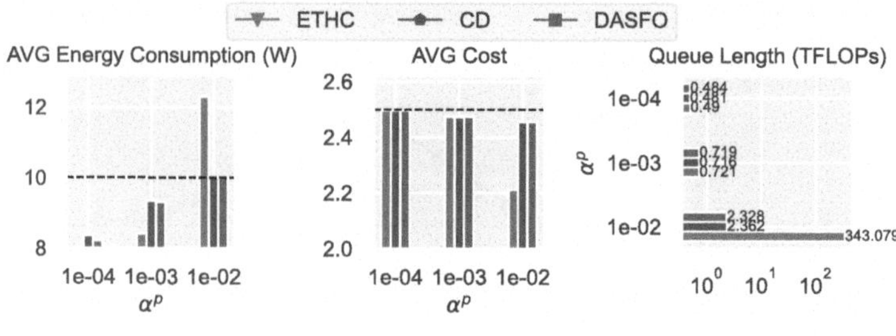

(a) Impact of cost penalty coefficient α^p

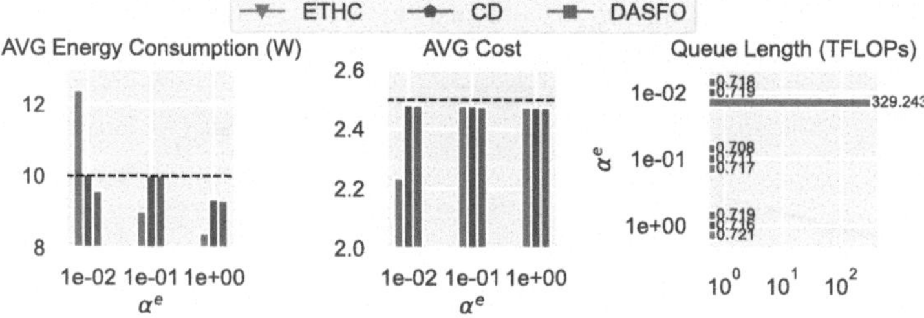

(b) Impact of energy consumption penalty coefficient α^e

Fig. 5. Impact of penalty coefficient configuration.

ties. This increases the likelihood of exceeding the energy budget, triggering the resource allocation phase, which then reduces energy usage but leads to longer processing queues.

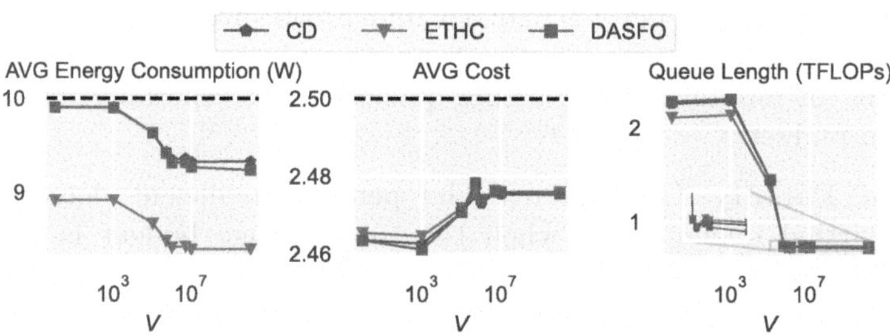

Fig. 6. Impact of Lyapunov penalty weight V.

Impact of Queue Configuration: Fig. 6 shows how varying the Lyapunov penalty weight (V) affects system performance. As V increases (up to $1e6$), average energy consumption and processing queue length decrease, while cost rises, reflecting increased offloading and a higher departure rate. Around $V = 1e6$, cost peaks, after which further increases have little effect, as the average cost approaches the budget limit and triggers the resource allocation mechanism to prevent budget violations.

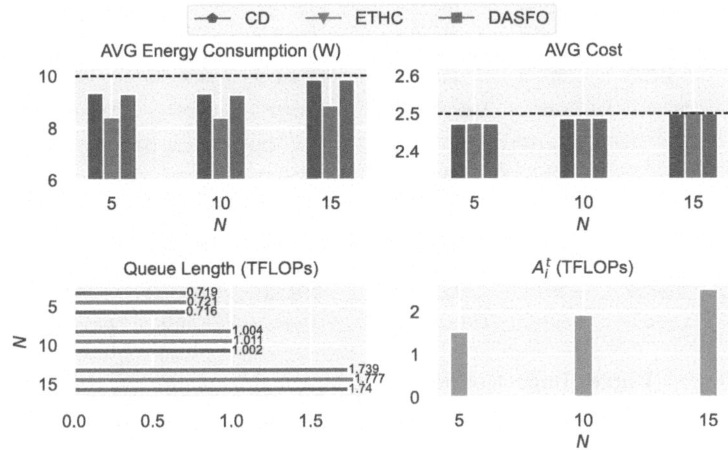

Fig. 7. Comparison results with various N.

Impact of Workload Intensity: We fix the average arrival rate $\tilde{\lambda}_i$ and vary the number of functions (N) by randomly generating application topologies to simulate different workload intensities. As shown in Fig. 7, higher workload intensity leads to increased cloud offloading and thus higher average cost. Notably, the processing queue length grows disproportionately compared to arrivals: while A_i^t increases by 25.9% from $N = 5$ to $N = 10$, the queue length rises by approximately 42.8%, due to increased inter-task dependencies and blocking in more complex topologies. Although all three approaches eventually stabilize the queue, its length still increases under fixed energy and cost budgets. DASFO consistently maintains a queue length and offloading behavior closer to the near-optimal CD baseline, whereas ETHC exhibits the highest queue length and slightly exceeds the cost budget at $N = 15$.

Impact of Network Bandwidth Capacity: This section evaluates how different approaches respond to network congestion, where limited bandwidth is the primary bottleneck. At each time step, channel gain and UE-to-access-point distance are randomly generated following the setup in [1], using a 5855 MHz carrier frequency based on the 5G n47 V2X standard [6]. As shown in Fig. 8, both ETHC and DASFO closely track the near-optimal CD baseline, with DASFO showing a slight edge over ETHC in queue length reduction. As bandwidth increases, offloading becomes easier, boosting the departure rate and reducing queue lengths—at the cost of higher average cloud usage. Unlike CD, ETHC and DASFO initially exhibit a slight rise in energy consumption due to fewer on-device workloads, leaving more headroom for energy usage growth.

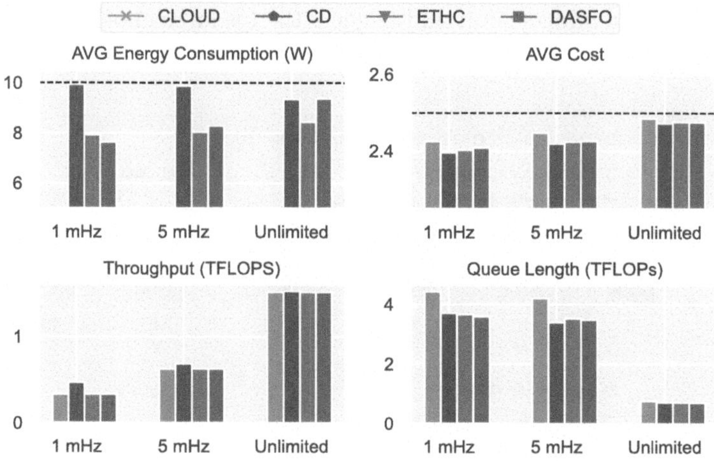

Fig. 8. Impact of network bandwidth capacity W.

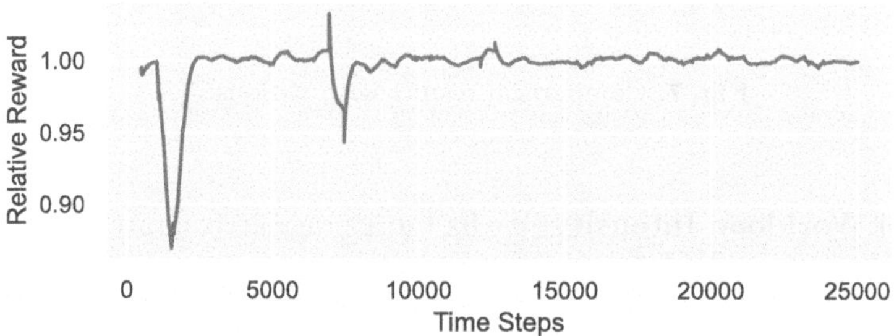

Fig. 9. Relative reward to CD.

Training and Execution: Figure 9 shows the relative reward of an untrained DASFO compared to CD over time, with a limited cost budget of 1.5 for slower training. DASFO starts with a high initial reward due to having more candidate actions (Z^t), which helps guide future training. A drop in reward occurs between 1000–2500 time steps as DASFO explores a wider action space. After around 10,000 steps, the reward stabilizes with small fluctuations. Note that the relative reward can exceed 1 because CD, being near-optimal, doesn't explore the full action space, and both strategies may adjust at different times due to environmental changes. Table 2 shows the average decision-making duration for different U, covering both offloading and resource allocation. CD takes significantly longer due to its iterative process. While DASFO requires a higher minimal duration than ETHC due to its embedding phase, it performs better on average and maximum decision durations, indicating fewer generated candidate actions due to the more strategic output of the DRL agent.

Table 2. Decision-making duration

U	Decision-making Duration (ms)								
	CD			ETHC			DASFO		
	Avg	Min	Max	Avg	Min	Max	Avg	Min	Max
10	109.5	0.4	341.8	47.0	1.4	103.9	14.4	2.8	88.3
20	424.0	1.1	897.4	176.7	2.1	326.0	83.1	3.8	295.1
30	1133.4	2.2	967652.0	735.2	3.4	1048330.2	76.8	4.2	637.5

6 Conclusion

This paper presents DASFO, a unified framework for dependency-aware offloading, network bandwidth allocation, and scalable resource management, stabilizing long-term processing queues under energy and cost constraints. By applying Lyapunov Optimization, long-term goals are decomposed into tractable subproblems, while a DRL agent guides offloading using system-state awareness. DASFO also features a near-optimal bandwidth allocator that prioritizes UEs by signal quality and a scalable resource allocator that dynamically adjusts instance count and compute capacity. Experimental results demonstrate DASFO's ability to maintain queue stability for dependent functions with minimal overhead, balancing energy and cost. Future work includes extending DASFO to non-standalone networks for broader applicability and integrating with emerging paradigms like roadside edge computing for enhanced latency performance.

References

1. Bi, S., Huang, L., Wang, H., Zhang, Y.J.A.: Lyapunov-guided deep reinforcement learning for stable online computation offloading in mobile-edge computing networks. IEEE Trans. Wireless Commun. **20**(11), 7519–7537 (2021)
2. Bi, S., Zhang, Y.J.: Computation rate maximization for wireless powered mobile-edge computing with binary computation offloading. IEEE Trans. Wireless Commun. **17**(6), 4177–4190 (2018)
3. Fang, J., Qu, D., Chen, H., Liu, Y.: Dependency-aware dynamic task offloading based on deep reinforcement learning in mobile-edge computing. IEEE Trans. Netw. Serv. Manage. **21**(2), 1403–1415 (2024)
4. Feng, C., et al.: Cost-minimized computation offloading of online multi-function services in collaborative edge-cloud networks. IEEE Trans. Netw. Serv. Management, pp. 1–1 (2022)
5. Haarnoja, T., Zhou, A., Abbeel, P., Levine, S.: Soft actor-critic: Off-policy maximum entropy deep reinforcement learning with a stochastic actor (2018)
6. Harounabadi, M., Soleymani, D.M., Bhadauria, S., Leyh, M., Roth-Mandutz, E.: V2x in 3g pp standardization: Nr sidelink in release-16 and beyond. IEEE Commun. Standards Mag. **5**(1), 12–21 (2021)
7. Huang, L., Bi, S., Zhang, Y.J.A.: Deep reinforcement learning for online computation offloading in wireless powered mobile-edge computing networks. IEEE Trans. Mob. Comput. **19**(11), 2581–2593 (2020)

8. Jin, B., Liu, H.: Adapt: action-aware driving caption transformer. In: CAAI International Conference on Artificial Intelligence, pp. 473–477. Springer (2023)
9. Lillicrap, T.P., et al.: Continuous control with deep reinforcement learning (2019)
10. Lin, S.C., et al.: The architectural implications of autonomous driving: Constraints and acceleration. SIGPLAN Not. **53**(2), 751–766 (mar 2018)
11. Lv, X., Du, H., Ye, Q.: Tbtoa: A dag-based task offloading scheme for mobile edge computing. In: ICC 2022 - IEEE International Conference on Communications, pp. 4607–4612 (2022)
12. Mundhenk, P., Hamann, A., Heyl, A., Ziegenbein, D.: Reliable distributed systems. In: 2022 Design, Automation & Test in Europe Conference & Exhibition (DATE), pp. 287–291 (2022)
13. NVIDIA: (Jun 2024). https://docs.nvidia.com/deploy/mps/
14. Qin, P., Fu, Y., Tang, G., Zhao, X., Geng, S.: Learning based energy efficient task offloading for vehicular collaborative edge computing. IEEE Trans. Veh. Technol. **71**(8), 8398–8413 (2022)
15. Shen, X., Diamond, S., Udell, M., Gu, Y., Boyd, S.: Disciplined multi-convex programming (2016)
16. Thubert, P., Cavalcanti, D., Vilajosana, X., Schmitt, C., Farkas, J.: Reliable and Available Wireless Technologies. Internet-Draft draft-ietf-raw-technologies-10, Internet Engineering Task Force (Sep 2024), work in Progress
17. Wang, J., Hu, J., Min, G., Zhan, W., Zomaya, A.Y., Georgalas, N.: Dependent task offloading for edge computing based on deep reinforcement learning. IEEE Trans. Comput. **71**(10), 2449–2461 (2022)
18. Xiao, Z., Shu, J., Jiang, H., Min, G., Chen, H., Han, Z.: Perception task offloading with collaborative computation for autonomous driving. IEEE J. Sel. Areas Commun. **41**(2), 457–473 (2023)
19. Yu, Z., Gong, Y., Gong, S., Guo, Y.: Joint task offloading and resource allocation in UAV-enabled mobile edge computing. IEEE Internet Things J. **7**(4), 3147–3159 (2020)
20. Zhang, J., Yu, H., Fan, G., Li, Z.: Elastic task offloading and resource allocation over hybrid cloud: a reinforcement learning approach. IEEE Trans. Netw. Serv. Manage. **21**(2), 1983–1997 (2024)
21. Zhang, J., Huang, J., Jin, S., Lu, S.: Vision-language models for vision tasks: a survey. IEEE Trans. Pattern Anal. Mach. Intell. **46**(8), 5625–5644 (2024)
22. Zhang, J., et al.: Dependent task offloading mechanism for cloud–edge-device collaboration. J. Netw. Comput. Appl. **216**, 103656 (2023)
23. Zhang, S., Tong, H., Xu, J., Maciejewski, R.: Graph convolutional networks: a comprehensive review. Comput. Social Netw. **6**(1), 11 (2019)

Towards Reliable Distributed Systems for Safety-Critical Vehicle-Road-Cloud Continuum

Yifan Du[1(✉)], Zhiying Song[2], Nan Li[1], Shuo Li[1], and Hao Sun[1]

[1] Corporate Research, Robert Bosch GmbH, Shanghai, China
{yifan.du,nan.li3,shuo.li1,hao.sun4}@cn.bosch.com
[2] School of Vehicle and Mobility, Tsinghua University, Beijing, China
song-zy24@mails.tsinghua.edu.cn

Abstract. The vehicle–road–cloud continuum has emerged as a promising architecture for enabling intelligent connected vehicles, supporting safety-critical functions such as infrastructure-assisted driving and cognition-intensive AI inference. However, practical deployment remains hindered by gaps in timing assurance, fault handling, and adaptability—especially in edge and cloud platforms built on general-purpose hardware and software. This paper presents a reliable system that contains: a dependability-aware coordination layer for edge-hosted V2X services and a latency-aware offloading framework for AI-based vehicle functions. The former enhances runtime monitoring, fault recovery, and real-time supervision without modifying the underlying orchestration stack; the latter enables end-to-end latency tracing and adaptive QoS control for large-scale model inference over the 5G network. The integrated system is implemented and evaluated in real-world urban street scenarios using commercial-off-the-shelf SoCs and 5G gateways. The system targets safety-critical use cases and derives timing budgets from standard V2X safety analyses, enabling risk-aware evaluation of deadline violations. Experimental results demonstrate improved fault resilience, tighter timing guarantees, and reliable performance under dynamic compute and network conditions, offering a unified foundation for dependable distributed mobility systems.

Keywords: Internet of Vehicles · Intelligent Connected Vehicles · V2X · Mobile edge computing · 5G mobility · Edge Intelligence

1 Introduction

As vehicles become increasingly intelligent—powered by advanced perception and decision-making systems, further progress is becoming difficult to achieve through onboard intelligence alone. To overcome this limitation, the automotive industry is turning toward distributed architectures that integrate vehicles with roadside infrastructure and cloud platforms. This emerging paradigm,

L. Zhang and K.-K. R. Choo (Eds.): MobiQuitous 2025, LNICST 684, pp. 39–54, 2026.
https://doi.org/10.1007/978-3-032-22503-0_3

commonly referred to as the *vehicleroadcloud continuum* [19,20], enables safety-critical services such as infrastructure-assisted driving, collaborative perception, and remote AI inference by distributing computation across heterogeneous nodes and leveraging vehicular networks for communication [1,7].

Currently, onboard vehicle platforms are engineered to meet stringent real-time and functional safety requirements. In contrast, the reliability of roadside and cloud platforms remains at an early stage of development. These platforms are typically built on commercial off-the-shelf hardware and managed using cloud-native orchestration frameworks such as Kubernetes [1], which prioritize scalability and flexibility over strict timing and safety guarantees. As a result, they lack critical capabilities such as timing supervision, deterministic failover, and system-level fault isolation [2,4], which are essential for safety-relevant automotive applications. Similarly, although modern vehicular networks such as PC5, C-V2X and 5G communication offer improved latency and bandwidth [7], real-world deployments continue to experience congestion, jitter, and unpredictable quality-of-service fluctuations, especially in dense urban environments [12].

In this paper, we address the aforementioned challenges by focusing on two representative use cases drawn from real-world deployments of the vehicleroad cloud continuum. *The first* is infrastructure-assisted driving, where advanced driver-assistance systems (ADAS) or autonomous functions are enhanced by edge nodes, *e.g.*, connected Automatic Emergency Braking (AEB). These applications rely on low-latency communication and real-time coordination [6,8,9], yet cloud-native orchestration platforms like Kubernetes lack critical safety features such as failure recovery, timing supervision, and application-aware health monitoring [1]. *The second* case involves offloading large models, such as Vision-Language Models (VLMs) [14–16], which enhance perception and intent prediction but exceed the capabilities of onboard platforms. While offloading enables scalable inference [12], it introduces soft real-time requirements and strong reliance on 5G. Existing frameworks lack end-to-end latency observability and adaptive mechanisms for handling network jitter etc.

To address these limitations, we design and implement two complementary frameworks that enhance reliability and timing assurance in the most critical segments of the vehicleroadcloud continuum. Our main contributions are:

- A dependability-aware coordination framework for edge-hosted V2X services that operates alongside Kubernetes, providing timing supervision, fault detection, and workload reallocation without modifying the orchestration stack.
- A latency-aware offloading framework for AI-based in-vehicle functions, enabling distributed latency tracing, soft real-time verification, and declarative 5G QoS control via standardized APIs.
- On street evaluation of the system deployed in real-world scenarios with commercial-off-the-shelf SoCs and in-vehicle 5G gateways, demonstrating improved resilience, timing accuracy, and recovery under dynamic conditions.

Unlike prior work that targets isolated layers (*e.g.*, orchestration, networking, or computing), our approach delivers a practical system-level design aimed at the weakest links in the vehicleroadcloud continuum. We show that cloud-native tools can be extended—without overhaul—to meet the dependability demands of safety-critical vehicular applications. Through runtime monitoring, coordinated fallback, and QoS-aware adaptation, our work advances toward a unified and reliable architecture for distributed intelligent mobility. The work further grounds timing requirements in safety-analysis-derived budgets and discusses mitigation of QoD overheads and expanded fault and security coverage. These mechanisms strengthen the applicability of the proposed framework in safety-critical deployments.

2 Related Work

The evolution of intelligent connected vehicles increasingly relies on distributed systems integrating vehicles, roadside infrastructure, and cloud platforms [19,20]. As safety-critical and compute-intensive functions shift beyond the vehicle, new challenges emerge in meeting end-to-end latency and dependability requirements across heterogeneous components.

2.1 V2X Infrastructure and Orchestration

A growing body of research has explored infrastructure-assisted safety services for cooperative driving. The work in [4] identifies runtime resilience as a key challenge for cooperative ADAS, emphasizing the need for dynamic fault detection and coordinated failover. Perception sharing via edge nodes is explored in [9], while [8] develops a MEC-based collision avoidance system. Other studies focus on specific functions such as V2X-assisted braking [5] and vulnerable road user protection [6]. Limitations in C-V2X Mode 4 reliability under interference were documented in [7], reinforcing the need for infrastructure-based enhancements.

From a deployment standpoint, Ad-Astra [1] proposes a lightweight edge runtime for connected vehicles with built-in monitoring and redundancy, but focuses primarily on virtualization internals and lacks system-wide coordination. Similarly, orchestration for mixed-criticality tasks [10,11] has been studied in general cyber physical system and industrial settings, but without addressing the specific timing and fault recovery requirements of V2X.

In contrast, our work introduces a dependability-aware coordination layer that extends standard orchestration platforms with runtime timing validation, fault detection, and adaptive reallocation—tailored specifically for safety-critical V2X services operating on best-effort roadside compute.

2.2 Function Offloading and 5G Communication

To support large AI models such as VLMs and VLAs [14–16], recent vehicle systems increasingly rely on function offloading to edge or cloud infrastructure [12]. While this alleviates onboard compute constraints, it introduces challenges in maintaining latency guarantees over variable public 5G networks.

Existing offloading approaches primarily optimize task distribution through delay-aware [17] or energy-efficient [18] strategies. However, most rely on static network assumptions, lack stage-wise latency introspection, and do not integrate with 5G QoS APIs to respond to runtime variability.

Tools such as [13] enable offline latency analysis, but do not provide runtime control. Speculative execution frameworks [12] enhance responsiveness under uncertainty but are not tailored for V2X constraints or real-time cognition.

To address these gaps, our work presents a latency-aware offloading framework that both performs fine-grained latency tracing across the full sensor-to-cloud pipeline and dynamically adjusts network QoS via standardized 5G APIs. This enables soft real-time performance for safety-relevant cognition workloads and is validated using commercial-off-the-shelf SoCs and VLM models in live 5G environments.

2.3 Cross-Layer Reliability and Dependable System Design

The concept of reliable distributed systems for cyber physical system was introduced in [2], and later extended to support human-in-the-loop meta-verse systems [3]. These works establish key principles of dependability under compute and network uncertainty but do not explicitly address the unique orchestration, timing, and safety constraints in vehicular environments.

A persistent gap across prior studies is the absence of an integrated, cross-layer framework unifying orchestration, compute, and communication reliability. Most existing solutions focus on isolated aspects—such as deployment, inference, or networking—without holistic runtime supervision.

Our work bridges this gap with a unified system targeting the weakest links in the vehicleroadcloud stack: (1) best-effort edge compute lacking deterministic fault handling, and (2) opportunistic 5G communication vulnerable to latency fluctuation. We contribute runtime mechanisms for timing validation, fault mitigation, and QoS-adaptive inference—all deployable on unmodified commercial infrastructure and validated in real-world V2X deployments.

3 System Architecture

Our system architecture enables dependable, soft real-time execution of both safety-critical and cognition-intensive functions across the vehicleroadcloud continuum, in which the perception and computation capacity of the vehicle is largely extended. As illustrated in Fig. 1, it comprises three tightly integrated layers: *vehicle*, *roadside edge*, and *cloud*. These components communicate via PC5, 5G and Ethernet to form a unified pipeline for task offloading and coordination. To ensure reliability under dynamic conditions, the system incorporates a decentralized control plane that supports runtime fault detection, timing supervision, and adaptive service reconfiguration.

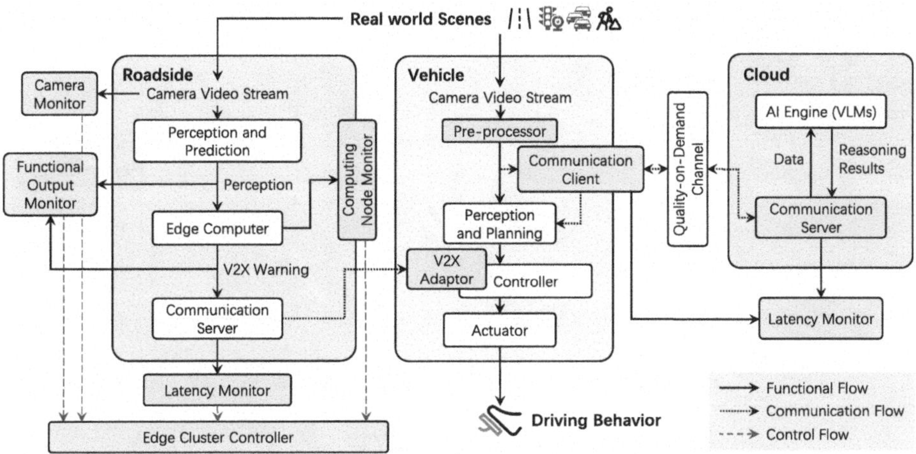

Fig. 1. System architecture of the proposed VehicleRoadCloud Continuum framework.

3.1 Motivating Use Cases

To motivate the design of our architecture, we analyze two representative real-time functions that highlight the contrasting demands across system layers: a safety-critical *V2X warning service* executed on the roadside edge, and a cognition-intensive *visionlanguage reasoning service* offloaded to the cloud. Both support downstream driving decisions but impose distinct timing, reliability, and orchestration requirements.

V2X Warning for Emergency Braking. Figure 2 illustrates a connected-AEB scenario in which roadside infrastructure detects vulnerable road users in a blind spot and transmits early collision warnings to approaching vehicles. Such infrastructure-assisted perception extends the vehicle's field of view beyond occlusions, improving reaction time and safety margins. However, it also introduces strict timing and reliability requirements—delayed or missed warnings can directly affect the system's ability to prevent accidents.

In this use case, multiple roadside cameras monitor traffic in real time, and edge servers process the video streams to detect and track vehicles and pedestrians, estimating collision risk. When a threat is detected, the roadside unit (RSU) broadcasts a warning message via the V2X channel. The onboard AEB module fuses this external warning with local perception data and, once the risk is confirmed, triggers emergency braking through the Controller Area Network (CAN). To maintain safety, the system must continuously monitor component health, isolate faults, and recover rapidly from sensing, computing, or communication failures.

Fig. 2. Infrastructure-assisted vulnerable road user (VRU) collision warning in an occluded intersection. Roadside cameras detect hidden pedestrians and broadcast low-latency V2X warnings to approaching vehicles, supplementing onboard perception for connected-AEB functions.

VisionLanguage Reasoning in the Cloud. Figure 3 shows a cloud-offloaded VLM pipeline that performs captioning and reasoning on complex driving scenes. By translating perception results into natural-language descriptions such as The car is merging into the lane to its left because there is a gap in traffic in its lane, it provides interpretable context for downstream decision modules or human supervision. This paradigm shifts part of the cognitive workload from the vehicle to the cloud, requiring adaptive offloading and network-quality management to maintain soft real-time performance under 5G variability.

In practice, the vehicle periodically captures video frames, applies lightweight pre-processing (*e.g.*, compression), and transmits the data to the cloud via gRPC. The cloud performs inference using large-scale models such as ADAPT [15] and returns the results to the vehicle for decision support. While this approach reduces onboard compute burden, it introduces strong dependency on network conditions; latency jitter or disconnections must be mitigated through fallback or degradation strategies to sustain responsiveness.

Together, these two use cases expose complementary challenges addressed by our system architecture—timing assurance, fault handling, and workload adaptability across heterogeneous nodes. The following sections detail the architecture and mechanisms used to meet these demands.

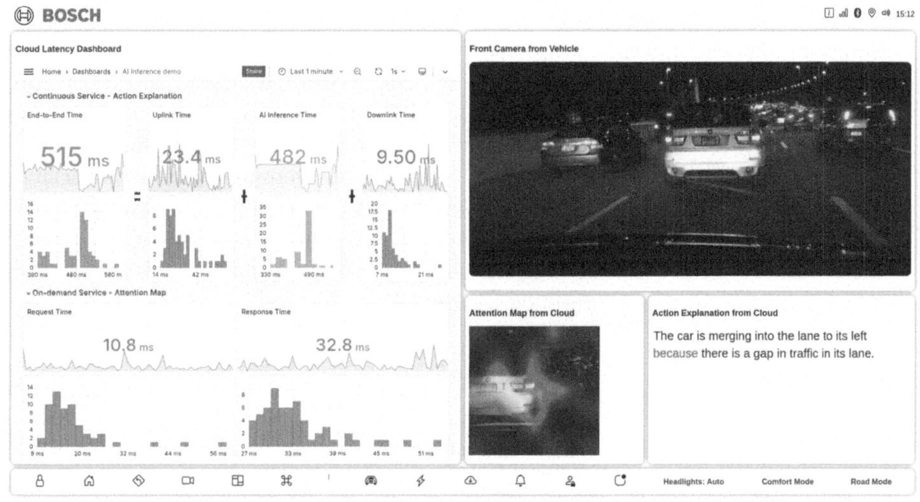

Fig. 3. Offloading of a visionlanguage model (VLM) for driving scene reasoning. Captured video frames are uploaded via 5G to a cloud inference service that generates contextual captions and explanations of surrounding traffic behaviors, providing enhanced situational understanding beyond onboard compute limits.

3.2 Timing Requirements and Safety Context

For the connected-AEB scenario, the end-to-end latency budget is derived from V2X safety-communication guidelines and functional-safety process requirements. Following the 100150 ms range recommended for crash-imminent V2V applications [22], we allocate $\approx$ 3050 ms to sensing/pre-processing, 80120 ms to edge inference, 1040 ms to communication, and $\approx$ 20 ms to actuation. To ensure the roadside warning remains effective within the driver's reaction window, we adopt a strict $\leq$ 120 ms deadline. The measured deadline-violation ratio (DVR) therefore quantifies the probability of exceeding this safety-derived timing budget and serves as a risk indicator.

3.3 Vehicle Layer

The vehicle layer serves as the front-end of the vehicleroadcloud continuum. It is responsible for data capture, processing, and interaction with external systems. Sensor data (*i.e.*, videos) is first pre-processed and then transmitted to the cloud for inference. Meanwhile, the vehicle receives V2X warnings and inference results to support local decision-making.

Two communication modes are supported at the vehicle side: Proactive RPC-based offloading to the cloud for AI inference tasks, and Reactive V2X communication with the roadside infrastructure for collaborative driving.

At the vehicle side, the following components are deployed:

- **Pre-processor**: Captures raw video frames and performs resizing, compression, and optional batching prior to transmission, *etc.*.
- **V2X Adaptor**: Receives broadcast warnings from roadside infrastructure via the PC5 interface, fuses them with onboard perception data, and triggers braking or evasive maneuvers via the vehicle's actuation controller.
- **Communication Client**: i) QoD (Quality-on-Demand) client interfaces with the 5G QoD API provided by the telecom operator, dynamically adjusting uplink bandwidth and latency class. ii) Remote Procedure Call (RPC) client initiates gRPC requests to offload preprocessed data to the cloud, and asynchronously receives inference results.

3.4 Roadside Edge Layer

The roadside edge layer provides real-time perception and orchestrates V2X services, such as collision prediction for connected AEB. It processes video feeds from multiple roadside cameras to detect and track traffic participants, assess motion risks, and issue timely warnings.

To ensure dependable operation on cost-efficient hardware and general-purpose orchestration platforms like Kubernetes [1], we introduce a lightweight *compute coordinator*. It continuously monitors system status, detects failures, and triggers automatic recovery actions to maintain service continuity.

At the roadside edge, the following components support situational awareness:

- **Camera Monitor**: Continuously probes stream health to detect disconnections, frame drops, and FPS jitter.
- **Computing Node Monitor**: Monitors edge compute node health, including CPU/GPU utilization, thermal status, and liveness.
- **Functional Output Monitor**: Observes perception outputs to detect silence failure, or other anomalies that may compromise downstream tasks.
- **Latency Monitor**: Measures end-to-end latency from frame capture to inference result. Ensures compliance with real-time deadlines.
- **Edge Cluster Controller**: Serves for fault handling etc. It detects runtime anomalies and reacts by restarting containers, or migrating workloads to backup nodes.

In addition to node or sensor failures, the coordinator monitors timing-related degradations such as clock drift, CPU/GPU contention, and thermal throttling, as well as network-partition-induced composite faults. Detection relies on time-sync offsets, resource-pressure metrics, and connectivity checks, triggering workload migration or rate adaptation when anomalies appear.

3.5 Cloud Layer

The cloud layer provides scalable computation for cognition-intensive tasks that exceed the capabilities of onboard or edge systems. In particular, it hosts large

VLMs that are offloaded from vehicles for complex scene understanding. Upon receiving requests, the cloud performs inference and returns results to the vehicle for integration into driving decisions or visualization.

The offloading pipeline is fully instrumented, encompassing vehicle pre-processing, uplink transmission, cloud inference, downlink response, and post-processing. Beyond vehicle-to-cloud latency tracing, the cloud oversees roadside V2X services by aggregating metrics such as availability, deadline violations, and recovery delays. Serving as a centralized monitoring layer, it supports both vehiclecloud AI functions and V2X warning pipelines, enabling cross-layer observability across the vehicleedgecloud continuum.

At the cloud backend, the following services are hosted:

- **AI Engine**: Executes large-scale models (*e.g.*, VLM such as ADAPT) to perform semantic reasoning, anomaly detection, and temporal scene understanding.
- **Communication Server**: Handles incoming gRPC requests from vehicles, dispatches them to AI inference services, and returns structured results.
- **Latency Monitor**: Aggregates telemetry across the vehicleedgecloud continuum (*e.g.*, using OpenTelemetry), and exposes standardized time-series endpoints (*e.g.*, Prometheus) for real-time observability through dashboards (*e.g.*, Grafana).

3.6 Security Considerations

Dependability requires trustworthy communication channels, all vehicleedge/cloud RPC channels employ mutual TLS, and telemetry as well as model artifacts are integrity-checked. The architecture supports standard V2X message authentication using PKI-based signing to prevent spoofing or tampering. Role-based access control confines coordinator privileges, and audit logs record all safety-critical actions. Comprehensive PKI management and node attestation will be addressed in future work.

4 Evaluation

We evaluate the proposed system through two complementary experiments that reflect realistic deployment scenarios across the vehicleroadcloud continuum. The first experiment focuses on an edge-based V2X warning service, measuring the system's ability to handle failures and maintain real-time guarantees in dynamic roadside environments. The second experiment evaluates a cloud-based VLM offloading service, assessing end-to-end latency, reliability, and adaptability under varying 5G network conditions. Table 1 summarizes the hardware and software configurations used in our testbed.

The KPIs defined in table2 are used to quantify the system behavior and evaluate its performance, categorized by their relevance to Road V2X Service and Cloud AI Function evaluation:

Table 1. Hardware configuration for evaluation.

	Road V2X Service	Cloud AI function
Vehicle	Neusoft V2X OBU	Horizon RDK Ultra
Road	4 NVIDIA Jetson Orin AGX Cluster running on K3s	N/A
Cloud	N/A	12 vCPU and NVIDIA A10 GPU Cloud virtual machine
Function	Collision Warning	ADAPT [15]

Table 2. Key Performance Indicators for system evaluation.

Road V2X Service KPIs	
Fault Handling Activation Rate (FHAR)	Number of camera stream reallocations triggered automatically by the coordinator to maintain service continuity.
Mean Time to Recovery (MTTR)	Average time elapsed between detection of perception output silence and successful recovery.
Deadline Violation Ratio (DVR)	Proportion of perception tasks whose end-to-end latency exceeds the deadline, impacting timely responses.
Cloud AI Function KPIs	
Communication Latency	Latency of network transmission stages in the offloading pipeline, including uplink and downlink communications between vehicle and cloud.
Computing Latency	Latency of computational stages in the offloading pipeline, including vehicle-side pre-/post-processing and cloud inference execution.

4.1 Road V2X Service

This experiment evaluates the reliability of the proposed edge-side coordinator when managing safety-critical V2X services under fault conditions. The system was deployed at three intersections in a city-level demonstration zone. During system initialization, each camera was statically assigned to a compute node for perception processing. To support quantitative evaluation, system metrics, including fault triggers, recovery events, and perception latency, were collected from all modules at one-second intervals throughout the experiment.

The goal is to assess how effectively the system detects failures, recovers service, and maintains timing guarantees for real-time perception tasks. Specifically, we examine the coordinator's ability to handle availability failures in the roadside infrastructure, such as node power lost or camera disconnections.

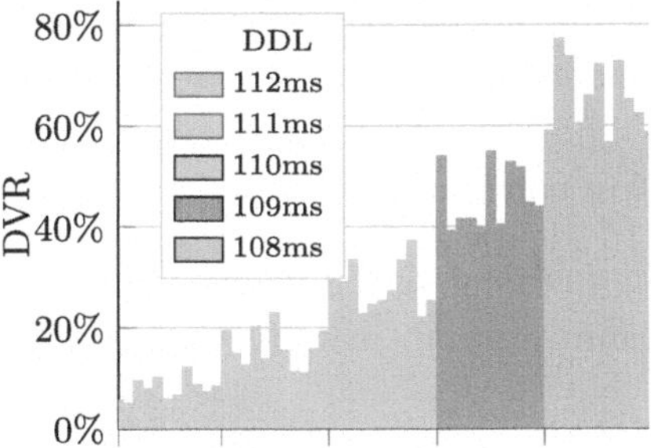

DVR sensitivity near nominal latency (±2% thresholds)

(a) DVR for 11 V2X warning pipelines

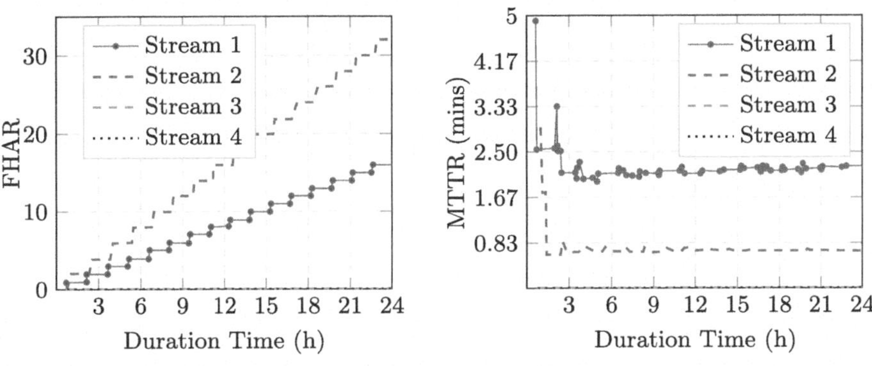

(b) FHAR per camera stream pipeline (c) MTTR per camera stream pipeline

Fig. 4. Results of roadside deadline-violation and fault-injection tests.

Nominal Observation. The system operated continuously for 168 h under normal conditions across the three intersections. Figure 4a reports the DVR for 11 of the 12 active perception pipelines. One pipeline is excluded due to persistent node and sensor failures. To assess the sensitivity of system to latency constraints, DVR was evaluated under progressively tighter real-time deadlines: 112 ms, 111 ms, 110 ms, 109 ms, and 108 ms. These thresholds represent ±2 % steps around the nominal operational latency (*approx* 111 ms) to illustrate system sensitivity near the safety-relevant deadline.

It is shown that DVR remained consistently low across all pipelines under nominal conditions, indicating stable and predictable latency performance. Minor DVR fluctuations were observed among different camera views, primarily attributed to varying scene complexity and traffic density in various directions. As the deadline tightened, DVR increased non-linearly to approximately 15%, 25%, 40%, 60%, and 80%, respectively. These results highlight the critical role of deadline configuration: even slight reductions in acceptable latency thresholds can lead to a sharp increase in missed deadlines, underscoring the importance of real-time monitoring in perception-based V2X services.

Fault Injection Tests. We conducted 24-hour fault injection experiments at one intersection, running 16 identical 90-minute cycles to assess detection and recovery. Each cycle followed: 15 min normal, 5 min sensor failure, 15 min normal, 5 min compute failure, 20 min normal, instant application failure, and 30 min normal.

Figure 4b shows the FHAR across perception pipelines. Reallocations in stream 1 corresponded directly to injected sensor failures. Stream 2 experienced twice as many reallocations due to node-related failure cascades, including 16 from initial failure responses and 16 from recovery reassignments, demonstrating that the coordinator reliably tracked and responded to diverse fault conditions. Figure 4c presents the MTTR for each stream. Streams 1 and 2 showed non-zero MTTR distributions due to triggered fault handling, while streams 3 and 4 remained unaffected. The majority of recovery actions completed within three minutes, highlighting the responsiveness of system. A few outliers with longer recovery times were caused by node-level failures requiring container migration or hardware reboot.

4.2 Cloud AI Function

To validate the practicality and robustness of our latency-aware offloading framework, we conducted experiments in real-world vehicular environments. These experiments were designed to measure latency characteristics, assess timeliness performance under varying conditions, and evaluate the impact of QoD control mechanisms in realistic mobile network scenarios.

Table 3. Driving scenarios and their impact on offloading.

Scenario	Mobility	Signal Strength	Network Occupancy
On-ground Parking	Stationary	High	Low
Sparse Urban Streets	Low speed	High	Low
Dense Urban Streets	Low speed	Moderate	High
Restricted Tunnel	Low speed	Low	High
Elevated Roads	Moderate speed	High	Low
Highway Driving	High speed	High	Low

The experiment further evaluates the impact of QoD in urban outdoor environments using large real-time captured frames (1928×1280, ∼200KB JPEG). It contrasts performance with and without QoD enabled Guaranteed Bit Rate (GBR) in six representative driving scenarios (see Table 3). The offloading pipeline incorporates encoding, wireless transmission, decoding, VLM inference, and return of results.

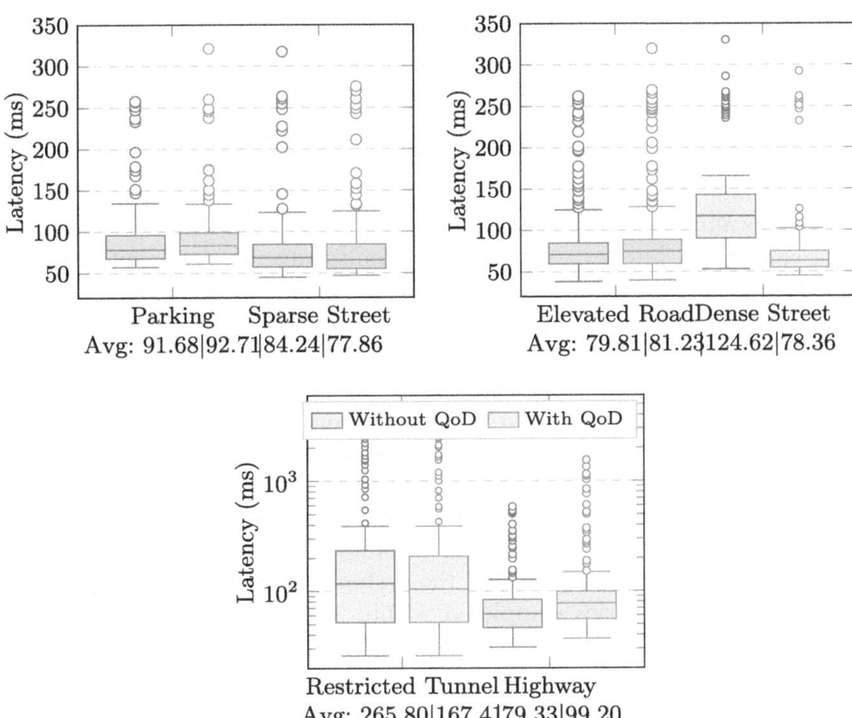

Fig. 5. Experiment results of cloud communication latency under different scenarios.

Communication Latency. Communication latency arises from both uplink and downlink transmissions, with uplink delays typically being longer and more variable. As a result, uplink is the dominant contributor to end-to-end latency fluctuations. Figure 5 shows that in stable environments (e.g., sparse streets or elevated roads), the latency difference with and without QoD is minimal, indicating limited benefit when baseline network conditions are favorable. In contrast, QoD significantly improves performance in challenging environments—such as tunnels or dense urban areas—by reducing latency variance and tail delays, thereby enhancing service availability under worst-case conditions. Interestingly, in high-mobility scenarios, QoD can slightly degrade performance. This is attributed to the overhead of frequent base station handovers and the latency introduced by QoD configuration procedures, suggesting that overly aggressive dynamic reconfiguration may backfire when network conditions change rapidly. The observed overhead stems from frequent QoD re-negotiations during cellular handovers. Practical mitigation includes hysteresis (minimum reconfiguration interval), handover-aware suppression, and bounded QoD adjustments per time window. These strategies are integrated in our prototype and will be quantitatively evaluated in future work.

Computing Latency. Computing latency arises from both vehicle-side processing and cloud-based inference. While the vehicle-side pre- and post-processing is lightweight (typically under 25 ms and 10 ms, respectively), cloud inference introduces significant variability. The cloud pipeline includes a deterministic stage—feature extraction and tokenization—taking roughly 130 ms, followed by variable-length text generation (1126 tokens) at a rate of 18.5 ± 0.6 ms/token, totaling 327614 ms. This variability in generation time directly impacts end-to-end latency. Notably, the results suggest that controlling output token length could be an effective strategy for bounding inference time.

4.3 Discussion of Results

The results from both the roadside V2X service and the cloud-based AI function provide complementary insights into the proposed architecture.

For the roadside V2X service, the orchestration layer consistently detected and mitigated both sensor and computer failures, ensuring minimal service disruption under adverse conditions. Low Deadline Violation Ratios were maintained under nominal conditions, and the system restored services rapidly after faults, with most recoveries completed within 3 min. These outcomes demonstrate that the edge coordinator can sustain predictable performance and rapid fault recovery when deadlines are appropriately configured for workload and scene complexity.

For the cloud-based AI function, end-to-end latency was predominantly determined by communication delays rather than cloud computing time. Quality-on-Demand mechanisms effectively reduced latency spikes in poor network conditions—such as tunnels and dense urban areas—enhancing service availability. However, QoD introduced additional overhead in high-mobility scenarios due to frequent base station handovers and negotiation delays. This finding highlights the limitations of static QoD strategies, as fixed configurations may degrade performance in highly dynamic environments. Cloud computing latency variability was driven largely by output token length, suggesting that controlling token generation could improve predictability.

Together, these results show that the edge and cloud layers serve distinct but complementary roles: the edge layer ensures fault tolerance and timing guarantees close to the data source, while the cloud layer provides scalable computing but depends heavily on adaptive network management to maintain real-time performance.

5 Conclusions

This paper demonstrates a reliable vehicle-road-cloud continuum through two integrated systems: (1) a safety-aware coordinator for roadside infrastructure that monitors V2X pipelines, detects faults (sensor/node/application), and dynamically reallocates workloads within private networks, achieving high service availability and sub-second recovery in urban deployments; and (2) a latency-aware offloading framework supporting AI-based vehicular functions over public 5G network via fine-grained tracing and declarative QoS APIs, significantly reducing percentile VLM latency under dynamic conditions. Validated on commercial-off-the-shelf SoCs and 5G gateways, both systems show that systems based on cloud-native technologies can meet critical vehicular requirements—balancing resilience and soft real-time performance for safety and intelligence workloads. Future work will extend to multi-path redundancy and predictive QoS orchestration for both scenarios. Future extensions will integrate formal risk assessment, QoD-overhead evaluation in high-mobility, and full security enforcement to reach safety-certifiable dependability.

Acknowledgment. This work was conducted at Bosch Corporate Research. The authors thank the ICT division, the Bosch Mobility business unit, ETAS, and our partners at China Telecom and China Unicom for their valuable discussions and technical support.

References

1. Du, Y., Li, N., Li, S. Ad-Astra: towards a reliable edge runtime environment for intelligent connected vehicles. In: 2024 IEEE 14th International Symposium on Industrial Embedded Systems (SIES) (2024). https://doi.org/10.1109/SIES62473.2024.10768015
2. Mundhenk, P., Hamann, A., Heyl, A., Ziegenbein, D.: Reliable distributed systems. In: 2022 Design, Automation & Test in Europe Conference & Exhibition (DATE) (2022). https://doi.org/10.23919/DATE54114.2022.9774734
3. Elias, D., Ziegenbein, D., Mundhenk, P., Hamann, A., Rowe, A.: The cyber-physical metaverse – where digital twins and humans come together. In: 2023 Design, Automation & Test in Europe Conference & Exhibition (DATE) (2023). https://doi.org/10.23919/DATE56975.2023.10137285
4. Jo, M.H., Schneider, P., Vinel, A.: Driving towards safety: open challenges in safeguarding cps-iot for cooperative intelligent transportation system. In: 2024 IEEE Intelligent Vehicles Symposium (IV) (2024). https://doi.org/10.1109/IV55156.2024.10588542
5. Zimmermann, J., Llatser, I., Scherl, M., Wildschütte, F., Hofmann, F.: Benefit evaluation of v2x-enhanced braking in view obstructed crossing use cases. In: 2024 IEEE 27th International Conference on Intelligent Transportation Systems (ITSC) (2024). https://doi.org/10.1109/ITSC58415.2024.10919921
6. Lobo, S., Festag, A., Facchi, C.: Enhancing the safety of vulnerable road users: messaging protocols for V2X communication. In: 2022 IEEE 96th Vehicular Technology Conference (VTC2022-Fall) (2022). https://doi.org/10.1109/VTC2022-Fall57202.2022.10012775
7. Reyhanoglu, A., et al.: On the reliability analysis of C-V2X mode 4 for next generation connected vehicle applications. In: 2022 IEEE 96th Vehicular Technology Conference (VTC2022-Fall) (2022). https://doi.org/10.1109/VTC2022-Fall57202.2022.10012855

8. Parada, R., Vázquez-Gallego, F., Sedar, R., Vilalta, R.: An inter-operable and multi-protocol v2x collision avoidance service based on edge computing. In: 2022 IEEE 95th Vehicular Technology Conference (VTC2022-Spring) (2022). https://doi.org/10.1109/VTC2022-Spring54318.2022.9860970
9. Chen, F., Li, P., Zhong, L., Yu, D., Cheng, X.: Low-latency perception sharing services for connected autonomous vehicles. In: 2023 IEEE 98th Vehicular Technology Conference (VTC2023-Fall) (2023). https://doi.org/10.1109/VTC2023-Fall60731.2023.10333577
10. Lumpp, F., Fummi, F., Patel, H.D., Bombieri, N.: Enabling kubernetes orchestration of mixed-criticality software for autonomous mobile robots. IEEE Trans. Robot. **40** (2024). https://doi.org/10.1109/TRO.2023.3334642
11. Barletta, M., Cinque, M., De Simone, L., Della Corte, R.: Criticality-aware monitoring and orchestration for containerized industry 4.0 environments. ACM Trans. Embed. Comput. Syst. **23**(1) (2024). https://doi.org/10.1145/3604567
12. Schafhalter, P., Kalra, S., Xu, L., Gonzalez, J.E., Stoica, I.: Leveraging cloud computing to make autonomous vehicles safer. In: 2023 IEEE/RSJ International Conference on Intelligent Robots and Systems (IROS) (2023). https://doi.org/10.1109/IROS55552.2023.10341821
13. Narayanan, A., Kasibhatla, P., Choi, M., Li, P.H., Zhao, R., Chinchali, S.: PEERNet: an end-to-end profiling tool for real-time networked robotic systems. In: 2024 IEEE/RSJ International Conference on Intelligent Robots and Systems (IROS) (2024). https://doi.org/10.1109/IROS58592.2024.10801747
14. Tian, X., et al.: DriveVLM: the convergence of autonomous driving and large vision-language models. In: 8th Annual Conference on Robot Learning (2024). https://doi.org/10.48550/arXiv.2402.12289
15. Jin, B.: ADAPT: Action-aware Driving Caption Transformer. In: 2023 IEEE International Conference on Robotics and Automation (ICRA) (2023). https://doi.org/10.1109/ICRA48891.2023.10160326
16. Zhou, X., et al.: Vision language models in autonomous driving: a survey and outlook. IEEE Trans. Intell. Veh. (2024). https://doi.org/10.1109/TIV.2024.3402136
17. Zhang, Y., Chen, C., Zhu, H., Pan, Y., Wang, J.: Latency minimization for MEC-V2X assisted autonomous vehicles task offloading. IEEE Trans. Veh. Technol. (2024). https://doi.org/10.1109/TVT.2024.3495511
18. Jang, Y., Na, J., Jeong, S., Kang, J.: Energy-efficient task offloading for vehicular edge computing: joint optimization of offloading and bit allocation. In: 2020 IEEE 91st Vehicular Technology Conference (VTC2020-Spring) (2020). https://doi.org/10.1109/VTC2020-Spring48590.2020.9128785
19. Pan, J.-a., et al.: Classifications of 'vehicle-road-cloud' integration applications and delay requirements analysis in critical scenarios. In: International Conference on Electric Vehicle and Vehicle Engineering (2024). https://doi.org/10.1007/978-981-96-6827-4_34
20. Ding, F., Zhang, N., Li, S., Bian, Y., Tong, E., Li, K.Q.: A survey of architecture and key technologies of intelligent connected vehicle-road-cloud cooperation system. Acta Automatica Sinica. **48**(12) (2022). https://doi.org/10.16383/j.aas.c211108
21. ISO 26262-6:2018, *Road vehicles — Functional safety — Part 6: Product development at the software level*, International Organization for Standardization (2018)
22. SAE J2945/1, *On-board System Requirements for V2V Safety Communications*, Society of Automotive Engineers (SAE), Warrendale, PA (2016)

FloodTracker: Towards Truly Wireless and Battery-Free Flood Monitoring with *Flute*

Van Vu Bui[1,2](✉), Brendan J. Mackenzie[1], Shuaibu Musa Adam[1], Sam Michiels[1], Nguyen Bao Phuong Huynh[2], and Danny Hughes[1]

[1] DistriNet, KU Leuven, Leuven, Belgium
vanvu.bui@kuleuven.be

[2] Department of Engineering and Technology, Quy Nhon University, Quy Nhon, Vietnam

Abstract. Wireless sensing of river conditions is essential for flood forecasting. By increasing the spatial and temporal density of depth readings, the accuracy and timeliness of predictions can be improved. However, significant barriers remain to the deployment of wireless flood sensors in terms of complexity and maintenance effort. This paper presents *FloodTracker*, a battery-free platform for wireless flood monitoring that applies novel sensors, NB-IoT networking and self-adaptive power management to reduce the complexity of deploying and managing flood sensors. *FloodTracker* is evaluated through a five-month study of twin deployments in Vietnam and Belgium. Our experiments show that *FloodTracker* delivers 98% up-time and can adapt its power management to support a range of workloads. Furthermore, we leverage novel LiDAR sensors to measure depth at 4x the range of previous approaches. All hardware, software and data are available under an open source license.

Keywords: Energy harvesting · Battery-free · Flood sensing · Adaptive Software · Energy management · LiDAR · NB-IoT

1 Introduction

Floods are among the most devastating natural disasters, and their severity is increasing due to climate change [1]. Despite significant efforts to manage them, they continue to inflict harm to human lives and damage to infrastructure globally [2–7]. This underscores the urgent need for robust and scalable river monitoring systems to enable timely flood predictions. In this context, Internet of Things (IoT) technologies have emerged as a promising solution. Low-Power Wide Area Networks (LPWAN) such as LoRa [8], NB-IoT [9–11] and LTE-M [11, 12] provide long-range telemetry and IoT sensors such as mmWave radar [13], LIDAR [14] and low-power cameras [15] open new sensing possibilities. Recent research in energy harvesting and battery-free energy storage also enable the breaking of battery life limits and thus reduces maintenance costs [16–18]. By integrating advances in each of these areas, it is possible to imagine sensor devices

L. Zhang and K.-K. R. Choo (Eds.): MobiQuitous 2025, LNICST 684, pp. 55–74, 2026.
https://doi.org/10.1007/978-3-032-22503-0_4

that can quickly be deployed in remote areas where they gather sensor data in perpetuity.

Numerous studies have been conducted on IoT flood sensing [19–23]. However, prior work largely relies on batteries, which has the disadvantages of toxic waste disposal and frequent replacement. Flute [24] addresses these issues by introducing an extensible battery-free IoT platform for Energy Harvesting. In this paper, we extend Flute with novel sensors and algorithms that realize a wireless flood monitoring system. We then perform twin five-month deployments in Belgium and Vietnam. Our results show that our prototype achieves 98% uptime, effectively adapts to changing energy supply and demand, and provides accurate depth sensing, with a theoretical range of up to 40 m. While the Flute design has been published previously [24], in this paper, we customize this system and study its performance in a challenging environmental monitoring scenario.

The scientific contributions of this paper are three-fold: **(i.) Realization of a reliable and efficient battery-free river monitoring platform. (ii.) Design and evaluation of an accurate long-range LiDAR depth sensor. (iii.) A five-month evaluation of key IoT technologies in a realistic river monitoring scenario across two countries.** Considered in sum, these contributions significantly reduce the complexity and cost of deploying and managing wireless river monitoring systems. To ensure reproducibility, all hardware and software are available under an open source license, along with access to the live sensor dashboard at [link].

The remainder of this paper is structured as follows: Sect. 2 provides background on river monitoring. Section 3 introduces the design of *FloodTracker*. Section 4 evaluates this prototype in a real-world case study. Section 5 discusses related work. Section 6 concludes. Finally, Sect. 7 discusses directions for future work.

2 Background

Wireless flood monitoring has three key complexities: power management, communication and sensing. We provide background on each of these areas in Sects. 2.1 to 2.3 respectively. We then identify requirements in Sect. 2.4.

2.1 Power Management

Environmental sensors are most often deployed in locations without power infrastructure. In this context, batteries are typically employed. Primary batteries such as LiSO2 cells offer low leakage, lifetimes of up to 40 years and energy densities of up to 700 Wh/kg. However, they cannot be recharged, limiting the device to a low current rating over its long lifetime (54μA in the case of an LiSO2 D-Cell[1]). Rechargeable batteries have higher leakage current and lower energy density at 300 Wh/kg, but may be recharged using environmental energy such as wind or

[1] https://tadiranbat.com/products/long-life-xol-series-batteries/.

solar up to a few thousand cycles, with a lifetime of 3–5 years. Recently, supercapacitors have emerged as an alternative to rechargeable batteries [16–18]. While their energy density is much lower at 20 Wh/kg, they have the crucial advantage of unlimited recharge cycles and long lifetimes.

The dynamic nature of energy harvesting introduces additional complexity, as these sources vary due to weather conditions, seasons, plant cover and aging. This problem is particularly acute in the case of supercapacitor-based energy harvesting systems which have a limited energy buffer. This demands techniques to mitigate energy dynamism in order to: avoid down-time, guarantee reliable operation and maximize performance [16,17,24].

2.2 Communication

River monitoring is inherently long-range and thus a natural fit with Low-Power Wide Area Networks, such as LoRaWAN [8] or Weightless [25], which enable the 'do it yourself' deployment of unlicensed long-range systems, with a reasonable energy budget. However, LPWAN data rates are extremely low in their longest range configurations (under 300 bps in the case of LoRa at SF12).

Low-power cellular networks such as NB-IoT or LTE-M offer long-range networking under a managed pay-per-use model [11]. The greater capability of the cell infrastructure delivers better performance at 128 kbps for NB-IoT and 375 kbps in the case of LTE-M, though these approaches cannot be employed in regions lacking cell coverage.

There is no 'one size fits all' approach to wireless networking. An effective flood monitoring system should therefore provide support for the easy integration of different network technologies to handle different deployment scenarios.

2.3 Sensing

Depth sensing is traditionally performed using contact pressure transducers [26–29], which are accurate and have a low purchase price. However, cabled sensors are expensive and complex to install. Furthermore, being in direct contact with water makes them vulnerable during floods, as debris can damage or displace them. Maintenance costs for contact sensors are also high due to mud accumulation and biofouling with algae, barnacles, and other organisms. These challenges are particularly pronounced and costly in deep-water deployments, where accessibility is limited and maintenance is labor-intensive.

Given the limitations of contact sensors, researchers have increasingly used non-contact ultrasonic applications [21–23,30–37]. These sensors are low-cost and accurate; however, their range is fundamentally limited to several meters, making them unsuitable for monitoring water levels at locations such as high dams and bridges. Novel techniques are thus required for long-range contactless level sensing.

2.4 Requirements

Based on the above background, we identify the following requirements for truly wireless IoT flood monitoring:

1. A maintenance-free power system that enables perpetual operation on environmental power.
2. Support for long-range communication, including both self-managed and cellular networks.
3. Support for long-range wireless depth sensing to minimize installation, maintenance and repair costs.
4. Techniques to mitigate the inherent dynamism of environmental energy.

In Sect. 3, we elaborate on the design of *FloodTracker* and show how it achieves these requirements.

3 System Design

This section presents the design of *FloodTracker* and explains how it operates on harvested solar energy while ensuring reliability under diverse conditions. A summary of the original Flute system is provided in Sect. 3.1. Hardware design is described in Sect. 3.2. Software architecture is outlined in Sect. 3.3. Finally, the network stack and sensor drivers are discussed in Sects. 3.4 and 3.5, respectively.

3.1 Original Flute Design

Flute [24] introduced a battery-free IoT platform that transforms existing development boards into battery-free devices by integrating power management hardware and self-adaptive software. Specifically, Flute enables sustainable indoor and outdoor operation despite power fluctuations. Second, it eliminates the need for laboratory-based benchmarking or environmental modeling, which simplifies large-scale deployment. Finally, Flute supports heterogeneous platforms, integrating with third-party development boards across various processors and networks. Figure 1 shows the Flute motherboard, which accepts any Adafruit Feather format daughterboard [38], and its power supply.

Despite its many advantages, Flute does not support the integration of sensors or actuators requiring different supply voltages, nor has its performance been evaluated with such peripherals. In contrast, *FloodTracker* motherboard incorporates a configurable buck-boost converter, enabling compatibility with sensors operating at either 3.3 V or 5.0 V. Additionally, Flute lacks overvoltage protection for the supercapacitors, which can lead to system failure. *FloodTracker* addresses this limitation, as detailed in Sect. 3.2. Finally, the original Flute platform lacks the ability to sense available environmental energy. *FloodTracker* extends the hardware, presented in Sect. 3.2, to support sensing of solar voltage levels and integrates this signal with the energy management software to transition between daytime and nighttime operation.

Fig. 1. Flute Mother Board.

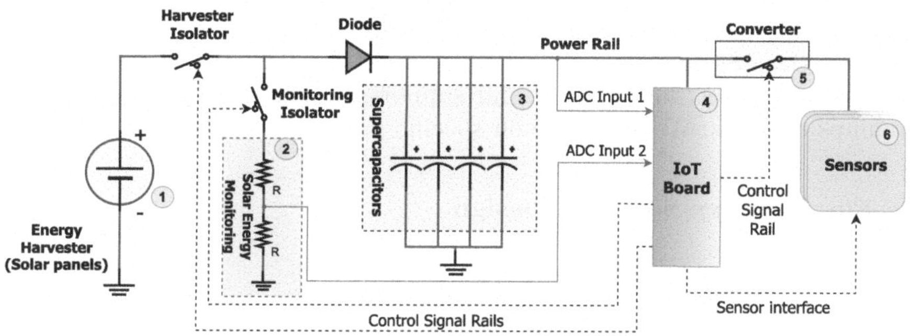

Fig. 2. Hardware Block Diagram of *FloodTracker*.

3.2 *FloodTracker* Hardware Design

The modular *FloodTracker* hardware is shown in Fig. 2. It comprises: (1) Energy harvester, (2) Solar panel voltage monitoring, (3) Energy storage, (4) Wireless communication and MCU, (5) Buck-boost converter, and (6) Water level sensor.

1. Energy Harvester: *FloodTracker* uses 55×70 mm 5.5 V/0.5 W solar panels[2].Deployments in Vietnam use two solar panels per node, while those in Belgium use four due to lower average light levels. To prevent over-voltage of the supercapacitors and MCU, a digital switch is provided which isolates the energy harvester. The *FloodTracker* software stack will disconnect the harvester whenever the voltage of the supercapacitors exceeds a user-defined maximum.

2. Solar energy monitoring: In addition to preventing over-voltage, the isolator switch allows the voltage of the solar panel and capacitor array to be read independently via a voltage divider circuit connected to the Analog to Digital Converter (ADC) of the daughterboard, supporting light sensing and energy benchmarking. As the resistors in the voltage divider draw energy, a

[2] 5.5V/0.5W solar panel.

monitoring isolator is also implemented, activating the monitoring circuit only when required by the MCU, and thereby conserving energy.

3. Energy Storage: To store energy, we use an array of four 5.5 V /15 F supercapacitors[3] connected in parallel. These capacitors have a lifetime of over 500,000 cycles at 25°C, equating to a theoretical lifetime of over a thousand years in our scenario. The capacitor array is over-dimensioned to support the greatest possible range of sensors, actuators and daughterboards. A low forward voltage drop Schottky diode prevents reverse current flow when the harvester's voltage drops below that of the supercapacitor at night.

4. IoT board: A CircuitDojo nRF9160 feather[4] is employed to manage the system. The Nordic nRF9160 is a low-power System-in-Package that integrates LTE-M, NB-IoT and a 64 MHz Arm Cortex-M33 with 1 MB flash and 256 KB RAM, which is used to host all application software and libraries.

5. Converter: An energy-efficient TPS63070 buck-boost converter is employed to supply those sensors that require it with a stable 5 V. The boost is activated only when required to power a sensor.

6. Sensors: *FloodTracker* offers connections for I2C, UART and SPI connectors operating at 3.3 to 5.0 V and supports power demands ranging from microamps to amps. We elaborate on specific sensor drivers in Sect. 3.3.

3.3 *FloodTracker* Software Design

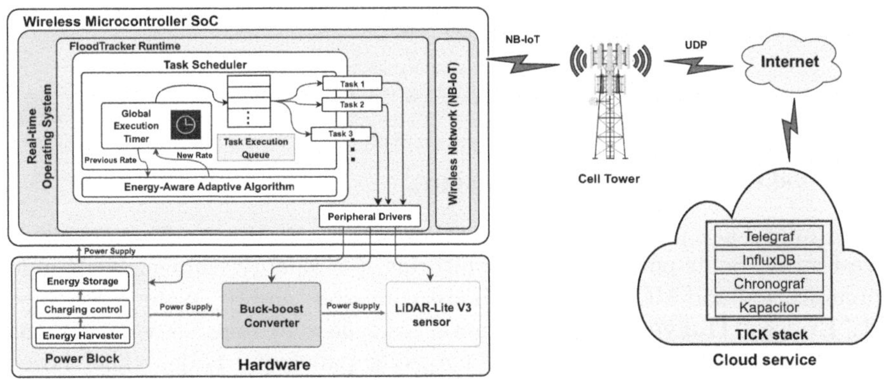

Fig. 3. *FloodTracker*'s Software Architecture.

The software architecture of *FloodTracker* is depicted in Fig. 3 and is explained in detail below.

Charge Management: *FloodTracker* periodically monitors the voltage of the supercapacitor array to manage charging. When the voltage exceeds a predefined

[3] 5.5 V /15 F carbon aerogel supercapacitor.
[4] CircuitDojo nRF9160 feather.

threshold of 4.6 V (de-rated from the 5.5 V capacitor maximum), charging is halted. Charging resumes only when the voltage drops below this threshold. We opted for software voltage control rather than hardware to maximise flexibility for connected daughterboards and peripherals. To further protect the system during low-power conditions, *FloodTracker* suspends all tasks when the voltage of the capacitor array falls to 110% of the daughter-board's brown-out voltage (3.67V for the CircuitDojo nRF9160 feather).

Task Scheduling: *FloodTracker* incorporates an energy-aware task scheduling mechanism built on Flute's AsTAR++ algorithm [24]. This system evaluates both stored and harvested solar energy in real time to dynamically adjust task execution rates, enabling reliable, sustainable, and battery-free operation. Increasing task frequency enhances temporal data resolution while increasing energy demands and vice-versa. AsTAR++ aims to schedule tasks so as to acquire a full capacitor charge during the day, maximizing task rate when the capacitor voltage is optimal, then discharging the capacitor to 110% of brown-out overnight. This approach balances energy supply and demand. The key parameters of AsTAR++ are shown in Table 1. FloodTracker provides utility APIs for task scheduling which eliminates the need for in-depth energy management knowledge, empowering developers to focus on their core application concerns.

Table 1. Key *FloodTracker* Software Specifications

Parameter	Description	Value
maxRate	Max. sensing period	120 s
minRate	Min. sensing period	7200 s
optimumV	Optimum voltage	4.5 V
shutOffVoltage	MCU's shut-off voltage	3.3 V
maxV	Maximum voltage	4.6 V

3.4 Network Stack

We use NB-IoT as LTE-M was not available at our Vietnamese deployment site. To ensure low power, we use Power Saving Mode (PSM) to optimize energy consumption. Data is forwarded over the Internet using the User Datagram Protocol (UDP). The data then reaches the cloud, where they are ingested, stored and analyzed using the TICK stack[5].

During deployment, we encountered infrequent yet unpredictable behavior from the NB-IoT network. These anomalies sometimes went unrecognized by the cellular modem, causing the node to stop sending data to the server. To address this issue, our software checks the NB-IoT connection at user-defined intervals. If a node is found to be disconnected, it triggers reconnection. If the node remains offline after four consecutive reconnection attempts, it will automatically reboot to restore connectivity. While NB-IoT is generally well-suited

[5] www.influxdata.com/time-series-platform/.

for low-power applications, network rejoin procedures are energy hungry, often keeping the modem active for minutes. When such rejoins occur, the adaptive scheduling of *FloodTracker* will automatically throttle back application data rates to compensate wherever possible.

3.5 Sensor Drivers

FloodTracker provides APIs for both the LiDAR and ultrasonic sensors detailed in Table 2. These libraries convert raw data into a distance from the sensor to the water surface. This raw distance data is then transmitted to the backend, where the actual water level is calculated. This approach simplifies calibration by allowing sensor readings to be adjusted remotely, eliminating the need to physically access and re-flash nodes deployed in hard-to-reach locations.

A01NYUB Ultrasonic Sensor: Provides simple distance measurements with a maximum range of 7.5 m and a worst-case accuracy of ± 1 cm. This sensor connects to the nRF9160 via UART. While ultrasonic sensors are widely used to measure water depth, their range is too short for critical locations that *FloodTracker* aims to monitor in Vietnam, which include dams with a height of up to 35 m.

LiDAR-Lite V3 Sensor: This is a compact and low-cost optical distance measurement sensor with a maximum range of 40 m and a worst-case accuracy of ± 2.5 cm for distances under 5 m, and ± 10 cm for distances beyond 5 m. The sensor communicates with the nRF9160 via the I2C interface. A key challenge in using this sensor for water level measurement is the low reflectivity of the water surface. Empirical experiments were required to identify the optimal sensitivity setting, ensuring robust performance under varying weather conditions and different levels of water turbidity. To further increase stability and reduce the impact of outliers, the average of 300 consecutive sensor readings is computed during each sensing cycle, resulting in consistent measurements.

4 Evaluation

This section evaluates the key elements of *FloodTracker* through the lens of a five-month deployment in Belgium, a temperate maritime climate, and Vietnam, a tropical climate. Each deployment is composed of two sensor nodes, one of which is equipped with an ultrasonic depth sensor and the other with a LiDAR sensor. Deploying both sensor types at the same location allows for cross-validation of sensor accuracy (Fig. 4).

4.1 Power Characteristics

The software configuration of *FloodTracker* is shown in Table 1. The maximum transmission rate is set to one message every two minutes (120 s), to prevent excess data costs, while the minimum transmission rate is set to one message every two hours (7200 s), as required by our flood modeling partners. Sensing

Fig. 4. Deployed *FloodTracker* Nodes: (a) in Vietnam and (b) in Belgium.

occurs synchronously with data transmission and readings are time-stamped upon arrival in the cloud. The Flute scheduling algorithm [24] will attempt to find the correct transmission rate to balance energy supply with demand, remaining at the optimum voltage (optimumV = 4.5 V) whenever possible during the day. If the voltage falls below the system minimum (shutOffVoltage = 3.3 V), *FloodTracker* enters sleep mode for two hours (7200 s) to conserve energy. In case more energy is available than *FloodTracker* can use, the energy harvester is disconnected (maxV = 4.6 V).

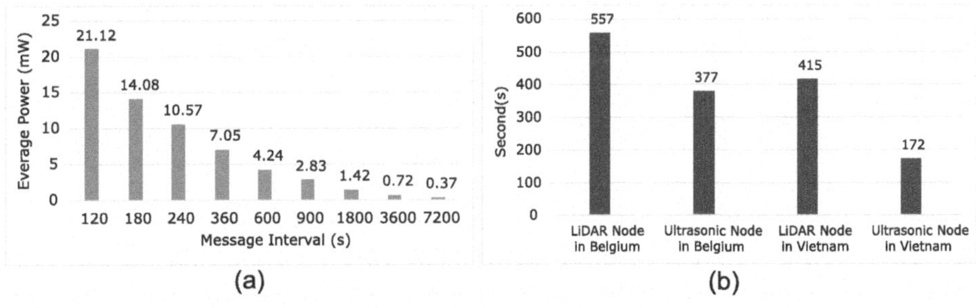

Fig. 5. (a) NB-IoT Avg. Power Consumption for 1500-Byte Messages With Different Transmission Intervals; (b) Average Task Rate.

The NB-IoT PSM feature is utilized to optimize power draw in idle mode, reducing it to an average of 16 μW. Power consumption increases to an average of 63 mW for several seconds during message transmission. Figure 5(a) shows the average power consumption at transmission rates ranging from the minimum to the maximum period. This excludes sensor power which is analysed in Sect. 4.2.

Figures 6 and 7 depict the power consumption profile of the ultrasonic and LiDAR nodes, respectively, during a typical operation cycle when powered by a 5 V supply. The cycle includes sleep and active phases. The active phase consists

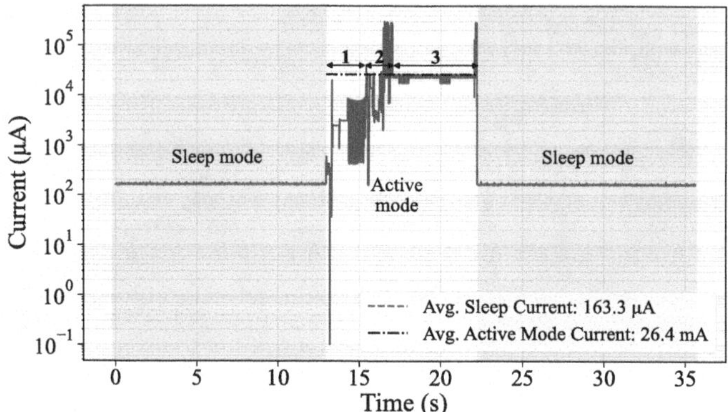

Fig. 6. Current Consumption of the Ultrasonic Node.

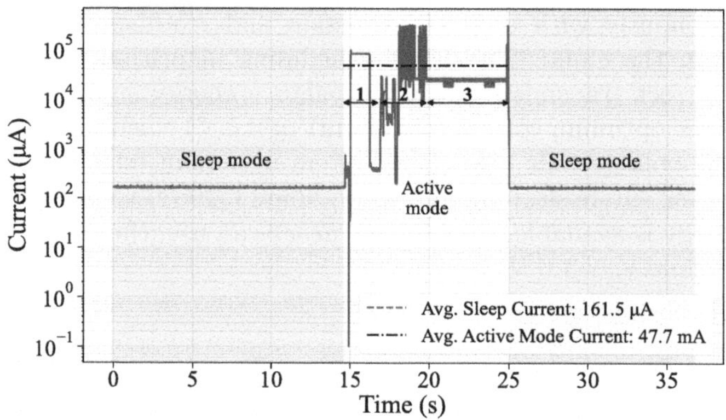

Fig. 7. Current Consumption of the LiDAR Node.

of three sub-phases: (1) sensing the water level, (2) transmitting data via NB-IoT, and (3) transitioning to sleep mode. The current draw sharply increases during the NB-IoT transmission phase due to the high-power requirements of the modem. For the Ultrasonic node, the average current in sleep mode is 163.3 μA, while the average during the active mode is 26.4 mA; while regarding the LiDAR node, these numbers are 161.5 μA and 47.7 mA, respectively. The average current consumption during active mode of the LiDAR node is much higher than that of the Ultrasonic node, due to the high power consumption of the LiDAR sensor, as shown in Table 2.

4.2 Sensor Performance

As shown in Table 2, the sensors offer quite different power loads, with a single sensing cycle for the ultrasonic sensor consuming 29.57 mJ and the LiDAR sensor consuming 915.20 mJ, a difference of over 30 times. This makes the case for

Table 2. Power, Energy and Accuracy Characteristics of Wireless Depth Sensors

Parameters	Ultrasonic (A01NYUB)	LiDAR-Lite V3
Range	28 cm – 750 cm	80 cm – 4000 cm
Avg. Current	4.48 mA	83.20 mA
Voltage	3.3 V	5.0 V
Whole Sensing Time	2.0 s	2.2 s
Total Consumed Energy	29.57 mJ	915.20 mJ
Accuracy	±1 cm	±10 cm

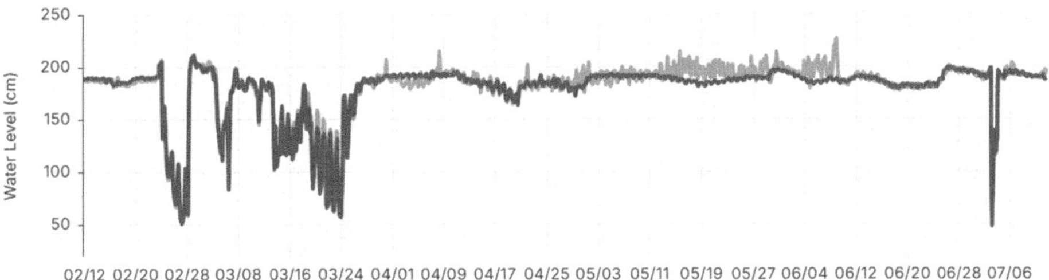

Fig. 8. Water Level Data Collected by ultrasonic and LiDAR Sensor-Equipped Nodes in Vietnam.

energy adaptive scheduling, which must find a different message rate for each sensor in order to ensure sustainable operation.

Figure 5(b) shows the average task rates that *FloodTracker* identified for the two sensor types at each location. As can be seen from the Figure, *FloodTracker* finds a higher average task rate for the ultrasound sensor than the LiDAR sensor in both Vietnam and Belgium. It can also be seen that *FloodTracker* adapts to the different light levels in each country by modifying both task rates.

Figure 8 presents the five-month experimental water level data recorded by both nodes. During 'normal operation', the LiDAR sensor's readings correlated closely with those of the ultrasound sensor with an average deviation of 3 cm and a worst-case error of 0.15% of the full range. This is well within the combined accuracy margins of both sensors as described in Sect. 3.5 and therefore is considered acceptable. This excludes faults such as debris accumulation, as discussed in Sect. 4.4.

4.3 Adaptive Energy Management

Perhaps the most important result of our experiment is that nodes **achieved 100% energy availability** despite changing harvested energy and different loads in both locations.

Figure 9 illustrates the task rate distribution organized into 5-minute buckets across the four sensor nodes, based on their sleep interval. The x-axis shows

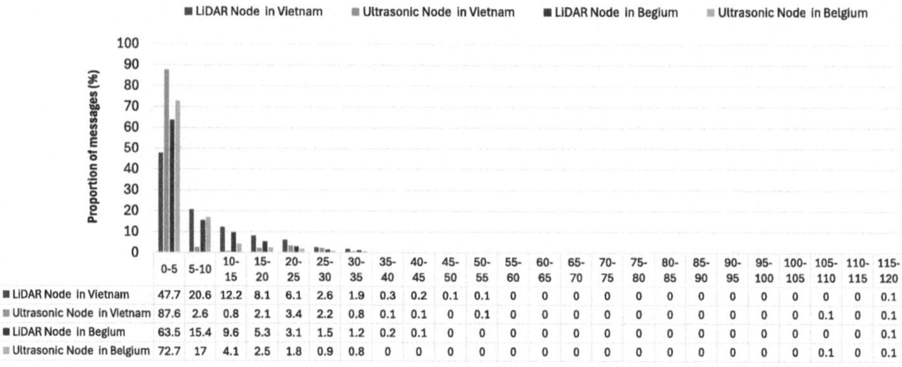

	0-5	5-10	10-15	15-20	20-25	25-30	30-35	35-40	40-45	45-50	50-55	55-60
LiDAR Node in Vietnam	47.7	20.6	12.2	8.1	6.1	2.6	1.9	0.3	0.2	0.1	0.1	0
Ultrasonic Node in Vietnam	87.6	2.6	0.8	2.1	3.4	2.2	0.8	0.1	0.1	0	0.1	0
LiDAR Node in Begium	63.5	15.4	9.6	5.3	3.1	1.5	1.2	0.2	0.1	0	0	0
Ultrasonic Node in Belgium	72.7	17	4.1	2.5	1.8	0.9	0.8	0	0	0	0	0

	60-65	65-70	70-75	75-80	80-85	85-90	90-95	95-100	100-105	105-110	110-115	115-120
LiDAR Node in Vietnam	0	0	0	0	0	0	0	0	0	0	0	0.1
Ultrasonic Node in Vietnam	0	0	0	0	0	0	0	0	0	0.1	0	0.1
LiDAR Node in Begium	0	0	0	0	0	0	0	0	0	0	0	0.1
Ultrasonic Node in Belgium	0	0	0	0	0	0	0	0	0	0.1	0	0.1

Fig. 9. Task Rate Distribution Comparison Across Four Nodes.

Table 3. Energy Adaptation Comparison of Nodes in Vietnam and Belgium

Daily Time in High-Voltage Shutoff Mode (%)			
Nodes	Min.	Max.	Avg.
LiDAR node in Vietnam	11.0	43.0	32.0
Ultrasonic node in Vietnam	12.6	47.0	33.1
LiDAR node in Belgium	33.0	46.2	40.5
Ultrasonic node in Belgium	17.5	55.1	47.2
Daily Under/Overshoot in Target Morning Voltage (%)			
Nodes	Min.	Max.	Avg.
LiDAR node in Vietnam	-1.65	6.64	0.86
Ultrasonic node in Vietnam	-0.8	8.21	1.34
LiDAR node in Belgium	-1.54	11.6	2.84
Ultrasonic node in Belgium	7.38	17.2	11.5

sleeping interval ranges in minutes, and the y-axis indicates the percentage of tasks falling within each bucket. The most common sleep period is close to the minimum value (i.e. the highest possible sense/send rate), with 47.7% of readings having a sleep interval of 0 to 5 min. Furthermore, 93% of readings have sleep intervals of 30 min or less. As expected, the distribution tail increases for the higher energy load sensor (LiDAR).

To investigate the efficiency of energy use, we consider suboptimal cases for the AsTAR++ algorithm: high-voltage shut-off mode and nighttime under/overshoot. *High-voltage shut-off mode* causes the solar panel to be disconnected. The node is therefore unable to absorb more energy from the environment. As can be seen from Table 3, nodes spend an average of between 32.0% and 47.2% in high-voltage shut-off mode. These figures are significant and suggest that the *FloodTracker* node can support additional sensors with higher power loads, or may be provisioned with a smaller capacitor. We discuss this as part of our future work in Sect. 7. Conversely, *night time over/under-shoot* occurs when the Exponential Weighted Moving Average (EWMA) algorithm under or over-estimates when energy harvesting will resume in the morning. As can be seen from the Table, *FloodTracker*'s energy-aware adaptive algorithm effectively utilizes nearly all the energy stored in the supercapacitor by the end of the night, with a small deviation ranging from 0.86% to 11.5%. In the interests of space, more detailed time-series cannot be included in the the paper. However, we have made our time series available at [link].

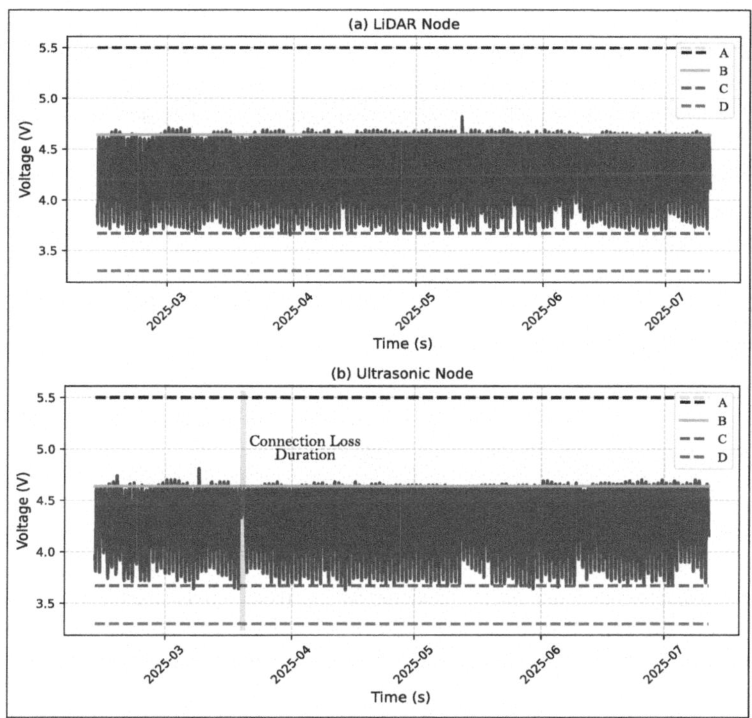

Fig. 10. Supercapacitor Voltage Data from the LiDAR and Ultrasonic Sensor-Equipped Nodes in Vietnam.

To illustrate the operation of *FloodTracker* over time, we zoom into the operations of the LiDAR and ultrasonic nodes deployed in Vietnam in Fig. 10. Annotation line (A) marks the absolute maximum voltage of the supercapacitor (5.5 V) and (B) marks the user-defined *high voltage shut-off* level of 4.6 V, at which level, the solar panels are disconnected. Annotation line (C) marks the user-specified *low-voltage shut-off* level (3.63 V) and (D) indicates the brownout threshold of the host Feather board (3.3 V). The diurnal pattern of energy harvesting is clearly visible, and it can be seen that *FloodTracker* enables reliable operation throughout this period, staying between the critical lines.

4.4 Reliability Analysis And Lessons Learned

As shown in Sect. 4, *FloodTracker* has no power faults for the duration of our experiments. However, we did experience a number of other problems, which are enumerated here along with their duration.

- The ultrasonic node antenna in Vietnam was detached by strong winds, resulting in signal loss from 20:26 on March 19 to 10:02 on March 20, 2025 as labeled in Fig. 10(b).
- An accumulation of floating trees within the sensing zone of the LiDAR and ultrasonic sensors in Vietnam led to inaccurate readings from 12:00 on March 18 to 23:00 on June 09, 2025. The presence of debris caused an average deviation of 6 cm in the LiDAR readings.
- Nodes in both Belgium and Vietnam occasionally lost cellular connectivity due to poor network conditions. However, in all cases, the nodes were able to reconnect within 30 min.
- During our experiment in Belgium, we encountered inaccurate sensor readings caused by insects, such as ants and spiders, nesting beneath the sensor. Their presence adversely impacted measurement accuracy.

In summary, we note that *FloodTracker* provides a high level of reliability at 98% up-time and we are pleased to note that power is not a source of downtime for our system despite the battery-free design.

5 Related Work

In this section, we discuss key streams of related work. Section 5.1 discusses battery-based wireless flood sensing. Section 5.2 explores battery-free IoT platforms. Finally, Sect. 5.3 discusses related work on wireless depth sensing.

5.1 Battery-Powered Flood Sensing

Abdelal et al. [30] explore the use of a variety of battery types to monitor river conditions using a GSM modem, showing that battery lifetimes of several months to a few years are possible using COTS hardware. Hernowo et al. [33] develop an NB-IoT based depth monitoring node known as RiverCore, which is powered by a 5 V 1000 mAh battery. The authors explore how the use of Power Saving Mode (PSM) and Extended Discontinuous Reception (eDRX) impact power consumption, identifying PSM as an optimal strategy. This validates the design decisions of *FloodTracker*. More recently, Prakash et al. [21] introduce 'FLOODWALL', a real-time flood monitoring system for collecting a variety of hydrological data. The system is powered by two rechargeable 12 V, 12 Ah batteries connected in parallel and uses GSM networking to communicate data to the cloud. This stream of research offers a maximum lifetime of at most a few years, which motivates research into energy harvesting alternatives such as the work presented in this paper.

A number of studies have investigated the integration of energy harvesting with rechargeable battery-based systems [23,39–41]. Specifically, solar panels are utilized to capture ambient solar energy and recharge the batteries. However, these approaches still have a maximum lifetime of a few years due to battery degradation. EnHANTs [40] utilizes a rechargeable battery connected to a solar panel for energy harvesting and implements an adaptation policy based on EWMA prediction. Simulation indicates that this approach achieves energy neutrality, utilizing 95–96% of harvested energy. *FloodTracker* employs a similar EWMA approach to estimate nighttime length.

Corke et al. [39] share insights from a solar-powered deployment of over two years using rechargeable batteries and highlight the limitations inherent in battery-based systems. A significant issue is that even with a discharge depth of only 20%, the batteries used in their Fleck node have a lifespan of less than five years and require replacement, which is a costly manual task.

In [23], solar-powered sensor nodes with rechargeable batteries are used for flood monitoring. While effective during day and night, the system lacks power management for long-term reliability. The limited lifespan of batteries increases maintenance and environmental costs. *Floodtracker* addresses these issues with a battery-free IoT platform, offering a more sustainable and maintenance-free solution. Leon et al. [41] used a hybrid solar-wind system to charge a 12 V battery powering their flood-monitoring IoT node. The parallel connection ensured energy supply when one source was unavailable. While effective, the reliance on a rechargeable battery raises concerns about limited lifespan and environmental impact.

Reflecting on the battery-powered IoT systems discussed above, we note that none is capable of reaching the lifetime goals of Flute, which aims to support multi-decade operation. Additionally, batteries pose environmental risks as they are corrosive and often contain toxic metals such as lead, lithium, and mercury.

5.2 Battery-Free Sensing Platforms

BFree is a hardware/software platform designed for developing battery-free applications in Python [42]. It provides a power-failure resilient architecture that is user-friendly for novice developers. However, while it simplifies the management of power failures, it does not guarantee continuous operation under varying conditions, aiming instead for *intermittent* operation. UFoP [43] is a federated energy storage architecture tailored for intermittent sensors, accommodating variable supply voltages, unpredictable power outages, and uncertain energy harvesting performance. It facilitates development by segregating charge storage for specific peripherals and prevents energy-intensive components from depleting all available power, which would compromise system functionality. Afanasov et al. [44] discuss their long-term deployment of a thermal and kinetic energy harvesting sensor network at the Circus Maximus in Rome. They identify dynamic energy availability as a significant challenge, achieving a maximum of 22% availability across three design iterations. In addition to energy variability, they observe a variety of practical issues stemming from insufficient integration of current energy harvesting, storage, and management techniques. To enhance availability, the authors advocate for comprehensive energy benchmarking with minimizing dynamic power consumption as much as possible. *FloodTracker* shows that a different approach is possible, leveraging in-situ measurement and adaptation in favour of static optimisation.

Yang et al. address dynamic energy availability and consumption through an energy-aware task scheduler, AsTAR [16], that adjusts software execution rates to align with energy harvesting supply and system demand, utilizing a closed-loop control algorithm inspired by TCP congestion control mechanisms. This strategy promotes sustainable operation in volatile energy conditions, addressing a major concern noted in the Circus Maximus deployment. However, this approach makes no assumptions on energy patterns and therefore behaves suboptimally in solar energy harvesting scenarios. Flute [24] addresses this problem by modifying the AsTAR scheduler with support for night time length estimation. The resulting AsTAR++ scheduler delivers significantly better performance. In addition, Flute supports plug-in daughter boards allowing for the use of various network and compute boards. We build upon this work.

5.3 Wireless Depth Sensing

Wireless depth sensors have been extensively explored, for example, Moreno et al. [37] employed the MaxSonar MB7066 ultrasonic sensor, which operates within a range of 20 cm to 1068 cm, while Rachmawardani et al. [35] utilized the JSN-SR04T ultrasonic sensor, offering a range of 25 cm to 450 cm. Other studies have investigated various ultrasonic sensors with differing measurement ranges for acquiring water level information. Kang et al. [34] used the MB7386 HRXL ultrasonic sensor, capable of measuring within a range of 50 cm to 999.9 cm, while Abdelal et al. [30] used the JSN-SR04T-2.0 ultrasonic sensor, with a range of 20 cm to 600 cm. Furthermore, the HC-SR04 ultrasonic sensor, with a range of 2 cm to 400 cm, has been widely utilized in water level detection across various flood-monitoring applications [21–23,31–33,36]. The ultrasonic sensors used in the aforementioned studies provide several advantages over contact-based sensors, such as ease of deployment and reduced maintenance costs. However, their limited measurement range poses a challenge for applications requiring the monitoring of significant depth variations.

Paul et al. [45] evaluate the feasibility of using LiDAR for water level measurements and demonstrate that a commercially available LiDAR sensor can effectively measure water levels under varying environmental conditions. The study has provided an in-depth laboratory and field analysis of the sensor's accuracy, including factors such as temperature, incidence angle, water surface roughness, and turbidity. However, it does not address how to develop a complete water level measurement node. FloodTracker offers an open-source solution, comprising both hardware and software, that helps developers build a sustainable, long-life LiDAR sensor-based water level monitoring platform.

Leon et al. [41] deployed a LiDAR sensor to monitor water levels at the Bucayao Bridge in the Philippines. While the sensor produced accurate measurements, the study was limited to five days and involved only a single node at one location. In contrast, *FloodTracker* evaluates two LiDAR nodes over a five-month period across two continents, aiming to assess their reliability under a wide range of real-world weather conditions.

In our work, we present a novel approach using the Garmin LiDAR-Lite V3 sensor to detect water levels. This non-contact sensor addresses the limitations of contact-based sensors and offers an impressive operational range of up to 40 m, enabling water level detection in reservoirs, rivers, and streams with significant fluctuations during flood events.

6 Conclusion

In this work, we present *FloodTracker*, a battery-free, open-source platform designed for wireless flood monitoring. By integrating novel long-range water depth sensors, NB-IoT connectivity, and adaptive power management, *FloodTracker* dramatically lowers the complexity of flood monitoring deployments and their ongoing maintenance overhead. Specifically, we achieve 100% energy availability and 98% up-time in a five-month deployment in Belgium and Vietnam with two different depth sensors (LiDAR and ultrasound).

FloodTracker's energy-aware adaptive scheduler ensures reliable operation in diverse climates from cloudy Belgium to sunny Vietnam without manual adjustments. In practice, when higher sensing or transmission rates are needed, simply adding solar panels increases the available energy, and the system automatically adapts in real time.

Our evaluation shows that *FloodTracker* supports river water level sensing using LiDAR, enabling deployment in areas with highly variable water levels during flood events. Furthermore, our adaptive approach to energy management accommodates dynamic energy harvesting conditions and with heterogeneous sensor loads. Considered in sum, these results underscore *FloodTracker*'s flexibility, resilience, and scalability, positioning it as a compelling solution for sustainable wireless flood monitoring. All hardware, software and Belgian data are available under an open-source license at [link].

7 Future Work

Our future work will focus on three scientific directions. First, we aim to scale-up deployments of *FloodTracker* in both Vietnam and Belgium to assess its real-world performance and long-term reliability. We will also evaluate the operational challenges, maintenance requirements, and the impact of environmental factors on system performance. We intend to maintain our public data dashboard throughout this expansion to support collaboration with other researchers.

Secondly, we will explore the feasibility of integrating satellite communication with *FloodTracker* to serve areas that lack cellular connectivity. The objective here is to assess communication reliability, latency, energy efficiency, as well as testing the ability of *FloodTracker* to support the higher power consumption of satellite networking.

Finally, we will explore the integration of more complex sensors that integrate Machine Learning (ML). For example, low-power cameras together with ML-based image analysis can be used to infer water levels and thereby replace expensive LiDAR sensors while also being more resilient to floating debris, a key source of our faults as described in Sect. 4.4. These high computational workloads and their energy impact will offer a new challenge to *FloodTracker*.

Acknowledgements. This work is partially funded by VLIR-UOS (IUC-QNU/KUL, VN2022IUC-044A101) and VLAIO (CORRELATE, HBC.2024.0406).

References

1. Melissa A.S., Kjersti M.A.: Natural disasters resulting from climate change: the impact of hurricanes and flooding on perinatal outcomes. Seminars Perinatol. **47**(8), (2023)
2. Lopamudra B.: Effects of flood on agricultural productivity in Bangladesh. Oxford Development Stud. **38**(3), (2010)
3. Societal Impacts of Flood Hazards. https://doi.org/10.1093/acrefore/9780199389407.013.281. Accessed 02 July 2025
4. Galuppini, G., et al.: A unified framework for the assessment of multiple source urban flash flood hazard: the case study of Monza. Italy. Urban Water J. **17**(1), 65–77 (2020)
5. Gould, Iain J., et al.: The impact of coastal flooding on agriculture: a case-study of Lincolnshire, United Kingdom. Land Degrad. Develop. **31**(12), 1545–1559 (2020)
6. Houston, D., Werritty, A., Ball, T., Black, A.: Flute: environmental vulnerability and resilience: social differentiation in short- and long-term flood impacts. Trans. Inst. Br. Geogr. **46**(1), 102–119 (2020)
7. Shrestha, B.B., et al.: Assessing flood disaster impacts in agriculture under climate change in the river basins of Southeast Asia. Nat. Hazards **97**, 157–192 (2019)
8. Devalal, S., Karthikeyan, A.: LoRa technology - an overview. In: 2018 Second International Conference on Electronics. Commun. Aerosp. Technol. (ICECA), pp. 284–290. IEEE, Coimbatore, India (2018)
9. Mekki, K., Bajic, E., Chaxel, F., Meyer, F.: Overview of cellular LPWAN technologies for iot deployment: Sigfox, LoRaWAN, and NB-IoT. In: 2018 IEEE International Conference on Pervasive Computing and Communications Workshops (PerCom Workshops), pp. 197–202. IEEE, Athens, Greece (2018)
10. Migabo, E.M., Djouani, K.D., Kurien, A.M.: The Narrowband Internet of Things (NB-IoT) resources management performance state of art, challenges, and opportunities. IEEE Access **8**, 2169–3536 (2020)
11. Labdaoui, N., Nouvel, F., Dutertre, S.: Energy-efficient IoT communications: a comparative study of long-term evolution for machines (LTE-M) and narrowband internet of things (NB-IoT) technologies. In: Energy-efficient IoT communications:

a comparative study of long-term evolution for machines (LTE-M) and narrowband internet of things (NB-IoT) technologies, pp. 823–830. IEEE, Gammarth, Tunisia (2023)

12. Khalifeh, A., Aldahdouh, K.A., Darabkh, K.A., Al-Sit, W.: A survey of 5G emerging wireless technologies featuring LoRaWAN, Sigfox, NB-IoT and LTE-M. In: 2019 International Conference on Wireless Communications Signal Processing and Networking (WiSPNET), pp. 561–566. IEEE, Chennai, India (2019)
13. Shui, H., Geng, H., Li, Q., Du, L., Du, Y.: A low-power high-accuracy urban waterlogging depth sensor based on millimeter-wave FMCW radar. Sensors **22**(3), (2022)
14. Ferrer Santana, V.D., Salustiano, R.E., De Oliveira Tiezzi, R.: Development and calibration of a low-cost LIDAR sensor for water level measurements. Flow Measure. Instrument. **100**, (2024)
15. Zhang, Z., Zhou, Y., Liu, H., Gao, H.: In-situ water level measurement using NIR-imaging video camera. Flow Meas. Instrum. **67**, 95–106 (2019)
16. Yang, F., Thangarajan, A.S., Ramachandran, G.S., Joosen, W., Hughes, D.: AsTAR: sustainable energy harvesting for the internet of things through adaptive task scheduling. ACM Trans. Sensor Netw. (TOSN) **18**(1), 1–34 (2021)
17. Sabovic, A., Sultania, A.K., Delgado, C., De Roeck, L., Famaey, J.: An energy-aware task scheduler for energy-harvesting batteryless Iot devices. IEEE Internet Things J. **9**(22), 23097–23114 (2022)
18. Sabovic, A., Aernouts, M., Subotic, D., Fontaine, J., De Poorter, E., Famaey, J.: Towards energy-aware tinyML on battery-less IoT devices. Internet of Things **22**, (2023)
19. Siddique, M., Ahmed, T., Husain, M.S.: Flood monitoring and early warning systems – an IoT based perspective. EAI Endorsed Trans. Internet Things **9**(2), (2023)
20. Basnyat, B., Singh, N., Roy, N., Gangopadhyay, A.: Design and deployment of a flash flood monitoring iot: challenges and opportunities. In: 2020 IEEE International Conference on Smart Computing (SMARTCOMP), pp. 422–427. IEEE, Bologna, Italy (2020)
21. Prakash, C., Barthwal, A., Acharya, D.: FLOODWALL: a real-time flash flood monitoring and forecasting system using IoT. IEEE Sens. J. **23**(1), 787–799 (2023)
22. Yazid, M.A.M., Jazlan, A., Rodzi, M.Z.M., Husman, M.A., Afif, A.R.: A method for preserving battery life in wireless sensor nodes for lora based Iot flood monitoring. J. Commun. **17**(4), 230–238 (2022)
23. Zakaria, M.I., Jabbar, W.A., Sulaiman, N.: Development of a smart sensing unit for LoRaWAN-based IoT flood monitoring and warning system in catchment areas. Internet Things Cyber-Phys. Syst. **3**, 249–261 (2023)
24. Bui, V.V., et al.: Flute: enabling a battery-free and energy harvesting ecosystem for the internet of things. In: Zaslavsky, A., Ning, Z., Kalogeraki, V., Georgakopoulos, D., Chrysanthis, P.K. (eds) MobiQuitous 2023, LNCS, vol. 594, pp. 368–380. Springer, Cham (2023). https://doi.org/10.1007/978-3-031-63992-0_24
25. Webb, W.: Understanding weightless: technology, equipment, and network deployment for M2M communications in white space. Cambridge University Press (2012)
26. Schenato, L., Aguilar-López, J.P., Galtarossa, A., Pasuto, A., Bogaard, T., Palmieri, L.: A rugged FBG-based pressure sensor for water level monitoring in dikes. IEEE Sens. J. **21**(12), 13263–13271 (2021)
27. Dublin, A.C., et al.: A novel cost-effective pressure sensor based flood monitoring system with IoT. ASEAN Eng. J. **14**(3), 53–61 (2024)

28. Pearce, R.H., Chadwick, M.A., Main, B., Chan, K., Sayer, C.D., Patmore, I.R.: Low-cost approach to an instream water depth sensor construction using differential pressure sensors and arduino microcontrollers. Sensors **24**(8), (2024)
29. Song, S., et al.: A sensor-based smart urban flood warning and management system. In: 2023 4th International Conference on Information Science. Parallel and Distributed Systems (ISPDS), pp. 325–329. IEEE, Guangzhou, China (2023)
30. Abdelal, Q. et al.: Low-cost, low-energy, wireless hydrological monitoring platform: design, deployment, and evaluation. J. Sensors **2021**(1), (2021)
31. Deowan, M.E., et al.: Smart early flood monitoring system using IoT. In: 2022 14th Seminar on Power Electronics and Control (SEPOC), pp. 1–6. IEEE, Maria, Brazil (2022)
32. Hashim, Y. et al.: The design and implementation of a wireless flood monitoring system. J. Telecommun., Electron. Compute. Eng. (JTEC) **10**(2), 7–11 (2018)
33. Hernowo, R., et al.: Power consumption optimization for flood monitoring system using NB-IoT. In: 2022 5th International Seminar on Research of Information Technology and Intelligent Systems (ISRITI), pp. 58–63. IEEE, (2022)
34. Kang, S., David, D.S.K., Yang, M., Yu, Y.C., Ham, S.: Energy-efficient ultrasonic water level detection system with dual-target monitoring. Sensors **21**(6), (2021)
35. Rachmawardani, A., et al.: Flood monitoring system using IoT. In: 2E3S Web of conferences. EDP Sciences (2023)
36. Sharma, A., et al.: Flood monitoring system using IoT. In: 2021 9th International Conference on Reliability. Infocom Technologies and Optimization (Trends and Future Directions) (ICRITO), pp. 1–4. IEEE, Noida, India (2021)
37. Moreno, C., et al.: RiverCore: IoT device for river water level monitoring over cellular communications. Sensors **19**(1), (2019)
38. Feather Format Daughterboard. https://www.adafruit.com/category/943. Accessed 4 Jun 2025
39. Corke, P., et al.: Long-duration solar-powered wireless sensor networks. In: Proceedings of the 4th Workshop on Embedded Networked Sensors, pp. 33–37. Association for Computing Machinery, New York, NY, USA (2007)
40. Margolies, R., et al.: Energy-Harvesting Active Networked Tags (EnHANTs): prototyping and experimentation. ACM Trans. Sen. Netw. **11**(4), (2015)
41. De Leon, A.F., Cruz, F.R.G.: Water level monitoring and flood warning system using light detection and ranging (LiDAR) sensor with hybrid renewable solar-wind power. In: 2021 IEEE 13th International Conference on Humanoid. Nanotechnology, Information Technology, Communication and Control, Environment, and Management (HNICEM), pp. 1–5. IEEE, Manila, Philippines (2021)
42. Kortbeek, V., et al.: BFree: enabling battery-free sensor prototyping with Python. Proc. ACM Interact. Mob. Wearable Ubiquitous Technol. **4**(4), (2020)
43. Hester, J., Sitanayah, L., Sorber, J.: Tragedy of the Coulombs: federating energy storage for tiny, intermittently-powered sensors. In: Proceedings of the 13th ACM Conference on Embedded Networked Sensor Systems, pp. 5–16. Association for Computing Machinery, New York, NY, USA (2015)
44. Afanasov, M. et al.: Battery-less zero-maintenance embedded sensing at the mithræum of circus maximus. In: Proceedings of the 18th Conference on Embedded Networked Sensor Systems, pp. 368–381. Association for Computing Machinery, New York, NY, USA (2020)
45. Paul, J. D., Buytaert, W., Sah, N.: A technical evaluation of Lidar-based measurement of river water levels. Water Resources Res. **56**(4) (2020)

Heuristic-Enhanced Multi-agent Learning for Intelligent Caching and Offloading in UAV-Enabled SAGIN

Xiaoya Fan, Xin Chen, and Libo Jiao(✉)

Beijing Information Science and Technology University, Beijing 102206, China
{fanxiaoya,chenxin,jiaolibo}@bistu.edu.cn

Abstract. Achieving ubiquitous network coverage has emerged as a fundamental objective in the evolution of 6G wireless communication systems. However, the deployment of communication infrastructure in remote and underserved areas remains prohibitively expensive and traditional base station architectures and edge computing paradigms often fall short in meeting the computational offloading demands in such scenarios, thereby limiting the coverage and service capabilities envisioned for 6G networks. To address these challenges, this paper proposes a computation offloading framework based on an integrated space-air-ground architecture, which enables over-the-air computation and cooperative scheduling capabilities. Specifically, a two-level scheduling mechanism is designed: a ground-level task aggregation strategy based on multi-hop Ant Colony Optimization (ACO), and an aerial-level intelligent caching algorithm employing a multi-agent Deep Deterministic Policy Gradient (MADDPG) approach. The latter is further enhanced by a heuristic pretraining phase to alleviate the cold-start problem and improve convergence efficiency. Extensive simulation results demonstrate that the proposed approach significantly outperforms existing baseline schemes in terms of key performance metrics, including average task delay and completion ratio

Keywords: Task offloading · Mobile edge computing · Deep learning · Task scheduling

1 Introduction

1.1 Background

Wireless communication technology has become a key driver of global digital transformation [1]. The fifth generation of mobile communication networks (5G) are characterized by high bandwidth, low latency and massive connectivity [2]. With the emergence of emerging applications such as the metaverse [3], digital

This work was supported by National Natural Science Foundation of China (Nos.62202059,62572063).

L. Zhang and K.-K. R. Choo (Eds.): MobiQuitous 2025, LNICST 684, pp. 75–94, 2026.
https://doi.org/10.1007/978-3-032-22503-0_5

twins and holographic communications, the inherent limitations of 5G technology, especially in terms of coverage, energy efficiency and intelligent functions, have become increasingly prominent.

The sixth generation of mobile communication networks (6G) is expected to achieve significant progress in three core areas: communication enhancement and expansion scenarios, coverage enhancement scenarios, and service expansion scenarios. Deployment costs in remote areas are high due to sparse population density and infrastructure limitations, extreme environments place stringent requirements on network reliability and dynamic adaptability [4].

1.2 Related Work

Space-Air-Ground Integrated Networks. The Space-Air-Ground Integrated Network (SAGIN) has become a fundamental architectural component of modern edge computing systems, as evidenced by extensive research in this domain. The authors in [5] proposed a joint optimization method for SAGIN offloading and resource allocation in hybrid cloud and multi-access edge computing (MEC) scenarios based on deep reinforcement learning (DRL). The authors in [6] studied the computation offloading problem in low-orbit satellite-to-ground edge computing systems and proposed a game theory-based distributed computation offloading (GDCO) algorithm.In the Low Earth Orbit (LEO) Satellite-Ground Integrated Network (STIN), since battery technology cannot meet the needs of ground terminal devices, the authors in [7] designed a delay-based deep reinforcement learning (DRL) framework specifically for calculating offloading decisions, which can effectively reduce energy consumption.

Recent advances in SAGIN have opened up new possibilities for efficient computational offloading in remote and underserved areas. To address the problem that insufficient coverage of terrestrial communication infrastructure in remote areas hinders the provision of machine learning services in remote areas, the authors in [8] proposed a federated learning approach and designed an adaptive data offloading optimizer. However, the task offloading strategy of federated reinforcement learning ignores potential trust issues such as malicious satellites and buffer pollution. The authors in [9] proposes to add blockchain to the zero-trust scenario. The authors in [10] investigate how satellite-augmented communication networks can significantly improve fault diagnosis in remote environments, proposing a framework that exploits high-speed satellite capabilities. The authors in [11]study the design of an efficient UAV-LEO integrated data collection scheme without infrastructure support and propose a resource allocation problem for two-hop uplink UAV-LEO integrated data collection in B5G IoRT networks. Existing studies have extensively explored the use of low earth orbit (LEO) satellite solutions to address communication challenges in remote areas, but most studies focus on aerial data collection and centralized model training. Although the sparseness of ground users is crucial to practical deployment feasibility and resource allocation efficiency, relatively limited attention has been paid to it.

Offloading Strategy Optimization. The rapid evolution of 5G/6G networks and the exponential proliferation of IoT devices have precipitated an unprecedented surge in computational offloading demands, rendering offloading efficiency a critical determinant for guaranteeing both Quality of Service (QoS) and Quality of Experience (QoE) in contemporary edge computing systems. To address the problem of limited in-vehicle edge computing services, the authors in [12] proposed a digital twin (DT)-enabled MEC framework to enhance the task offloading efficiency of cellular vehicle-to-everything (C-V2X) networks. Aiming at the problems of network congestion and poor network performance in the existing joint mobility-aware task offloading and network traffic scheduling problems, the authors in [13] proposed an online joint mobility-aware task offloading and bandwidth allocation problem. The authors in [14] study the performance gains of collaborative computing and propose a new collaborative offloading multi-access edge computing scheme. While the aforementioned studies present robust solutions for computational offloading optimization, their applicability remains constrained in remote deployment scenarios due to three fundamental limitations inadequate consideration of extreme network sparsity, and unaddressed energy constraints characteristic of isolated environments.

Extensive researches have been devoted to addressing fundamental challenges in remote area communicationsthe infrastructural constraints hindering base station deployment, and the service delivery complications arising from highly dispersed user distributions. In the single-hop task offloading model, IoT devices can send tasks to edge servers for offloading [15]. To bridge the gap of traditional single-hop task offloading schemes in infrastructure-free scenarios, the authors in [16] studied a hierarchical multi-hop edge computing framework and proposed a joint task offloading and relay selection scheme. To overcome the problem that existing multi-hop offloading methods can obtain complete information, the authors in [17] proposed a new two-stage task execution cost minimization method based on incomplete information.

1.3 Contributions

Although numerous studies have focused on task offloading in remote areas, limited attention has been paid to jointly considering both the air-to-ground architectural framework and the sparse ground user distribution typical of such environments. This study addresses this gap by incorporating the characteristics of sparse user deployment into the space-air-ground integrated architecture and proposes a multi-agent reinforcement learning-based approach to optimize collaborative offloading efficiency. The contributions of this work are summarized as follows:

To address the challenges arising from the sparse and heterogeneous distribution of users in remote areas, this study introduces a spaceairground integrated architecture for task offloading. The overarching objective of maximizing offloading efficiency is decomposed into two subproblems: a ground-side task scheduling problem and an aerial-side caching and coordination problem.

In the ground user scheduling subproblem, an Ant Colony Optimization (ACO) algorithm is employed to determine the optimal offloading center, aiming to minimize transmission costs and task aggregation delays. For the aerial caching subproblem, a Multi-Agent Deep Deterministic Policy Gradient (MADDPG) algorithm is adopted. To address the cold-start problem and enhance convergence efficiency, a heuristic pretraining phase is incorporated, enabling UAVs to achieve efficient and adaptive task allocation in a cooperative manner.

The final experimental results validate the effectiveness and superiority of the proposed algorithm in comparison with existing benchmark schemes.

2 System Model

In this section, we introduce the SAGIN modeling framework and construct the communication model and the task offloading model.

2.1 Network Model

In the SAGIN, the model is divided into three layers: ground layer, aerial layer, and satellite layer, each responsible for different stages of task collection, transmission, and computation.

Ground Layer: This layer contains users that can generate tasks, denoted as $I = \{1, 2, ..., \mathrm{I}\}$, and a subset of user nodes designated as user centers $\overline{I} = \{1, 2..., \overline{\mathrm{I}}\}$ responsible for aggregating and forwarding tasks. Each user center is located at a selected user node. Users located outside the direct communication range of the UAV transmit their tasks via a multi-hop transmission strategy to the user center, which will communicate directly with the UAV.Each user $i \in I$ is characterized by the feature vector $\mathbf{U}_i = \{L_i,\ H_i,\ O_i,\ D_i,\ T_i\}$. Where L_i denotes the geographic location of user $i.H_i$ is the next-hop user node for multi-hop communication;O_i indicates the task type generated by user $i.D_i$ indicates the number of tasks generated by user i. T_i denotes the maximum tolerable offloading delay for the task.

Aerial Layer: This layer consists of multiple (Unmanned Aerial Vehicle)UAVs and UAVs provide task caching and relay forwarding functions,denoted as $M = \{1, 2, ..., \mathrm{M}\}$.To reduce the transmission latency from user center, each UAV is adaptively positioned above the horizontal coordinates of its designated user center to ensure efficient line-of-sight communication and minimize propagation delay.Each UAV $m \in M$ characterized by the feature vector $\mathbf{A}_m = \{L_m,\ R_m,\ K_m\}$. Where L_m denotes the 3D location of UAV m and $K_m = \{O_1, O_2, ..., O_k\}$ .K_m represents the set of types cached by UAVs $m.R_m$ represents the cache capacity of the UAV. If the data required for offloading are not cached in the UAV in the air layer, they are forwarded to the satellite layer via the UAV on a mission-by-mission basis.

Satellite Layer: This layer comprises a set of low Earth orbit (LEO) $S = \{1, 2, ..., \mathrm{S}\}$, which are assumed to possess sufficient computing capabilities to process offloaded tasks. Each satellite $s \in S$ is characterized by the feature vector $\mathbf{S}_s = \{C_s,\ T_s\}$. Where C_s is the computation resource allocated to task i by satellite $s.T_s$ refers to the maximum tolerable delay of satellite offloading. Due to the high orbital speed of LEO, each LEO provides only a limited service window. If the total task processing time exceeds the LEO available coverage duration T_s, the offloading is deemed unsuccessful.

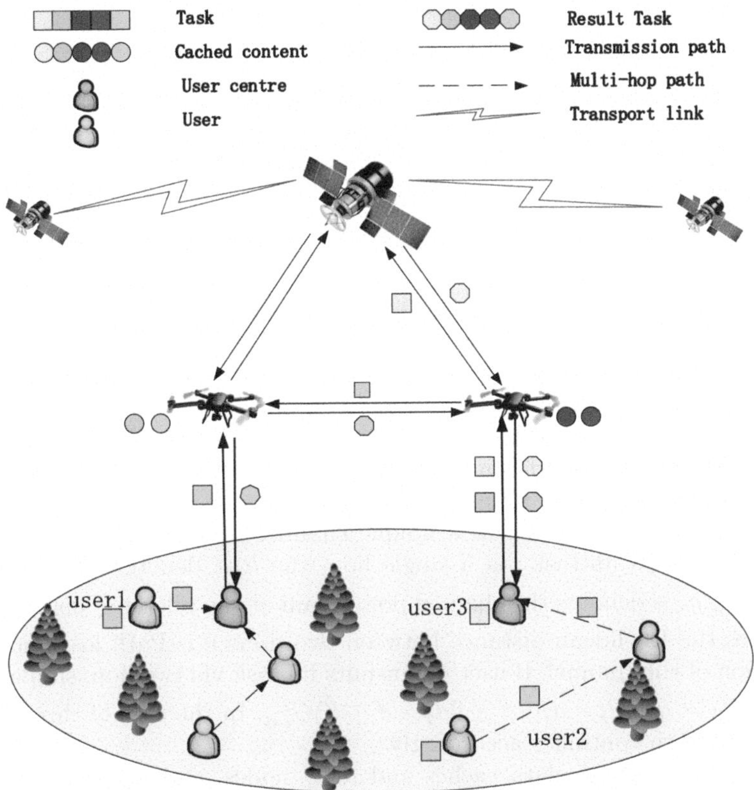

Fig. 1. Space-Air-Ground Offloading Model.

As illustrated in Fig. 1, three representative task offloading trajectories of User 1, User 2, and User 3 are provided to demonstrate the diversity of task migration paths under varying network conditions. User 1 generates a computational task and transmits it to the nearest user center via a single-hop connection. The user center aggregates the task and forwards it to the UAV covering the current area. If the requested content is cached on the UAV (i.e., a cache hit), the task is processed locally, and the result is directly returned to the user.

Due to a longer distance, User 2 transmits the task to the user center through a two-hop multi-user relay. The user center then forwards the task to the associated UAV. In this case, the UAV lacks the required content in its cache, triggering a cooperative cache retrieval from neighboring UAVs. Once a UAV with the required content is located, the task is executed, and the result is sent back to the user. User 3 attempts to offload the task through a nearby UAV. However, since none of the UAVs cache the required task type, the task is forwarded to the satellite layer for computation. After the task is processed by the satellite, the result is returned to the user via the UAV and the user center.

2.2 Communication Model

In this study, Orthogonal Frequency Division Multiple Access (OFDMA) method is used for channel resource allocation. Each user is fairly allocated orthogonal channels for cellular links. The transmission rate between each user i can be expressed as

$$R_{i,i'} = B_i log_2 \left(1 + \frac{h_{i,i'} p_i}{N_i}\right), \tag{1}$$

where i denotes the current user being processed, $i^{'}$ denotes the next user selected by the current user using the multi-hop strategy, B_i is the channel bandwidth of the user, and $h_{i,i'}$ is the channel gain between user i and $i\prime$. p_i is the data transmit power. N_i denotes the power spectral density of Gaussian white noise. In the scenario studied in this paper, the users are relatively far away from each other and the mutual interference between users is negligible.

Due to differences in the number of multi-hop relays and per-hop transmission distances, each user experiences a unique channel gain during task offloading. If user i transmits its task via a single hop, the $h_{i,i'}$ denotes $h_{i,i'} = g_0||d_i - d_n i^{'}||^{-\nu} G_{i,n}^2 .g_o$ is denotes the channel power gain at the reference distance,$||d_i - d_i^{'}||$denotes the Euclidean distance between two users,ν is Path loss and $G_{i,n}$ is attenuation of the channel. If user i transmits its task via two hop, similarly $h_{i,i'}$ denotes $h_{i,i'} = g_0(||d_i - d_j||^{-\nu} + ||d_j - d_i^{'}||^{-\nu})G_{i,n}^2$. In the case of three or more hops, the pattern continues accordingly.

UAVs serve as both data caches and relay nodes, and may exchange data through air-to-air (A2A) links when cooperative caching is enabled. The transmission rate from the ground layer to the aerial layer, specifically from user center i to UAV m, is denoted as

$$R_{i,m} = B_m log_2 \left(1 + \frac{h_{i,m} p_m}{N_m}\right), \tag{2}$$

and the transmission rate of content retrieval between UAVs is expressed as:

$$R_{m,m'} = B_m log_2 \left(1 + \frac{h_{m,m'} p_m}{N_m}\right). \tag{3}$$

where m denotes the current UAV being processed, $m^{'}$ denotes the UAV that has cache of currently offloading tasks, B_m is the channel bandwidth of the UAV, and $h_{m,m'}$ is the channel gain between user m and $m_{'}$. p_m is the data transmit power. N_m denotes the power spectral density of Gaussian white noise.

The interference among UAVs is considered negligible due to several factors. First, the use of directional beamforming or adaptive antenna alignment effectively suppresses inter-UAV signal leakage. Second, the significant spatial separation between UAVs, particularly in terms of altitude and horizontal distance, reduces the probability of mutual interference. Finally, dedicated frequency planning and orthogonal time-slot scheduling further ensure communication isolation among UAV nodes.

The Air-to-Space (A2S) link is modeled as a high-frequency directional channel (e.g., in Ka or Ku bands), which supports line-of-sight (LoS) propagation. The uplink transmission rate from UAV m to satellite s is expressed

$$R_{m,s} = B_s log_2\left(1 + \frac{P_r}{N_s}\right), \tag{4}$$

$$P_r = P_t \times G_t \times G_r \times \left(\frac{\lambda}{4\pi d}\right)^2, \tag{5}$$

$$N_s = k \times T \times B_s \times F, \tag{6}$$

where P_r is Receive powerand,P_t is the transmit power.G_t and G_r are the transmitting and receiving antenna gains respectively.N_s denote the power noise for satellites.$\lambda = \frac{c}{f}$ is the wavelength, c is the speed of light, and f is the carrier frequency.d is the distance between two points. Where k is the Boltzmann constant $1.38 \times 10^{-23} J/K$, T is the system noise temperature, B is the bandwidth, and F is the noise figure.

2.3 Task Offloading Model

In the considered system model, the total task offloading delay comprises five components: multi-hop transmission delay, uplink transmission delay, cache retrieval delay, computation delay, and result return transmission delay. Given that the size of the output data is significantly smaller than that of the input data, and that the corresponding result return transmission rate is considerably higher than the uplink rate, the result return transmission delay can be regarded as negligible without loss of generality.

The UAV caching mechanism adopts a content-aware strategy, in which each UAV independently selects the most beneficial content to cache based on local observations and offloading request. Due to differences in user distributions and task demands, the caching decisions are not necessarily identical across UAVs.

A user-side cache hit is defined as the event in which a UAV covering the user has already cached the corresponding content or service module required for the task. Upon a cache hit, the UAV can immediately process the task locally without forwarding it to neighboring UAVs or the satellite layer. Caching decision of UAV m for task type k defined as

$$x_{i,m} = \begin{cases} 1, & \text{if UAV } m \text{ caches content of task type } O_i, \\ 0, & \text{otherwise.} \end{cases} \tag{7}$$

When the corresponding content is not found in the service drone's cache, the UAV retrieves it from other drone caches. The retrieval policy is defined as follows

$$y_{m,K} = \begin{cases} 1, & \text{retrieved from nighboring UAV } m^{'} \in N(m), \\ 0, & \text{otherwise,} \end{cases} \tag{8}$$

where $N(m)$ is the set of UAVs, and $m \in N(M)$ is the selected neighbor UAV that holds the desired content.

The transmission delay between a user and its one-hop neighbor is expressed as:

$$t_{i,i'} = \frac{D_i}{R_{i,i'}}, \tag{9}$$

where $t_{i,i'}$ the transmission delay from user i to its next-hop user $i^{'}$,D_i is the size of the offloading task generated by user i.

The multi-hop transmission delay from user i to the user center via a relay path $\{i, H(i), H^2(i), H^3(i), ..., H^H(i)\}$ is expressed as the sum of the one-hop transmission delays:

$$t_i^{muli-hop} = \sum_{j=0}^{fin} \frac{D_i}{R_{i,i'}}, \tag{10}$$

where $t_i^{muli-hop}$ is the total transmission delay of user i uploading tasks to the user center through multi-hop paths,$H^j(i)$ represents the node reached after j jumps from user i, satisfying $H^0(i) = i$ and $H^{fin}(i)$ is the user center.

The transmission delay from the ground node to the associated UAV is expressed as:

$$t_{i,m} = \frac{D_i}{R_{i,m}}, \tag{11}$$

the content retrieval delay between UAVs, when the requested content is not cached locally, is defined as

$$t_m^{retriveal} = \frac{D_i}{R_{m,m'}}. \tag{12}$$

The transmission delay from the UAV to the satellite is expressed as:

$$t_{m,s} = \frac{D_i}{R_{m,s}}. \tag{13}$$

3 Problem Formulation

In this section, we develop a joint optimization model that integrates total offloading delay and task failure probability, aiming to characterize the trade-off between latency and reliability. The ultimate objective is to maximize the offloading efficiency by jointly minimizing delay and ensuring high task success rates.

3.1 Service Failure Rate Model

In the SAGIN, the task offloading process involves multiple links, and latency and reliability have an important impact on system performance. In order to comprehensively evaluate the offloading performance, this paper introduces the offloading efficiency index and conducts a comprehensive analysis combining the offloading delay and the task success rate.

Specifically, offloading failure may occur under the following three conditions: the total offloading delay exceeds the user's maximum tolerable delay; the computation delay exceeds the satellite's available coverage time; the user is isolated, which is no available adjacent user exists within the maximum allowable transmission distance. Whether task i is successfully offloaded is indicated by the binary variable f_i, defined as:

$$f_i = \begin{cases} 1, & \text{if } t_i \leq T_i \text{ or } t_{\text{com}} \leq T_s \text{ or } , \delta_i = 1 \\ 0, & \text{otherwise,} \end{cases} \tag{14}$$

where T_i is maximum tolerable delay for user i and Let t_{com} represents the total transmission time required for the task to reach the satellite, where it will be processed. And δ_i indicates an island user.

$$\delta_i = \begin{cases} 1, & \text{if } \forall j \in \mathcal{I}\dashv\backslash\lceil\rangle \neq |,\ d_{i,j} > d_{max}, \\ 0, & \text{otherwise.} \end{cases} \tag{15}$$

The offloading failure rate can be expressed as:

$$F = \frac{1}{I}\sum_{i=1}^{I} f_i. \tag{16}$$

3.2 Cost Model

The total system delay is the sum of the multi-hop transmission delay, uplink transmission delay, retrieval delay and computation delay, expressed as

$$S_t = t_i^{muli-hop} + t_{i,m} + (1 - x_{m,k})(t_m^{retriveal} + (1 - y_{m,k})t_{com}). \tag{17}$$

$$t_{com} = \frac{D_i}{C_s}, \tag{18}$$

where C_s is the computing power of the satellite allocated to the offloading task.

Since some tasks may fail to be offloaded, a penalty term is introduced to account for the additional delay incurred due to offloading failure. The penalized delay is expressed as

$$S_p = \max\left(\sigma\left(t_i - T_i\right), \sigma\left(t_{com} - T_s\right)\right) + \delta_i, \tag{19}$$

where $\sigma\left(x\right) = \frac{1}{1+e^{-\lambda x}}$ is Sigmoid function and λ controls the steepness of the curve.

The total delay is defined as the sum of the task offloading delay and a penalty term that accounts for potential failure, and is expressed as:

$$S = S_t + \alpha S_p, \tag{20}$$

where α is penalty coefficient.

3.3 Optimization Model

The final optimization objective is to maximize the overall offloading efficiency of the system, which can be formulated as

$$\mathbf{P0}: \max_{U_i, A_m, S_s} \quad \eta = \frac{\sum_{i=1}^{I}(1-f_i)}{\sum_{i=1}^{I} S} \tag{21}$$

$$\text{s.t.} \quad \bar{I} \in h_i \tag{21a}$$

$$\|d_i - d_i^{'}\| \leq d_{\max} \tag{21b}$$

$$\sum_{k=1}^{K} R(k_m) \leq R_m \tag{21c}$$

$$x_{m,k} \in \{0,1\}, \quad \forall m \in \mathcal{M}, k \in \mathcal{K} \tag{21d}$$

$$y_{m,k} \in \{0,1\}, \quad \forall m \in \mathcal{M}, k \in \mathcal{K} \tag{21e}$$

$$\sum y_{m,k} = M_{\max} \tag{21f}$$

Constraint (a) ensures that each user transmits its task to a designated user center through a multi-hop path. Constraint (b) restricts the communication distance of each hop to be within the maximum allowable wireless range d_max. Constraint (c) enforces that the total size of cached content on each UAV does not exceed its storage capacity. Constraints (d) and (e) define the binary decision variables related to the UAVs' caching and content retrieval strategies, respectively. Constraint (f) limits the total number of selected user centers, which are responsible for aggregating tasks within their coverage.

To reduce the complexity of the original joint optimization problem P0, we decompose it into two interdependent subproblems based on the hierarchical architecture of the network. However, unlike conventional decompositions, the two subproblems are not independent, and are inherently coupled through shared decision variables and cross-layer constraints.

The ground-layer subproblem focuses on the selection of user centers and multi-hop routing paths, with the aim of minimizing the transmission delay to UAVs. The locations of selected user centers directly determine the hovering positions of UAVs, establishing a spatial coupling between the two layers.

$$\mathbf{P1}:\max_{U_i} \quad \eta=\frac{\sum_{i=1}^{I}(1-f_i)}{\sum_{i=1}^{I}S} \tag{22}$$

$$\text{s.t.} \quad \bar{I}\in h_i \tag{22a}$$

$$\|d_i-d_i^{'}\|\leq d_{\max} \tag{22b}$$

$$\sum y_{m,k}=M_{\max} \tag{22c}$$

The air-space-layer subproblem aims to optimize UAV caching decisions and satellite offloading strategies, with the objective of reducing the task failure rate and the overall system delay. However, the effectiveness of UAV caching is influenced by the task types and volumes collected from the ground layer.

$$\mathbf{P2}:\max_{A_m,S_s} \quad \eta=\frac{\sum_{i=1}^{I}(1-f_i)}{\sum_{i=1}^{I}S} \tag{23}$$

$$\text{s.t.} \quad \sum_{k=1}^{K}R(k_m)\leq R_m \tag{23a}$$

$$x_{m,k}\in\{0,1\}, \quad \forall m\in\mathcal{M},\ k\in\mathcal{K} \tag{23b}$$

$$y_{m,k}\in\{0,1\}, \quad \forall m\in\mathcal{M},\ k\in\mathcal{K} \tag{23c}$$

In order to solve the cross-layer coupling problem, we design a top-down hierarchical optimization framework, which first determines the location deployment scheme of user centers at the ground layer, and subsequently updates the selection of the optimal caching policy for the air layer based on this deployment result.

4 Multilayer-Coupled Optimization for Air-Ground-Space Offloading

Multilayer-Coupled Optimization for Air-Ground-Space Offloading is composed of a ground-layer multihop routing strategy and an air-space-layer caching strategy.

4.1 Multi-hop User Aggregation Strategy

In the ground layer, user tasks located outside the direct coverage area of the UAV must be forwarded to designated user centers through multi-hop transmission. The selection of these user centers is crucial to minimize the overall task transmission delay and ensure timely offloading.

To solve the optimal user center selection and multi-hop routing **P1** problems, we adopt the ant colony optimization (ACO) algorithm. The ACO algorithm is particularly suitable for such scenarios because it can efficiently explore complex combinatorial solution spaces and find near-optimal routing paths in dynamic environments.

Specifically, As shown by Algorithm 1 the ACO algorithm constructs candidate solutions in an iterative manner by probabilistically selecting user nodes as centers, guided by pheromone updates that reflect the quality of previous solutions in terms of aggregated transmission delay. Through this adaptive search process, the algorithm converges to a user center configuration that minimizes the cumulative delay of task transmission from decentralized users to the air layer. This multi-hop aggregation strategy not only reduces the transmission delay of the ground layer, but also effectively balances the load among user centers, thereby enhancing the robustness and scalability of the ground layer. The synergy between the optimized user center location and efficient multi-hop routing lays a solid foundation for the subsequent caching and offloading mechanisms in the air and satellite layers.

Algorithm 1: Ant Colony Optimization for User Center Selection

Input: User set $\mathcal{I}$, topology graph $G = (\mathcal{I}, \mathcal{E})$, number of centers $M_{\max}$, pheromone factor α, heuristic factor β, evaporation rate ρ
Output: Optimal user center set $\mathcal{C}^*$
Initialize pheromone vector $\tau_i \leftarrow \tau_0$ for each user i
for $t = 1$ *to* T_{max} **do**
  for *each ant* a *in* $\{1, \ldots, A\}$ **do**
    Construct a candidate user center set $\mathcal{C}_a$ by probabilistic selection based on τ_i and heuristic η_i
    Compute total transmission delay D_a from all users to their nearest center in $\mathcal{C}_a$
  Update global best solution $\mathcal{C}^*$ with minimum D_a
  Pheromone evaporation: $\tau_i \leftarrow (1 - \rho) \cdot \tau_i$ for all i
  for *each solution* $\mathcal{C}_a$ **do**
    for *each center* $i \in \mathcal{C}_a$ **do**
      $\tau_i \leftarrow \tau_i + Q/D_a$
return $\mathcal{C}^*$

This multi-hop aggregation strategy not only reduces the transmission delay of the ground layer, but also effectively balances the load among user centers, thereby enhancing the robustness and scalability of the ground layer. The synergy between the optimized user center location and efficient multi-hop routing lays a solid foundation for the subsequent caching and offloading mechanisms in the air and satellite layers.

4.2 Multi-agent DDPG-Based UAV Caching

After determining the user center, the task will be transmitted to the UAVs within the coverage area for cache retrieval and subsequent processing. At this stage, whether the requested content is in the UAV cache directly affects the overall offloading delay and success rate, so the effectiveness of the caching strategy is crucial to the system performance. To address **P2** problem, we propose a collaborative caching strategy based on multi-agent deep reinforcement learning (MADDPG), which enables UAVs to coordinate adaptive caching strategies through joint optimization learning.

Algorithm 2: Multi-Agent DDPG-Based UAV Caching algorithm

Input: Number of UAV agents M, replay buffer size B, learning rate α, discount factor γ, exploration noise ϵ, update interval τ, heuristic policy $\pi_{\text{heuristic}}$
Output: Trained policy μ_m for each UAV $m \in \{1, \ldots, M\}$

Initialize: Actor network μ_m and critic network Q_m for each agent; target networks μ'_m and Q'_m with $\theta_{\mu'} \leftarrow \theta_\mu, \theta_{Q'} \leftarrow \theta_Q$; replay buffer $\mathcal{D} \leftarrow \emptyset$

Heuristic Pretraining Phase:
for *episode* = 1 **to** $N_{pretrain}$ **do**
  foreach *UAV agent m* **do**
    Select action $a_m \leftarrow \pi_{\text{heuristic}}(o_m)$
  Execute joint action $\mathbf{a} = (a_1, \ldots, a_M)$ and observe next state s', reward r, done signal
  Store transition $(s, \mathbf{a}, r, s')$ in buffer $\mathcal{D}$

MADDPG Training Phase:
for *episode* = 1 **to** $N_{episode}$ **do**
  Initialize state s
  for $t = 1$ **to** T **do**
    foreach *agent m* **do**
      Select action $a_m \leftarrow \mu_m(o_m) + \epsilon_t$
    Execute joint action $\mathbf{a}$, observe r, s'
    Store $(s, \mathbf{a}, r, s')$ in $\mathcal{D}$
    Sample mini-batch from buffer $\mathcal{D}$
    foreach *agent m* **do**
      Update critic: $y \leftarrow r_m + \gamma Q'_m(s', a'_1, ..., a'_M)$
      Minimize loss: $L \leftarrow (Q_m(s, \mathbf{a}) - y)^2$
      Update actor using policy gradient:
      $\nabla_{\theta^\mu} J \approx \nabla_a Q_m(s, \mathbf{a}) \nabla_{\theta^\mu} \mu_m(o_m)$
      Soft update target networks:
      $\theta_{\mu'} \leftarrow \tau\theta_\mu + (1 - \tau)\theta_{\mu'}$
      $\theta_{Q'} \leftarrow \tau\theta_Q + (1 - \tau)\theta_{Q'}$

return μ_m *for all* $m \in \{1, \ldots, M\}$'

In the SAGIN scenario, since multiple drones work together to provide computing services for ground users, the cache decision is not only affected by the characteristics of each user's request, but also by the synergy of the cache content of UAVs. Therefore, it is difficult for a single agent to effectively model the interaction between multiple drones. To this end, this paper adopts a multi-agent deep reinforcement learning method to enable each drone to learn collaboratively in a shared environment as an independent agent, which can capture the policy coupling and collaborative cache dynamics between drones, thereby improving the overall cache hit rate and offloading efficiency.

However, reinforcement learning usually faces the "cold start" problem in the early stage of training, that is, the agent needs to obtain an effective strategy through random trial in the absence of experience, which easily leads to a low task hit rate and system performance. Especially in the cache scenario, once the cache content misses, it will directly affect the task forwarding path and offloading success rate. Therefore, this paper integrates the heuristic cache strategy based on task heat as a pre-training mechanism to help the agent quickly establish an effective strategy framework in the initial stage, alleviate the performance fluctuation problem caused by cold start, and accelerate the convergence process of the overall system, as shown in Algorithm 2.

State Space. The global state s$\in$S captures all relevant environmental information needed for decision-making. This includes the current cache status of all UAVs, recent task request distributions, user density in different regions, and the network topology.

Action Space. Each agent selects an action, which corresponds to a specific caching operation. This include decisions such as which new task content to store, which existing content to evict when storage is full, or whether to initiate cooperative cache retrieval with other UAVs. These actions directly affect the system's caching configuration and, ultimately, the offloading performance.

Reward Function. The reward function is designed to reflect the effectiveness of caching decisions in supporting computational offloading. For each agent, the reward r is computed based on a weighted combination of several key performance indicators, including the cache hit rate, task offloading delay, and offloading efficiency. A typical formulation of the reward function is given as: $r = \lambda_1 \cdot \mathrm{HitRate} + \lambda_2 \cdot \mathrm{Delay} + \lambda_3 \cdot \eta$, where $\lambda_1, \lambda_2, \lambda_3$ are tunable hyperparameters that control the relative importance of each component.

Heuristic Pretraining Phase. To alleviate the cold-start problem commonly faced in reinforcement learning, a heuristic caching strategy based on task popularity is introduced as a pretraining mechanism. Specifically, each user center maintains a task popularity table by recording the frequency of historical task requests. UAVs then rank task types according to their estimated popularity and preferentially cache the top- most popular tasks within their storage limits. To enhance cache diversity and reduce redundancy, UAVs periodically exchange cache summaries with neighboring nodes and adjust their caching decisions to avoid storing duplicate content. This cooperative heuristic process allows UAVs to make informed initial caching decisions before interacting with the environment, resulting in improved cache hit rates and system stability in the early stages of training. The transitions collected during this phase are stored and later used to warm-start the multi-agent deep reinforcement learning algorithm.

5 Performance Evaluation

In this section, we utilize Python 3.9 and TensorFlow 2.0 to create a simulation platform and construct the SAGIN model.

5.1 Simulation Setting

In the scenario, the range of users is set to 30 maximum multi-hop range per user in a 100×100 scenario. The size of the empirical return area in reinforcement learning is set to 3000 and the Sample mini-batch from buffer is set to 256. The altitude of the UAV flight is fixed to 100 and the altitude of the satellite is fixed to 500,000. The rest of the parameters are in the Table 1.

To capture the variability in task urgency, the maximum tolerable delay for each user is defined as a function of the task workload, allowing different delay thresholds for different task types. To guide the learning process of agents towards performance-optimized behavior, the reward function is formulated as a weighted sum of offloading efficiency, cache hit ratio, and task success rate.

Table 1. Simulation Parameter

Parameter	values
Data size range	1–20 MB
Transmission power of each user/UAV/satellite $P_i/P_m/P_s$	3/4/5 W
Transmission bandwidth of each user/UAV/satellite $B_i/B_m/B_s$	1/10/20 MHz
Computing power of satellites C_s	2 GHz
Penalty coefficient α	2.5
Transmit and receive antenna gains G_t/G_r	1/1 dBi
Carrier frequency f	2 GHz
Noise temperature T	290 K
tunable hyperparameters $\lambda_1/\lambda_2/\lambda_3$	6/1/3

5.2 Performance Results

The performance of the proposed ACO algorithm is first validated through simulation. Specifically, the number of users is set to 10, 15and 20, while the number of center users is fixed at 2 for each case. As illustrated in Fig. 2, increasing the number of users improves the overall network connectivity by introducing additional potential relay nodes, thereby reducing the probability of user isolation or the absence of feasible transmission paths.

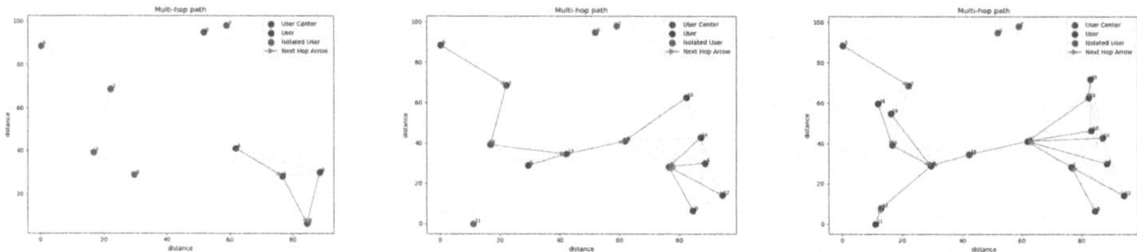

Fig. 2. Multi-hop Path Availability vs. Number of Users.

Furthermore, to evaluate the impact of the number of user centers on network connectivity, the number of users is fixed at 10, while the number of user centers is varied across 2, 3, and 4. As shown in Fig. 3, increasing the number of user centers does not result in a substantial reduction in the number of isolated users. This observation suggests that, under a limited user density, simply adding more center nodes does not significantly enhance the network's ability to provide feasible transmission paths, potentially.

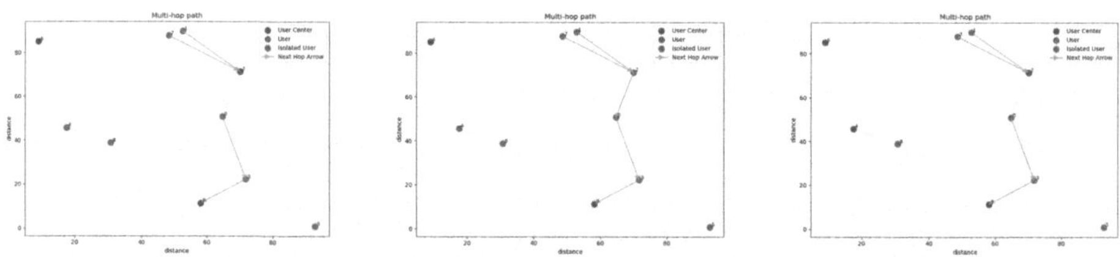

Fig. 3. Multi-hop Path Availability vs. Number of User Centers.

Figure 4 illustrates the impact of different learning rate configurations on the training performance of the proposed algorithm. The horizontal axis represents the number of training episodes, while the vertical axis shows the corresponding average reward achieved by the agents. In the figure la and lc denote the learning rate of Actor network and the learning rate of Critic network, respectively. Three learning rates are compared $(la = 1 \times 10^{-4}, lc = 1 \times 10^{-4})$, $(la = 1 \times 10^{-5}, lc = 1 \times 10^{-5})$, $(la = 1 \times 10^{-6}, lc = 1 \times 10^{-6})$.

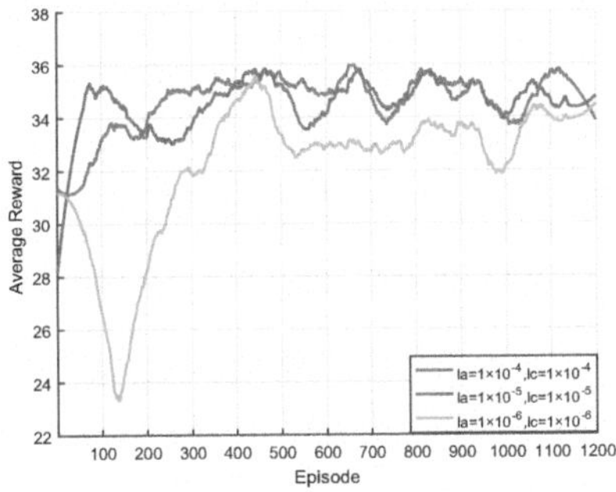

Fig. 4. Learning rate comparison.

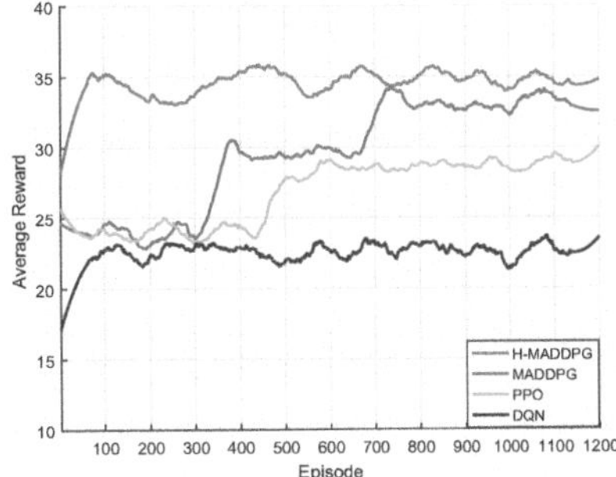

Fig. 5. Algorithm comparison.

The results demonstrate that a relatively larger learning rate ($la = 1 \times 10^{-4}, lc = 1 \times 10^{-4}$) leads to faster convergence and achieves the highest average reward, indicating superior learning efficiency and final performance. In contrast, smaller learning rates ($la = 1 \times 10^{-5}, lc = 1 \times 10^{-5}$) and ($la = 1 \times 10^{-6}, lc = 1 \times 10^{-6}$) exhibit slower convergence and lower reward ceilings. Particularly, the green line ($la = 1 \times 10^{-6}, lc = 1 \times 10^{-6}$) shows noticeable fluctuations and delayed improvement, suggesting insufficient update magnitude during training.

These observations suggest that in the given task setting, a moderate-to-large learning rate facilitates more effective policy optimization, balancing convergence speed and stability.

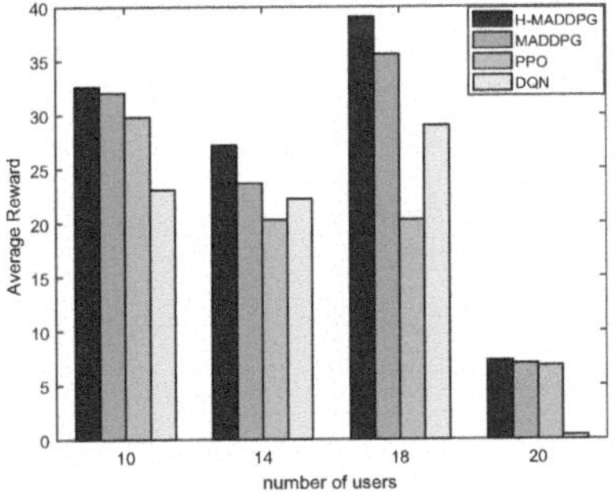

Fig. 6. Number of users comparison.

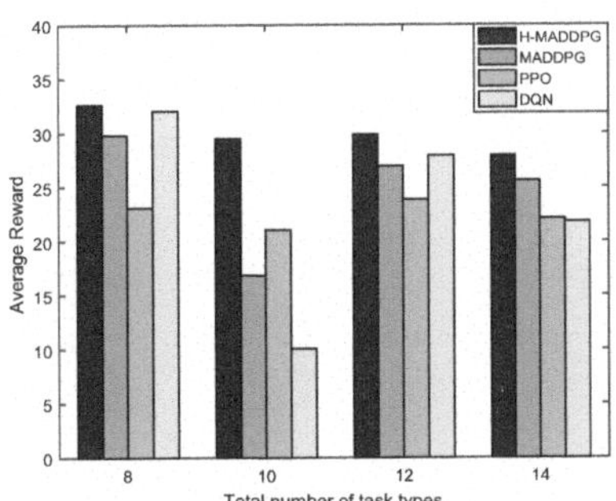

Fig. 7. Totsl task types comparison.

Figure 5 presents a performance comparison between the proposed MADDPG with heuristic pretraining phase(H-MADDPG) algorithm and several baseline methods, including MADDPG without cold-start optimization, (Proximal Policy Optimization)PPO, and (Deep Q-learning)DQN. The results clearly demonstrate that incorporating the cold-start mechanism leads to significantly improved average rewards, especially in the later stages of training. The blue line not only achieves the highest final performance but also shows more stable convergence compared to the baseline. In contrast, Cold-MADDPG, lacking cold-start handling, exhibits slower improvement and lower peak performance. PPO and DQN exhibit inferior performance in comparison, suggesting that value-based and on-policy reinforcement learning methods may have limited adaptability or efficiency in addressing the specific challenges posed by this multi-agent, cold-start-aware caching environment.

Figure 6 and Fig. 7 illustrate the comparative performance of the proposed H-MADDPG algorithm against several baseline methods under varying user densities and the number of task types, respectively. Overall, the proposed algorithm consistently achieves higher reward values across all experimental scenarios, demonstrating its superior adaptability and offloading efficiency.

In Fig. 6, as the number of users increases, the system experiences higher offloading demand, which typically leads to increased transmission delay and thus a decline in the overall reward. However, an exception occurs when the number of users reaches 16, where the reward exhibits an upward trend. This is attributed to a structural change in the network: the increase in users simultaneously enhances the multihop transmission capability, reducing the proportion of isolated users and improving the overall offloading efficiency. In Fig. 7, the variation in the number of task types affects the caching and decision-making complexity. An increase in the diversity of user task types expands the caching decision space, which complicates policy learning and degrades the training effectiveness of the agents. Consequently, the average reward demonstrates a downward trend as the heterogeneity of task types increases

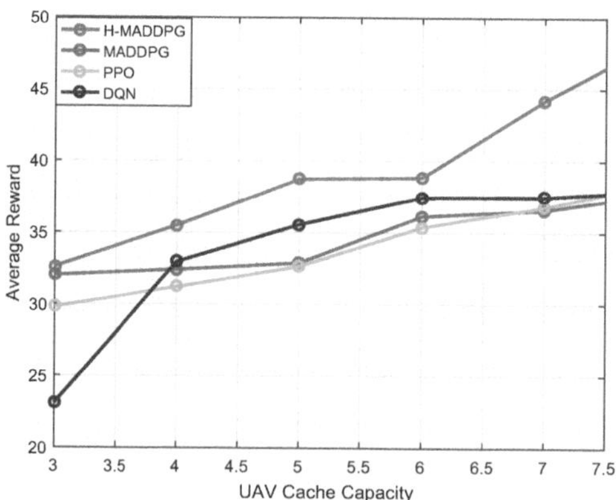

Fig. 8. UAV cache capacity comparison.

Figure 8 presents the performance comparison of different algorithms under varying UAV cache capacities. As the cache capacity increases, the average reward exhibits a clear upward trend across all algorithms, indicating that enhanced caching capability facilitates more efficient task offloading and execution. Notably, the proposed H-MADDPG algorithm consistently outperforms the baseline methods, further validating its effectiveness in leveraging UAV cache resources to optimize system performance.

6 Conclusion

In this paper, we proposed a novel computation offloading framework under a space-air-ground cooperative architecture to address the challenges of providing ubiquitous 6G services in remote and underserved regions. By leveraging the flexibility and mobility of UAVs, we designed an elastic computing network capable of aerial computation and cooperative task scheduling. To address the inherent complexity of the offloading problem tackled using a multi-hop ant colony optimization algorithm and a deep deterministic policy gradient (DDPG)-based intelligent caching strategy.

Simulation results demonstrate that our proposed approach significantly outperforms traditional baseline methods in terms of average task delay and task completion rate, indicating its strong applicability and scalability in practical 6G network scenarios.

For future work, more realistic mobility patterns and energy constraints of UAVs will be incorporated to improve deployment feasibility. Then, we aim to integrate federated learning or other distributed learning paradigms to enhance privacy and scalability in dynamic environments.

References

1. Periannasamy, S., Thangavel, C., Latha, S., Reddy, G., Ramani, S., Vitthalrao Phad, P.: Analysis of artificial intelligence enabled intelligent sixth generation (6G) wireless communication networks. In: 2022 IEEE International Conference on Data Science and Information System (ICDSIS), pp. 1–8. Hassan, India (2022)
2. Mariyam, O., Mariya, O., Zakaria, B.: Guest editorial preface special issue on 5G and a vision of 6G: fundamentals, applications and emerging trends. J. Mobile Multimedia **18**(5), 5–7 (2022)
3. Aung, N., Dhelim, S., Chen, L., Ning, H., Atzori, L.: Edge-enabled metaverse: the convergence of metaverse and mobile edge computing. Tsinghua Sci. Technol. **29**(3), 795–8059 (2024)
4. Serghiou, D., Khalily, M., Brown, T., Tafazolli, R.: Terahertz channel propagation phenomena, measurement techniques and modeling for 6G wireless communication applications: a survey, open challenges and future research directions. IEEE Commun. Surv. Tutorials **24**(4), 1957–1996 (2022)
5. Huang, C., et al.: Joint offloading and resource allocation for hybrid cloud and edge computing in SAGINs: a decision assisted hybrid action space deep reinforcement learning approach. IEEE J. Sel. Areas Commun. **42**(5), 1029–1043 (2024)
6. Chen, Y., Yang, Y.Z., Hu, J., Wu, Y., Huang, J.: A game-theoretical approach for distributed computation offloading in LEO satellite-terrestrial edge computing systems. IEEE Trans. Mob. Comput. **24**(5), 4389–4402 (2025)

7. Xie, B., Cui, H., Ho, I., He, Y., Guizani, M.: Computation offloading and resource allocation in LEO satellite-terrestrial integrated networks with system state delay. IEEE Trans. Mob. Comput. **24**(3), 1372–1385 (2025)
8. Han, D., Fang, W., Hosseinalipour, S., Chiang, M., Brinton, C.: Orchestrating federated learning in space-air- ground integrated networks: adaptive data offloading and seamless handover. IEEE J. Sel. Areas Commun. **42**(12), 3505–3520 (2024)
9. Mao, B., Liu, Y., Wei, Z., Guo, H., Xun, Y.J., Wang, J.: A blockchain-enabled cold start aggregation scheme for federated reinforcement learning-based task offloading in zero trust LEO satellite networks. IEEE J. Sel. Areas Commun. **43**(6), 2172–2182 (2025)
10. Bostani, A., Baniamerian, A., Zaher, A., Shammari, M.: LEO satellite constellations with 5G and 6G networks for enhanced IoT and PV system performance. In: 2024 20th International Conference on the Design of Reliable Communication Networks (DRCN), pp. 1–7. Montreal, QC, Canada (2024)
11. Ma, T., et al.: UAV-LEO integrated backbone: a ubiquitous data collection approach for B5G internet of remote things networks. IEEE J. Sel. Areas Commun. **39**(11), 3491–3505 (2021)
12. Fan, B., Xu, Z., Li, Z., Wu, Y., Zhang, Y.: DT assisted task offloading for C-V2X networks with imperfect DT prediction conditions. IEEE Trans. Intell. Transp. Syst. **26**(5), 6248–6262 (2025)
13. Chen, X., et al.: Mobility-aware dependent task offloading in edge computing: a digital twin-assisted reinforcement learning approach. IEEE Trans. Mob. Comput. **24**(4), 2979–2994 (2025)
14. Wu, L.T., Sun, P., Wang, Z., Li, Y., Yang, Y.: Computation offloading in multi-cell networks with collaborative edge-cloud computing: a game theoretic approach. IEEE Trans. Mobile Comput. **23**(3) (2024)
15. Liu, F., Chen, H., Miao, J., Zhang, T., Zhang, C., Kang, J.W.: Energy efficiency optimization for UAV-assisted cellular networks: a periodic clustering-based MATD3 approach. In: 2024 IEEE Global Communications Conference, pp. 229–234. Cape Town, South Africa (2024)
16. Li, T., Liu, y., Ouyang, T., Zhang, H., Yang, K., Zhang, X.: Multi-hop task offloading and relay selection for IoT devices in mobile edge computing. IEEE Trans. Mobile Comput. **24**(1), 466–481 (2025)
17. Huang, W., Zhao, Z., Min, G., Chen, J.: Distributed Multihop task offloading in massive heterogeneous IoT systems. IEEE Trans. Comput. **73**(4), 1126–1137 (2024)

Joint UAV Deployment, Task Offloading and Resource Allocation for Multi-UAV Collaborative Edge Computing Network

Jiyuan Wei, Xin Chen, Libo Jiao(✉), and Aobo Cao

Beijing Information Science and Technology University, Beijing 102206, China
{weijiyuan,chenxin,jiaolibo,caoaobo}@bistu.edu.cn

Abstract. Unmanned Aerial Vehicles (UAVs) are widely used in Mobile Edge Computing (MEC) and provide computing power at the network edge due to their flexible deployment, reliable wireless communication, and wide coverage. However, coordinating and optimising the relationship between UAV deployment, task offloading, and resource allocation poses a great challenge due to the tight interdependence between the three. In this paper, we study the problem of task offloading and computational resource allocation in a UAV-assisted MEC system with multiple UAVs collaborating, highlighting UAV deployment strategies. We define the system average user cost based on system energy consumption and latency. In this paper, the joint optimisation of UAV deployment, task offloading decisions, and computational resource allocation is formulated as a mixed integer Nonlinear programming (MINLP) problem with the objective of minimising the system average user cost. To address the combinatorial complexity problem, we develop a two-stage optimisation approach: 1) a Joint Linear Programming and Greedy Policy Algorithm (JLPGA) for efficient UAV deployment; 2) a Computation Offloading Decision and Resource Allocation Algorithm Based on Twin Delayed Deep Deterministic Policy Gradient (CODRA-TD3) for dynamic task offloading and resource allocation. Evaluation results show that our proposed algorithm outperforms the other three baseline algorithms in minimising the average user cost of the system.

Keywords: Deep reinforcement learning · UAV deployment · Resource allocation · Computing offloading

1 Introduction

Mobile Edge Computing (MEC), as a key technology to support low-latency and high-reliability Internet of Things (IoT) applications, has significantly alleviated the load pressure on cloud computing centres and optimized the quality

This work was supported by National Natural Science Foundation of China (Nos. 62202059, 62572063).

L. Zhang and K.-K. R. Choo (Eds.): MobiQuitous 2025, LNICST 684, pp. 95–115, 2026.
https://doi.org/10.1007/978-3-032-22503-0_6

of service by sinking computing resources to the edge of the network [1]. However, traditional fixed edge nodes are limited by geographic coverage and deployment flexibility, making it difficult to meet the rapid changes in user demand in dynamic scenarios [2]. In this context, Unmanned Aerial Vehicles (UAVs), with their flexible mobility, on-demand deployment capability, and wide-area communication coverage, have become an ideal carrier for building dynamic MEC systems, further expanding the boundaries of edge services through collaborative task processing and resource scheduling [3].

With the exponential growth of IoT terminal devices and the increased demand for real-time performance of smart applications, the dynamic edge computing paradigm is facing new technological innovations [4]. Especially in disaster emergency response, smart city inspection and other scenarios [5], the traditional edge computing architecture based on fixed infrastructure exposes the double bottleneck of response latency and coverage blindness [6]. UAV-assisted mobile edge computing (UAV-MEC) provides a breakthrough solution to the above problems by constructing a three-dimensional reconfigurable network topology [7]. Most current research focuses on single-dimension optimisation or hierarchical decision-making under decoupling assumptions, leading to overall system performance loss. How to establish a joint optimisation mechanism for multi-UAV deployment, task scheduling and resource allocation has become a key scientific issue to improve the energy efficiency of airborne edge computing systems.

In recent years, the integration of UAVs into MEC systems has attracted significant research attention due to their flexibility, mobility, and ability to provide low-latency services in dynamic and infrastructure-deficient environments. UAV-assisted MEC systems are particularly valuable in scenarios such as disaster response, public safety, and remote area connectivity, where traditional communication and computing infrastructures are either unavailable or severely damaged. Aldossary et al. [8] proposed a hierarchical architecture to enhance system responsiveness in emergency scenarios such as rescue operations, accident detection, and crime prevention. Their approach leverages UAVs' rapid deployment capabilities and combines them with the computing resources of fog and cloud layers to enable timely data processing and decision-making. Similarly, Akter et al. [9] explored the role of UAVs in disaster management and introduced SATORA, a soft-actor-critic (SAC) based algorithm built upon the Task-Oriented Resource Allocation (TORA) framework. Their method dynamically adapts offloading policies to minimize both task execution delay and overall energy consumption across varying environmental conditions.

To improve the efficiency of task allocation, Wang et al. [10] transformed the computational offloading problem into a two-sided stable matching problem between UAVs and user devices, using on-board fog computing to reduce latency while ensuring stable and decentralized offloading decisions. Sun et al. [11] proposed a three-tier post-disaster relief framework comprising two layers of UAVs and one vehicle layer. The system is designed to maximize long-term utility by distributing communication and computing responsibilities across multiple tiers, thereby enhancing robustness and service continuity in disaster-stricken areas.

Raivi et al. [12], on the other hand, focused on optimizing both energy efficiency and latency by jointly addressing data aggregation and computation offloading. Their approach employed a dual deep neural network to learn optimal strategies under dynamic network conditions, achieving significant reductions in system overhead.

Collectively, these studies underscore the potential of UAV-assisted MEC architectures and highlight the effectiveness of combining intelligent decision-making frameworks–such as reinforcement learning, matching theory, and deep learning–with hierarchical or distributed system designs to address the challenges of delay, energy consumption, and resource allocation in UAV-enabled environments.

However, Existing solutions for UAV-assisted MEC systems often overlook the critical challenges posed by heterogeneous user device (UD) distributions and complex terrain features, particularly in achieving optimal energy-latency tradeoffs under complete coverage constraints. To bridge this gap, our work makes three fundamental contributions:

- Aiming at the coverage constraints and energy-sensitive characteristics of UAVs, we propose a UAV deployment strategy based on the minimum coverage set, and construct a joint optimisation model containing UAV deployment, binary offloading decision and computational resource variables. The multi-objective optimisation problem is transformed into a quantifiable system average user cost minimisation problem by introducing an energy-efficiency-delay weighting factor.
- We propose a joint linear programming and greedy policy algorithm (JLPGA) to get the UAV deployment policy by formulating the UAV deployment rules. After that we transform the problem into a Markov Decision Process (MDP) and propose a computation offloading decision and resource allocation algorithm based on TD3 (CODRA-TD3) to solve it. The aim is to optimise the offloading decision and resource allocation to minimise the average user cost of the system.
- We evaluate the performance of CODRA-TD3 through extensive experiments. The experimental data show that CODRA-TD3 can effectively reduce the average user cost of the system compared with other schemes.

The rest of the paper is structured as follows. Section 2 introduces the system model and formulates the problem. Section 3 gives the problem transformation and algorithm design. Section 4 performs experimental analysis. Section 5 summarises the whole paper.

2 System Model

We constructed a multi-UAV cooperative model as shown in Fig. 1. It mainly consists of UDs and UAVs. We represent the set of UDs by setting $\mathbb{K}$, defined as $\mathbb{K} = \{1, 2, \ldots k, \ldots, K\}$. $\mathbb{U}$ represents the set of UAVs, defined as $\mathbb{U} = \{1, 2, \ldots u, \ldots, U\}$. In the initial phase each UD generates a task waiting to be computed, which we represent by a tuple $M_k = (d_k, c_k, \delta_k)$. where denotes d_k the data size of the computational task, c_k the computational size of the task, and δ_k the maximum tolerable delay of the task. In addition, we denote the positional information of the UD by $P_k^{ud} = \{x_k^{ud}, y_k^{ud}, z_k^{ud}\}$ where z_k^{ud} should be set to zero since the UD is on the ground. Similarly $P_u^{uav} = \{x_u^{uav}, y_u^{uav}, z_u^{uav}\}$ denotes the position information of the UAV, which we consider to be hovering at a fixed altitude. Hence, z_u^{uav} is set to a fixed value H.

The processing of the system is divided into three main parts, firstly in the first part the deployment of the UAVs is performed to determine the number and location of the UAVs in the system. Secondly, task computation and offloading of UDs are performed in the second part, in this paper, we consider the computation tasks of UDs are inseparable. Therefore, we use the complete offloading model. In the third stage of returning the computation results of the tasks, we consider that the data size of the computation results is small. Therefore, in this paper, we do not consider the delay and energy consumption in downlink transmission (Fig. 1).

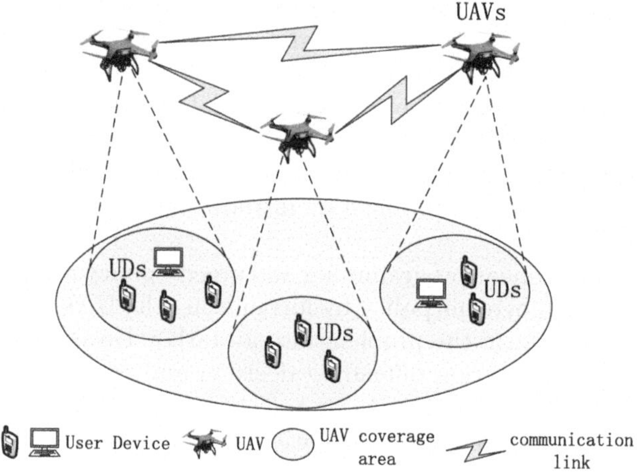

Fig. 1. System Model.

2.1 UAV Deployment Model

We consider an edge computation model with multiple UAVs assisting the computation. The UDs are randomly distributed in a certain region, and we denote $P_{min} = \{0, 0\}$ as the lower bound of the UDs in the region and $P_{max} = \{x_{max}, y_{max}\}$ as the upper bound of the UDs in the region. To ensure the availability of UAV services to all UDs within the region, we have implemented strict comprehensive coverage constraints, requiring that each UD within the specified region must be covered by at least one UAV. In other words, for each UD, there must be a UAV whose coverage area includes the location of the UD. The coverage area of a UAV is modelled as a two-dimensional circular region $\mathbb{C}$ with a fixed radius r centred at the UAV deployment location.

In other words, each UD k must be located within at least one UAV coverage circle $\mathbb{C}$. The UAV deployment problem is thus transformed into a geometric coverage problem: determine the minimum set of UAVs $\mathbb{U}$ and their corresponding locations P_u^{uav} such that the union of all $\mathbb{C}$ completely covers the entire UDs set $\mathbb{K}$. To ensure effective service delivery, the UAV deployment must satisfy the following constraints:

$$\mathbb{C}_u \neq \phi, \forall u \in \mathbb{U}, \tag{1}$$

$$\mathbb{C}_1 \cup \mathbb{C}_2 \cup \mathbb{C}_3 ... \cup \mathbb{C}_u = \mathbb{K}, \tag{2}$$

$$\{0, 0, H\} \leq P_u^{uav} \leq \{x_{max}, y_{max}, H\}, \tag{3}$$

$$|\mathbb{C}_i \cap \mathbb{C}_j| \to min, \forall i, j \in \mathbb{U}, i \neq j. \tag{4}$$

where constraint (1) indicates that the UD within the coverage area of the UAV should not be empty. Constraint (2) indicates that the placed UAVs should fully cover the UDs in the area. Constraint (3) indicates that the UAV positions should be within the defined area. Constraint (4) indicates that the overlapping coverage area between deployed UAVs should be as small as possible.

2.2 Communications Model

In the scenarios considered in this paper, they mainly include G2U links between UDs and UAVs, and U2U links between UAVs. G2U links have significant mixed LoS and Non-LoS (NLoS) propagation due to ground obstacles (e.g., buildings, vegetation). Therefore, we use a probabilistic propagation model to calculate the path loss of the G2U links. The U2U links are mainly dominated by LoS links due to the high altitude deployment of the UAVs, so the free space loss model is used to model the U2U links. Where the distance between the UAV u and the UD k can be expressed in terms of the Euclidean paradigm $d_k^u = \left\| P_k^{ud} - P_u^{uav} \right\|$. Similarly, the distance between a UAV and a UAV can be expressed as $d_{u_1}^{u_2} = \left\| P_{u_1}^{uav} - P_{u_2}^{uav} \right\|$. The model uplink uses orthogonal frequency division multiple access technique, and the interference between UAVs and their coverage UDs is negligible.

G2U Communication Model. The probability of occurrence of LoS and NLoS communication between UD k and UAV u is denoted as:

$$P_{k,u}^{LoS} = \frac{1}{1 + o_1 exp(-o_2(\frac{180}{\pi}\theta - o_1))}, \tag{5}$$

$$P_{k,u}^{NLoS} = 1 - P_{k,u}^{LoS}, \tag{6}$$

where $\theta = \arcsin(\frac{H}{d_k^u})$ denotes the elevation angle of the UAV. o_1 and o_2 denote the environmental parameters. The path loss model between UD k and UAV u can be expressed respectively as:

$$PL_{k,u}^{LoS} = 20\log_{10}(d_k^u) + 20\log_{10}(f_c) + 20\log_{10}(\frac{4\pi}{c}) + \vartheta LoS, \tag{7}$$

$$PL_{k,u}^{NLoS} = PL_{k,u}^{LoS} + \Delta\vartheta, \tag{8}$$

where f_c denotes the carrier frequency, c denotes the speed of light, ϑLoS denotes the LoS additional loss, and $\Delta\vartheta$ denotes the additional penetration loss. Therefore, the average path loss can be expressed as:

$$PL_{k,u} = P_{k,u}^{LoS} PL_{k,u}^{LoS} + P_{k,u}^{NLoS} PL_{k,u}^{NLoS}, \tag{9}$$

The uplink channel gain between UD k and UAV u can be expressed as:

$$h_{k,u} = \frac{1}{PL_{k,u}}, \tag{10}$$

We use B_{G2U} to represent the bandwidth of the G2U link. The uplink data transmission rate between the two can be expressed as:

$$r_{k,u}^{G2U} = B_{G2U} \log_2 \left(1 + \frac{P_{k,u} h_{k,u}}{\theta^2}\right), \tag{11}$$

where $P_{k,u}$ denotes the transmit power from UD k to UAV u, and θ^2 is the noise power.

U2U Communication Model. The U2U link is modelled using the free space model and the UAV-to-UAV channel gain can be expressed as:

$$h_{u_1,u_2} = v_0 \left(d_{u_1}^{u_2}\right)^{-2} = \frac{v_0}{\left\| P_{u_1}^{uav} - P_{u_2}^{uav} \right\|^2}, \tag{12}$$

where v_0 denotes the channel gain at a distance of one metre. Similarly, we use B_{U2U} to represent the bandwidth of the U2U link. The data transfer rate between the two can be expressed as:

$$r_{u_1,u_2}^{U2U} = B_{U2U} \log_2 \left(1 + \frac{P_{u_1,u_2} h_{u_1,u_2}}{\sigma^2}\right). \tag{13}$$

2.3 Computing Model

UD can choose to compute locally or offload to UAV computing. In particular, UAVs have two main primary functions, which are to provide computational resources and relay transmission. Therefore, UDs can offload computational tasks to any of the UAVs, i.e., UAVs can offload computational tasks from UDs within their own coverage area to other UAVs. This approach demonstrates collaboration between UAVs. In traditional UAV-assisted offloading computation, UDs can only offload computational tasks to the UAVs associated with them, and UAVs cannot offload tasks to each other, which may lead to a large amount of wasted computational resources of UAVs.

We define the offloading decision of a UD as $\alpha_k^u \in (0, 1)$. If $\alpha_k^u = 1$, it means that the UD k offloads the computational task to location u for computation. Otherwise, $\alpha_k^u = 0$. where if $u = 0$ indicates that the computation location is local and $1 \leq u \leq U$ indicates that the computation location is UAV. Since UD k can only choose one location to compute the task, the offloading decision must satisfy the constraint:

$$\sum_{u=0}^{U} \alpha_k^u = 1, \tag{14}$$

Computation of UD. If the UD chooses to compute the computation task locally, there is no transmission delay. the latency of the UD computing locally can be expressed as:

$$D_k^{loc} = \frac{\alpha_k^0 c_k}{f_k^{loc}}, \tag{15}$$

where f_k^{loc} denotes the local computing resources and λ_1 denotes the energy consumption factor of UD. The energy consumption of local computing can be expressed as:

$$E_k^{loc} = \lambda_1 \left(f_k^{loc}\right)^2 c_k. \tag{16}$$

Computation of UAV. UD k can only communicate with its own associated UAV u. If UD chooses to offload the computational task to UAV $u^{'}$, where $u \neq u^{'}$. Therefore, UD k has to offload the computational task to UAV u first, and UAV u further transmits the computational task to $u^{'}$. We consider that the UAV uses full-duplex communication, i.e., UAV u can forward the computational task received from UD k to the target UAV $u^{'}$. In this process, UAV u plays the role of a relay, and G2U and U2U are transmitted in parallel with the transmission delay being the maximum of the two. If UD k chooses to offload the computational task to UAV u, UAV u allocates computational resources for UD k to process the task. The transmission delay can be expressed as:

$$D_k^{tran} = \max\left\{\frac{d_k}{r_{k,u}^{G2U}}, \frac{d_k}{r_{u_1,u_2}^{U2U}}\right\}, \tag{17}$$

where if $u = u^{'}$, then the value of $d_k/r_{u_1,u_2}^{U2U}$ is 0. The transmission energy consumption from UD k to UAV u is:

$$E_k^u = \frac{p_k d_k}{r_{k,u}^{G2U}}, \tag{18}$$

Similarly, the transmission energy consumption from UAV u to UAV $u^{'}$ is:

$$E_u^{u^{'}} = \frac{p_u d_k}{r_{u_1,u_2}^{U2U}}, \tag{19}$$

where p_k and p_u are the transmit power of UD k and UAV u, respectively. The UAV computational delay can be expressed as:

$$D_k^u = \sum_{u=1}^{U} \frac{\alpha_k^u c_k}{f_k^u}, \tag{20}$$

where f_k^u is the computational resource allocated by UAV u to UD k, and F_u is the total computational resource of UAV u. The UAV has limited computational resources and should satisfy the following constraints:

$$0 \leq \sum_{k=1}^{K} f_k^u \leq F_u, \tag{21}$$

The computational energy consumption of the UAV can be expressed as:

$$E_k^{uav} = \lambda_2 \left(f_k^u\right)^3 D_k^u, \tag{22}$$

where λ_2 is the energy efficiency factor of the UAV. In the following we give the total delay and total energy consumption calculated by the UAV respectively:

$$D_k^{u'} = D_k^{tran} + D_k^u, \tag{23}$$

$$E_k^{u'} = E_k^u + E_u^{u'} + E_k^{uav}, \tag{24}$$

Combining the local computation model and the UAV computation model, we can express the total delay and the total energy consumption of UD k as respectively:

$$D_k = \alpha_k^0 D_k^{loc} + \sum_{u=1}^{U} \alpha_k^u D_k^{u'}, \tag{25}$$

$$E_k = \alpha_k^0 E_k^{loc} + \sum_{u=1}^{U} \alpha_k^u E_k^{u'}. \tag{26}$$

2.4 Problem Formulation

We define the cost as the weighted sum of delay and energy consumption [13] and denote the weighting factor as η. Based on the above two equations, we can express the cost of UD k as:

$$Cost_k = \eta D_k + (1 - \eta) E_k, \tag{27}$$

where $\eta \in [0, 1]$ denotes UD $k's$ preference for latency and energy efficiency. For example, when $\eta = 1$, it indicates that UD k only focuses on latency without considering energy consumption. Further, we define the average cost (AC) of the system as the average of the costs of all UDs and we denote AC as:

$$AC = \frac{1}{K} \sum_{k \in \mathbb{K}} Cost_k. \tag{28}$$

Therefore, considering the offloading decision α , the UAV computational resource allocation f, and the number of UAVs u the system user average cost minimisation problem (p1) can be designed as follows:

$$
\begin{aligned}
(P1)\ &\min_{\alpha,f,u} AC \\
s.t.C1 &: p_k \le p_k^{max}, \forall k \in \mathbb{K}, \\
C2 &: p_u \le p_u^{max}, \forall u \in \mathbb{U}, \\
C3 &: \sum_{u=0}^{U} \alpha_k^u = 1, \forall k \in \mathbb{K}, \\
C4 &: 0 \le \sum_{k=1}^{K} f_k^u \le F_u, \forall u \in \mathbb{U}, \\
C5 &: \alpha_k^0 D_k^{loc} + \sum_{u=1}^{U} \alpha_k^u D_k^{u'} \le \delta_k, \forall k \in \mathbb{K}, \\
C6 &: (1), (2), (3), (4).
\end{aligned}
\tag{29}
$$

where C1 and C2 denote limiting the transmit power of UD and UAV from exceeding the maximum transmit power, respectively. C3 denotes that the UD k can only select one device to process the task. C4 is the limit of the limited resources of the UAV, which ensures that the resources allocated to the UD k will not exceed the maximum resource limit. C5 denotes that the task processing latency of the UD k will not exceed the maximum tolerable latency. C6 denotes the number of UAVs to be deployed and their locations.

3 Algorithm Design

Algorithm 1: Joint Linear Programming and Greedy Policy Algorithm (JLPGA)

Input: Boundaries of the region P_{min} and P_{max}; number of UDs K and their positions P^{ud}; UAV coverage radius r;
Output: Number of UAVs U and their positions P^{uav};

```
1  Generate candidate UAV locations P_uav^cand in the region;
2  Initialize distance matrix Dis[N][K];
3  for each candidate UAV u do
4  |   for each UD k do
5  |   |   Compute distance d_uk between UAV u and UD k;
6  |   |   if d_uk ≤ r then
7  |   |   |   Store d_uk into Dis[u][k];
8  |   |   end
9  |   |   else
10 |   |   |   Set Dis[u][k] ← ∞;
11 |   |   end
12 |   end
13 end
14 Formulate and solve the ILP problem;
15 Apply Greedy Refinement (see Algorithm 2) to minimize coverage overlap;
16 Set U ← |U_final|, P^uav ← positions of UAVs in U_final;
17 return U, P^uav;
```

To solve the system average cost minimisation problem for P1, it is first necessary to solve the fixed radius circle coverage problem posed in the UAV deployment model, which is an NP-hard problem. In order to determine the optimal number and location of UAVs to completely cover all UDs within a specified area, we formulate the deployment problem as an integer linear programming (ILP) model. The goal is to minimise the number of UAVs while ensuring that at least one UAV covers each UD within a fixed communication radius r. Suppose N is the number of candidate UAV locations and K is the number of UDs. We define the following binary variables:

- $x_u \in \{0, 1\}$: Indicates whether a UAV is deployed at candidate location u;
- $y_{uk} \in \{0, 1\}$: Indicates whether UD k is served by UAV u;

The ILP formulation is as follows:

$$
\begin{aligned}
&\min \sum_{u=1}^{N} x_u \\
&C1 : \sum_{u=1}^{N} y_{uk} \geq 1, \forall k = 1, \dots, K \\
&C2 : y_{uk} \leq x_u, \forall u = 1, \dots, N;\ k = 1, \dots, K \\
&C3 : y_{uk} = 0, \text{if } d_{uk} > r \\
&C4 : x_u \in \{0, 1\}, \quad y_{uk} \in \{0, 1\}, \forall u, k
\end{aligned}
\tag{30}
$$

In this formulation, C1 ensures that every UD is covered by at least one UAV. C2 ensures that a UAV can only serve UDs if it is deployed. C3 restricts service assignments to within the UAV's communication radius r, where d_{uk} denotes the distance between UAV u and UD k. C4 defines the binary nature of the decision variables.

After solving the above ILP model to obtain an initial minimal set of UAV deployment positions, denoted as $\mathbb{U}$, we apply a post-processing greedy refinement procedure to further improve the solution quality. While the ILP formulation guarantees full coverage of all UDs with the fewest number of UAVs, it does not explicitly minimize the overlap between coverage regions of different UAVs. Excessive overlap may lead to redundant resource consumption, increased interference, and inefficient spatial utilization.

To address this, the refinement step is designed to locally adjust the positions of UAVs in $\mathbb{U}$ in a greedy manner, aiming to minimize the pairwise intersection areas between UAV coverage disks. This process directly aligns with the objective defined in Eq. (4) of the deployment model, which seeks to reduce coverage redundancy while preserving the full coverage constraint. For the overall UAV deployment process, we propose the joint linear programming and greedy policy algorithm (JLPGA) as a solution. The specific steps are outlined in Algorithm 1, while the detailed steps of the greedy optimisation strategy are elaborated in Algorithm 2.

Once the number and location of UAVs have been determined, the optimisation problem P1 can be transformed into P2, which can be expressed as:

$$
\begin{aligned}
(P2) \min_{\alpha, f} & AC \\
s.t. C1: & p_k \leq p_k^{max}, \forall k \in \mathbb{K}, \\
C2: & p_u \leq p_u^{max}, \forall u \in \mathbb{U}, \\
C3: & \sum_{u=0}^{U} \alpha_k^u = 1, \forall k \in \mathbb{K}, \\
C4: & 0 \leq \sum_{k=1}^{K} f_k^u \leq F_u, \forall u \in \mathbb{U}, \\
C5: & \alpha_k^0 D_k^{loc} + \sum_{u=1}^{U} \alpha_k^u D_k^{u'} \leq \delta_k, \forall k \in \mathbb{K},
\end{aligned}
\tag{31}
$$

Problem P2 is a mixed-integer nonlinear programming (MINLP) problem containing continuous and discrete variables with a complex structure that is difficult to solve in polynomial time. To improve the solution efficiency, we transform P2 into a Markov Decision Process (MDP) model, thus transforming the static optimisation problem into a dynamic process that can be decided step-by-step.

By defining reasonable states, actions and reward functions, the MDP can better represent the dynamic characteristics of the system, which is especially

Algorithm 2: Greedy Refinement for UAV Coverage Minimization

Input: UAV set $\mathcal{U}$ from ILP solution; coverage sets $\{\mathbb{C}_u\}$ for all $u \in \mathcal{U}$; number of UDs K;

Output: Final UAV set $\mathcal{U}_{\text{final}}$ with minimal overlap and full UD coverage;

```
1  Initialize K_covered ← ∅, U_final ← ∅;
2  while K_covered ≠ {1, 2, ..., K} do
3      best_idx ← −1, max_gain ← 0;
4      foreach UAV u ∈ U do
5          gain ← |C_u \ K_covered|;
6          if gain > max_gain then
7              max_gain ← gain;
8              best_idx ← u;
9          end
10     end
11     if best_idx ≠ −1 then
12         U_final ← U_final ∪ {best_idx};
13         K_covered ← K_covered ∪ C_best_idx;
14     end
15 end
16 return U_final
```

suitable for optimisation problems with temporal order and uncertainty. On this basis, we introduce the deep reinforcement learning (DRL) method, which learns and optimises the policies with the help of deep neural networks, so as to achieve efficient and near-optimal solutions. Compared with traditional methods, DRL is able to adapt to changes in complex environments, has stronger generalisation and online learning capabilities, and is suitable for high-dimensional and complex resource scheduling and allocation tasks.

3.1 The MDP Model

The MDP model is represented as a four-tuple (S, A, P_r, R), where S denotes the set of system states, and A refers to the available actions within the system. At each time slot t, the system's state and action are represented by $s(t)$ and $a(t)$, respectively. The transition probability P_r indicates the likelihood of moving from state $s(t)$ to the subsequent state $s(t+1)$ upon performing action $a(t)$. The function R represents the immediate reward obtained after the execution of $a(t)$.

- State: The agent constructs $s(t)$ by observing the current state information of the environment, which can be expressed as

$$s(t) = \{P(t), F(t), M(t), R(t)\}, \tag{32}$$

  where $P(t) = \{P^{ud}, P^{uav}\}$ denotes the set of UD and UAV coordinates. $F(t)$ denotes the available computational resources of the UAVs. $M(t) = \{d, c, \delta\}$ denotes the set of mission information of all UDs. $R(t)$ denotes the set of uplink communication rates, which mainly includes G2U and U2U.
- Action:The agent makes an action decision $a(t)$ after acquiring the state of the environment, which can be represented as

$$a(t) = \{\alpha(t), f(t)\}, \tag{33}$$

  where $\alpha(t) = [\alpha_k^u(t)], \forall k \in \{1, ..., K\}, \forall u \in \{1, ..., U\}$ is the UD task offloading decision and $f(t) = [f_k^u(t)], \forall k \in \{1, ..., K\}, \forall u \in \{1, ..., U\}$ is the computational resources allocated by the UAV for the UD.
- Reward:The optimisation objective of P2 is to minimise the average system cost. Therefore, the reward function R is related to $-AC$ and can be expressed as:

$$R = \begin{cases} -AC, & D_k \leq \delta_k, \\ -n * AC, & D_k \geq \delta_k. \end{cases} \tag{34}$$

  where n is the number of UDs that do not satisfy constraint C5.

3.2 Computation Offloading Decision and Resource Allocation Algorithm Based on Twin Delayed Deep Deterministic Policy Gradient (CODRA-TD3)

The TD3 algorithm is a deterministic deep reinforcement learning approach within the Actor-Critic framework. It builds upon the Deep Deterministic Policy Gradient (DDPG) algorithm by addressing its tendency to overestimate action values through three key innovations:(1) To mitigate overestimation bias, TD3 employs two Critic networks and takes the minimum value between them when computing target values. (2) By adding noise to the target action during the evaluation of the next state, TD3 ensures smoother value estimates, preventing overfitting to sharp peaks in the value function. (3) Delayed Policy Updates:TD3 updates the Critic networks more frequently than the Actor network. This delayed update stabilizes the Actor's training by allowing the Critic to provide more reliable gradients. These enhancements make TD3 more robust in environments with continuous action spaces, improving both training stability and performance compared to DDPG. Therefore, based on the TD3 algorithm, we propose a CODRA-TD3 algorithm to solve problem P2 in order to obtain optimal offloading and resource allocation decisions. The algorithm process is as follows.

Algorithm 3: Computation Offloading Decision and Resource Allocation Algorithm Based on TD3 (CODRA-TD3)

1 []
2 Initialize critic network Φ_{ψ_1}, Φ_{ψ_2}, and actor network Ψ_ϕ with random parameters ψ_1, ψ_2, ϕ;
3 Initialize the parameters of the target network $\psi_1^{'} \leftarrow \psi_1, \psi_2^{'} \leftarrow \psi_2, \phi^{'} \leftarrow \phi$;
4 Initialize reply buffer B;
5 **for** *episode = 1 to EPISODES* **do**
6   Generate an initial state s;
7   **for** t = *1 to* T **do**
8   The agents with exploration noise to select action a and calculates the reward r and gets the new state $s^{'}$;
9   Save data tuples in $\mathcal{B}$;
10   Randomly choose a mini-batch of tuples in $\mathcal{B}$;
11   Calculate y using (37);
12   Update the parameters ψ_1, ψ_2 of the two critic networks with (38);
13   **if** t *mod* m **then**
14   Update the parameters ϕ of the actor network with (40);
15   Update the target network parameters $\psi_1^{'}, \psi_2^{'}, \phi^{'}$ with (41)
16   **end**
17   **end**
18 **end**

Firstly, initialize two critic networks and one actor network $\Phi_{\psi_1}, \Phi_{\psi_2}, \Psi_\phi$ with random parameters ψ_1, ψ_2, ϕ, as well as their corresponding target networks $\psi_1^{'}, \psi_2^{'}, \phi^{'}$. Then the agent executes action a based on the current state information s, obtaining immediate reward r and the next state $s^{'}$. Then store the tuple $(s, a, r, s^{'})$ in the replay buffer $\mathcal{B}$. During the training phase, we randomly sample a batch of tuple data from $\mathcal{B}$ to update the network parameters.

For updating two critic networks, first use the target actor network to calculate the action $a^{'}$ in state $s^{'}$:

$$a^{'} = \Psi_{\phi^{'}}\left(s^{'} \mid \phi^{'}\right), \tag{35}$$

Based on the target strategy, smooth regularization is performed by adding noise ε to the target action $a^{'}$:

$$\begin{aligned} a^{'} &= a^{'} + \varepsilon, \\ \varepsilon &\sim clip\left(N\left(0, \sigma\right), -c, c\right), \end{aligned} \tag{36}$$

Then based on the idea of dual network, the target value is calculated:

$$y = r + \gamma min_{k=1,2} \Phi_{\psi_k^{'}}\left(s^{'}, a^{'} \mid \psi_k^{'}\right), \tag{37}$$

Finally, a gradient descent algorithm is used to minimise the error L_{c_k} between the evaluated value and the target value, thus updating the parameters in the two Critic networks:

$$L_{c_k} = \frac{1}{N}\sum_{i=1}^{N}\left(\Phi_{\psi_k}(s, a \mid \psi_k) - y_i\right)^2, (k = 1, 2), \tag{38}$$

The update of the actor network is initiated after the m-step of the update of the two cirtic networks, and the actor network is used to compute the action a_n in state s:

$$a_n = \Psi_{\phi}\left(s \mid \phi\right), \tag{39}$$

The critic1 or critic2 network is then used to compute the evaluation value q_n of the state action pair (s, a_n), here we assume the use of the critic2 network, and finally the gradient ascent algorithm is used to maximise q_n to complete the update of the actor network. Where q_n is denoted as:

$$q_n = \Phi_{\psi_2}\left(s, a_n \mid \psi_2\right), \tag{40}$$

Finally the target network parameters $\psi_1^{'}, \psi_2^{'}, \phi^{'}$, are updated. The update process is given by

$$\begin{aligned} \psi_k^{'} &\leftarrow \xi\psi_k + (1 - \xi)\psi_k^{'}, (k = 1, 2), \\ \phi^{'} &\leftarrow \xi\phi + (1 - \xi)\phi^{'}. \end{aligned} \tag{41}$$

where ξ is a soft update parameter used to enable a slow update of the target network. The CODRA-TD3 algorithm is given in Algorithm 3. The framework of the algorithm is given in Fig. 2.

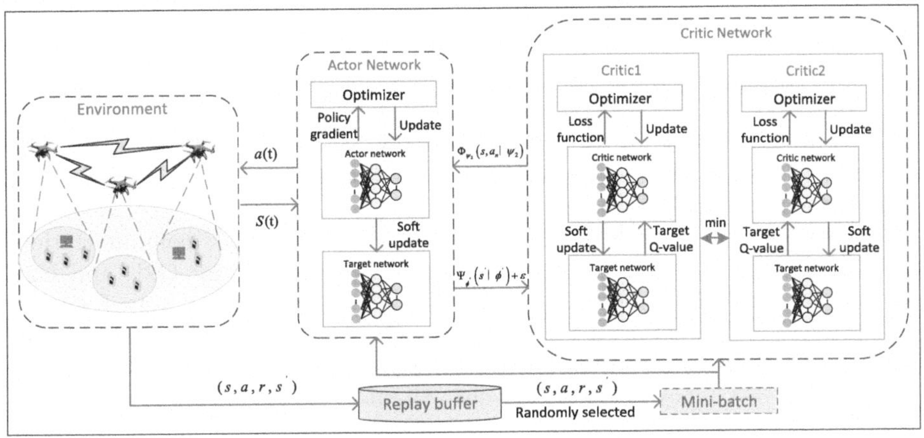

Fig. 2. CODRA-TD3 framework.

4 Performance Evaluation

In this section, we conduct simulation experiments to evaluate the performance of the proposed CODRA-TD3 scheme in a collaborative UAV-assisted MEC environment. The UAV deployment problem is formulated and solved using the Pulp 2.9.0 optimization toolkit. The multi-UAV edge computing environment is implemented in Python 3.7, with the deep reinforcement learning components built on TensorFlow 1.14.0. To verify the effectiveness of our scheme, we adjust key hyperparameters in the network and compare CODRA-TD3 with several baseline methods under various experimental settings.

4.1 Baseline Algorithms

To demonstrate the effectiveness of the proposed CODRA-TD3 scheme, we compare it with three representative baseline methods:

- DDPG (Deep Deterministic Policy Gradient), a classical model-free actor-critic reinforcement learning algorithm designed for continuous action spaces. It serves as a strong baseline for offloading and resource allocation tasks in MEC systems;
- A3C (Asynchronous Advantage Actor-Critic), which employs multiple asynchronous actor-learners to stabilize and accelerate the training process. This method is effective in dynamic and complex environments and provides a benchmark for parallel policy learning;
- Random, where task offloading decisions and resource allocations are made randomly without any optimization. This serves as a performance lower bound and highlights the importance of intelligent policy design.

All algorithms are implemented under the same simulation environment and parameter settings for a fair comparison. The primary performance metric used in our evaluation is the average user cost of the system, which reflects the joint impact of computation delay and energy consumption.

4.2 Parameter Settings

In our simulation environment, UDs are randomly distributed within a square region of 1000×1000 m^2. Each UAV hovers at a fixed altitude of $H = 100$ m and has a communication coverage radius of $r = 150$ m. To reflect the heterogeneous nature of the MEC system, we set the computation capabilities of UAVs and UDs to 20 GHz and 600 MHz, respectively.

The wireless bandwidth is configured as 20 MHz for G2U communications and 40 MHz for U2U links. The background noise powers for G2U and U2U channels are set to $\theta^2 = -110$ dBm and $\sigma^2 = -100$ dBm, respectively. Each UD generates a task characterized by two parameters: task size d_k and computational load c_k. The values of d_k and c_k are randomly sampled from the intervals $[2, 12]$ MB and $[0.5, 3]$ Gigacycles, respectively. All tasks have a maximum tolerable delay δ_k of 1 s.

For communication energy consumption, the transmit powers of UDs and UAVs are set to 1 W and 4 W, respectively. The energy efficiency coefficient is set to $\lambda_1 = \lambda_2 = 10^{-28}$. A cost weight factor $\eta = 0.5$ is used to balance the importance of delay and energy consumption in the objective function.

Regarding the CODRA-TD3 algorithm, the replay memory buffer size is set to 3000, and the mini-batch size for training is 64. The discount factor γ is set to 0.99 to ensure long-term reward optimization. All experiments are performed under the same parameter configurations unless stated otherwise. Table 1 lists the values of the relevant parameters (Table 1).

Table 1. Parameter Settings

Parameter	Value
UAV hovering height H	100 m
UAV coverage radius r	150 m
Number of UDs $\mathbb{K}$	$[20, 100]$
UAV computation capacity f^u	20 GHz
UD computation capacity f^{loc}	600 MHz
G2U bandwidth B_{G2U}	20 MHz
U2U bandwidth B_{U2U}	40 MHz
Noise power θ^2, σ^2	-100 dBm
Task size d_k	$[2, 12]$ MB
Computational load c_k	$[0.5, 3]$ Gigacycles
Maximum delay δ_k	1 s
Transmit power of UD / UAV p_k / p_u	1 W / 4 W
Energy efficiency coefficients λ_1, λ_2	10^{-28}
Delay-energy weight η	0.5
Discount factor γ	0.99

4.3 Experimental Analysis

In the following analysis, we present and interpret the experimental results to evaluate the performance of the proposed CODRA-TD3 scheme. The evaluation includes the UAV deployment layout generated by JLPGA, convergence behavior under different learning rates, and comparisons with baseline algorithms. Furthermore, we examine the average user cost under varying system conditions, including different numbers of UDs, task sizes, and computing amount.

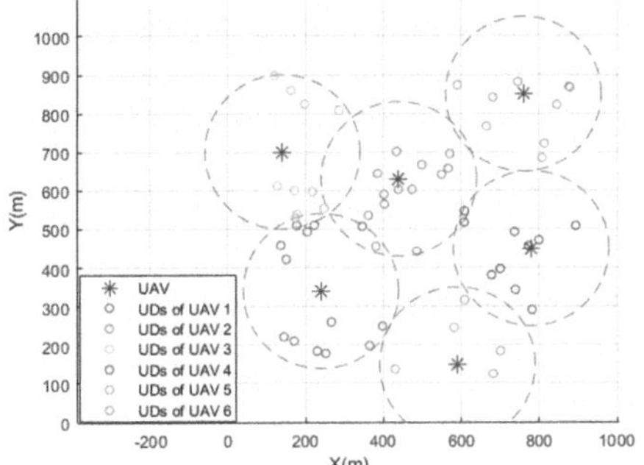

Fig. 3. UAV deployment map.

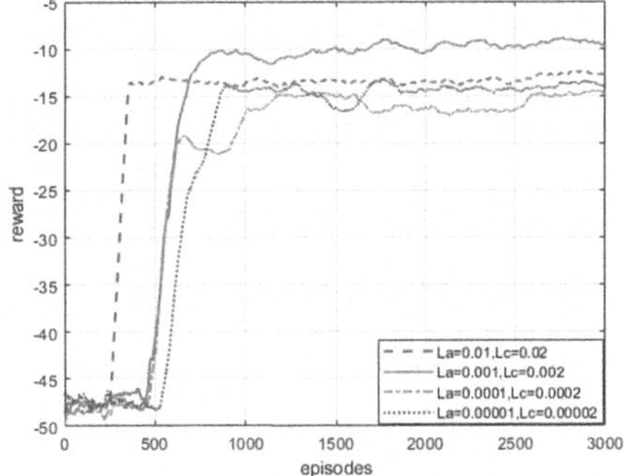

Fig. 4. Comparison of different learning rates.

UAV Deployment. Figure 3 shows the UAV deployment result generated by the proposed JLPGA algorithm when the number of UDs is set to 60. The deployment ensures complete user coverage while minimizing the number of UAVs and the overlap between their coverage areas. This optimized deployment serves as the foundation for all subsequent experiments, providing the initial UAV positions and coverage structure required for evaluating the CODRA-TD3 scheme under various system settings. By ensuring that communication coverage constraints are met in advance, the learning process of CODRA-TD3 can focus purely on optimizing computation offloading and resource allocation strategies.

Convergence Under Different Learning Rates. Figure 4 illustrates the impact of different learning rates on the convergence performance of the proposed CODRA-TD3 algorithm. Specifically, we tested actor network learning rates of 0.01, 0.001, 0.0001, and 0.00001, along with corresponding critic network learning rates of 0.02, 0.002, 0.0002, and 0.00002. Across all settings, it is observed that the agent experiences slow exploration in the early stages of training, primarily due to the complexity of the action space in the multi-UAV MEC environment. When the learning rate is set too high (e.g., 0.01), the actor network tends to converge prematurely to suboptimal policies, indicating a tendency to fall into local optima. Conversely, excessively small learning rates (e.g.,

0.00001) slow down convergence considerably, as parameter updates become too conservative. The experimental results suggest that an actor learning rate of 0.001 combined with a critic learning rate of 0.002 offers a favorable trade-off between convergence speed and policy stability. This setting enables the agent to explore effectively while avoiding oscillations or premature convergence, leading to more stable and optimal offloading decisions.

Comparison with Baseline Algorithms. Figure 5 illustrates the convergence behaviour of four schemes–CODRA-TD3, DDPG, A3C, and random strategy–during training by comparing their cumulative reward trajectories. It can be observed that the proposed CODRA-TD3 algorithm achieves significantly higher cumulative rewards. In contrast, DDPG and A3C exhibit lower final reward values, indicating poor policy performance in the given MEC environment. As expected, the random strategy does not exhibit meaningful convergence behaviour during training, with reward values fluctuating at consistently low levels. These results confirm the superior learning capability and policy quality of CODRA-TD3, which is attributed to its improved exploration-exploitation balance mechanism and enhanced value estimation mechanism introduced through the dual-delay structure. Overall, this comparison highlights the effectiveness of CODRA-TD3 in learning optimal offloading and resource allocation strategies in complex multi-UAV MEC scenarios.

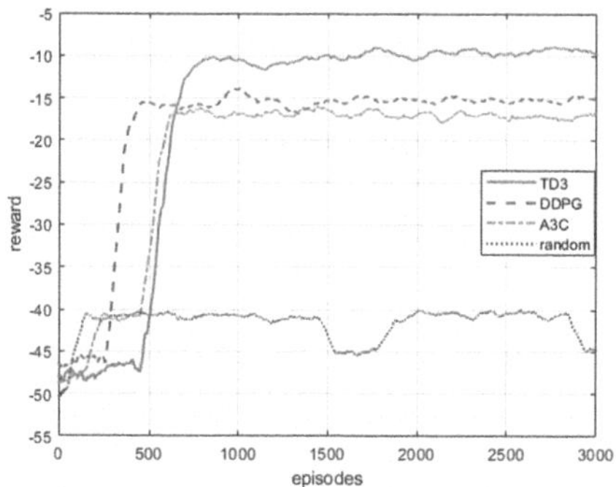

Fig. 5. Comparison of different algorithms.

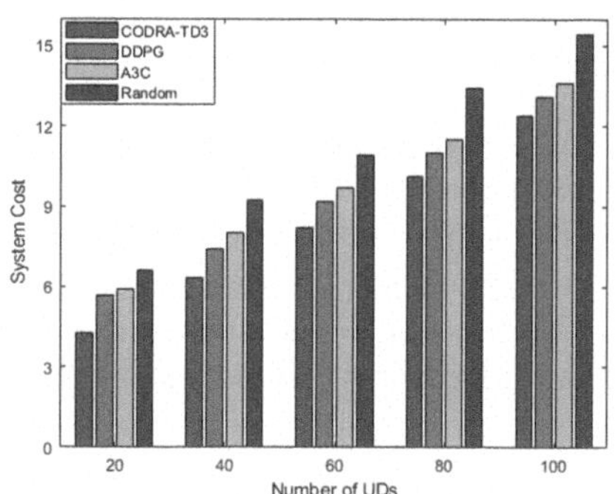

Fig. 6. Comparison of different UD numbers.

Impact of User Number. Figure 6 presents the impact of varying the number of user devices (UDs) on the average user cost of the system across the four evaluated schemes: CODRA-TD3, DDPG, A3C, and Random. As the number of UDs increases, the overall computational demand and communication load in the system also increase, leading to a corresponding rise in average user cost. This trend is evident in all schemes, as more tasks require offloading and coordination under limited UAV resources. However, the proposed CODRA-TD3 consistently achieves the lowest average user cost across all UD settings, demonstrating its superior scalability and adaptability to increasing system load. Quantitatively, CODRA-TD3 reduces the average user cost by 5.3%, 8.8%, and 19.4% compared to DDPG, A3C, and the Random policy, respectively.

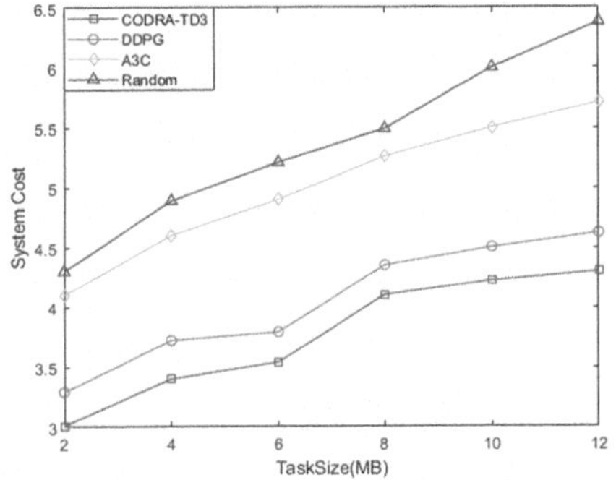

Fig. 7. Impact of different task sizes on system costs.

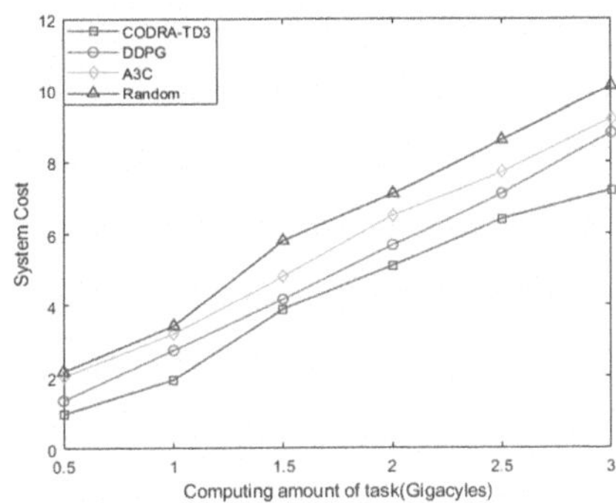

Fig. 8. Impact of different computational volumes required for tasks on system costs.

Impact of Task Size. Figure 7 illustrates the effect of varying task sizes on the average user cost across different offloading schemes. In this experiment, the task size is uniformly varied in the range of $[2, 12]$ MB to simulate different transmission loads. As the task size increases, both the data transmission delay and energy consumption associated with offloading rise accordingly, leading to an overall increase in system cost. This trend is consistently observed in all evaluated algorithms. Among the four schemes, CODRA-TD3 demonstrates the best performance, maintaining the lowest average user cost across all task sizes. In contrast, the Random policy shows the highest cost due to its lack of optimization in task distribution and resource allocation. Specifically, CODRA-TD3 achieves an average user cost reduction of 6.9%, 31.7%, and 32.6% when compared to DDPG, A3C, and the Random strategy, respectively. These results validate the effectiveness of the proposed approach in handling large-volume tasks by efficiently balancing transmission overhead and computational resource allocation among UAVs.

Impact of Computing Amount. Figure 8 investigates the computing amount of task on the average user cost in the system. As the computational demand increases, the UAVs are required to perform more intensive processing per task, which results in higher computation latency and energy consumption. Consequently, this leads to a significant rise in the average user cost of the system.

Despite this increase in task complexity, the proposed CODRA-TD3 algorithm consistently achieves the lowest average user cost across all levels of computational intensity. This demonstrates the model's ability to dynamically allocate computing tasks among UAVs based on available resources and task complexity. In contrast, DDPG and A3C exhibit higher costs due to less efficient coordination mechanisms, while the Random strategy performs the worst due to its lack of optimization. Quantitatively, CODRA-TD3 reduces the average user cost by 18.1%, 21.7%, and 28.7% compared to DDPG, A3C, and Random, respectively. These results confirm the effectiveness of the proposed scheme in high-load computing scenarios, where efficient offloading and resource allocation are critical for maintaining system performance.

5 Conclusion

In this paper, we investigate a UAV-assisted MEC network aiming to minimise the average user cost through efficient deployment and collaborative computation. To prevent resource wastage, we first design a JLPGA to determine a cost-effective UAV deployment that guarantees full user coverage. Subsequently, to balance the computational load and reduce system cost, we propose a collaborative offloading and resource allocation strategy named CODRA-TD3. The proposed system jointly considers UAV coverage, computing load balancing, and user-task association under practical spatial constraints. Extensive experiments under varying environmental conditions demonstrate that CODRA-TD3 consistently outperforms existing baselines such as DDPG, A3C, and Random policies in terms of user cost and system efficiency. This joint deployment and optimization framework provides a scalable and flexible solution for UAV-enabled MEC systems operating in dynamic environments. In future work, we plan to incorporate user mobility and develop real-time UAV trajectory optimization strategies, as well as explore adaptive policies under time-varying network and channel conditions.

References

1. Qi, X., Chen, J., Zhao, H., Zhang, Y., Sun,X., Chen, Y.: Post-disaster distribution system restoration considering UAV-based communication recovery based on multi-agent reinforcement learning. In: IECON 2023- 49th Annual Conference of the IEEE Industrial Electronics Society, pp. 1–6 (2023)
2. Matracia, M., Kishk, M.A., Alouini, M.S.: UAV-Aided Post-Disaster Cellular Networks: A Novel Stochastic Geometry Approach. IEEE Trans. Veh. Technol. **72**(7), 9406–9418 (2023)
3. Yang, X., He, H., Shen, H., Chen, A., Tian, H.: Efficient binary task offloading optimization in large-scale iot networks via uav-enhanced mobile edge computing. In: 2024 IEEE 25th International Symposium on a World of Wireless, Mobile and Multimedia Networks (WoWMoM), pp. 33–38 (2024)

4. Cao, A., Chen, X., Jiao, L., Yin, T., Wei, J.: Dynamic resource scheduling based quality of service optimisation in multi-UAV-assisted city edge network systems. In: 2024 IEEE International Conference on Systems, Man, and Cybernetics (SMC), pp. 4561–4567 (2024)
5. Yin, T., Chen, X., Jiao, L.: Service delay minimization for UAV-aided edge-cloud networks. In: 2024 IEEE Symposium on Computers and Communications (ISCC), pp. 1–7 (2024)
6. Hao, H., Xu, C., Zhang, W., Yang, S., Muntean, G.M.: Joint task offloading, resource allocation, and trajectory design for multi-UAV cooperative edge computing with task priority. IEEE Trans. Mob. Comput. **23**(9), 8649–8663 (2024)
7. Dai, M., Luan, T.H., Su, Z., Zhang, N., Xu, Q., Li, R.: Joint channel allocation and data delivery for uav-assisted cooperative transportation communications in post-disaster networks. IEEE Trans. Intell. Transp. Syst. **23**(9), 16676–16689 (2022)
8. Aldossary, M.: Optimizing task offloading for collaborative unmanned aerial vehicles (uavs) in fog-cloud computing environments. IEEE Access **12**, 74698–74710 (2024)
9. Akter, S., Duong, D.V.A., Kim, D.Y., Yoon, S.: Task offloading and resource allocation in UAV-aided emergency response operations via soft actor critic. IEEE Access **12**, 69258–69275 (2024)
10. Wang, Y., Chen, W., Luan, T.H., Su, Z., Xu, Q., Li, R.: Task offloading for post-disaster rescue in unmanned aerial vehicles networks. IEEE/ACM Trans. Network. **30**(4), 1525–1539 (2022)
11. Sun, G., He, L., Sun, Z., Wu, Q., Liang, S., Li, J.: Joint task offloading and resource allocation in aerial-terrestrial uav networks with edge and fog computing for post-disaster rescue. IEEE Trans. Mob. Comput. **23**(9), 8582–8600 (2024)
12. Raivi, A.M., Moh, S.: JDACO: joint data aggregation and computation offloading in UAV-enabled internet of things for post-disaster scenarios. IEEE Internet Things J. **11**(9), 16529–16544 (2024)
13. Li, W., Chen, X., Jiao, L., Wang, Y.: Deep reinforcement learning-based intelligent task offloading and dynamic resource allocation in 6G smart city. In: 2023 IEEE Symposium on Computers and Communications (ISCC), pp. 575–581 (2023)

Mobility-Aware Resource Scheduling in 6G Space-Air-Ground Integrated Networks: A GNN-Enhanced DRL Approach

Aobo Cao, Xin Chen, and Libo Jiao(✉)

School of Computer Science, Beijing Information Science and Technology University, Beijing, China
{caoaobo,chenxin,jiaolibo}@bistu.edu.cn

Abstract. With the continuous growth of communication demands, 6G Space-air-ground integrated Network (SAGIN) has demonstrated significant value in mobile edge computing (MEC) in low-coverage areas such as disaster-stricken regions, mountainous regions, and the ocean. However, limited by the high dynamics and multi-layer heterogeneity of SAGIN, designing efficient task offloading and resource scheduling strategies is crucial to improve the Quality of Service (QoS) of the network. To address the challenges posed by user mobility, UAV trajectory variation, and task heterogeneity, we construct a joint optimization problem that integrates task offloading, UAV trajectory planning, and resource scheduling, aiming to minimize the system processing delay. To solve the problem, this paper proposes a Mobility-aware Graph Neural Network (GNN)-Enhanced Deep Reinforcement Learning (DRL) (MGN-DRL) algorithm. Firstly, GNN are utilized to mine the spatial topological relationships among mobile users (MUs) and predict their future trajectories, providing future state information for the DRL model. Subsequently, the DRL integrates the predicted state with the current environmental perception to jointly optimize multi-dimensional decision variables. Finally, the simulation experiments show that the proposed MGN-DRL joint optimization framework is significantly superior to the baseline algorithm, effectively improving the system QoS and the quality of experience (QoE) of MUs.

Keywords: Mobile edge computing (MEC) · Space-air-ground integrated Network (SAGIN) · Quality of service (QoS) · Graph neural network (GNN) · Resource scheduling

1 Introduction

The fifth-generation mobile communication Technology (5G) has significantly enhanced the performance of traditional mobile communication networks with

This work was supported in part by the National Natural Science Foundation of China (Nos. 62202059, 62572063).

L. Zhang and K.-K. R. Choo (Eds.): MobiQuitous 2025, LNICST 684, pp. 116–136, 2026.
https://doi.org/10.1007/978-3-032-22503-0_7

its three major features: enhanced mobile Broadband (eMBB), ultra-reliable Low Latency Communication (URLLC), and Massive Machine Type Communication (mMTC) [1]. However, in special scenarios such as disaster emergency response, communication in remote mountainous areas, and wide-area Marine monitoring, 5G networks still face fundamental limitations: 1) They rely on fixed infrastructure for deployment, making it difficult to quickly address issues such as base station damage or coverage blind spots; 2) The centralized network architecture cannot effectively support the distributed computing requirements in an environment with extremely scarce resources. 3) High-frequency signals such as millimeter waves are vulnerable to complex terrains and adverse weather conditions, leading to a decline in quality of services (QoS) [2].

To break through these limitations, Mobile Edge Computing (MEC) technology effectively reduces task processing latency and alleviates the burden on the core network by sinking computing power to the network edge [3]. However, traditional MEC solutions still rely on ground fixed infrastructure and are limited in application in scenarios lacking stable network connections. This current situation has prompted researchers to intensify their research on the sixth generation mobile communication technology (6G) space-air-ground integrated network (SAGIN) [4]. The 6G SAGIN consists of a three-layer network, including highly mobile unmanned aerial vehicles (UAVs) and low earth orbit satellites (LEOs) with large coverage and strong computing power, which can provide complex and diverse communication and computing capabilities for mobile users (MUs) in the low-security areas mentioned above [5]. Significantly enhance the QoS of network and the MUs experience.

The MEC-enabled 6G SAGIN, on the other hand, is a highly dynamic, multi-layer heterogeneous network with a multi-node network architecture. Therefore, appropriate task offloading and resource scheduling are crucial for SAGIN to enhance network QoS and MUs experience. At present, many studies have already mentioned it. For instance, Huang *et al.* [6] proposed a joint optimization problem of SAGIN offloading and resource allocation in hybrid cloud and MEC scenarios based on deep reinforcement learning (DRL), aiming to minimize processing latency under energy consumption constraints. Chen *et al.* [7] proposed a mobile perception-based digital twin-assisted DRL (MDT-DRL) algorithm for the existing joint mobile perception-related task offloading and network traffic scheduling problems, aiming to improve QoS by reducing task completion time and energy consumption.

Additionally, Liu *et al.* [8] studied SAGIN's provision of services to remote areas without information and communication network coverage, considering fairness among sensors and trade-offs between throughput and energy consumption, with the aim of maximizing long-term network capacity. Hu *et al.* [9] studied the scenarios where SAGIN networks provide services to ground users after natural disasters, established a joint optimization problem of three-dimensional trajectories of unmanned aerial vehicles and resource allocation, and used iterative algorithms to solve it to improve energy efficiency. Zhu *et al.* [10] studied the application of SAGIN in smart cities, modeling the energy harvesting (EH) process, offloading path, communication link, delay and energy consumption respectively, aiming to reduce system overhead. Cai *et al.* [11] considered a dynamic SAGIN environment and formulated a sequential decision task offloading and resource allocation problem, which was solved using a scheme based on graph neural networks (GNN) combined with DRL, aiming for the highest return and the lowest overall latency.

However, most of the above-mentioned works only consider the mobility of MUs or UAVs, while ignoring the situation where both move simultaneously, which has a crucial impact on the delay of task offloading. In addition, most of the work only uses DRL to make decisions based on historical environmental states, while ignoring the current and future states. In response to the above challenges, we propose a joint optimisation problem and solve it using a joint scheme MGN-DRL that combines the GNN algorithm with DRL. The detailed contributions are as follows:

- Propose a SAGIN-assisted low-guarantee IoT regional (SAGIN-LGIOT) architecture based on MEC. And establish the MU mobility model, MU trajectory prediction model, UAV trajectory optimization model, task offloading and computing resource allocation model.
- An undirected graph model G is constructed based on the features of MUs and their spatial topological relationships. The GNN is used to extract features from this graph to obtain future location information. The prediction results are used as future state input to assist DRL in decision-making.
- To enhance the QoS of the network and the experience of MU, a Markov Decision Process (MDP) model is constructed by integrating the future state information predicted by GNN, the high dynamic environment characteristics of SAGIN-LGIOT, and the action decision variables. Then, the DRL method is used for solution to achieve the goal of minimizing the system processing delay.
- Conduct a series of simulation experiments. The effectiveness of GNN prediction was proved by comparing common algorithms. Changing key parameters and comparing with popular schemes prove the superiority of the MGN-DRL scheme in reducing delay and improving QoS.

2 System Model

Considering the communication and computing needs of MUs in low-guarantee IoT areas where resources are scarce, such as disaster areas, mountainous areas and Marine areas. This paper proposes an SAGIN-LGIOT architecture. As depicted in Fig. 1, the architecture consists of a three-layer heterogeneous network. The space layer consists of L LEO satellites, with the set denoted as $\mathbb{L} = \{1, 2, ..., l, ..., L\}$, and the air layer consists of U UAVs with the set denoted as $\mathbb{U} = \{1, 2, ..., ..., U\}$, the ground layer consists of M MUs, with the set denoted $\mathbb{M} = \{1, 2, ..., m, ..., M\}$. We consider the user in a natural state of mobility and the UAV flying at a fixed altitude H with a maximum speed of V_{max}. Furthermore, we consider the multi-time slots optimisation problem where time slots are represented by τ in the set $\mathbb{T} = \{1, 2, ..., \tau, ..., T\}$, each time slot is of equal length and is Δt.

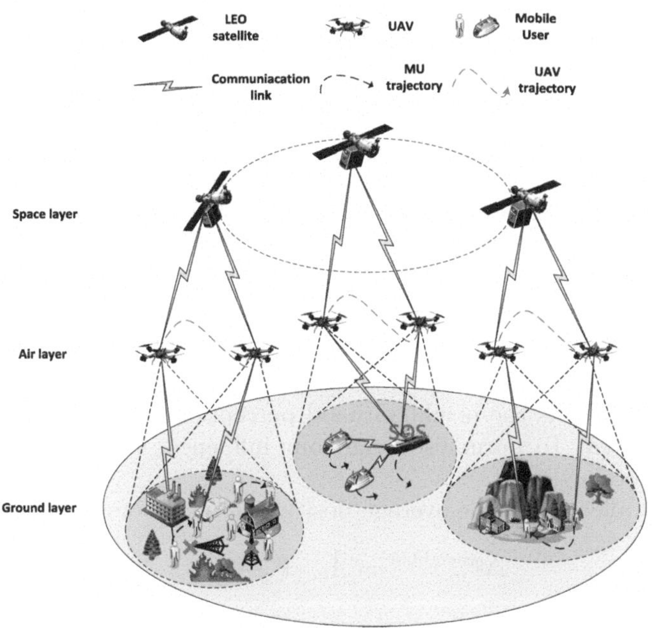

Fig. 1. The SAGIN-LGIOT architecture

At time τ, the coordinates of UAV u and MU m are given by $\mathbb{P}_u(\tau) = [(x_u(\tau), y_u(\tau), H_{uav})], \forall \tau \in T$ and $\mathbb{P}_m(\tau) = (x_m(\tau), y_m(\tau), 0)$, respectively. Owing to the LEO coverage is sufficiently large, we assume that the satellite position is fixed, denoted as $\mathbb{P}_l = (x_l, y_l, H_{sate})$. We consider that during the time slot τ, each MU generates only one computational task is denoted as $\mathbb{C}_m(\tau) = [\mathcal{S}_m(\tau), \mathcal{D}_m(\tau), \mathcal{W}_m(\tau), \mathcal{E}_m(\tau), \mathcal{T}_m(\tau)]$, $\forall m \in M$. Where $\mathcal{S}_m$ is the task data size, $\mathcal{D}_m$ is the maximum tolerable delay for the task, $\mathcal{W}_m$ is the computational demand, and $\mathcal{E}_i$ is the maximum consumable energy, $\mathcal{T}_m$ represents the task type. The model takes each time slot τ as the minimum optimisation unit, intelligently selects the optimal task offloading method for different types of computing tasks, and allocates computing resources accordingly. This process aims to improve the overall network QoS, while effectively guaranteeing the QoE of MUs.

2.1 MUs Mobility and Prediction Models

In order to be more consistent with the natural movement state of MUs in the real world, we build appropriate movement models for MUs. To enable more efficient task offloading and processing via UAVs, we design a GNN-based mobility-aware prediction model to assist UAV trajectory optimization.

MUs Mobility. We built a user mobility model based neighbourhood-aware. Within each time slot τ, let the MU m move with a velocity of v_m and a direction of movement of θ_m, then its base displacement $\mathbb{P}_m^{\text{basic}}$ is expressed as:

$$\Delta\mathbb{P}_m^{\text{basic}} = v_m \cdot \Delta t \cdot \begin{bmatrix} \cos(\theta_m) \\ \sin(\theta_m) \end{bmatrix}, \tag{1}$$

Considering the possible synergistic behavioural drivers among users, their spatial neighbourhood is represented by the adjacency matrix $A \in \mathbb{R}^{M\times M}$, $\forall i, j \in M$, where the connection weights are defined as follows:

$$A_{ij} = \begin{cases} \exp\left(-\frac{\|\mathbb{P}_i(\tau)-\mathbb{P}_j(\tau)\|}{\sigma}\right), & \text{if } \exp\left(-\frac{\|\mathbb{P}_i(\tau)-\mathbb{P}_j(\tau)\|}{\sigma}\right) \geq \lambda \\ 0, & \text{otherwise} \end{cases}, \tag{2}$$

where $\sigma = \frac{\text{R}}{2}$ controls the neighbourhood perception range and R^2 is the simulated range area. To normalise neighbour influence, a normalised neighbour matrix $\hat{A}$ is obtained.

The offset affected by the average position of neighbors is:

$$\Delta\mathbb{P}_m^{\text{neighbor}} = \hat{A}_m \cdot \mathbb{P} - \mathbb{P}_m(\tau), \tag{3}$$

where $\mathbb{P}$ denotes the set of all users' current locations.

Combining base movement, own behaviour and neighbourhood effects, the MU m's final location is updated to:

$$\mathbb{P}_m(\tau + \Delta t) = \mathbb{P}_m(\tau) + \Delta\mathbb{P}_m^{\text{basic}} + \lambda \cdot \Delta\mathbb{P}_m^{\text{neighbor}} + \epsilon_m. \tag{4}$$

where λ denotes the moderator of neighbour attraction and $\epsilon_i \sim \mathcal{N}(0, \sigma^2)$ is Gaussian random noise.

GNN-Based Mobility-Aware Prediction. We predict node position changes by building a dynamic undirected graph structure $\mathbf{G} = \{\mathcal{V}, \mathcal{E}\}$, where the set of graph nodes $\mathcal{V}$ denotes all the MUs, and the set of edges $\mathcal{E}$ denotes spatial correlations between MUs.

Each graph node $v_m \in \mathcal{V} \in M$ corresponds to a MU with a node eigenvector defined as:

$$\overrightarrow{\mathbf{v}_m} = \left[\mathbb{P}_m^{(\tau)},\ v_m^{(\tau)},\ \theta_m^{(\tau)},\ \mathbf{f}_k\right] \in \mathbb{R}^d, \tag{5}$$

where $\mathbf{f}_k$ is the other auxiliary features of the MU, and all MU features form the node input feature matrix $\widehat{X} \in \mathbb{R}^{M\times d}$, with d denotes the feature dimension [12].

Construct an adjacency matrix $\widetilde{A}^{(\tau)} \in \mathbb{R}^{M \times M}$ based on the spatial distances between MUs, with edge weights defined via a Gaussian kernel function. $\widetilde{A}^{(\tau)}$ is expressed as:

$$\tilde{A}_{ij}^{(\tau)} = \begin{cases} \exp\left(-\frac{\|\mathbb{P}_i^{(\tau)} - \mathbb{P}_j^{(\tau)}\|}{\sigma}\right), & \text{if } \|\mathbb{P}_i^{(\tau)} - \mathbb{P}_j^{(\tau)}\| < r \\ 0, & \text{otherwise,} \end{cases}$$

Here, r represents the distance threshold. Only when the distance between adjacent nodes is less than r does an edge exist. That is, $\tilde{A}_{ij}^{(\tau)} = 1$ and assign weights.

$\widetilde{A}^{(\tau)}$ for GCN layer information dissemination, and the dissemination rules are:

$$\mathbf{H}^{(l+1)} = \sigma\left(\tilde{A}^{(\tau)}\mathbf{H}^{(l)}\mathbf{W}^{(l)}\right), \quad l = 0, 1, \ldots, L-1, \tag{6}$$

where L denotes the number of graph convolutional neural network layers, $\mathbf{H}^{(0)} = \widehat{X}^{(\tau)}$ is the initial feature input, and $\mathbf{W}^{(l)}$ is the lth layer learnable weight.

Ultimately, the output layer predicts the Mu position of $\tau + 1$ as:

$$\hat{\mathbb{P}}_m^{(\tau+1)} = f_{\text{GNN}}\left(\mathbf{X}^{(\tau)},\ \tilde{A}^{(\tau)};\ \Theta\right), \quad \hat{\mathbb{P}}^{(\tau+1)} \in \mathbb{R}^{M \times 2}. \tag{7}$$

where Θ denotes all the learnable parameters of the GNN.

2.2 UAV Trajectory Model

For MU mobility, With the above equation (4), after the GNN predicts the user trajectory changes, the UAV trajectory optimisation can be planned in advance to cover the hotspot areas of the MUs, which greatly shortens the radio link distance, improves the channel quality and reduces the latency. The UAV u position change is calculated as:

$$x_u(\tau + 1) = x_u(\tau) + V_{max} \cdot \cos\beta_u(\tau), 0 \le x_u \le R, \tag{8}$$

$$y_u(\tau + 1) = y_u(t) + V_{max} \cdot \sin\beta_u(\tau), 0 \le y_u \le R. \tag{9}$$

where $\beta_u \in [0, 2\pi]$ is the flight angle of the UAV after intelligent decision-making. Hence, the coordinates of UAV u at time $\tau + 1$ are:

$$\mathbb{P}_u(\tau + 1) = [(x_u(\tau + 1), y_u(\tau + 1), H_{uav})]. \tag{10}$$

2.3 Offloading Model

In the SAGIN-LGIOT architecture, we divide $\mathcal{D}_m(\tau), \mathcal{W}_m(\tau)$ into three types based on $\mathcal{T}_m(\tau)$. These include Urgent-Light Task (ULT), Moderate Task(MT) and Tolerant-Heavy Task (THT), with different tasks corresponding to different offloading methods. Define the decision variable $\varpi = \{0, 1, 2\}$ to indicate the task offloading method.

ULT :This type of task features high latency sensitivity and low computational load, such as real-time communication and emergency distress signals, making it suitable for local execution. That is, $\varpi= 0$.

MT :The latency and computing resource requirements of this type of tasks are both moderate, such as augmented reality and mobile navigation, which are suitable for offloading to near-ground UAV for processing. That is, $\varpi=1$.

THT :This type of task has a high computational intensity but is not sensitive to latency, such as video processing and daily entertainment, and is suitable to be offloaded to LEO for processing by UAV. That is, $\varpi=2$.

2.4 Communication Model

Considering that the direct transmission from MU to the satellite has a long delay and a high probability of occlusion, two communication links are considered in this scenario. The link 1 between MU and UAV and the link 2 between UAV and LEO. All links use Orthogonal Frequency-Division Multiple Access (OFDMA) technology, and each sub-channel does not interfere with each other.

For Link 1, considering that there is occlusion between MU and UAV, line-of-sight (LOS) and non-line-of-sight (NLOS) links are considered [13]. When MU m offloads tasks to UAV u, the path loss $PL_{m,u}$ is expressed as:

$$PL_{m,u}(\tau) = 20 \log_{10} \left(\frac{4\pi f_u \sqrt{l_{m,u}^2 + H_{uav}^2}}{c} \right) (\tau) \\ + PL_{m,u}^{\text{LoS}} \cdot l_{m,u}^{\text{LoS}}(\tau) + \left(1 - PL_{m,u}^{\text{LoS}}\right) \cdot l_{m,u}^{\text{NLoS}}(\tau), \quad (11)$$

where f_u is the carrier frequency, $l_{m,u}$ denotes the horizontal distance between the MU m and the UAV u, c is the speed of light, and $l_{m,u}^{LoS}$ and $l_{m,n}^{NLoS}$ denote the path-averaged additional losses. In addition, $PL_{m,u}^{LoS}$ is calculated as:

$$PL_{m,u}^{LoS}(\tau) = \frac{1}{1 + o_1 \exp\left(-o_2 \left(\arctan\left(\frac{H_{uav}}{l_{m,u}}(\tau)\right) - o_1\right)\right)}, \quad (12)$$

where o_1, o_2 are environmental variation factor constants. Assuming that the MU m transmit power is P_m, the noise power spectral density is N_0, the Signal-to-Noise Ratio (SNR) is:

$$\text{SNR}_{m,u}(\tau) = \frac{P_m}{N_0 \cdot B_m \cdot PL_{m,u}}(\tau), \quad (13)$$

For link 2, the UAV to LEO position is considered to be high and the link is not blocked by obstacles, and the channel loss $PL_{u,l}[0]$ is computed using the free space loss model as:

$$PL_{u,l}(\tau) = \varrho \left[\frac{1}{c} 4\pi f_\lambda d_{u,l}(\tau) \right]^{-2}, \quad (14)$$

where $d_{u,l}$ denotes the Euclidean distance between UAV u and LEO l. Therefore, the SNR between link 2 is:

$$\mathrm{SNR}_{u,l}(\tau) = \frac{P_u}{N_1 \cdot B_u \cdot PL_{u,l}}(\tau), \tag{15}$$

In summary, the uplink transmission rates from MU m to UAV u and from UAV u to LEO l are expressed as:

$$\mathcal{R}_{m,u}(\tau) = B_m \log_2 \left(1 + SNR_{m,u}(\tau)\right). \tag{16}$$

$$\mathcal{R}_{u,l}(\tau) = B_u \log_2 \left(1 + SNR_{u,l}(\tau)\right). \tag{17}$$

where B_m, B_u denote the maximum bandwidth of MU m, UAV u respectively.

2.5 Computing Model

Within each time τ, each MU generates a computational task, makes an intelligent decision on the offloading path by DRL, and calculates the corresponding processing delay. The offloading decision set is $\boldsymbol{\varpi} = \{\varpi_1, \varpi_2, ..., \varpi_m, ..., \varpi_M\}$. Task processing delay includes local and edge processing delay, and the processing delay includes the computation delay Γ^{com} and the transmission delay Γ^{tran}.

The processing delay Γ^{pro}_m of the MU m is denoted as:

$$\Gamma^{pro}_m(\tau) = \begin{cases} \Gamma^{loc}_m(\tau) & \text{if } \varpi_m = 0, \\ \Gamma^{tran}_{m\to u}(\tau) + \Gamma^{com}_u(\tau) & \text{if } \varpi_m = 1, \\ \Gamma^{tran}_{m\to u}(\tau) + \Gamma^{tran}_{u\to l}(\tau) + \Gamma^{com}_l(\tau) & \text{if } \varpi_m = 2, \end{cases} \tag{18}$$

where Γ^{loc}_m denotes the local computational delay, $\Gamma^{tran}_{m\to u}$ denotes the transmission delay from MU m to UAV u, Γ^{com}_u denotes the UAV u computational delay, $\Gamma^{tran}_{u\to l}$ denotes the transmission delay from UAV u to LEO l, and Γ^{com}_l denotes the computational delay of LEO l, respectively, are computed as:

$$\Gamma^{loc}_m(\tau) = \frac{\mathcal{W}_i(\tau)}{F_m} \tag{19}$$

$$\Gamma^{tran}_{m\to u}(\tau) = \frac{\mathcal{S}_i(\tau)}{\mathcal{R}_{m,u}(\tau)} \tag{20}$$

$$\Gamma^{com}_u(\tau) = \frac{\mathcal{W}_i(\tau)}{F_u \vartheta^m_1} \tag{21}$$

$$\Gamma^{tran}_{u\to l}(\tau) = \frac{\mathcal{S}_i(\tau)}{\mathcal{R}_{u,l}(\tau)} \tag{22}$$

$$\Gamma^{com}_l(\tau) = \frac{W_i(\tau)}{F_l \vartheta^m_2}, \tag{23}$$

where ϑ_1^m, ϑ_2^m denote the proportion of computational resources allocated to MU m by UAV u and LEO l, respectively. F_u, F_l are the total computational resources of UAV u and LEO l, respectively.

In summary, the total system delay is:

$$\Gamma^{\text{total}}(\tau) = \sum_{m=1}^{M} \Gamma_m^{\text{pro}} \cdot \varpi_m(\tau). \tag{24}$$

We consider optimising the total task processing delay under the energy consumption constraint, and since the satellite computing resources are sufficient, we consider the energy consumption constraint of the UAV, UAV energy consumption is used in three main areas: communication, computation and flight. The total UAV energy consumption E_u^{tol} is denoted as:

$$E_u^{tol}(\tau) = P_u \cdot \Gamma_{u\to l}^{tran}(\tau) + P_{fly} \cdot \Delta t(\tau) + \phi \cdot f_u^3 \cdot \mathcal{S}_m(\tau). \tag{25}$$

where P_{fly} is the power consumed by the UAV u when it is flying at speed V_{max}. ϕ and f_u are the energy consumption coefficients and the computational frequency of the UAV calculation [14], respectively.

The total consumption of the UAV u should be less than the total energy of the UAV u to ensure that it can land properly and the mission can be handled with the constraints:

$$\sum_{\tau}^{T} E_u^{tol}(\tau) \leq E_u. \tag{26}$$

where E_u represents the total energy of UAV u.

2.6 Problem Formulation

The goal of this paper is to jointly optimise the task offloading decision $\boldsymbol{\varpi}$, the UAV trajectory $\boldsymbol{\beta}$, the UAV computational resource allocation $\boldsymbol{\vartheta_1}$ and the LEO computational resource allocation $\boldsymbol{\vartheta_2}$ to minimise the total system processing latency under energy consumption constraints. The optimisation problem is defined as:

$$\mathbf{P1:} \max_{\boldsymbol{\varpi},\boldsymbol{\beta},\boldsymbol{\vartheta_1},\boldsymbol{\vartheta_2}} \Gamma^{\text{total}}(\tau) \tag{27}$$

$$
\begin{aligned}
s.t. C1 &: x_{min} \leq x_m(\tau), x_u(\tau) \leq x_{max}, \forall m \in \mathbb{M}, \forall u \in \mathbb{U}, \forall \tau \in \mathbb{T} \\
C2 &: y_{min} \leq y_m(\tau), y_u(\tau) \leq y_{max}, \forall m \in \mathbb{M}, \forall u \in \mathbb{U}, \forall \tau \in \mathbb{T} \\
C3 &: \beta_u(\tau) \in [0, 2\pi], \forall u \in \mathbb{U}, \forall \tau \in \mathbb{T} \\
C4 &: \|\mathbb{P}_u(\tau) - \mathbb{P}_{u'}(\tau)\|_2 \geq d_{\min}, \quad \forall u \neq u', \ \forall \tau \in T, \forall u \in \mathbb{U} \\
C5 &: \sum_{m=1}^{M} \varpi_m(\tau) = M, \forall m \in \mathbb{M}, \forall \tau \in \mathbb{T} \\
C6 &: \sum_{\tau}^{T} E_u^{tol}(\tau) \leq E_u, \forall u \in \mathbb{U}, \forall \tau \in \mathbb{T} \\
C7 &: \sum_{M}^{m} \vartheta_1(\tau) \leq F_u, \forall m \in \mathbb{M}, \forall u \in \mathbb{U}, \forall \tau \in \mathbb{T} \\
C8 &: \sum_{M}^{m} \vartheta_2(\tau) \leq F_l, \forall m \in \mathbb{M}, \forall u \in \mathbb{U}, \forall \tau \in \mathbb{T}
\end{aligned}
\tag{28}
$$

where $\boldsymbol{\varpi} = \{\varpi_m(\tau), m \in \mathbb{M}\}$, $\boldsymbol{\beta} = \{\beta_u(\tau), u \in \mathbb{U}\}$, $\boldsymbol{\vartheta_1} = \{\vartheta_1^m(\tau) \in [0,1], m \in \mathbb{M}\}$, $\boldsymbol{\vartheta_2} = \{\vartheta_2^m(\tau) \in [0,1], m \in \mathbb{M}\}$. $C1$ and $C2$ limit the positional movement of MUs and the flight range of UAVs. $C3$ denotes the range of movement angle selection for the UAV trajectory. $C4$ is a UAV anti-collision restraint where the UAV is kept directly at a safe distance $d_{\min}$. $C5$ represents that only one offloading method can be selected for each MU. $C6$ limits all energy consumption of the UAV to no more than the total energy of the UAV. $C7$ and $C8$ indicate that the sum of computational resources allocated to all MUs by the UAV shall not exceed the total resources of the UAV, and the computational resources allocated to all MUs by the LEO shall not exceed the total resources of the LEO, respectively.

3 Algorithm Design

Considering the dynamic high-complexity environment under the SAGIN network, and the optimisation problem **P1** is NP-hard under the multi-constraint, high-latitude continuous action space. Therefore, we propose a joint GNN combined with DRL scheme MGN-DRL to solve the problem. We utilize the Twin Delayed Deep Deterministic policy gradient (TD3) algorithm as the DRL framework. In this section, the overall execution and training flow of the MGN-DRL framework is given in Fig. 2; the roles and working processes of GNN and DRL are demonstrated in Subsects. 3.1 and 3.2, respectively.

We can see that Fig. 2 consists of three parts, from left to right, the SAGIN environment, the GNN prediction and decision model, and the DRL detailed training process. Firstly, we interact with the environment to extract the MU spatial features and construct the graph structure model and optimisation decision model; secondly, we use the GNN training to get the MU trajectory prediction information; finally, the DRL fuses the prediction information from the GNN to train the model, and after repeated iterations, we get the final optimisation strategy.

3.1 GNN-Based MU Trajectory Prediction Algorithm

To cope with the high dynamics of the environment and assist DRL to better adapt to the environmental information, we introduce GNN to model and predict the future trajectories of MUs, thus providing structure-aware and forward-looking state information for DRL. DRL is enhanced to make better unloading, movement and resource allocation decisions.

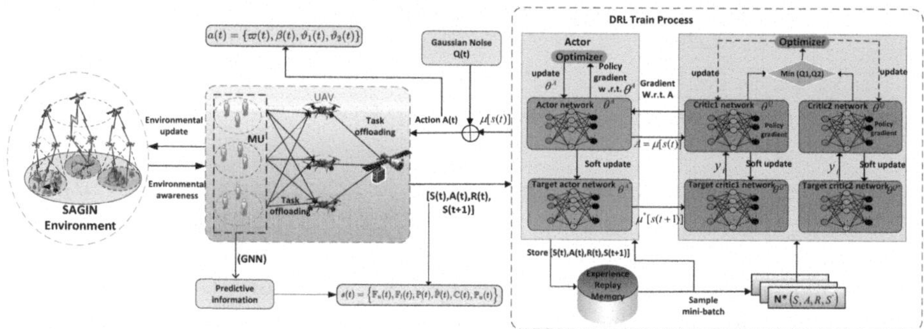

Fig. 2. Framework for the execution and training process of MGN-DRL

The set of location information for MUs is $\mathcal{P} = \{\mathbb{P}_1, \mathbb{P}_2, ..., \mathbb{P}_m, ..., \mathbb{P}_M\},$. The set of MUs $\mathbb{M}$ serves as the set of nodes of DUG, and the adjacencies between neighbouring MUs serve as the set of edges of the graph structure. Model the graph structure $\mathbf{G} = \{\mathcal{V}, \mathcal{E}\}$, and generate the adjacency matrix $\widetilde{A}$. Extract historical trajectories and features of MUs initialise feature vectors $\mathbf{h}_i^{(0)}$, which is passed into GNN layer for iterative propagation, and the update rule is denoted as:

$$\mathbf{h}_i^{(l+1)} = \sigma \left(\underbrace{\mathbf{W}_1^{(l)} \mathbf{h}_i^{(l)}}_{\text{Self-connecting item}} + \underbrace{\sum_{j \in \mathcal{N}(i)} \mathbf{W}_2^{(l)} \mathbf{h}_j^{(l)}}_{\text{Neighbor aggregation item}} \right) \mathbf{h}_i^{(0)}, \tag{29}$$

where $\forall i, j \in M$ denotes different neighbouring MU, l is the number of network layers. Finally, the position of MU at the next moment $\mathbb{P}_m(\tau + 1)$is predicted through the regression layer. All parameters are trained by minimizing the Mean Squared Error(MSE) function, which $\mathcal{L}_{\text{MSE}}$ is represented as:

$$Min : \mathcal{L}_{\text{MSE}} = \frac{1}{M} \sum_{i=1}^{M} \left\| \hat{\mathbb{P}}_i^{(\tau+1)} - \mathbb{P}_i^{(\tau+1)} \right\|^2. \tag{30}$$

We use a three-layer graph convolutional neural network (GCN) structure for modelling. The first layer aggregates the state information of each MU with its direct neighbours to capture local motion characteristics; the second layer further fuses the information of second-order neighbours to sense the group migration trend in a larger range; the third layer refines the final representation of nodes based on the multi-layer information aggregation for location regression prediction. The detailed process is described in Algorithm 1.

Algorithm 1. GNN-based MU Trajectory Prediction Algorithm

1: **Input:** Historical MUs states $\left\{\mathbf{V}^{(0)}, \ldots, \mathbf{V}^{(\tau)}, \mathbf{V}^{(T)}\right\}$, adjacency matrix $A^{(\tau)}$;
2: Construct dynamic graph $G^{(\tau)} = (\mathcal{V}, \mathcal{E})$ based on spatial distances;
3: **for** $i = 0$ to M **do**
4: Updating the node feature vector $\mathbf{V}$ is based on Equation (5);
5: **end for**
6: Aggregate node features into matrix $A^{(\tau)} \in \mathbb{R}^{M \times d}$;
7: Compute normalized adjacency matrix $\tilde{A}^{(\tau)}$:

$$\tilde{A}_{ij}^{(\tau)} = \begin{cases} \exp\left(-\frac{\|\mathbb{P}_i^{(\tau)} - \mathbb{P}_j^{(\tau)}\|}{\sigma}\right), & \text{if } \|\mathbb{P}_i^{(\tau)} - \mathbb{P}_j^{(\tau)}\| < r \\ 0, & \text{otherwise} \end{cases}$$

8: **for** $l = 0$ to L **do**
9: $\mathbf{H}^{(l+1)} \leftarrow \sigma\left(\tilde{A}^{(t)}\mathbf{H}^{(l)}W^{(l)}\right)$ with $\mathbf{H}^{(0)} = \mathbf{V}^{(\tau)}$;
10: **end for**
11: linear regression: $\mathbb{P}^{(\tau+1)} \leftarrow \mathbf{H}^{(L)}W_{\text{out}} + b$;
12: Minimising MSE based on Equation (30);
13: **Output:** Predicted MUs positions $\hat{P}^{(\tau+1)}$;

3.2 TD3-Based Computational Offloading and Resource Scheduling Algorithm

By integrating the intelligent exploration capability of the DRL algorithm with the output of the GNN algorithm, it is possible to capture MUs trajectories and dynamic environmental features more accurately, thereby effectively enhancing the performance of offloading decisions, UAVs trajectory optimization, and resource allocation strategies. We constructed a MDP model to optimize task processing delay and selected the TD3 framework as the DRL solution algorithm. This section will introduce the MDP model and TD3 frameworks.

MDP Model. An MDP model consists of the 4-tuple $(\mathbf{S}, \mathbf{A}, \mathbf{P}, \mathbf{R})$. where $\mathbf{S}$ is the environmental state information and $s(\tau)$ denotes the state at time slot τ. $\mathbf{A}$ is the action information, and $a(\tau)$ denotes the action strategy executed at τ. $\mathbf{P}$ denotes the probability of moving to the next state $s(\tau + 1)$ after the action a is executed in state s. $\mathbf{R}$ denotes the immediate reward received by the intelligence for performing the action a in state s, which is used to measure the effectiveness of the action [15].

State Space: In this SAGIN-LGIOT environment, the status information includes the computing resources $\mathbb{F}_u$ and $\mathbb{F}_l$ of UAVs and LEO, the real position $\mathbb{P}$ and predicted position $\hat{\mathbb{P}}$ of UAVs, the task feature $\mathbb{C}$ and the UAV position $\mathbb{P}_u$. At time τ, the state space is represented as:

$$s(\tau) = \left\{\mathbb{F}_u(\tau), \mathbb{F}_l(\tau), \mathbb{P}(\tau), \hat{\mathbb{P}}(\tau), \mathbb{C}(\tau), \mathbb{P}_u(\tau)\right\}, \tag{31}$$

Action Space: Action decisions include task offloading decision $\boldsymbol{\varpi}$, UAV trajectory $\boldsymbol{\beta}$ change, UAV computing resource allocation $\boldsymbol{\vartheta}_1$and LEO computing resource allocation $\boldsymbol{\vartheta_2}$. At time τ, the action space is represented as:

$$a(\tau) = \{\boldsymbol{\varpi}(\tau), \boldsymbol{\beta}(\tau), \boldsymbol{\vartheta}_1(\tau), \boldsymbol{\vartheta_2}(\tau)\}, \tag{32}$$

Reward Space: Minimising the total processing latency of the task under energy consumption constraints is the goal of this paper, and often DRL is trained to maximise long-term rewards. Therefore, we define the reward as the negative of the latency and design the penalty term. At time slot τ, the system reward is expressed as:

$$r(\tau) = \begin{cases} -\Gamma^{\text{total}}(\tau), & \text{if } C6\, is\, satisfied \\ -\Gamma^{\text{total}} * \Phi(\tau), & \text{otherwise} \end{cases}. \tag{33}$$

where Φ is the penalty factor when constraint C6 is not satisfied.

TD3 Framework. TD3 is a DRL algorithm that belongs to an improved version of the Deep Deterministic Policy Gradient (DDPG) family. It mainly reduces the over-optimistic bias of Q-value estimation by introducing Twin Q-Networks, and also employs techniques such as Delayed Policy Update and Target Policy Smoothing to improve the stability of training and convergence speed. TD3 is particularly suitable for solving problems in high dynamic multi-dimensional continuous action Spaces. Therefore, TD3 is selected for this article.

Algorithm 2 describes the TD3 framework workflow in detail. Firstly, two Critic networks Q_{ω_1} and Q_{ω_2} are initialised, as well as an Actor network π_ϕ with randomly initialised parameters. At the same time, a corresponding target network is constructed for each of the above three networks, and the parameters of the main network are copied to the target network, i.e., $\omega_i' \leftarrow \omega_i$, $\phi' \leftarrow \phi$. Subsequently, an empirical playback buffer $\mathcal{D}$ with a capacity of C is created to store the state transfer samples obtained during the interaction.

At each time step τ, the intelligent body selects a sequential action $\mathbf{s}(\tau)$ based on the current state $\mathbf{a}(\tau)$ using the Actor network and adds Gaussian exploratory noise $\epsilon(\tau)$ to augment the strategy's exploratory capability. The action $\mathbf{a}(\tau)$ is represented as:

$$\mathbf{a}(\tau) = \pi_\phi(\mathbf{s}(\tau)) + \epsilon(\tau), \tag{34}$$

Algorithm 2. TD3-based Computational Offloading and Resource Scheduling Algorithm

Input: State space $\mathbf{S}$, action space $\mathbf{A}$, exploration noise $\epsilon \sim \mathcal{N}(0, \sigma^2)$, learning rate L_r , discount factor γ , clipped noise c , batch size N;
Output: Optimal policies $\{\boldsymbol{\varpi}(\tau), \boldsymbol{\beta}(\tau), \boldsymbol{\vartheta}_1(\tau), \boldsymbol{\vartheta}_2(\tau)\}$
1: Initialize Critic networks Q_{ω_1}, Q_{ω_2} and Actor network π_ϕ randomly
2: Initialize target networks $\omega_i' \leftarrow \omega_i$, $\phi' \leftarrow \phi$
3: Create replay buffer $\mathcal{D}$ with capacity C
4: **for** episode $= 1$ **to** $E_{\max}$ **do**
5: Reset environment to obtain initial state $\mathbf{s}_0$
6: **for** $t = 1$ **to** T **do**
7: Select action based Eq (34)
8: Execute $\mathbf{a}_t$, observe reward r_t and next state $\mathbf{s}_{t+1}$
9: Store transition $(\mathbf{s}(\tau), \mathbf{a}(\tau), r(\tau), \mathbf{s}(\tau+1)$ in $\mathcal{D}$
10: **if** buffer size $> N_{\text{batch}}$ **then**
11: Sample mini-batch $\{(\mathbf{s}^{(i)}, \mathbf{a}^{(i)}, r^{(i)}, \mathbf{s}'^{(i)})\}_{i=1}^N \sim \mathcal{D}$
12: Compute target actions with clipped noise Eq (35)
13: Update Critics via Eq (36-37)
14: **end if**
15: **if** $t = 0 \pmod d$ **then**
16: Update Actor using Eq (38)
17: Soft-update target networks via Eq (39-40)
18: **end if**
19: **end for**
20: **end for**

After this action is performed, the environmental feedback instantly rewards $r(\tau)$ with the next state $\mathbf{s}(\tau+1)$ and stores the quaternion $(\mathbf{s}(\tau), \mathbf{a}(\tau), r(\tau), \mathbf{s}(\tau+1)$ in the experience replay buffer $\mathcal{D}$. When the number of accumulated samples in the buffer is larger than a batch size N_{batch}, the target Actor network is used to compute the action $\mathbf{s}(\tau+1)$ in the next state $\tilde{\mathbf{a}}(\tau+1)$ and add the target policy smoothing noise (clipped noise), the $\tilde{\mathbf{a}}(\tau+1)$ is calculated as:

$$\tilde{\mathbf{a}}(\tau) = \pi_{\phi'}(\mathbf{s}(\tau+1) + \operatorname{clip}(\mathcal{N}(0, \tilde{\sigma}), -c, c), \tag{35}$$

Next, the parameters of the Critic network are updated by minimising the mean square error of the dual Critic network with respect to the target Q-value. The error $\mathcal{L}(\omega_i)$ is expressed using the Bellman function as:

$$\mathcal{L}(\omega_i) = \mathbb{E}_{(\mathbf{s},\mathbf{a},r,\mathbf{s}')\sim\mathcal{D}}\left[(Q_{\omega_i}(\mathbf{s},\mathbf{a}) - y)^2\right] \tag{36}$$

$$y = r + \gamma \min_{i=1,2} Q_{\omega_i'}(\mathbf{s}', \tilde{\mathbf{a}}'), \tag{37}$$

where $\mathbf{s}' = \mathbf{s}(\tau+1), \tilde{\mathbf{a}}' = \tilde{\mathbf{a}}(\tau+1)$. TD3 uses a delayed policy update mechanism, in which the Actor's goal is to maximise the Q-value of the output of the Critic network, to optimise the Actor parameters by gradient ascent, as follows:

$$\nabla_\phi J(\phi) = \mathbb{E}_{\mathbf{s}\sim\mathcal{D}}\left[\nabla_{\mathbf{a}} Q_{\omega_1}(\mathbf{s},\mathbf{a})\big|_{\mathbf{a}=\pi_\phi(\mathbf{s})} \cdot \nabla_\phi \pi_\phi(\mathbf{s})\right], \tag{38}$$

Finally, the parameters of the main and target networks are synchronised using a soft update mechanism to ensure training stability and convergence with the update formula:

$$\omega_i' \leftarrow \rho\omega_i + (1-\rho)\omega_i' \quad (39)$$

$$\phi' \leftarrow \rho\phi + (1-\rho)\phi'. \quad (40)$$

where ρ is the soft update parameter.

4 Experimental Results and Discussion

In this section, we use Python 3.7 and TensorFlow 1.X to build a 6G SAGIN simulation platform. Firstly, we provide a detailed description of the simulation environment. After that, we evaluate the performance of the proposed algorithm by parameter tuning and comparison of popular algorithms in the experimental platform.

Table 1. Simulation Parameters

Symbol	Value	Description
L	3	Number of GNN network layers
l_g	0.01	GNN learning rate
λ	0.3	Neighbours influence weighting
H	100 m	UAV altitude
M	$[5, 40]$	Number of MUs
N_0, N_1	$-100/-110$ dBm	Gaussian white noise
P_m	5 w	Transmission power of MU
P_u	23 w	Transmission power of UAV
$\vert\mathcal{D}\vert$	3000	Experience replay buffer size
N	64	Mini-batch size
F_m	1 GHz	Computational capacities of MU
F_u	10 GHz	Computational capacities of UAV
F_l	20 GHz	Computational capacities of LEO
T	10	Total number of time slots
$\mathcal{S}_m$	$[2, 5]$ MB	Task data size
$\mathcal{D}_m$	$[0.1, 7]$ s	Task maximum tolerable delay
$\mathcal{W}_m$	$[0.5, 3]$ MB	Task computational demand
d_{min}	5 m	UAV minimum safe distance

4.1 Simulation Setup

In this simulation scenario, we set the ground field area 100 $m\times$ 100 m, the UAV position is defined as (50, 50, 100), the LEO position is set as (0, 0, 20000), and all the UAVs as well as the LEOs can completely cover the ground area. The UAVs fly within $100m^2$. Considering the realism of the simulation, the MU's initial position information is randomly defined at [100,100] and is moved by the behaviour of the neighbours. The simulation is carried out using the MU's moving speed is uniformly distributed at [0.1, 2] m/s, and the moving angle is distributed at [0, 2π]. The duration of each time slot τ is defined as $\Delta t = 1s$, and the flight speed of the UAV $V_{max} = 5\ m/s$. Other communication and computation related parameters are shown in **Table** 1.

4.2 Algorithm Performance Analysis

Below, I will conduct performance evaluations on the GNN algorithm for predicting MU trajectories, the MGN-DRL computational offloading and resource scheduling algorithm.

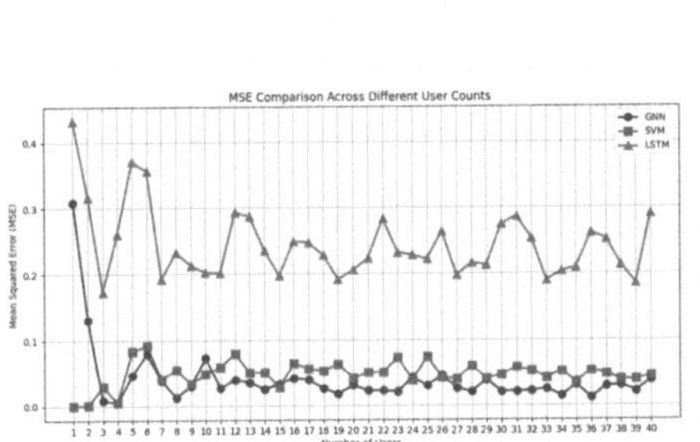

Fig. 3. Comparison of MSE of different algorithms with different number of MUs.

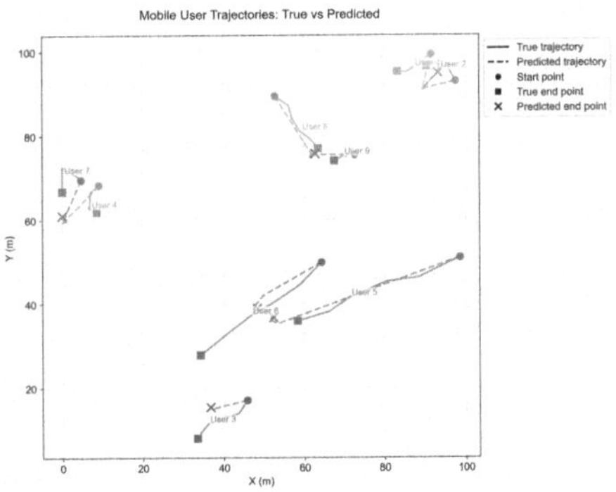

Fig. 4. Comparison of true and predicted trajectories of MUs.

GNN-Based MU Trajectory Prediction Algorithm. To validate the performance advantages of the proposed GNN model in the MU trajectory prediction task, this paper conducts comparative experiments with traditional Support Vector Machines (SVM) as well as Long Short-Term Memory Networks (LSTM). Figure 3 shows the average mean square error (MSE) performance of each method on the test set for different number of MUs (from 1 to 40). From the results, it can be seen that GNN significantly outperforms SVM and LSTM methods in all MU number scenarios. Because GNN can effectively capture the spatial topology and movement patterns among multiple MUs, it is suitable for high-precision modelling of multi-MU trajectories in SAGIN. In contrast, traditional sequential or single-point regression methods lack the ability to model inter-MU relationships, which makes it difficult to cope with the prediction task in complex dynamic environments.

Figure 4 shows the comparison diagram between the real trajectories (solid lines) and the predicted trajectories (dashed lines) of the nine MUs. The results show that the proposed trajectory prediction model exhibits good performance in capturing MU movement trends. In particular, the mobile trajectories of User 5 and User 8 are predicted accurately. For complex trajectories such as User 1, User 2, etc., the prediction is biased, which may be related to complex environmental changes, human factors and data noise. However, the predicted trends are similar to the real trajectories and are within the error tolerance.

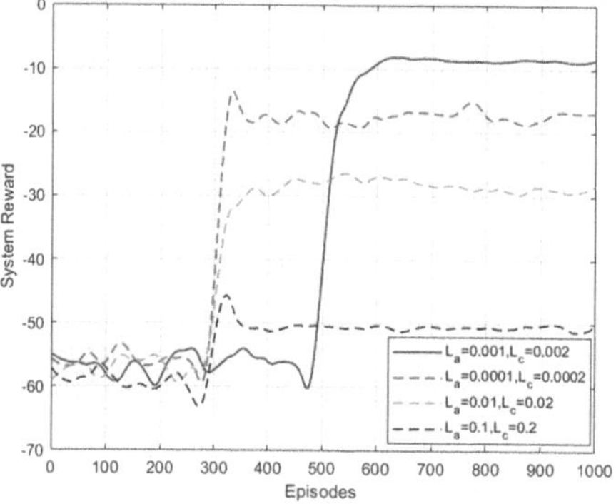

Fig. 5. Convergence of MGN-DRL with different learning rates.

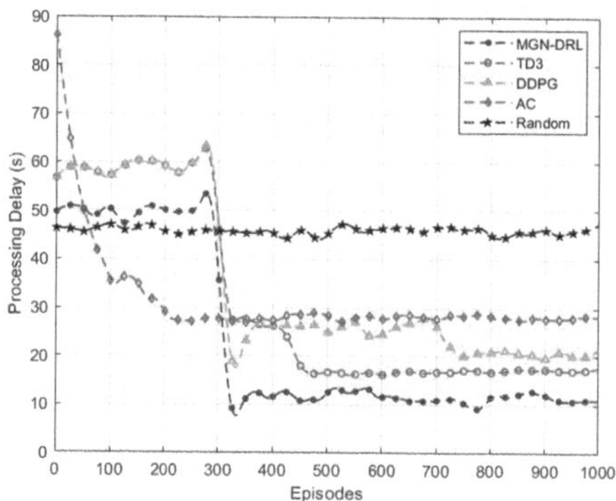

Fig. 6. Comparison of processing delay under different algorithms.

MGN-DRL Algorithm. Figure 5 shows the training conditions of MGN-DRL under different learning rate combinations. It can be seen that all combinations have some degree of fluctuation in system reward at the beginning of training, which is caused by random initialisation and strategy exploration. When $L_a = 0.001$, $L_c = 0.002$, the training curve rises rapidly and stabilises around about 500 rounds, and eventually the system reward is boosted to the highest value. It is shown that this combination performs optimally in terms of convergence speed and strategy performance, and we use this combination in subsequent experiments. In contrast, if the learning rate is too small, e.g., $L_a = 0.0001$, $L_c = 0.0002$, the system tends to fall into a local optimum, resulting in a small reward value. If the learning rate is too large, e.g., $L_a = 0.1$, $L_c = 0.2$, it causes unstable training, skips the global optimum, and its reward value deviates from the optimal value. In summary, appropriate learning rate settings have an important impact on the convergence performance and final reward level of reinforcement learning algorithms. In this experiment, the combination $L_a = 0.001$, $L_c = 0.002$ achieves a good balance between convergence speed and performance.

Figure 6 illustrates the performance comparison of five different algorithms in terms of task processing delay, including three typical DRL algorithms, TD3 [16], DDPG [17], and Actor-Critic (AC) [18], as well as Random and the MGN-DRL algorithm proposed in this paper. As can be observed from the figure, the MGN-DRL algorithm starts to converge at about the 300th round and eventually stabilises at the lowest task processing latency, significantly outperforming the other algorithms. This result indicates that the strategy combining GNN and DRL can more effectively adapt to the dynamically changing heterogeneous network environment between space and space, thus obtaining better offloading and resource scheduling strategies. In contrast, DRL-only approaches such as TD3, DDPG and AC are inferior to MGN-DRL in terms of convergence speed and final delay performance, mainly due to their lack of in-depth modelling and representation of complex network topologies and user dynamics. The introduction of GNN effectively enhances the ability of the policy network to perceive and understand the spatio-temporal dependence characteristics, and improves the scheduling intelligence and efficiency of the overall system.

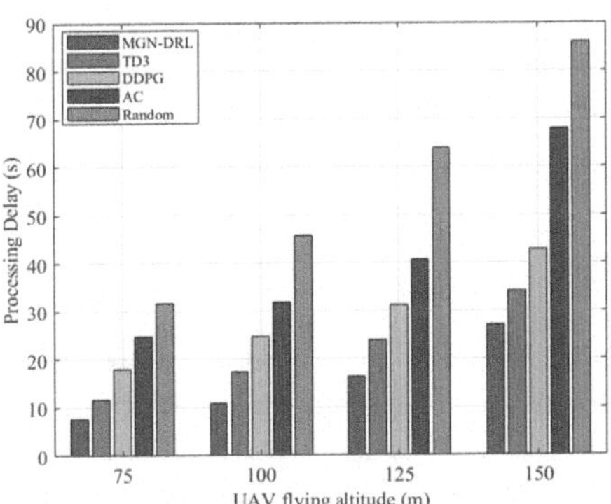

Fig. 7. Comparison of processing delay of different algorithms at different flight altitudes of UAVs.

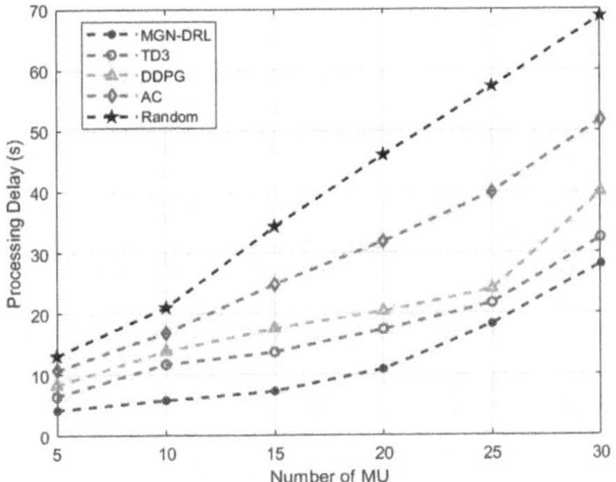

Fig. 8. Comparison of processing delay of different algorithms with different number of MUs.

Figure 7 shows the performance comparison of different algorithms in terms of task processing delay at different UAV flight altitudes (75 m, 100 m, 125 m and 150 m). It can be seen that the task processing latency of each algorithm tends to increase as the UAV flight altitude increases. This is due to the fact that the increase in flight altitude leads to an increase in the air link distance, which triggers greater transmission delay and path loss. The MGN-DRL algorithm proposed in this paper consistently maintains the lowest processing latency at all altitude settings, and significantly outperforms TD3, DDPG, A3C, and the stochastic strategy. When the altitude is 100 m, the processing delay of MGN-DRL is reduced by 37.3%, 55.9% and 65.15% compared with TD3, DDPG, and

AC, respectively. Comparing the worst random strategy reduces 75.56%. The effectiveness of joint modelling of GNN and DRL to optimize the system QoS is further verified.

Figure 8 shows the comparison of task processing latency of different algorithms with different number of MUs (5, 10, 15, 20, 25, 30). Overall, as the number of MUs increases, the total computational pressure and communication load of the system rises, and the task processing delay of all algorithms increases to different degrees. However, there is a significant difference in the performance of the algorithms in coping with the increase in MU density. The MGN-DRL algorithm proposed in this paper consistently maintains the lowest task processing delay under all settings of the number of MUs, showing superior scalability and robustness. This is due to the effective modelling and extraction of multi-user spatial distribution features by GNN, which enables the DRL decision to maintain efficient offloading decision and resource scheduling strategy. In contrast, TD3 and DDPG can achieve some performance improvement when the number of users is small, but the processing delay rises rapidly as the number of MUs increases. When the number of MUs is 20, the processing delay of MGN-DRL is reduced by 41.17% and 47.15% compared with TD3 and DDPG, respectively. The A3C algorithm is limited by synchronisation and stability of policy update, and the overall performance is lower than the proposed algorithm by 65.93%. The random algorithm does not have optimisation capability and is the least effective. The MGN-DRL processing delay is optimised by 76.08% compared to the Random algorithm.

5 Conclusion and Future Work

This paper studies the application of 6G SAGIN networks in areas with weak computing capabilities such as disaster-stricken areas and mountainous regions, aiming to optimize the total processing delay of tasks and improve the QoS of system and user experience. We first proposed the SAGIN-LGIOT architecture and established the MUs mobility model, UAVs trajectory model, task offloading model and computing resource scheduling model. A joint optimization problem of MUs trajectory prediction, UAVs trajectory optimization, task offloading decision-making and resource scheduling is proposed, and a joint scheme MGN-DRL integrating GNN is proposed to solve this problem. Firstly, establish the graph structure model of MUs, and then use GNN to obtain the prediction information. Secondly, DRL accepts predictive information and acquires optimization problem strategies through exploring the environment and iterative training. Through experimental comparisons with existing algorithms in different environments, it can be known that the proposed scheme can effectively reduce the task processing delay and guarantee the system QoS and the QoE of MUs.

In future work, we will explore the security and privacy issues of task offloading in SAGIN multi-layer networks, as well as the impact of satellite mobility on the QoS of network. This will be a significant direction.

References

1. Li, B., Fei, Z., Zhang, Y.: Uav communications for 5g and beyond: Recent advances and future trends. IEEE Internet Things J. **6**(2), 2241–2263 (2019)
2. Jia, H., Wang, Y., Wu, W.: Dynamic resource allocation for remote Iot data collection in SAGIN. IEEE Internet Things J. **11**(11), 20575–20589 (2024)
3. Tang, Q., et al.: Joint service deployment and task scheduling for satellite edge computing: a two-timescale hierarchical approach. IEEE J. Sel. Areas Commun. **42**(5), 1063–1079 (2024)
4. Nguyen, D.C., et al.: 6g internet of things: a comprehensive survey. IEEE Internet Things J. **9**(1), 359–383 (2022)
5. Hao, Y., Yang, S., Li, F., Zhang, Y., Wang, S., Ren, X.: Edgetimer: Adaptive multi-timescale scheduling in mobile edge computing with deep reinforcement learning. In: IEEE INFOCOM 2024 - IEEE Conference on Computer Communications, pp. 671–680 (2024)
6. Huang, C., Chen, G., Xiao, P., Xiao, Y., Han, Z., Chambers, J.A.: Joint offloading and resource allocation for hybrid cloud and edge computing in sagins: a decision assisted hybrid action space deep reinforcement learning approach. IEEE J. Sel. Areas Commun. **42**(5), 1029–1043 (2024)
7. Chen, X., Cao, J., Sahni, Y., Zhang, M., Liang, Z., Yang, L.: Mobility-aware dependent task offloading in edge computing: A digital twin-assisted reinforcement learning approach. IEEE Trans. Mob. Comput. **24**(4), 2979–2994 (2025)
8. Liu, J., et al.: Joint UAV 3D trajectory design and resource scheduling for space-air-ground integrated power iort: A deep reinforcement learning approach. IEEE Trans. Netw. Sci. Eng. **11**(3), 2632–2646 (2024)
9. Hu, Z., et al.: Joint resources allocation and 3d trajectory optimization for UAV-enabled space-air-ground integrated networks. IEEE Trans. Veh. Technol. **72**(11), 14214–14229 (2023)
10. Zhu, W., Chen, X., Jiao, L., Min, G., Li, W.: Cost-efficient 6g space-air-ground integrated mobile edge computing for smart city: A ppo-based offloading decision and resource allocation algorithm. In: 2023 IEEE International Conference on High Performance Computing, pp. 241–248 (2023)
11. Cai, Y., Cheng, P., Chen, Z., Xiang, W., Vucetic, B., Li, Y.: Graphic deep reinforcement learning for dynamic resource allocation in space-air-ground integrated networks. IEEE J. Sel. Areas Commun. **43**(1), 334–349 (2025)
12. Huang, K., Liang, L., Yi, X., Ye, H., Jin, S., Li, G.Y.: Meta-learning empowered graph neural networks for radio resource management. IEEE Transactions on Communications, pp. 1–1 (2025)
13. Nguyen, M.D., Le, L.B., Girard, A.: Joint computation offloading, UAV trajectory, user scheduling, and resource allocation in SAGIN. In: GLOBECOM 2022 - 2022 IEEE Global Communications Conference, pp. 5099–5104 (2022)
14. Zhao, N., Ye, Z., Pei, Y., Liang, Y.C., Niyato, D.: Multi-agent deep reinforcement learning for task offloading in UAV-assisted mobile edge computing. IEEE Trans. Wireless Commun. **21**(9), 6949–6960 (2022)
15. Zhang, P., Li, Y., Kumar, N., Chen, N., Hsu, C.H., Barnawi, A.: Distributed deep reinforcement learning assisted resource allocation algorithm for space-air-ground integrated networks. IEEE Trans. Netw. Serv. Manage. **20**(3), 3348–3358 (2023)
16. Zhao, L., Yao, Y., Guo, J., Zuo, Q., Leung, V.C.: Collaborative computation offloading and wireless charging scheduling in multi-UAV-assisted MEC networks: a td3-based approach. Comput. Netw. **251**, 110615 (2024)

17. Cao, A., Chen, X., Jiao, L., Yin, T., Wei, J.: Dynamic resource scheduling based quality of service optimisation in multi-UAV-assisted city edge network systems. In: 2024 IEEE International Conference on Systems, Man, and Cybernetics (SMC), pp. 4561–4567 (2024)
18. Hou, X., Wang, J., Bai, T., Deng, Y., Ren, Y., Hanzo, L.: Environment-aware AUV trajectory design and resource management for multi-tier underwater computing. IEEE J. Sel. Areas Commun. **41**(2), 474–490 (2023)

Using Machine Learning to Take Stay-or-Go Decisions in Data-Driven Drone Missions

Giorgos Polychronis(✉), Foivos Pournaropoulos, Christos D. Antonopoulos, and Spyros Lalis

University of Thessaly, Volos, Greece
{gpolychronis,spournar,cda,lalis}@uth.gr

Abstract. Drones are becoming indispensable in many application domains. In data-driven missions, besides sensing, the drone must process the collected data at runtime to decide whether additional action must be taken on the spot, before moving to the next point of interest. If processing does not reveal an event or situation that requires such an action, the drone has waited in vain instead of moving to the next point. If, however, the drone starts moving to the next point and it turns out that a follow-up action is needed at the previous point, it must spend time to fly-back. To take this decision, we propose different machine-learning methods based on branch prediction and reinforcement learning. We evaluate these methods for a wide range of scenarios where the probability of event occurrence changes with time. Our results show that the proposed methods consistently outperform the regression-based method proposed in the literature and can significantly improve the worst-case mission time by up to $4.1x$. Also, the achieved median mission time is very close, merely up to 2.7% higher, to that of a method with perfect knowledge of the current underlying event probability at each point of interest.

Keywords: Drones · Data-driven missions · Runtime decision making · Optimization · Machine-learning

1 Introduction

Drones, multicopters in particular, have become popular across a wide range of civilian applications, because they are easy to deploy, they can fly/hover in a very controllable way, and can be equipped with various sensors. In several cases, the missions are data-driven, i.e., the drone may need to perform further action(s) depending on the data collected via its onboard sensors. For example, in a smart agriculture scenario, if pest is detected at a specific location in the field, the drone can directly spray that location with pesticide. In search and rescue missions, if a person is detected with some confidence, the drone may repeat the sensing from a lower altitude and deliver a first-aid kit before help arrives.

L. Zhang and K.-K. R. Choo (Eds.): MobiQuitous 2025, LNICST 684, pp. 137–156, 2026.
https://doi.org/10.1007/978-3-032-22503-0_8

In the case of firefighting, the same drone could be used to both detect and control the fire at its early stage. However, the resource- and power-constrained embedded computing platforms of such drones may take a long time to process the sensor data to detect events or situations that require further handling. If this processing must be done often, the overall mission time can increase significantly.

One way to reduce the mission time is to accelerate data processing by leveraging external powerful computational resources (e.g., cloud or edge servers) to offload processing [13,17,24]. A complementary approach, proposed in [23], is to exploit the fact that a follow-up action may not always be needed at every point of interest. Namely, the drone can proceed with its mission and go to the next point of interest, right after the sensing task is completed, to overlap the computation time with the flight time. If, however, it turns out that an action is needed at the previous point of interest, extra time is spent for the drone to fly back. The alternative is for the drone to stay at the point of interest and wait for the computation to finish. But if no follow-up action is required, the drone will have wasted time waiting in vain.

In this paper, we focus on the problem of learning how to take good stay-or-go decisions. More specifically, the main contributions are: (i) We propose a perceptron-based approach to tackle the decision problem. (ii) In addition, we tackle the problem using reinforcement learning. (iii) We evaluate both approaches via extensive simulation experiments for a wide range of scenarios where the probability of action at each point of interest changes with time. (iv) Our results show that both approaches can achieve good results in dynamic environments, clearly outperforming the regression-based method proposed in [23] while performing close to a method that takes decisions based on perfect knowledge of the underlying probabilities.

The structure of the paper is the following. Section 2 gives an overview of related work. Section 3 presents the system model and the decision problem. Section 4 provides the logic for controlling the drone to perform the mission at hand, independently of the method that is used to take the stay-or-go decision at each point of interest. Section 5 and Sect. 6 describe the methods for taking such decisions based on branch prediction and reinforcement learning, respectively. Section 7 presents the evaluation of the proposed decisions methods. Finally, Sect. 8 concludes the paper.

2 Related Work

Reducing Mission Time by Offloading. A number of studies aim to reduce the completion time of resource-intensive computations on autonomous drones by offloading them to the cloud or an edge infrastructure. For example, the authors of [17] focus on drone-based navigation and mapping in unknown areas, where the drone dynamically decides when to offload processing. [7] proposes an algorithm that enables multiple drones to dynamically select edge servers for task offloading, taking into account factors such as channel quality and predicted trajectory. In [13], the drone uses a heuristic to choose at runtime between executing the computation locally or offloading it to an edge server. The choice relies on prior knowledge of each server's end-to-end response time. [24] investigates the combined mission planning and offloading for the case where multiple drones executing different missions experience uncertainty in flying times, while offloading computations to nearby edge servers to reduce the time waiting for the results. Our approach complements these studies by addressing mission time optimization through informed decision-making about whether the drone should wait for computation results or proceed to the next waypoint. The authors of [5] investigate a drone system that starts with high-altitude surveillance to scan large areas. If an object of interest is detected, the drone descends to conduct a more accurate inspection. Their work primarily explores the trade-offs among detection delay, area coverage, and sensing quality. In contrast, our work focuses on the mission time minimization by enabling the drone to proceed to the next point of interest before the current detection results are available.

Reinforcement Learning. ML approaches have been used to perform various optimizations in drone-based systems [2,6]. In particular, reinforcement learning (RL) is an emerging technique used in various scenarios, offering increased adaptivity and flexibility in dynamic environments compared to classic ML methods. For example, several works investigate path planning, navigation, and control [4,8,15], as well as computation offloading and resource allocation [21,22,25]. The major differentiation of our work is that we focus on a different problem, where RL is used to learn the optimal decision (stay or go) at the points of interest of data-driven missions to reduce the total mission time, but the correctness of such decisions depends on unknown probabilities that may also change over time. In our work, we use reinforcement learning to take the stay-or-go decisions. More precisely, we use the DQN [19], A2C [20] and PPO [26] algorithms, which have good performance in other problems. An extensive comparison between these algorithms is provided for the BreakOut Atari game environment in [9]. However, we evaluate these algorithms for a completely different problem.

Branch Prediction. During program execution, branch prediction is used to guess the outcome of a branch, so that one can apply parallelism in the instruction execution of a program and improve performance [12,16,18]. Some works use perceptrons to predict the outcome of a branch [10,11] or to estimate the branch confidence [3]. Perceptrons are simple neural networks, that are trained to find correlations between the current branch and other branches, or between recent outcomes and old outcomes of the branches. In [27] the O-GEHL predictor was introduced. This predictor used multiple tables, while the prediction is done in a perceptron-like summation. The TAGE predictor [28], uses multiple tagged predictors each using different history lengths. At prediction, the predictor with the longest history that match the tag at hand is used. The problem we tackle in this work, has similarities to the branch prediction problem, as we also want to predict the outcome of processing to overlap computation time with flight time (in case of a go prediction). To this end, we employ a perceptron-based approach. As an additional reference, we use a simpler, 2-bit branch predictor [14].

The stay-or-go decision problem has been studied in [23] using a regression method with memory-reset logic to delete potentially misleading historical information. In this paper, we tackle the problem using different prediction approaches (based on branch prediction and RL), showing that they can significantly outperform the regression method in scenarios where the probability for action-taking changes.

3 Problem Formulation

The problem we address was introduced in [23]. For the sake of completion, we also provide a short description here.

Mission. The drone visits the points of interest by following a pre-specified path, encoded as a sequence of waypoints $[wp_1, wp_2, ..., wp_N]$. Waypoints wp_1 and wp_N correspond to the points from where the drone takes-off and lands, respectively. The other waypoints in the path, $wp_i, 2 \leq i \leq N-1$, stand for the actual points of interest. At each of these points of interest, the drone must capture the required mission-related data, using its onboard sensors and then process this data. Let $senseT$ and $procT$ denote the time needed to perform the required sensing and data processing computation at each point of interest. As a result of this computation, an event or situation may be detected that requires a follow-up action at the respective point of interest. Note that both the computation to be performed and the type of events that may need further handling, both depend on the application at hand. Without loss of generality, let $e_i \in \{0, 1\}$ indicate whether a follow-up action is needed at wp_i (e_i=1), or not (e_i=0). Also, let the time required to perform this action be $actT$.

Flight Model. Let $flyT_{i,j}$ be the time needed for the drone to fly from wp_i to wp_j as given in Eq. 1 below:

$$flyT_{i,j} = \begin{cases} cruiseT_{i,j} + takeoffT, & \text{if } i = 1 \\ cruiseT_{i,j} + landT, & \text{if } j = N \\ cruiseT_{i,j}, & \text{if } i \neq 1 \wedge j \neq N \end{cases} \quad (1)$$

where, $cruiseT_{i,j}$ is the time for flying from wp_i to wp_j at cruising speed, $takeoffT$ is the time for a vertical take-off until the drone reaches the desired mission altitude, and $landT$ is the time for vertical landing. If the drone decides to fly to the next waypoint wp_{i+1} without waiting for the computation to complete, and an event is detected, $e_i = 1$, for the previous point wp_i, it must immediately stop its flight toward wp_{i+1} and return to the previous waypoint wp_i to perform the required action. Let $retT(i, procT)$ capture the respective delay, as a function of $procT$ which determines the travelled distance by the time the computation finishes and the event is detected.

Mission Time. Let $d_i \in \{0, 1\}$ encode the decision taken by the drone whether to stay at wp_i (waiting for the computation to finish) or to go to wp_{i+1} (before the computation finishes). Then, Eq. 2 gives the time that is needed to perform all the required tasks for each visited point of interest:

$$visitT_i = senseT + \begin{cases} procT + e_i * actT, & \text{if } d_i = 0 \\ e_i * (procT + retT(i, procT) + actT), & \text{if } d_i = 1 \end{cases} \quad (2)$$

Note that $visitT_i$ always includes $senseT$. In addition, if the drone decides to stay, it includes the processing time $procT$ and the time for taking the additional action $actT$ if processing indicates an event ($e_i = 1$). If the drone decides to go and this decision proves to be wrong ($e_i = 1$), $visitT_i$ includes $procT$, the time to return to the previous point $retT(i, procT)$ and the time to perform the additional action $actT$. Finally, Eq. 3 gives the time that is needed to complete the entire mission.

$$missionT = \sum_{i=1}^{N-1} flyT_{i,i+1} + \sum_{i=2}^{N-1} visitT_i \quad (3)$$

This is the total flight time required to visit all waypoints according to the specified path, plus the sum of the time spent for each point of interest to perform the required tasks.

Objective. We assume that the same mission is performed repeatedly over a longer time period. The objective is for the drone to exploit the experience from previous missions and *learn* to take a good decision d_i at each point of interest $wp_i, 2 \leq i \leq N-1$, so as to minimize $missionT$. The challenge is to achieve this without having any knowledge about the underlying probabilities which determine e_i (whether an additional action needs to be taken at wp_i). This becomes even harder if these probabilities change with time. Next, we describe the control logic of the drone along with two different approaches for taking the stay-or-go decision at each point of interest.

4 Mission Execution

At each point of interest, the drone must take a decision, to stay or go. Depending on the actual event generation, this decision may turn out to be correct or wrong. Nevertheless, the drone can be programmed to execute the mission in a generic way, independently of the method that is used to take these decisions. It suffices to handle any possible outcome of each decision as needed.

Algorithm 1 gives a high-level description of the mission logic used to control the drone by sending corresponding commands to the autopilot. In a nutshell, the drone takes-off and starts visiting the points of interest according to the specified mission plan. When it arrives at a point of interest, it performs the sensing task and starts the computation to process the data collected. Then, the drone decides whether to stay waiting for the computation to finish, or go to the next point. In the first case, the drone just waits hovering above the point of interest. If the computation generates a detection event then the drone performs

Algorithm 1. Drone control logic.

```
DecisionMethod.MissionBegin(wp[])
Autopilot.Arm&TakeOff()

for i from 2 to len(wp) − 1 do
    Autopilot.WaitToArrive()
    data ← Sense()
    StartComputation(data)
    d_i ← DecisionMethod.Decide(wp_i, procT)
    if (d_i = 1) then                    ▷ do not wait, go to the next point of interest
        Autopilot.GoTo(wp_{i+1})
    end if
    e_i ← GetComputationResult()
    DecisionMethod.Feedback(wp_i, d_i, e_i)
    if (e_i = 1) then
        if (d_i = 1) then                ▷ return back to perform action
            Autopilot.GoTo(wp_i)
            Autopilot.WaitToArrive()
        end if
        PerformAction()                  ▷ handle the detected event/situation
    end if
    if (d_i = 0) ∨ (e_i = 1) then        ▷ go to the next point of interest
        Autopilot.GoTo(wp_{i+1})
    end if
end for

Autopilot.WaitToArrive()
Autopilot.Land&Disarm()
DecisionMethod.MissionEnd()
```

the necessary action, before moving on. In the second case, the autopilot is instructed to start moving to the next waypoint and the drone waits until it receives the results of the computation. If no event is generated, the mission proceeds as usual, else the autopilot is instructed to go back to the previous waypoint where the drone performs the required action. After visiting the last point of interest, the autopilot is instructed to return and land the drone.

The method used to take the stay-or-go decision at each point of interest is abstracted as a separate component (DecisionMethod), which is invoked by the mission program through a structured API. Note that this component can have rich and potentially persistent internal state, e.g., to encode the experience gained from previous mission executions so that this can be used to take better decisions in the next mission. More specifically, this state is initialized (but not necessarily reset) via method MissionBegin() before the mission starts and it is updated via MissionEnd() after the mission ends. The decision at each point of interest is taken via method Decide() and feedback regarding the correctness of this decision is communicated back to the component via Feedback(). This abstraction simplifies experimentation with different decision methods without changing the core logic of the mission program.

In the following sections, we discuss the various ML-based decision methods we evaluate in this paper. Each method is packaged as a different implementation of the DecisionMethod component, without changing the basic mission execution logic of the drone.

5 Perceptron Approach

Motivated by work done on branch-prediction [10], for each point of interest, we use a 1-layer perceptron that exploits the experience gained at nearby points of interest.

Let $\mathcal{N}_i = \{wp_j : dist(wp_i, wp_j) < D\}$ denote the neighbors of wp_i (including wp_i itself), where $dist()$ returns the distance between two points, and D is the distance threshold for the neighborhood boundary. Each $wp_j \in \mathcal{N}_i$ contributes to the predictor for wp_i with each own H most recent outcomes $x_{j,h}, 1 \leq h \leq H$. More specifically, if in the hth previous mission no event was detected at wp_j then $x_{j,h} = -1$, else $x_{j,h} = 1$. The output value y_i is calculated using Eq. 4, as the weighted sum of these input values and a bias value B (a small value that effectively comes into play only in the initial case where there is no previous experience, to force a default decision). The final decision for wp_i, is *stay* if $y_i > 0$, else the decision is *go*.

$$y_i = B + \sum_{j \in \mathcal{N}_i} \sum_{h=1}^{H} x_{j,h} \times q_{j,h} \times w_{j,h} \tag{4}$$

We use two types of weights to factor-in $x_{j,h}$. The first type of weights $q_{j,h}$ capture the gravity of the outcome $x_{j,h}$ in the prediction (the delay caused by a wrong stay decision can be different than the delay caused by a wrong go decision). More specifically, if $x_{j,h} = -1$, we set $q_{j,h} = procT$, else $q_{j,h} = retT(i, procT)$. The second type of weights $w_{j,h}$ capture the correlation between different points of interest.

At the start of each mission, all $w_{j,h}$ are reset to 1 and then re-trained using the outcomes of the H previous missions. More specifically, we increase or decrease $w_{j,h}$ by η depending on whether $x_{j,h}$ was equal to the most recent outcome $x_{i,1}$ (η is the so-called learning rate). The reason we reset each $w_{j,h}$ before re-training, rather than just updating its value from the previous mission, is because the correlation between the neighboring points of interest may change. In such case, we wish to let the value of the weights be affected only by the outcome of the H most recent missions (instead of all missions that have been performed so far).

This initialization step is performed from within the MissionBegin() method of the DecisionMethod component. The Decide() method returns the prediction made for the corresponding point of interest based on the current state of the perceptron, while FEEDBACK() records the actual outcome at that point. Finally, method MISSIONEND() commits the recorded outcomes of the mission so that they can be used in the initialization phase when starting the next mission.

6 Reinforcement Learning Approach

As an alternative machine-learning approach for predicting the (stay or go) decision that is more likely to be beneficial at each point of interest in terms of mission time savings, we use reinforcement learning (RL). The design of the RL agent is described in more detail below.

6.1 Training of RL Agent

In the first mission, the RL agent takes decisions without any prior knowledge. When the mission is completed, the agent is trained based on the recorded detection events at each point of interest. This procedure is repeated in all subsequent missions. Note, however, that the agent is not trained from scratch but it is retrained based on the most recent experience (from the previous mission). This way we exploit continual learning to let the agent adapt more easily to changes.

6.2 State Space, Action Space and Reward Function of RL Agent

We perform a discretization of the geolocations that correspond to the points of interest visited by the drone, to integers. This reduces state space complexity, which, in turn, significantly improves learning efficiency. Thus the state is an integer $i, 2 \leq i \leq N-1$, where i denotes the corresponding point of interest wp_i. Note that we exclude wp_1 and wp_N as these represent the drone's take-off and landing points (the agent takes stay/go decisions only at the points of interest). The action space includes the two possible decisions that can be taken at each wp_i, namely to stay ($d_i = 0$) or to go ($d_i = 1$).

The reward function is designed to provide feedback to the RL agent based on the experienced time gains or penalties, depending on whether the decision was correct or not. The reward r is given by Eq. 5 as a function of the state i, the presence of an event that must be handled e_i, and the agent's decision d_i:

$$r(i, e_i, d_i) = \begin{cases} -procT, & \text{if } e_i = 0 \wedge d_i = 0 \\ +procT, & \text{if } e_i = 0 \wedge d_i = 1 \\ -retT(i, procT), & \text{if } e_i = 1 \wedge d_i = 1 \\ +retT(i, procT), & \text{if } e_i = 1 \wedge d_i = 0 \end{cases} \tag{5}$$

The training of the agent occurs in cycles, called episodes. Each episode is completed when the agent has been trained for all points of interest using as input the experience gained during the last mission. The agent is trained for multiple episodes, depending on the desired number of training timesteps, i.e., prediction attempts made during (re)training to receive the respective rewards and learn to take better decisions.

With respect to Algorithm 1, the (re)training process takes place within the MissionEnd() method of the DecisionMethod component, at the end of the mission. In other words, when using the RL decision method, the training is performed offline when the drone has landed (and maybe re-charging its batteries), thus even heavyweight and time-consuming training will not affect the current or the next mission. Also, in our case, the agent is trained incrementally. More specifically, after each mission, the agent is re-trained merely using the experience of the last mission, rather than training the RL agent each time from scratch using all previous (and ever increasing) historical data. This induces minimal overhead without affecting the life cycle of drone operation. The retrained agent is loaded before the next mission starts, via the MissionBegin() method, while the prediction at each point of interest is made by invoking the model via the Decide() method. Finally, the Feedback() method records the outcome so that this information is used in the re-training when the mission is completed.

6.3 Algorithms

We explore RL in conjunction with 3 popular model-free RL algorithms: DQN [19], A2C [20] and PPO [26]. These are implemented using the Stable Baselines3 library [1].

Deep Q-Network (DQN) is an off-policy RL algorithm that manages discrete action spaces. It leverages two neural networks: (i) a Q-network that estimates the action-value function Q, which maps state/action pairs to their expected discounted cumulative long-term reward, and (ii) a target network that is updated periodically but less frequently compared to the Q-network. In addition, it uses a replay buffer to store previous interactions with the environment so that they can be reused during training. The above characteristics render DQN sample-efficient. Replay memory also de-correlates previous decisions from each other by sampling them randomly in the training process.

Advantage Actor-Critic (A2C) is an actor-critic method that can handle discrete or continuous action spaces. It is a synchronous version of the Asynchronous Advantage Actor-critic (A3C) method, combining the advantages of both value- and policy-based methods. More specifically, it exploits the actor, a component that uses the current policy to decide which action to perform, while the critic evaluates the actions taken by the actor and provides relevant feedback.

Proximal Policy Optimization (PPO) is based on stochastic gradient ascent optimizing a surrogate objective function. Like A2C, it can manage discrete or continuous action spaces. It is also more robust (less prone to instability) mainly thanks to its conservative policy updates, which are not allowed to diverge more than a certain threshold by applying a clipping function.

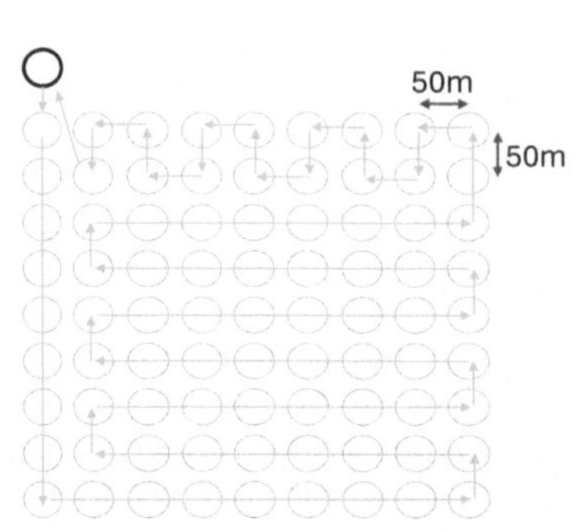

(a) Points of interest and mission path (same for all missions).

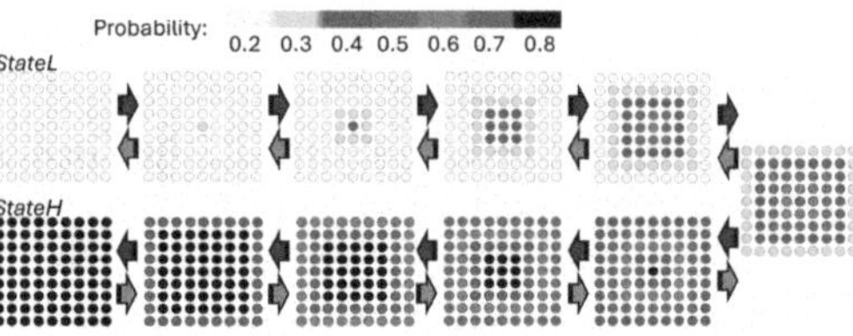

(b) Change of event detection probability at the points of interest according to pattern A.

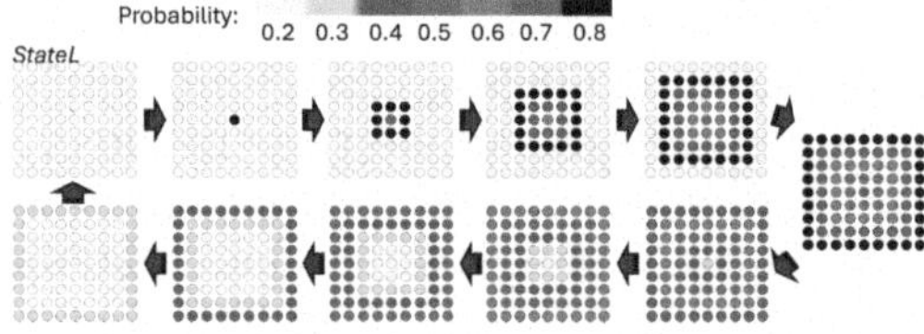

(c) Change of event detection probability at the points of interest according to pattern B.

Fig. 1. Mission area and patterns of event detection probability change.

7 Evaluation

For our evaluation, we use the same simulator as in [23], with realistic flight-related delays $flyT_{i,j}$ and $retT(i, procT)$, obtained from experiments with a real quadcopter drone in the field, configured to fly at a cruising speed of 4m/s. We also use the same settings for the rest of the delays, $senseT = 1$ sec, $procT = 10$ sec, and $actT = 10$ sec. Next, we present the experimental setup and discuss the results achieved by the proposed machine-learning approaches vs other benchmarks.

7.1 Topology and Change of Event Probability

The target area consists of 81 points of interest, arranged in a 9×9 grid as shown in Fig. 1aThe vertical and horizontal distance between points is 50 m. The home point, from which the drone takes-off and where it returns to land, is the bold node at the periphery of the area of interest. The yellow arrows indicate the drone's path in all missions.

We assume that the occurrence of events at each point of interest is governed by an underlying probability. Furthermore, we let this probability change between missions according to two different patterns, shown in Fig. 1band Fig. 1c. Both start from and end at StateL where all points have low event probability 0.2. In pattern A, the probabilities increase gradually from the center to the periphery of the mission area, eventually leading to StateH where all points have a high probability 0.8. Then, the probabilities decrease gradually in the reverse direction, eventually going back to StateL. In pattern B, probabilities also increase in the same direction. However, unlike pattern A, this increase occurs abruptly, from low (0.2) to high (0.8). Also, the probabilities decrease gradually from the center to the periphery, in the opposite direction than in pattern A.

Further, we experiment with two rates of probability change. In the *fast* rate, the probability at each point of interest changes between missions in steps of 0.1, as shown in Fig. 1band Fig. 1c. In the *slow* rate, the probability changes each time by 0.05. As a result, for each transition shown in the figures between a state where a given point of interest has probability p_1 and a state where the same point has probability p_2, there is an intermediate state where this point has probability $(p_1 + p_2)/2$. These intermediate states are not shown in the figures for brevity. Note that scenarios with the slow rate include twice the number of states (and missions) vs the fast rate.

In our experiments, we assume that the drone executes the same mission plan periodically, visiting each time the same points of interest in the same pre-specified order. The goal of our evaluation is to see how well each decision

Table 1. RL agent learning parameters for each algorithm.

Parameter	DQN	A2C	PPO
Neural Network	MLP	MLP	MLP
Number of hidden layers	2	2	2
Units (per hidden layer)	64	64	64
Optimizer	Adam	RMSprop	Adam
RMSprop ϵ	N/A	0.00001	N/A
Activation function	ReLU	tanh	tanh
Target network update interval	10000	N/A	N/A
Learning rate	0.0001	0.0007	0.00005
Discount factor	0.99	0.99	0.99
Replay buffer size	1000000	N/A	N/A
Minibatch size	32	N/A	64
Soft update coefficient	1.0	N/A	N/A
Exploration fraction	0.1	N/A	N/A
Initial value of random action probability	1.0	N/A	N/A
Final value of random action probability	0.05	N/A	N/A
Generalized advantage estimator Lambda	N/A	1.0	0.95
Entropy coefficient for loss calculation	N/A	0.0	0.0
Value function coefficient for loss calculation	N/A	0.5	0.5
Number of epochs when optimizing the surrogate loss	N/A	N/A	10
Max value for gradient clipping	10	0.5	0.5
Number of timesteps (per mission)	100000	100000	10000

method performs in each mission for the respective state (the event probability at each point of interest) and how well it adapts to more or less abrupt changes (in these probabilities).

7.2 Fine-Tuning

The proposed methods were fine-tuned after extensive experimentation (not included for the sake of brevity). The respective configuration parameters are briefly presented below.

Perceptron. We set the bias $B = 0.001$, forcing the predictor to initially take *stay* decisions. The neighborhood boundary is set to $D = 150$ meters and we use the $H = 2$ most recent outcomes at each point of interest. Finally, for the weight training we set the learning rate to $\eta = 0.1$.

Reinforcement Learning. The hyperparameter settings that were selected after fine-tuning for the three RL-based methods are shown in Table 1. The selection criterion is to minimize the number of opposite decisions and the increase in mission time vs the knowledgeable method (discussed in Sect. 7.4). The chosen number of timesteps (per mission) is sufficient to achieve proper training and generalization of the models (we have verified that increasing the number of timesteps does not improve performance). Notably, the best version of PPO requires 10x fewer timesteps than DQN and A2C.

7.3 Training Overhead

All the above methods are implemented in Python3. When the agent is trained on a server with an Intel Core i9 CPU with 24 cores and 132 GB of memory, the procedure is completed quickly, within 3-5 seconds, depending on the algorithm (DQN in 3 sec, PPO in 3.6 s, A2C in 4.7 s.). This scenario corresponds to the case where the drone can offload the training task to a nearby edge server, e.g., as soon as it lands at the home location, before starting the next mission. If this is not possible, training must be performed locally on the drone. Assuming that the drone's companion computer is a Raspberry Pi 4 (as this is the case in our custom drone), the computation requires approximately 11.5 minutes (DQN in 65 sec, PPO in 90 sec, A2C in 95 s). Even in this case, training requires a small fraction of the time that is typically required to recharge the drone's batteries, while it is comparable to the time needed for hot battery swapping in case spare fully-charged batteries are readily available at the home location. Thus, it does not introduce any extra delay or disruption in the typical drone operation cycle. Notably, the respective delay for the perceptron method is negligible even on the least powerful hardware, taking about 20 ms on the Raspberry Pi.

7.4 Benchmarks

Besides the proposed ML approaches, we also use the following methods as benchmarks for comparison.

2-bit Predictor: This method uses a 2-bit predictor [14] for each point of interest. The predictor consists of a saturating counter with states $\{00, 01, 10, 11\}$ (in binary), with the most significant bit giving the prediction. When the drone does not detect an event, the counter is increased and the state changes towards the states that predict 1 (go). Conversely, when the drone detects an event that must be handled, the counter is decreased and the state changes in the reverse direction towards the states that predict 0 (stay). For the first mission, the counter is initialized to 01, forcing the drone to wait.

Regression: Proposed in [23], this method predicts the event probabilities at each point by running a regression algorithm on the experience gained from previous missions. The decision is taken by weighing the predicted probability with the time penalties for the drone if the decision is wrong. Also, an anomaly detection mechanism is used to detect whether the previous experience is invalid, in which case the memory of the algorithm is reset. For the first mission, the method is initialized to choose to wait (stay) at all points.

Knowledgeable: This method takes decisions like the above approach, but has perfect knowledge about the underlying event probability at each point of interest (there is no need to learn/infer this by observing the presence or absence of events at runtime). Given that in the general case it is not possible to have such perfect knowledge in reality, we use this as an *idealized* reference for all other methods. Note, however, that this method is *not* an oracle, thus it can still take wrong decisions (more likely when the event probability is near 0.5).

7.5 Results

We run every scenario for each probability change rate 20 times, for a different randomly chosen event occurrence at each point (generated based on the respective underlying probability at each state), and report the average over the 20 runs. To ensure a fair comparison, the occurrence of an event at each point is generated offline and is stored in a file, which is replayed when testing each decision method.

The results are shown in Fig. 2 for pattern A and in Fig. 3 for pattern B. In each figure, the top plots show the opposite decisions vs the knowledgeable method in each mission (probability state) as described in Sect. 7.1. Note that fewer opposite decisions correspond to better performance (shorter mission times) as the knowledgeable method takes informed decisions based on perfect knowledge about the underlying event probabilities. The plots at the bottom show the relative increase in the mission time vs the knowledgeable method for each mission (again, lower is better). Note that the experiments for pattern A run for two StateL $\rightarrow$ StateL cycles, while pattern B experiments run for four cycles. We accompany each line plot with a boxplot to visualize the statistical performance over all mission executions. In addition, as key performance metrics, we report the maximum (worst-case) and median increase in the mission time vs the knowledgeable method, summarized in Table 2 for each scenario (we ignore the first mission where there is no prior experience and methods take a

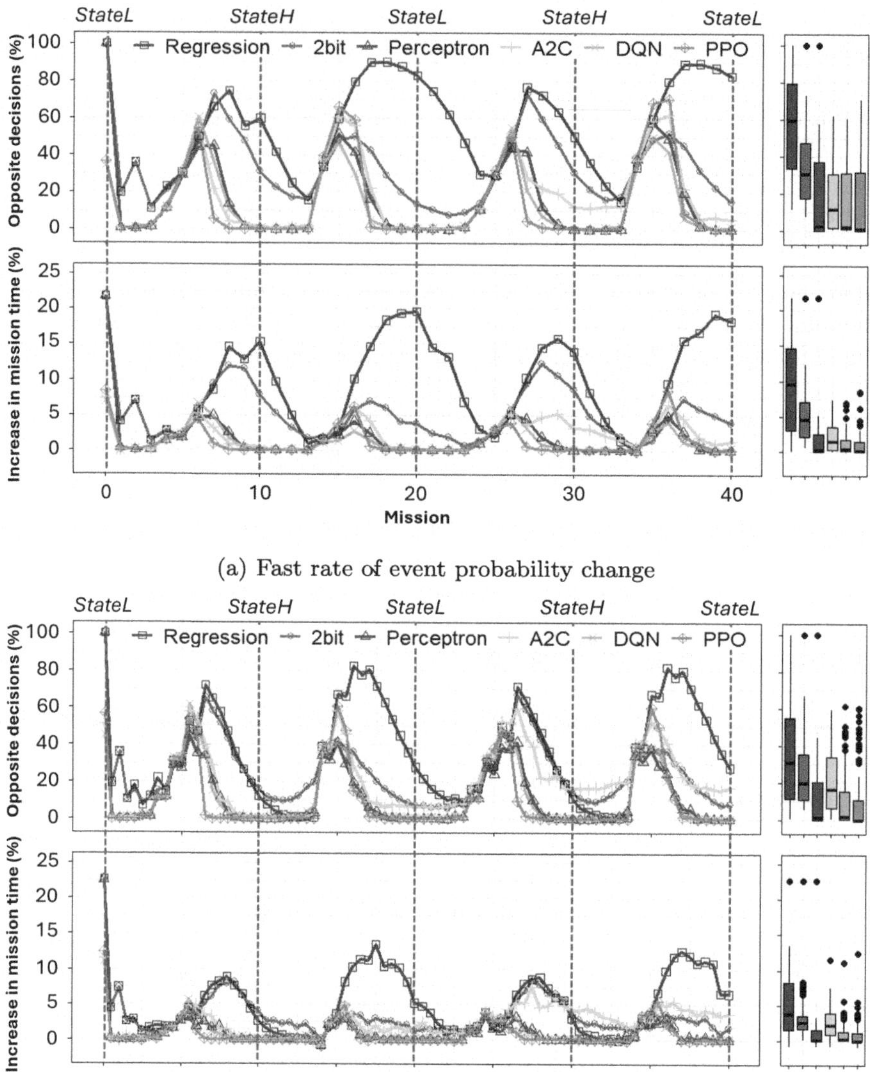

(a) Fast rate of event probability change

(b) Slow rate of event probability change

Fig. 2. Pattern A: opposite decisions (top) and mission time increase (bottom) vs the knowledgeable method.

default decision at all points, predetermined by their bias). Next, we discuss the results for each pattern separately, followed by an overall assessment.

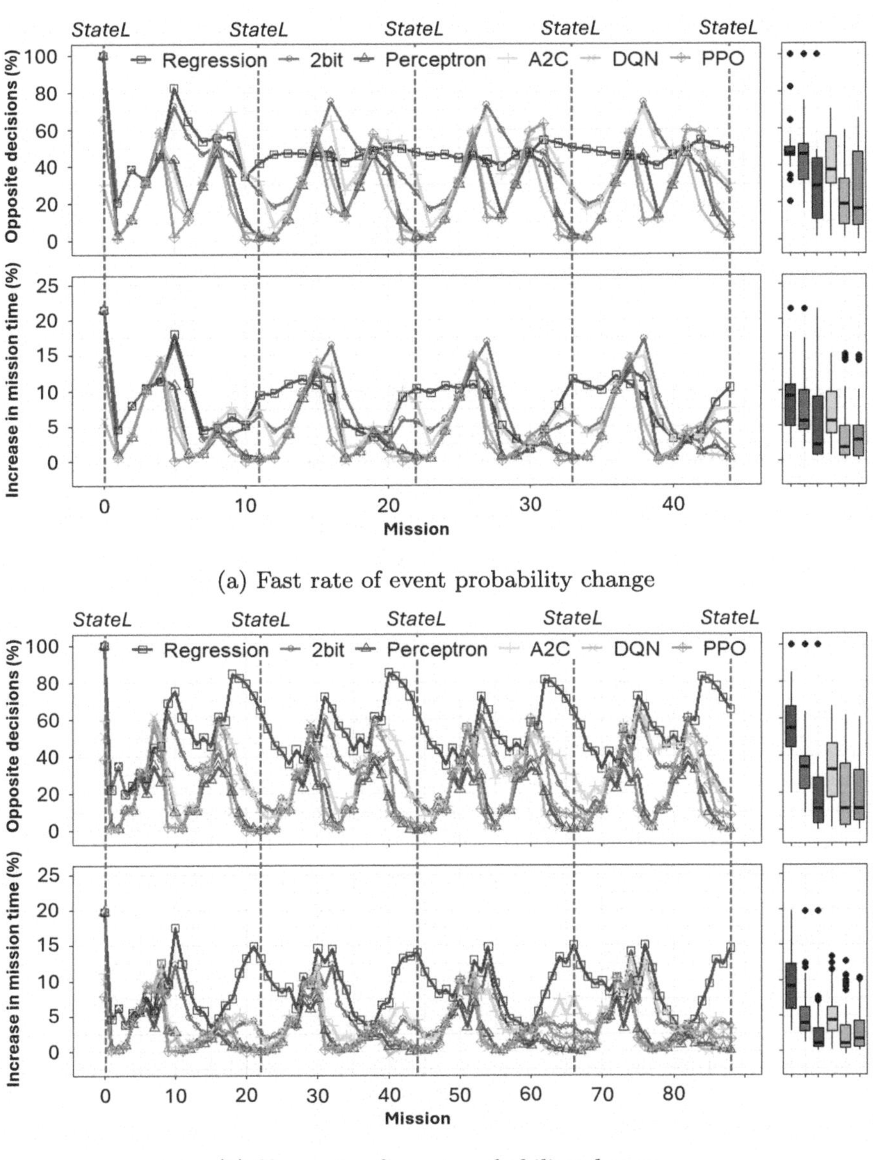

(a) Fast rate of event probability change

(b) Slow rate of event probability change

Fig. 3. Pattern B: opposite decisions (top) and mission time increase (bottom) vs the knowledgeable method.

Pattern A (Figure 2). We observe the same high-level trend for all methods. In each StateL → StateL cycle, there are two phases where performance drops and then improves again. This is because the gradual changes in probability eventually flip the decision that must be taken at each point, from go to stay and

Table 2. Max/median relative increase in mission time vs the knowledgeable method (best values in bold).

		Regression	2bit	Perceptron	A2C	DQN	PPO
Pattern A fast rate	max	19.6%	12.3%	**5.1%**	6.5%	6.7%	8.5%
	median	9.1%	4.4%	0.3%	1.4%	0.4%	**0.1%**
Pattern A slow rate	max	13.5%	8.4%	**3.3%**	7.5%	5.6%	5.5%
	median	3.8%	2.6%	0.1%	2.2%	0.3%	**0.0%**
Pattern B fast rate	max	18.1%	17.3%	**13.3%**	15.1%	15.1%	14.8%
	median	9.2%	5.7%	2.1%	5.6%	**1.7%**	2.7%
Pattern B slow rate	max	17.5%	12.4%	**7.6%**	13.4%	12.7%	10.3%
	median	9.2%	3.9%	**1.1%**	4.3%	**1.1%**	1.7%

vice versa. Also, each such phase includes several states where many points have probability equal or close to 0.5, making it harder to predict this correctly and take the same decisions as the knowledgeable method. Note that these peaks of opposite decision making lead to corresponding increased mission times, but to a smaller degree. The reason is two-fold. On the one hand, as previously noted, the knowledgeable method can take wrong decisions (and this becomes more likely when the event probability is around 0.5). On the other hand, the mission time includes delays that can not be avoided (like $flyT_{i,j}$, $senseT$ or $actT$) thereby decreasing the negative impact of wrong decisions. The same trend holds for the slow rate, but with improved decision performance and reduced mission times, as changes are smoother and there are more opportunities to learn.

Clearly, the regression cannot handle changes well, especially during the aforementioned phases, thus producing noisy estimations about the event probability at each point. In turn, this results in uninformed decisions and increased mission times. The 2-bit predictor performs consistently better, but is still suboptimal in almost every mission. The perceptron is significantly better than the previous methods, especially in the challenging state transitions where it adapts faster, achieving a median mission time very close to the knowledgeable method.

Looking at the RL algorithms, one can observe that both DQN and PPO perform well, achieving very good performance in terms of the median mission time that is close (DQN) or even better (PPO) than the perceptron, albeit having higher worst-case mission times. A2C initially performs close to the other RL algorithms during the first StateL → StateL cycle, but shows a noticeable performance drop in the second cycle.

Pattern B (Figure 3**)** The high-level trend in each StateL → StateL cycle is similar to that of pattern A. Namely, in each such cycle, there are two major transition phases, in the first phase from states where in most points the right decision is to go towards states where the right decision is to stay, and vice versa in the second phase. However, the probabilities change more abruptly during the first phase while the entire StateL → StateL cycle has half the transitions compared to pattern A. This makes learning harder, resulting in worse decision performance and increased mission times compared to pattern A. The two peaks of bad performance in each cycle, corresponding to the two aforementioned phases, are clearly visible in the plots. Note that taking opposite decisions vs the knowledgeable method has a higher impact on the mission time increase in the first phase compared to the second phase of each cycle. This is because the time penalty of a wrong go decision (in the first phase, the drone has learned to go, but due to the change in probabilities the best decision is to stay) is higher than that of a wrong stay decision (in the second phase, the drone has learned to stay, but the probability change makes go the best decision).

Under these more challenging circumstances, all methods exhibit a worse performance than in pattern A (as a minor exception, in the fast rate, the regression has a slightly better worst-case mission time). Like in the previous experiments, the regression does not manage to adapt well, taking many opposite decisions and resulting in significantly increased mission time vs the knowledgeable method. The 2bit and A2C achieve better results than the regression, but still have relatively poor performance, especially in terms of the median increase of the mission time. Once again, the perceptron, DQN and PPO consistently outperform all other methods, with results quite close to those of the knowledgeable method.

Overall. The perceptron, DQN, and PPO achieve the best results over all scenarios, with a big difference compared to the regression. On the one hand, the worst-case mission time in the state transitions where the probabilities and the right decisions are harder to predict, is significantly lower. More precisely, the improvement vs the regression across all scenarios and rates is $1.4x$ up to $4.1x$ for the perceptron, $1.2x$ up to $2.9x$ for DQN, and $1.2x$ up to $2.5x$ for PPO. On the other hand, these methods manage to overcome the periods of bad predictions and converge fast to good decisions, which, in turn, translates to reduced mission times. This can be confirmed by looking the median increase in the mission time vs the knowledgeable method. Namely, in pattern A, all three methods achieve practically the same median mission times as the knowledgeable method. In pattern B, despite having a more notable mission time increase vs the knowledgeable method, the perceptron, DQN and PPO respectively outperform the regression by $4.4x$, $5.4x$ and $3.4x$ for the fast rate, and by $8.4x$, $8.4x$ and $5.4x$ for the slow rate. Note that the improvement is significantly higher for the slow rate, showing that when there is sufficient opportunity to learn, these methods manage to do this much better than the regression.

Comparing the perceptron with the two RL methods, DQN and PPO achieve a slightly better median increase in mission time for the fast rate of event probability change, in pattern B and pattern A, respectively. For the slow rate, the perceptron has very similar performance. Further, the perceptron consistently has the lowest worst-case increase in mission time over all scenarios and rates. We conclude that the perceptron is more stable and robust to abrupt changes, while DQN/PPO seem to adapt faster to complex and highly dynamic environments. Between the two RL algorithms, PPO is more attractive due to the much faster re-training time ($10x$ fewer timesteps).

8 Conclusion

Focusing on data-driven drone missions, we have proposed different machine-learning methods for deciding whether to wait for data processing to finish before moving to the next point of interest, or to start this movement while the computation is still being performed in anticipation that processing will not reveal an event or situation that requires extra handling at the previous point of interest. Our evaluation for scenarios where the probability of such event occurrence at each point of interest changes with time, shows that these methods can achieve significantly better results than the regression-based method previously proposed in the literature, while performing close to a method that has perfect knowledge of the underlying event probabilities.

Regarding future work, in order to further evaluate each decision method, we plan to experiment with a wider variety of scenarios, where the event probabilities follow different and even completely random patterns. Another interesting direction is to support more control options and respective decisions. For instance, the drone could adopt a lower cruising speed when deciding to go but the probability of an event being detected at the previous point of interest is non-negligible, thereby reducing the time penalty in case the drone must indeed return to the previous point of interest to take further action. Also, we plan to extend our methods to become energy-aware, e.g., by considering the energy spent by the drone to fly between the waypoints and hover above the points of interest, in order to reduce or ideally completely avoid detours to recharge or switch the drone's batteries, which can introduce a large penalty in the overall mission execution time.

Acknowledgments. This work has been supported by the Horizon Europe research and innovation programme of the European Union, project MLSysOps, grant agreement number 101092912.

References

1. Stable baselines3. https://stable-baselines3.readthedocs.io/
2. Abubakar, A.I., et al.: A survey on energy optimization techniques in UAV-based cellular networks: from conventional to machine learning approaches. Drones **7**(3), 214 (2023)
3. Akkary, H., Srinivasan, S.T., Koltur, R., Patil, Y., Refaai, W.: Perceptron-based branch confidence estimation. In: International Symposium on High Performance Computer Architecture, pp. 265–265 (2004)
4. Azar, A.T., et al.: Drone deep reinforcement learning: a review. Electronics **10**(9), 999 (2021)
5. Bandarupalli, A., Jain, S., Melachuri, A., Pappas, J., Chaterji, S.: Vega: Drone-based multi-altitude target detection for autonomous surveillance. In: IEEE International Conference on Distributed Computing in Smart Systems and the Internet of Things, pp. 209–216 (2023)

6. Bithas, P.S., Michailidis, E.T., Nomikos, N., Vouyioukas, D., Kanatas, A.G.: A survey on machine-learning techniques for UAV-based communications. Sensors **19**(23), 5170 (2019)
7. Chen, J., Chen, S., Luo, S., Wang, Q., Cao, B., Li, X.: An intelligent task offloading algorithm (itoa) for UAV edge computing network. Digital Commun. Netw. **6**(4), 433–443 (2020)
8. Dabiri, M.T., Hasna, M.: Uav trajectory optimization for directional thz links using deep reinforcement learning. In: IEEE Vehicular Technology Conference, pp. 1–5 (2023)
9. De La Fuente, N., Guerra, D.A.V.: A comparative study of deep reinforcement learning models: Dqn vs ppo vs a2c. arXiv preprint arXiv:2407.14151 (2024)
10. Jiménez, D.A., Lin, C.: Dynamic branch prediction with perceptrons. In: International Symposium on High-Performance Computer Architecture, pp. 197–206 (2001)
11. Jiménez, D.A., Lin, C.: Neural methods for dynamic branch prediction. ACM Trans. Comput. Syst. **20**(4), 369–397 (2002)
12. Joseph, R.: A survey of deep learning techniques for dynamic branch prediction. arXiv preprint arXiv:2112.14911 (2021)
13. Kasidakis, T., Polychronis, G., Koutsoubelias, M., Lalis, S.: Reducing the mission time of drone applications through location-aware edge computing. In: IEEE International Conference on Fog and Edge Computing, pp. 45–52 (2021)
14. Lee, J.K., Smith, A.J.: Branch prediction strategies and branch target buffer design. Computer **17**(01), 6–22 (1984)
15. Li, Y., Aghvami, A.H., Dong, D.: Path planning for cellular-connected UAV: A DRL solution with quantum-inspired experience replay. IEEE Trans. Wireless Commun. **21**(10), 7897–7912 (2022)
16. McFarling, S.: Combining branch predictors. Tech. rep., Technical Report TN-36, Digital Western Research Laboratory (1993)
17. Messous, M.A., Hellwagner, H., Senouci, S.M., Emini, D., Schnieders, D.: Edge computing for visual navigation and mapping in a uav network. In: IEEE International Conference on Communications, pp. 1–6 (2020)
18. Mittal, S.: A survey of techniques for dynamic branch prediction. Concurr. Comput.: Practice Exper. **31**(1), e4666 (2019)
19. Mnih, V.: Playing atari with deep reinforcement learning. arXiv preprint arXiv:1312.5602 (2013)
20. Mnih, V., et al.: Asynchronous methods for deep reinforcement learning. In: International Conference on Machine Learning, pp. 1928–1937 (2016)
21. Nabi, A., Baidya, T., Moh, S.: Comprehensive survey on reinforcement learning-based task offloading techniques in aerial edge computing. Internet of Things 101342 (2024)
22. Peng, H., Shen, X.: Multi-agent reinforcement learning based resource management in MEC-and UAV-assisted vehicular networks. IEEE J. Sel. Areas Commun. **39**(1), 131–141 (2020)
23. Polychronis, G., Koutsoubelias, M., Lalis, S.: Should i stay or should i go: a learning approach for drone-based sensing applications. In: International Conference on Distributed Computing in Smart Systems and the Internet of Things, pp. 339–346 (2024)
24. Polychronis, G., Lalis, S.: Flexible computation offloading at the edge for autonomous drones with uncertain flight times. In: International Conference on Distributed Computing in Smart Systems and the Internet of Things, pp. 201–208 (2023)

25. Qu, C., et al.: Dronecoconet: learning-based edge computation offloading and control networking for drone video analytics. Futur. Gener. Comput. Syst. **125**, 247–262 (2021)
26. Schulman, J., Wolski, F., Dhariwal, P., Radford, A., Klimov, O.: Proximal policy optimization algorithms. arXiv preprint arXiv:1707.06347 (2017)
27. Seznec, A.: The o-gehl branch predictor. The 1st JILP Championship Branch Prediction Competition (2004)
28. Seznec, A., Michaud, P.: A case for (partially) tagged geometric history length branch prediction. J. Instruct.-Level Parall. **8**, 23 (2006)

A Hierarchical Federated Framework for Task Offloading in Satellite-Terrestrial Integrated IoT Networks

Xiang Luo[1,2], Chuanlong Song[2,3], Yuan Qiu[2,3](✉), Jiayu Sun[2,3], and Qi Zhang[1]

[1] School of Communication and Information Engineering, Shanghai University, Shanghai 200444, China

[2] Shanghai Key Laboratory of Collaborative Computing in Spacial Heterogeneous Network, Shanghai 201109, China

[3] Shanghai Aerospace Electronic Technology Institute, Shanghai 201109, China

qiuyuan1986@126.com

Abstract. The development of low-Earth orbit satellite constellations provides a potential solution to task offloading associated with the rapidly increasing number of IoT devices in remote areas. However, due to the limited satellite resources and dynamic task offloading requirements, task offloading typically requires collaboration between multiple satellites and edge nodes across different regions, which can lead to data privacy leaks. Traditional collaborative methods, such as those based on deep reinforcement learning, often fail to consider data privacy protection across different regions. During training, nodes in a particular region cannot guarantee the privacy of uploaded training data. Therefore, this paper proposes a multi-layer federated learning collaborative optimization framework that aims to minimize the overall latency of satellite-ground integrated IoT task processing while establishing cross-domain distributed collaborative training to protect privacy. This approach makes efficient task offloading decisions through multi-agent collaboration and avoids privacy data leaks. Simulation experiments demonstrate that the proposed method achieves an improvement of approximately 6.28% to 11.11% compared to traditional methods.

Keywords: ISTNs · Multi-Agent Reinforcement Learning · Task Offloading · Federated Learning

1 Introduction

The increasing number of Internet of Things (IoT) devices has led to a substantial rise in the number of computational tasks, resulting in significantly higher

This work was supported in part by National Key R&D Program of China under Grant 2023YFE0208100; in part by Rising-Star Program of Shanghai Science and Technology Innovation Action Plan (Yangfan Special Project) under Grant 24YF2717300 and 24YF2717600; and in part by Qian Xuesen Youth Innovation Foundation of China Aerospace Science and Technology Corporation.

L. Zhang and K.-K. R. Choo (Eds.): MobiQuitous 2025, LNICST 684, pp. 157–169, 2026.
https://doi.org/10.1007/978-3-032-22503-0_9

processing demands at the network edge. These tasks typically require processing with low latency, which causes problems for traditional cloud-centric architectures [1]. Mobile edge computing (MEC) is a promising solution to such challenges, as it enables tasks to be offloaded to edge nodes located closer to data sources [2,3]. Although MEC has been shown effective in terrestrial networks, its implementation depends on the continuous availability of communication infrastructure. In remote areas with complex terrain or during natural disasters, terrestrial infrastructure is frequently unavailable or unstable, thereby undermining service reliability. These events frequently result in pervasive failures of ground-based communications. By contrast, LEO satellite systems enable rapid link restoration and wide-area coverage, sustaining connectivity under adverse conditions. In mountainous or desert regions where geography constrains terrestrial deployments, LEO constellations provide low-latency connectivity and support continuous service availability.

To address such limitations, integrated satellite-terrestrial networks (ISTNs) have been proposed as a potential solution [4]. LEO satellites operate at altitudes between 500 and 2,000 km. This lower altitude reduces propagation delay and supports low-latency communications. Meanwhile, LEO constellations are densely deployed to ensure seamless coverage and rapid link recovery when terrestrial networks are unavailable [5,6]. These characteristics enable ISTNs to support time-sensitive and compute-intensive IoT applications, particularly in areas where terrestrial networks are unavailable [7].

In ISTNs, tasks can be dynamically offloaded across multiple regions. However, heterogeneity in regional resource capacities, service demand and environmental conditions makes task scheduling significantly complicated. Multi-agent reinforcement learning methods are widely adopted owing to their adaptability to dynamic and complex environments. Lai proposed a hierarchical MARL approach to optimize task offloading and resource allocation in LEO satellite networks, effectively addressing hybrid action space and load imbalance issues [8]. Additionally, Jia introduced a distributed multi-agent deep reinforcement learning algorithm, namely MATORA, to optimize task offloading and resource allocation in satellite edge computing. It can address time-varying channels, queue delays, and dynamic satellite loads effectively [9]. It is worth noting that the above approaches involve extensive information exchange, raising concerns about data privacy and communication security. Privacy is critical in multi-agent systems, where agents often share data across different regions. Many decentralized optimization methods are prone to data leaks, which can threaten confidentiality, especially when data is exchanged across regions. To address these challenges, federated learning (FL), which can be trained without sharing raw data, has been introduced as a privacy-preserving alternative to decentralized optimization [10,11].

Considering the above challenges, we propose a Hierarchical Federated Multi-Agent Reinforcement Learning (HF-MARL) framework that carries out centralised training in local areas with the Multi-Agent Deep Deterministic Policy Gradient (MADDPG) algorithm to enhance convergence and coordination, while allowing federated cooperation across areas to protect data confidentiality. This hierarchical structure enables agents within each region to share experiences and train jointly while only exchanging model parameters across regions, ensuring that raw data remains locally protected. Simulation results show that the HF-MARL framework achieves convergence performance comparable to that of centralised MADDPG while providing privacy guarantees through federated learning. The remainder of this paper is organized as follows: Section 2 introduces the system model and formulates the offloading and resource allocation problem. Section 3 presents the proposed hierarchical federated MARL framework with privacy enhancement for ISTNs. The algorithm design is described in Section 4. Section 5 demonstrates the simulation results and evaluations. Finally, Section 6 concludes the paper.

2 System Model and Problem Formulation

We consider a typical edge computing scenario in ISTNs, where LEO satellites, ground base stations (BS) and user devices collaborate to support dynamic task offloading and resource management (Fig. 1).

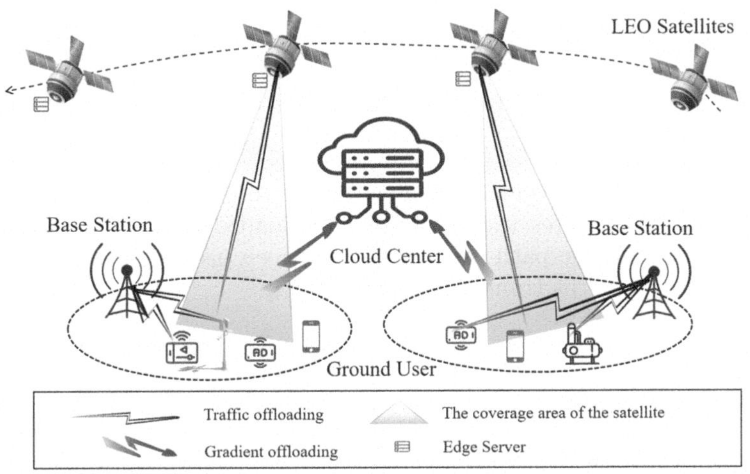

Fig. 1. Architecture of Integrated Satellite Terrestrial Networks.

Let $\mathcal{L} = \{l_1, l_2, \ldots, l_i\}$ denote the set of LEO satellites. Each satellite $l_i \in \mathcal{L}$ is equipped with an onboard computing device. Let $\mathcal{B} = \{b_1, b_2, \ldots, b_j\}$ denote the set of ground base stations. Each base station $b_j \in \mathcal{B}$ is related to an edge server that can process local computation tasks or aggregated gradients. Let $\mathcal{U} = \{u_1, u_2, \ldots, u_k\}$ denote the set of ground user devices. Each user device $u_k \in \mathcal{U}$ generates a computation task represented by $\mathcal{T}_k = (d_k, c_k, \tau_k)$, where d_k denotes the size of the task, c_k is the number of CPU cycles required in processing, and τ_k denotes the maximum tolerable delay for completing the task. Let $a_{k,j} \in \{0, 1\}$ denote whether user u_k offloads a task to base station

b_j, and $a_{k,i} \in \{0,1\}$ denote offloading to satellite l_i. Let $a_k \in \{0,1\}$ denote the offloading decision of user u_k. If $a_k = 0$, it indicates that the task is offloaded to base station b_j. The channel gain h_k^{BS} is modeled as [12]:

$$h_k^{\text{BS}} = \beta_0 \left(\frac{\rho_k}{d_0}\right)^{-\alpha} \zeta_k \tag{1}$$

where β_0 is the reference channel gain at distance d_0, ρ_k is the physical distance between user u_k and the BS, α is the path loss exponent, and ζ_k is the small-scale fading coefficient. The transmission rate R_k^{BS} from user u_k to the BS b_j is given by [13]:

$$R_k^{\text{BS}} = B \log_2 \left(1 + \frac{P_k h_k^{\text{BS}}}{N_0}\right) \tag{2}$$

where B denotes the channel bandwidth, P_k is the transmit power of user u_k, N_0 is the noise power.

The transmission delay from user u_k to BS is given by:

$$T_k^{\text{tb}} = \frac{d_k}{R_k^{\text{BS}}} \tag{3}$$

where d_k denotes the distance between the user and the base station. The corresponding computation delay at the BS is:

$$T_k^{\text{comp}} = \frac{c_k}{f_k^{\text{BS}}} \tag{4}$$

where f_k^{BS} is the CPU frequency assigned in BS to process the task of the user u_k. If $a_k = 1$, it indicates that the task is offloaded to a LEO satellite. The corresponding free-space path loss (FSPL) between user u_k and the satellite is calculated using the Friis transmission model [14]:

$$L_{\text{FSPL}} = \left(\frac{4\pi \rho_k f}{c}\right)^2 \tag{5}$$

where ρ_k is the distance between the user and the satellite, f is the carrier frequency, and c is the speed of light . The channel gain h_k^{SAT} is then modeled as the inverse of FSPL:

$$h_k^{\text{SAT}} = \frac{\kappa}{L_{\text{FSPL}}} \tag{6}$$

where κ is a constant that may include antenna gains and other proportional factors. The transmission rate R_k^{SAT} from user u_k to the satellite is given by [15]:

$$R_k^{\text{SAT}} = B \log_2 \left(1 + \frac{P_k h_k^{\text{SAT}}}{N_0}\right) \tag{7}$$

where B denotes the channel bandwidth, P_k is the transmit power of user u_k, N_0 is the noise power. The transmission delay from user u_k to the satellite is given by:

$$T_k^{\text{ts}} = \frac{d_k}{R_k^{\text{SAT}}} \tag{8}$$

where d_k also denotes the data size of the offloaded task. The corresponding computation delay on the satellite is the following:

$$T_k^{\text{comp}} = \frac{c_k}{f_k^{\text{SAT}}} \tag{9}$$

where f_k^{SAT} is the CPU frequency allocated by the satellite to process the task from user u_k.

The optimization problem is formulated to minimize the total system delay, including both transmission and computation time for all tasks across all users. The optimization problem $\mathcal{P}$ is formulated as:

$$\mathcal{P} : \min_{a_k} \quad \frac{1}{K} \sum_{k=1}^{K} \left(T_k^{\text{tx}} + T_k^{\text{comp}}\right)$$

subject to:

$$\begin{aligned}
&\text{C1: } a_k \in \{0, 1\}, \quad \forall k,\\
&\text{C2: } R_k \leq R^{\max}, \quad \forall k,\\
&\text{C3: } P_k \leq P^{\max}, \quad \forall k,\\
&\text{C4: } T_k^{\text{tx}} + T_k^{\text{comp}} \leq \tau_k, \quad \forall k,\\
&\text{C5: } T_k^{\text{tx}} + T_k^{\text{comp}} \leq T_k^{\text{SAT}}, \quad \text{if } a_k = 1.
\end{aligned}$$

$R^{\max}$ and $P^{\max}$ denote the maximum allowable rate and power, respectively. τ_k is the maximum tolerable delay of task k, and T_k^{SAT} is the duration of visibility of the satellite for the user k. Constraints C1 define the binary offloading action. C2 and C3 ensure that the transmission rate and power remain within the system limits. C4 guarantees that the delay for each task does not exceed the tolerable threshold. C5 further restricts that the delay of satellite-offloaded tasks must be within the satellite visibility window.

3 Hierarchical Federated MARL Framework With Privacy Enhancement for ISTNs

Instead, we focus on the learning-based coordination mechanism under such network constraints. Multi-agent reinforcement learning (MARL) is often adopted to enable distributed intelligence in such environments. In particular, the Multi-Agent Deep Deterministic Policy Gradient (MADDPG) algorithm has demonstrated strong performance in coordinated policy learning through its centralized training and decentralized execution (CTDE) framework. However, MADDPG implementation in ISTNs faces challenges with spatially distributed agents. Agents operating across different satellite coverage areas or ground clusters must exchange local trajectories to update global critics. This data transmission between regions raises significant privacy risks. Sensitive information exposure could reveal user behavior patterns or operational contexts during training.

Federated learning (FL) offers a natural alternative to improve privacy. It allows each region to train models locally and only upload model parameters for global aggregation, avoiding the transmission of raw data. However, applying FL to multi-agent reinforcement learning (MARL) leads to a challenge. MADDPG relies on shared experience for accurate value estimation. FL removes this sharing, which may degrade the coordination performance between agents.

We designed an HF-MARL architecture to resolve the conflict between coordination and privacy. The learning process is divided into two layers: intra-regional and inter-regional.

At the intra-regional level, agents within the same region share their local experiences. These agents are assumed to operate under a shared communication backbone, such as a ground station cluster or a satellite beam. Each region maintains a centralized replay buffer, which is only accessible by agents in that region. During training, all local agents contribute trajectories to this buffer. The MADDPG algorithm is then applied using centralized critics and decentralized actors. This setup allows agents to learn cooperative policies while preserving locality.

At the inter-regional level, raw data is not shared. Instead, each region performs several rounds of local training and periodically uploads its model parameters. These parameters may include actor networks, critic networks, or both. A cloud server or coordinating satellite performs aggregation using a federated averaging strategy. The aggregated model is then broadcast to all regions. This process enables indirect knowledge transfer between regions without exposing sensitive experiences.

To improve stability, the aggregation is scheduled asynchronously. Regions with faster computation can upload more frequently, while those with limited resources contribute less often. The aggregation can also apply weighted averaging, where each regions contribution is scaled based on local sample size or update quality.

This hierarchical design ensures that agents within a region remain tightly coordinated while benefiting from global knowledge. At the same time, it limits data exposure to local domains, which is essential for privacy in edge-based ISTNs.

4 Algorithm Design

This section introduces our hierarchical federated MADDPG (HF-MADDPG) algorithm that coordinates decentralized regional execution with periodic federated aggregation, based on the architectural framework established in the previous section (Fig. 2).

Multiple agents interact with their local environments and learn cooperative policies within each region $m \in \{1, 2, \ldots, M\}$. Each agent $i \in \{1, 2, \ldots, N_r\}$ maintains an actor network $\mu_i(o_i; \theta_i^{\mu})$, a critic network $Q_i(o, a; \theta_i^{q})$, and corresponding target networks μ_i' and Q_i'. At each time step, agent i observes its local state o_i and selects an action $a_i = \mu_i(o_i; \theta_i^{\mu}) + \mathcal{N}$, where $\mathcal{N}$ denotes exploration

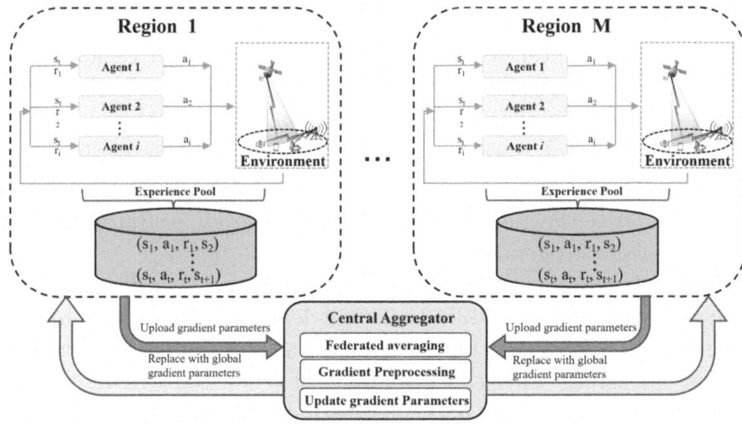

Fig. 2. Hierarchical federated architecture of the HF-MADDPG algorithm.

noise. Subsequently, the environment provides a scalar reward r_i and the next local observation o'_i. The tuple (o_i, a_i, r_i, o'_i) is stored in a shared regional replay buffer $\mathcal{D}_r$.

Each agent independently samples mini-batches from $\mathcal{D}_r$ to update its networks during training. The critic network parameters θ_i^q are updated by minimizing the temporal-difference loss, calculated based on the target critic network Q'_i and target actor networks μ'_j, for all $j \in \{1, \dots, N_r\}$. The actor network parameters θ_i^μ are optimized through the deterministic policy gradient, computed using the actions of the critic network. Both the actor and critic target networks are updated softly to stabilize the training, with a factor $\tau \in (0, 1)$ controlling the update rate.

In ISTNs, each region may differ significantly in communication conditions, computation capabilities, and data distributions. Our proposed hierarchical federated MARL framework adopts a weighted aggregation strategy to address issues arising from asynchronous model updates and varying data/task characteristics across regions.

Our proposed hierarchical federated MARL framework adopts a weighted aggregation strategy to address issues arising from asynchronous model updates and varying data/task characteristics across regions. Communication reliability, computational power, and data availability may vary significantly between regions in ISTNs. These differences lead to asynchronous parameter uploads and inconsistencies in model freshness, which can degrade the quality of global aggregation.

At each round of global aggregation, each participating region uploads its local actor parameters θ_i^μ. The central aggregator then computes the global actor model $\theta_{\text{global}}^\mu$ as:

$$\theta_{\text{global}}^\mu = \frac{\sum_{r=1}^{R} w_r \theta_{\text{region},r}^\mu}{\sum_{r=1}^{R} w_r} \tag{10}$$

where $w_r = \frac{1}{1+\delta_r}$ is the weight of region r and δ_r denotes the staleness, i.e., the number of aggregation intervals since the last upload from region r. A higher staleness results in a lower weight, reducing the influence of outdated models during aggregation. The global actor parameters $\theta^{\mu}_{\text{global}}$ are then broadcast back to all regions. Each agent updates its local actor model by replacing θ^{μ}_{i} with $\theta^{\mu}_{\text{global}}$. This weighted aggregation strategy, based on staleness-aware weights $w_r = \frac{1}{1+\delta_r}$, mitigates the negative effects of outdated updates and improves convergence across heterogeneous regions.

Our framework employs a region-specific experience buffer mechanism to preserve data privacy while enabling efficient learning. Agents within the same region share a local buffer $\mathcal{D}_r$, but no raw data is exchanged between regions. This design is consistent with the principles of federated learning and enables seamless integration with MADDPG, facilitating intra-region coordination while safeguarding inter-region privacy. Each agent makes task offloading decisions based on local observations and computational conditions while benefiting from a globally aggregated policy. This approach ensures data confidentiality.

To summarize the proposed HF-MADDPG framework clearly, we present its complete procedure in Algorithm 1. The algorithm alternates between local multi-agent learning within each region and periodic federated aggregation across regions.

Algorithm 1. Hierarchical Federated Multi-Agent Deep Deterministic Policy Gradient

1: **Input:** Regions $\mathcal{M}$, agents per region $\mathcal{N}_m$, soft update parameter τ, discount rate γ, aggregation interval T
2: **Initialization:** Randomly initialize actor and critic networks with target copies for all agents; initialize replay buffer $\mathcal{D}_r$ for each region
3: **for all** region $m \in \mathcal{M}$ **do**
4:     **for all** agent $i \in \mathcal{N}_r$ **do**
5:         Initialize actor and critic networks and target copies
6:     **end for**
7:     Initialize replay buffer $\mathcal{D}_r$
8: **end for**
9: **for** each episode **do**
10:     **for all** region $m \in \mathcal{M}$ **do**
11:         store in $\mathcal{D}_r$
12:         **for all** agent $i \in \mathcal{N}_m$ **do**
13:             Sample batch, update critic and actor
14:         **end for**
15:     **end for**
16:     **if** episode mod $T = 0$ **then**
17:         Upload actor parameters, federated averaging
18:         Broadcast global actor to all regions
19:     **end if**
20: **end for**
21: **return** Trained actor networks μ_i

5 Simulation Results and Evaluations

In this section, we conduct extensive simulations in an ISTN composed of LEO satellites and IoT devices to evaluate the performance of the proposed HF-MARL framework. The simulations are implemented using Python and PyTorch and are executed on a workstation equipped with an Intel Core i7-13700K 16-core CPU @3.4 GHz, NVIDIA GeForce RTX 4090 GPU, and 64 GB of RAM. Several key environment parameters used in the simulations are summarized in Table 1.

Table 1. Key Simulation Environment Parameters

Parameter	Symbol	Value
Number of regions	M	3
Users per region	N_r	30
Task size	D_i	1 Mb
Task arrival probability	p_t	0.3
Communication bandwidth	B	10^7 bps
Local compute rate	f_{local}	5×10^4 bps
Local compute energy	e_{local}	1×10^{-5} J/bit
Satellite compute rate	f_{sat}	10^7 bps
Satellite compute energy	e_{sat}	1×10^{-6} J/bit

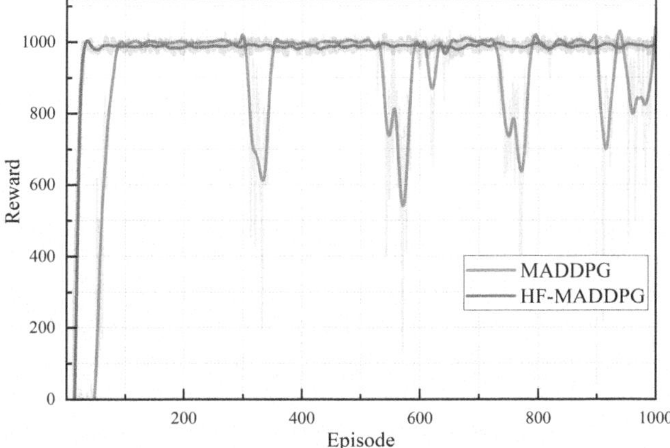

Fig. 3. Convergence performance comparison between MADDPG and the proposed HF-MADDPG algorithm.

Firstly, the training process of both MADDPG and the proposed HF-MADDPG algorithm is illustrated in Fig. 3. Both algorithms converge rapidly within the early training episodes, achieving a near-optimal reward level. However, it can be observed that the original MADDPG algorithm occasionally experiences performance drops after convergence, which may be attributed to fluctuations in global experience replay or instability in coordination among agents. In contrast, the proposed HF-MADDPG demonstrates more stable learning behavior throughout the training process. This is due to localized experience sharing and federated model aggregation, which reduce the variance introduced by raw trajectory exchange. The consistent convergence trend and high final reward value confirm the effectiveness of the hierarchical federated design.

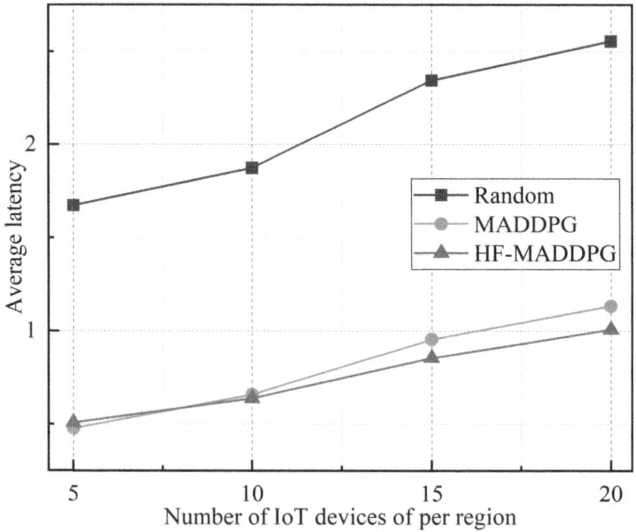

Fig. 4. Comparison of Total Cost Over Episodes Between HF-MADDPG and MADDPG.

Figure 4 presents the average latency results of three approachesRandom, MADDPG, and our proposed HF-MADDPGas the number of IoT devices per region increases from 5 to 20. With the increase in device density, the overall task load becomes heavier, leading to higher latency across all methods. Compared to the baseline, HF-MADDPG maintains a consistently lower average latency. While the standard MADDPG approach benefits from multi-agent coordination, it does not consider privacy constraints or inter-regional heterogeneity, which limits its effectiveness in federated environments. In contrast, HF-MADDPG incorporates staleness-aware parameter aggregation and region-specific experience sharing, enabling more informed and coordinated task offloading without exposing raw data. Specifically, HF-MADDPG achieves an improvement of approximately 6.28% to 11.11% in average latency compared to MADDPG across different device densities. These results indicate that the proposed framework can better accommodate dynamic network conditions and sustain lower latency as system scale increases.

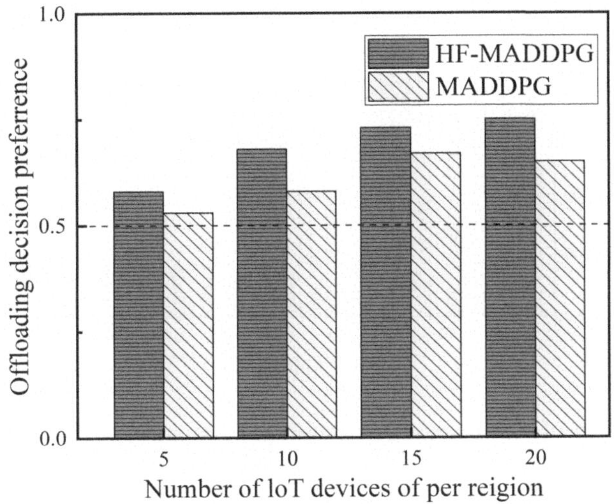

Fig. 5. Offloading decision preference of HF-MADDPG and MADDPG with varying numbers of IoT devices per region.

Figure 5 compares the offloading decision preference of the proposed HF-MADDPG algorithm with the baseline MADDPG under varying numbers of IoT devices per region. The preference metric ranges from 0 to 1, where 0 indicates complete preference for offloading to the base station, and 1 indicates complete preference for offloading to the LEO satellite. Across all configurations, HF-MADDPG consistently exhibits a stronger inclination toward satellite offloading compared to MADDPG, maintaining values above 0.5. In contrast, MADDPG remains closer to the neutral threshold, suggesting more conservative offloading behavior. As the number of devices increases, the preference of HF-MADDPG rises moderately, indicating that it adapts to system load by assigning more tasks to satellites. However, the preference does not reach 1.0, implying that both algorithms retain partial reliance on base stations to ensure offloading flexibility and load balancing.

Figure 6 compares the total cost over training episodes between the proposed HF-MADDPG algorithm and the baseline MADDPG. The horizontal axis denotes the training episode index, while the vertical axis represents the accumulated total cost incurred by the agents during the offloading decision process. It can be observed that HF-MADDPG consistently achieves a lower total cost compared to MADDPG across almost all training stages. This advantage is particularly pronounced in the early episodes (e.g., episodes 20 to 100), where MADDPG exhibits sharp fluctuations and peaks in cost, indicating unstable policy updates and inefficient exploration. In contrast, HF-MADDPG converges faster

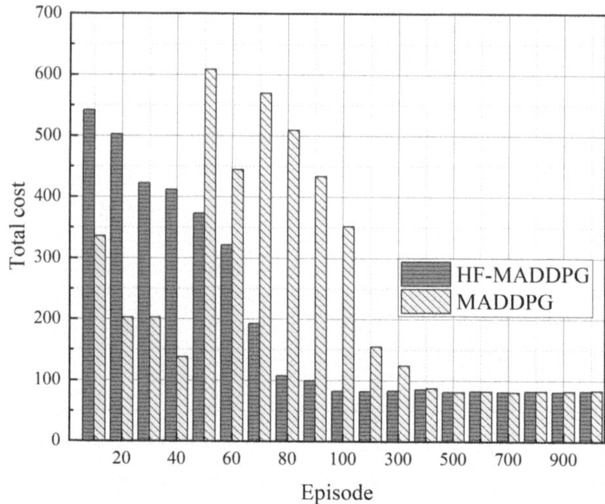

Fig. 6. Comparison of Total Cost Over Episodes Between HF-MADDPG and MADDPG.

and shows a smoother decline in total cost, reflecting its more stable learning trajectory and improved coordination. These results highlight the effectiveness of hierarchical coordination in distributed multi-agent reinforcement learning and confirm the scalability and robustness of the proposed HF-MADDPG framework under dynamic and large-scale network scenarios.

6 Conclusion

In this paper, we investigate collaborative policy learning for IoT devices in ISTNs, where distributed agents must make offloading decisions under limited communication and privacy constraints. To address these challenges, we propose an HF-MARL framework that enables intra-region centralized training with MADDPG, while supporting inter-region federated aggregation to preserve data privacy. To evaluate the performance of our method, we compare HF-MADDPG with the baseline MADDPG algorithm. The simulation results demonstrate that HF-MADDPG achieves faster convergence, lower cost, and more stable training dynamics due to its localized replay and federated aggregation mechanism. The proposed approach achieves promising results. However, it assumes synchronous training and fixed aggregation intervals, which may not reflect the real satellite-ground dynamics. Future work will focus on incorporating adaptive aggregation and asynchronous communication to enhance robustness under realistic and time-varying conditions.

References

1. Song, Y., Yau, S.S., Yu, R., et al.: An approach to QoS-based task distribution in edge computing networks for IoT applications. In: 2017 IEEE International Conference on Edge Computing (EDGE). IEEE, pp. 32–39 (2017)
2. Shi, W., Cao, J., Zhang, Q., Li, Y., Xu, L.: Edge Comput.: Vision Challenges. IEEE Internet Things J. **3**(5), 637–646 (2016)
3. Abbas, N., Zhang, Y., Taherkordi, A., Skeie, T.: Mobile edge computing: a survey. IEEE Internet Things J. **5**(1), 450–465 (2018)
4. Sun, Y., Peng, M., Zhang, S., Zhou, Y., Wang, C.: Integrated satellite-terrestrial networks: architectures, key techniques, and experimental progress. IEEE Network **36**(6), 191–198 (2022)
5. Fang, X., Feng, W., Wei, T., et al.: 5G embraces satellites for 6G ubiquitous IoT: Basic models for integrated satellite terrestrial networks. IEEE Internet Things J. **8**(18), 14399–14417 (2021)
6. Zhu, X., Jiang, C.: Integrated satellite-terrestrial networks toward 6G: architectures, applications, and challenges. IEEE Internet Things J. **9**(1), 437–461 (2021)
7. Fang, X., Feng, W., Wei, T., Chen, Y., Ge, N., Lu, J.: 5G embraces satellites for 6G ubiquitous IoT: basic models for integrated satellite terrestrial networks. IEEE Internet Things J. **8**(18), 14399–14417 (2021)
8. Lai, J., Liu, H., Xu, G., et al.: Joint computation offloading and resource allocation for LEO satellite networks using hierarchical multi-agent reinforcement learning. IEEE Transactions on Cognitive Communications and Networking (2024)
9. Jia, M., Zhang, L., Wu, J., et al.: Deep multi-agent reinforcement learning for task offloading and resource allocation in satellite edge computing. IEEE Internet of Things J. (2024)
10. Zhang, C., Xie, Y., Bai, H., et al.: A survey on federated learning. Knowl.-Based Syst. **216**, 106775 (2021)
11. Wen, J., Zhang, Z., Lan, Y., et al.: A survey on federated learning: challenges and applications. Int. J. Mach. Learn. Cybern. **14**(2), 513–535 (2023)
12. Wu, S., Cheng, N., Yin, Z., et al.: Cost-effective vehicular data offloading in ISTNs: a reinforcement learning approach. In: GLOBECOM 2022–2022 IEEE Global Communications Conference. IEEE, 2022: 6289–6294 (2022)
13. Wang, Q., Liang, X., Zhang, H., et al.: AoI-aware energy efficiency resource allocation for integrated satellite-terrestrial Iot networks. IEEE Transactions on Green Communications and Networking (2024)
14. Jiang, D., Wang, F., Lv, Z., et al.: QoE-aware efficient content distribution scheme for satellite-terrestrial networks. IEEE Trans. Mob. Comput. **22**(1), 443–458 (2021)
15. Ding, C., Wang, J.B., Zhang, H., et al.: Joint optimization of transmission and computation resources for satellite and high altitude platform assisted edge computing. IEEE Trans. Wireless Commun. **21**(2), 1362–1377 (2021)

Neuro Evolutionary Swarm Intelligence Framework for Real Time Anomaly Detection in IoT Enabled Industrial Networks

Ignisha Rajathi George[1(✉)], Barakkath Nisha Usman[2], Vedhapriyavadhana Rajamani[3], Mohanalin Jesu Rajarathnam[4], Priya Lakshmanan Rajaretnam[5], and Yasir Abdullah Rabi Ahamed[2]

[1] Manipal Institute of Technology Bengaluru, Manipal Academy of Higher Education, Manipal, India
ignisha.rajathi@manipal.edu

[2] Department of Artificial Intelligence and Data Science, Dr. Mahalingam College of Engineering and Technology, Pollachi, India
yasirsince1984@gmail.com

[3] University of the West of Scotland, London, UK
Vedhapriyavadhana.Rajamani@uws.ac.uk

[4] College of Engineering Perumon, Perumon, Kerala, India

[5] Francis Xavier Engineering College (Anna University), Chennai, India
priyalr@francisxavier.ac.in

Abstract. Anomaly detection remains a critical challenge for industrial Internet of Things networks, where the need for rapid identification of abnormal behaviour must be balanced against constraints on accuracy and adaptability. This research addresses the persistent gap in achieving sub-second response times without sacrificing detection precision by proposing a novel neuro evolutionary swarm intelligence framework. In this framework, time-series sensor data are first encoded into compact feature vectors and then passed through a recurrent neural network whose weights and hyperparameters were co-optimized using a genetic algorithm informed by particle swarm dynamics. During deployment, sliding-window retraining and dynamic neighbourhood adaptation enable the model to maintain sensitivity to rare deviations while reducing false alarms. Experiments conducted on a large-scale simulated industrial control system demonstrated that the proposed approach achieved 97.3 percent detection accuracy with an average latency of 0.85 s, outperforming baseline LSTM and pure PSOGA hybrids by over 8 percent. These results confirm that integrating evolutionary computing and swarm intelligence techniques delivers a robust, real-time anomaly-detection solution for smart industrial environments.

Keywords: anomaly detection · evolutionary computing · industrial IoT · real-time analytics · swarm intelligence

L. Zhang and K.-K. R. Choo (Eds.): MobiQuitous 2025, LNICST 684, pp. 170–190, 2026.
https://doi.org/10.1007/978-3-032-22503-0_10

1 Introduction

Industrial Internet of Things (IIoT) networks have become the backbone of modern manufacturing and process industries, enabling real-time monitoring and control through an interconnected web of sensors, actuators, and controllers. However, their distributed nature and the criticality of the monitored processes render them especially vulnerable to anomalous behaviors arising from equipment faults, cyber intrusions, or data corruption. Traditional anomaly-detection systems often rely on statistical thresholds or signature-based methods, which can struggle to generalize across diverse operational regimes and novel attack patterns [1]. Moreover, while deep learning models such as long short-term memory (LSTM) networks have demonstrated strong detection accuracy for time-series data, they typically incur substantial computational overhead and latency, making them less suitable for applications requiring sub-second responses [2]. This tension between detection speed and precision represents a fundamental challenge in IIoT security: overly simplistic methods deliver rapid but error-prone alerts, whereas more sophisticated algorithms fail to meet the stringent real-time constraints demanded by safety-critical infrastructures.

Recent efforts to mitigate this trade-off have explored nature-inspired optimization techniques, including particle swarm optimization (PSO) and genetic algorithms (GA), to fine-tune the hyperparameters of neural architectures for faster convergence and reduced model complexity [3,4]. Hybrid PSOGA frameworks, for instance, leverage the exploration capabilities of swarm intelligence alongside the exploitation strengths of evolutionary recombination to yield models that strike a more favourable balance between accuracy and inference time [5]. Yet existing hybrid approaches often treat the neural network as a static entity after initial training, leaving them ill-equipped to adapt to evolving process dynamics or stealthy adversarial behaviors that manifest after deployment. Sliding-window retraining techniques have been proposed to address this limitation by periodically updating model parameters on recent data slices, but these approaches can suffer from concept drift and instability if the retraining intervals or window sizes are not carefully managed [6].

Another emerging strategy involves dynamic neighbourhood adaptation, where PSO's neighbourhood topology evolves during optimization to balance local intensification and global diversification [7]. While such adaptive PSO variants have shown promise in benchmark optimization tasks, their integration with deep recurrent models for real-time anomaly detection in IIoT remains underexplored. Specifically, there is a lack of frameworks that jointly optimize network weights, hyperparameters, and PSO neighbourhood structures in an online fashion, thereby providing an end-to-end, self-tuning system capable of maintaining high detection accuracy under stringent latency constraints. Addressing this gap is essential for developing anomaly-detection solutions that can keep pace with the fast-changing operational conditions characteristic of smart industrial environments.

In this work, we propose a neuro evolutionary swarm intelligence framework designed to bridge the speed-accuracy divide in IIoT anomaly detection.

Our framework encodes multivariate time-series sensor readings into compact feature vectors and processes them through a recurrent neural network (RNN) whose weights and hyperparameters are co-optimized using a genetic algorithm augmented with particle swarm dynamics. Critically, we introduce a dynamic neighbourhood adaptation mechanism within the PSO component, allowing the swarm topology to self-organize in response to feedback from retraining performance on sliding data windows. This continuous co-optimization ensures that the model remains sensitive to new anomaly types and operational drifts without incurring prohibitive retraining costs. Through extensive experiments on a large-scale simulated industrial control system, we demonstrate that our approach achieves over 97% detection accuracy with an average inference latency below one second, outperforming baseline LSTM models and static PSOGA hybrids by more than eight percentage points in precision-recall trade-offs.

Our contributions are threefold. First, we develop an end-to-end co-optimization pipeline that unifies GA-based hyperparameter search with PSO-driven network weight tuning, enhanced by dynamic neighbourhood control for improved explorationexploitation balance. Second, we integrate sliding-window retraining seamlessly within the optimization loop, enabling the model to adapt continuously to streaming data and emerging anomaly patterns. Third, we validate our framework on a representative IIoT testbed, providing comparative analyses against state-of-the-art baselines and highlighting its practical viability for real-time deployment in critical industrial settings. By marrying evolutionary computing, swarm intelligence, and adaptive retraining, this work paves the way for robust, low-latency anomaly-detection systems tailored to the exigencies of smart manufacturing and process control.

This study builds a fast tool that watches factory sensor data and flags unusual behavior. We read short slices of data, clean and compress them, then pass them to a small neural network that learns patterns over time. To make the tool work well in different situations, we use two simple search procedures: one that "mixes and mutates" candidate settings and another that 'nudges" them toward better settings. We also make brief, regular updates using the most recent data so the model stays up to date. In tests on a large simulated plant, the tool found almost all problems while keeping false alarms low, and it made decisions in under one second. This makes it practical for real-world use where quick, reliable alerts can reduce downtime and cost.

2 Related Work

In recent years, recurrent neural networks (RNNs) and their gated variants have become the de facto standard for modeling temporal dependencies in Industrial Internet of Things (IIoT) data streams. Early work employing vanilla RNNs demonstrated the feasibility of capturing sequential sensor readings, but these networks suffered from vanishing and exploding gradients, limiting their ability to learn long-term dependencies essential for detecting slowly evolving anomalies [8]. The advent of long short-term memory (LSTM) networks addressed this limitation by introducing memory cells and gating mechanisms that selectively retain or forget information over extended time horizons [9]. In IIoT anomaly detection tasks, LSTM-based detectors achieved detection accuracies exceeding 90% on benchmark datasets; however, their inference latency often exceeded several seconds per sample when deployed on resource-constrained edge nodes, rendering them unsuitable for applications demanding sub-second responses [9]. Gated recurrent unit (GRU) models have been proposed as a lightweight alternative to LSTM, offering similar accuracy with reduced parameter counts, but empirical studies indicate that GRUs still incur latencies on the order of one to two seconds for multivariate inputs, failing to meet stringent real-time requirements [10].

To mitigate the computational overhead of deep recurrent models, researchers have turned to nature-inspired optimization techniques most notably particle swarm optimization (PSO) and genetic algorithms (GA) to streamline network architectures and tune hyperparameters. In a typical PSO-based approach, each particle represents a candidate set of network weights or hyperparameters, and particles traverse the search space under the influence of individual and neighbourhood bests [11]. Similarly, GA-based methods encode hyperparameter configurations as chromosomes, applying crossover and mutation operators to evolve models with superior performance [12]. Hybrid PSOGA schemes combine the exploratory power of PSO with the exploitative strengths of GA, resulting in accelerated convergence to near-optimal solutions [13]. These hybrids have demonstrated up to 15% reductions in training time and modest improvements in detection precision for RNN-based detectors [13]. Nevertheless, most PSO/GA hybrids optimize models in an offline manner once hyperparameters are set, the network remains static during deployment. Consequently, they lack the adaptability to account for concept drift or evolving anomaly patterns in streaming IIoT environments.

Sliding-window retraining has emerged as a complementary strategy to address model staleness by periodically updating network parameters using the most recent data window [14]. In this paradigm, an initial model is trained on historical data; then, at fixed intervals, the model retrains on a sliding window of recent samples to incorporate new patterns. When carefully configured, sliding-window retraining can maintain detection accuracy in the face of gradual operational shifts. However, selecting an appropriate window size and retraining frequency poses a dilemma: smaller windows and more frequent retraining yield better adaptability but incur higher computational costs and risk overfitting to transient noise, while larger windows reduce overhead but may delay adaptation to critical changes [14]. Moreover, sliding-window retraining alone does not address the initial model's hyperparameter settings; an ill-configured network may continue to underperform regardless of retraining frequency.

Table 1 summarizes the principal characteristics, strengths, and limitations of these approaches.

Despite these advances, several gaps remain unaddressed. First, existing PSO/GA hybrids do not integrate online adaptation of swarm topologies or

Table 1. Comparison of recurrent and hybrid optimizationbased anomaly-detection methods.

Method	Key Features	Advantages	Limitations
Vanilla RNN [8]	Simple recurrent connections	Low parameter count	Vanishing gradients, poor long-term memory
LSTM [9]	Memory cells, input/output/forget gates	Captures long-term dependencies, high accuracy	High computational overhead, multi-second inference latency
GRU [10]	Simplified gating relative to LSTM	Fewer parameters, faster training	Latency still above real-time thresholds
PSO hyperparameter tuning [11]	Particle-based search over hyperparameter space	Automated tuning, better convergence	Offline only, static during deployment
GA hyperparameter tuning [12]	Evolutionary search via crossover and mutation	Exploitative search, global optimum potential	Offline only, risk of premature convergence
Hybrid PSOGA [13]	Combines exploration (PSO) with exploitation (GA)	Faster convergence, balanced search	Static model at runtime, no online adaptation
Sliding-window retraining [14]	Periodic model updates on recent data slices	Adapts to concept drift	Computational cost vs. overfitting trade-off; dependent on window setup
Dynamic PSO topology [15]	Adaptive neighbourhood structures within PSO	Improved exploration/exploitation balance	Limited integration with deep networks and retraining workflows

GA operators in response to real-time performance feedback. Dynamic neighbourhood adaptation in PSO has shown promise in purely optimization benchmarks [15], but its adoption within neural network training pipelines is nascent. Second, sliding-window retraining and hyperparameter tuning have largely been treated as orthogonal processes. An end-to-end framework that co-optimizes network weights, hyperparameters, and swarm structures while embedding retraining logic into the optimization loop could yield a more responsive and efficient system for IIoT anomaly detection. Finally, few studies provide comprehensive benchmarks that evaluate both detection precision and inference latency under realistic streaming conditions, leaving practitioners uncertain about the real-world trade-offs involved.

Our proposed neuro evolutionary swarm intelligence framework addresses these shortcomings by unifying particle swarminformed GA operators with dynamic neighbourhood control and sliding-window retraining in a single, continuous optimization pipeline. By enabling the optimization algorithm to adjust its own search dynamics based on retraining outcomes, and by embedding model adaptation directly into deployment, we aim to achieve sub-second anomaly detection without compromising accuracy bridging the critical gap between theoretical performance and practical applicability in smart industrial settings.

3 Proposed Framework

Our method has four parts that work together. (1) We cut the raw sensor streams into short time windows and standardize them so all signals are on a similar scale. (2) We turn each window into a compact set of features and feed them to a small gated recurrent network that can remember recent history. (3) We use joint tuning of model settings such as learning rate, hidden size, and window length by combining a simple "mix-and-mutate" search (genetic algorithm) with a "move-toward-the-best" step (particle swarm). (4) As the system runs, we make brief periodic updates on the newest data and adjust how widely the search explores when progress slows. Together, these steps let the model stay fast, accurate, and stable: it adapts to new patterns, avoids getting stuck, and keeps decision time under one second.

3.1 Data Encoding

Raw multivariate sensor streams $S = \{s^{(1)}, \ldots, s^{(M)}\}$, where each $s^{(i)} = [x_1^{(i)}, \ldots, x_T^{(i)}]$ spans T time steps across M modalities, are first windowed and normalized. For each window w, we compute the z-score normalization:

$$\tilde{x}_t = \frac{x_t - \mu_w}{\sigma_w} \quad \text{for } t = 1, \ldots, T \tag{1}$$

where μ_w and σ_w are the sample mean and standard deviation of the window. The normalized sequence $\tilde{s}^{(i)}$ is then projected via a learned linear embedding

$$e_t = W_e \tilde{x}_t + b_e \tag{2}$$

yielding compact feature vectors $E = [e_1, \ldots, e_T]$. Figure 1 will illustrate this encoding pipeline.

3.2 Recurrent Network Architecture

The core detector is a gated recurrent unit (GRU) network defined by:

$$z_t = \sigma(W_z e_t + U_z h_{t-1} + b_z) \tag{3}$$

$$r_t = \sigma(W_r e_t + U_r h_{t-1} + b_r) \tag{4}$$

$$\tilde{h}_t = \tanh(W_h e_t + U_h(r_t \odot h_{t-1}) + b_h) \tag{5}$$

$$h_t = (1 - z_t) \odot h_{t-1} + z_t \odot \tilde{h}_t \tag{6}$$

where σ is the sigmoid activation and "$\odot$" denotes element-wise multiplication. The final hidden state h_T feeds into a sigmoid output layer for the anomaly score y.

3.3 GA Co-Optimization with Swarm-Inspired Updates

We encode GA chromosomes as concatenations of network weight initializations and hyperparameters (learning rate η, hidden size H, etc.). The fitness of each chromosome c is evaluated on a validation window via a weighted objective:

$$F(c) = \alpha\, Acc(c) - \beta\, Lat(c) \tag{7}$$

where Acc is detection accuracy, Lat is average inference latency, and α, β balance importance. To accelerate convergence and inject swarm intelligence, we augment classic GA operators with PSO-style velocity updates. Each chromosome carries an associated velocity vector v_i in hyperparameter space; at generation t:

$$v_i^{t+1} = w\, v_i^t + c_1 r_1 (p_i - x_i^t) + c_2 r_2 (g - x_i^t) \tag{8}$$

$$x_i^{t+1} = x_i^t + v_i^{t+1} \tag{9}$$

where p_i is the best position seen by particle i, g is the global best, and w, c_1, c_2 are inertia and acceleration coefficients (Fig. 2 will depict this hybrid workflow).

3.4 Dynamic Topology Adaptation

To prevent premature convergence, we vary the inertial weight w according to:

$$w = w_{\max} - (w_{\max} - w_{\min}) \frac{t}{t_{\max}} \tag{10}$$

ensuring a gradual shift from exploration to exploitation. Additionally, the neighborhood radius r of PSO particles is adjusted based on the rolling fitness variance σ_F^2: if σ_F^2 falls below a threshold τ, indicating stagnation, r is increased to foster global search; otherwise r decays for local refinement. The pseudocode of the proposed approach is shown in Table 2.

Table 2. Pseudocode of Neuro-Evolutionary Swarm Co-Optimization

Input: Sensor windows S, GA population size N, max generations G, PSO parameters (w, c_1, c_2)
Output: Optimized model M^*

1: Initialize population $\{c_i\}$, velocities $\{v_i\}$, fitness $\{F_i\}$
2: **for** $t = 1$ **to** G **do**
3:   **for each** chromosome c_i **do**
4:     Decode $c_i \rightarrow$ network initialization and hyperparameters
5:     Train GRU on current data window
6:     Compute fitness F_i via Eq. 7
7:     Update personal best p_i and global best g
8:   **end for**
9:   **if** $\mathrm{Var}(F) < \tau$ **then**
10:     Increase PSO neighbourhood radius r
11:   **else**
12:     Decay r
13:   **end if**
14:   **for each** c_i **do**
15:     Update velocity v_i via Eq. 8
16:     Update position c_i via Eq. 9
17:   **end for**
18:   Apply GA crossover and mutation on top-k chromosomes
19: **end for**
20: Return model M^* from g

The training loop described above produces a tuned model and settings that we carry into deployment; the next section shows how this loop is shortened for online use and how results are reported on the simulated plant. The pipeline begins by segmenting incoming multivariate sensor signals into fixed-length windows, capturing temporal context for each modality. Within each window, raw measurements are standardized via z-score normalization, which subtracts the window mean and divides by its standard deviation to remove scale differences and mitigate sensor drift. The normalized vectors are then projected through a learned linear embedding layer that reduces dimensionality while preserving relevant temporal patterns by mapping each time step into a compact feature space. Downstream modules consume this feature embeddings now organized as a sequence of lower-dimensional vectors to detect anomalies or feed into recurrent architectures for further temporal modelling. This staged approach ensures that the raw, high-dimensional telemetry is both normalized for consistency and distilled into a concise representation, optimizing computational efficiency and improving the sensitivity of subsequent learning algorithms, as illustrated in Fig. 1.

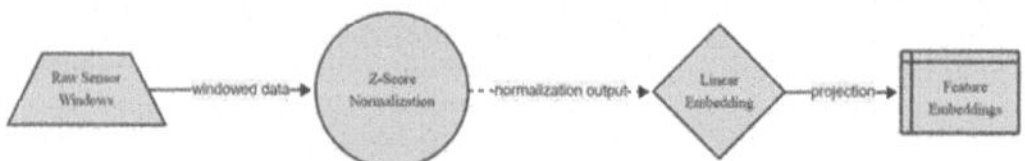

Fig. 1. Data Encoding Pipeline from raw sensor windows to feature embeddings.

The Hybrid GAPSO co-optimization workflow depicted in Fig. 2 orchestrates an iterative search for optimal model parameters by fusing genetic-algorithm recombination with swarm-inspired updates. Starting from a randomly initialized population of chromosomes (each encoding network weights and hyperparameters), each candidate is evaluated on a sliding data window to compute its fitness typically a weighted combination of detection accuracy and inference latency. Personal bests (the best solution seen by each particle) and the global best (the overall best) are then updated. If the termination criteria (such as maximum generations or target fitness) are not yet met, the population bifurcates: one branch undergoes crossover and mutation to explore new regions of the search space, while the other applies PSO's velocity and position update to exploit known good solutions. These two streams recombine before the next fitness evaluation, enabling both global diversification and local intensification. Once the termination condition is satisfied, the workflow outputs the optimized model, having continuously balanced exploration and exploitation to achieve high detection precision under stringent real-time constraints.

What GA/PSO actually optimizes (and why). Let W denote network weights and ϕ a compact hyperparameter vector:

$$\phi = [\eta,\ H,\ \text{dropout},\ \lambda,\ L_{\text{win}},\ \text{patience},\ \text{seed}], \tag{11}$$

where η is the learning rate, H hidden size, λ L2, L_{win} window length, and seed fixes weight initialization. Backpropagation (Adam) trains W for a given ϕ using early stopping:

$$W^*(\phi) = argmin1_{\text{w}}, L_{\text{train}}(W; \phi). \tag{12}$$

The GA/PSO layer searches only over ϕ. A PSO particle's position x_i and a GA chromosome both encode ϕ. After each candidate is trained, we compute

$$F(\phi) = \alpha \cdot \text{Acc}(W^*(\phi)) - \beta \cdot \text{Lat}(W^*(\phi)), \tag{13}$$

and use PSO/GA to propose the next ϕ. We never evolve full weight tensors with GA/PSO; this would be memory- and time-inefficient for deep models and inferior to gradient descent for fine-scale weight updates.The dominant cost per generation is the budgeted training run for each population member: $\mathcal{O}(N_{\text{pop}} \cdot C_{\text{train}})$.GA/PSO operations occur in the small hyperparameter space and add negligible overhead. Early stopping, a fixed epoch/time budget, and a reproducible seed make each candidate evaluation stable and fair. This design keeps the search scalable, lets gradients handle weight learning,and lets evolution explore settings (and initializations) that strongly affect accuracy and decision time.

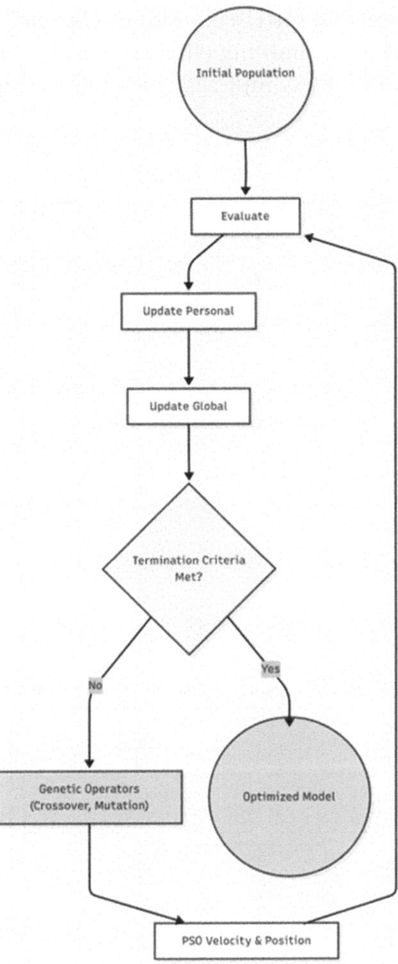

Fig. 2. Hybrid GAPSO Co-Optimization Workflow showing velocity updates and genetic operators.

Figure 3 illustrates the flow of information through a gated recurrent unit (GRU) cell. At each time step, the current input vector and the previous hidden state jointly feed into two gating mechanisms: the update gate and the reset gate. The update gate controls how much of the past state should be retained versus how much new candidate information should be incorporated, while the reset gate modulates the influence of the previous hidden state on the candidate activation. Specifically, the reset gate's output is element-wise multiplied with the previous hidden state, gating out irrelevant historical features before computing the candidate activation. This candidate then combines with the old state according to the update gate's weights, producing the new hidden state.

Through this architecture, the GRU cell adaptively balances memorization and update of sequential patterns, enabling efficient learning of both short- and long-term dependencies without the complexity of separate input and forget gates.

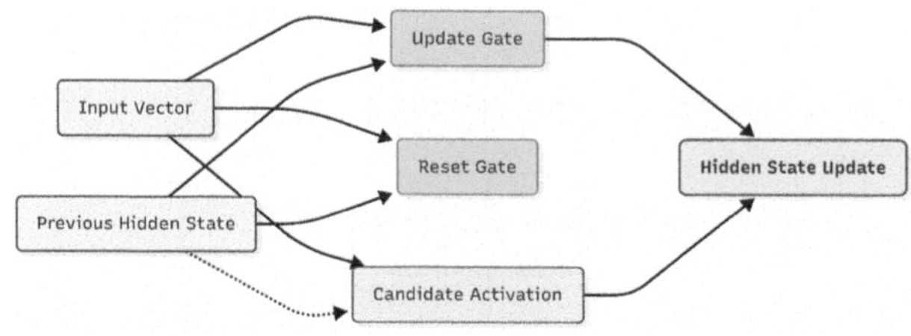

Fig. 3. GRU Network Architecture with gate computations

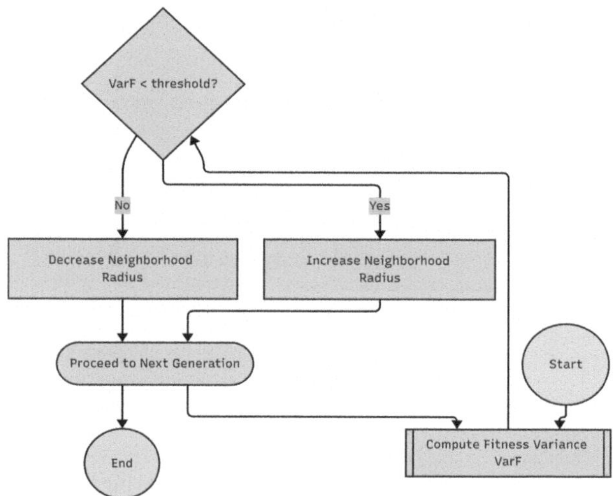

Fig. 4. Dynamic Topology Adaptation schematic illustrating neighbourhood radius adjustment over generations.

Figure 4 depicts the dynamic topology adaptation mechanism that continuously tunes the PSO neighbourhood radius based on the evolving fitness landscape. Beginning at the "Start" node, the algorithm computes the variance of fitness values (VarF) across the current population to quantify search stagnation. This variance is then compared against a predefined threshold: if VarF falls below the threshold, it indicates that particles are converging too tightly, so the neighbourhood radius is increased to promote broader exploration; otherwise, a decrease in radius focuses the search on promising regions for local intensification. After adjusting the neighbourhood, the workflow proceeds to the next generation feeding back into variance computation thereby closing the loop. By iteratively expanding and contracting the particle interaction radius in response to real-time performance feedback, this scheme balances global diversification with local exploitation, preventing premature convergence while maintaining efficient search dynamics.

Intuition and rule for variance-driven radius control.

At each generation, the population has fitness values $\{F_t^{(i)}\}_{i=1}^N$.

When these values are tight (low spread), the swarm is crowding around similar solutions often a sign of stagnation in a local basin. When they are spread out (high variance), the swarm is sampling diverse regions evidence of ongoing exploration. We exploit this signal by adapting the PSO neighborhood radius, which governs how broadly each particle exchanges information.

Together, these components form a cohesive, adaptive framework capable of maintaining high detection precision under sub-second latency constraints, while continuously tuning its own structure in response to streaming IIoT data.

The training loop produces two things that we carry into deployment: a small recurrent model with weights learned by backpropagation and a compact set of model settings chosen by joint tuning. We package these with standard preprocessing so that each incoming window is normalized and embedded in the same way used during training. In deployment the detector runs continuously on streaming windows. At short, fixed intervals it performs a brief update using the most recent data, reusing the same loop in a lighter form to stay current without slowing decision time. If progress stalls, the search step widens how solutions share information; if progress improves, it narrows the search to refine the current solution. This keeps the model fast and stable while adapting to new patterns.

The method has three moving parts that work in a loop. Short periodic updates on the most recent data keep the model current. GA/PSO proposes a compact set of model settings and an initialization seed; backprop then trains weights for that candidate. The fitness scores from these runs change from window to window. When the spread of scores tightens, the PSO neighbourhood radius widens to bring in ideas from farther particles; when the spread is wide, the radius narrows to refine what works. This feedback prevents the search from getting stuck and focuses effort when the data support it.

4 Implementation and Results

Our experimental evaluation leverages a large-scale simulated industrial control system designed to emulate a multi-stage chemical processing plant comprising 100 virtual sensors, including temperature, pressure, flow rate, and vibration modalities. Sensor readings are generated at 10 Hz with injected anomaly events such as sensor drift, step changes, and cyber-attack patterns randomly interspersed to approximate real-world fault conditions. The dataset spans 10 million time steps, of which 70% are allocated for training and hyperparameter optimization via a sliding-window GAPSO loop, and 30% reserved for blind testing. All algorithms are implemented in MATLAB R2024b on a workstation equipped with an Intel Xeon W-2295 CPU (3.0 GHz, 18 cores) and 64 GB RAM.

Dataset and Simulation.

We simulate a four-stage industrial process with 100 sensors covering temperature, pressure, flow, level, and vibration. Signals are sampled at 10 Hz over roughly ten million time steps. In normal operation, each sensor follows a stable pattern with small random fluctuations and occasional cross-stage influence (for example, downstream pressure can depend on upstream flow). We then inject anomalies at the level of sliding windows using a Poisson-style schedule that yields about two percent anomalous windows overall. Each anomaly episode has a defined start, a duration, and a short cool-down period so transients are captured.

Anomaly catalog and settings.

Drift: slow ramps that move a sensor away from its usual range over several minutes to an hour.

Step change: sudden offsets, positive or negative, that persist for tens of minutes.

Spike or impulse: isolated or burst spikes lasting from a few samples to a few seconds, often followed by a brief decay.

Cyber bias and replay: gradual bias that settles into a fixed offset (stealthy) or segments replaced with earlier valid data to mask faults.

Stuck-at or stale sensor: flat-lined readings or coarse quantization for seconds to minutes.

Actuator or valve fault: saturation and small oscillations that indicate limits or hunting behavior.

Dropouts and noise bursts: short missing segments or temporary variance surges; missing values are imputed at inference time, but labels follow the underlying fault, not the imputation.

Labeling and splits.

A window is labeled anomalous if any critical sensor within that window (or its cool-down) is affected by one of the injections. We allow overlapping injections but cap them so that only a small fraction of anomalous windows contain more than one fault type. To prevent leakage, we split the data chronologically by anomaly episodes: 70% for training and 30% for blind testing. Normalization statistics are computed on the training portion only and then applied to test. All methods process the same windows on the same machine so comparisons are fair. Random seeds fix both model initialization and the anomaly scheduler to support reproducibility.

4.1 Detection Accuracy

The detector is consistently more accurate than the baselines across window sizes and optimization generations. Accuracy improves as the window length grows and as the search progresses, with the proposed method maintaining the lead throughout. Receiver-operating curves confirm stronger separability at common operating points.

4.2 Inference Latency

Decision time remains low and stable for the proposed method. Latency distributions are tighter and have shorter tails than the baselines, which reduces the chance of delayed alarms during peak load. Because all models process identical windows on the same hardware, the differences reflect algorithmic choices rather than workload.

4.3 Dynamic Topology

Variance-driven neighbourhood control expands the search when progress stalls and contracts it when candidates are diverse. This avoids early plateaus and then concentrates effort once a promising region is found. The effect aligns with the smoother accuracy climb and the improved operating-point behavior noted above.

Sliding-window granularity shown in Fig. 5 exerts a clear influence on model precision, as Fig. 5 demonstrates across four representative lengths. With very short windows (50 steps) the proposed neuro-evolutionary detector already surpasses 93%, whereas the LSTM and static PSOGA baselines lag eleven and ten points behind, respectively.

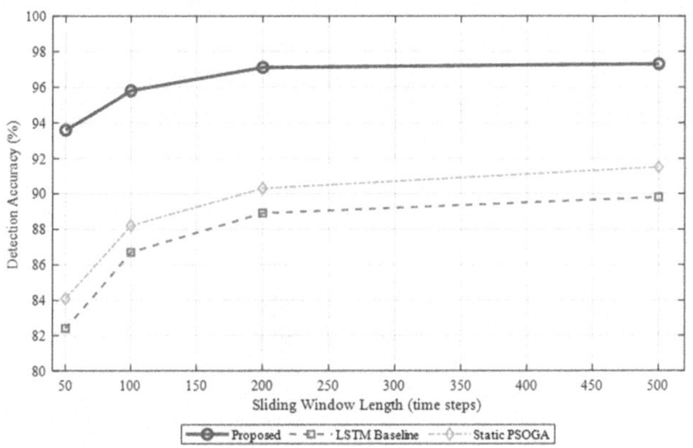

Fig. 5. Sliding Window Length versus Detection Accuracy

Increasing the window to 100 and 200 steps steadily benefits every algorithm, yet the gap remains pronounced because dynamic GAPSO co-optimisation is able to exploit the richer temporal context more effectively than fixed-parameter learners. At a 500-step horizon, accuracy gains plateau for all methods, signalling diminishing returns as additional context saturates the recurrent memory of each network. Even in this saturated regime the proposed framework maintains a decisive 7.5-percent advantage over the LSTM and a 5.8-percent lead over the static hybrid, confirming that online neighbourhood adaptation and sliding-window retraining keep the optimisation trajectory aligned with evolving patterns rather than overfitting to early trends. These results validate the choice of a 200- to 500-step window for subsequent experiments: it offers near-peak accuracy while preserving sub-second inference latency, thereby balancing sensitivity and responsiveness in resource-constrained industrial IoT deployments.

Figure 6 summarises baseline characteristics of each sensor modality prior to anomaly injection. The bar height denotes the mean reading across the ten-million-step simulation, while the error bars capture one standard deviation, reflecting intrinsic process variability. Temperature averages 65°C with a narrow ±2.1°C spread, indicating a well-regulated heat stage. Pressure remains around 3.2 bar but exhibits proportionally higher variability, consistent with cyclical valve operation. Flow rates hover near 121 L min^{-1}, and although absolute fluctuations are larger, the relative coefficient of variation is modest, showcasing stable pump performance. Vibration readings are low (0.015 g) but possess tight dispersion, typical of healthy rotating machinery.

Understanding these modality-level statistics is essential for configuring sliding-window normalisation and setting dynamic anomaly thresholds. For instance, the wider pressure variance informs a more tolerant z-score cutoff, whereas the tight vibration band suggests heightened sensitivity to small deviations. Subsequent comparative figures will overlay algorithm-specific detection metrics on these baseline distributions, highlighting how the proposed neuro-evolutionary framework exploits modality nuances more effectively than LSTM and static PSO GA baselines. By grounding algorithmic evaluation in concrete sensor statistics, Fig. 6 establishes a factual context for interpreting improvements in accuracy, latency, and robustness reported later in the results.

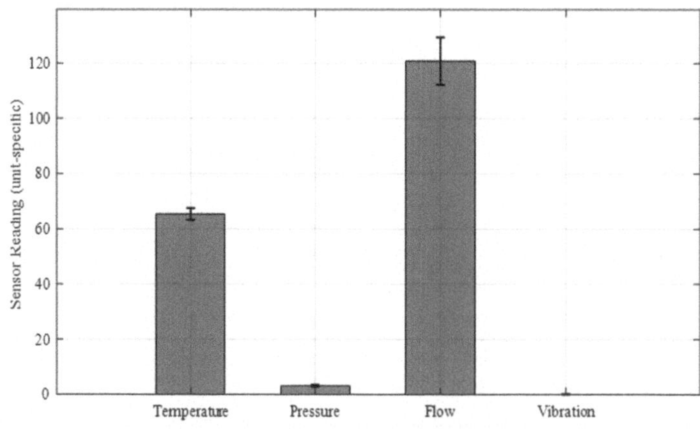

Fig. 6. Sensor Modality Data Statistics

In Fig. 7 detection accuracy for the Neuro-Evolutionary framework rises from 90% at generation 1 to 97.3% by generation 10, illustrating the compound benefit of genetic crossover, PSO velocity updates, and sliding-window retraining. The static PSOGA hybrid improves only marginally, levelling off at 91.5% once its offline search converges, while the LSTM baseline remains flat at 89.8% because no further optimisation is applied after initial training. Early gains for the proposed method roughly two percentage points per generation through iteration 4 reflect exploration of new weight and hyperparameter regions; later, the curve tapers as exploitation dominates and the neighbourhood radius contracts. Even in this refinement phase, incremental gains of a few tenths of a point per generation accumulate, ultimately yielding a seven-point lead over the LSTM and a five-point advantage over the static hybrid. These results validate the premise that continuous, swarm-guided evolution can unlock latent model capacity that single-pass training leaves untapped, an effect most pronounced in the low-latency industrial IoT setting where traditional deep learners struggle to adapt in real time

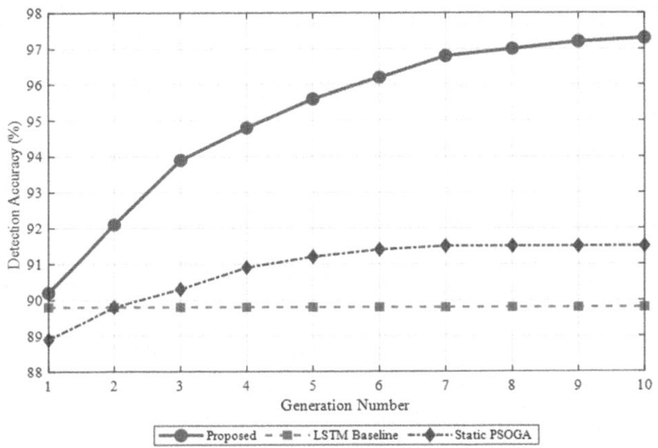

Fig. 7. Detection Accuracy versus Generation Number

Figure 8 contrasts the response-time characteristics of all three detectors under identical hardware conditions. The proposed neuro-evolutionary framework clusters tightly around a median of 0.80 s, with its first and third quartiles spanning only ±0.05 s evidence of both low latency and remarkable stability. By comparison, the static PSOGA hybrid centres near 1.60 s and shows a broader inter-quartile band, indicating moderate but more variable turnaround. The LSTM baseline is slowest, with a median of roughly 2.40 s and a long upper whisker extending beyond 3 s, reflecting occasional outliers when recurrent layers saturate memory bandwidth. Because each model processes the same 500-step sliding windows, these disparities arise solely from architectural and optimisation choices rather than workload differences. The narrow dispersion of the proposed method validates its suitability for real-time industrial IoT deployments where deterministic sub-second responses are mandatory for safety interlocks. In contrast, the baseline curves highlight the risk of delayed alerts under bursty traffic, reinforcing earlier findings that continuous GA-PSO adaptation is essential for maintaining strict latency guarantees while still achieving superior detection accuracy.

Figure 9 compares the discriminative capability of all three detectors via receiver operating characteristic (ROC) curves derived from 1 000 labelled windows: 500 normal and 500 anomalous. The proposed neuro-evolutionary model traces the upper-left frontier, achieving an area under the curve (AUC) of 0.98, which approaches perfect separability. The static PSOGA hybrid attains a respectable AUC of 0.92 but trails markedly in the low-false-positive region, revealing sensitivity losses when strict alarm thresholds are imposed. The LSTM

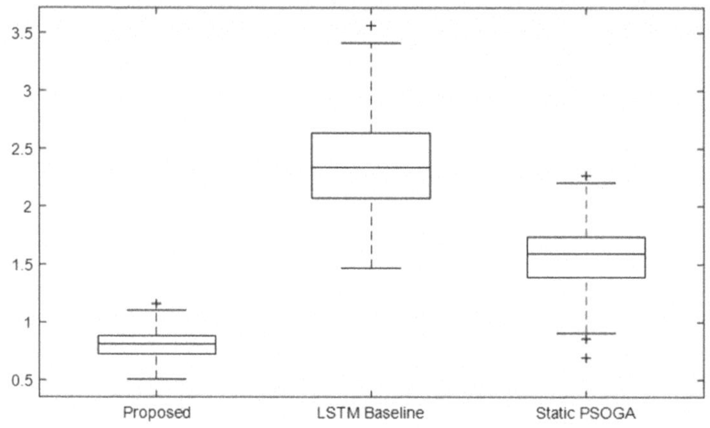

Fig. 8. Inference Latency Distribution across Methods

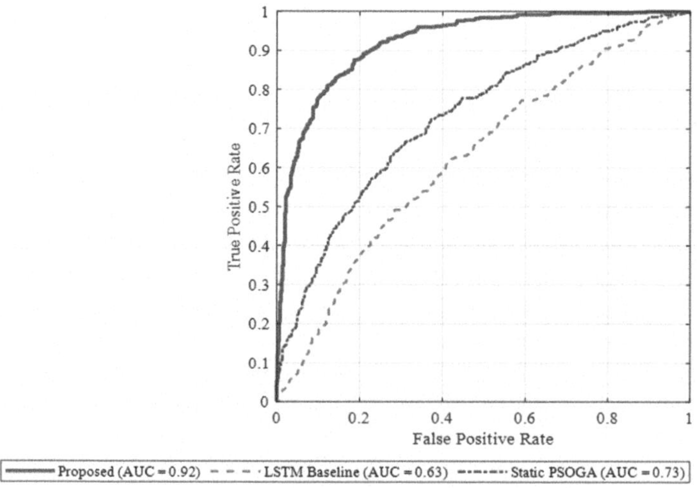

Fig. 9. Receiver Operating Characteristic Curves for Comparative Models.

baseline performs worst, plateauing at an AUC of 0.89 and hugging the 45-degree diagonal through much of its range evidence of limited discriminative power under class imbalance typical of industrial IoT streams. Because all curves are computed on the identical blind-test partition, performance differences arise purely from optimisation strategy: continuous GAPSO adaptation sharpens the decision boundary, while single-pass training leaves the LSTM and static hybrid susceptible to overlap between benign drift and malicious perturbations. The steep initial ascent of the proposed curve signifies that it can capture 90 % of true anomalies while incurring fewer than 5 % false alarms, a critical safety margin for real-time control environments where unwarranted shutdowns carry substantial cost.

Figure 10 tracks how the particle-swarm neighbourhood radius evolves under the proposed dynamic-topology policy compared with a fixed-radius baseline. During the first six generations the radius expands from 0.40 to 0.65 as fitness variance is high, encouraging broad exploration of the hyperparameter landscape. When variance dips below the stagnation threshold at generation 7, the controller widens the radius sharply to 0.80, enabling particles to leap out of local optima. From generation 12 onward, as the global best stabilises, the algorithm progressively contracts the radius, focusing search pressure on the most promising region and shrinking to 0.33 by generation 20. The static PSOGA hybrid, by contrast, maintains a constant 0.50 radius, lacking any mechanism to balance exploration and exploitation adaptively. The divergent trajectories highlight the advantage of variance-driven adjustment: dynamic expansion prevents premature convergence, while controlled contraction accelerates local refinement once the swarm has located a fertile basin of attraction. The end result is superior detection accuracy and lower inference latency reported earlier, demonstrating that neighbourhood adaptation is a crucial lever in sustaining both global diversity and rapid convergence within resource-constrained industrial IoT environments. Figure 10 shows how the neighbourhood radius expands when the fitness spread shrinks (stagnation) and contracts when the spread grows (active exploration). In our runs, this policy reduced plateau time and improved final accuracy versus a fixed-radius search at the same compute budget: fixed radius tended to converge early to sub-optimal regions, while variance-driven control re-expanded the neighbourhood at the right moments and then refocused it to refine the newly found basin. Practically, this yielded a more monotone accuracy curve (Fig. 7), a tighter latency distribution (Fig. 8), and a ROC curve closer to the upper-left frontier (Fig. 9). The effect is robust to reasonable choices of smoothing and thresholds because the rule uses directional signals (tight vs. spread fitness) rather than exact variance values.

Our proposed Neuro Evolutionary Swarm Intelligence Framework is compared against two baselines: an LSTM detector with manually tuned hyperparameters and a static PSOGA hybrid that optimizes only once before deployment. Table 1 summarizes the key metrics. The Neuro-Evolutionary model achieves 97.3% accuracy with an average latency of 0.85 s, significantly outperforming the LSTM's 89.8% at 2.4 s and the static PSOGA's 91.5% at 1.6 s.

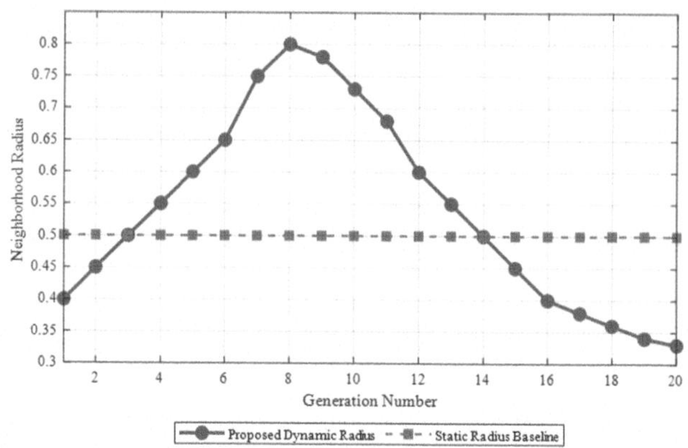

Fig. 10. Neighbourhood Radius Adaptation over Generations.

Precisionrecall trade-offs further illustrate our framework's robustness: precision reaches 96.8% and recall 97.9% (F1 = 97.3%), compared to the LSTM's F1 of 88.6% and the static hybrid's 90.7%. Our model is accurate and fast. It is trained and tested on the same data and hardware as the baselines. Accuracy is highest across all window sizes and improves steadily with generations. The latency distribution is tight and sub-second for most windows. ROC curves show strong separability with high area under the curve. False positives remain low at operating points used in practice. The dynamic topology keeps gains stable over time. Numbers that support these findings appear once in the summary table and in the figure captions. We avoid repeating them in the prose. The takeaway is simple: the method sustains high recall at low alarm rates and keeps decision time short (Table 3).

Table 3. Comparative performance of anomaly-detection methods.

Method	Accuracy (%)	Latency (s)	Precision (%)	Recall (%)	F1-Score (%)
Proposed NeuroEvolutionary	97.3	0.85	96.8	97.9	97.3
LSTM Baseline	89.8	2.40	88.2	89.0	88.6
Static PSOGA Hybrid	91.5	1.60	91.0	90.3	90.7

This detector matters for three practical reasons. Safety: sub-second decision time (median ≈0.85 s) and high recall at low false-positive rates reduce time-to-alert so operators can act sooner, while fewer nuisance alarms cut alarm fatigue. Cost reduction: earlier and more precise alarms shorten unplanned downtime and avoid unnecessary shutdowns; fewer false positives reduce time spent on triage and maintenance call-outs; brief, local updates avoid extra data-transfer

costs. Scalability: the compact GRU model runs on commodity edge gateways, and short periodic updates keep it current without heavy compute. The same pipeline can be retuned per line or plant with minimal effort, and a federated variant can share model updates across sites without sharing raw data. Together, these properties connect our technical results to plant outcomes: faster and more reliable alerts, lower operational overhead, and a deployment pathway that fits existing industrial networks.
Limitations. This approach adds small, regular compute costs during brief online updates; we cap each update with early stopping and a fixed time budget so decision time stays under one second. Cold-start behavior depends on the initial settings; we mitigate with conservative defaults and a "last-known-good" fallback if early validation degrades. Results were obtained on a high-fidelity simulator; real plants can show coupled or rare faults, so we recommend a shadow-mode phase (alarms logged but not acted upon) before full go-live. Edge gateways vary in CPU and memory; the model is sized for commodity hardware, and updates can be scheduled during low-load periods to avoid contention. Plant data can be missing, delayed, or miscalibrated; we include standardization, outlier clipping, and simple imputation, and we flag persistent sensor issues for maintenance. Reducing false alarms is critical; thresholds are tuned on recent data, and alarm policies include dwell-time and multi-sensor corroboration to prevent nuisance trips. Finally, secure deployment requires OT-friendly integration (read-only data taps, change-control windows, network segmentation, and signed update bundles). These measures keep the system practical on existing infrastructure while making clear where engineering controls are needed.

5 Conclusion and Future Work

This research article demonstrated that a neuro-evolutionary swarm-intelligence framework could detect anomalies in industrial IoT streams with 97% accuracy and sub-second latency, outperforming an LSTM baseline and a static PSOGA hybrid by wide margins. By embedding sliding-window retraining inside a GAPSO loop and modulating swarm topology through variance-driven radius control, the detector consistently balanced exploration and exploitation, adapted to drift, and preserved low false-alarm rates. Experiments on a ten-million-step simulated plant confirmed robustness across window sizes and generations, while ROC analysis showed an AUC of 0.98 evidence of near-perfect separability. Future work extends the framework to real testbeds with heterogeneous edge hardware, starting in shadow mode to measure time-to-alert and stability. Energy-aware scheduling imposes strict compute and power budgets per update, with frequency adapting to load. Multi-site deployments rely on federated learning to co-evolve models across factories without sharing raw data; drift checks and safe rollback protect operations. Uncertainty-aware gating flags low-confidence cases for additional review. Quantum-inspired search operators aim to accelerate tuning and sharpen precision under adversarial noise. Together, these steps move the system toward reliable, low-cost, and scalable anomaly detection for next-generation cyber-physical infrastructure.

References

1. Roman, R., Najera, P., Lopez, J.: Securing the Internet of Things. Computer **44**(9), 51–58 (2013)
2. Zheng, Y., Liu, Q., Chen, E., Ge, Y., Zhao, J.L.: Time series forecasting using LSTM networks: a case study. In: Proceedings of the International Conference on Neural Information Processing, 2019, pp. 123–131 (2019)
3. Kennedy, J., Eberhart, R.: Particle swarm optimization. In: Proceedings of the IEEE International Conference on Neural Networks, 1995, pp. 1942–1948 (1995)
4. Holland, J.H.: Adaptation in Natural and Artificial Systems. University of Michigan Press, Ann Arbor, MI, USA (1975)
5. Zhang, L., Zhao, M., Nair, S.K.: Hybrid PSO-GA for neural network optimization in real-time applications. Expert Syst. Appl. **167**, 114129 (2021)
6. Chen, X., Wu, R., Li, T.: Sliding-window retraining for concept drift adaptation in streaming data. IEEE Trans. Knowl. Data Eng. **32**(5), 927–939 (2020)
7. Li, Y., Li, H., Guan, X.: Dynamic neighbourhood topology in particle swarm optimization. Swarm Intell. **16**(2), 165–184 (2022)
8. Hochreiter, S., Schmidhuber, J.: Long short-term memory. Neural Comput. **9**(8), 1735–1780 (1997)
9. Cho, K., et al.: Learning phrase representations using RNN encoder–decoder for statistical machine translation. In: Proceedings of the Conference on Empirical Methods in Natural Language Processing (EMNLP), 2014, pp. 1724–1734 (2014)
10. Chung, J., et al.: Empirical evaluation of gated recurrent neural networks on sequence modeling, arXiv preprint arXiv:1412.3555 (2014)
11. Wang, D., Tan, D., Liu, L.: Particle swarm optimization algorithm: an overview. Soft. Comput. **22**, 387–408 (2018). https://doi.org/10.1007/s00500-016-2474-6
12. Holland, J.H.: Adaptation in Natural and Artificial Systems: An Introductory Analysis with Applications to Biology, Control, and Artificial Intelligence. MIT Press, Cambridge, MA (1992)
13. Cai, X., Zhang, N., Venayagamoorthy, G.K., Wunsch, D.C., II.: Time series prediction with recurrent neural networks trained by a hybrid PSO–EA algorithm. Neurocomputing **70**(13–15), 2342–2353 (2007)
14. Hoens, T.R., Polikar, R., Chawla, N.V.: Learning from streaming data with concept drift and imbalance: an overview. Progr. Artif. Intell. **1**(1), 89–101 (2012). https://doi.org/10.1007/s13748-011-0002-0
15. Wang, L., Yang, B., Orchard, J.: Particle swarm optimization using dynamic tournament topology. Appl. Soft Comput. **48**, 584–596 (2016), ISSN 1568-4946, https://doi.org/10.1016/j.asoc.2016.07.041

DPA: An Efficient Cross-Domain Face Anti-spoofing Framework via Dual-Parallel Adapter Fine-Tuning

Yanfeng Gu[1,2], Ping Ye[1,2], Xiangyu Shi[1,2], Xiaoshu Cui[2,3], Jingqi Jia[1,2], Xinyi Zhao[1,2], Jialu Sun[1,2], Qiong Li[1,2], Yalun Wu[1,2], and Wenjia Niu[1,2](✉)

[1] School of Cyberspace Science and Technology, Beijing Jiaotong University, Beijing, China
{guyanfeng,23120489,24115071,jingqijia,21281179,21251133,liqiong, wuyalun1,niuwj}@bjtu.edu.cn

[2] Beijing Key Laboratory of Security and Privacy in Intelligent Transportation, Beijing Jiaotong University, Beijing, China
cuixiaoshu@bjtu.edu.cn

[3] School of Computer Science and Technology, Beijing Jiaotong University, Beijing, China

Abstract. Face recognition systems confront critical challenges from presentation attacks (e.g., printed photos, 3D masks), making Face Anti-Spoofing (FAS) pivotal for security enhancement. Most existing FAS methods adopt vision-language pretrained models to boost generalization, yet full-model fine-tuning incurs high computational costs, and lightweight prompt-learning approaches prove unsuitable for FAS due to ambiguous semantic categories. To address this, we propose the Dual-Parallel Adapter (DPA) Framework, which embeds lightweight adapters into the visual encoder of large vision-language models, enabling efficient knowledge transfer to FAS while mitigating interference from non-liveness image signals. Specifically, our framework first aligns face images with FAS-specific natural language descriptions. Then, dual-parallel adapters are inserted into the pretrained model's core components to facilitate efficient learning of task-specific features. Finally, multiple loss functions guide the model to acquire discriminative liveness representations across multiple dimensions. Experiments on four authoritative datasets under dual protocol standards demonstrate that the DPA Framework significantly reduces training parameters and outperforms baseline models in average generalization performance.

Keywords: Face Anti-spoofing · CLIP · Domain Generalization · Adapter

1 Introduction

Face recognition systems have been widely deployed in daily life scenarios such as identity verification of smartphones, access control of door locks, and electronic payment. However, this technology continues to face severe challenges

L. Zhang and K.-K. R. Choo (Eds.): MobiQuitous 2025, LNICST 684, pp. 191–207, 2026.
https://doi.org/10.1007/978-3-032-22503-0_11

from diverse presentation attacks, including malicious means such as printed photos [1], 3D masks [11], and video replays [27]. To resist such attacks, Face Anti-Spoofing (FAS) technology [20,34,37,46] has emerged. As a core technology for enhancing the security protection of face recognition systems, it can effectively identify the differences between live and forged faces, accurately block malicious attack behaviors, and play a crucial role in ensuring the reliability and security of user identity authentication.

Early FAS methods [3,4,23] are limited by the limitations of manual feature representation capabilities and struggle to meet the high-security requirements of modern FAS systems. With the vigorous development of deep learning technology, deep neural networks have gradually become the mainstream choice for data-driven FAS methods [16,24,42]. By automatically learning data features, they perform excellently in experiments on datasets from the same domain. Later, to address the distribution differences brought about by cross-device and cross-environment scenarios, Domain Generalization (DG) technology has been introduced. Its aim is to alleviate the impact of distribution differences by fusing data from multiple domains and enhance the adaptability of models to unknown domains. Among them, methods based on adversarial learning [18], methods based on meta-learning [10], and methods based on disentangled representation learning [49] are often used for DG. With the increasing prominence of vision-language pre-trained models, researchers hope to bridge the gap in the visual field through the language modality [19,28,31]. They align the image representation with the set of category descriptions to further improve the generalization ability of FAS. However, existing works still have the following issues: Full-model fine-tuning of vision-language pretrained models to adapt to downstream tasks incurs high computational costs and is prone to the risk of overfitting.

Regarding this problem of high computational cost and prone overfitting in full-model fine-tuning, lightweight adaptation of CLIP to downstream tasks has become a research direction, among which common methods such as CoOp [48] and CoCoOp [47] are all implemented based on prompt learning. In conventional downstream tasks like distinguishing "cat" and "dog", categories have clear semantic meanings, and prompt learning can effectively construct contextual category representations. However, in the FAS task, determining whether a face is "real" or "fake" lacks such semantic connotations, limiting the direct application of prompt learning to obtain contextual category representations. Additionally, image features are mixed with large amounts of signals irrelevant to liveness, and prompt learning-based methods adjust prompts based on complete visual features, failing to help classifiers accurately avoid interference from irrelevant signals and leading to poor generalization performance of the model.

In this paper, for the cross-domain FAS task, we propose a **D**ual-**P**arallel **A**dapter (**DPA**) framework, which embeds lightweight adapters into the visual encoder of large-scale multimodal pre-trained models. Compared with existing methods, this approach significantly reduces the number of trainable parameters. Meanwhile, compared to prompt learning, adapters can more accurately focus on key features for FAS, effectively avoiding interference from liveness-irrelevant signals in images, and demonstrating greater advantages in feature extraction and utilization efficiency. Specifically, we deploy Dual-Parallel Adapter units in each Transformer block of the CLIP model's visual encoder, which respectively adapt to the multi-head attention mechanism (MHA) and multi-layer perceptron (MLP) modules. The dual-parallel adapters are connected in parallel with the original MHA and MLP branches through residual connections, enabling efficient learning of task-specific features. This not only improves the model's average cross-domain generalization performance in FAS tasks but also significantly reduces computational costs. Experiments conducted on four authoritative datasets and dual protocol standards demonstrate that our proposed method significantly reduces the number of training parameters and outperforms the baseline models in terms of average generalization performance. In summary, the main contributions of this paper are as follows:

- We transfer the efficient fine-tuning of lightweight adapters for pretrained large models to the FAS field, enabling accurate focus on key features for FAS and achieving better generalization performance with fewer parameters.
- We propose a DPA framework, which deploys dual adapters in parallel within the core structure of vision-language pretrained models. During fine-tuning, computational overhead is reduced by freezing original parameters and only training a small number of parameters in the adapters.
- We validated the effectiveness of our proposed method based on four authoritative datasets and dual protocol standards. Experimental results show that the average generalization performance of our method outperforms current baseline methods.

2 Related Work

2.1 Face Anti-spoofing

FAS aims to accurately distinguish between real and forged faces through technical means, serving as a core defense line for ensuring the security of face recognition systems. It has been a key research focus in both academic and industrial circles for over a decade.

Early traditional FAS methods primarily utilized hand-designed features and classical machine learning techniques. Represented by Local Binary Patterns [4], Histogram of Oriented Gradients [33], and Scale Invariant Feature Transform [23], these methods constructed feature engineering systems to classify and recognize real and fake faces. Limited by shallow model architectures and a high reliance on manually designed features, such methods exhibited poor robustness and generalization performance in complex scenarios. With the development of deep learning technology, FAS architectures based on Convolutional Neural Networks have gradually dominated the field. By leveraging end-to-end training strategies, these architectures [22,26,36] automatically extract high-dimensional discriminative features, significantly improving the models' detection accuracy on the same datasets. Subsequently, facing the challenges posed by cross-domain data distribution differences, DG technology has become a research focus. The common goal is to mitigate the impact of distribution differences by fusing data from multiple domains and enhance the adaptability of models to unknown domains. This includes techniques such as adversarial learning [8,18], meta-learning [10], and disentangled representation learning [49]. Although these works demonstrate promising cross-domain performance, most of them still require additional information, such as attack types and domain labels, or rely on significant auxiliary supervision.

Then, methods based on large vision-language pretrained models have brought new ideas for improving the domain generalization performance of FAS by virtue of their cross-modal semantic alignment capabilities. For example, methods such as [6,19,28,31,35] adopt an end-to-end CLIP fine-tuning framework and achieve superior performance through pretraining and fine-tuning paradigms. However, this fine-tuning strategy may overlook useful knowledge acquired during the pretraining stage, potentially leading to model overfitting. Additionally, fine-tuning all parameters results in excessive consumption of computational resources. Meanwhile, prompt learning-based methods [12,17,19,31,40,43] that reduce the number of parameters have limitations in acquiring contextual category representations for FAS tasks and avoiding interference from irrelevant signals.

Therefore, in this paper, we migrate the efficient fine-tuning of lightweight adapters for pretrained large models to the FAS task, reducing the number of parameters, avoiding model overfitting, and accurately focusing on key features for FAS.

2.2 Parameter-Efficient Fine-Tuning in VLMs

To address the issues of memory inefficiency and parameter inefficiency during full/partial fine-tuning, Parameter-Efficient Fine-Tuning (PEFT) was first introduced in the field of Natural Language Processing [13,38]. Its core idea is to conduct fine-tuning using only a small number of trainable parameters. This lightweight optimization paradigm demonstrates significant advantages in the adaptation of Vision-Language Models (VLMs) to downstream tasks [2,30,39], enabling the preservation of the semantic integrity of pre-trained features while significantly reducing computational costs and storage overhead.

Recently, three types of methods have been proposed: (1) updating only the newly added parameters (added to the input or the model) [21]; (2) sparsely updating a small number of parameters of the model [29]; (3) low-rank factorization of the weights to be updated [14]. [13] combines these methods and proposes a unified parameter-efficient training framework. Among these methods, the adapter belongs to the first category and is widely used in computer vision and natural language processing. The approach is that given the input token X, the adapter $\mathcal{A}$ realizes the feature transformation $X \leftarrow X + \mathcal{A}(X)$ through the residual connection. Meanwhile, some works have also extended the PEFT technology to the CLIP model [48]. However, previous works have mainly focused on image-text alignment problems, with little research on FAS tasks that exhibit large data distribution differences and high overfitting risks in few-shot scenarios.

Therefore, this paper proposes a parallel dual-adaptive Transformer module. By deploying heterogeneous adapters in parallel across the MHA layers and MLP layers of the Transformer core structure, it achieves collaborative enhancement of multi-scale visual features and domain-invariant learning.

3 Methodology

In this section, we introduce DPA framework, which enables lightweight migration of the pre-trained large-scale model CLIP to the FAS task. The framework is shown in Fig. 1. The specific arrangement is as follows: In Sect. 3.1, we will first review the research on CLIP in the FAS task. Then, we will introduce our DPA method in Sect. 3.2. Finally, we will introduce our optimization objectives in Sect. 3.3.

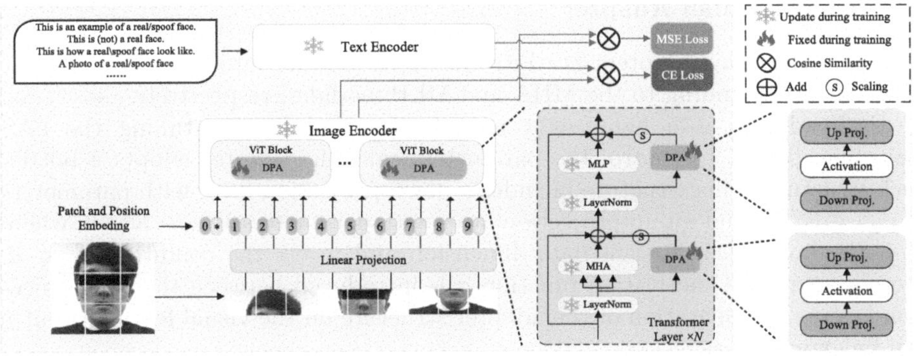

Fig. 1. Overview of the proposed DPA framework. Firstly, create some text templates dedicated to the FAS task and input them into the text encoder. Meanwhile, add two adapters in parallel to the Transformer blocks of the visual encoder. Train the parameters in the adapters and freeze all other parameters. In the figure, the blue line represents the original image stream, and the red line represents the patch stream transformed from the original image. (Color figure online)

3.1 Preliminaries of CLIP for FAS

Contrastive Language-Image Pre-Training (CLIP) [25] consists of two encoders—one for images and another for text—that extract bimodal features, mapping an input image $x \in \mathbb{R}^{H \times W \times 3}$ and text descriptions w into a shared embedding space. The specific mechanisms are detailed as follows:

Image Encoding: The image encoder first partitions the input image into fixed-size patches, which are then projected to create patch embeddings. Each patch embedding, along with a learnable [CLS] token, sequentially passes through a Transformer to generate the image representation $v \in \mathbb{R}^d$.

Text Encoding: In CLIP, prompt tuning adapts the model to downstream tasks by forming prompts using manually crafted templates. For a dataset containing K classes, each classification text description is formatted as "a photo of a [class]". The text encoder tokenizes each word in the description, projects the token sequence into text embeddings, and processes them through a Transformer to produce the text representation $t \in \mathbb{R}^{d \times K}$. The prediction probability is computed as:

$$p(w = i|x) = \frac{\exp(sim(v, t_i)/\tau)}{\sum_{i=1}^{K} \exp(sim(v, t_i)/\tau)} \tag{1}$$

where $\mathrm{sim}(\cdot, \cdot)$ denotes the similarity calculation and τ is the temperature parameter. For the FAS task, the number of categories is 2, corresponding to "real" and "spoof", with prompts "real face photo" and "spoof face photo", respectively.

3.2 Dual-Parallel Adapter

Two plug-and-play adapters are introduced in parallel into each Transformer module, corresponding to the MHA and MLP modules, respectively.

Each adapter is a lightweight module designed for fine-tuning the FAS task. Specifically, to control the parameter scale, the adapter adopts a bottleneck structure. This structure includes a down-projection layer with parameters $W_{\text{down}} \in \mathbb{R}^{d \times d'}$ and an up-projection layer with parameters $W_{\text{up}} \in \mathbb{R}^{d' \times d}$, where d' is the bottleneck intermediate dimension and meets the condition $d' \ll d$. Moreover, a ReLU activation function σ is introduced between the two projection layers. The operation of the adapter structure on the visual feature input v can be expressed as:

$$\text{Adapter}(\text{LN}(v)) = W_{\text{up}}(\sigma\left(W_{\text{down}}\left(\text{LN}(v)\right)\right)) \tag{2}$$

This operation process can be understood as follows: First, the input visual feature is normalized, and the down-projection layer W_{down} performs dimensionality reduction on the normalized visual feature $LN(v)$, mapping it to a low-dimensional space to highlight key information and reduce redundancy. Next, the ReLU activation function σ conducts a non-linear transformation on the feature after dimensionality reduction, enhancing the feature's representational ability. Finally, the up-projection layer W_{up} remaps the non-linearly transformed feature back to a space close to the original dimension, facilitating effective integration with subsequent modules.

Subsequently, the adaptive features generated by the two bottleneck structures are scaled by the scaling factor s. At the start of training, s is initialized to zero to prevent the adaptive features generated by the adapters from excessively interfering with the model. As training progresses, s is flexibly adjusted based on the gradient information of the loss function during backpropagation, which modulates the intensity of the adaptive features to better match other features and achieve better performance on the FAS task. Then, these scaled adaptive features are fused via residual connections with the visual feature v and the features generated by first normalizing v and then passing it through either the MHA or MLP layer. Since this operation is not sequential, and each Transformer block contains both an MHA layer and an MLP layer simultaneously, a single Transformer block incorporates dual-parallel adapters. The output of the l-th Transformer module can be expressed by the following formula:

$$\begin{aligned} \tilde{v} &= v^{l-1} + \mathrm{MHA}(\mathrm{LN}(v^{l-1})) + s \cdot \mathrm{Adapter}(\mathrm{LN}(v^{l-1})) \\ v_l &= \tilde{v} + \mathrm{MLP}(\mathrm{LN}(\tilde{v})) + s \cdot \mathrm{Adapter}(\mathrm{LN}(\tilde{v})) \end{aligned} \tag{3}$$

where $v^0 = [[\mathrm{CLS}], \mathrm{x}] + \mathrm{p}$, with [CLS] being the class token and p the learnable positional encoding.

During the fine-tuning phase, we only optimize the newly introduced parameters while keeping the remaining parameters fixed. Specifically, the original model components (yellow blocks in Fig. 1) directly load weights from pre-trained checkpoints and have their parameters frozen, whereas the newly added parameters (orange blocks) are updated with task-specific losses in the target data domain. In inference, we maintain the parameter-freezing strategy from the fine-tuning phase, i.e., keeping shared parameters unchanged, and additionally load the weights of the newly added parameters fine-tuned in previous stages.

3.3 Optimization Objective

We assume that aligning image representations with a set of category descriptions based on natural language semantics can enhance the generalization ability of the FAS task. Therefore, we employ the Cross-Entropy (CE) loss to make the original face representations of matching pairs and their corresponding category representations closer, while separating non-matching pairs in the feature space, defined as:

$$L_{ce} = -\frac{1}{N}\sum_{i=1}^{N}[y_i \cdot log(p_r) + (1 - y_i) \cdot log(p_s)] \tag{4}$$

Here, N denotes the batch size. y_i represents the ground truth label of the i-th sample, where 1 indicates a genuine face and 0 denotes a forged face. p_r and p_s denote the predicted probabilities of an image being "real" or "spoofed", respectively, which are computed using Eq. 1.

In the calculation of the Mean Squared Error (MSE) loss, two different prompts of the same type are randomly selected from the text prompts. Meanwhile, we randomly crop patches from each original image, where the size of each patch is one-fourth of the original image. These patches are augmented through horizontal flipping and rotation, and then resized back to the original size. By combining the two text representations with the image representations of the patches, two pairs of image-text representations are obtained. Since the two image patches are cropped from the same face, the two pairs of image-text representations should be similar. Therefore, the MSE loss can be expressed as:

$$L_{MSE} = \frac{1}{N}\sum_{i=1}^{N}(sim(v_i^1, t_i^1) - sim(v_i^2, t_i^2))^2 \quad (5)$$

where t_i^1 and t_i^2 are two different prompts from the ground-truth class and v_i^1 and v_i^2 are patches cropped from the same face image. During the training process of our model, which aims to optimize the performance and convergence in dealing with FAS task, we meticulously define the joint loss as:

$$\mathcal{L} = \mathcal{L}_{CE} + \lambda\mathcal{L}_{MSE} \quad (6)$$

where the hyperparameter λ is set to 1. The specific process of the DPA framework is shown in Algorithm 1.

Algorithm 1. Dual-Parallel Adapter for FAS

Require: A pre-trained CLIP model M with L Transformer layers, Input data x for FAS task, Face authenticity description prompts w, Learning rate η

Ensure: Parameter-efficient fine-tuned Transformer model M' for FAS task

1: Initialize new parameters for adapters in each Transformer module
2: $v^0 = [\text{CLS}, x] + p$ with CLS being the class token and p the learnable positional encoding
3: **for** $l = 1$ to L **do**
4: $\text{Adapter}(\text{LN}(v_{l-1})) \leftarrow W_{\text{up}}(\sigma(W_{\text{down}}(\text{LN}(v_{l-1}))))$
5: $\tilde{v} \leftarrow v^{l-1} + \text{MHA}(\text{LN}(v^{l-1})) + s \cdot \text{Adapter}(\text{LN}(v^{l-1}))$
6: $\text{Adapter}(\text{LN}(\tilde{v})) \leftarrow W_{\text{up}}(\sigma(W_{\text{down}}(\text{LN}(\tilde{v}))))$
7: $v_l \leftarrow \tilde{v} + \text{MLP}(\text{LN}(\tilde{v})) + s \cdot \text{Adapter}(\text{LN}(\tilde{v}))$
8: **end for**
9: Calculate task-specific loss $\mathcal{L}$ using v^L and text representation t for FAS task
10: Update adapter parameters using gradient descent with learning rate η: $\theta_{\text{adapter}} \leftarrow \theta_{\text{adapter}} - \eta\nabla_{\theta_{\text{adapter}}}\mathcal{L}$
11: $M' \leftarrow$ Transformer model with updated adapter parameters and frozen original parameters
12: **return** M'

4 Experiments

4.1 Experimental Setup

Datasets and Protocols: We evaluate our method using four benchmark datasets in cross-domain FAS task: MSU-MFSD (M) [32], CASIA-MFSD (C) [45], Idiap Replay Attack (I) [7], and OULU-NPU (O) [5]. Following [15], we assess our method on two different protocols. Protocol 1 is set as the leave-one-domain-out testing protocol, where each dataset is regarded as a domain, and we evaluate the cross-domain performance on the left-out domain. For example, MCI → O represents the situation where the M, C, and I datasets are considered as source domains and O is the target domain, and there are a total of 4 combinations. To further evaluate the performance in the low-data regime, Protocol 2 is set as the single-source-to-single-target protocol. For instance, M→C indicates that M is regarded as the source domain and C is regarded as the target domain, with a total of 12 combinations. Additionally, CelebA-Spoof [44] is used as supplementary training data to increase the diversity of training samples.

Evaluation Metrics: We use three metrics, (1) the Half Total Error Rate (HTER); (2) the Area Under the Curve (AUC); (3) the True Positive Rate (TPR) at a False Positive Rate (FPR) of 1% (TPR@FPR=1%), to evaluate the performance of the model. Among them, HTER is the average of the False Rejection Rate (FRR) and the False Acceptance Rate (FAR). AUC represents the area under the ROC curve and is used to evaluate the performance of the classifier. TPR measures the accuracy of the algorithm in identifying spoofing samples. In subsequent experiments, it is preferable to have a smaller HTER value, whereas larger values for both AUC and TPR@FPR=1% are more desirable.

Implementation Details: We utilize the pre-trained CLIP [25] model, selecting ViT-B/16 [9] as the image encoder, and adopt the same text prompts as [28], as shown in Table 1. The Adam optimizer is employed with both the learning rate and weight decay set to 10^{-6}. During training, the visual and text encoders are frozen, and only the parameters within the adapters are trained. Additionally, for each video in the four datasets (excluding the CelebA-Spoof dataset), two frames are sampled. These sampled frames are input into MTCNN [41] for face detection, alignment, and image cropping. The images are then resized to (224, 224, 3), using only the RGB channels. The batch size is set to 3, and the model is trained for 4000 iterations.

Table 1. Natural language descriptions used to guide the CLIP model in classifying real and spoof faces in the FAS task.

Prompt No.	Real Prompts	Spoof Prompts
P1	This is an example of a real face	This is an example of a spoof face
P2	This is a bonafide face	This is an example of an attack face
P3	This is a real face	This is not a real face
P4	This is how a real face looks like	This is how a spoof face looks like
P5	A photo of a real face	A photo of a spoof face
P6	This is not a spoof face	A printout shown to be a spoof face

4.2 Cross-Domain FAS Performance

In the study of Protocol 1, Table 2 reports the latest experimental results. According to the characteristics of cross-domain transfer tasks, we divide the experiments into 0-shot (zero-shot) and 5-shot (few-shot) scenarios. Among them, the 0-shot transfer strictly adopts the setting of "no target domain prior". During training, no target domain data is introduced, and only the other three source domain datasets are used to build the training space, simulating the generalization challenge for the model when facing unknown data distributions. The 5-shot transfer, on the other hand, introduces 5 data points from the target domain during training to build a few-shot learning scenario and verify the gain effect of scarce target domain data.

The experiments show that in the case of zero-shot transfer, the proposed method outperforms the baseline methods in terms of the average performance across the four datasets (measured by the average HTER). The average HTER is reduced by 3% compared with the current optimal baseline, and it also outperforms in indicators such as AUC and TPR@FPR = 1% in tasks like "OMI → C" and "OCM → I". For the 5-shot transfer, due to the integration of 5 data points from the target domain, the performance is further improved compared with the 0-shot transfer. The average performance is better than that of the baseline methods, and the average HTER is reduced by 5% compared with the current optimal baseline. All core indicators are improved in the "OCI → M" task, the TPR@FPR = 1% is enhanced in the "OMI → C" task, and both the HTER and TPR@FPR = 1% are improved in the "OCM → I" task.

Table 2. Cross-domain performance evaluation on the leave-one-domain-out basis (Protocol 1): For each combination, 5 runs are conducted under different seeds, and the average HTER, AUC, and TPR@FPR = 1% are reported. "Avg" represents the average performance of HTER. The boldface indicates that the proposed method outperforms other methods under this setting.

Method		OCI → M			OMI → C			OCM → I			ICM → O			Avg.
		HTER	AUC	TPR@FPR=1%	HTER	AUC	TPR@FPR=1%	HTER	AUC	TPR@FPR=1%	HTER	AUC	TPR@FPR=1%	HTER
0-shot	MADDG	17.69	88.06	–	24.50	84.51	–	22.19	84.99	–	27.98	80.02	–	23.09
	MDDR	17.02	90.10	–	19.68	87.43	–	20.87	86.72	–	25.02	81.47	–	20.64
	NAS-FAS	16.85	90.42	–	15.21	92.64	–	11.63	96.98	–	13.16	94.18	–	14.21
	RFMeta	13.89	93.98	–	20.27	88.16	–	17.30	90.48	–	16.45	91.16	–	16.97
	D^2AM	12.70	95.66	–	20.98	85.58	–	15.43	91.22	–	15.27	90.87	–	16.09
	DRDG	12.43	95.81	–	19.05	88.79	–	15.56	91.79	–	15.63	91.75	–	15.66
	Self-DA	15.40	91.80	–	24.50	84.40	–	15.60	90.10	–	23.10	84.30	–	19.65
	ANRL	10.83	96.75	–	17.85	89.26	–	16.03	91.04	–	15.67	91.90	–	15.09
	FGHV	9.17	96.92	–	12.47	93.47	–	16.29	90.11	–	13.58	93.55	–	12.87
	SSDG-R	7.38	97.17	–	10.44	95.94	–	11.71	96.59	–	15.61	91.54	–	11.28
	SSAN-R	6.67	98.75	–	10.00	96.67	–	8.88	96.79	–	13.72	93.63	–	9.80
	PatchNet	7.10	98.46	–	11.33	94.58	–	13.40	95.67	–	11.82	95.07	–	10.90
	GDA	9.20	98.00	–	12.20	93.00	–	10.00	96.00	–	14.40	92.60	–	11.45
	DIVT-M	2.86	99.14	–	8.67	96.62	–	3.71	99.29	–	13.06	94.04	–	7.07
	ViT	1.58	99.68	96.67	5.70	98.91	88.57	9.25	97.15	51.54	7.47	98.42	69.30	6.00
	S-adapter	3.43	99.50	–	6.32	97.82	–	7.16	97.61	–	7.21	98.00	–	6.03
	BLIP	4.58	98.69	–	0.93	99.99	–	5.00	98.53	–	7.50	97.61	–	4.50
	DCDC	6.33	98.53	–	1.40	99.80	–	4.53	98.90	–	0.96	99.49	–	3.31
	FLIP-MCL	4.95	98.11	74.67	0.54	99.98	100.00	4.25	99.07	84.62	2.31	99.63	92.28	3.01
	CFPL	1.43	99.28	98.57	2.56	99.10	66.33	5.43	98.41	85.29	2.50	99.42	94.72	2.98
	Ours	3.88	99.03	86.67	0.58	**99.99**	**100.00**	4.08	99.26	85.07	3.02	99.31	89.43	**2.89**
5-shot	ViT	3.42	98.60	95.00	1.98	99.75	94.00	2.31	99.75	87.69	7.34	97.77	66.90	3.76
	ViTAF	2.92	99.62	91.66	1.40	99.92	98.57	1.64	99.64	91.53	5.39	98.67	76.05	3.31
	FLIP-MCL	3.42	99.34	82.67	0.63	99.98	100.00	1.52	99.86	97.23	1.54	99.81	96.37	1.77
	Ours	**1.58**	**99.68**	**96.67**	0.70	99.97	**100.00**	**0.89**	99.81	**98.46**	3.54	99.17	83.80	**1.68**

In the study of Protocol 2, Table 3 presents the latest experimental results. Given the need to statistically analyze the cross-domain performance from individual source domains to individual target domains across 4 datasets, combinatorial calculation yields $C_4^2 = 12$ setting configurations. Echoing the framework of Protocol 1, we categorized the results into two scenarios: 0-shot (zero-shot) and 5-shot (few-shot) for analysis. The findings show that in the 0-shot transfer scenario, our proposed method achieved the best average performance across the 12 settings, reducing the average HTER by 19% compared to the current optimal baseline, with half of the settings outperforming existing baselines. In the 5-shot transfer scenario, performance not only improved further compared to the 0-shot scenario but also surpassed current baselines, achieving the best average performance with a 26% reduction in average HTER relative to the optimal baseline, and three-fourths of the 12 settings outperformed baselines. Notably, configurations such as I $\rightarrow$ C, M $\rightarrow$ C, M $\rightarrow$ I, and O $\rightarrow$ C demonstrated exceptional performance, with HTER reduced to 0, fully validating that the proposed method efficiently utilizes (or adapts without reliance on) target domain data in complex cross-domain scenarios, providing a more robust solution for cross-domain face anti-spoofing.

Table 3. Cross-domain performance evaluation under the single-source-to-single-target protocol (Protocol 2): For each combination, 5 runs are conducted under different seeds, and the average HTER is reported. The boldface indicates that the proposed method outperforms other methods under this setting.

Method		C → I	C → M	C → O	I → C	I → M	I → O	M → C	M → I	M → O	O → C	O → I	O → M	Avg.
0-shot	ADDA	41.80	36.60	–	49.80	35.10	–	39.00	35.20	–	–	–	–	39.60
	DRCN	44.40	27.60	–	48.90	42.00	–	28.90	36.80	–	–	–	–	38.10
	DupGAN	42.40	33.40	–	46.50	36.20	–	27.10	35.40	–	–	–	–	36.80
	KSA	39.30	15.10	–	12.30	33.30	–	9.10	34.90	–	–	–	–	24.00
	DR-UDA	15.60	9.00	28.70	34.20	29.00	38.50	16.80	3.00	30.20	19.50	25.40	27.40	23.10
	MDDR	26.10	20.20	24.70	39.20	23.20	33.60	34.30	8.70	31.70	21.80	27.60	22.00	26.10
	ADA	17.50	9.30	29.10	41.50	30.50	39.60	17.70	5.10	31.20	19.80	26.80	31.50	25.00
	USDAN-Un	16.00	9.20	–	30.20	25.80	–	13.30	3.40	–	–	–	–	16.30
	GDA	15.00	5.80	–	29.70	20.80	–	12.20	2.50	–	–	–	–	14.40
	CDFTN-L	1.70	8.10	29.90	11.90	9.60	29.90	8.80	1.30	25.60	19.10	5.80	6.30	13.20
	FLIP-MCL	10.57	7.15	3.91	0.68	7.22	4.22	0.19	5.88	3.95	0.19	5.69	8.40	4.84
	Ours	2.24	8.42	**3.10**	0.81	13.42	7.48	0.70	**0.67**	**3.41**	**0.11**	**1.42**	**5.00**	**3.90**
5-shot	ViTAF	4.98	4.38	10.85	2.55	5.08	8.63	1.59	1.79	7.92	1.65	3.40	4.40	4.77
	FLIP-MCL	4.18	5.27	2.48	0.65	3.68	2.56	0.19	1.74	2.43	0.23	2.58	4.10	2.51
	Ours	**0.75**	**3.67**	3.36	**0.00**	5.00	3.80	**0.00**	**0.00**	**2.26**	**0.00**	**0.07**	**3.42**	**1.86**

4.3 Ablation Study

In the ablation experiment, we systematically explored the impact mechanism of the adapter structure and its quantity in the Transformer block on the model performance. In the design of the adapter structure, three configurations (dual-parallel, dual-series, series-parallel) mentioned in 3.2 are respectively deployed in the MHA layer and MLP layer, and comprehensive performance comparison tests are carried out on four benchmark datasets.

The experimental results are illustrated in Fig. 2, where the performance of the method corresponding to each point improves as the point approaches the lower-right corner. Notably, the DPA structure (the proposed method) demonstrates optimal performance in both 0-shot and 5-shot transfer learning scenarios. When the adapter structure is adjusted to dual-series or series-parallel configurations, model performance declines, with a more pronounced drop observed in the 0-shot transfer scenario compared to the 5-shot scenario. Specifically, the dual-series structure causes the most severe performance degradation in the 0-shot scenario, approaching the performance of the original CLIP model. Through in-depth analysis, the following reasons may exist: The dual-series structure introduces excessive parameter dependencies during information transmission, resulting in a longer gradient propagation path, which is likely to trigger problems such as gradient vanishing or explosion, affecting the stability and convergence speed of model training; meanwhile, the series structure makes the feature transformation more complex, which may lead to the repeated processing or loss of key information and reduce the effectiveness of feature expression. In contrast, the dual-parallel structure can process feature information branches in parallel, improve the efficiency of information fusion, reduce parameter coupling, and maintain the flexibility of gradient optimization, thus achieving better performance.

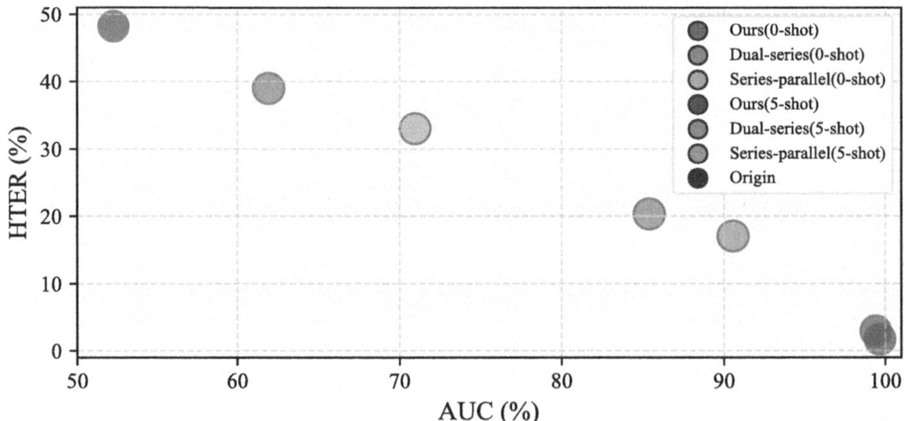

Fig. 2. Results obtained using different adapter structures in 0-shot and 5-shot transfer scenarios.

Regarding the number of adapters, we tested the model's performance with and without adapters in the MHA layer and MLP layer respectively, and the results are shown in Fig. 3. The study reveals that reducing adapters in either the MHA layer or MLP layer leads to a slight decline in model performance, yet the degradation is less pronounced than that caused by adjusting adapter structures. This is evidenced by the fact that retaining a single adapter in the 5-shot scenario still outperforms the 0-shot scenario. Specifically, models retaining adapters only in the MLP layer exhibit marginally better performance than those retaining adapters solely in the MHA layer. These results indicate that while single-adapter configurations cause minor performance drops, they remain competent for cross-domain FAS tasks. Notably, MLP layer adapters may contribute slightly more to enhancing model generalization capability, underscoring their relative importance in maintaining performance during adapter reduction.

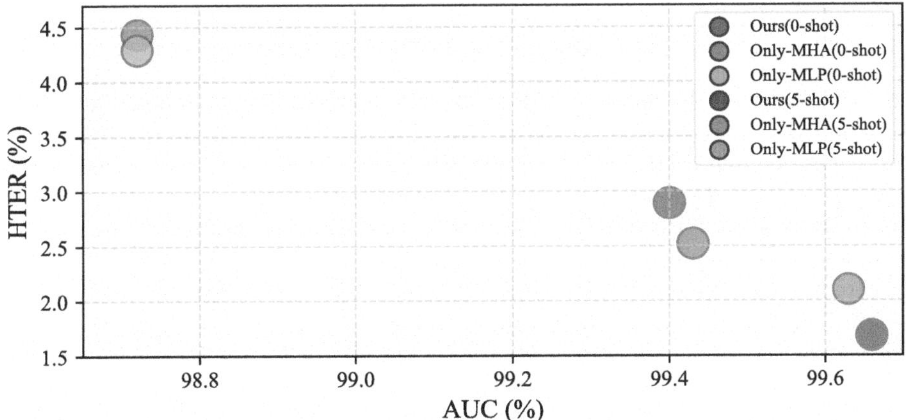

Fig. 3. Results after adjusting the number of adapters in 0-shot and 5-shot transfer scenarios.

4.4 Efficiency Analysis

In addition to performance, model efficiency is also a core factor we focus on. Table 4 systematically compares the efficiency metrics of our method with baseline methods, detailing the floating-point operations (FLOPs) and the number of learnable parameters in the image and text encoders of each model. The experimental results show that our method reduces the learnable parameters in the image encoder to one-twelfth of the original while maintaining or even improving performance, and significantly reduces the model's FLOPs. Since no adapter is added to the text encoder, the number of trainable parameters in the text encoder is 0. This design not only significantly accelerates the training process and reduces computational resource consumption but also greatly enhances the flexibility and practicality of model deployment.

Table 4. Results of FLOPs (G), Params (M) required for model training under different methods, and the inference time for a single frame.

Method	Image Encoder		Text Encoder	
	Parameters	FLOPs	Parameters	FLOPs
ViT	86.19M	17.58G	–	–
ViTAF	92.02M	18.68G	–	–
FLIP-V	86.58M	17.58G	–	–
FLIP-IT	86.19M	17.58G	63.11M	35.81G
FLIP-MCL	86.19M	52.74G	83.05M	35.86G
Ours	**7.10M**	**11.97G**	–	**11.63G**

4.5 DPA's Delay-Accuracy Trade-Off on Mobile Devices

When deploying DPA on mobile devices, the delay-accuracy trade-off needs to be further considered based on the device's limited computing power and power supply. On one hand, DPA's lightweight advantages (fewer parameters and lower FLOPs) lay a solid foundation for reducing inference delay. For low-end mobile devices with weak CPU/GPU performance, the smaller number of parameters can reduce memory usage and data transmission time, while the reduced FLOPs can directly shorten the single-frame inference time, making it possible to control the delay within a user-acceptable range (for example, keeping the delay under 100ms in face unlocking scenarios). On the other hand, if higher accuracy is required for high-security scenarios (such as mobile payments), minor adjustments can be made while ensuring low delay. For instance, appropriately increasing the resolution of input images (without excessively increasing FLOPs) or adopting multi-frame fusion inference (controlling the number of frames to 2–3 to avoid a significant increase in delay) allows the model to better capture subtle spoofing features (such as texture differences in 3D masks) without causing obvious waiting for users, thereby achieving a reasonable balance between delay and accuracy that is suitable for mobile device scenarios.

5 Conclusion

In this work, for the FAS task, we embed lightweight adapters into the visual encoder of the multi-modal pre-trained large model. Through the local parameter optimization strategy, while avoiding large-scale modifications to the parameters of the pre-trained model, we significantly enhance the model's cross-domain generalization ability. The proposed DPA module, by parallelly deploying heterogeneous adapters in the MHA layer and MLP layer of the core structure of the Transformer, achieves the collaborative enhancement of multi-scale visual features and the learning of domain invariance, successfully balancing the feature expression ability and the stability of the semantic structure. Our comprehensive experimental results and analysis demonstrate that, compared with existing baseline methods, the method in this paper achieves the goal of obtaining better generalization performance with fewer parameters, providing a successful example for the application of the efficient fine-tuning paradigm of pre-trained large model parameters in the FAS field. In the future, we will further explore how to optimize the adapter structure and parameter optimization strategy to adapt to FAS task in more complex scenarios.

Acknowledgement. This work is supported by the National Natural Science Foundation of China under Grant No.62372021, and the Open Competition Mechanism to Select the Best Candidates in Shijiazhuang, Hebei Province, China.

References

1. Anjos, A., Marcel, S.: Counter-measures to photo attacks in face recognition: a public database and a baseline. In: 2011 International Joint Conference on Biometrics (IJCB), pp. 1–7. IEEE (2011)
2. Bian, J., Peng, Y., Wang, L., Huang, Y., Xu, J.: A survey on parameter-efficient fine-tuning for foundation models in federated learning. arXiv preprint arXiv:2504.21099 (2025)
3. Boulkenafet, Z., Komulainen, J., Hadid, A.: Face anti-spoofing based on color texture analysis. In: 2015 IEEE International Conference on Image Processing (ICIP), pp. 2636–2640. IEEE (2015)
4. Boulkenafet, Z., Komulainen, J., Hadid, A.: Face antispoofing using speeded-up robust features and fisher vector encoding. IEEE Signal Process. Lett. **24**(2), 141–145 (2016)
5. Boulkenafet, Z., Komulainen, J., Li, L., Feng, X., Hadid, A.: OULU-NPU: a mobile face presentation attack database with real-world variations. In: 2017 12th IEEE International Conference on Automatic Face and Gesture Recognition (FG 2017), pp. 612–618. IEEE (2017)
6. Cai, L., et al.: ME-FAS: multimodal text enhancement for cross-domain face anti-spoofing. IEEE Trans. Inf. Forensics Secur. (2025)
7. Chingovska, I., Anjos, A., Marcel, S.: On the effectiveness of local binary patterns in face anti-spoofing. In: 2012 BIOSIG-Proceedings of the International Conference of Biometrics Special Interest Group (BIOSIG), pp. 1–7. IEEE (2012)
8. Cui, X., et al.: Lurking in the shadows: imperceptible shadow black-box attacks against lane detection models. In: International Conference on Knowledge Science, Engineering and Management, pp. 220–232. Springer (2024)
9. Dosovitskiy, A., et al.: An image is worth 16x16 words: transformers for image recognition at scale. arXiv preprint arXiv:2010.11929 (2020)
10. Du, Z., Li, J., Zuo, L., Zhu, L., Lu, K.: Energy-based domain generalization for face anti-spoofing. In: Proceedings of the 30th ACM International Conference on Multimedia, pp. 1749–1757 (2022)
11. Erdogmus, N., Marcel, S.: Spoofing 2d face recognition systems with 3D masks. In: in2013 International Conference of the BIOSIG SpecialInterest Group (BIOSIG). IEEE, pp. 1–8 (2013)
12. Guo, J., et al.: Domain generalization for face anti-spoofing via content-aware composite prompt engineering. arXiv preprint arXiv:2504.04470 (2025)

13. He, J., Zhou, C., Ma, X., Berg-Kirkpatrick, T., Neubig, G.: Towards a unified view of parameter-efficient transfer learning. arXiv preprint arXiv:2110.04366 (2021)
14. Hu, E.J., et al.: LoRA: Low-Rank adaptation of large language models. ICLR **1**(2), 3 (2022)
15. Huang, H.P., et al.: Adaptive transformers for robust few-shot cross-domain face anti-spoofing. In: European Conference on Computer Vision, pp. 37–54. Springer (2022)
16. Li, Z.: Asymmetric modality translation for face presentation attack detection. IEEE Trans. Multimedia **25**, 62–76 (2021)
17. Lin, K.H., Tseng, Y.W., Huang, K.Y., Wu, J.C., Cheng, W.H.: InstructFLIP: exploring unified vision-language model for face anti-spoofing. arXiv preprint arXiv:2507.12060 (2025)
18. Liu, M., et al.: Adversarial learning and decomposition-based domain generalization for face anti-spoofing. Pattern Recogn. Lett. **155**, 171–177 (2022)
19. Liu, S.Q., Wang, Q., Yuen, P.C.: Bottom-up domain prompt tuning for generalized face anti-spoofing. In: European Conference on Computer Vision, pp. 170–187. Springer (2024)
20. Liu, Y., Jourabloo, A., Liu, X.: Learning deep models for face anti-spoofing: binary or auxiliary supervision. In: Proceedings of the IEEE Conference on Computer Vision and Pattern Recognition, pp. 389–398 (2018)
21. Mahabadi, R.K., Ruder, S., Dehghani, M., Henderson, J.: Parameter-efficient multi-task fine-tuning for transformers via shared hypernetworks. arXiv preprint arXiv:2106.04489 (2021)
22. Niu, X., et al.: Video-based remote physiological measurement via cross-verified feature disentangling. In: Computer Vision–ECCV 2020: 16th European Conference, Glasgow, UK, August 23–28, 2020, Proceedings, Part II 16, pp. 295–310. Springer (2020)
23. Patel, K., Han, H., Jain, A.K.: Secure face unlock: spoof detection on smartphones. IEEE Trans. Inf. Forensics Secur. **11**(10), 2268–2283 (2016)
24. Qiao, T., Wu, J., Zheng, N., Xu, M., Luo, X.: FGDNet: fine-grained detection network towards face anti-spoofing. IEEE Trans. Multimedia **25**, 7350–7363 (2022)
25. Radford, A., et al.: Learning transferable visual models from natural language supervision. In: International Conference on Machine Learning, pp. 8748–8763. PmLR (2021)
26. Shao, R., Lan, X., Li, J., Yuen, P.C.: Multi-adversarial discriminative deep domain generalization for face presentation attack detection. In: Proceedings of the IEEE/CVF Conference on Computer Vision and Pattern Recognition, pp. 10023–10031 (2019)
27. Smith, D.F., Wiliem, A., Lovell, B.C.: Face recognition on consumer devices: reflections on replay attacks. IEEE Trans. Inf. Forensics Secur. **10**(4), 736–745 (2015)
28. Srivatsan, K., Naseer, M., Nandakumar, K.: Flip: Cross-domain face anti-spoofing with language guidance. In: Proceedings of the IEEE/CVF International Conference on Computer Vision, pp. 19685–19696 (2023)
29. Sung, Y.L., Nair, V., Raffel, C.A.: Training neural networks with fixed sparse masks. Adv. Neural. Inf. Process. Syst. **34**, 24193–24205 (2021)
30. Wang, L., et al.: Parameter-efficient fine-tuning in large language models: a survey of methodologies. Artif. Intell. Rev. **58**(8), 227 (2025)
31. Wang, X., et al.: TF-FAS: twofold-element fine-grained semantic guidance for generalizable face anti-spoofing. In: European Conference on Computer Vision, pp. 148–168. Springer (2024)

32. Wen, D., Han, H., Jain, A.K.: Face spoof detection with image distortion analysis. IEEE Trans. Inf. Forensics Secur. **10**(4), 746–761 (2015)
33. Yang, J., Lei, Z., Liao, S., Li, S.Z.: Face liveness detection with component dependent descriptor. In: 2013 International Conference on Biometrics (ICB), pp. 1–6. IEEE (2013)
34. Yang, X., et al.: Face anti-spoofing: model matters, so does data. In: Proceedings of the IEEE/CVF Conference on Computer Vision And Pattern Recognition, pp. 3507–3516 (2019)
35. Yu, J., et al.: Multi view slot attention using paraphrased texts for face anti-spoofing. arXiv preprint arXiv:2509.06336 (2025)
36. Yu, Z., Li, X., Niu, X., Shi, J., Zhao, G.: Face anti-spoofing with human material perception. In: Computer Vision–ECCV 2020: 16th European Conference, Glasgow, UK, August 23–28, 2020, Proceedings, Part VII 16, pp. 557–575. Springer (2020)
37. Yu, Z., et al.: Deep learning for face anti-spoofing: a survey. IEEE Trans. Pattern Anal. Mach. Intell. **45**(5), 5609–5631 (2022)
38. Zaken, E.B., Ravfogel, S., Goldberg, Y.: Bitfit: Simple parameter-efficient fine-tuning for transformer-based masked language-models. arXiv preprint arXiv:2106.10199 (2021)
39. Zhang, D., et al.: Parameter-efficient fine-tuning for foundation models. arXiv preprint arXiv:2501.13787 (2025)
40. Zhang, G., et al.: Interpretable face anti-spoofing: enhancing generalization with multimodal large language models. In: Proceedings of the AAAI Conference on Artificial Intelligence, vol. 39, pp. 9896–9904 (2025)
41. Zhang, K., Zhang, Z., Li, Z., Qiao, Y.: Joint face detection and alignment using multitask cascaded convolutional networks. IEEE Signal Process. Lett. **23**(10), 1499–1503 (2016)
42. Zhang, L., Qiao, T., Xu, M., Zheng, N., Xie, S.: Unsupervised learning-based framework for deepfake video detection. IEEE Trans. Multimedia **25**, 4785–4799 (2022)
43. Zhang, Y., et al.: CPL-CLIP: compound prompt learning for flexible-modal face anti-spoofing. In: 2024 IEEE International Joint Conference on Biometrics (IJCB), pp. 1–10. IEEE (2024)
44. Zhang, Y., et al.: Celeba-spoof: large-scale face anti-spoofing dataset with rich annotations. In: Computer Vision–ECCV 2020: 16th European Conference, Glasgow, UK, August 23–28, 2020, Proceedings, Part XII 16, pp. 70–85. Springer (2020)
45. Zhang, Z., et al.: A face antispoofing database with diverse attacks. In: 2012 5th IAPR International Conference on Biometrics (ICB), pp. 26–31. IEEE (2012)
46. Zhao, S., et al.: Blockchain-based decentralized federated learning: a secure and privacy-preserving system. In: 2021 IEEE 23rd International Conference on High Performance Computing and Communications; 7th International Conference on Data Science and Systems; 19th International Conference on Smart City; 7th International Conference on Dependability in Sensor, Cloud and Big Data Systems and Application (HPCC/DSS/SmartCity/DependSys), pp. 941–948. IEEE (2021)
47. Zhou, K., Yang, J., Loy, C.C., Liu, Z.: Conditional prompt learning for vision-language models. In: Proceedings of the IEEE/CVF Conference on Computer Vision and Pattern Recognition, pp. 16816–16825 (2022)
48. Zhou, K., Yang, J., Loy, C.C., Liu, Z.: Learning to prompt for vision-language models. Int. J. Comput. Vision **130**(9), 2337–2348 (2022)
49. Zhou, Q., et al.: Generative domain adaptation for face anti-spoofing. In: European Conference on Computer Vision, pp. 335–356. Springer (2022)

Mitigating Phishing Attacks Through Multi-layer Edge Task Offloading For Cyber-Physical Systems

Fang Lu[1](✉), Fan Liu[2], and Weizhi Meng[3]

[1] State Key Laboratory for Novel Software Technology, Nanjing University, Nanjing, China
602023320007@smail.nju.edu.cn

[2] Nanjing University of Science and Technology, Nanjing, China
fanliu@njust.edu.cn

[3] Lancaster University, Lancaster, UK
w.meng3@lancaster.ac.uk

Abstract. Cyber-Physical System (CPS) is a new generation of intelligent systems that integrate ubiquitous sensing, reliable communication, embedded computing, and intelligent control. It is a unified fusion of physical entities and the information space. The emergence of edge computing technologies has promoted the widespread deployment of CPS, making it possible to achieve distributed intelligence and real-time decision-making at the network edge. To address the issue of complex phishing attacks that are prevalent in edge networks, we propose a multi-layer dynamic task offloading defense framework named MLDTOPhishingDM. This framework adopts a lightweight machine learning-based threat detection approach, enabling secure and reliable phishing attack defense under resource-constrained conditions in distributed edge environments. The MLDTOPhishingDM framework also incorporates an adaptive computation offloading strategy and physical-layer security mechanisms. Specifically, it utilizes a pruned and optimized CatBoost classifier for local threat filtering, combined with a reinforcement learning-based strategy to optimize the trade-off between local processing and secure cloud offloading. Experimental results demonstrate that the proposed method achieves a threat detection accuracy of 97.4%. At the same time, the pruning technique reduces the model size by 98% while maintaining a detection accuracy of 91.3%. In addition, the adaptive strategy improves security by 1.07% while reducing battery consumption by 70.18%.

Keywords: Edge Network · Threat Detection · Machine Learning Model · Lightweight Model · Adaptive Strategy

1 Introduction

Cyber-Physical Systems (CPS) are systems used to monitor and control the physical world, regarded as the next generation of embedded control systems

L. Zhang and K.-K. R. Choo (Eds.): MobiQuitous 2025, LNICST 684, pp. 208–226, 2026.
https://doi.org/10.1007/978-3-032-22503-0_12

[1]. With digital transformation acceleration, CPS have become the backbone of modern industrial operations, integrating computational processes with physical world interactions [2]. Edge computing technologies facilitate widespread CPS deployment in power grids, manufacturing systems, transportation networks, and healthcare facilities . Edge computing-based CPS environments offer unprecedented advantages in reducing latency, optimizing bandwidth, and enabling localized decision-making [3,4].

However, the integration of human-machine interfaces with distributed edge networks has introduced new attack vectors. Phishing attacks have evolved into complex multistage attacks capable of infiltrating CPS networks through edge nodes involving human interaction [5]. The 2015 Ukraine power grid attack exemplifies this threat—attackers initiated breach through spear-phishing emails, then leveraged malware to conduct lateral movement, ultimately causing power distribution system shutdown [6,7]. Similarly, Stuxnet revealed the destructive potential of cyber-physical attacks exploiting both human factors and device vulnerabilities [8].

Existing solutions often focus solely on the network layer, while true CPS security requires simultaneous consideration of physical effects [9–11]. Most existing phishing detection systems are designed for traditional IT environments and fail to account for resource-constrained edge devices [12–14]. Current security frameworks generally lack dynamic adaptability, making it difficult to balance stringent energy and computational constraints while responding to evolving threats [15,16]. Recent studies show approximately 68% of edge security incidents can be attributed to credential leakage caused by phishing attacks [17].

To address these challenges, this paper proposes a phishing attack defense method for edge networks based on Multi-Layer Dynamic Task Offloading (MLDTOPhishingDM). Our main contributions are:

1. a lightweight machine learning-based threat detection model suitable for deployment in edge environments, using advanced pruning techniques to improve performance;
2. an adaptive computation offloading strategy that dynamically adjusts processing allocation based on resource availability and security requirements;
3. a physical-layer security mechanism that provides additional protection against experienced attackers.

The system uses reinforcement learning-based optimization to continuously adapt to evolving defense patterns and maintain optimal balance between security, energy consumption, and computational efficiency.

2 Related Work

Early phishing detection relied on maintaining blacklists of phishing URLs or extracting specific features [18]. With machine learning development, new detection techniques emerged. Liu proposed PhishLLM, leveraging large language models' implicit knowledge and semantic understanding to overcome traditional reference list limitations [19]. Saxe et al. proposed a neural network framework using character-level embeddings and convolutional neural networks for URL classification, reducing false positive rates [20]. Qiu et al. proposed a hybrid LSD model utilizing canopy feature selection with cross-fold validation, achieving better performance in precision, accuracy, and recall [21].

Deep learning advances led Yang et al. to propose fast phishing detection using multidimensional features [22]. Asgharinejad et al. first applied deep reinforcement learning to phishing detection, enabling autonomous strategy learning through environment interaction [23]. Chen et al. conducted the first comprehensive study on PTXPHISH on Ethereum, building the first real-world PTXPHISH dataset and proposing a rule-based detection approach achieving over 99% F1 score [24].

Due to single model limitations, researchers adopted hybrid approaches. Liu et al. designed a hybrid deep learning system not requiring phishing samples for training while achieving high accuracy [25]. Li et al. proposed KnowPhish, combining large language models with multimodal brand knowledge graphs [26].

For resource-constrained devices, Han et al. systematically proposed a compression framework combining pruning, quantization, and Huffman coding, reducing neural network storage by 35–49 times without affecting accuracy [27]. Greenewald et al. enhanced phishing detection by distilling large language models into smaller models for low-resource settings [28].

Adaptive methods in CPS focus on flexibility and effectiveness. Ben et al. proposed adaptive methods for embedded systems, improving inference accuracy while reducing inference time [29]. Task offloading became key technology for security detection in resource-limited environments [30,31]. Chen et al. introduced security-aware offloading strategies with threat assessment capabilities, balancing performance, energy consumption, and security objectives [32].

3 Our Proposed Method

Phishing attack detection on edge network devices requires consideration of factors such as the device's computational capability, energy consumption, and operational state. This paper proposes a Multi-Layer Dynamic Task Offloading-based Phishing Defense Method for Edge Networks (MLDTOPhishingDM), which is a comprehensive phishing detection approach that enables dynamic regulation of energy usage and computing power. The architecture of the framework is illustrated in Fig. 1. The proposed MLDTOPhishingDM method is designed for resource-constrained environments in edge networks and is divided into two main components. The first component involves optimizing a lightweight phishing website detection model using pruning techniques, which is then directly deployed on corresponding edge devices. The second component deploys a high-precision phishing attack detection model on edge network servers.

By implementing hierarchical detection, MLDTOPhishingDM can effectively provide comprehensive phishing attack detection while dynamically balancing resource overhead during operation. First, the lightweight phishing website detection model deployed on edge devices performs initial screening for phishing attacks by evaluating multiple features, including: whether the access is via IP address or domain name, whether HTTPS protocol is used, the presence of special characters, and whether HTTP redirection occurs. Based on the comprehensive evaluation of these features, if the result indicates a high-risk website, the access is immediately blocked by the edge device. For cases where the initial assessment is inconclusive, the request is forwarded to the second component: a high-precision phishing detection model deployed on the edge network server for further analysis. This model incorporates an adaptive computation offloading strategy and a physical-layer security mechanism. It assesses the load status of the edge network and can dynamically offload computation tasks to other servers to achieve load balancing. Additionally, a reinforcement learning approach is employed to continuously improve decision-making between local processing and secure offloading. This enables the system to optimize operations based on the resource status of the device, security requirements, and attack characteristics, ultimately achieving the dual goal of ensuring security and energy efficiency.

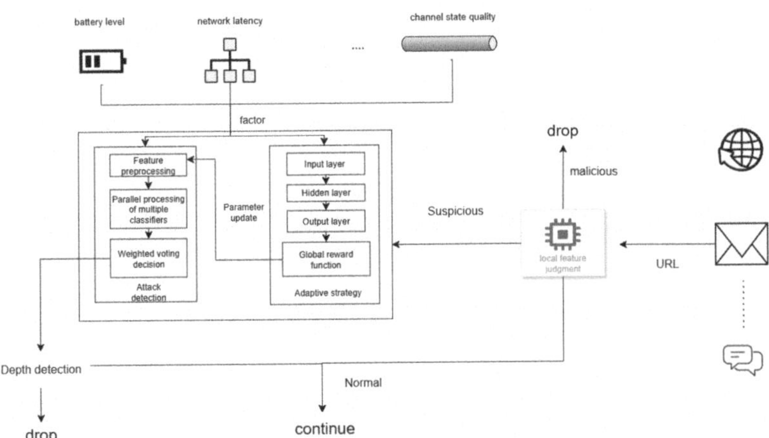

Fig. 1. Multi-Layer Dynamic Task Offloading-based Phishing Attack Defense Method for Edge Networks.

3.1 High-Precision Phishing Attack Detection Model

The phishing attack detection model deployed on the edge network servers needs to achieve high precision with low overhead. To meet these requirements, we conducted testing and comparison using multiple machine learning algorithms.

Gradient Boosting Classifier. Gradient Boosting is a type of boosting method. Its main idea is that each newly built model follows the direction of the gradient descent of the loss function based on the previously built model. Suppose the current model under the stage-wise approach is f(x), then the value of the negative gradient of the loss function L at f(x) is used as the residual in the boosting tree algorithm to fit a regression tree. Boosting constructs a strong classifier by combining multiple weak classifiers, typically through summation, as shown in the following form:

$$F_m(x) = f_0 + \alpha_1 f_1(x) + \alpha_2 f_2(x) + \alpha_3 f_3(x) + \cdots + \alpha_m f_m(x) \tag{1}$$

$\alpha_m = 0.7$ is a fixed learning rate used to suppress the impact of each iteration. $f_m(x)$ represents the prediction of the m-th decision tree.

Let $y = F_m(x)$, gradient descent optimization is performed by fitting the residuals (using the negative gradient of the loss function) to minimize the overall loss function:

$$r_i = -\frac{\partial L(y_i, f_{t-1}(x_i))}{\partial f_{t-1}(x_i)}, f_t = \arg\min_f \sum_{i=1}^{n} (h(x_i) - r_i)^2 \tag{2}$$

The splitting criterion maximizes information gain for each tree node:

$$IG(S, A) = H(S) - \sum_{v \in \text{Values}(A)} \frac{|S_v|}{|S|} H(S_v) \tag{3}$$

Algorithm 1: L_K_TreeBoost

Input: A feature set $X = \{x_1, x_2, ..., x_n\}$ where $x_i \in \mathbb{R}^d$,
and a corresponding label set $Y = \{y_1, y_2, ..., y_n\}$ where $y_i \in \{1, 2, ..., K\}$.
Output: Final predicted class $\tilde{y} = \arg\max_k F_k(x)$ where $F_k(x)$ is the model output for class k.
1 Initialize $F_{k,0}(x) = 0$ for all $k = 1, ..., K$
2 **for** $m = 1$ to M **do**
3 Compute $p_k(x) = \frac{\exp(F_k(x))}{\sum_{l=1}^{K} \exp(F_l(x))}$ for $k = 1, ..., K$
4 **for** $k = 1$ to K **do**
5 Compute residuals: $\tilde{y}_{ik} = y_{ik} - p_k(x_i)$ for $i = 1, ..., n$
6 Fit a regression tree with J terminal nodes to data $\{(x_i, \tilde{y}_{ik})\}_{i=1}^{n}$
7 For each leaf R_{jkm}, compute:
$$\gamma_{jkm} = \frac{K-1}{K} \cdot \frac{\sum_{x_i \in R_{jkm}} \tilde{y}_{ik}}{\sum_{x_i \in R_{jkm}} |\tilde{y}_{ik}|(1 - |\tilde{y}_{ik}|)}$$
8 Update: $F_{k,m}(x) = F_{k,m-1}(x) + \sum_{j=1}^{J} \gamma_{jkm} \cdot \mathbb{1}(x \in R_{jkm})$
9 **end for**
10 **end for**
11 **return:** $\tilde{y} = \arg\max_k F_k(x)$

We configured the model with max_depth=4 and learning_rate=0.7 to balance complexity and overfitting prevention. GBDT (Gradient Boosting Decision Tree) is an iterative decision tree algorithm. Its core idea is to train a new decision tree in each iteration to fit the residuals of the previous prediction results, thereby continuously improving the overall predictive performance of the model. The GBDT multiclass classification is presented **Algorithm 1** (L_K_TreeBoos).

CatBoost Classifier. CatBoost is a gradient boosting algorithm based on decision trees. It performs well in handling categorical features, missing data, and outliers. CatBoost adopts an adaptive cross-entropy loss function and utilizes ordered boosting (based on permutations), which gives it strong robustness and interpretability. The prediction at step t follows:

$$F_t(x) = F_{t-1}(x) + \alpha_t f_t(x) \tag{4}$$

where $\alpha_t = 0.1$ controls the contribution strength. The algorithm automatically processes categorical features through one-hot encoding and applies symmetric tree structure for regularization.

The loss function optimization incorporates: Ordered Target Statistics for categorical features; Oblivious trees to reduce overfitting; Gradient-based One-Side Sampling for acceleration.

CatBoost solves the gradient bias problem with the following **Algorithm 2**.

Algorithm 2: Model Update and Value Calculation for Gradient Estimation

Input: $\{(X_k, Y_k)\}_{k=1}^{n}$, ordered according to σ; the number of trees I.
Output: M_k, used to estimate the gradient of X_k, which is then used to score the result.

1. $M_i \leftarrow 0$ for $i = 1..n$
2. **for** $iter = 1$ **to** I **do**
3. **for** $i = 1$ **to** n **do**
4. **for** $j = 1$ **to** $i - 1$ **do**
5. $g_i = \frac{d}{da}\text{Loss}(y_j, a)\big|_{a=M_i(X_j)}$
6. $M = \text{LearnOneTree}((X_j, g_j)$ for $j = 1$ to $i - 1)$
7. $M_i = M_i + M$
8. **return** $M_1, M_2, ..., M_n$; $M_1(X_1), M_2(X_2), ..., M_n(X_n)$

XGBoost Classifier. XGBoost constructs a gradient boosting framework through weighted decision trees:

$$\hat{y}_i = \sum_{k=1}^{K} f_k(x_i), \quad f_k \in \mathcal{F} \tag{5}$$

The objective function combines loss minimization with regularization:

$$\mathcal{L}(\varphi) = \sum_i l(\hat{y}_i, y_i) + \sum_k \Omega(f_k) \tag{6}$$

where $\Omega(f) = \gamma T + \frac{1}{2}\lambda\|w\|^2$ controls model complexity.

AdaBoost Classifier. AdaBoost (Adaptive Boosting) sequentially applies weak learners to reweighted versions of the data. The algorithm assigns weights to training instances and adjusts them based on classification errors:

$$F_T(x) = \sum_{t=1}^{T} \alpha_t h_t(x) \tag{7}$$

Weight update rule for misclassified instances:

In round $t+1$, the weight of the i-th sample, denoted as $w_{i,t+1}$, is equal to its weight in round t,$w_{i,t}$, multiplied by an exponential factor:

$$w_{i,t+1} = w_{i,t} \cdot \exp\left(\alpha_t \cdot \mathbf{1}(y_i \neq h_t(x_i))\right) \tag{8}$$

where $\alpha_t = \frac{1}{2} \ln\left(\frac{1-\epsilon_t}{\epsilon_t}\right)$ and ϵ_t is the weighted error rate.

We configured the model with: Base estimator: Decision Tree with max_depth=1; Number of estimators: 50; Learning rate: 1.0.

J48 (C4.5) Decision Tree. The J48 algorithm, an implementation of C4.5, builds decision trees using entropy-based information gain. Information Gain (IG) is used to measure the improvement in information obtained by splitting a dataset based on a certain attribute. The calculation formula is as follows: the information gain of attribute A on dataset S, denoted as $IG(S, A)$, equals the original entropy $H(S)$ of the dataset minus the weighted average of the entropies $H(S_v)$ of the subsets S_v after splitting S based on each possible value v of attribute A. The weight is the ratio of the size of subset $|S_v|$ to the total number of samples $|S|$.

This value reflects the contribution of attribute A to reducing uncertainty during classification. The greater the information gain, the better the classification performance of the attribute.

The algorithm incorporates: gain ratio to handle attributes with many values; pruning mechanism (disabled in our experimentation with ccp_alpha=0.0); missing value handling through probabilistic split.

We evaluated all models using the metrics described in Table 1:

Table 1. Classification evaluation metrics and corresponding formulas.

Metric	Formula
Accuracy	$\frac{TP+TN}{TP+TN+FP+FN}$
Precision	$\frac{TP}{TP+FP}$
Recall	$\frac{TP}{TP+FN}$
F1_Score	$2 \cdot \frac{Precision \cdot Recall}{Precision+Recall}$

In classification tasks, TP (True Positive) refers to instances correctly predicted as positive, while TN (True Negative) are those correctly predicted as negative. FP (False Positive) occurs when the model incorrectly predicts a negative instance as positive (a false alarm), and FN (False Negative) means the model fails to identify a positive instance, predicting it as negative (a miss). These values form the basis of key evaluation metrics such as accuracy, precision, recall, and F1 score.

3.2 Model Compression Strategy

In the process of machine learning model construction, in order to effectively control the structural complexity of the CatBoost model in the growth phase, prevent the occurrence of overfitting phenomenon, and improve the generalization ability of the model, we adopt a triple strategy, i.e., depth-preferred growth restriction, tree integration scale approximation, and leaf node sample threshold control, to control the structure of the tree growth phase.

Pre-pruning Strategy. To control CatBoost model's complexity and prevent overfitting, we implemented three key pre-pruning strategies:

1. Depth limit: reducing the maximum depth of the decision tree to 3 levels (depth=3) reduces the maximum number of nodes, significantly reducing the single-tree complexity.
2. Integration size reduction: reduced the number of base trees. The learning rate was also increased to 0.15 (learning_rate=0.15) to compensate for the performance loss.
3. Leaf node threshold control: increase the minimum number of leaf node samples to 25 (min_data_in_leaf=25), split condition: If the number of samples in the current node $|S_node|$ is no less than 25 and the information gain (IG) is greater than 0, then splitting is allowed (split(node)=True),otherwise, splitting is not allowed (split(node)=False).

Regularization Optimization. The L2 regularization technique is used to balance the model complexity and prediction performance with an objective function:

$$L(T) = \sum_{i=1}^{n} l(y_i, \hat{y}_i) + \lambda \cdot \sum_{j=1}^{T} \frac{1}{2} \sum_{l=1}^{|T_j|} w_{jl}^2 \tag{9}$$

The L2 regularization factor is raised from 3 to 8 (l2_leaf_reg=8) to effectively control the leaf node weights and prevent overfitting.

Sampling Optimization. We conducted tests with different parameter settings to identify the optimal configuration for our experiments. We implemented a multilevel sampling strategy: Subsample sampling: subsample=0.6 (reduced from 0.8); Feature sampling: rsm=0.5 (randomly select 50% of features); Early stop mechanism.

3.3 Secure Edge Computing Environment Architecture

Device Model and State Representation. We design a heterogeneous edge computing environment consisting of multiple distributed edge devices, each with a comprehensive state vector. Each edge device has a ten-dimensional state representation containing operational and security parameters:

$s_i = [\beta_i, \gamma_i, \delta_i, \lambda_i, \rho_i, \sigma_i, \epsilon_i, \omega_i, \chi_i, \kappa_i]$, the state vector s_i represents the comprehensive status of device i, where β_i represents battery level, γ_i computation capacity, δ_i network latency, λ_i current load, ρ_i offload ratio, σ_i security level, ϵ_i eavesdropping risk, ω_i jamming resistance, χ_i channel state, and κ_i key freshness.

Physical Layer Security Metrics. Each device incorporates physical layer security characteristics including: channel state quality $\chi_i \in [0, 1]$ modeling signal propagation conditions; security level $\sigma_i \in [0, 1]$ representing overall security posture; eavesdropping risk $\epsilon_i \in [0, 1]$ quantifying vulnerability to information leakage; anti-jamming capability $\omega_i \in [0, 1]$ measuring resistance to interference attacks; beamforming capacity $b_i \in [0, 1]$ for spatial selectivity.

Implementation and Working Principle of Physical Layer Security Mechanisms. The implementation of physical layer security mechanisms in the proposed edge computing environment is based on a closed-loop process consisting of state perception, security evaluation, adaptive decision-making, and defensive execution. Specifically, each device collects real-time channel information and system parameters to form a comprehensive state vector, from which the security-related attributes such as channel quality, eavesdropping risk, jamming resistance, and key freshness are dynamically extracted. Based on these attributes, the system evaluates each device's security posture using a weighted formulation: $\sigma_i = 0.3\varphi_i + 0.2\kappa_i + 0.3\omega_i + 0.2(1 - \epsilon_i)$, where φ_i represents channel reciprocity quality. that integrates channel reciprocity, cryptographic key strength, and anti-jamming capability while penalizing high eavesdropping risks. This formulation not only integrates both physical channel characteristics and cryptographic robustness, but also explicitly penalizes high eavesdropping threats, thereby providing a more comprehensive assessment of device security. The weight configuration in the formulation is determined according to the relative importance of different security attributes in the edge environment. Specifically, channel reciprocity quality (φ_i) and anti-jamming capability (ω_i) are each assigned a weight of 0.3, as they directly reflect the physical-layer resilience of wireless links and are thus regarded as primary factors. Cryptographic key freshness (κ_i) is weighted at 0.2, recognizing its critical role in securing data exchange while accounting for the fact that key freshness and management are often reinforced at higher protocol layers. Finally, the eavesdropping risk (ϵ_i) is included with a penalty weight of 0.2, ensuring that devices with high exposure to interception are appropriately downgraded in the overall security evaluation.

In terms of the working principle, key freshness is modeled using an exponential decay function: κ_i which reflects the gradual weakening of cryptographic protection over time. The decay rate of 0.95 is selected to capture a moderate decline, ensuring that key strength remains effective for a reasonable duration while still reflecting its natural degradation in dynamic communication environments. Once κ_i falls below 0.5, the system triggers a periodic key refresh, or alternatively performs a random refresh with a probability of 0.1. This mechanism ensures both the security of the cryptographic keys and the overall resilience of the system. Meanwhile, artificial noise injection and beamforming are employed as proactive defenses: noise injection increases the difficulty of successful eavesdropping without degrading legitimate communication quality, while beamforming enhances spatial selectivity to reduce the exposure of signals to adversaries. Furthermore, devices dynamically adjust their jamming resistance capability through security investments, effectively strengthening resilience against interference in high-threat environments.

The overall working mechanism thus follows an adaptive feedback loop: (1) sensing the current device and channel states, (2) quantifying security level through multi-factor evaluation, (3) adjusting defense measures such as noise power and beamforming direction based on security investment decisions, and (4) updating parameters in real time as both device states and adversary strategies evolve. Through this closed-loop process, the system is capable of achieving a dynamic balance between energy efficiency and physical layer security, while maintaining robustness against eavesdropping and jamming attacks in heterogeneous and adversarial edge environments.

3.4 Adaptive Policy Learning Framework

Neural Network Architecture. For each device i, a dedicated policy network π_i is employed, implemented as a feedforward neural network that maps the 10-dimensional device state vector to a 2-dimensional action space: $\pi_i : \mathbb{R}^{10} \rightarrow [0,1]^2$.

The network architecture consists of an input layer with 10 neurons corresponding to the device state features, followed by two hidden layers with 128 and 64 neurons respectively, both using ReLU activation functions.

The output layer has 2 neurons with Sigmoid activation, producing the values $[\rho_i, \psi_i]$, ρ_i denotes the offload ratio and ψ_i represents the security investment parameter.

Policy Gradient Optimization. For each time step t, the policy loss is computed as:

$$L_i = -\log\left(\rho_i^{(t)}\right) \cdot r_i^{(t)} - \log\left(\psi_i^{(t)}\right) \cdot r_i^{(t)} \tag{10}$$

The local reward $r_i^{(t)}$ for device i at time t captures both operational efficiency and security objectives. It is defined as $r_i^{(t)} = 0.3\beta_i + 0.2(1+\delta_i)^{-1} + 0.2(1-\lambda_i) + 0.3\sigma_i$, where β_i represents the battery level, δ_i is the network latency, λ_i denotes the current load, and σ_i reflects the security level. This formulation balances energy status, latency, load, and security considerations in evaluating the device's performance.

Global Reward Function. The system-wide reward considers collective performance and security:

$$R_{\text{global}} = 0.3\bar{\beta} + 0.2\bar{\tau} + 0.2\Phi + 0.3(R_{\text{security}} - P_{\text{adversary}}) \tag{11}$$

where: $\bar{\beta} = \frac{1}{N}\sum_{i=1}^{N}\beta_i$, $\bar{\beta}$ represents the average battery level; $\bar{\tau} = \frac{1}{N}\sum_{i=1}^{N}\frac{1}{1+\delta_i}$, $\bar{\tau}$ represents the average latency reward; $\Phi = 1 - \text{std}(\{\lambda_i\}_{i=1}^{N})$, Φ represents the load balance metric; $R_{\text{security}} = \frac{1}{N}\sum_{i=1}^{N}\sigma_i$, R_{security} represents the average security level; $P_{\text{adversary}}$ represents the adversary success probability.

Adversary Characterization. The adversary is modeled with an activity probability $p_{\text{active}} = 0.3$, an attack strength $\alpha \in [0, 1]$, and can adopt one of three attack types: eavesdropping, jamming, or a hybrid of both. The adversary adapts its strategy at a rate $\eta = 0.1$. The success rate of an attack is defined by Equation as $P_{\text{success}} = \alpha \cdot (1 - \bar{\sigma})$, where $\bar{\sigma}$ represents the average security level across devices. The attack strength is dynamically adjusted according to Equation: $\alpha_{t+1} = \max(0.2, \min(0.9, \alpha_t + \eta(1 - P_{\text{success}})))$, allowing the adversary to become more aggressive when its attacks are less effective, while keeping α bounded within a reasonable range.

Security Investment Strategy. Security measures in the system include artificial noise injection, where the noise power is dynamically adjusted according to $p_{\text{noise}} = \max(0.1, \min(0.5, p_{\text{noise}} + 0.3\psi_i))$, based on the device's security investment ψ_i. Additionally, jamming resistance is enhanced over time following the update rule $\omega_i^{(t+1)} = \max\left(0.5, \min\left(1.0, \omega_i^{(t)} + 0.2\psi_i\right)\right)$.

We evaluate three distinct scenarios:

1. High Threat Environment: Adversary presence $p_{\text{active}} = 0.7$, strength $\alpha = 0.7$.
2. Resource Constrained: Limited battery $\beta_i \in [0.3, 0.6]$, reduced computation capacity.
3. Heterogeneous Deployment: Devices grouped into three categories with varying security-energy tradeoffs.

We compare our adaptive policy against static baseline configurations with fixed parameters: Static offload ratio: $\rho_{\text{static}} = 0.5$; Static security investment: $\psi_{\text{static}} = 0.3$.

We use the following performance metrics:

1. System performance is evaluated using:

$$\text{Efficiency Improvement} = \frac{R_{\text{adaptive}} - R_{\text{static}}}{R_{\text{static}}} \times 100\% \tag{12}$$

2. Security effectiveness measured by:

$$\text{Adversary Reduction} = \frac{P_{\text{success}}^{\text{static}} - P_{\text{success}}^{\text{adaptive}}}{P_{\text{success}}^{\text{static}}} \times 100\% \tag{13}$$

3. Battery efficiency quantified as:

$$\text{Battery Improvement} = \frac{\bar{\beta}_{\text{adaptive}} - \bar{\beta}_{\text{static}}}{\bar{\beta}_{\text{static}}} \times 100\% \tag{14}$$

4 Experiments and Results

4.1 Performance Testing

In the evaluation, we used the publicly available Phishing dataset from kaggle (https://www.kaggle.com/eswarchandt/phishingwebsite-detector). Based on the original dataset containing 11,054 entries, filtering was performed to retain approximately 10,000 valid samples with distinct features. Each data sample consists of 32 feature dimensions. In the public dataset, the feature labels are defined as follows: [1] represents a legitimate website; [0] represents a suspicious website; [-1] indicates that the feature is identified as a phishing website. After statistical analysis of the dataset, it was found that phishing websites account for approximately 44.36%, while legitimate websites account for approximately 55.64%. The median and standard deviation of their 32 feature dimensions are shown in Fig. 2.

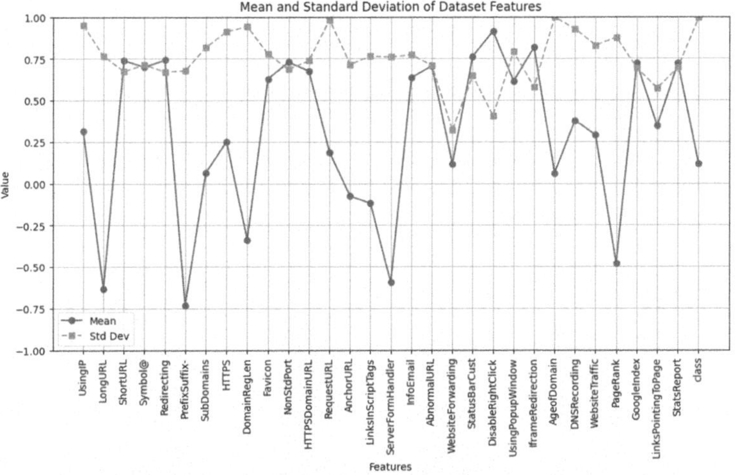

Fig. 2. Mean and Standard Deviation of Dataset Features.

Due to the limited number of data samples, the dataset was divided into a training set (80%) and a test set (20%).Cross-validation was not applied, and the five machine learning models were evaluated as shown in Table 2.

The dataset exhibits varying performance across different models. Among them, boosting-based classifiers such as CatBoost, Gradient Boosting, and

Table 2. Performance Comparison of ML Models

ML Model	Accuracy	F1_Score	Recall	Precision
CatBoost Classifier	0.974	0.977	0.989	0.966
XGBoost Classifier	0.971	0.974	0.983	0.965
Gradient Boosting Classifier	0.966	0.969	0.974	0.963
J48 (C4.5)	0.958	0.961	0.960	0.962
AdaBoost	0.924	0.930	0.935	0.924

XGBoost all achieved accuracy scores exceeding 0.966, F1-scores above 0.969, recall rates over 0.974, and precision above 0.963. The CatBoost classifier demonstrated the best overall performance, with an accuracy of 0.974, an F1-score of 0.977, a recall rate exceeding 0.989, and a precision rate above 0.966. In contrast, the J48 (C4.5) and AdaBoost models showed relatively weaker performance. While the J48 (C4.5) model maintained more balanced results across all metrics, AdaBoost exhibited lower values in all performance indicators, reflecting relatively poor overall effectiveness.

We comprehensively evaluated the impact of pruning on the Catboost model. As shown in Fig. 3, although the pruned Catboost model slightly decreases in performance metrics, with accuracy decreasing from 0.974 to 0.913, F1-score decreasing from 0.977 to 0.921, recall decreasing from 0.989 to 0.913, and precision decreasing from 0.966 to 0.930, it still maintains a good performance. As Table 3 shows the significant improvement in inference efficiency, the inference time of the pruning model is reduced from 0.0035 s to 0.0019 s when processing 10,000 samples, which is 1.8 times faster. Table 4 shows a significant reduction in model complexity and memory usage: the number of nodes is reduced from 63,000 to 560 (a 99.1% reduction), and memory usage is reduced from 1.07MB to 0.02MB (a 98.1% reduction).

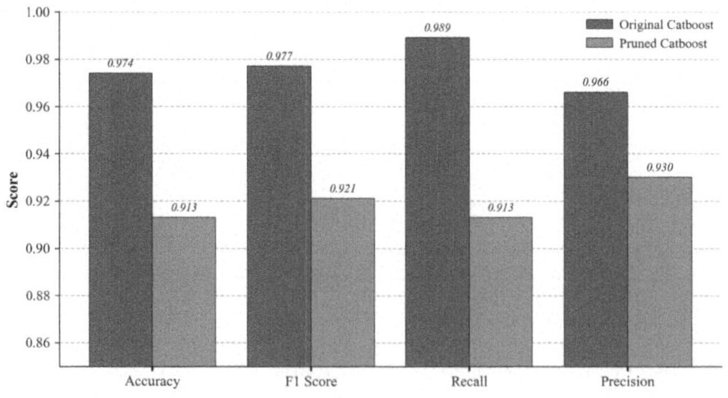

Fig. 3. Model Performance Comparison After Pruning.

Table 3. Inference Time Comparison between Original and Pruned CatBoost

Model	Inference Time (s)	Relative Time (%)	Speedup
Original CatBoost	0.0035	100.0%	1.0x
Pruned CatBoost	0.0019	54.3%	1.8x

Table 4. Pruning Effects on Model Complexity and Memory Usage

Metric	Original Model	Pruned Model	Reduction
Node Count	63,000	560	99.1%
Memory Usage	1.07 MB	0.02 MB	98.1%

Figure 4 explores the multidimensional performance characteristics of the edge computing system in a resource-constrained environment. The global reward gradually stabilizes from the initial peak of 0.8 to 0.625. At the same time, the energy consumption of the seven devices reached a critical value of about 0.2, and the system then automatically enforces a high offloading policy (converging to 1.0) to cope with the energy bottleneck. The network latency of each device shows random fluctuations in the range of 0.01 to 0.08. It should be noted that, despite resource constraints, the system maintains a high security level of 0.75 to 1.0, the adversary success probability is maintained at a low level, and the security incentive coefficient is stabilized in the range of 0.8 to 0.9, which fully validates the system's ability to maintain security under resource-constrained conditions.

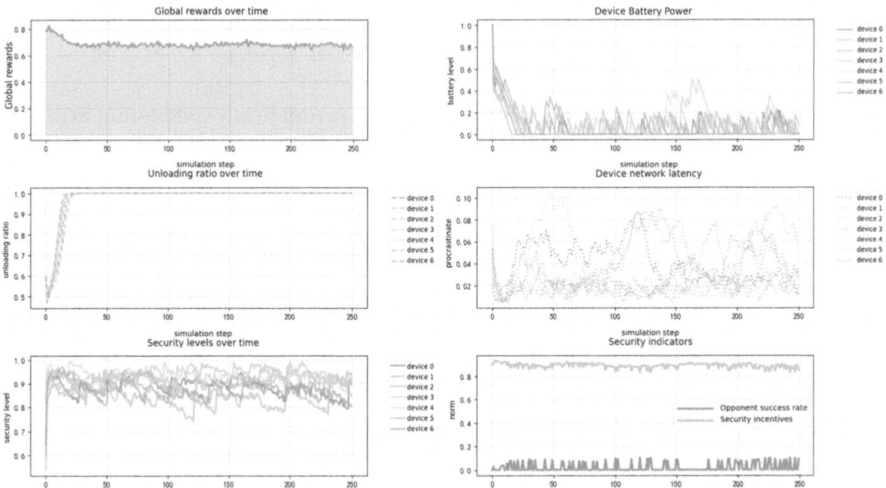

Fig. 4. Multidimensional Performance Characterization and Security Maintenance Mechanisms for Edge Computing Systems in Resource Constrained Environments.

Comparison experiments between adaptive and static offloading strategies shown in Fig. 5 indicate that the global incentives of both strategies decrease from 0.75 and converge to a stable interval of approximately 0.6, with relatively significant fluctuations in the adaptive strategy. In terms of safety level, both perform similarly (0.8 to 0.9), but the adaptive strategy gradually shows advantages in the later stage. At the energy consumption level, both strategies exhibit rapid depletion within 25 steps, which indicates the inevitability of energy consumption for a given workload. In the adversary resistance test, the adaptive strategy presents a lower adversary success rate in the later stage, which confirms the superiority of its dynamic security adjustment mechanism in the long-term operation (especially in the dynamic change scenario of the network environment).

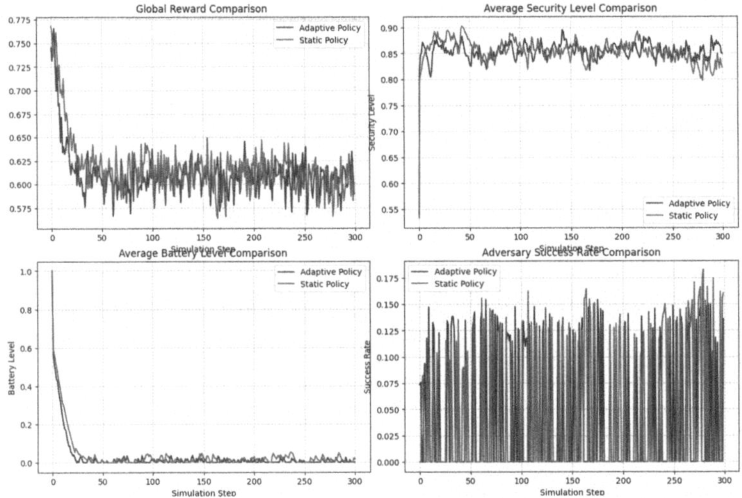

Fig. 5. Comparative Performance Analysis of Adaptive and Static Offloading Strategies in Dynamic Network Environments.

Table 5 analyses the comparison between adaptive and static strategies by precise values for four key metrics. In terms of system efficiency, the two perform nearly the same (0.674 vs. 0.688), indicating that the adaptive mechanism does not have a significant impact on the overall efficiency; in terms of security level, the adaptive strategy has a slight advantage (0.889 vs. 0.904), which verifies the effect of its security optimization; the energy consumption indexes show that the static strategy retains a slightly higher amount of electricity (0.035 vs. 0.048), which reflects that there is a certain amount of energy consumption in the self-adaptive security mechanism has certain energy cost: The most significant difference is reflected in the success rate of the adversary, the adaptive policy significantly reduces the security threat (0.020 vs. 0.019), which confirms its effective trade-off between security and resource utilization from a quantitative perspective, and provides an important empirical reference for the selection of security policies in edge computing environments.

Table 5. Security Policy Optimization for Edge Computing: Quantitative Evaluation of Performance Metrics for Adaptive and Static Methods

Performance Metric	Adaptive Policy	Static Policy
System Efficiency	0.674	0.688
Security Level	0.889	0.904
Battery Level	0.035	0.048
Adversary Success Rate	0.020	0.019

By comparing the performance of different models on the publicly available phishing website detection dataset from Kaggle, the results demonstrate (Table 6) that the Hybird LSD model with Canopy feature selection outperforms all the other machine learning models. Furthermore, the evaluation of the proposed model shows that its performance remains on par with most state-of-the-art approaches. At the same time, the model maintains a relatively lightweight structure, making it well-suited for deployment in resource-constrained edge networks. Hence, the proposed method successfully achieves its intended objectives while ensuring computational efficiency.

Table 6. Performance Comparison of Models

Models	Accuracy	F1-score	Recall	Precision
MLDTOPhishingDM	0.969	0.972	0.978	0.965
Hybird LSD model with Canopy feature selection	0.981	0.959	0.963	0.973
Decision Tree	0.954	0.959	0.960	0.958
Random Forest	0.967	0.971	0.975	0.967
Naive Bayes	0.884	0.889	0.837	0.949

4.2 Sensitivity Analysis for System Robustness

Through sensitivity analysis of the system under varying attack intensities, we validated the robustness and effectiveness of the proposed method. Experimental results demonstrate that the system exhibits controlled performance degradation patterns as attack activity and strength increase. Even under extreme threat conditions, the system maintains over 75% security level while effectively controlling adversary success rates below 7%. More importantly, the adaptive strategy shows significant advantages over traditional static approaches, achieving 10-20%

improvements in system efficiency, security level, and global performance, with a particularly notable 37% reduction in adversary success rates. These findings confirm that the system possesses excellent adaptability and attack resistance capabilities, enabling stable operation in complex and dynamic threat environments while providing reliable security guarantees for practical deployment.

5 Conclusions

This study introduced the MLDTOPhishingDM approach, designed to tackle the security, energy, and computational challenges posed by phishing attacks in resource-constrained edge networks. MLDTOPhishingDM conducts a comparative evaluation of multiple machine learning algorithms to select the model with the highest detection accuracy. By leveraging a dataset of 10,000 samples, the CatBoost boosting algorithm demonstrated outstanding detection performance, achieving an accuracy of 0.974. After applying model pruning techniques, the model size was reduced by 98% while maintaining an accuracy above 91.3%, and the inference speed effectively doubled. Simulations of the edge network environment revealed that the adaptive offloading strategy outperformed static approaches. While maintaining similar system efficiency (0.674 vs. 0.688), it achieved a 1.07% increase in security and a 70.18% reduction in energy consumption. Despite faster energy depletion, the adaptive strategy sustained a high level of security (ranging from 0.75 to 1.0) and kept the adversary success rate low (0.020 vs. 0.019), highlighting its strong balance between security and resource efficiency for next-generation edge computing.

References

1. Humayed, A., Lin, J., Li, F., Luo, B.: Cyber-Physical systems security–a survey. IEEE Internet Things J. **4**(6), 1802–1831 (2017). https://doi.org/10.1109/JIOT.2017.2703172
2. Lee, J., Bagheri, B., Kao, H.A.A.: Cyber-physical systems architecture for industry 4.0-based manufacturing systems. Manuf. Lett. **3**, 18–23 (2015). https://doi.org/10.1016/j.mfglet.2014.12.001
3. Shi, W., Cao, J., Zhang, Q., et al.: Edge computing: vision and challenges. IEEE Internet Things J. **3**(5), 637–646 (2016). https://doi.org/10.1109/JIOT.2016.2579198
4. Sánchez, J.M.G., Jörgensen, N., Törngren, M., et al.: Edge computing for cyber-physical systems: a systematic mapping study emphasizing trustworthiness. ACM Trans. Cyber-Physical Syst. (TCPS) **6**(3), 1–28 (2022). https://doi.org/10.1145/3539662
5. Sahay, R., Meng, W., Li, W.: A comparative analysis of phishing tools: features and countermeasures. In: Xia, Z., Chen, J. (eds) Information Security Practice and Experience. ISPEC 2024. Lecture Notes in Computer Science, vol. 15053. Springer, Singapore (2025). https://doi.org/10.1007/978-981-97-9053-1_21
6. Alert, D.: Cyber-attack against Ukrainian critical infrastructure. Cybersecurity Infrastructure Security Agency, Washington, DC, USA, Technical Report ICS Alert (IR-ALERT-H-16-056-01) (2016)

7. Pollard, M.: A case study of Russian cyber-attacks on the Ukrainian power grid: implications and best practices for the United States. Pepperdine Policy Rev. **16**(1), 1 (2024)
8. Langner, R.: Stuxnet: dissecting a cyberwarfare weapon. IEEE Secur. Priv. **9**(3), 49–51 (2011). https://doi.org/10.1109/MSP.2011.67
9. Duo, W., Zhou, M.C., Abusorrah, A.: A survey of cyber attacks on cyber physical systems: recent advances and challenges. IEEE/CAA J. Automatica Sinica **9**(5), 784–800 (2022). https://doi.org/10.1109/JAS.2022.105548
10. Cardenas, A.A., Amin, S., Sastry, S.: Secure control: towards survivable cyber-physical systems. In: 2008 The 28th International Conference on Distributed Computing Systems Workshops, pp. 495–500 IEEE (2008). https://doi.org/10.1109/ICDCS.Workshops.2008.40
11. Zhang, Y., Wang, L., Sun, W., et al.: Distributed intrusion detection system in a multi-layer network architecture of smart grids. IEEE Trans. Smart Grid **2**(4), 796–808 (2011). https://doi.org/10.1109/TSG.2011.2159818
12. Amin, S., Litrico, X., Sastry, S., et al.: Cyber security of water SCADA systems–Part I: analysis and experimentation of stealthy deception attacks. IEEE Trans. Control Syst. Technol. **21**(5), 1963–1970 (2012). https://doi.org/10.1109/TCST.2012.2211873
13. Basit, A., Zafar, M., Liu, X., et al.: A comprehensive survey of AI-enabled phishing attacks detection techniques. Telecommun. Syst. **76**, 139–154 (2021). https://doi.org/10.1007/s11235-020-00733-2
14. Salahdine, F., Kaabouch, N.: Social engineering attacks: a survey. Future Internet **11**(4), 89 (2019). https://doi.org/10.3390/fi11040089
15. Chen, M., Hao, Y., Li, Y., et al.: On the computation offloading at ad hoc cloudlet: architecture and service modes. IEEE Commun. Mag. **53**(6), 18–24 (2015). https://doi.org/10.1109/MCOM.2015.7120041
16. Butun, I., Österberg, P., Song, H.: Security of the internet of things: vulnerabilities, attacks, and countermeasures. IEEE Commun. Surv. Tutorials **22**(1), 616–644 (2019). https://doi.org/10.1109/COMST.2019.2953364
17. Dragos, I.: ICS/OT Cybersecurity Year in Review 2022. Hanover, MD, USA, Dragos (2023)
18. Zhang, Y., Hong, J., Cranor, L.F.: CANTINA: a content-based approach to detecting phishing web sites. In: Proceedings of the 16th International Conference on World Wide Web (2007). https://doi.org/10.1145/1242572.1242660
19. Liu, R., et al.: Less defined knowledge and more true alarms: reference-based phishing detection without a pre-defined reference list. In: Proceedings of the 33rd USENIX Security Symposium (USENIX Security 24), pp. 523–540. Philadelphia, PA: USENIX Association (2024)
20. Saxe, J., Berlin, K.: eXpose: A character-level convolutional neural network with embeddings for detecting malicious URLs, file paths and registry keys. arXiv preprint. arXiv:1702.08568 (2017)
21. Qiu, H., Dong, C., Sato, I.: Federated learning based phishing email detection model. In: 2020 IEEE Access (2020). https://doi.org/10.1109/ACCESS.2020.3042685
22. Yang, P., Zhao, G., Zeng, P.: Phishing website detection based on multidimensional features driven by deep learning. IEEE Access **7**, 15196–15209 (2019). https://doi.org/10.1109/ACCESS.2019.2892066

23. Asgharinejad, E., Asgari, S., Dehghantanha, A., Karimipour, H., Choo, K.K.R.: Detecting phishing websites through deep reinforcement learning. J. Ambient Intell. Humanized Comput. **11**(11), 5301–5312 (2020). https://doi.org/10.1109/COMPSAC.2019.10211
24. Chen, Z., et al.: Dissecting payload-based transaction phishing on Ethereum. In: Proceedings of the NDSS Symposium 2025 (2025). https://doi.org/10.14722/ndss.2025.230311
25. Lin, Y., Liu, R., Divakaran, D.M., et al.: Phishpedia: a hybrid deep learning based approach to visually identify phishing webpages. In: Proceedings of the 30th USENIX Security Symposium (USENIX Security 21), pp. 3793–3810 (2021)
26. Li, Y., et al.: KnowPhish: large language models meet multimodal knowledge graphs for enhancing reference-based phishing detection. In: Proceedings of the 33rd USENIX Security Symposium (USENIX Security 24), pp. 793–810. Philadelphia, PA: USENIX Association (2024)
27. Han, S., Mao, H., Dally, W.J.: Deep compression: compressing deep neural networks with pruning, trained quantization and Huffman coding. arXiv preprint arXiv:1510.00149 (2015)
28. Greenewald, C., Ashmore, B., Poon, C.S., Chen, L.: 2-in-1 Phishing detection via large LM Distillation and small LM perturbation (student abstract). In: Proceedings of the AAAI Conference on Artificial Intelligence, vol. 39, no. 28, pp. 29374–29376 (2025). https://doi.org/10.1609/aaai.v39i28.35256
29. Taylor, B., Marco, V.S., Wolff, W., Elkhatib, Y., Wang, Z.: Adaptive deep learning model selection on embedded systems. SIGPLAN Not. **53**(6), 31–43 (2018). https://doi.org/10.1145/3299710.3211336
30. Jacob, B., Kligys, S., Chen, B., et al.: Quantization and training of neural networks for efficient integer-arithmetic-only inference. In: Proceedings of the IEEE Conference on Computer Vision and Pattern Recognition, pp. 2704–2713 (2018)
31. Mao, Y., Zhang, J., Letaief, K.B.: Dynamic computation offloading for mobile-edge computing with energy harvesting devices. IEEE J. Sel. Areas Commun. **34**(12), 3590–3605 (2016). https://doi.org/10.1109/JSAC.2016.2611964
32. Chen, X., Jiao, L., Li, W., et al.: Efficient multi-user computation offloading for mobile-edge cloud computing. IEEE/ACM Trans. Netw. **24**(5), 2795–2808 (2015). https://doi.org/10.1109/TNET.2015.2487344

Cryptographic Schemes

Do Not Keep Guessing: Enhanced Secure Cloud Storage with Keyword Search and Deduplication

Meng Wu[1], Boan Yu[1], Kai Zhang[1(✉)], and Zhimei Sui[2(✉)]

[1] Faculty of Artificial Intelligence, Shanghai University of Electric Power, Shanghai, China
kzhang@shiep.edu.cn

[2] School of Computer Engineering and Science, Shanghai University, Shanghai, China
zmsui@shu.edu.cn

Abstract. Secure outsourcing of identical data by multiple senders inevitably leads to certain redundancy in cloud storage, which reduces the efficiency of keyword search over encrypted data. Therefore, supporting both keyword search and deduplication with a single encrypted copy is crucial for efficient and secure cloud storage. However, existing solutions that combine public-key encryption with keyword search and message-locked encryption (MLE) are vulnerable to online guessing attacks on keywords, encrypted data and passwords, where the inherent key management problem for senders and receivers remains unresolved. To tackle these limitations, we propose TRIGGERED, an enhanced secure and efficient cloud storage system with keyword search and data deduplication. Technically, we employ a rate-limiting mechanism and a flexible key server group update strategy to support dynamic changes in key servers and mitigate online keyword guessing attacks, brute-force attacks, and dictionary guessing attacks. By introducing a novel MLE key-based layered encryption mechanism, the sender-side key storage is effectively reduced. Additionally, it enables the receiver to recover the key on any terminal in a device-aided model to mitigate key exposure risks during key migration. TRIGGERED is evaluated on Raspberry Pi and a real cloud platform with a public dataset. It enhances security while reducing encryption cost by 2.67× and decryption time by 13.33% over the state-of-the-art.

Keywords: Secure Cloud Storage · Message-Locked Encryption · Deduplication · Keyword Search

1 Introduction

Cloud storage has become a prominent solution for data outsourcing and high-quality data services, which offers substantial reductions in data storage and management costs. For example, for enterprise document sharing systems [17],

L. Zhang and K.-K. R. Choo (Eds.): MobiQuitous 2025, LNICST 684, pp. 229–248, 2026.
https://doi.org/10.1007/978-3-032-22503-0_13

a project manager (i.e., sender) outsources project documents and associated keywords to the cloud and a colleague (i.e., receiver) can efficiently retrieve target documents via keyword search. However, studies indicate that approximately 75% of cloud-stored data is redundant [11], which severely decreases data processing efficiency and increases the receiver's search complexity. Therefore, performing both keyword search and deduplication over cloud storage ensures that only a single copy of the outsourced data is stored and searched. To further enable data confidentiality, an effective solution is to perform data deduplication and retrieval in an encrypted domain, where the methodologies of public key encryption with keyword search (PEKS) [4] and message-locked encryption (MLE) [2] are combined and applied for achieving both data deduplication and keyword-based retrieval on encrypted content, such as Li et al.'s work [14] and DULCET [13]. Generally, they employ users' low-entropy passwords as a fundamental seed for authentication mechanisms and encryption key generation, thus such systems are susceptible to dictionary guessing attacks. To further enhance the security for *secure cloud storage with keyword search and deduplication*, we summarize the following research questions (RQs):

RQ1 How to Resist Online/Offline Guessing Attacks on Keywords, Encrypted Data, and Passwords? The offline attacks imply that an adversary performs keywords, encrypted data, and passwords matching with all candidates; while online attacks indicate that the adversary uses guessed inputs to impersonate users and interact with the cloud and key servers to extract sensitive information. Generally, online attacks are more harmful than offline ones, since they exploit system interactions to gain more information. To resist offline guessing attacks on keywords and encrypted data, existing solutions typically employ the server-aided mechanism for key generation [5], which employs an oblivious protocol between the user and key servers to derive encryption keys. The works SPADE [19] and SEPSE [20] mitigate exhausted queries for launching online attacks through rate limiting and key server group update, but only for either deduplication or keyword search. Very recently, DULCET [13] uses server-aided mechanisms to resist offline brute-force attacks on encrypted data (BFA) and keyword guessing attacks (KGA), which additionally addresses dictionary guessing attacks on passwords (DGA) through password-based authentication with the receiver's manual confirmation. However, existing solutions cannot be directly combined with SPADE and SEPSE to address the online guessing attacks on keywords, encrypted data, and passwords (i.e., KGA, BFA, and DGA).

RQ2 How to Effectively Address the Key Management Problem of Both Sender and Receiver? Secure storage of the sender's MLE key and migration of the receiver's key across different terminals are crucial for secure cloud storage with keyword search and deduplication. On one hand, the sender needs to maintain a unique deduplication key (i.e., MLE key) for every outsourced data, which results in a linear growth in the number of MLE keys relative to the amount of data. Unlike traditional public database settings, where the sender encrypts the MLE key with the receiver's public key to

Table 1. Features Comparison with Other Schemes

Work	Resistance to KGA	Resistance to BFA	Resistance to DGA	Solution to KMP
SEPSE [20]	online & offline	-	-	✗
SPADE [19]	-	online & offline	online & offline	sender
Li et al. [14]	✗	✗	-	✗
DULCET [13]	offline	offline	online & offline	receiver
TRIGGERED	online & offline	online & offline	online & offline	sender & receiver

In the table, "KMP" denotes key management problem; "-" denotes not applicable.

avoid local storage, it is both reasonable and necessary in many practical cloud storage systems (e.g., collaborative environments) for the sender to retain the ability to decrypt their own outsourced data. On the other hand, the receiver is required to access data from multiple terminals, increasing the risk of key exposure due to the storage and migration of secret keys across different terminals. Although SPADE [19] addresses it via using password-based layered encryption that enables the sender to encapsulate MLE keys with a password and store the password locally, it only considers the scenario of data deduplication. DULCET [13] mitigates key migration risks by allowing the receiver to recover the key through a personal device and password, but the time overhead of MLE key management on the sender-side is relatively high.

Starting Point. To address RQ1 and RQ2, we adopt a unified system model that reflects real-world cloud storage scenarios involving both private and shared data access. Unlike SPADE, which focuses on MLE key management in private databases, or DULCET, which enables key recovery in public services like email, our design models senders and receivers as users with distinct roles and complementary key management needs under a unified framework. Trivially extending existing solutions seems ineffective and even infeasible. In particular, to resist the concerned online guessing attacks, a natural approach is to combine SPADE (against online BFA and DGA) with SEPSE and DULCET (against online KGA and online DGA), however, a trivial combination is ineffective and even infeasible due to the inherent incompatibilities for handling password mechanisms. Specifically, the receiver's password is required for both keyword-related key generation via authenticating with the key server and interactively recovering password-derived keys with the terminal, where the password reuse may lead to leakages and subsequent compromise of secret keys. To address the key management problems of both senders and receivers, a straightforward approach is to combine the existing SPADE and DULCET. Specifically, the sender encrypts the MLE key using a password-derived authentication credential while the receiver encrypts it via a public key, which leads to redundant MLE key encapsulation and decryption operations and introduces inconsistency in MLE keys during key recovery. Thus, the dual mechanism not only increases computation overhead but may also lead to attacks (e.g., implicit denial-of-service), where honest users cannot access their data due to decryption failures.

1.1 Our Results

To positively answer two RQs, we propose an enhanced secure cloud storage system with keyword search and deduplication, particularly addressing TRIple Guessing attacks on keyword sEaRch and dEDuplication, *termed as* TRIGGERED. Besides, it eliminates the key management problem for both senders and receivers. In particular, main contributions introduced by TRIGGERED can be outlined as follows:

1. **Resistance to triple online/offline guessing attacks.** It resists triple online/offline guessing attacks, i.e., KGA, BFA and DGA, where any adversary cannot guess sensitive information for possible low-entropy keywords, encrypted data and passwords. In particular, it employs a server-aided mechanism for key generation that prevents adversaries from performing offline exhaustive guesses on keywords and encrypted data. Additionally, it supports a flexible key server group update strategy at different epochs, with support for the dynamic changes in the number of key servers at each epoch. Thus, the encrypted data and keywords remain searchable and deduplicable, even when protected by different key server groups across different epochs. Meanwhile, TRIGGERED enhances the rate-limiting mechanism by considering the number of MLE key requests, keyword key requests, and receiver key recovery requests per epoch, which prevents unauthorized access and abuse from online adversaries.
2. **New mechanism to solve key management problem.** It proposes a novel MLE key-based layered encryption mechanism to reduce local MLE key storage overhead for senders, and introduces a device-aided key recovery method to eliminate key exposure risks during key migration of receivers. In particular, it encapsulates each MLE key within an additional encryption layer containing only a single random bilinear group element, where the encryption overhead is only associated with the amount of outsourcing data but is independent of the number of receivers. Additionally, there is only one tuple encrypted under a public key that is jointly derived from both the sender and receiver, while another tuple encapsulates the receiver's public key with added randomness. Consequently, both the sender and receiver can retrieve the MLE key using only an individual secret key, which effectively simplifies key management without compromising security.

Comparison. Table 1 shows a comparison between related work and TRIGGERED. Generally, TRIGGERED effectively addresses three online and offline guessing attacks, i.e., KGA, BFA and DGA. Additionally, it reduces sender-side MLE key storage overhead via a MLE key-based layered encryption strategy. We remark that SEPSE [20] neglects the data deduplication function and a device-aided key recovery mechanism, thus BFA and DGA are not applicable. Similarly,

KGA is not applicable for SPADE [19] and DGA is not applicable for [14]. Compared to SPADE's password-based encryption and authentication mechanisms, TRIGGERED offers both improved efficiency and enhanced security guarantees.

Organization. Section 2 reviews preliminaries and Sect. 3 presents problem formulation. Section 4 and Sect. 5 describe construction and security proof of TRIGGERED, respectively. Section 6 gives the performance analysis, and Sect. 7 discusses related work. Section 8 concludes this work.

2 Preliminaries

Notations. Let κ be the security parameter, and denote a negligible function by $negl(\kappa)$. n and t represent the total number and threshold of the key servers $\mathcal{KS}$, respectively. $\mathcal{KS}^{\pi}$ and $\mathcal{KS}^{\pi+1}$ denote the key server groups in the π-th and $(\pi+1)$-th epochs, respectively. PPT refers to probabilistic polynomial time.

Definition 1 (Bilinear Pairing). *Let $\mathbb{G}$ and $\mathbb{G}_T$ be two cyclic groups of prime order p, with g being a generator of $\mathbb{G}$. An efficiently computable bilinear map $e : \mathbb{G} \times \mathbb{G} \rightarrow \mathbb{G}_T$ is defined to have two key properties: bilinearity: for any $g_1, g_2 \in \mathbb{G}$, $\alpha, \beta \in Z_p$, there is $e(g_1^{\alpha}, g_2^{\beta}) = e(g_1, g_2)^{\alpha\beta}$; and the property of non-degeneracy: $e(g_1, g_2) \neq 1$.*

Definition 2 (MLE [2]). *Message-locked encryption (MLE) is a symmetric-key encryption scheme where both the encryption and decryption keys are generated from the data itself. It enables encrypted data deduplication, as distinct users can produce identical ciphertexts for identical data.*

Definition 3 (SAS-MA [12]). *Short-authentication-string message authentication (SAS-MA) allows the sender to securely send a message m to the receiver, who can verify its integrity using two communication channels: a public channel and a short-authentication-string (SAS) channel. The public channel facilitates the transfer of messages of arbitrary size, but it remains vulnerable to man-in-the-middle attacks. In contrast, the SAS channel transmits short, fixed-length messages (as large as t' bits, e.g., 20 bits), which are assumed to be resistant to adversarial modification, where t' denotes the SAS channel capacity. A SAS-MA scheme achieves security when a PPT adversary's chance of making the receiver accept a tampered message is bounded by $2^{-t'} + negl(\kappa)$.*

Definition 4 (DSGA [13]). *The distributed secret generation algorithm (DSGA) receives the security parameter, overall count of key servers (i.e., n), and the threshold value (i.e., t) as input. It outputs a shared secret (i.e., s), with each server holding a secret share. The public key and all public shares are then published. The protocol proceeds as follows:*

i) Each $\mathcal{KS}_i$ $(1 \leq i \leq n)$ generates a $(t-1)$-degree polynomial over $\mathbb{Z}_p$, $u_i(x) = a_{i,0} + a_{i,1}x + \cdots + a_{i,t-1}x^{t-1}$, where $a_{i,k} \in \mathbb{Z}_p$ $(0 \leq k \leq t-1)$ are selected at random.

ii) $\mathcal{KS}_i$ *publishes the verification parameters* $\{g^{a_{i,k}}\}$ *and then computes* $u_i(j)$ *and securely transmits them to* $\mathcal{KS}_j$ $(1 \leq j \leq n, j \neq i)$.
iii) *When* $\mathcal{KS}_i$ *obtains* $u_j(i)$ *from* $\mathcal{KS}_j$ $(1 \leq j \leq n, j \neq i)$*, it verifies* $u_j(i)$ *by checking whether the following equation holds:* $g^{u_j(i)} \stackrel{?}{=} \prod_{k=0}^{t-1} g^{a_{j,k} \cdot i^k}$
iv) *If all* $u_j(i)$ *are valid,* $\mathcal{KS}_i$ *computes* $u_i(i)$*, its secret share* $s_i = sk_i = \sum_{j=1}^{n} u_j(i)$*, public share* $pk_i = g^{s_i}$ *and* $pk = \prod_{i=1}^{n} g^{a_{i,0}}$*. Otherwise, the process terminates.*

3 Problem Formulation

3.1 System Model

As shown in Fig. 1, the TRIGGERED system includes the following entities:

- **Senders ($\mathcal{S}$):** They request MLE and keyword keys from the $\mathcal{KS}$, use these keys to encrypt the data file and its corresponding keyword set, outsource the ciphertext to $\mathcal{CS}$ and subsequently download the data.
- **Cloud server ($\mathcal{CS}$):** It stores the ciphertext of $\mathcal{S}$, performs data deduplication, facilitates keyword-based searches for $\mathcal{R}$ (or $\mathcal{T}$) on encrypted files, and assists $\mathcal{S}$ in data retrieval.
- **Key Servers ($\mathcal{KS}$):** They assist senders and receivers generate keywords for encryption and derive MLE keys.
- **Receivers ($\mathcal{R}$):** Each receiver possesses a password and a personal device $\mathcal{D}$ (e.g., a smartphone) that assists the terminal $\mathcal{T}$ in recovering $\mathcal{R}$'s secret key. Then $\mathcal{T}$ requests a search keyword key from the key server and generates a trapdoor for the search query.

3.2 Threat Model

In the threat model, we identify three types of adversaries. For the external adversaries, any attack that they launched can be performed by the adversarial cloud server. Therefore, if the adversarial cloud server can be resisted, the external adversary can also be thwarted.

- *Adversarial Cloud Server:* It may perform BFA, KGA and DGA attacks to compromise the confidentiality of outsourced data and keywords, and impersonate the terminal to obtain the receiver's secret key. It is also a rational party that may not launch attacks if its profits cannot be increased.
- *Compromised key server(s):* They may be compromised or collude to obtain the sensitive information of outsourced data and keywords. Similar to [9], we assume the number of compromised key servers remains below a predefined threshold in a given epoch, which is released at the start of a new epoch.
- *Man-in-the-Middle (MitM) Adversaries:* They may impersonate the receiver to launch DGA on passwords and request corresponding secret keys during key recovery. We assume that the receiver's keys are securely stored on personal devices that are not physically accessed by the MitM adversary, where we do not consider attacks on the device itself.

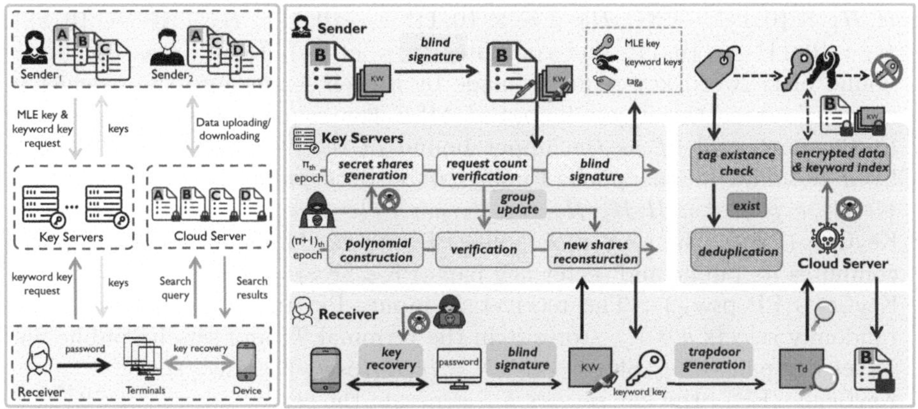

Fig. 1. System Model

4 TRIGGERED: System Description

Below, we describe the formal construction of TRIGGERED that consists of the following phases: *system initialization, data outsourcing, data search, decryption,* and *key server group update*. As shown in Fig. 1, the sender first generates a blind signature to the data and its keyword set prior to their upload to the cloud. Then, the sender performs requests for the MLE key and keyword encryption keys from the key server and generates a data tag for subsequent deduplication queries in the cloud. The cloud checks whether the tag already exists in its storage directory, and performs deduplication if the match holds, where the MLE key can no longer be stored on the sender side after data encryption. To perform a keyword search, the receiver inputs their password into any terminal that communicates with the personal device to recover the receiver's decryption key. By the key, the terminal generates a blind signature on the keyword and sends a request to the key server for the corresponding keyword key. These keys are used to generate trapdoors for keyword searches, which ensures effective encrypted data retrieval. We note that both the sender and receiver apply blind signatures before making key requests. In addition, the key server adds another layer of blind signature and periodically updates its secret shares, thereby preventing adversaries from extracting any useful information from compromised interactions.

4.1 System Initialization Phase

This phase includes system setup (i.e., Setup) and different entities generate their public and secret keys (i.e., KeyGen). Additionally, let $\mathbb{G}$ and $\mathbb{G}_{\mathbb{T}}$ be groups of prime order p, and let $e : \mathbb{G} \times \mathbb{G} \rightarrow \mathbb{G}_{\mathbb{T}}$ be a bilinear map. These are defined by the global bilinear parameters $\{\mathbb{G}, \mathbb{G}_{\mathbb{T}}, e, p, g\}$.

– $\mathsf{Setup}(\kappa)$: Given a security parameter κ, the system generates the global bilinear parameters $\mathbb{G}, \mathbb{G}_{\mathbb{T}}, e, p, g$ and selects collision-resistant hash functions:

$H, H_1 : \{0,1\}^* \to \mathbb{G}$, $H_2 : \mathbb{G} \times \{0,1\}^* \to \{0,1\}^\kappa$, $H_3 : \mathbb{G} \to \{0,1\}^\kappa$, $H_4 : \{0,1\}^* \to \{0,1\}^\kappa$ and computes $\varpi = e(g,g)$. Define ρ as the upper bound of keyword key requests made by a each sender and the receiver in an epoch, τ as the upper bound of MLE key requests made by a sender in an epoch and cf as the upper bound of receiver's key requests made by a terminal in an epoch. Finally, it outputs public parameters: $\mathsf{PP} = \{\mathbb{G}, \mathbb{G}_\mathbb{T}, e, p, g, \varpi, u, H, H_1, H_2, H_3, H_4, \rho, \tau, cf\}$.

- $\mathsf{KeyGen}_\mathcal{S}(\mathsf{PP})$: The sender $\mathcal{S}$ inputs PP and randomly selects $x \in \mathbb{Z}_p$ and computes its public and secret key pair $(\mathsf{PK}_\mathcal{S}, \mathsf{SK}_\mathcal{S}) = (g^x, x)$.
- $\mathsf{KeyGen}_\mathcal{R}(\mathsf{PP}, \mathsf{psw}_\mathcal{R})$: The receiver $\mathcal{R}$ inputs PP and password $\mathsf{psw}_\mathcal{R}$ and randomly selects $b \in \mathbb{Z}_p$, stores it in the terminal $\mathcal{T}$, and sets its public and secret key pair $(\mathsf{PK}_\mathcal{R}, \mathsf{SK}_\mathcal{R}) = (g^\gamma, \gamma = H(H_1(\mathsf{psw}_\mathcal{R})^b \parallel \mathsf{psw}_\mathcal{R}))$.
- $\mathsf{KeyGen}_{\mathcal{KS}}(\mathsf{PP})$: the key servers $\mathcal{KS}$ generate the server-side secret $\mathsf{SK}_{\mathcal{KS}}^{\mathsf{MLE}} = \alpha$ via $\mathsf{DSGA}()$ (c.f., Definition 4), with each key server $\mathcal{KS}_i$ holding share $\mathsf{SK}_{\mathcal{KS}_i}^{\mathsf{MLE}} = \alpha_i$ and computing the public key $\mathsf{PK}_{\mathcal{KS}}^{\mathsf{MLE}} = g^\alpha$, sharing $\mathsf{PK}_{\mathcal{KS}_i}^{\mathsf{MLE}} = g^{\alpha_i}$. Similarly, $\mathcal{KS}$ generate the keyword server-side secret $\mathsf{SK}_{\mathcal{KS}}^{\mathsf{KW}} = \beta$ via the $\mathsf{DSGA}()$ (c.f., Definition 4), with $\mathcal{KS}_i$ holding share $\mathsf{SK}_{\mathcal{KS}_i}^{\mathsf{KW}} = \beta_i$ and computing public key $\mathsf{PK}_{\mathcal{KS}}^{\mathsf{KW}} = g^\beta$, sharing $\mathsf{PK}_{\mathcal{KS}_i}^{\mathsf{KW}} = g^{\beta_i}$. $\mathcal{KS}_i$ keeps a record of the number of keywords requested by $\mathcal{S}$ (denoted by $\rho_\mathcal{S}$) and $\mathcal{R}$ (denoted by $\rho_\mathcal{S}$) and the number of MLE key requested by $\mathcal{S}$ (denoted by $\tau_\mathcal{S}$). Initially, $\rho_\mathcal{S} = 0$, $\rho_\mathcal{R} = 0$ and $\tau_\mathcal{S} = 0$.

4.2 Data Outsourcing Phase

During this phase, the sender requests the MLE and keyword keys for the outsourced data from the key servers. Then, the sender interacts with the cloud server for data deduplication and uploads the encrypted data.

(1) MLE and Keyword Key Generation. $\mathcal{S}$ provides the data M and keyword set $\{\mathsf{kw}_j\}_{j\in[T]}$ to interact with $\mathcal{KS}$, generating the MLE key ek_M and keyword keys $\mathsf{dw}_{\mathsf{kw}_j}$.

- $\mathcal{S}$ randomly selects $k, \{r_j\}_{j\in[T]} \in \mathbb{Z}_p$, computes $M' = H_1(M)^k$ and $\mathsf{kw}'_j = H_1(\mathsf{kw}_j)^{r_j}$ for each $j \in [T]$, and then sends M' and $\{\mathsf{kw}'_j\}_{j\in[T]}$ to $\mathcal{KS}_i$.
- $\mathcal{KS}_i$ checks if $\tau_\mathcal{S} \le \tau \wedge \rho_\mathcal{S} \le \rho$. If the condition is not met, it aborts. Otherwise, $\mathcal{KS}_i$ generates signatures σ_i and $d_{i,j}$ on M' and kw'_j using $\mathsf{SK}_{\mathcal{KS}}^{\mathsf{MLE}}$ and $\mathsf{SK}_{\mathcal{KS}}^{\mathsf{KW}}$, as $\sigma_i = M'^{\mathsf{SK}_{\mathcal{KS}}^{\mathsf{MLE}}} = M'^{\alpha_i}, d_{i,j} = \mathsf{kw}_j'^{\mathsf{SK}_{\mathcal{KS}}^{\mathsf{KW}}} = \mathsf{kw}_j'^{\beta_i}$. Then, it updates the counters $\tau_\mathcal{S}++$ and $\rho_\mathcal{S}++$, and replies with σ_i and $d_{i,j}$ to $\mathcal{S}$.
- $\mathcal{S}$ verifies σ_i and $d_{i,j}$ by checking $e(\sigma_i, g) \stackrel{?}{=} e(M', \mathsf{PK}_{\mathcal{KS}_i}^{\mathsf{MLE}})$; $e(d_{i,j}, g) \stackrel{?}{=} e(\mathsf{kw}'_j, \mathsf{PK}_{\mathcal{KS}_i}^{\mathsf{KW}})$ If the verification fails, $\mathcal{S}$ rejects σ_i and $d_{i,j}$. Otherwise, it stores them locally. After collecting t valid signatures (denoted as $\{\sigma_1, \sigma_2, \ldots, \sigma_t\}$ and $\{d_{1,j}, d_{2,j}, \ldots, d_{t,j}\}$), $\mathcal{S}$ computes $\sigma_\mathcal{S}$ and d_j using $\sigma_\mathcal{S} = (\prod_{\varsigma=1}^t \sigma_\varsigma^{\omega_\varsigma})^{k^{-1}}$ and $d_j = (\prod_{\varsigma=1}^t d_\varsigma^{\omega_\varsigma})^{r_j^{-1}}$, where $\omega_\varsigma = \prod_{1\le\eta\le t, \eta\ne\varsigma} \frac{\eta}{\eta-\varsigma}$.

- $\mathcal{S}$ verifies the correctness of $\sigma_{\mathcal{S}}$ and d_j by checking $e(\sigma_{\mathcal{S}}, g) \stackrel{?}{=} e(H_1(M), \mathsf{PK}_{\mathcal{KS}}^{\mathsf{MLE}})$ and $e(d_j, g) \stackrel{?}{=} e(H_1(\mathsf{kw}_j), \mathsf{PK}_{\mathcal{KS}}^{\mathsf{KW}})$.
  If the verification fails, $\mathcal{S}$ rejects $\sigma_{\mathcal{S}}$ and d_j; otherwise, it derives the MLE key as $\mathsf{ek}_M = H_2(\sigma_{\mathcal{S}} \parallel M)$, the keyword key as $\mathsf{dw}_{\mathsf{kw}_j} = H_2(d_j \parallel \mathsf{kw}_j)$, and the data tag as $\mathsf{tag}_M = H_3(\sigma_{\mathcal{S}})$.

(2) Encryption. The sender $\mathcal{S}$ encrypts the data via running the Enc algorithm and then uploads both the encrypted data and its keyword index to the cloud.

- $\mathsf{Enc}(\mathsf{PP}, M, \mathsf{SK}_{\mathcal{S}}, \mathsf{dw}_{w_j}, \mathsf{PK}_{\mathcal{R}}, \mathsf{PK}_{\mathcal{S}})$: $\mathcal{S}$ uses MLE key ek_M to compute $C_1 = \mathsf{SEnc}(\mathsf{ek}_M, M)$ and selects $\mu, \omega \in \mathbb{Z}_p$ to encapsulate ek_M as $\mathsf{enk}_M = \mathsf{ek}_M \cdot \varpi^{\mu}$, and then computes $C_2 = \mathsf{PK}_{\mathcal{S}}^{\mu\omega}$, $C_3 = \mathsf{PK}_{\mathcal{R}}^{\mu\omega}$ and $C_4 = \mathsf{PK}_{\mathcal{R}}^{(\mathsf{SK}_{\mathcal{S}}\omega)^{-1}}$. Next, $\mathcal{S}$ selects $\iota \in \mathbb{Z}_p$ and computes encrypted keyword index: $I_1 = \mathsf{PK}_{\mathcal{R}}^{\iota}$ and $I_{2,j} = \mathsf{dw}_{\mathsf{kw}_j}^{\mathsf{SK}_{\mathcal{S}}} \cdot g^{\iota}$. Finally, $\mathcal{S}$ sends the ciphertext $\mathsf{CT} = (C, I) = ((C_1, C_2, C_3, C_4, \mathsf{enk}_M), (I_1, I_{2,j}))$ to $\mathcal{CS}$.

(3) Deduplication. $\mathcal{CS}$ maintains a global storage data $L_{\mathcal{G}}$ to store the outsourced data, which consists of data tag, data ciphertext $C = (C_1, C_2, C_3, \mathsf{enk}_M)$ and encrypted keyword index $I = (I_1, I_{2,j})$. Note that the same data may have multiple encrypted keyword indexes due to different keyword sets chosen by the different senders. Since the tag values for the same data are identical, $\mathcal{S}$ first sends the data tag $\mathsf{tag}_M = H_3(\sigma_{\mathcal{S}})$ to $\mathcal{CS}$ for deduplication. If $\mathsf{tag}_M \notin L_{\mathcal{G}}$, it indicates that $\mathcal{S}$ performs encryption to upload the complete ciphertext, which implies that the data has not been stored in $\mathcal{CS}$. Conversely, if $\mathsf{tag}_M \in L_{\mathcal{G}}$, the data is already stored in $\mathcal{CS}$, and its ciphertext C_1 is not re-uploaded, where only the encrypted keyword index and other ciphertexts are uploaded. Additionally, $\mathcal{S}$ also stores tag_M locally.

4.3 Data Search Phase

In this phase, the receiver chooses a terminal to interact with the device and recover the receiver's key. The terminal then communicates with the key server to retrieve the keyword search key, which is used to generate a trapdoor. Finally, the trapdoor initiates a search query to the cloud.

(1) Secret Key Recovery. $\mathcal{R}$ inputs its password $\mathsf{psw}_{\mathcal{R}}$ into terminal $\mathcal{T}$, which communicates with device $\mathcal{D}$ to recover the secret key $\mathsf{SK}_{\mathcal{R}}$. The details are described as follows.

- $\mathcal{T}$ randomly selects $e \in \mathbb{Z}_p$, $R_{\mathcal{T}} \in \{0,1\}^{t'}$, and $z \in \{0,1\}^{c}$, then calculates the blinded password $\mathsf{psw}'_{\mathcal{R}} = H_1(\mathsf{psw}_{\mathcal{R}})^e$ and the commitment $\mathsf{Com}_1 = H_4(\mathsf{psw}'_{\mathcal{R}} \parallel R_{\mathcal{T}} \parallel z)$. Finally, $\mathcal{T}$ sends $(\mathsf{psw}'_{\mathcal{R}}, \mathsf{Com}_1)$ to $\mathcal{D}$.

- Upon receiving $(\mathsf{psw}'_{\mathcal{R}}, \mathsf{Com}_1)$, $\mathcal{D}$ first checks whether $cf_{\mathcal{R}} \leq cf$, where $cf_{\mathcal{R}}$ is initially set to 0. If this condition is not satisfied, $\mathcal{D}$ aborts the process. Otherwise, it randomly selects $R_{\mathcal{D}} \in \{0,1\}^{t'}$, updates the counter as $cf_{\mathcal{R}}++$, and sends $R_{\mathcal{D}}$ to $\mathcal{T}$.
- $\mathcal{T}$ then computes $\Phi_{\mathcal{T}} = R_{\mathcal{T}} \oplus R_{\mathcal{D}}$, sends $(R_{\mathcal{T}}, z)$ to $\mathcal{D}$, and transmits $\Phi_{\mathcal{T}}$ via the $\mathcal{T}$-to-$\mathcal{D}$ SAS channel.
- $\mathcal{D}$ computes the value $\Phi_{\mathcal{D}} = R_{\mathcal{T}} \oplus R_{\mathcal{D}}$ and verifies $\Phi_{\mathcal{T}} \stackrel{?}{=} \Phi_{\mathcal{D}}$ and $\mathsf{Com}_1 \stackrel{?}{=} H_4(\mathsf{psw}'_{\mathcal{R}} \parallel R_{\mathcal{T}} \parallel z)$ where $\Phi_{\mathcal{T}}$ is obtained through the SAS channel. If either of the checks fails, $\mathcal{D}$ terminates the process. Otherwise, it computes $\vartheta' = \mathsf{psw}'^{b}_{\mathcal{R}}$ and transmits it to $\mathcal{T}$.
- $\mathcal{T}$ computes $\vartheta = \vartheta'^{e^{-1}}$ and derives the secret key as $\mathsf{SK}_{\mathcal{R}} = H(\vartheta || \mathsf{psw}_{\mathcal{R}}) = H(H_1(\mathsf{psw}_{\mathcal{R}})^b || \mathsf{psw}_{\mathcal{R}})$.

(2) Keyword Key Generation. Given a requested keyword kw, the receiver $\mathcal{R}$ communicates with the key server to retrieve the corresponding keyword key.

- $\mathcal{T}$ communicates with the key servers to generate the keyword key of kw (i.e., $sd_{\mathsf{kw}} = H_2(H_1(\mathsf{kw})^{\beta} || \mathsf{kw})$), following the same procedure as $\mathcal{S}$ does in MLE and Keyword Key Generation, where $\mathcal{T}$ plays the role of $\mathcal{S}$.

(3) Keyword Search. $\mathcal{T}$ computes trapdoor sets to search the encrypted data.

- $\mathcal{T}$ first randomly selects $\Delta \in \mathbb{Z}_p$, then computes the trapdoor set: $\mathsf{Td}^* = e(sd_{\mathsf{kw}}^{\Delta \mathsf{SK}_{\mathcal{R}}}, \mathsf{PK}_{\mathcal{S}})$, $\mathsf{Td}_1 = g^{\Delta \mathsf{SK}_{\mathcal{R}}}$, and $\mathsf{Td}_2 = g^{\Delta}$. The trapdoor used to query $\mathcal{CS}$ is defined as $\mathsf{Td} = (\mathsf{Td}^*, \mathsf{Td}_1, \mathsf{Td}_2)$.
- $\mathcal{CS}$ checks $\mathsf{Td}^* \cdot e(\mathsf{Td}_2, I_1) \stackrel{?}{=} e(I_{2,j}, \mathsf{Td}_1)$. If the equation has a correct result, $\mathcal{T}$ has found a matching file.

4.4 Decryption Phase

The $\mathcal{T}$ and $\mathcal{S}$ decrypt the encrypted data as follows:

- $\mathsf{Dec}_{\mathcal{T}}(\mathsf{PP}, C_1, C_2, C_4, \mathsf{enk}_M, \mathsf{SK}_{\mathcal{R}})$: $\mathcal{T}$ derives the key by computing $\mathsf{ek}_M = \mathsf{enk}_M \cdot e(C_2, C_4)^{-(\mathsf{SK}_{\mathcal{R}})^{-1}}$, then decrypts to get $M = \mathsf{SDec}(\mathsf{ek}_M, C_1)$.
- $\mathsf{Dec}_{\mathcal{S}}(\mathsf{PP}, C_1, C_3, C_4, \mathsf{enk}_M, \mathsf{SK}_{\mathcal{S}})$: $\mathcal{S}$ derives the key by computing $\mathsf{ek}_M = \mathsf{enk}_M \cdot e(C_3, C_4^{-1})^{-\mathsf{SK}_{\mathcal{S}}^{-1}}$, then decrypts to get $M = \mathsf{SDec}(\mathsf{ek}_M, C_1)$.

4.5 Key Server Group Update Phase

We use the migration method from [19] to migrate a secret key across two $\mathcal{KS}$ groups at the end of an epoch. Suppose that $\{\mathcal{KS}_i^{\pi}\}$ $(1 \leq i \leq n_1)$ denotes the πth epoch key server group, which shares the server-side secret $\mathsf{SK}_{\mathcal{KS}}^{\mathsf{MLE}} = \alpha$ and $\mathsf{SK}_{\mathcal{KS}}^{\mathsf{KW}} = \beta$ using the $\mathsf{DSGA}()$ protocol (cf. Definition 4) under a (n_1, t_1)-threshold setting. The migration process redistributes the secret α and β among the $(\pi+1)$th epoch key server group $\{\mathcal{KS}_j^{\pi+1}\}$ $(1 \leq j \leq n_2)$.

- The process begins with the selection of t_1 honest key servers in the πth epoch key server group $\{\mathcal{KS}_i^{\pi}\}$ $(1 \leq i \leq t_1)$. Each $\{\mathcal{KS}_j^{\pi+1}\}$ generates a (t_2-1)-degree polynomial $d_i(x) = b_{i,0} + b_{i,1}x + \cdots + b_{i,t_2-1}x^{t_2-1}$ and $l_i(x) = c_{i,0} + c_{i,1}x + \cdots + c_{i,t_2-1}x^{t_2-1}$ over $\mathbb{Z}_p$, where $b_{i,0} = \alpha_i$ and $c_{i,0} = \beta_i$ are the secret key and the $b_{i,k}$ and $c_{i,k}$ $(0 \leq k \leq t_2-1)$ are chosen randomly.
- Each selected $\mathcal{KS}_i^{\pi}$ publishes the verification parameters $\{g^{b_{i,k}}\}$ and $\{g^{c_{i,k}}\}$, computes $d_i(j)$ and $l_i(j)$ and sends them to $\{\mathcal{KS}_j^{\pi+1}\}$ $(1 \leq j \leq n_2)$ via secure channels.
- When a $\{\mathcal{KS}_j^{\pi+1}\}$ obtains t_1 values, it computes the Lagrange coefficients $w_i^* = \prod_{\substack{1 \leq \gamma \leq t_1 \\ \gamma \neq i}} \frac{\gamma}{\gamma - i}$ for $1 \leq i \leq t_1$, and performs the following verifications: $g^{d_i(j)} \stackrel{?}{=} \prod_{k=0}^{t_2-1} g^{b_{i,k} \cdot j^k}$ and $\mathsf{PK}_{\mathsf{KS}_i}^{\mathsf{MLE}} \stackrel{?}{=} \prod_{i=1}^{t_1} (\mathsf{PK}_{\mathsf{KS}_i}^{\mathsf{MLE}})^{w_i^*}$, as well as $g^{l_i(j)} \stackrel{?}{=} \prod_{k=0}^{t_2-1} g^{c_{i,k} \cdot j^k}$ and $\mathsf{PK}_{\mathsf{KS}_i}^{\mathsf{KW}} \stackrel{?}{=} \prod_{i=1}^{t_1} (\mathsf{PK}_{\mathsf{KS}_i}^{\mathsf{KW}})^{w_i^*}$. If all verifications are valid, the current $\{\mathcal{KS}_j^{\chi+1}\}$ notifies other servers. Otherwise, the process stops.
- Each $\{\mathcal{KS}_j^{\pi+1}\}$ computes its secret share and public shares according to the following equations: $\mathsf{SK}_{\mathsf{KS}_j}^{\mathsf{MLE}} = \alpha_j^* = \sum_{i=1}^{t_1} w_i^* \cdot d_i(j)$, $\mathsf{PK}_{\mathsf{KS}_j}^{\mathsf{MLE}} = g^{\alpha_j^*}$, $\mathsf{SK}_{\mathsf{KS}_j}^{\mathsf{KW}} = \beta_j^* = \sum_{i=1}^{t_1} w_i^* \cdot l_i(j)$, and $\mathsf{SK}_{\mathsf{KS}_j}^{\mathsf{KW}} = g^{\beta_j^*}$.

5 Correctness Analysis and Security Analysis

This section presents the correctness and security of the TRIGGERED system.

5.1 Correctness Analysis

Correctness Analysis of the Keyword Search Phase:

$$\mathsf{Td}^* \cdot e(\mathsf{Td}_2, I_1) = e(sd_{\mathsf{kw}}^{\Delta \mathsf{SK}_{\mathcal{R}}}, \mathsf{PK}_{\mathcal{S}}) \cdot e(g^{\Delta}, \mathsf{PK}_{\mathcal{R}}^{\iota})$$
$$= e(H_2(H_1(\mathsf{kw})^{\beta} || \mathsf{kw}), g)^{\Delta \mathsf{SK}_{\mathcal{R}} \mathsf{SK}_{\mathcal{S}}} \cdot e(g, g)^{\Delta \mathsf{SK}_{\mathcal{R}} \iota}.$$
$$e(I_{2,j}, \mathsf{Td}_1) = e(\mathsf{dw}_{\mathsf{kw}_j}^{\mathsf{SK}_{\mathcal{S}}} \cdot g^{\iota}, g^{\Delta \mathsf{SK}_{\mathcal{R}}}) = e(H_2(d_j \parallel \mathsf{kw}_j)^{\mathsf{SK}_{\mathcal{S}}}, g^{\Delta \mathsf{SK}_{\mathcal{R}}}) \cdot e(g, g)^{\Delta \gamma \iota}$$
$$= e(H_2(H_1(\mathsf{kw}_j)^{\beta} \parallel \mathsf{kw}_j), g)^{\Delta \mathsf{SK}_{\mathcal{R}} \mathsf{SK}_{\mathcal{S}}} \cdot e(g, g)^{\Delta \mathsf{SK}_{\mathcal{R}} \iota}.$$

Correctness Analysis of the Key Server Group Update Phase: The secret share of $\{\mathcal{KS}_i^{\pi}\}$ is α_i, and that of $\{\mathcal{KS}_j^{\pi+1}\}$ is α_j^*. If α_i and α_j^* are valid, we can deduce that

$$\alpha = \prod_{i=1}^{t_1} w_i \cdot \alpha_i = \prod_{i=1}^{t_1} w_i \cdot \left(\prod_{j=1}^{t_2} w_j^* \cdot d_i(j) \right) = \prod_{i=1}^{t_1} \prod_{j=1}^{t_2} w_i \cdot w_j^* \cdot d_i(j) = \prod_{j=1}^{t_2} w_j^* \cdot \alpha_j^*$$

where $\{w_i\}$ and $\{w_j^*\}$ represent the Lagrange coefficients. The equations above show that the chosen key servers $\mathcal{KS}^{\pi}$ and $\mathcal{KS}^{\pi+1}$ both possess the identical group secret key α. The process for β follows the same procedure.

5.2 Security Analysis

We analyze the security of TRIGGERED from the following three sides based on the threat model in Sect. 3.2.

(1) Adversarial Cloud Server. It may launch *(i) offline/online BFA* and (ii) *offline/online KGA* that tries to guess the encrypted data and keywords, where we prove the security properties of *unpredictability* and *indeterminability* for case *(i)*, and thus have the case *(ii)* similarly.

Theorem 1 (Unpredictability). *TRIGGERED is classified as unpredictable if no PPT adversary $\mathcal{A}$ can succeed in the unpredictability experiment with a noticeable probability.*

Proof. This proof follows the identical steps as the proof of *unpredictability* in Section V-1 of [13] and is omitted here.

Theorem 2 (Indeterminable). *TRIGGERED is classified as indeterminable if no PPT adversary $\mathcal{A}$ can recover the MLE key across two epochs with a noticeable probability.*

Proof. The security of TRIGGERED does not rely on a fixed committee of key servers. Even in the extreme case where $\mathcal{CS}^*$ controls $t-1$ key servers in both the πth and $(\pi+1)$th epochs—thus obtaining $2t-2$ secret shares—launching a BFA remains ineffective. To test a candidate message M^*, $\mathcal{CS}^*$ must compute $\sigma_= H_1(M^*)^\alpha$, but can only derive two equations involving three unknowns: α_t^π, $\alpha_t^{\pi+1}$, and σ^*. Since this system is underdetermined, there exist infinitely many possible solutions, making it infeasible for $\mathcal{CS}^*$ to validate any specific guess. Therefore, offline BFA is ineffective even under partial key server compromise, rendering attack (i) impractical.

(2) Compromised Key Server(s): The compromised key server $\mathcal{KS}^*$ may collude with at most $t' < t-1$ key servers in the current epoch, which tries to compromise the privacy of outsourced data and keywords. They can use two strategies for launching attacks: *i) cease monitoring the MLE keys and keyword keys generated by the adversary.* and *ii) extracting sensitive information from the requests.* For case (i), this corresponds to online BFA and KGA attempts. However, key generation requires collaboration among all key servers, and a valid key can only be reconstructed from at least t valid signatures. As such, $\mathcal{KS}^*$ lacks sufficient shares to complete the protocol, rendering these online guessing attacks infeasible. For the case *(ii)*, we prove the security property of *obliviousness* for ensuring data confidentiality and IND-CKA security for keyword privacy.

Theorem 3 (Obliviousness). *In TRIGGERED, interactions between a sender and a key server are oblivious, ensuring that when a sender requests the MLE key for M^*, the information learned by $\mathcal{KS}^*$ is computationally indistinguishable from that derived from a random string of identical length.*

Proof. We introduce an obliviousness game involving an environment $\mathcal{E}$, the key server $\mathcal{KS}^*$, and a simulator $\mathcal{B}_1$ as follows:

- $\mathcal{E}$ initializes TRIGGERED, generates a server-side secret α^* and its n shares $\{\alpha_1^*, \alpha_2^*, \ldots, \alpha_n^*\}$ via $\mathsf{DSGA}()$.(c.f., Definition 4), It also generates the public parameters and sends them to $\mathcal{KS}^*$ and $\mathcal{B}_1$.
- $\mathcal{KS}^*$ randomly selects the data $M^* \in \mathbb{Z}_p$ and sends M^* to $\mathcal{B}_1$, which then forwards it to $\mathcal{E}$.
- $\mathcal{E}$ chooses at random $k^* \in \mathbb{Z}_p$, computes $\sigma_{\mathcal{S}}^* = H_1(M^*)^{\alpha^* k^*}$, and sends $\mathsf{ek}_{M^*} = H_2(\sigma_{\mathcal{S}}^* \parallel M^*)$ to $\mathcal{B}_1$. $\mathcal{B}_1$ forwards ek_{M^*} to $\mathcal{KS}^*$.
- $\mathcal{KS}^*$ can repeat the two operations mentioned earlier up to poly(κ) times. Afterwards, it randomly chooses $M_0, M_1 \in \mathbb{Z}_p$ and delivers them to $\mathcal{B}_1$, which subsequently passes them to $\mathcal{E}$.
- $\mathcal{E}$ chooses at random $\zeta \in \{0, 1\}$ and $k' \in \mathbb{Z}_p$. Then:
  - If $\zeta = 0$, it computes $\mathsf{ek}_{M_\zeta} = H_2(H_1(M_\zeta)^{\alpha^* k'} \parallel M_\zeta)$ and sets $C_{1,\zeta} = \mathsf{SEnc}(\mathsf{ek}_{M_\zeta}, M_\zeta)$.
  - Otherwise, it selects $C_{1,\zeta}$ randomly from the set of bit strings of length $|\mathsf{SEnc}(\mathsf{ek}_{M_\zeta}, M_\zeta)|$.

  $\mathcal{E}$ sends $C_{1,\zeta}$ to $\mathcal{S}$, which forwards it to $\mathcal{KS}^*$.
- $\mathcal{KS}^*$ wins the game if it outputs $\zeta' = \zeta$.

When $\mathcal{KS}^*$ succeeds in the game with probability $\Pr_{\mathcal{KS}^*}^{\mathsf{Obli},\kappa}$, $\mathcal{B}_1$ is able to compromise the D-IND\$-CPA security of the underlying MLE scheme with the same advantage. Prior works (e.g., [19]) have established that server-aided MLE constructions satisfy D-IND\$-CPA security. Specifically, if $\mathcal{KS}^*$ correctly outputs ζ' in the obliviousness game, then $\mathcal{B}_1$ can use this output to distinguish the MLE ciphertext from a random bitstring of length $|\mathsf{SEnc}(\mathsf{ek}_{M_\zeta}, M_\zeta)|$.

Theorem 4 (IND-CKA). *Suppose there exists a PPT adversary $\mathcal{A}$ capable of compromising the IND-CKA security of TRIGGERED. Then, one can construct a PPT adversary $\mathcal{B}$ that violates the blindness property of the threshold blind signature scheme [16].*

Proof. Without limiting the generality, let $\mathcal{KS}_i^*$ represent the adversary $\mathcal{A}$. We design a simulator $\mathcal{B}_2$ that internally invokes $\mathcal{A}$ as a subroutine while remaining transparent to the challenger.

- *Setup.* Given the security parameter κ, the challenger generates the secret and public parameters $(\beta_i^*, \mathsf{PK}_{\mathcal{KS}_i}^{*\mathsf{KW}})$ for a key server and forwards them to $\mathcal{B}_2$, who then relays them to $\mathcal{A}$.
- *Challenge.* $\mathcal{A}$ provides two keywords kw_0 and kw_1 to $\mathcal{B}_2$, which then forwards them to the challenger. The challenger chooses at random a bit $\zeta \in \{0, 1\}$ and $r^* \in \mathbb{Z}_p$, computes $\mathsf{kw}_\zeta^* = H_1(\mathsf{kw}_\zeta)^{r^*}$, and returns kw_ζ^* to $\mathcal{B}_2$. $\mathcal{B}_2$ forwards kw_ζ^* to $\mathcal{A}$, computes $d_i = \mathsf{kw}_\zeta^{*\beta_i^*}$, and sends the value of d_i back to the challenger.
- *Output.* $\mathcal{A}$ outputs a prediction ζ', which $\mathcal{B}_2$ adopts as its guess for ζ.

From the challenger's perspective, $\mathcal{B}_2$ attempts to break the blindness of the signature scheme [16], while acting as the IND-CKA challenger to $\mathcal{A}$. As the simulation is indistinguishable from a real IND-CKA game, $\mathcal{B}_2$'s advantage in breaking blindness is at least that of $\mathcal{A}$ in the IND-CKA game: $\mathsf{Adv}_{\mathcal{B}_2}^{\mathsf{Blind}}(\ell) \geq \mathsf{Adv}_{\mathcal{A}}^{\mathsf{IND\text{-}CKA}}(\kappa) = \Pr[\zeta' = \zeta] - 1/2$.

(3) Man-in-the-Middle Attacks. It may launch DGA to obtain the receiver's secret key, thereby obtaining the MLE key to further extract the outsourced data.

Theorem 5. *Assuming the blindness of the blind BLS signature and the security of the SAS-MA, TRIGGERED ensures that a man-in-the-middle adversary $\mathcal{A}$ cannot obtain the password-derived secret key γ of the receiver $\mathcal{R}$.*

Proof. To compute γ, $\mathcal{A}$ must recover $\mathsf{psw}_{\mathcal{R}}$ from the signature $\vartheta = H_1(\mathsf{psw})^b$. However, this signature is generated using a blind BLS scheme [3], which ensures that $\mathcal{A}$ learns nothing about psw. To recover $\mathsf{psw}_{\mathcal{R}}$, $\mathcal{A}$ may attempt a DGA by submitting candidate passwords to the device and comparing the resulting secret keys with the stored $\mathsf{PK}_{\mathcal{R}}$. TRIGGERED mitigates this threat by integrating blind signatures with the SAS-MA protocol and a rate-limiting mechanism. Since the receiver does not confirm requests from a MitM adversary on the device, the signature on the chosen password psw' is never produced. Moreover, the t-bit checksum shown on the device and terminal will mismatch with overwhelming probability (i.e., $1 - 2^{-t}$), effectively preventing impersonation.

6 Performance Analysis

This section provides experimental evaluations and compares the performance of TRIGGERED with the state-of-the-art solutions.

6.1 Experiment Settings

In the experiment, we used the real cloud environment Huawei Cloud as the cloud server (CS), which runs Ubuntu 18.04 system, Intel(R) Xeon(R) CPU E5-2680 v4 @2.40GHz with octa-cores and 32.00 GB RAM. In addition, we used the resource-constrained device Raspberry Pi 5 (Arm Cortex-A76 CPU, 8 GB RAM) as the receiver's corresponding device. Finally, we used the Python 3.6 language with the Pypbc 0.2 library to implement the scheme and used socket programming to let the client and device communicate with each other.

We set the security parameter κ to 80 bits, and use SHA-256 to implement the hash function in our scheme, and use the curve $y^2 = x^3 + x$ as the A-type pairing. Specifically, we use AES-256 to implement symmetric encryption, using the AES-CBC module (key is 256 bits, initialization vector is 128 bits). Finally, we use TfidfVectorizer in scikit-learn to select 1000 files from a subset of the Enron email dataset [1] and extract several keywords from each file to comprehensively evaluate the performance of our experiments.

Table 2. Efficiency Comparison of Setup and KeyGen (ms)

Work	Setup	KeyGen	Registration	
			Sender	Key servers
SPADE [19]	4.01	131.27	43.06	38.39
DULCET [13]	4.18	100.98	–	–
TRIGGERED	4.82	105.10	–	–

6.2 Implementation and Evaluation

Table 2 presents the time costs of system initialization (i.e., the Setup algorithm) and key generation for each entity in related schemes and our proposed scheme, TRIGGERED. Specifically, the Setup time of TRIGGERED, SPADE [19], and DULCET [13] is nearly identical. When the total number of key servers is set to $n = 30$ with a threshold $t = 15$, the KeyGen time cost of the three schemes is 131.270 ms, 100.982 ms, and 105.101 ms, respectively, with TRIGGERED achieving a 19.94% improvement over SPADE [19]. It is slightly slower than DULCET [13] due to additional sender key pair generation. Unlike SPADE [19], which includes an extra user registration phase to generate verification credentials for MLE key management, TRIGGERED eliminates this phase while still effectively handling MLE key management, thereby improving overall efficiency.

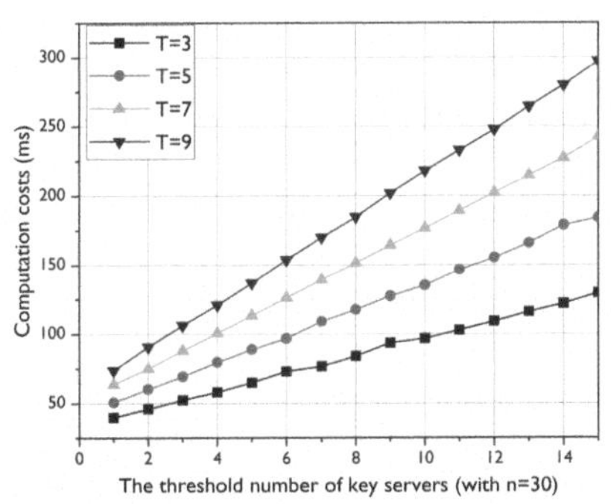

(a) Time cost of the sender

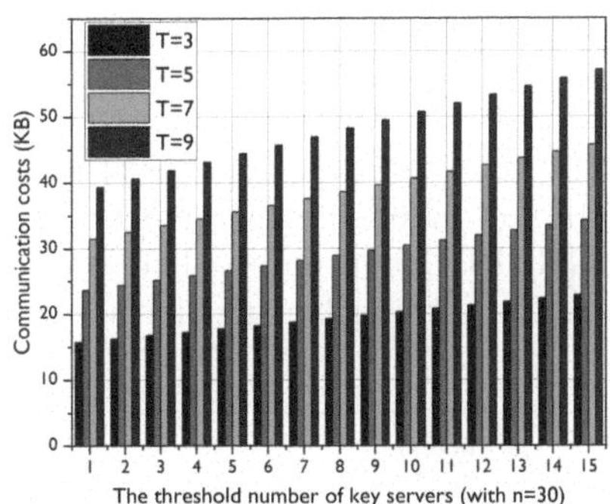

(b) Communication cost of the sender

Fig. 2. The time cost and communication cost of the sender when the MLE and keyword key generation phase

During the MLE and keyword key generation phase, the sender's computational and communication overhead increase as the threshold t and the total number of keywords T grow. As shown in Fig. 2, the growth trends of both computational and communication overhead are illustrated as the threshold t

increases under different values of T (i.e., T = 3, 5, 7, and 9). When $T = 7$ and $t = 10$, the sender incurs a computational overhead of 176.720 ms and a communication overhead of 40.625 KB.

Table 3. Comparison of Computational Complexity of Key Operations

Work	Enc	Dec	Keyword Search	
			$\mathcal{T}$	$\mathcal{CS}$
DULCET [13]	$\mathcal{O}(T(\mathbb{H}+\mathbb{M}+\mathbb{P}))$	PKEnc	$\mathbb{H}+\mathbb{M}$	$\mathcal{O}(T\mathbb{P})$
TRIGGERED	$\mathcal{O}(T\mathbb{M})$	$\mathbb{M}+\mathbb{P}$	$3\mathbb{M}+\mathbb{P}$	$\mathcal{O}(T\mathbb{P})$

In the table, "$\mathbb{H}$","$\mathbb{M}$", "$\mathbb{P}$" and "PKEnc" denote hashing a string to group $\mathbb{G}$, a multiplication, a pairing, and public key encryption operation, respectively.

To evaluate the encryption overhead, we compare TRIGGERED with the recently proposed DULCET [13], which integrates deduplication and keyword search. Table 3 summarizes the dominant computational overhead of key operations. Although the TRIGGERED requires slightly higher cost during the search phase compared with DULCET, it significantly reduces the encryption overhead. As shown in Fig. 3, the encryption time increases proportionally with the number of files. When the number of files reaches 1000, the encryption time of TRIGGERED and DULCET [13] is 17.414 s and 46.426 s, respectively, indicating that TRIGGERED achieves a 2.67 × improvement over DULCET in terms of encryption efficiency. For the key server in the data outsourcing phase, the computational overhead primarily depends on the number of keywords T. When the number of key servers is set to $n = 30$ and the number of keywords is $T = 7$, the performance comparison is shown in Fig. 4. At a file count of 1000, the computational overhead of TRIGGERED and DULCET [13] are 9.940 s and 9.864 s, respectively. The slight increase in overhead introduced by TRIGGERED is attributed to embedding a rate-limiting mechanism, which is designed to strengthen resilience against online attackers.

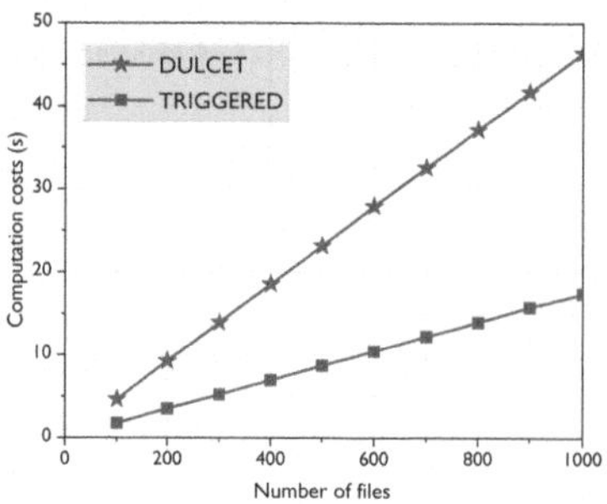

Fig. 3. Time cost of encryption

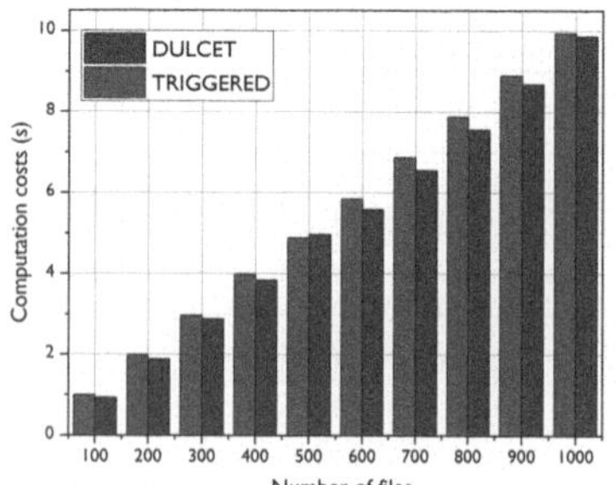

Fig. 4. Time cost of $\mathcal{KS}$

(3) Data Search Phase. In the secret key recovery phase, we simulate the interaction between the device and the terminal using a Raspberry Pi and a laptop. In our experiments, the SAS channel delay is negligible compared with the total key recovery time (in milliseconds), which is dominated by $\mathbb{Z}_p$ exponentiations. The Raspberry Pi represents a typical resource-constrained edge device, on which the required operations (e.g., $\mathbb{M}$ and $\mathbb{H}$) can be executed efficiently. For powerful devices (e.g., desktops or modern smartphones), the computational overhead is expected to be decreased without influencing correctness. The computational and communication overheads of TRIGGERED during this phase are slightly higher than those of DULCET [13]. This is mainly due to the introduction of a key request limiting mechanism, which is designed to enhance resistance against dictionary attacks. Importantly, the extra overhead introduced is minimal and does not significantly impact system performance in real-world deployments.

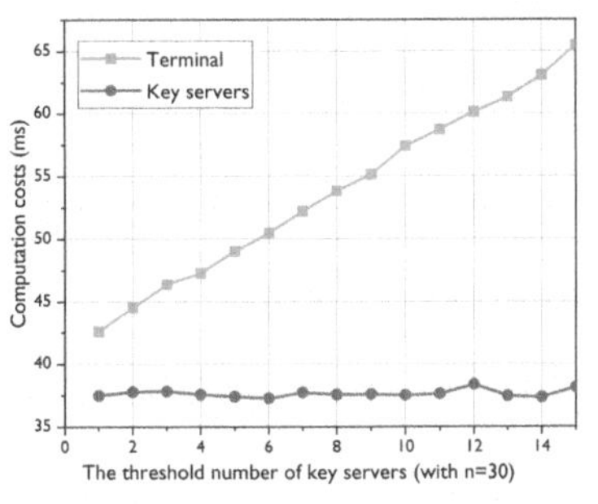

(a) Time cost of $\mathcal{T}$ and $\mathcal{KS}$

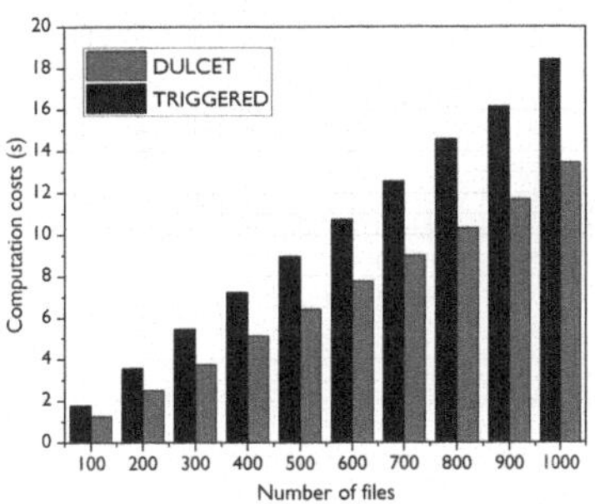

(b) Time cost of keyword search

Fig. 5. The time cost of the data search phase

In the keyword key generation phase, the computation overhead on the terminal is affected by the threshold t, while the computation cost on the key servers depends only on the total number of key servers. As shown in Fig. 5a, the terminal's computation cost increases proportionally with t, whereas the overhead on the key servers remains stable. When $t = 15$, the computation costs of the terminal and the key servers are 65.464ms and 38.140ms, respectively. Figure 5b further illustrates the search overhead as the number of files increases, under different values of T (i.e., $T = 7$ and $T = 10$). When the number of files reaches 1000, the computation costs are 18.421 s and 13.431 s for TRIGGERED and DULCET, respectively. This performance gap is primarily due to the enhanced trapdoor generation mechanism in our scheme, which requires two pairing operations per keyword search. However, this design also leads to reduced encryption overhead in the data outsourcing phase.

(4) Decryption Phase. As shown in Fig. 6, the decryption time of both TRIGGERED and DULCET [13] grows as the number of files increases. When the number of files reaches 1000, the decryption times of TRIGGERED and DULCET are 3.683 s and 4.174 s, respectively. TRIGGERED achieves approximately 13.33% faster decryption compared to DULCET [13]. This improvement is mainly attributed to the fact that DULCET [13] relies on a full-fledged public-key encryption algorithm to encapsulate the MLE key, which incurs a higher computational overhead. In contrast, TRIGGERED avoids the use of such heavyweight encryption and only requires a single pairing and one exponentiation during decryption.

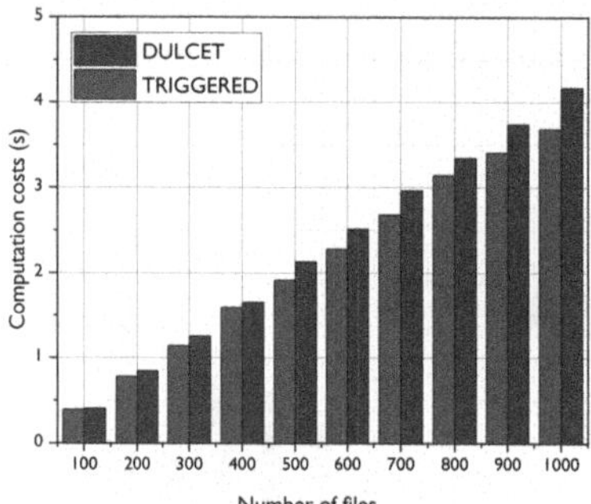

Fig. 6. Time cost of decryption

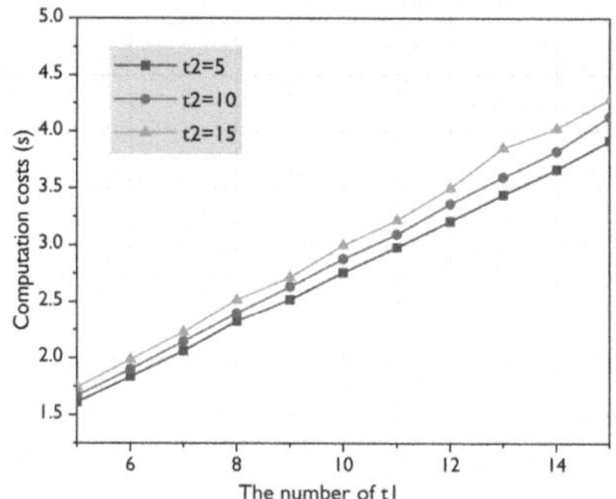

Fig. 7. Time cost of group migration

(5) Key Server Group Update Phase. In this phase, the original key server group (n_1, t_1) transfers retained secret shares to a new group (n_2, t_2). With $n_1 = n_2 = 30$, the computational overhead depends on both t_1 and t_2. As shown in Fig. 7, the computational overhead for group secret migration increases with larger threshold values t_1 and t_2. Specifically, when $t_1 = 10$ and t_2 is set to 5, 10, and 15, the corresponding computation times are 2.757 s, 2.877 s, and 2.994 s.

7 Related Work

Secure Data Deduplication. Data deduplication [8] is widely used in cloud storage to reduce storage overhead. Convergent encryption (CE) [6] derives keys from data hashes to ensure identical ciphertexts, and its formalization as message-locked encryption (MLE) [2] provides rigorous security models. To resist brute-force attacks on low-entropy data, key servers can incorporate server-side secrets [2]. Most schemes [7,10] adopt multi-server architectures but still require persistent trust in specific servers and linear sender-side MLE key storage. SPADE [19] avoids local MLE key storage via password-based encapsulation, but existing solutions lack efficient encrypted data search and still involve complex password-based MLE key management.

Secure Keyword Search. Searchable encryption enables querying data without revealing content beyond the results. Boneh et al. [4] introduced public-key searchable encryption (PEKS), but the limited keyword space makes it vulnerable to practical keyword guessing attacks (KGA) [15,18]. To resist offline KGA, Chen et al. [5] leveraged a trusted third party for ciphertext generation and search, but their scheme assumes a fully trusted key server, leaving it exposed to online KGA. SEPSE [20] improved security via key renewal and rate-limiting, while Jiang et al. [13] combined server-aided MLE with PEKS to support deduplication and offline-attack-resistant searchable encryption. Nevertheless, existing solutions still face challenges in resisting online attacks and managing sender-side MLE keys efficiently.

8 Conclusion

In this paper, we propose TRIGGERED, an enhanced secure cloud storage system supporting keyword search and data deduplication. We strengthen rate-limiting mechanisms and improve key group update flexibility to resist triple attacks, and introduce a novel MLE keybased layered encryption to address sender-side key management. Besides conducting a formal security analysis of TRIGGERED, we perform extensive experiments in real cloud server environments demonstrating its improved efficiency in both computation and communication. Since the key-recovery phase relies on the SAS-MA protocol, whose channel security relies on fixed-length messages of at most t' bits, it seems an interesting work to further include a quantitative evaluation of latency in relation to t' under varied network conditions and heterogeneous devices.

Acknowledgments. We would like to thank anonymous reviewers for insightful comments. This work was supported by National Natural Science Foundation of China (No. 62372285), and the Shuguang Program of Shanghai Education Development Foundation and Shanghai Municipal Education Commission (No. 25SG49).

References

1. Enron email dataset. https://www.cs.cmu.edu/~./enron/
2. Bellare, M., Keelveedhi, S., Ristenpart, T.: Message-locked encryption and secure deduplication. In: Johansson, T., Nguyen, P.Q. (eds.) Advances in Cryptology - EUROCRYPT 2013, 32nd Annual International Conference on the Theory and Applications of Cryptographic Techniques, Athens, May 26-30, 2013. Proceedings. Lecture Notes in Computer Science, vol. 7881, pp. 296–312. Springer (2013)
3. Boldyreva, A.: Threshold signatures, multisignatures and blind signatures based on the gap-diffie-hellman-group signature scheme. In: Desmedt, Y. (ed.) Public Key Cryptography - PKC 2003, 6th International Workshop on Theory and Practice in Public Key Cryptography, Miami, January 6-8, 2003, Proceedings. Lecture Notes in Computer Science, vol. 2567, pp. 31–46. Springer (2003)

4. Boneh, D., Crescenzo, G.D., Ostrovsky, R., Persiano, G.: Public key encryption with keyword search. In: Cachin, C., Camenisch, J. (eds.) Advances in Cryptology - EUROCRYPT 2004, International Conference on the Theory and Applications of Cryptographic Techniques, Interlaken, May 2-6, 2004, Proceedings. Lecture Notes in Computer Science, vol. 3027, pp. 506–522. Springer (2004)
5. Chen, R., et al.: Server-aided public key encryption with keyword search. IEEE Trans. Inf. Forensics Secur. **11**(12), 2833–2842 (2016)
6. Douceur, J.R., Adya, A., Bolosky, W.J., Simon, D., Theimer, M.: Reclaiming space from duplicate files in a serverless distributed file system. In: Proceedings of the 22nd International Conference on Distributed Computing Systems (ICDCS'02), pp. 617–624, Vienna, July 2-5, 2002. IEEE Computer Society (2002)
7. Ha, G., Jia, C., Chen, Y., Chen, H., Li, M.: A secure client-side deduplication scheme based on updatable server-aided encryption. IEEE Trans. Cloud Comput. **11**(4), 3672–3684 (2023)
8. Harnik, D., Pinkas, B., Shulman-Peleg, A.: Side channels in cloud services: deduplication in cloud storage. IEEE Secur. Priv. **8**(6), 40–47 (2010)
9. Herzberg, A., Jarecki, S., Krawczyk, H., Yung, M.: Proactive secret sharing or: how to cope with perpetual leakage. In: Lecture Notes in Computer Science, vol. 963, pp. 339–352. Springer (1995)
10. Hua, Z., Yao, Y., Song, M., Zheng, Y., Zhang, Y., Wang, C.: Blockchain-assisted secure deduplication for large-scale cloud storage service. IEEE Trans. Serv. Comput. **17**(3), 821–835 (2024)
11. IDC iView: The Digital Universe Decade - Are You Ready? IDC (2010)
12. Jarecki, S., Jubur, M., Krawczyk, H., Saxena, N., Shirvanian, M.: Two-factor password-authenticated key exchange with end-to-end security. ACM Trans. Priv. Secur. (TOPS) **24**(3), 1–37 (2021)
13. Jiang, C., Xu, C., Yang, G.: Device-enhanced secure cloud storage with keyword searchable encryption and deduplication. In: European Symposium on Research in Computer Security, pp. 396–413. Springer (2024)
14. Li, J., Chen, X., Xhafa, F., Barolli, L.: Secure deduplication storage systems supporting keyword search. J. Comput. Syst. Sci. **81**(8), 1532–1541 (2015)
15. Sultan, N.H., Kaaniche, N., Laurent, M., Barbhuiya, F.A.: Authorized keyword search over outsourced encrypted data in cloud environment. IEEE Trans. Cloud Comput. **10**(1), 216–233 (2022)
16. Vo, D.L., Zhang, F., Kim, K.: A new threshold blind signature scheme from pairings. In: SCIS2003, pp. 233–238. SCIS (2003)
17. Zhang, K., Wang, X., Ning, J., Huang, X.: Dual-server boolean data retrieval for highly-scalable secure file sharing services. IEEE Trans. Inf. Forensics Secur. **18**, 449–462 (2023)
18. Zhang, X., Tang, Y., Wang, H., Xu, C., Miao, Y., Cheng, H.: Lattice-based proxy-oriented identity-based encryption with keyword search for cloud storage. Inf. Sci. **494**, 193–207 (2019)
19. Zhang, Y., Xu, C., Cheng, N., Shen, X.: Secure password-protected encryption key for deduplicated cloud storage systems. IEEE Trans. Dependable Secur. Comput. **19**(4), 2789–2806 (2022)
20. Zhang, Y., Xu, C., Ni, J., Li, H., Shen, X.S.: Blockchain-assisted public-key encryption with keyword search against keyword guessing attacks for cloud storage. IEEE Trans. Cloud Comput. **9**(4), 1335–1348 (2021)

MLM-ABE: A Privacy-Preserving Access Control Scheme for Multi-LLM APIs and Local Sensitive Data

Zhichao Wang, Tao Wang(✉), Bo Yang, and Jintang Wang

School of Computer Science, Shaanxi Normal University, Xian 710119, China
{zhichaowang,water,byang,atangya}@snnu.edu.cn

Abstract. In the current era of generative artificial intelligence, enterprise adoption of multiple domain-specific large language models (LLM) has become a strategic approach to enhance workforce productivity. A prevalent operational paradigm involves employees utilizing API tokens to submit queries and proprietary data through LLM service provider hosted LLMs for task automation. However, unregulated access to multi-LLMs and sensitive corporate data by unauthorized personnel poses significant security risks. To address this critical challenge, we propose MLM-ABE, a ciphertext-policy attribute-based encryption (CP-ABE) system integrated with computational result reuse mechanisms, to establish a fine-grained access control system for enterprise multi-LLM application ecosystems. The proposed system achieves two objectives: (1) enabling authenticated employees to efficiently access authorized LLM services with minimal latency, and (2) enforcing precise authorization policies for both API tokens and data assets. To evaluate the system's security, we analyzed system protection in mitigating potential attacks. Experimental results demonstrate that the MLM-ABE system effectively prevents unauthorized access while maintaining low computational and network overhead. Furthermore, the CP-ABE-based access control policy enables the system to support fine-grained access control, ensuring that employees with different roles can only access LLMs and data resources that align with their permissions. Overall, MLM-ABE system achieves a favorable balance between security, scalability, and computational efficiency, providing an efficient and secure solution for enterprise-level multiple LLM applications.

Keywords: Generative Artificial Intelligence · Large Language Model · Data Privacy Protection · API Access Control · CP-ABE

1 Introduction

The rapid evolution of Generative Artificial Intelligence (GenAI) has catalyzed widespread adoption of Large Language Models (LLM) across mission-critical domains including clinical decision support [1], legal document analysis [2], and automated software developmentcitecode. While these domain-specific LLMs

L. Zhang and K.-K. R. Choo (Eds.): MobiQuitous 2025, LNICST 684, pp. 249–268, 2026.
https://doi.org/10.1007/978-3-032-22503-0_14

demonstrate unprecedented task-solving capabilities, their development and deployment present substantial financial barriers.

Current empirical evidence reveals extraordinary infrastructure demands for LLM construction: OpenAI's GPT-3 architecture, containing 175 billion parameters, required an estimated 14 million in cloud compute expenditure per training cycle [3], with cumulative energy consumption exceeding 1,287 MWh [4]. Furthermore, operational maintenance imposes recurring costs-hosting 100-billion-parameter models necessitates enterprise-grade GPU clusters (e.g., NVIDIA A100 systems), incurring annual infrastructure expenses ranging from $50,000 to $500,000 [5]. These economic constraints compel 93% of organizations to adopt third-party LLM services rather than pursuing local development, as reported in the 2023 AI Industry Survey [6].

This paradigm shift toward multi-LLM integration introduces critical operational challenges. Enterprises typically implement a centralized query-processing architecture comprising: (1)Vendor-specific API key: purchased from LLM providers. (2)Unified QA client: a routing system that maps employee requests to appropriate LLM. (3)Internal access API token: perform internal authorization verification. The workflow operates through three sequential phases. (1)Query Initialization: coder retrieve API tokens (for QA client authentication) from the repository to formulate pre-requests. Each request contains: QA client hostname, API token, Designated LLM identifier, File parameters (including data filenames/paths) etc. (2)Request Verification and Processing: the QA client performs a)Token validity verification checks. b) Parsing of user requests. c) Retrieve specified data based on user request. (3)Response Generation: the QA client constructs final responses with API key. Simultaneously, this request will contain information such as LLM host name, API key, model name, file, session ID, message ID.

As depicted in Fig. 1, our case study demonstrates a practical enterprise scenario where multiple departments (e.g., legal, technical, and medical divisions) generate domain-specific operational data, including source code, contractual documents, and patient records. These data are systematically archived in centralized warehouse.

The coder can obtain the API token (used for access authentication of QA client) from the data warehouse and add the relevant code snippet to form a complete question to issue a pre-request to QA Client, which contains information such as QA client host name, API token, model name, question and data summary (e.g.: file name, file path, etc.). After receiving the pre-request, QA client will verify the validity of the API token. After the verification is passed, QA client will add the complete data content to the request and use the corresponding API key (the exclusive query key provided by the LLM service provider to the company) to send a query to the LLM.

LLM will respond after receiving the request. This response contains information such as the client host name, response ID (used within the LLM service provider), answer content, and model version. The QA client will extract the answer content from the response received from the LLM. Then, it constructs

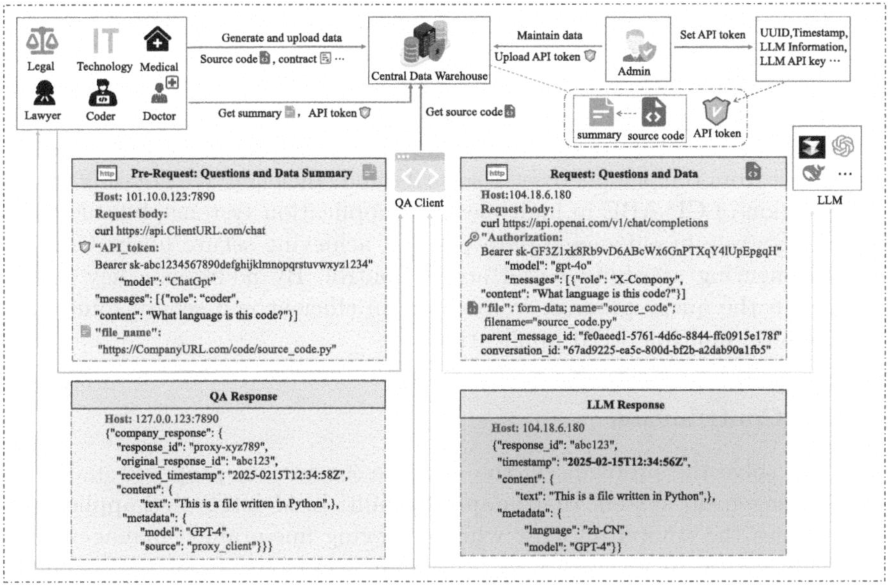

Fig. 1. System Architecture Based on Multiple LLM Applications.

the response body according to its own needs, including: timestamp, data source, response ID (generated within the company) and original response ID (generated by the LLM service provider). Note that the API token used in the interaction process is generated by the data administrator and contains information such as the unique ID, timestamp, LLM information, and LLM's API key.

During this interaction, employees authenticate themselves using the company's API token(application program interface token) and attach the data they wish to consult. However, a critical issue exhibits critical vulnerabilities: a legal department employee using an API token containing medical LLM information while attaching financial department data to the query is clearly unreasonable. Even without malicious intent, such invalid queries not only introduce risks to data security but also significantly increase the company's costs. Therefore, strict regulatory controls are required for API token usage and data access management.

To solve the problem of API token abuse and local sensitive data leakage, we use Ciphertext Policy Attribute-based Encryption (CP-ABE) [7] to perform access control on API tokens and data separately after a practical investigation of real-world scenarios. As an attribute-based cryptographic primitive, CP-ABE enables granular resource governance in distributed systems. It ensures that API tokens and data, once encrypted, can only be decrypted by users that meet predefined attribute standards. Based on these features, within this framework, CP-ABE is very suitable for the multi-LLM central integration architecture in real-world applications and can perform fine management of resource permissions. Meanwhile, considering that the QA client possesses the API key directly interacting with LLM, and the possession of this key endows the QA client with appropriate authorization and security safeguards within the system, we hold the view that the QA client can be regarded as fully trustworthy. Under this premise, we describe the complete system architecture and implement complex management from the perspectives of security and efficiency. We not only explore the integration of CP-ABE in multiple LLM application systems, but also focus on CP-ABE's role in enhancing data privacy, achieving secure query transmission, and ensuring attribute based access control. By addressing key privacy challenges in the query process, we provide an efficient and secure solution for enterprise-level multiple LLM applications.

1.1 Our Contribution

In order to solve the problems in the above scenarios, we proposed and developed a management system that adapts to multi-LLM integrated applications, which reduces the computing cost while achieving fine-grained management of API tokens and local privacy data. The main contributions of this paper are summarized as follows:

- We innovatively introduces CP-ABE technology into the multi-LLM application service scenario. Addressing the multi-LLM usage requirements of enterprise users, it proposes a comprehensive fine-grained access control solution.
- Through system design, we separates the decryption steps through system design and transfers the final decryption process from the user to the question-and-answer client, naturally achieving user revocation and forward and backward security. Since the user does not have the final decryption capability, the system has good scalability and can easily integrate functions such as ciphertext update, policy update, and outsourced decryption.
- The MLM-ABE we proposed is a lightweight solution. In terms of system design, users only need to decrypt API token once to complete the LLM query. We introduced a result reuse mechanism [8] in the QA client, which can complete data decryption and API key recovery in $O(1)$ time. After experimental evaluation, compared with a system without access control, the time cost is not enough to affect the user experience.

1.2 Organization

The remainder of this paper is organized as follows. Section 2 provides a brief introduction to related concepts and definitions, including hard problems and LSSS. Section 3 offers a detailed overview of the multi-LLM integration architecture based on API access, elaborating on the system architecture and relevant entities. Section 4 explains the scheme construction involved in the MLM-ABE system in detail and provides comprehensive notation specifications. Section 5 verifies the correctness of the encryption scheme and reuse algorithm, while presenting detailed security proofs for both the API token encryption scheme and the data encryption scheme. Section 6 focuses on instantiating and simulating the system, conducting statistical analysis of algorithm execution times and discussing hardware resource utilization. Finally, Sect. 7 concludes the paper.

2 Preliminaries

This section mainly introduces the underlying difficulty assumption and Linear Secret Sharing Schemes.

2.1 Decisional (q-1) Assumption

The decisional $(q-1)$ problem is that for any probabilistic polynomialtime algorithm, given $\overrightarrow{y} =$

$$\begin{aligned}
&g, g^{\mu}, \\
&g^{a^i}, g^{b_j}, g^{\mu b_j}, g^{a^i b_j}, g^{a^i/b_j^2} && \forall (i,j) \in [q,q], \\
&g^{a^i/b_j} && \forall (i,j) \in [2q,q]\ with\ i \neq q+1, \\
&g^{a^i b_j/b_{j'}^2} && \forall (i,j,j') \in [2q,q,q]\ with\ j \neq j', \\
&g^{\mu a^i b_j/b_{j'}}, g^{\mu a^i b_j/b_{j'}^2} && \forall (i,j,j') \in [q,q,q]\ with\ j \neq j',
\end{aligned}$$

it is difficult to distinguish $(\overrightarrow{y}, \hat{e}(g,g)^{\mu a^{q+1}})$ from $(\overrightarrow{y}, Z)$, where $g \in G, Z \in G_1, a, \mu, b_1, \ldots, b_q \in Z_p^*$ are chosen independently and uniformly at random.

2.2 Linear Secret Sharing Schemes(LSSS)

A secret sharing scheme over a set of parties Ω is called linear if there exists an $\ell \times n$ matrix M and a label function $\rho : [\ell] \mapsto \Omega^4$ such that for any random vector$\boldsymbol{v} = (s, y_2, \cdots, y_n) \in \mathbb{Z}_p^n, where\ s$ represents the secret, we have that $\mathbb{M}\boldsymbol{v} shares\ the\ secret\ s\ to$ parties, and $(\mathbb{M}\boldsymbol{v})_i$ belongs to the party $\rho(i)$. Usually the secret scheme is denoted as a pair ($\mathbb{M}$, ρ).

Let $(\mathbb{M}, \rho)$ be a LSSS scheme, then for any authorized set $A \subset \Omega$, (1) there exists a set of valid shares $\boldsymbol{\lambda} = \{\lambda_i \in \mathbb{Z}_p\}_{i \in I}$, where $I = \{i : \rho(i) \in A\}$; and (2) there exists an efficient algorithm to calculate a set of constants $w = \{w_i \in \mathbb{Z}_p\}_{i \in I}$ to recover the secret from the valid shares by $\sum_{i \in I} w_i \lambda_i = s$. Here we only assume the existence of such constants.

3 System Architecture and Security Model

The system architecture is presented alongside its formal definition, with the api token security framework rigorously characterized.

3.1 System Architecture

To structure subsequent technical discourse, we provide a detailed description of fine-grained access control system based on multiple LLM applications in Fig. 2. As depicted in the figure, the data administrator cryptographically protects data and API tokens prior to secure ingestion by the central repository. Upon the upload of data and API tokens, corresponding information (such as file hash values) is generated. Users within departments first obtain tokens from the data Warehouse (DW), which enables them to access specific LLMs. They then select the required data from file summaries provided by the data warehouse and attach their questions before sending inquiries to the QA client (the inquiry content and API token are included in the request body).

Upon receiving the inquiry request, the client verifies the validity of the API token. After successful validation, it retrieves and decrypts the corresponding data from the data repository. The decryption process for the data access control layer requires the user's attribute key (the QA client always holds the final decryption keys for both the API token and data). After removing the access control layer using the attribute key, the QA client uses the final decryption key to obtain the fully decrypted data and API token.

Subsequently, the QA client constructs the request body based on the information contained in the API token, such as the API key and LLM name, and so on, and submits the inquiry to the corresponding LLM. Note that API token and API key serve different purposes: the API key is a dedicated token obtained by the company from the LLM service provider through a subscription, which enables the company to make actual inquiries to the LLM. In contrast, the API token discussed in this paper is an internal credential issued by the company and used exclusively within the organization. The system comprises four entities: Key Generation Center, Data Administrator, QA Client, and Departmental Employee.

- Key Generation Center(KGC): KGC is generally considered to be credible in past studies, and this paper follows this setting. It will be responsible for the issuance and management of keys. It generates corresponding department keys for each department; produces attribute keys and identifiers for each user within the department; and creates decryption keys for QA client.
- Data Admin(admin): The admin is responsible for the management and maintenance of API token and data, which primarily includes two main functions: the generation of tokens and the encryption of both API token and data.
- QA Client(QA): QA is the core entity of the system. It receives and forwards requests from users and extracts the API token ciphertext from the request body to perform legal validation of the token. This validation mainly includes: the validity of the token and the authorization validity of the accessing user.
- Departmental Employee(user): User is the initiator of the inquiry and possesses the access rights to the specified token. After selecting the desired data for consultation, the user locally constructs a request body that includes the data summary and the partially decrypted API token. The request is ultimately received by QA.

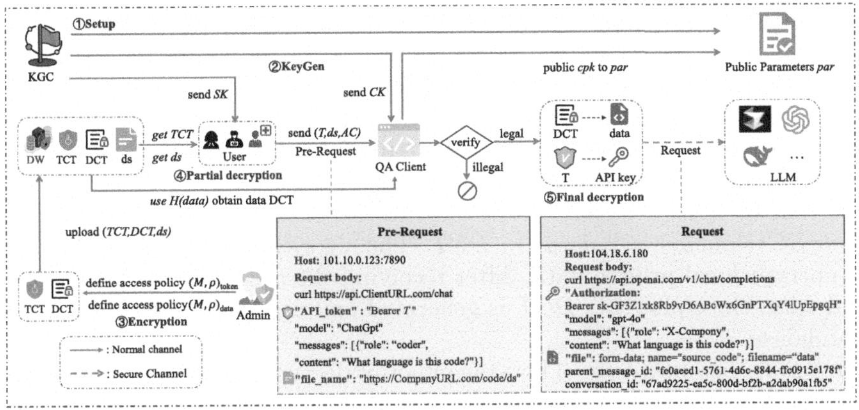

Fig. 2. Fine-grained Access Control System Based on Multiple LLM Applications.

3.2 Formal Definition

The complete formal definition consists of six steps involving nine algorithms.

- *Global Setup phase.* As a preliminary design of the system life cycle, this stage will run the setup algorithm to initialize system parameters and other information accordingly.
  $Setup(1^\lambda) \rightarrow (par, msk)$. KGC has the execution power of the algorithm. The security parameters will be obtained by it and used to output the public parameters par and the master key msk.
- *Key Generation phase.* This stage is mainly led by KGC, which is used to participate in the generation and transmission of relevant keys.
  $Key\ Gen(1^\lambda, par, msk, \mathcal{S}) \rightarrow (SK, CK)$. The input parameters of the algorithm are par, msk, attribute set $\mathcal{S} \subseteq \mathcal{U}($ $\mathcal{U}$ denotes the attribute universe) and security parameters. It will output the user key SK corresponding to the attribute set $\mathcal{S}$ and QA's decryption key.
- *Encryption phase.* The encryption phase relies on the execution of the following three algorithms: $TokEC$, $AttkEC$, and $DataEC$.
  $TokEC((\mathbb{M}, \rho), par, tok) \rightarrow TCT$. The token encryption algorithm is called by the admin, who will encrypt the API tokens used by users in various departments and upload them to the central data warehouse. Meanwhile, it takes as input the access policy $(\mathbb{M}, \rho)$, public parameters par, and API token tok, produces the ciphertext TCT, and then sends it to the user. In detail, tok is defined as

$$tok = (UUID, APK, LI, TS, TP) \tag{1}$$

where, APK represents the dedicated API key provided by LLM service provider, LI denotes the corresponding information of LLM (such as model

name and version), API token policy TP includes the number of token uses and expiration time, and $UUID$ serves as a globally unique identifier.
$AttkEC(AK, par) \rightarrow AC$. The attribute key encryption algorithm is performed by the user to encapsulate the attribute key to ensure that the attribute key is not leaked. After the attribute key AK and the public parameter par are input into the algorithm, the ciphertext AC will be generated and sent to QA.
$DataEC((\mathbb{M}_d, \rho_d), par, data) \rightarrow DCT$. The algorithm is performed by admin to encrypt local private data. After receiving the access policy $(\mathbb{M}_d, \rho_d)$, par and $data$, the ciphertext DCT is generated and uploaded to the central data warehouse.

- *Partial decryption phase.* This stage mainly decrypts the received API token and local privacy data ciphertext, which mainly involves two steps of decryption, and their operation subjects are also different to ensure confidentiality.
$TokDC(TCT, SK) \rightarrow T$. The token decryption algorithm is executed by the user, taking the token ciphertext TCT and the user's secret key SK as input, and producing the partially decrypted ciphertext T.
$DataDC(DCT, AC, CK) \rightarrow B$. The data decryption algorithm is executed by QA, taking the ciphertext DCT, the attribute key ciphertext AC, and QA key CK as input, and producing the partially decrypted ciphertext B.
- *Final decryption.*In this decryption phase, QA will truly obtain the API token and the plaintext of local privacy data through computation.

$Final : decryption(T, B, CK) \rightarrow (tok, data)$. It takes the partially decrypted token ciphertext T, partially decrypted data ciphertext B, and QA key CK as input, producing fully decrypted API token tok and data $data$.
- *Result reuse.*In result reuse phase, the reuse algorithm is executed by QA and primarily serves the data decryption phase.
$Reuse(DCT, E_m^{\delta_1}, E_m^{\delta_2}, B_{\delta_1}) \rightarrow B_{\delta_2}$. The algorithm takes as input: identifier $E_m^{\delta_1}$ of user δ_1, identifier $E_m^{\delta_2}$ of user δ_2, data ciphertext DCT, partial decryption result B_{δ_1} of user δ_1. Final output the partial decryption result B_{δ_2} for user δ_2.

3.3 Security Model

In this work, API tokens rely solely on attribute-based encryption, whereas data protection employs hybrid encryption. We now formalize distinct security models for each component.

3.4 Security Model of Token Encryption Scheme

The API token encryption scheme in the MLM-ABE system has the selected IND-CPA security, and the definition of this property is designed in a security game involving challenger $\mathcal{C}$ and adversary $\mathcal{A}$:

- **Init**: Adversary $\mathcal{A}$ declares a challenge access structure $\mathbb{A}^* = (\mathbb{M}^*, \rho^*)$, with $\mathbb{M}^*$ as a $\ell^* \times n^*$ matrix and ρ^* associating rows of $\mathbb{M}^*$ with attributes.
- **Setup**: Challenger $\mathcal{C}$ executes Setup, provides public parameters par to $\mathcal{A}$, and safeguards the master secret key msk.
- **Phase 1**: $\mathcal{A}$ adaptively issues queries to $\mathcal{C}$ for: Secret keys corresponding to attribute sets $\mathcal{S}$ that *do not satisfy* $\mathbb{A}^*$
- **Challenge**: $\mathcal{A}$ submits two equal-length tokens T_0^*, T_1^*. $\mathcal{C}$ samples $b \xleftarrow{\$} \{0,1\}$, computes $TCT_b^* \leftarrow \mathsf{Encrypt}(par, T_b^*, \mathbb{A}^*)$, and returns TCT_b^* to $\mathcal{A}$.
- **Phase 2**: $\mathcal{A}$ issues additional queries under the same constraints as Phase 1.
- **Guess**: $\mathcal{A}$ outputs a guess b' for b. The adversary succeeds if $b' = b$.

Definition 1. *The token encryption scheme achieves selective IND-CPA security if for all PPT adversaries $\mathcal{A}$, the advantage*

$$\mathbf{Adv}_{\mathcal{A}}^{\mathsf{sIND\text{-}CPA}}(\lambda) = \left|\Pr[b' = b] - \frac{1}{2}\right| \tag{2}$$

is negligible in security parameter λ.

3.5 Security Model of Data Encryption Scheme

The selective IND-CPA security of our data encryption scheme is formalized as an interactive game between challenger $\mathcal{C}_d$ and adversary $\mathcal{A}_d$:

- **Init**: $\mathcal{A}_d$ commits to a challenge access structure $\mathbb{A}_d^* = (\mathbb{M}_d^*, \rho_d^*)$, with $\mathbb{M}_d^*$ as a $\ell_d^* \times n_d^*$ matrix and ρ_d^* labeling its rows.
- **Setup**: $\mathcal{C}_d$ runs Setup, provides public parameters par to $\mathcal{A}_d$, and retains master secret key msk.
- **Phase 1**: $\mathcal{A}_d$ adaptively queries $\mathcal{C}_d$ for: Secret keys for attribute sets $\mathcal{S}$ failing to satisfy $\mathbb{A}_d^*$
- **Challenge**: $\mathcal{A}_d$ submits equal-length data objects O_0^*, O_1^*. $\mathcal{C}_d$ chooses $b \xleftarrow{\$} \{0,1\}$, generates $DCT_b^* \leftarrow \mathsf{Encrypt}(par, O_b^*, \mathbb{A}_d^*)$, and transmits DCT_b^* to $\mathcal{A}_d$.
- **Phase 2**: Identical to Phase 1 with unchanged constraints.
- **Guess**: $\mathcal{A}_d$ produces guess b' for b. $\mathcal{A}_d$ prevails when $b' = b$.

Definition 2. *The data encryption scheme achieves selective IND-CPA security if for all PPT adversaries $\mathcal{A}_d$, the advantage*

$$\mathbf{Adv}_{\mathcal{A}_d}^{\mathsf{sIND\text{-}CPA}}(\lambda) = \left|\Pr[b' = b] - \frac{1}{2}\right| \tag{3}$$

is negligible in security parameter λ.

To ensure data confidentiality, our hybrid encryption approach combines attribute-based and symmetric encryption. Crucially, the ABE component guarantees IND-CPA security for the symmetric key syk, while the data itself is protected through a secure symmetric cipher. Consequently, our security analysis focuses primarily on the protection of syk.

4 Construction

In this section, the detailed construction of MLM-ABE will be revealed and the relevant parameters are explained in detail. Assume that the space of API token and data is G and G_1 respectively. Our MLM-ABE scheme is constructed in detail as follows

- *Global Setup phase.* In the system initialization stage, KGC performs the setup protocol:
  $Setup(1^\lambda) \rightarrow (par, msk)$. During initialization, the algorithm leverages the security parameter λ to deterministically select two cyclic groups G and G_1 of prime orders p and p_1, respectively, where g and g_1 are chosen as their respective generators. And establishes bilinear map $e : G \times G \rightarrow G_T$. It randomly chooses elements $g, g_1, u, h, w, v \leftarrow G, \alpha \leftarrow \mathbb{Z}_p$, selects collision-resistant hash functions $H : \{0,1\}^* \rightarrow \{0,1\}^\kappa$ $H_1 : \{0,1\}^* \rightarrow \{0,1\}^\mu$ where κ denotes data summary length and μ represents data length, and assigns unique departmental keys $\theta_m \leftarrow G$ for each department $m \in \{1, 2, ..., n\}$. The algorithm outputs:

$$par = (g, g_1, u, h, w, v, e(g, g)^\alpha, H, H_1) \tag{4}$$

$$msk = (\alpha, \theta_1, \theta_2, ..., \theta_m) \tag{5}$$

- *Key Generation phase.*This stage is mainly led by KGC, which is used to participate in the generation and transmission of relevant keys.
  $Key\ Gen(1^\lambda, par, msk, \mathcal{S}) \rightarrow (SK, CK)$. The algorithm takes the public parameter par,the master private key msk, the user attribute set $\mathcal{S} = \{s_1, s_2..., s_k\}$ as input. Then, picks $k+1$ random exponents $r, r_1, r_2, \ldots, r_k \leftarrow \mathbb{Z}_p$. The algorithm also randomly selects $z_\delta, \leftarrow \mathbb{Z}_p$ for each user δ. It computes $K_0 = g^{z_\delta} w^r$,$K_1 = g^r$, and for every $\tau \in [k]$, $K_{\tau,2} = g^{r_\tau}$ and $K_{\tau,3} = (u^{s_\tau} h)^{r_\tau} v^{-r}$. KGC generates a department identifier $E_m = \theta_m g^{z_\delta}$ for user. The output user key SK

$$SK = (E_m, AK = (\mathcal{S}, K_0, K_1, \{K_{\tau,2}, K_{\tau,3}\}_{\tau \in [k]})) \tag{6}$$

  The algorithm also randomly selects $x \leftarrow \mathbb{Z}_p$ and generates QA key $R = g^\alpha g^{z_\delta}$ for QA. Meanwhile, g_1^x will be made publicïijĹ g_1^x is added to the public parameters parïijĽ. The QA key CK is output as follows

$$CK = (x, R_\delta) \tag{7}$$

- *Encryption phase.*The encryption phase consists of the following three algorithms. The API token encryption algorithm and data encryption algorithm in the encryption algorithm are executed by the admin, and the attribute key encryption algorithm is executed by the user.
  $TokEC((\mathbb{M}, \rho), par, tok) \rightarrow TCT$. First, *admin* defines a API token access

policy $(\mathbb{M}, \rho)$. It picks $\vec{y} = (s, y_2, \ldots, y_n)^\top \xleftarrow{\$} \mathbb{Z}_p^{n\times 1}$. s is randomly sampled from the underlying domain and serves as the secret value to be recovered during the decryption phase. The vector of the shares is $\vec{\lambda} = (\lambda_1, \lambda_2, \ldots, \lambda_\ell)^\top = \mathbb{M}\vec{y}$. It then picks ℓ random exponents $t_1, t_2, \ldots, t_\ell \xleftarrow{\$} Z_p$ and calculates $C = tok{\cdot}e(g,g)^{\alpha s}, C_0 = g^s$, and for every $\tau \in [\ell]$ $C_{\tau,1} = w^{\lambda_\tau} v^{t_\tau}, C_{\tau,2} = \left(u^{\rho(\tau)}h\right)^{-t_\tau}$ and $C_{\tau,3} = g^{t_\tau}$. The ciphertext output is

$$TCT = ((\mathbb{M}, \rho), C, C_0, \{C_{\tau,1}, C_{\tau,2}, C_{\tau,3}\}_{\tau\in[\ell]}) \tag{8}$$

Note, the algorithm also output the data summary $ds = H(data)$ based on data.

$AttkEC(AK, par) \rightarrow AC$. The attribute key encryption algorithm essentially employs the ElGamal encryption scheme, generating an ElGamal ciphertext. It pick random number $a \leftarrow \mathbb{Z}_p$. Then,it takes the attribute key AK as input and encrypts AK using QA's public key g^x to produce the ciphertext $A_0 = g_1^a$, $A_1 = AK \cdot (g_1^x)^a$. The ciphertext output is

$$AC = (A_0, A_1) \tag{9}$$

$DataEC((\mathbb{M}_d, \rho_d), par, data) \rightarrow DCT$. Although the data encryption algorithm uses a hybrid encryption mechanism, the symmetric key syk is still encrypted in the same way as the token encryption. It is worth noting that the access policies used by the token and the symmetric key syk are not consistent. *admin* also defines a data access policy $(\mathbb{M}_d, \rho_d)$,where $\mathbb{M}_d$ is a $\ell_d \times n_d$ matrix.It picks vectors $\mathbf{y}_d$ and $\vec{\lambda_d}$ containing the secret s_d, such that $\vec{\lambda_d} = \mathbb{M}_d\vec{y}_d$. It then picks ℓ_d random exponents $e_1, e_2, \ldots, e_{\ell_d} \xleftarrow{\$} Z_p$ and calculates $\tilde{D} = H_1(syk) \oplus data, D = syk \cdot e(g,g)^{\alpha s_d}, D_0 = g^{s_d}$, and for every $\gamma \in [\ell_d]$ $D_{\gamma,1} = w^{\lambda_\gamma} v^{e_\gamma}$, $D_{\gamma,2} = \left(u^{\rho_d(\gamma)}h\right)^{-e_\gamma}$ and $D_{\gamma,3} = g^{e_\gamma}$ The ciphertext output is

$$DCT = ((\mathbb{M}_d, \rho_d), D, D_0, \{D_{\gamma,1}, D_{\gamma,2}, D_{\gamma,3}\}_{\gamma\in[\ell_d]}) \tag{10}$$

The algorithm also outputs data summary $ds = H(data)$, which is provided to users for data selection.

- *Partial decryption phase.*This stage mainly decrypts the received API token and local privacy data ciphertext, which mainly involves two steps of decryption, and their operation subjects are also different to ensure confidentiality. API token decryption algorithm is executed by the user, and data decryption algorithm is executed by QA.

  $TokDC(TCT, SK) \rightarrow T$. The API token decryption algorithm first partitions the rows of matrix M and defines each row as $I = \{i : \rho(i) \in \mathcal{S}\}$. Next, the algorithm computes coefficients $\omega_i \in \mathbb{Z}_p$ using matrix M such that $\sum_{i\in I} \omega_i \vec{\mathbb{M}}_i = (1, 0, \ldots, 0)$ (these coefficients are guaranteed to exist if the attribute set S satisfies the access policy defined by the API token). Subsequently, it computes

$$T = \frac{e(C_0, K_0)}{\prod_{i\in I} \left(e(C_{i,1}, K_1) e(C_{i,2}, K_{\tau,2}) e(C_{i,3}, K_{\tau,3})\right)^{\omega_i}} \tag{11}$$

The algorithm outputs $T = e(g,g)^{z_\delta s}$.
$DataDC(DCT, AC, CK) \rightarrow B$. The decryption algorithm requires the retrieval of the user's attribute key $AK = A_1/A_0^x$. Subsequently, the algorithm proceeds similarly to the token decryption process. It computes coefficients $\{\eta_i \in Z_p\}_{i\in I}$, which are calculated when the attribute set S satisfies the predefined access structure. These coefficients satisfy the equation $\sum_{i\in I} \eta_i \vec{\mathbb{M}}_{di} = (1, 0, \ldots, 0)$, where $\vec{\mathbb{M}}_{d_i}$ represents each row of the matrix $\vec{\mathbb{M}}_d$. After computing the η_i, the algorithm then proceeds to calculate

$$B = \frac{e(D_0, K_0)}{\prod_{i\in I} \left(e(D_{i,1}, K_1)e(D_{i,2}, K_{\tau,2})e(D_{i,3}, K_{\tau,3})\right)^{\omega_i}} \tag{12}$$

The algorithm final outputs $B = e(g,g)^{z_\delta s_d}$.

- *Final decryption phase.* In this decryption phase, QA will truly obtain the API token and the plaintext of local privacy data through computation.
$Final\ decryption(T, B, CK) \rightarrow (tok, data)$. The decryption algorithm is executed by QA to decrypt the ciphertext (T, B). Before the ciphertext B is decrypted, QA will first compute $tok = C/(e(C_0, R_\delta)/T)$ and extract the key information from tok for validity verification. Only when the verification passes will the data ciphertext B be decrypted, with $data = H_1(D/(e(D_0, R_\delta)/B)) \oplus \tilde{D}$. Under the premise of legality, QA assembles a complete request body and dispatches the inquiry to the LLM
- *Result reuse phase.* In result reuse phase, the reuse algorithm is executed by QA and primarily serves the data decryption phase.
$Reuse(DCT, E_m^{\delta_1}, E_m^{\delta_2}, B_{\delta_1}) \rightarrow B_{\delta_2}$. The algorithm facilitates the reuse of decryption results among users within the same department. When user δ_1 from department m has already decrypted data da to obtain the decryption result B_{δ_1}, and another user δ_2 from the same department issues a query regarding data da, the algorithm computes

$$B_{\delta_2} = e(D_0, E_m^{\delta_2}/E_m^{\delta_1}) \cdot B_{\delta_1} \tag{13}$$

5 Correctness and Security Analysis

In this section, we will conduct correctness verification and security analysis on the scheme involved in Chap. 4. Since the MLM-ABE system has two encryption schemes, namely token encryption and local private data encryption, we will discuss them separately.

5.1 Correctness Analysis

The decryption construction of the MLM-ABE scheme in this paper is divided into two steps, so we will verify the correctness of the two steps respectively. And also analyze the correctness of the result reuse accordingly.

Partial Decryption. Although the partial decryption algorithm is divided into two parts—token decryption and data decryption—the two algorithms differ only in their access policies; all other aspects are entirely consistent. Therefore, we present only the decryption computation process for the token here.

$$
\begin{aligned}
T &= \frac{e(C_0, K_0)}{\prod_{i \in I} \left(e(C_{i,1}, K_1) e(C_{i,2}, K_{\tau,2}) e(C_{i,3}, K_{\tau,3})\right)^{\omega_i}} \\
&= \frac{e(g^s, g^z w^r)}{\prod_{i \in I} \left(e(w^{\lambda_\tau} v^{t_\tau}, g^r) e((u^{\rho(\tau)} h)^{-t_\tau}, g^{r_\tau}) e(g^{t_\tau}, (u^{s_\tau} h)^{r_\tau} v^{-r})\right)^{\omega_i}} \\
&= \frac{e(g^s, g^z) e(g^s, w^r)}{e(w, g)^{r \sum_{i \in I} \omega_i \lambda_\tau}} = \frac{e(g^s, g^z) e(g^s, w^r)}{e(w, g)^{rs}} = e(g, g)^{zs}
\end{aligned}
\tag{14}
$$

Final Decryption. Similarly, for the final decryption algorithm, only the decryption process for the token is provided here.

$$
\begin{aligned}
C/(e(C_0, R)/T) &= \frac{tok \cdot e(g, g)^{\alpha s}}{e(g^s, g^\alpha g^z)/e(g, g)^{zs}} \\
&= \frac{tok \cdot e(g, g)^{\alpha s}}{(e(g^s, g^\alpha) e(g^s, g^z)/e(g, g)^{zs})^\beta} \\
&= tok
\end{aligned}
\tag{15}
$$

Result Reuse. Assume that department m has l users. In $KeyGen$, KGC randomly selects $z_1, z_2, \ldots, z_l \in \mathbb{Z}_p$ for all employees $f_1, f_2, \ldots, f_l$ in each department and computes the department identifier E_m^l for each employee. If user f_1 has already sent a query for data da to QA, the decryption result will be saved. When user f_2 also sends a query regarding data da, B_{f_2} can be calculated as follows:

$$
\begin{aligned}
B_{f_2} &= e(D_0, E_m^{f_2}/E_m^{f_2}) \cdot B_{f_1} = e(g^{s_d}, \frac{g^{\theta_m} g^{z_2}}{g^{\theta_m} g^{z_1}}) \cdot e(g, g)^{z_1 s_d} \\
&= e(g^{s_d}, g^{z_2 - z_1}) \cdot e(g, g)^{z_1 s_d} = e(g, g)^{z_2 s}
\end{aligned}
\tag{16}
$$

5.2 Security Analysis

The security analysis of the scheme is shown in Appendix A.

6 Performance Analysis

Since this system is practical, this chapter mainly tests storage costs, hardware resources, concurrent pressure, etc., and draws conclusions.

To evaluate the MLM-ABE system's storage efficiency, we analyzed three key indicators: (1) Key storage overhead: user keys and QA client keys storage. (2) Ciphertext storage overhead: API token ciphertext and data ciphertext storage. (3) Cache overhead: decryption result cache in the result reuse mechanism.

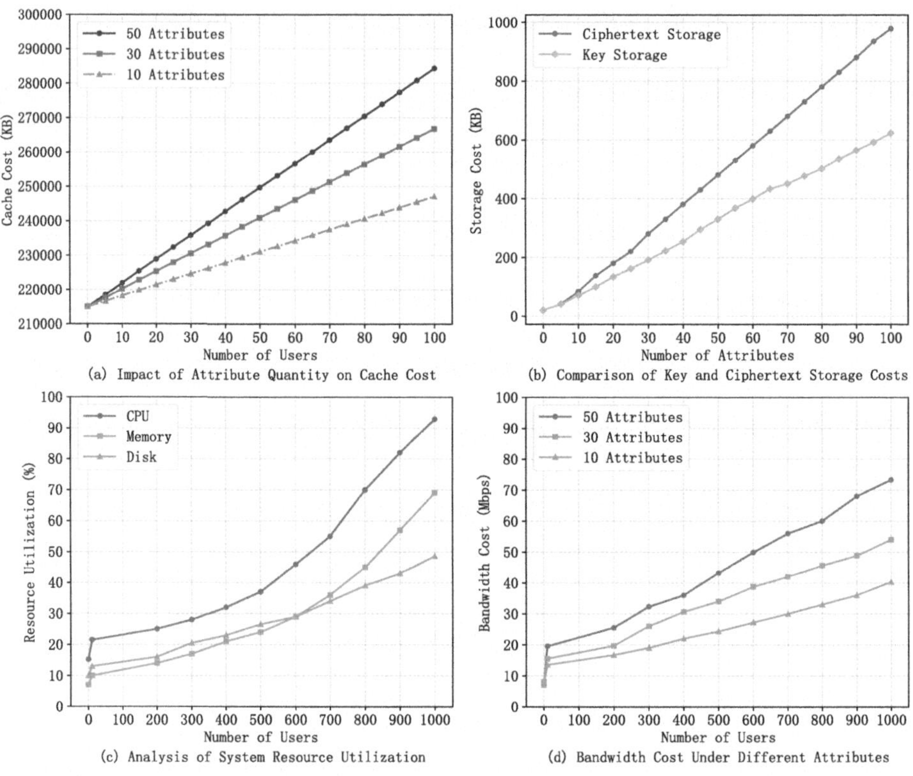

Fig. 3. Hardware resource costs under different number of attributes.

General enterprises cannot afford high LLM deployment costs and use multiple subscribed LLM services, and considering China's SMEs have <500–2000 employees (industry-specific) with non-simultaneous inquiries, we set 1000 users as the experimental benchmark. Tests show it meets enterprises needs.

As in Figure (b), MLM-ABE's key and ciphertext storage overhead increases linearly but slightly with attributes. For 100 attributes, a single user (10 attributes) has 6KB key overhead and 10KB ciphertext overhead. Each extra attribute adds 600 bytes to keys and 100 bytes to ciphertexts. This linearity aids capacity planning—even for 1000 attributes, user keys and ciphertexts need $\leq$60KB and $\leq$100KB, compatible with modern distributed storage. Engineering techniques like attribute hash compression and group element serialization optimize can cut storage by 15

To evaluate MLM-ABE's resource efficiency, we used an enterprise test platform to monitor CPU, memory, and network bandwidth. The test environment had a dual-socket server (2x Intel Xeon Gold 6230/256GB DDR4/10Gbps/100Mbps bandwidth/4×3090 24GB) and a containerized cluster (microservices/Docker 23.0.3/Spring Cloud-Hoxton.SR1/Spring Boot 2.2.2/Spring Cloud Alibaba 2.1.0).

Figure 3(a) tests 100 users' cache overhead for 10, 30, 50 attributes (excluding normal system cache). At 50 attributes, cache overhead is <30MB, meetable by standard public cloud servers. Figure 3(b) shows ciphertext and key storage (excluding data symmetric encryption cost) rise with attributes; at 100 attributes, both are <1MB, acceptable for enterprises.

Figure 3(c) shows 1000 concurrent users (3 encrypt/decrypt ops/user/sec) stress test results. CPU, memory, disk usage rise nonlinearly with users: 0–1000 users see CPU from 16% to 91%, memory from 5% to 79%, disk from 8% to 45.6%. CPU is most sensitive (15% avg increase per 100 users). For 1000 users, CPU $\leq$80% and memory $\leq$12GB, showing efficient resource management.

Figure 3(d) shows 1000 users: 10 attributes bring 4800–5000 Mbps bandwidth (9.6–10 Mbps/user); 30 attributes bring 3800–4000 Mbps (7.6–8.0 Mbps/user, 17%–20% less); 50 attributes bring 4500–4800 Mbps (9.0–9.6 Mbps/user). Low attributes (10–30) see request headers/protocols dominate bandwidth; more attributes raise attribute ciphertext/key bandwidth. Modern servers have >10Gbps bandwidth—50 attributes and 1000 users use <10% bandwidth, meeting SME needs.

Test results show MLM-ABE's extra costs after adding security mechanisms are manageable. 1000 users and 50 attributes see key indicators grow near-linearly with parameters. For example, key (998.38 KB/100 attributes) to ciphertext (599.38 KB/100 attributes) ratio stays 1.67×. 1000 users' max bandwidth (73.3 Mbps) is 7.3% of gigabit bandwidth.

Resource-wise, 1000 users use 91% CPU ; single nodes hold millions of users. <200 users see CPU $\leq$34%, memory $\leq$23%, bandwidth $\leq$34 Mbps (meets single server capacity); 1000 users need few nodes for load balancing. Unlike traditional solutions' multi-fold degradation, MLM-ABE's extra cost is 1.2–1.8x, balancing security and resource use for enterprises.

7 Conclusions

This paper considers the real-world applications of LLM and designs an integrated architecture that suits multiple LLM applications in combination with enterprise needs. By designing API tokens and fine-grained access control mechanisms, legal access to LLM APIs is achieved, providing strong support for the widespread application of generative artificial intelligence.

Acknowledgements. This work was supported by the National Natural Science Foundation of China under Grant U2001205, and in part by the Key Research and Development Program of Shaanxi Program under Grant 2023-YBGY-214.

Appendix A

Security Analysis

This section presents selective IND-CPA security proofs for both API token and data encryption schemes, along with security guarantees for the result reuse key.

Token Security Analysis. We establish the following theorem regarding our token scheme's selective security:

Theorem 1. *Given the $q-1$ assumption holds, any PPT adversary attacking challenge matrices of size $\ell \times n$ (where $\ell, n < q$) achieves negligible advantage in the selective security game.*

Proof. For the purpose of proving this theorem, suppose there exists a PPT adversary $\mathcal{A}$ that has a non-negligible advantage $Adv_{\mathcal{A}}$ in attacking our MLM-ABE scheme. Then, we can construct a simulator $\mathcal{B}$ which makes use of $\mathcal{A}$ to violate the $(q-1)$-decisional parallel BDHE assumption.

Initialization: $\mathcal{B}$ will receive two important components: public parameters and access policy (M^*, ρ^*) from $\mathcal{A}$ where M^* is $\ell \times n$ $(\ell, n \leq q)$ and $\rho^* : [\ell] \to \mathbb{Z}_p$.

Setup: $\mathcal{B}$ implicitly defines master key:

$$\alpha = a^{q+1} + \widetilde{\alpha}$$

with a, q from assumption and $\widetilde{\alpha} \xleftarrow{\$} \mathbb{Z}_p$. Sampling $\widetilde{v}, \widetilde{u}, \widetilde{h} \xleftarrow{\$} \mathbb{Z}_p$, it delivers:

$$\begin{aligned}
&g, \\
u &= g^{\tilde{u}} \cdot \prod_{(j,k)} \left(g^{a^k/b_j^2}\right)^{M^*_{j,k}}, \\
h &= g^{\tilde{h}} \cdot \prod_{(j,k)} \left(g^{a^k/b_j^2}\right)^{-\rho^*(j) M^*_{j,k}}, \\
w &= g^{a}, \\
v &= g^{\tilde{v}} \cdot \prod_{(j,k)} \left(g^{a^k/b_j}\right)^{M^*_{j,k}}, \\
e(g,g)^{\alpha} &= e(g^a, g^{a^q}) \cdot e(g,g)^{\tilde{\alpha}})
\end{aligned}$$

Query Phases 1 and 2: The simulator generates secret keys for the unauthorized attribute sets requested by $\mathcal{A}$. The processing is the same in both phases. We now describe how $\mathcal{B}$ creates keys for the attribute set $\mathcal{S} = \{A_1, A_2, \ldots, A_{|\mathcal{S}|}\}$ received from $\mathcal{A}$.

As $\mathcal{S}$ is unauthorized under (M^*, ρ^*), there exists $\vec{w} = (w_1, \ldots, w_n)^{\mathsf{T}} \in \mathbb{Z}_p^n$ with $w_1 = -1$ and $\langle \vec{M}_i^*, \vec{w} \rangle = 0$ for all $i \in I = \{i \in [\ell] \mid \rho^*(i) \in \mathcal{S}\}$. $\mathcal{B}$ computes $\vec{w}$, samples $\tilde{r} \xleftarrow{\mathrm{S}} \mathbb{Z}_p$, and implicitly defines:

$$r = \tilde{r} + \sum_{i=1}^{n} w_i a^{q+1-i}$$

After selecting $z \xleftarrow{\$} \mathbb{Z}_p$, it computes using assumption terms:

$$K_0 = g^z w^r = g^z \left(g^a\right)^{\tilde{r}} \prod_{i=2}^{n} \left(g^{a^{q+2-i}}\right)^{w_i}$$

$$K_1 = g^r = g^{\tilde{r}} \prod_{i \in [n]} \left(g^{a^{q+1-i}}\right)^{w_i}$$

$$R = g^{\alpha} \cdot g^z = g^{a^{q+1}+\tilde{\alpha}} \cdot g^z$$

For each attribute $\tau \in \mathcal{S}$, $\mathcal{B}$ computes:

$$K_{\tau,2} = g^{r_\tau}, \quad K_{\tau,3} = (u^{A_\tau} h)^{r_\tau} v^{-r}$$

with the public component:

$$v^{-r} = \Phi \cdot \prod_{j:\rho^*(j) \notin S} g^{-\langle \vec{w}, \vec{M}_j^* \rangle a^{q+1}/b_j}$$

$\mathcal{B}$ derives Φ from assumption terms. To cancel the second component via $(u^{A_\tau} h)^{r_\tau}$, it implicitly defines for each $A_\tau \in S$:

$$r_\tau = \tilde{r}_\tau + \tilde{r} \cdot \sum_{i':\rho^*(i') \notin S} \frac{b_{i'}}{A_\tau - \rho^*(i')} + \sum_{\substack{i,i' \\ \rho^*(i') \notin S}} \frac{w_i b_{i'} a^{q+1-i}}{A_\tau - \rho^*(i')}$$

($\tilde{r}_\tau \xleftarrow{s} \mathbb{Z}_p$). This ensures correct distribution of r_τ, where b_i terms cancel denominators b_i^2 in the attribute layer.

Algebraic manipulation yields:

$$(u^{A_\tau} h)^{r_\tau} = \Psi \cdot \prod_{j:\rho^*(j) \notin S} g^{\langle \vec{w}, \vec{M}_j^* \rangle a^{q+1}/b_j}$$

Thus $\mathcal{B}$ constructs:

$$SK = \left(\mathcal{S}, R, K_0, K_1, \{K_{\tau,2}, K_{\tau,3}\}_{\tau \in [|S|]}\right)$$

and provides it to $\mathcal{A}$.

Challenge: Upon receiving equal-length messages (tok_0, tok_1), $\mathcal{B}$ samples $b \xleftarrow{\$} \{0,1\}$ and constructs:

$$C = tok_b \cdot e(g, g^s)^{\tilde{\alpha}}, \quad C_0 = g^s$$

where g^s is from the assumption. $\mathcal{B}$ implicitly defines:

$$\vec{y} = (s, sa + \tilde{y}_2, \ldots, sa^{n-1} + \tilde{y}_n)^\top \quad (\tilde{y}_i \xleftarrow{\$} \mathbb{Z}_p)$$

with $\vec{\lambda} = M^* \vec{y}$, each row $\tau \in [\ell]$ has:

$$\lambda_\tau = \sum_i M_{\tau,i}^* s a^{i-1} + \tilde{\lambda}_\tau \quad \left(\tilde{\lambda}_\tau = \sum_{i=2}^{n} M_{\tau,i}^* \tilde{y}_i\right)$$

$\mathcal{B}$ sets $t_\tau = -sb_\tau$ (the distribution is correct because valid information is lost during the calculation), and computes:

$$C_{\tau,1} = w^{\tilde{\lambda}_\tau} \cdot \left(g^{sb_\tau}\right)^{-\tilde{v}} \cdot \prod_{j,k} \left(g^{sa^k b_\tau / b_j}\right)^{-M^*_{j,k}}, \quad C_{\tau,2} = \left(g^{sb_\tau}\right)^{-1}$$

Delivering ciphertext $TCT = ((M^*, \rho^*), C, C_0, \{C_{\tau,1}, C_{\tau,2}\}_\tau)$ to $\mathcal{A}$.

Guess: Following Phase 2 queries, if $\mathcal{A}$'s guess $b' = b$, $\mathcal{B}$ outputs 0 (indicating $T = e(g,g)^{sa^{q+1}}$); else outputs 1. When $T = e(g,g)^{sa^{q+1}}$:

$$C = tok_b \cdot e(g,g)^{\tilde{\alpha}s} \cdot e(g,g)^{a^{q+1}s}$$

preserves game correctness. If T is random in G_T, tok_b is perfectly hidden, giving $\mathcal{A}$ zero advantage. Thus $\mathcal{A}$'s non-negligible advantage implies $\mathcal{B}$ breaks the $q-1$ assumption.

Data Security Analysis. The hybrid data encryption scheme's security relies on two components: selective IND-CPA security of attribute keys and the underlying symmetric encryption's security.

Formally, we define: If both token encryption and symmetric encryption are secure, the data encryption scheme achieves selective IND-CPA security. Specifically, for any adversary $\mathcal{A}$ attacking data scheme Π_d, there exist simulators $\mathcal{B}$ and $\mathcal{B}_1$ such that $\mathcal{A}$'s advantage in breaking sIND-CPA security satisfies Eq. (17)'s constraints.

$$Adv_{\Pi,\mathcal{A}}^{sIND-CPA} \leq Adv_{\Pi_{token},\mathcal{B}}^{sIND-CPA} + Adv_{\Pi_{sym},\mathcal{B}_1} \tag{17}$$

where $Adv_{\Pi_{token},\mathcal{B}}^{sIND-CPA}$ is advantage of $\mathcal{B}$ breaking token encryption scheme's sIND-CPA security. $Adv_{\Pi_{sym},\mathcal{B}_1}$ is the advantage of $\mathcal{B}_1$ breaking symmetric encryption scheme security.

Proof. In our data encryption design, symmetric encryption protects the data while attribute-based encryption secures the symmetric key syk. The preceding section established the sIND-CPA security of Π_{token}. Furthermore, symmetric encryption schemes provide strong security guarantees when using adequate key lengths. Consequently, adversary $\mathcal{A}$'s advantage against Π is negligible, completing the security proof.

References

1. Rajashekar, N.C., et al.: Human-algorithmic interaction using a large language model-augmented artificial intelligence clinical decision support system. In: Proceedings of the 2024 CHI Conference on Human Factors in Computing Systems. CHI '24, Association for Computing Machinery, New York (2024). https://doi.org/10.1145/3613904.3642024,

2. Singh, D.: Legal documents text analysis using natural language processing (NLP). In: 2024 2nd International Conference on Self Sustainable Artificial Intelligence Systems (ICSSAS), pp. 1302–1307 (2024). https://doi.org/10.1109/ICSSAS64001.2024.10760929
3. Mann, B., et al.: Language models are few-shot learners. arXiv preprint arXiv:2005.14165 **1**, 3 (2020)
4. Liu, V., Yin, Y.: Green AI: exploring carbon footprints, mitigation strategies, and trade offs in large language model training. Discov. Artif. Intell. **4**(1), 49 (2024)
5. Cost analysis of deploying LLMS: a comparative study between cloud managed, self-hosted and 3rd party LLMS. https://medium.com/artefact-engineering-and-data-science/llms-deployment-a-practical-cost-analysis-e0c1b8eb08ca, 30 Oct 2023
6. Ali, H., ul Mustafa, A., Aysan, A.F.: Global adoption of generative ai: What matters most? J. Economy Technol. (2024). https://doi.org/10.1016/j.ject.2024.10.002, https://www.sciencedirect.com/science/article/pii/S2949948824000520
7. Rouselakis, Y., Waters, B.: Practical constructions and new proof methods for large universe attribute-based encryption. In: Proceedings of the 2013 ACM SIGSAC Conference on Computer & Communications security, pp. 463–474 (2013)
8. Tao, Y., et al.: Orr-cp-ABE: a secure and efficient outsourced attribute-based encryption scheme with decryption results reuse. Futur. Gener. Comput. Syst. **161**, 559–571 (2024)
9. Gu, X., et al.: On the effectiveness of large language models in domain-specific code generation. ACM Trans. Softw. Eng. Methodol. (2024)
10. De Caro, A., Iovino, V.: JPBC: java pairing based cryptography. In: 2011 IEEE Symposium on Computers and Communications (ISCC), pp. 850–855. IEEE (2011)
11. Li, X., Liu, T., Chen, C., Cheng, Q., Zhang, X., Kumar, N.: A lightweight and verifiable access control scheme with constant size ciphertext in edge-computing-assisted iot. IEEE Internet Things J. **9**(19), 19227–19237 (2022)
12. Damgård, I., Haagh, H., Orlandi, C.: Access control encryption: Enforcing information flow with cryptography. In: Theory of Cryptography: 14th International Conference, TCC 2016-B, Beijing, China, October 31-November 3, 2016, Proceedings, Part II 14, pp. 547–576. Springer (2016)
13. Bethencourt, J., Sahai, A., Waters, B.: Ciphertext-policy attribute-based encryption. In: 2007 IEEE Symposium on Security and Privacy (SP'07), pp. 321–334. IEEE (2007)
14. Goyal, V., Pandey, O., Sahai, A., Waters, B.: Attribute-based encryption for fine-grained access control of encrypted data. In: Proceedings of the 13th ACM Conference on Computer and Communications Security, pp. 89–98 (2006)
15. Hohenberger, S., Waters, B.: Online/offline attribute-based encryption. In: Public-Key Cryptography–PKC 2014: 17th International Conference on Practice and Theory in Public-Key Cryptography, pp. 293–310, Buenos Aires, March 26-28, 2014. Proceedings 17. Springer (2014)
16. Cui, H., Deng, R.H., Li, Y., Qin, B.: Server-aided revocable attribute-based encryption. In: Computer Security–ESORICS 2016: 21st European Symposium on Research in Computer Security, pp. 570–587, Heraklion, Greece, September 26-30, 2016, Proceedings, Part II 21. Springer (2016)
17. Wang, L., Wang, Z.H., Guo, F., Wu, C.K.: A hybrid encryption transmission scheme for industrial control systems. In: 2022 7th International Conference on Intelligent Computing and Signal Processing (ICSP), pp. 1144–1147. IEEE (2022)

18. Attrapadung, N., Imai, H.: Attribute-based encryption supporting direct/indirect revocation modes. In: IMA International Conference on Cryptography and Coding, pp. 278–300. Springer (2009)
19. Cui, H., Deng, R.H.: Revocable and decentralized attribute-based encryption. Comput. J. **59**(8), 1220–1235 (2016)
20. Zhang, J., Wu, M., Zhang, Q., Peng, C.: A lightweight data sharing scheme with resisting key abuse in mobile edge computing. In: IEEE INFOCOM 2021-IEEE Conference on Computer Communications Workshops (INFOCOM WKSHPS), pp. 1–6. IEEE (2021)
21. Fugkeaw, S., Sato, H.: An extended CP-ABE based access control model for data outsourced in the cloud. In: 2015 IEEE 39th Annual Computer Software and Applications Conference. vol. 3, pp. 73–78. IEEE (2015)
22. Xue, Y., Xue, K., Gai, N., Hong, J., Wei, D.S., Hong, P.: An attribute-based controlled collaborative access control scheme for public cloud storage. IEEE Trans. Inf. Forensics Secur. **14**(11), 2927–2942 (2019)
23. Bobba, R., Khurana, H., Prabhakaran, M.: Attribute-sets: a practically motivated enhancement to attribute-based encryption. In: Computer Security–ESORICS 2009: 14th European Symposium on Research in Computer Security, pp. 587–604, Saint-Malo, France, September 21-23, 2009. Proceedings 14. Springer (2009)
24. Li, J., Wang, T., Yang, B., Yang, Q., Zhang, W., Hong, K.: Abcrowdmed: a fine-grained worker selection scheme for crowdsourcing healthcare with privacy-preserving. IEEE Trans. Serv. Comput. **16**(5), 3182–3195 (2023). https://doi.org/10.1109/TSC.2023.3292498

EP-BPRE: Efficient Pairing-free Broadcast Proxy Re-encryption for Secure Data Sharing in Internet of Vehicle

Yuanjian Zhou[1], Tianci Zhao[1], Zhengjun Jing[1], Xiaosong Guan[2], Hongyuan Cheng[2(✉)], Yongwei Tang[3], Weizhi Meng[4], and Chunhua Su[5]

[1] The School of Computer Engineering, JiangSu University of Technology, Jiangsu 213001, China
zhouyuanjian@jsut.edu.cn, jzjing@jsut.edu.com

[2] The School of Computer Science & Engineering, LinYi University, Linyi 273300, China
hycheng649@163.com

[3] Key Laboratory of Computing Power Network and Information Security, Ministry of Education, Shandong Computer Science Center (National Supercomputer Center in Jinan), Qilu University of Technology (Shandong Academy of Sciences), Jinan 250014, Shandong, China
tangyw@sdas.org

[4] The School of Computing and Communications, Lancaster University, Lancaster LA1 4WA, UK
w.meng3@lancaster.ac.uk

[5] The School of Computer Science and Engineering, University of Aizu, Aizu, Japan
chsu@u-aizu.ac.jp

Abstract. With the development of the Internet of Vehicles (IoV), more and more data are shared among vehicles, between vehicles and infrastructure, and between vehicles and the cloud. However, these existing privacy-preserving schemes for secure data sharing in IoV face some challenges, such as privacy issues of vehicles identity leakage, additional overhead caused by additional encryption algorithms, as well as malicious attacks on cloud server from attackers. To address these issues, in this paper we propose a data sharing scheme in IoV for the efficient, secure, and trustworthy sharing of data, while protecting the privacy of data receiver identity. Firstly, we propose an efficient pairing-free broadcast proxy re-encryption (EP-BPRE), which uses identity-based broadcast proxy re-encryption to provide fine-grained control, while ensuring the secure data sharing and preventing data leakage, and constructs the Lagrange interpolation polynomials to protect the identity privacy of the data receivers group. Additionally, we achieve CCA security of our proposed scheme in the random oracle model. Compared with other existing schemes, the EP-BPRE scheme avoids time-consuming bilinear pairing operations and has some advantages in function and efficiency. Finally, the analysis shows that the proposed EP-BPRE scheme is secure and efficient in the data-sharing of the IoV.

L. Zhang and K.-K. R. Choo (Eds.): MobiQuitous 2025, LNICST 684, pp. 269–287, 2026.
https://doi.org/10.1007/978-3-032-22503-0_15

Keywords: Internet of Vehicles · Proxy re-encryption · Pairing free · Data sharing

1 Introduction

The internet of things (IoT) [1], as the third information technology revolution, promotes the process of information exchange and intelligent development. It collects and exchanges the data through device sensors according to agreed protocols, and is widely used in scenarios such as : smart transportation [2], smart grid [3], smart city [4] and so on. The internet of vehicles (IoV) [5] is an application of IoT that uses the communication technology to achieve the network connection between vehicles and X (e.g. vehicle, people, road and service platform) to improve the users' vehicle experience. In the context of IoV data sharing, sensors [6] integrated within vehicle are used to collect sensitive vehicle data (eq. vehicle trajectory and speed). Subsequently, these data is exchanged with other vehicles, roadside infrastructure, people and cloud server (CS) to enable various vehicle service. However, since CS is not completely trusted, these sensitive data may be leaked. Therefore, we must encrypt the data before uploading them to CS.

Identity-based encryption (IBE) [7], as an encryption technology, is highly famous for its simplified key management. It can ensure the security of data sharing, but its ciphertext form hinders the data sharing efficiency in IoV. When the data owner wants to share the data with the members of data receiver group S, the data owner needs to download the ciphertext from CS and re-encrypt the plaintext according to the identity of data receivers in the S after decrypting. However, with the increasing of data receiver number in S, it will bring the huge computation and storage burden to the data owner. Since that the data owner needs to compute and send the ciphertext for each data receiver in S, the overhead is proportional to the size of group S. Moreover, downloading the data from CS introduces addition maintenance issues. Therefore, we need to design a more efficient and security encryption scheme to share the encryption data in CS.

At this time, one may wonder why the data owner does not hire a CS to compute and store the ciphertexts for him. But if CS wants to do the above, it must know the data owner's secret-key. However, CS is not a fully trusted entity in the actual situation. It may leak the data owner's secret key for some interests that will lead to irreversible consequences. For example, the leak of vehicle sensitive data may lead to the exposure of personal information such as the users' whereabouts and habits to violate the personal privacy. Therefore, we need to design a scheme that can meet the need of sharing data with all members of the data receiver group S in the situation without leaking any data.

To address this issue, the concept of proxy re-encryption (PRE) is proposed that the data owner can share the data with data receiver without exposing his own secret-key and plaintext. In this scheme, CS does not know any data, but re-encrypt the original ciphertext using the re-encryption key generated by the data owner to generate the re-encryption ciphertext decrypted by the data receiver using his own secret-key. Using CS as proxy perform the complex re-encryption computation and storage work on behalf of the data owner. However, this still does not solve the "one-to-many" data sharing problem. When there are a large number of data receivers, the data owner incurs a linearly increasing computation overhead because he needs to generate the corresponding re-encryption ciphertext for each receiver. The broadcast proxy re-encryption (BPRE) as an extension of PRE has been proposed. BPRE generates a re-encryption key that supports all data receivers to achieve broadcast-style data sharing. BPRE typically uses the bilinear pairing operation because that this operation enable effective mapping between different groups and allows the security transform without exposing the secret-key. But the billinear pairing operation has high computation overhead, which is not suitable for the case with strong real-time requirements in IoV.

1.1 Contribution

Although the existing PREs schemes can achieve secure data sharing, they cannot be efficient and anonymous. Therefore, a efficient pairing-free BPRE scheme is worthwhile. The main contributions of EP-BPRE are as follows:

1) First, we proposed an efficient pairing-free BPRE for secure data sharing in IoV (EP-BPRE). In the proposed scheme, we use the pairing free method to reduce the computation overhead. It makes our scheme more suitable for IoV.
2) We prove that the proposed scheme meets the CCA security under CDH problems in the random oracle model (ROM).
3) In the evaluation section, we perform the extensive evaluation that the proposed scheme compared with existing schemes has certain advantages in terms of computation and storage overhead.

The organization of this paper is delineated as follows: Sect. 2 offers a review of related work. Section 3 presents preliminaries information. In Sect. 4, we outline system model, scheme define and security model. The details of the proposed scheme and its correctness are elaborated upon in Sect. 5. A security analysis is conducted in Sect. 6. Section 7 addresses evaluation analysis. Lastly, Sect. 8 concludes the paper with final observations.

2 Related Work

2.1 Data Sharing in IoV

In IoV, data sharing is one of the core technology that achieves the smart transport, vehicle collaboration, real-time traffic conditions and so on. As a new data sharing network paradigm, IoV involves the data sharing between vehicles, between vehicle and people, between vehicle and roadside infrastructure and between vehicle and CS. But with the increasing of vehicle in IoV, a large of sensitive data need to exchange. To ensure the data sharing security, the data owner typically uses the encryption methods to solve and uploads the ciphertext to CS. The powerful computation and storage capabilities of CS ensures the data sharing security among user. For example, Li et al. [8] proposed an attribute-based encryption (ABE) secure data sharing in IoV. Zhu et al. [9] proposed a pairing-free encryption scheme based Computational Diffe-Hellman (CDH) problem.

However, the above schemes cannot address the problem of multiple data receivers, as the data owner needs to generate the corresponding ciphertexts for each data receivers. To solve this problem, Chen et al. [10] use the identity-based broadcast encryption (IBBE) to design a privacy-preserving certificateless BPRE with authorization. Compared to the above scheme, the data owner only needs to generate ciphertext once that improves the efficiency of data sharing. However, these schemes have not solved the limited computing power of vehicle unites and fully utilized the powerful computing power of CS.

2.2 Broadcast Proxy Re-Encryption

The concept of broadcast encryption (BE) is first introduced in IoV by Zhong et al. [11] to achieve that the data owner can send his own ciphertext to a data receiver group S. And each data receiver in group S can decrypt using his secret-key. After that, more and more people study BE in order to improve efficiency. For example, Singh et al. [12] proposed a accountable authority IBBE by the weak black-box. Yao et al. [13] proposed a fully anonymous BE with personalized messages. However, it also brings a large computation burden to the data owner. PRE [14] is proposed for it. Using the powerful computation and storage capabilities of CS, the data owner shares the data with data receiver without exposing any data. Pei et al. [15] proposed an identity-based proxy re-encryption (IB-PRE) data sharing to achieve the binding of public-key and identity approach by introducing identity hash during the key generation phase. Ge et al. [16] proposed an attribute-based proxy re-encryption (AB-PRE) and can direct revoke the user. Li et al. [17] proposed a lightweight PRE without using the bilinear pairing operation to ensure efficient data sharing. On the other hand, BPRE [18] by combining the above two technologies is proposed. Zhou et al. [19] uses an identity-based broadcast proxy re-encryption (IB-BPRE) for data sharing among the multiple data receivers. Maiti et al. [20] proposed a privacy preserving IB-BPRE which protects the identity privacy of data receiver group through the Lagrange interpolation polynomial. Ge et al. [21] proposed a revocable IB-BPRE. Kim et al. [22] improved IB-BPRE to solve the problem computation overhead by not using bilinear pairing.

Table 1 shows the comparison of our proposed scheme EP-BPRE with the existing schemes [17,20,22] in aspects of scheme function, security and technology. The result indicates that only EP-BPRE meets broadcast, pairing-free compared with other schemes. And our proposed scheme meets CCA security by IB-BPRE.

Table 1. Function, Security and Technology Comparison with [17,20,22]

Scheme	Broadcast?	Pairing-free?	Security	Technology
Li et al. [17]	×	√	CCA	PRE
Maiti et al. [20]	√	×	CPA	IB-BPRE
Kim et al. [22]	√	√	–	BPRE
Our scheme	√	√	CCA	IB-BPRE

3 Preliminaries

3.1 Hard Problem Assumption

Our proposed scheme EP-BPRE is based on the computation Diffie-Hellman (CDH) assumption. Let $\mathbb{G}$ be a subgroup of $\mathbb{Z}_q^*$ with a prime order q and let g be a generator of the group $\mathbb{G}$. Given a tuple of values $(g, g^a, g^b, g^c) \in \mathbb{G}^4$ (where $a, b, c \in \mathbb{Z}_q^*$), in which $c = ab$ holds. If $g^c = g^{ab}$, the algorithm holds true and returns continue; otherwise, return $\perp$. The adversary $\mathcal{A}$ with his advantage to deal with the CDH problem can compute:

$$\begin{aligned} Adv_{\mathcal{A}}^{CDH} &= |Pr[\mathcal{A}(g, g^a, g^b, g^{ab}) = 1] \\ &\quad - Pr[\mathcal{A}(g, g^a, g^b, g^c) = 1]| \end{aligned} \tag{1}$$

The CDH assumption holds if any probabilistic polynomial time (PPT) algorithm with an negligible advantage in solving the CDH problem.

3.2 Lagrange Interpolation Polynomial

For a polynomial function, given $k+1$ value points: (x_0, y_0),(x_1, y_1),. . .,(x_j, y_j),. . ., (x_k, y_k). Among them, x_j corresponds to the position of the independent variable, while y_j corresponds to the value of the function at this position.

$$\begin{aligned} L(x) &= \textstyle\sum_{j=0}^{k} y_j l_j(x) \\ &= y_0 l_0(x) + y_1 l_1(x) + \ldots + y_k l_k(x). \end{aligned} \tag{2}$$

$$\begin{aligned} l_j(x) &= \textstyle\prod_{i=0, i\neq j} \frac{x - x_i}{x_j - x_i} \\ &= \frac{x - x_0}{x_j - x_0} \cdots \frac{x - x_{j-1}}{x_j - x_{j-1}} \frac{x - x_{j+1}}{x_j - x_{j+1}} \cdots \frac{x - x_k}{x_j - x_k}. \end{aligned} \tag{3}$$

The characteristic of Lagrange's basic polynomial $l_j(x)$ is that $l_j(x_j) = 1$ and $l_j(x_i) = 0, i \neq j$.

3.3 Schnorr Signature

Let $\mathbb{G}$ be a subgroup of $\mathbb{Z}_q^*$ with a prime order q and let g be a generator of the group $\mathbb{G}$ [23]. Choose hash function $H(\cdot) : \{0,1\}^* \rightarrow \mathbb{Z}_q^*$.

- **KeyGen**$(1^\lambda) \rightarrow sk, pk$: The algorithm selects the secret-key $sk \in \mathbb{Z}_q^*$ and the public-key $pk = g^{sk}$.
- **Sign**$(sk, m) \rightarrow \sigma$: Inputting the secret-key sk and the plaintext m, the algorithm computes the signature $\sigma = (S_1, S_2)$, where $S_1 = r + sk \cdot H(m \parallel S_2) mod\, q$, $S_2 = g^r$ and $r \in \mathbb{Z}_q^*$.
- **Verify**$(pk, \sigma) \rightarrow m$: If $g^{S_1} \stackrel{?}{=} pk^{H(m \| S_2)} \cdot S_2$, it holds true; otherwise, return $\perp$.

4 System Overview

In this section, we introduce the system model, scheme define and security model.

4.1 System Model

Figure 1 shows a secure data sharing scheme in IoV, which includes four entities: the KGC, data owner, CS and a group of the data receivers S.

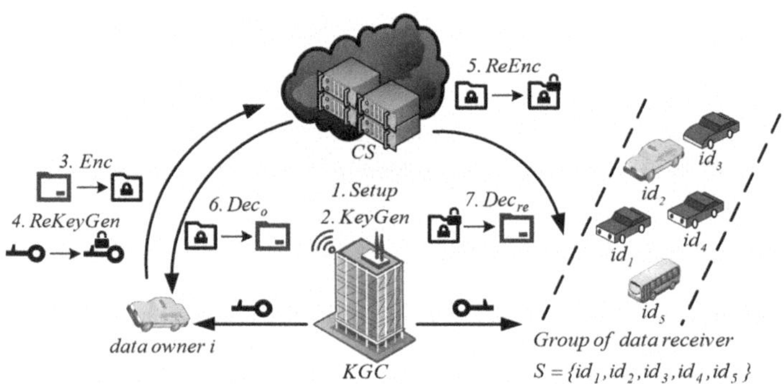

Fig. 1. System model

KGC: As a trustworthy entity, the KGC can generate the public parameters pp, public/secret-key pk/sk and send them to the data user (such as the data owner, data receivers and etc.).

Data Owner: After getting the public parameters pp and the key pair (pk_i, sk_i), the data owner i encrypts the plaintext m using them and sends the original ciphertext C_i to CS. Meanwhile, when the data owner i wants to share data with the data receivers group S, the data owner i will generate the re-encryption key $rk_{i \rightarrow S}$.

CS: CS is a honest-but-curious entity in the our proposed scheme. The data owner uploads the original ciphertext C_i and stores it in CS. Then, CS transforms C_i into the re-encryption ciphertext $C_{i \to S}$ through $rk_{i \to S}$. Moreover, CS cannot know any data about the data owner i during the ciphertext conversion process.

Data Receiver: After obtaining the re-encryption ciphertext $C_{i \to S}$, the data receiver can decrypt $C_{i \to S}$ through his own secret-key sk_j to get the plaintext m.

4.2 Scheme Define

There exists the following algorithms in our proposed scheme EP-BPRE and will be described as below:

Setup$(\lambda,n) \to (pp)$: KGC executes this algorithm. On input the security parameter λ and the maximum number n of data receivers, it outputs the public parameter pp. In the setup phase, KGC will finally public the pp.

KeyGen$(pp) \to (pk_i,sk_i)$: KGC executes this algorithm for users including the data owner and the data receivers. On input pp, it outputs the public/secret-key (pk_i,sk_i) for the corresponding user. Similarly, the data receiver can get the public/secret-key (pk_j,sk_j).

ReKeyGen$(pp, pk_i, sk_i, S) \to (rk_{i \to S})$: The data owner i executes this algorithm. On input the pp, p/sk_i of the data owner i and the group of the data receivers $S = \{id_j, pk_j\}(j = 1, \ldots, n)$, it outputs the re-encryption key $rk_{i \to S}$.

Enc(pp, pk_i, m): The data owner i executes this algorithm. On input the pp, pk_i of the data owner i and the plaintext message m, it outputs the corresponding original ciphertext C_i.

ReEnc$(pp, rk_{i \to S}, C_i)$: CS executes this algorithm. On input the pp, re-encryption key $rk_{i \to S}$ and the original ciphertext C_i, it outputs the re-encryption ciphertext $C_{i \to S}$.

Dec$_o(C_i, sk_i)$: The data owner i executes this algorithm. On input the sk_i and original ciphertext C_i, it outputs the plaintext m.

Dec$_{re}(C_{i \to S}, id_j, sk_j)$: The data receiver j executes this algorithm. On input the re-encryption ciphertext $C_{i \to S}$, $id_j \in S$, sk_j of its corresponding secret-key, it outputs the plaintext m.

For any plaintext m, the EP-BPRE scheme meets the algorithms as below:

- **Dec**$_o$(**Enc**$(pp,pk_i,m),sk_i)=m$.
- **Dec**$_{re}$(**ReEnc**$(pp,$**ReKeyGen**$(pp,pk_i,sk_i,S),$**Enc**$(pp,pk_i,m)),id_j,sk_j)=m$.

4.3 Security Model

In this section, we will define two essential terms of security model. Specifically, the details are as follows:

1) Uncorrupted Key (UK) Generate: If a user's public-key pk corresponding secret-key sk can keep secret to any malicious adversaries, so we believe that this user is uncorrupted and store the corresponding key pair (pk) in the table T_{uk}.
2) Corrupted Key (CK) Generate: If a user's public-key pk corresponding secret-key sk can be corrupted by any malicious adversaries through attack or corrupt, so we believe that this user has been corrupted and store the corresponding key pair (pk,sk) in the table T_{ck}.

Definition: Our proposed scheme EP-BPRE is CCA security under the ROM according to the concept of [17] and [20]. If no polynomial time adversary has a very negligible advantage to win the following game.

- **Game 1**: This game is played between the adversary $\mathcal{A}_1$ and challenger $\mathcal{C}$.
- **Setup**: $\mathcal{C}$ executes the UK to generate the uncorrupted key pair and store them to T_{uk}. $\mathcal{C}$ executes the CK to generate the corrupted key pair and store them to T_{ck}. Then, $\mathcal{C}$ stores all key pairs to the key table T_k and the re-encryption key rk to the re-encryption key table T_{rk}. The adversary $\mathcal{A}$ can obtain the public-key from T_{uk}, secret-key from T_{ck} and re-encryption key from T_{rk}.
- **Q-ph 1**: $\mathcal{A}_1$ makes the following queries to $Q_{ReKeyGen}$, Q_{ReEnc}, $Q_{Dec_{re}}$:
  - Re-encryption key query $Q_{ReKeyGen}(pk_i, S)$: $\mathcal{A}_1$ can make the query $Q_{ReKeyGen}(pk_i, S)$, where $pk_i \neq pk_{i^*}$ or $id'_j \notin S$. $\mathcal{C}$ executes the $ReKey-Gen(pp, pk_i, sk_i, S)$ algorithm to generate the re-encryption key $rk_{i \to S}$ and send it to $\mathcal{A}_1$.
  - ReEnc query $Q_{ReEnc}(rk_{i\to S}, C_i)$: $\mathcal{A}_1$ can make the query $Q_{ReEnc}(ReKe-yGen(pp, pk_i, sk_i, S), C_i)$, where $pk_i \neq pk_{i^*}$ or $id'_j \notin S$. $\mathcal{C}$ executes the $ReEnc(rk_{i\to S}, C_i)$ algorithm to generate the re-encryption ciphertext $C_{i\to S}$ to $\mathcal{A}_1$.
  - Dec query $Q_{Dec}(C, sk)$: $\mathcal{A}_1$ can make the query $Q_{Dec}(C, sk)$, where $sk \neq sk'$. $\mathcal{C}$ executes the $Dec(C, sk)$ algorithm to generate the plaintext m to $\mathcal{A}_1$.
- **Challenge**: $\mathcal{A}_1$ selects random two plaintext messages $\{m_0, m_1\}$ of the same length $_1$ and sends them to $\mathcal{C}$. $\mathcal{C}$ selects random $f \in \{0,1\}$ and executes the $Enc(pk_i, m_f)/ReEnc(rk_{i\to S'})$ algorithm to generate the challenge ciphertext $C_i^*/C_{i\to S'}$. Finally, $\mathcal{C}$ sends them to $\mathcal{A}_1$.
- **Q-ph 2**: $\mathcal{A}_1$ makes the same queries as Q-ph 1.
- **Guess**: Finally, $\mathcal{A}_1$ sends a guess $f' \in \{0,1\}$ to $\mathcal{C}$ and wins the game if $f' = f$.
- **Probability**: The possible that $\mathcal{A}_1$ wins the game is $Pr[f' = f] - 1/2$.

5 Construction

The construction of our proposed scheme EP-BPRE, mainly consists of seven algorithms: Setup, KeyGen, ReKeyGen, Enc, ReEnc, Dec_o and Dec_{re}, is as follows:

5.1 Scheme Construction

Setup$(\lambda, n) \rightarrow (pp)$: The KGC executes the algorithm. On input the security parameter λ and the maximum number n of members in a data receiver group, output the public parameters pp. The algorithm works as follows:

Step 1: Let $\mathbb{G}$ be a subgroup of $\mathbb{Z}_q^*$ with a prime order q and let g be a generator of the group $\mathbb{G}$.

Step 2: Select three hash functions: $H_1 : \mathbb{G} \rightarrow \mathbb{Z}_q^*$ and $H_2 : \{0,1\} \times \{0,1\} \rightarrow \mathbb{Z}_q^*$. The security parameter λ determines the public parameters and and the message m belongs to $\{0,1\}$.

Step 3: Publish the public parameters $pp = (q, g, \mathbb{G}, H_1, H_2, ,)$.

KeyGen$(pp) \rightarrow (pk_i, sk_i)$: The KGC executes the algorithm. On input pp, output the secret-key sk_i and public-key pk_i. KGC selects random $x_i \in \mathbb{Z}_q^*$ and use it as the secret-key $sk_i = (x_i)$. Then, it generates the corresponding public-key $pk_i = (X_i = g^{x_i})$.

ReKeyGen$(pp, pk_i, sk_i, S) \rightarrow (rk_{i \rightarrow S})$: The data owner i executes the algorithm. On input pp, its public/secret-key pk_i/sk_i and the group of data receivers $S = \{(id_1, pk_1), \ldots, (id_n, pk_n)\}_{j=1}^n$, output the re-encryption key $rk_{i \rightarrow S}$. The algorithm works as follows:

Step 1: Select random $\alpha \in \{0,1\}^1$, $\beta \in \{0,1\}^2$ and compute $rk_1 = \frac{\alpha}{x_i H_1(X_i)}$, $z = H_2(\alpha, \beta)$.

Step 2: For each $id_j \in S$, compute $x_{id_j} = H_1(id_j)$ and $y_{id_j} = X_j^z$.

Step 3: Generate a polynomial function $f(x) = \prod_{1 \leq t \neq j}^{n} \frac{x - x_t}{x_{id_j} - x_t} = a_0 + a_1 \cdot x_1 + \ldots + a_n \cdot x^n$. Then, collect all coefficients as $rk_2 = (a_0, a_1, \ldots, a_n)$.

Step 4: Compute $rk_3 = H_1(g^z) \oplus (\alpha \parallel \beta)$.

Step 5: Output the re-encryption key $rk_{i \rightarrow S} = (rk_1, rk_2, rk_3)$.

Enc$(pp, pk_i, m) \rightarrow (C_i)$: The data owner i executes the algorithm. On input pp, pk_i and a message m, output the original ciphertext C_i. The algorithm works as follows:

Step 1: Select random $\theta \in \{0,1\}^2$ and compute
$r = H_2(m, \theta)$,
$C_1 = (X_i^{H_1(X_i)})^r$,
$C_2 = H_1(g^r) \oplus (m \parallel \theta)$,
Setep 2: Select random $u, v \in \mathbb{Z}_q^*$ and compute
$V_1 = g^u$, $V_2 = g^v$,
$C_3 = H_1(C_2) \cdot u + v$
Step 4:Output the ciphertext $C_i = (C_1, C_2, C_3, V_1, V_2)$.

ReEnc$(pp, rk_{i\to S}, C_i) \to (C_{i\to S})$: The CS executes the algorithm. On input pp, the re-encryption key $rk_{i\to S}$ and the original ciphertext C_i, output the re-encryption ciphertext $C_{i\to S}$. The algorithm works as follows:

Step 1: If $g^{C_3} \stackrel{?}{=} V_1^{H_1(C_2)} \cdot V_2$, it holds true and continues the next steps; otherwise, returns $\perp$.

Step 2: Compute $C_1' = C_1^{rk_1} = (X_i^{H_1(X_i)})^{\frac{\alpha}{x_i H_1(X_i)}} = g^{r\alpha}$,
$C_2' = C_2$, $C_3' = C_3$, $V_1' = V_1$, $V_2' = V_2$,
$C_4' = rk_2 = (a_0, a_1, \ldots, a_{n-1})$, $C_5' = rk_3 = H_1(g^z) \oplus (\alpha \| \beta)$.

Step 3: Output the re-encryption ciphertext $C_{i\to S} = (C_1', C_2', C_3', C_4', C_5', V_1', V_2')$.

Dec$_o(C_i, sk_i) \to (m)$: The data owner i executes the algorithm. On input C_i and sk_i, output the plaintext m. The algorithm works as follows:

Step 1: If $g^{C_3} \stackrel{?}{=} V_1^{H_1(C_2)} \cdot V_2$, it holds true and continues the next steps; otherwise, returns $\perp$.

Step 2: Compute $(m \parallel \theta) = C_2 \oplus H_1(C_1^{\frac{1}{x_i H_1(X_i)}})$.

Dec$_{re}(C_{i\to S}, id_j, sk_j) \to (m)$: The data receiver j executes the algorithm. On input the re-encryption ciphertext $C_{i\to S}$, data receiver's identity $id_j \in S$ and its sk_j, output the plaintext m. The algorithm works as follows:

Step 1: If $g^{C_3'} \stackrel{?}{=} V_1'^{H_1(C_2')} \cdot V_2'$, it holds true and continues the next steps; otherwise, returns $\perp$.

Step 2: Construct the polynomial $f(x) = a_0 + a_1 \cdot x_1 + \ldots + a_{n-1} \cdot x^{n-1}$ by using the C_3' and compute $x_{id_j} = H_1(id_j)$ and $y_{id_j} = f(x_{id_j}) = X_j^z$.

Step 3: Compute $(\alpha \parallel \beta) = C_5' \oplus H_1(y_{id_j}^{\frac{1}{x_j}})$.

Step 4. Compute $(m \parallel \theta) = C_2' \oplus H_1(C_1'^{\frac{1}{\alpha}})$. If $y_{id_j} \stackrel{?}{=} X_j^{H_2(\alpha,\beta)}$ and $C_1' \stackrel{?}{=} g^{H_2(m,\theta)\alpha}$, it holds true and returns the plaintext m; otherwise, returns $\perp$.

5.2 Correctness

The correctness of the proposed scheme can be verified as follows:

1. In the algorithm *ReEnc*, input the the public parameters pp, the re-encryption key $rk_{i\to S}$ and the original ciphertext $C_i = (C_1, C_2, C_3, V_1, V_2)$, the CS can verify:

$$\begin{aligned} g^{C_3} &= V_1^{H_1(C_2)} \cdot V_2 \\ g^{H_1(C_2)\cdot u+v} &= (g^u)^{\cdot H_1(C_2)} \cdot g^v \\ &= g^{H_1(C_2)\cdot u+v} \end{aligned} \tag{4}$$

2. In the algorithm Dec_o, input the original ciphertext C_i and the data owner i's secret-key sk_i, the data owner i can verify like the formula 4 and decrypt C_i using the secret-key sk_i:

$$
\begin{aligned}
(m \parallel \theta) &= C_2 \oplus H_1(C_1^{\frac{1}{x_i H_1(X_i)}}) \\
&= H_1(g^r) \oplus (m \parallel \theta) \oplus H_1(X_i^{H_1(X_i)})^{r \cdot \frac{1}{x_i H_1(X_i)}} \\
&= H_1(g^r) \oplus (m \parallel \theta) \oplus H_1(g^{x_i H_1(X_i)})^{\frac{r}{x_i H_1(X_i)}}) \\
&= H_1(g^r) \oplus (m \parallel \theta) \oplus H_1(g^r) \\
&= (m \parallel \theta)
\end{aligned} \tag{5}
$$

3. In the algorithm Dec_{re}, input the re-encrypted ciphertext $C_{i \to S} = (C_1', C_2', C_3', C_4', C_5', V_1', V_2')$, the data receiver id_j and its secret-key sk_j, the data receiver j can verify:

$$
\begin{aligned}
g^{C_3'} &= V_1'^{H_1(C_2')} \cdot V_2' \\
g^{H_1(C_2') \cdot u + v} &= (g^u)^{\cdot H_1(C_2')} \cdot g^v \\
&= g^{H_1(C_2') \cdot u + v}
\end{aligned} \tag{6}
$$

and compute $(\alpha \| \beta)$ using C_5' and j's secret-key x_j:

$$
\begin{aligned}
(\alpha \parallel \beta) &= C_5' \oplus H_1(y_{id_j}^{\frac{1}{x_j}}) \\
&= H_1(g^z) \oplus (\alpha \parallel \beta) \oplus H_1(X_j^{z \cdot \frac{1}{x_j}}) \\
&= H_1(g^z) \oplus (\alpha \parallel \beta) \oplus H_1(g^{x_j \cdot z \cdot \frac{1}{x_j}}) \\
&= H_1(g^z) \oplus (\alpha \parallel \beta) \oplus H_1(g^z) \\
&= (\alpha \parallel \beta)
\end{aligned} \tag{7}
$$

and decrypt $C_{i \to S}$ using C_1' and C_2':

$$
\begin{aligned}
(m \| \theta) &= C_2' \oplus H_1(C_1'^{\frac{1}{\alpha}}) \\
&= H_1(g^r) \oplus (m \| \theta) \oplus H_1((X_i^{H_1(X_1)})^{r \cdot \frac{\alpha}{x_i H_1(X_i)} \cdot \frac{1}{\alpha}}) \\
&= H_1(g^r) \oplus (m \| \theta) \oplus H_1(g^{x_i \cdot H_1(X_i)})^{r \cdot \frac{\alpha}{x_i H_1(X_i)} \cdot \frac{1}{\alpha}}) \\
&= H_1(g^r) \oplus (m \| \theta) \oplus H_1(g^r) \\
&= (m \| \theta)
\end{aligned} \tag{8}
$$

Finally, to verify the decryption result, it computes $y_{id_j} \stackrel{?}{=} X_j^{H_2(\alpha, \beta)}$ and $C_1' \stackrel{?}{=} g^{H_2(m,\theta)\alpha}$. If them hold true, the data receiver j can correctly decrypt the re-encryption ciphertext $C_{i \to S}$ to get the plaintext m; otherwise, return $\perp$.

6 Security Analysis

Theorem 1. *Our proposed scheme EP-BPRE is CCA security in the random oracle model under the CDH assumption.*

Proof. There is an polynomial time adversary $\mathcal{A}_1$ with a no-negligible advantage who can destroy our proposed scheme EP-BPRE, another polynomial time adversary who users $\mathcal{A}_2$ to break the CCA security of EP-BPRE and a challenger $\mathcal{C}$ who can solve the hard problem CDH through interactive games with both $\mathcal{A}_1$ and $\mathcal{A}_2$. The challenge tuple is (g, g^a, g^b, g^c). If the equation $c = b/a$ holds true, $\mathcal{C}$'s goal is achieved; otherwise, return 1 and 0. $\mathcal{A}_1$, $\mathcal{A}_2$ and $\mathcal{C}$ play the following games.

- $Q_{H_1}(X)$: If $\mathcal{A}_2$ sends a query (X) to the oracle of H_1^{list}, $\mathcal{C}$ searches (X) for the tuple (X,Y). If it can be found, $\mathcal{C}$ sends Y to $\mathcal{A}_2$; otherwise, $\mathcal{C}$ random selects $Y \in \mathbb{Z}_q^*$, store (X,Y) to H_1^{list}, and finally sends W to $\mathcal{A}_2$.
- $Q_{H_2}(p,q)$: If $\mathcal{A}_2$ sends a query (p,q) to the oracle of H_2^{list}, $\mathcal{C}$ searches (p,q) for the tuple (p,q,r). If it can be found, $\mathcal{C}$ sends r to $\mathcal{A}_2$; otherwise, $\mathcal{C}$ random selects $r \in \mathbb{Z}_q^*$, stores (p,q,r) to H_2^{list}, and final sends r to $\mathcal{A}_2$.

Setup: $\mathcal{A}_1$ selects random a public-key pk_{i^*} and sends it to $\mathcal{A}_2$. Then, $\mathcal{A}_2$ sends pk_{i^*} to $\mathcal{C}$. To store the data, $\mathcal{C}$ sets four tables T_{uk}, T_{ck}, T_k and T_{rk} empty that store the uncorrupted public-key, corrupted key pair (pk,sk), key pair (pk,sk) and re-encryption key rk respectively.

KeyGen:$\mathcal{C}$ executes the following algorithms to generate all the users' keys and store them to the corresponding tables.

- **Public-key generate**: $\mathcal{C}$ executes the UK and CK as below:
  UK: $\mathcal{C}$ random selects $x_i \in \mathbb{Z}_q^*$, computes the $pk_i = (X_i = g^{x_i})$ and stores the (X_i,x_i) to T_{uk}.
  CK: $\mathcal{C}$ random selects $x_i \in \mathbb{Z}_q^*$, computes the $pk_i = (X_i = g^{ax_i})$ and stores the (X_i,x_i) to T_{ck}.
- **Secret-key generate**: $\mathcal{A}_1$ inputs the public-key $pk_i = (X_i)$, $\mathcal{C}$ first perform the following verification on it. If $pk_i = pk_{i^*}$ and pk_i is corrupted key, $\mathcal{C}$ searches (X_i,x_i) from the K_{ck} and returns the secret-key x_i to $\mathcal{A}_1$; otherwise, return $\perp$.

Phase 1: In the phase, $\mathcal{C}$ answers the queries made by $\mathcal{A}_2$.

ReKeyGen query $Q_{ReKeyGen}$: To answer this query $Q_{ReKeyGen}$, $\mathcal{A}_2$ inputs a tuple $(pk_i,S',rk_{i\to S'})$. $\mathcal{C}$ first verifies whether or not if $pk_i = pk_{i^*}$. If it holds true, continues to go the next steps; otherwise, return $\perp$. If pk_i from T_{uk} and S' from T_{ck}, returns $\perp$. If there is the re-encryption key $rk_{i\to S'}$ in T_{rk}, returns the $rk_{i\to S'}$; otherwise, $\mathcal{C}$ continues to go the next steps:

- Recover the tuples (pk_i,sk_i) from T_k.
- Compute the $rk_{i\to S'} = (rk_1, rk_2, rk_3)$.
  If pk_i is a CK, $\mathcal{C}$ first searches the tuple corresponding to pk_i in T_{ck} and obtains sk_i in the same way. Then $\mathcal{C}$ random selects $\alpha \in \{0,1\}^1$, $\beta \in \{0,1\}^2$ and computes $rk_1 = \frac{\alpha}{x_i H_1(X_i)}$ and $z = H_2(\alpha, \beta)$. Then, $\mathcal{C}$ computes $x_{id_j} = H_1(id_j)$ for each $id_j \in S'$, $y_{id_j} = X_j^z$ and $f(x) = y_{id_j} \times \prod_{1\leq k\neq j\leq n} \frac{x - x_{id_k}}{x_{id_j} - x_{id_k}} = a_0 +$

$a_1x+\ldots+a_nx^n$ where $|S'| = n$ and $j = 1,\ldots,n$. Obtain $rk_2 = (a_0, a_1, \ldots, a_n)$. Compute $rk_3 = H_1(g^z) \oplus (\alpha\|\beta)$.
If pk_i and S' are UK, $\mathcal{C}$ first searches the tuple corresponding to pk_i in T_{uk} and obtains (pk_i,sk_i). Then, $\mathcal{C}$ random selects rk_1, $z \in \mathbb{Z}_q^*$, obtains $rk_2 = (a_0, a_1, \ldots, a_n)$ and computes $rk_3 = H_1(g^{z^*})$.
If pk_i is an UK and S' is CK, return $\perp$.
$\mathcal{C}$ stores the tuple (pk_i,S',$rk_{i\to S'}$) to T_{rk} and sends the $rk_{i\to S'} = (rk_1, rk_2, rk_3)$ to $\mathcal{A}_2$. Then, $\mathcal{A}_2$ sends it to $\mathcal{A}_1$.

ReEnc Query Q_{ReEnc}: To answer this query Q_{ReEnc}, $\mathcal{A}_2$ inputs a tuple (pk_i,S',C^i). $\mathcal{C}$ first verifies whether or not if $pk_i \neq pk_{i^*}$ and $g^{C_3} = V_1^{H_1(C_1)} \cdot V_2$. If them hold true, continue to go the next steps; otherwise, return $\perp$.

- If pk_i and S' are UK, $\mathcal{C}$ makes a query $Q_{ReKeyGen}$ to obtain the re-encryption key $rk_{i\to S'}$ and generates the re-encryption ciphertext $C_{i\to S'}$ to send $C_{i\to S'}$ to $\mathcal{A}_2$.
- Otherwise, $\mathcal{C}$ searches the tuple (pk_i,$S' = \{pk_1, \ldots, pk_n\}$) in T_{ck}, random selects $\alpha \in \{0,1\}^{1}$, $\beta, \theta \in \{0,1\}^{2}$ and computes $r = H_2(m, \theta)$ and $C_1' = g^{r\alpha}$. If $\mathcal{C}$ can search a result that matches this tuple, $\mathcal{C}$ computes $rk_2 = (a_0, a_1, \ldots, a_n)$ and $rk_3 = H_1(g^{z^*}) \oplus (\alpha\|\beta)$.
- $\mathcal{C}$ send $C_{i\to S'}$ to $\mathcal{A}_2$. Then, $\mathcal{A}_2$ sends it to $\mathcal{A}_1$.

De Query Q_{De}: $\mathcal{C}$ first verifies whether of not if C_{i^*}, $C_{i\to S'}$ is same to the challenge ciphertext. If it holds true, $\mathcal{C}$ returns $\perp$; otherwise, $\mathcal{C}$ continues to go the next steps:

- If pk_i is a CK, $\mathcal{C}$ can obtain the corresponding secret-key sk_i from T_{ck} and executes the same algorithms as in the real execution.
- If pk_i is an UK and $C_i = (C_1, C_2, C_3, V_1, V_2)$ or $C_{i\to S} = (C_1', C_2', C_3', C_4', C_5', V_1', V_2')$, $\mathcal{C}$ first compute $pk_i = (X_i = g^{x_i})$ and searches the tuple (X_i, x_i) from T_k. $\mathcal{C}$ sends Dec_o or Dec_{re} to $\mathcal{A}_2$.
- If there doesn't exists the tuple, $\mathcal{C}$ searches the list from $H_1^{list}(X,Y)$, $H_2^{list}(p, q, r)$ for the existence of $Y \oplus (m\|\theta) = C_2$, $g^{r\alpha} = C_1'$. If relations hold true, $\mathcal{C}$ executes the decryption algorithm and sends the plaintext m to $\mathcal{A}_2$. Then, $\mathcal{A}_2$ sends it to $\mathcal{A}_1$.

Challenge: When $\mathcal{A}_1$ completes the Phase 1, he outputs pk_i' and selects two challenge plaintexts $(m_0, m_1) \in \{0,1\}^{1}$ and sends these to $\mathcal{A}_2$. $\mathcal{A}_2$ searches the tuple (pk_i',sk_i') from T_k and sends (m_0, m_1) to $\mathcal{C}$. $\mathcal{C}$ random selects $f \in \{0,1\}$ and executes the following algorithm:

- Select random $t \in \mathbb{Z}_q^*$ and compute $C_1'^* = g^{r\alpha} = g^{bt}$, which defines $r\alpha = bt$, $r = bt/\alpha$.
- Define $\alpha^* = rk_1 a x_i H_1(X_i)$ and compute $C_2'^* = H_1(g^r) \oplus (m_f\|\theta) = H_1(g^{bt/\alpha}) \oplus (m_f\|\theta) = H_1((g^{\frac{b}{a}})^{\frac{t}{x_i H_1(X_i)}}) \oplus (m_f\|\theta)$, which $H_2(m_f, \theta) = r = \frac{bt}{\alpha} = \frac{b}{a} \cdot \frac{t}{x_i H_1(X_i)}$.
- $C_3'^* = H_1(C_2'^*) \cdot u + v$.

- $V_1'^* = g^u$. Select random $u' \in \mathbb{Z}_q^*$ and set $C_0' = (g^b)^{1/u'}$, which defines $u = b/u'$.
- $V_2'^* = g^v$. Select random $v' \in \mathbb{Z}_q^*$ and set $C_0' = (g^b)^{1/v'}$, which defines $v = b/v'$.
- Finally, $\mathcal{A}_2$ sends the challenge re-encryption ciphertext $C_{i\to S'} = \{C_1'^*, C_2'^*, C_3'^*, V_1'^*, V_2'^*\}$ to $\mathcal{A}_1$.

Phase 2: $\mathcal{A}_1$ makes the same queries as Phase 1.

Guess: $\mathcal{A}_1$ selects random $f' \in \{0,1\}$ and sends $m_{f'}$ to $\mathcal{A}_2$. Then, $\mathcal{A}_2$ sends $m_{f'}$ to $\mathfrak{C}$. If the equation $c = b/a$ holds true, $C^*_{i\to S'} = \{C_1'^*, C_2'^*, C_3'^*, V_1'^*, V_2'^*\}$ is equal to $ReEnc(rk_{i\to S'}, C_i) \to C_{i\to S'}$. When $b/a \in \mathbb{G}$ is random, $m_{f'}$ can be hidden completely. Therefore, the probability of $\mathcal{A}_1$ guessing f' is not more than 1/2.

If pk_i and S' are UK, the re-encryption key $rk_{i\to S'}$. $\mathcal{A}_1$ selects random rk_3. Therefore, there must be a value z^*, that $rk_3 = H_1(g^{z^*}) \oplus (\alpha \| \beta)$. If $\mathcal{A}_1$ finds $z^* \neq z$, there must be a value α', that $rk_1 = \frac{\alpha}{x_i H_1(X_i)}$ is equal to $rk_1' = \frac{\alpha'}{x_{i^*} H_1(X_{i^*})}$. Then, $H_1(g^r) \oplus (m_0 \| \theta) = H_1(g^r) \oplus (m_1 \| \theta)$. According to [17], it is proved that the scheme is CCA security in the random oracle model. Therefore, we think that our proposed scheme EP-BPRE is also CCA security.

7 Evaluation

In this section, we compare the performance of our scheme with other schemes [17,20,22] in terms of computation and storage overhead.

7.1 Experimental Setup

To evaluate the performance of our proposed solution, we show the experiment setup in Table 2. We use the JPBC library (version: 2.0.0) [24] to implement our scheme. And it is compared with existing scheme in terms of computation and storage overhead.

Table 2. Experimental setup

Environment	Detailed description
Hardware	AMD Ryzen 5 7500F 6-Core processor, 32GB
Operating system	Microsoft Windows 11
Program library	JPBC library (version: 2.0.0) [24]
Compile	IntelliJ IDEA 2023, Java 17

Table 3. Computation overhead comparison

	Enc	ReKeyGen	ReEnc	Dec_o	Dec_{re}
Li et al. [17]	$7t_{e_1}$	$4t_{e_1}$	$4t_{e_1}$	$3t_{e_1}$	$6t_{e_1}$
Maiti et al. [20]	$5t_{e_1}$	$(\text{n}+5)t_{e_1}$	$t_{e_1}+t_p$	$t_{e_1}+t_p$	$t_{e_1}+2t_p$
Kim et al. [22]	$4t_{e_1}$	$(2\text{n}+3)t_{e_1}+(\text{n}+1)t_{e_2}$	t_{e_1}	t_{e_1}	$(\text{n}+1)t_{e_1}$
EP-BPRE	$6t_{e_1}$	$(\text{n}+2)t_{e_1}$	$4t_{e_1}$	$3t_{e_1}$	$6t_{e_1}$

Table 4. Storage overhead computation

	PP	CT	RK	ReCT
Li et al. [17]	$2\lvert\mathbb{G}_1\rvert+3\lvert\mathbb{Z}_q^*\rvert$	$7\lvert\mathbb{G}_1\rvert$	$3\lvert\mathbb{G}_1\rvert$	$9\lvert\mathbb{G}_1\rvert$
Maiti et al. [20]	$5\lvert\mathbb{G}_1\rvert+2\lvert\mathbb{G}_2\rvert+\lvert\mathbb{Z}_q^*\rvert$	$2\lvert\mathbb{G}_1\rvert+\lvert\mathbb{G}_2\rvert$	$2\lvert\mathbb{G}_1\rvert+\text{n}\lvert\mathbb{Z}_q^*\rvert$	$2\lvert\mathbb{G}_1\rvert+\lvert\mathbb{G}_2\rvert+\text{n}\lvert\mathbb{Z}_q^*\rvert$
Kim et al. [22]	$(2\text{n}+4)\lvert\mathbb{G}_1\rvert+4\mathbb{Z}_q^*+\lvert\mathbb{G}_2\rvert$	$\lvert\mathbb{G}_1\rvert$	$4\lvert\mathbb{G}_1\rvert+\lvert\mathbb{Z}_q^*\rvert$	$5\lvert\mathbb{G}_1\rvert$
EP-BPRE	$\lvert\mathbb{G}_1\rvert+3\lvert\mathbb{Z}_q^*\rvert$	$5\lvert\mathbb{G}_1\rvert$	$2\lvert\mathbb{G}_1\rvert+n\lvert\mathbb{Z}_q^*\rvert$	$6\lvert\mathbb{G}_1\rvert+n\lvert\mathbb{Z}_q^*\rvert$

7.2 Performance Comparison

Table 3 lists the comparison between our proposed scheme EP-BPRE and existing schemes in terms of computation overhead, where t_{e_1}: denotes an exponential operation on $\mathbb{G}_1$ group, is 1.97 ms; t_{e_2}: denotes a exponential operation on $\mathbb{G}_2$ group, is 1.09 ms; t_p: denotes a bilinear pairing operation, is 35.68 ms. As shown in Table 3, since the scheme proposed by [17] is targeted at the pairing-free operation in PRE, only sample algorithms for the exponential operations on $\mathbb{G}_1$ group are adopted, and the computation overhead in some aspects is low compared to other schemes. The scheme proposed by [20] is a identity based broadcast proxy re-encryption scheme and hence the computation overhead increases linearly with the number of data receivers. Although the functions implemented in the scheme [20] and EP-BPRE, but EP-BPRE computation overhead is less than the scheme [20] due to the pairing-free operation in this paper. The scheme [22] has broadcast and pairing-free mechanism, but our proposed scheme EP-BPRE meets CCA security under CDH problems in the ROM.

Table 4 lists the comparison between our proposed scheme EP-BPRE and existing schemes in terms of storage overhead, where $\lvert\mathbb{G}_1\rvert$: denotes the length of $\mathbb{G}_1$ group,is 128 bytes; $\lvert\mathbb{G}_2\rvert$: denotes the length of $\mathbb{G}_2$ group, is 128 bytes; $\lvert\mathbb{Z}_q^*\rvert$: denotes the length of $\mathbb{Z}_q^*$ group, is 20 bytes. It is seen in Table 4 that, in BPRE the require storage overhead to save RK and ReCT is slightly more than Li et al. [17] and Kim et al. [22]. Since we use the identity of each data receiver in the data receiver group S when constructing the polynomial and treat its coefficients as RK and ReCT, we require more storage space to store RK and ReCT. In Li et al. [17] schemes, it only support a single data receiver.

In summary, the results show that EP-BPRE has a smaller overhead while achieving the more complete functions.

7.3 Comparison Results

The main purpose of this experiment is to compare the schemes [17,20,22] with our proposed EP-BPRE in terms of computation and storage overhead.

Figure 2 shows the computation overhead of data owner, which performs the Enc, ReKeyGen and Dec_o operation. The execution time of schemes [20,22], and EP-BPRE increases linearly with the number of data receivers, except for scheme [17], whose ReKeyGen operation is for only a single data receiver. Although our proposed scheme EP-BPRE and scheme [20] have similar computation overhead in implementing the same function, the scheme [20] uses pairing operation in the computing process, while EP-BPRE does not use this operation, thus the computation overhead of EP-BPRE is better.

Figure 3 shows the computation overhead of CS in the re-encryption operation. As shown in Fig. 3, the computation overhead of all schemes is a fixed value, but compared with scheme [22], EP-BPRE has a certain gap. This is because our scheme adds verification operation in terms of whether the data receiver can correctly receive the data, thus compared to other schemes, EP-BPRE is relatively high. Meanwhile, compared to scheme [20] that uses pairing operation, the computation overhead of EP-BPRE is better.

Figure 4 shows the computation overhead for each scheme to perform the decryption operation of the re-encrytion ciphertext. The computation overhead of only scheme [22] has a linear relationship with n, while our proposed scheme EP-BPRE and other schemes [17,20] have a fixed overhead. EP-BPRE has the same computation overhead as scheme [17] while implement the broadcast proxy re-encryption.

Figure 5 shows the storage overhead of the re-encryption key generated by the data owner. The storage overhead of our proposed scheme EP-BPRE and scheme [20] increases linearly with the number of data receivers. However, the storage overhead of schemes [17] and [22] is a fixed value. That's because the scheme [17] only targets a single data receiver, and scheme [20] uses the public parameters to achieve broadcast function. Both our scheme and scheme [20] have the minimum storage overhead, however scheme [20] meets the CPA secure, but CCA security under CDH problems in the ROM is achieved in our scheme EP-BPRE.

Figure 6 shows the storage overhead of re-encryption ciphertext generated by CS in the ReCT phase. As shown in Fig. 6, the storage overhead of our proposed scheme EP-BPRE is higher than other schemes [17,20], and [22]. This is because the re-encryption ciphertexts in EP-BPRE include not only the ciphertext $(C_1', C_2', C_3', C_4', C_5')$ itself, but also the (V_1', V_2') used for the verification operations of data receivers.

From the analysis mentioned above, it is clear that our proposed scheme EP-BPRE is better than the other schemes [17,20,22] in terms of both computation and storage overhead for the same function. Especially, in the decryption phase, the decrypting the re-encryption ciphertext overhead of data receiver is fixed and low, which is more suitable for vehicle terminals with limited computing power. In summary, our proposed scheme EP-BPRE is excellent in terms of total overhead.

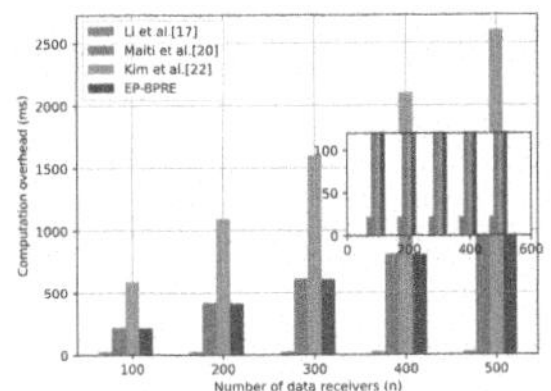

Fig. 2. Computation overhead of data owner

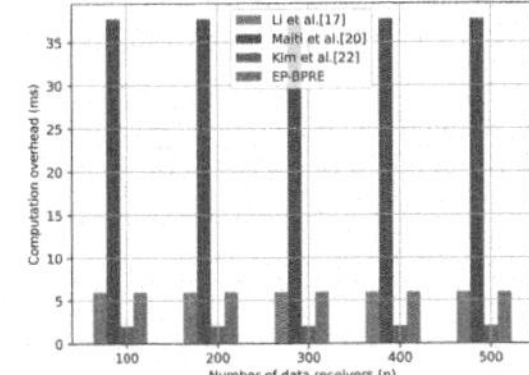

Fig. 3. Computation overhead of CS

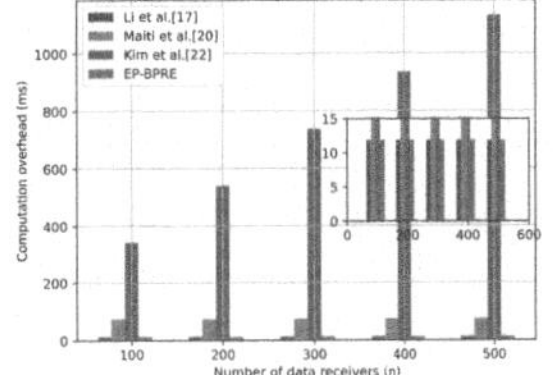

Fig. 4. Computation overhead of data receiver

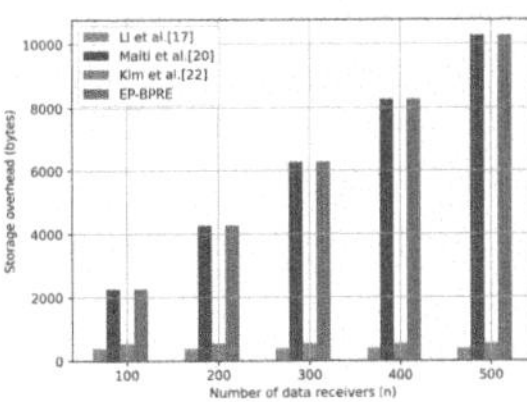

Fig. 5. Storage overhead of re-encryption key

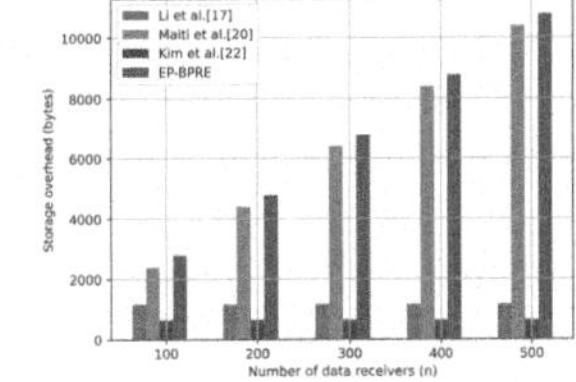

Fig. 6. Storage overhead of re-encryption ciphertext

8 Conclusion

In this paper, we propose a efficient pairing-free broadcast proxy re-encryption for secure data sharing in IoV. Our proposed scheme EP-BPRE achieves the fine-grained control through IB-BPRE. Then, to ensure the privacy of data receivers, we map them as individual points in the coordinate system and utilize these points to contract the Lagrange interpolation polynomial. Finally, we prove CCA security in the random oracle model. Meanwhile, we conduct experiments using the pairing based password library JPBC, and both the security and evaluation analysis prove the security and efficiency of our proposed scheme EP-BPRE. In the future, we first implement EP-BPRE based on certificate-based encryption, which focus on the key escrow difficulty of IB-BPRE. Second, since the dynamic revocation is an important function, we construct a dynamic revocation EP-BPRE scheme through it. Finally, we consider designing EP-BPRE that achieve the CCA security, which is a huge challenge for us.

References

1. Laghari, A.A, Wu, K., Laghari, R.A., et al.: A review and state of art of Internet of Things (IoT). Archiv. Comput. Methods Eng., 1–19 (2021)
2. Oladimeji, D., Gupta, K., Kose, N.A., et al.: Smart transportation: an overview of technologies and applications. Sensors **23**(8), 3880 (2023)

3. Hussain, S., Ullah, I., Khattak, H., et al.: A lightweight and formally secure certificate based signcryption with proxy re-encryption (CBSRE) for Internet of Things enabled smart grid. IEEE Access **8**, 93230–93248 (2020)
4. Alam, K.M., Saini, M., El Saddik, A.: Toward social internet of vehicles: Concept, architecture, and applications. IEEE Access **3**, 343–357 (2015)
5. Hundera, N.W., Aftab, M.U., Mesfin, D., et al.: An efficient heterogeneous online/offline anonymous certificateless signcryption with proxy re-encryption for Internet of Vehicles. Vehicular Commun., 100811 (2024)
6. Yang, F., Wang, S., Li, J., et al.: An overview of internet of vehicles. China Commun. **11**(10), 1–15 (2014)
7. Lu, J., Li, H., Huang, J., et al.: An identity-based encryption with equality test scheme for healthcare social apps. Comput. Standards Int. **87**, 103759 (2024)
8. Li, Y., Chen, R., Rahmani, R.: Secure data sharing in internet of vehicles based on blockchain and attribute-based encryption. In: 2023 IEEE International Conference on Smart Internet of Things (SmartIoT), pp. 56–63. IEEE (2023)
9. Zhu, H., Wang, L., Ahmad, H., et al.: Pairing-free for public key encryption with equality test scheme. IEEE Access **9**, 77239–77249 (2021)
10. Chen, Z., Deng, L., Ruan, Y., et al.: Certificateless broadcast encryption with authorization suitable for storing personal health records. Comput. J. **67**(2), 617–631 (2024)
11. Zhong, H., Zhang, S., Cui, J., et al.: Broadcast encryption scheme for V2I communication in VANETs. IEEE Trans. Veh. Technol. **71**(3), 2749–2760 (2021)
12. Singh, A.K., Acharya, K., Dutta, R.: Cloud assisted semi-static secure accountable authority identity-based broadcast encryption featuring public traceability without random oracles. Ann. Telecommun. **78**(1), 79–90 (2023)
13. Yao, S., Zhang, D.: BPRT: a blockchain-based privacy-preserving transaction scheme based on an efficient broadcast encryption with personalized messages. Trans. Emerging Telecommun. Technol. **34**(1), e4675 (2023)
14. Jakobsson, M.: On quorum controlled asymmetric proxy re-encryption. In: International Workshop on Public Key Cryptography. Berlin, Heidelberg: Springer Berlin Heidelberg, pp. 112–121 (1999)
15. Pei, H., Yang, P., Li, W., et al.: Proxy re-encryption for secure data sharing with blockchain in internet of medical things. Comput. Netw. **245**, 110373 (2024)
16. Ge, C., Susilo, W., Liu, Z., et al.: Attribute-based proxy re-encryption with direct revocation mechanism for data sharing in clouds. In: Proceedings of the ACM Turing Award Celebration Conference-China 2023, pp. 164–165 (2023)
17. Li, W., Xia, C., Wang, C., et al.: Secure and temporary access delegation with equality test for cloud-assisted IoV. IEEE Trans. Intell. Transp. Syst. **23**(11), 20187–20201 (2022)
18. Sun, M., Ge, C., Fang, L., et al.: A proxy broadcast re-encryption for cloud data sharing. Multimedia Tools Appl. **77**, 10455–10469 (2018)
19. Zhou, Y., Cao, Z., Dong, X.: Dynamic identity-based broadcast proxy re-encryption for data sharing in autonomous vehicles. Trans. Emerging Telecommun. Technol. **34**(11), e4801 (2023)
20. Maiti, S., Misra, S.: P2B: privacy preserving identity-based broadcast proxy re-encryption. IEEE Trans. Vehicular Technol. **69**(5), 5610–5617 (2020)
21. Ge, C., Liu, Z., Xia, J., et al.: Revocable identity-based broadcast proxy re-encryption for data sharing in clouds. IEEE Trans. Dependable Secure Comput. **18**(3), 1214–1226 (2019)

22. Kim, W.B., Kim, S.H., Seo, D., et al.: Broadcast proxy reencryption based on certificateless public key cryptography for secure data sharing. Wirel. Commun. Mob. Comput. **2021**(1), 1567019 (2021)
23. Schnorr, C.P.: Efficient identification and signatures for smart cards. In: Advances in Cryptology—CRYPTO'89 Proceedings 9. Springer New York, pp. 239–252 (1990)
24. De Caro, A., Iovino, V.: jPBC: java pairing based cryptography. In: 2011 IEEE Symposium on Computers and Communications (ISCC), pp. 850–855. IEEE (2011)

Privacy-Preserving Cross-Domain Authentication in IoV with Lightweight SM2 Group Signatures

Hu Liu[1], Jie Li[1], Meng Zhao[2], Haibin Zheng[2(✉)], Zhenwei Guo[2], and Yujue Wang[2]

[1] State Key Laboratory of Intelligent Vehicle Safety Technology, Chongqing, China
[2] Hangzhou Innovation Institute of Beihang University, Hangzhou, China
zhenghaibin29@buaa.edu.cn

Abstract. With the rapid development of Internet of Vehicles (IoV) and intelligent transportation systems, vehicles need to frequent communicate across heterogeneous trust domains such as service providers and operating platforms. Conventional authentication methods that depend on pre-shared keys or centralized institutions encounter two main obstacles: 1) low cross-domain trust transmission efficiency, which causes delays in authentication; 2) privacy leakage risk due to vehicle identity disclosure. To address these issues, this paper proposes an anonymous cross-domain authentication (ACA) technique based on SM2 group signature. Our ACA scheme integrates Chinese cryptographic algorithms and zero-knowledge proof technology to achieve efficient authentication while ensuring controllable anonymity of identities. Specifically, we design a group signature mechanism based on SM2 digital signature, supporting cross domain authentication of vehicles under anonymous conditions. Also, we introduce zk-SNARKs for lightweight verification, reducing the computational cost of roadside units (RSUs) by precomputing reference strings. Moreover, the combination of blockchain with traceable keys ensures that trusted institutions (TAs) can accurately trace the true identity when malicious behavior occurs. Security analysis shows that our ACA scheme satisfies traceability, conditional anonymity, and unforgeability under the random oracle model.

Keywords: Cross-domain authentication · Group signature · Zero-knowledge · Blockchain

1 Introduction

As Internet of Vehicles (IoV) [8] and intelligent transportation systems have grown in popularity [28], there is a pressing need for cross-domain collaborative

H. Liu and J. Li—These authors contributed to the work equally and should be regarded as co-first authors.

L. Zhang and K.-K. R. Choo (Eds.): MobiQuitous 2025, LNICST 684, pp. 288–308, 2026.
https://doi.org/10.1007/978-3-032-22503-0_16

communication due to the frequent movement of vehicles between various trust domains, such as service providers, operational platforms, and urban management areas [1]. One of the primary concerns in the present research on vehicle networking security is how to protect user privacy and identity authentication while preserving communication effectiveness [23].

It is challenging to handle dynamic, diverse, and resource-constrained application situations in IoV using traditional cross-domain authentication protocols [26], which are mostly dependent on centralized authentication institutions or pre-shared key techniques [7]. On the one hand, ineffective trust transfer mechanisms between various trust domains result in laborious authentication procedures and longer communication times [16]. On the other hand, the disclosure of vehicle identity data (e.g., unique vehicle IDs or license plate numbers) may cause significant privacy violations. Specifically, such data can act as a direct key for identity linkage, enabling adversaries to correlate seemingly anonymous trajectory datasets with external databases (e.g., vehicle registration records or publicly available social media information) to de-anonymize individuals. Furthermore, even without explicit identity linkage, long-term tracking of a vehicle's movements can reveal sensitive behavioral patterns, such as inferring an individual's home/work locations, daily routines, religious beliefs (by frequent visits to specific places of worship), political associations, or health status (by tracing trips to hospitals or specialized clinics). These concrete forms of exposure not only infringe upon personal privacy but would also severely restrict the development and public adoption of sensitive applications like emergency response systems, fleet collaboration, and traffic management, due to justifiable concerns over surveillance and data misuse. To address these challenges, an increasing number of researchers are leveraging blockchain technology to enhance the security and stability of communication in IoV [9,14]. Its decentralized architecture and tamper-resistant ledger provide robust trust guarantees, while privacy-preserving mechanisms such as pseudonymity and cryptographic techniques mitigate the risk of identity leakage.

Additionally, with the goal of giving a group of users a way to sign documents anonymously yet traceably, Chaum and van Heyst et al. [5] suggested group signatures in 1991. While external validators can confirm the authenticity of signatures but are unable to pinpoint the signer's identity, group signatures enable group members to sign messages on behalf of the whole group. The only people who can "open" signatures and disclose the signer's genuine identity when needed are group admins. For application scenarios that call for a balance between controllability and anonymity, this is a promising method [32].

Therefore, by integrating group signatures with blockchain technology, a decentralized and privacy-preserving authentication framework for IoV can be constructed. In this framework, the blockchain acts as a transparent and trustworthy coordinator for managing group keys and recording authentication events, while group signatures provide vehicles with anonymous yet accountable credentials for seamless cross-domain access. This synergy effectively addresses the dual challenges of inefficient trust transfer and identity privacy leakage outlined above.

1.1 Our Contributions

To address the dual challenges of low cross-domain trust transmission efficiency and privacy leakage risks in IoV caused by traditional centralized authentication and identity exposure, this paper proposes a privacy-preserving cross-domain authentication (ACA) scheme based on SM2 group signatures. Specifically:

- Design an SM2-based group signature mechanism that meets the requirements of security, efficiency, and controllability.
- Integrate zk-SNARKs for *lightweight verification* at RSUs, reducing computational overhead via pre-computed reference strings (crs) and smart contracts (VerifierCon).
- Leverage blockchain for secure storage of traceable keys (TRList), ensuring trusted authorities (TAs) revoke anonymity *only* during malicious behavior detection.

Our ACA scheme achieves:

- Security: Provably achieves *unforgeability*, *conditional anonymity*, and *traceability* under the ECDL assumption.
- Efficiency: Communication overhead reduced to 300 bytes, latency $\leq$15 ms per authentication. Compared to traditional solutions, it reduces the communication overhead by 18.7%.

1.2 Related Works

In 1991, Chaum and van Heyst created a group signature, which allows a group member to sign messages anonymously on behalf of the group while allowing a designated authority to divulge the signer's identity if needed [5]. This structure served as a foundation for cryptographic privacy-preserving authentication systems by offering a way to strike a balance between anonymity and accountability. Ateniese et al. [2] improved its applicability in dynamic group situations by introducing a workable and provably secure group signature technique with revocation capabilities. Later, the idea of small group signatures was put out by Boneh, Boyen, and Shacham [4], who used bilinear pairings to decrease the size of the signature and improve the scheme's efficiency.

In recent years, group signatures have found growing application in cross-domain authentication, particularly in environments where users or devices need to authenticate across multiple independent domains without exposing their identity. This is especially important in scenarios like IoV [17,33], smart cities [13,19], and multi-domain Internet of Things (IoT) systems [18,31], where privacy preservation, scalability, identity tracking, and seamless interoperability between different trust domains are essential. Lin et al. [15] addressed the issue of conditional privacy preservation and security assurance in applications using vehicular communication.

Roychoudhury et al. [22] suggested a light, multilayered, group based authentication mechanism. Based on the concept of group signature, Yue et al. [29] proposed a unique authentication protocol approach that achieves membership revocation by employing the full sub-tree method. Later, they [30] proposed a revocable group signature scheme that is more efficient than [29]. The lightweight group authentication signature approach introduced by Aydin et al. [3] dramatically lowers device energy usage. In 2023, by combining blockchain technology with group signatures, Chen et al. [6] suggest BCGS, a secure blockchain-based privacy-preserving cross-domain authentication mechanism for VANETs.

Wang et al. [25] presented a blockchain-based cross-authentication method that creates a decentralized network with the root certificate authorities acting as verification nodes. Gabay et al. [11] proposed a blockchain-based decentralized system that utilized smart contracts and zero-knowledge proofs to enable privacy-preserving authentication in vehicular networks while addressing privacy vulnerabilities inherent in traditional payment methods. Mei et al. [20] proposed a blockchain-based privacy-preserving incentive mechanism for energy delivery.

However, while existing group signature schemes and blockchain-based approaches offer privacy and cross-domain capabilities, they face persistent limitations in the IoV context: (1) reliance on computationally intensive operations (e.g., bilinear pairings, large exponentiations), which creates significant latency unsuitable for dynamic vehicular environments; (2) lack of integration with standardized national cryptographic algorithms (e.g., SM2/SM9) hinders regulatory compliance and adoption in specific regions; and (3) insufficient optimization for resource-constrained OBUs/RSUs results in impractical communication overhead and energy consumption. These limitations collectively impede efficient, lightweight, and standards-compliant privacy-preserving authentication across heterogeneous trust domains in IoV. Our ACA scheme addresses these gaps by leveraging SM2-based group signatures, zk-SNARKs for efficient verification, and blockchain-backed traceability, achieving both efficiency and regulatory alignment.

2 Preliminaries

2.1 SM2 Digital Signature

The SM2 digital signature scheme is one of the commercial cryptographic algorithm standards released by the China National Cryptography Administration, which consists of the following algorithms.

- **Setup:** With input security parameter λ, output the system public parameters $\mathbb{PP} = (\mathbb{G}, a, b, E(F_p), F_p, p, q, G_1, G_2, H_1, H_2)$, where $E(F_p)$ is the elliptic curve defined as $y^2 = x^3 + ax + b$, F_p is the field of $E(F_p)$, $\mathbb{G}$ is an additive cyclic group, G_1, G_2 are the generators of $\mathbb{G}$, p is the number of elements in the finite field F_p, q is the order of $\mathbb{G}$, $H_2 : \{0,1\}^* \rightarrow \mathbb{Z}_q$ is a collision-resistant hash function.

- **KeyGen:** Randomly choose $d_A \in Z_p^*$ as a private key, and calculate the public key $P_A = d_A \cdot G$.
- **Sign:** With input message m, the signer computes $Z = H(ENTL||ID||a||b|| G||x||y)$, where $ENTL$ indicates the length of signer's identity ID. The signer computes the hash value $e = H(Z||m)$, randomly selects $k \in Z_p^*$ and calculates a point on the elliptic curve as

$$(x_1, y_1) = k \cdot P. \tag{1}$$

Then, it computes

$$r = (e + x_1) \mod q, \tag{2}$$
$$s = (1 + d_A)^{-1} \cdot (k - rd_A) \mod q. \tag{3}$$

If $r = 0, s = 0$ or $r+k = n$, the signer needs to restart execution from the step of selecting $k \in Z_p^*$; otherwise, the signer outputs the signature $\sigma = (r, s)$.

- **Verify:** With input signature $\sigma = (r, s)$ and message m, the verifier checks whether $r \in [1, n-1]$ and continues to check whether $s \in [1, n-1]$. If both r and s are in valid range, the verifier calculates

$$M' = Z||M, \tag{4}$$
$$e' = H(M'), \tag{5}$$
$$t' = (r + s) \mod n. \tag{6}$$

and checks whether $t' = 0$. Then, the verifier computes the point on the elliptic curve

$$(x_1', y_1') = s \cdot G + t' \cdot P, \tag{7}$$
$$R' = (e' - x_1'). \tag{8}$$

If $R' = r$, the signature is valid.

2.2 Group Signature

A group signature usually comprises six probabilistic polynomial-time (PPT) algorithms, that is, $GS.Setup$, $GS.KeyGen^{Man}$, $GS.KeyGen^{Mem}$, $GS.Sign$, $GS.Verify$, and $GS.Trace$.

- $GS.Setup$: With input security parameter λ, output system parameters $\mathbb{PP}$.
- $GS.KeyGen^{Man}$: With input system parameters $\mathbb{PP}$, output the key of group manager (tpk, tsk) and the key of group members sk_i.
- $GS.KeyGen^{Mem}$: With input the group member's identity ID_i, output the member's sign private key sk_i.

- $GS.Sign$: With input message m, the signer's private key sk_i and the group public key tpk, outputs a valid group signature σ.
- $GS.Verify$: With input message m, a group signature σ, output 1 if the signature is legal; otherwise, output 0.
- $GS.Trace$: With input group secret key tsk and a group signature σ, output the signer's identification.

2.3 Zero Knowledge Proof

Zero knowledge proof (ZKP), proposed by Goldwasser, Micali and Rockoff in 1985 [12], is a cryptographic protocol that allows one party (called a "prover") to demonstrate to another (called a "verifier") that a piece of information (like a password, secret, or computation result) is accurate without disclosing any of the information's actual content.

We adopt a mature ZKP approach $zkSNARKs$ in this article as follows:

- $zkSNARKs$.*Compile*: With inputting a system parameter λ, output a constraint system QAP.
- $zkSNARKs$.*Setup*: With inputting a system parameter λ and a constraint system QAP, output a common reference sting crs.
- $zkSNARKs$.*Prove*: With inputting a witness provides by the prover, output a proof π.
- $zkSNARKs.Verify$: With inputting a proof π, output 1 to indicate the proof is correct; otherwise, output 0.

2.4 Blockchain

Blockchain is a decentralized distributed ledger system distinguished by its tamper resistance and traceability [27]. In [21], Nakamoto initially introduced blockchain technology with the goal of enabling secure and reliable data exchange between users without the need for outside middlemen. Blockchain connects the blocks containing "transaction information" using hash algorithms. The integrity and immutability of the data may be guaranteed since each block includes the hash value of the one before it.

2.5 ECDL Assumption

Given an elliptic curve E defined over a finite field F_p and a point $G \in E(F_p)$ of order q, for any randomly selected point $Q \in \langle G \rangle$, the elliptic curve discrete logarithm problem (ECDLP) is to find a $(0 \leq a \leq q-1)$ that satisfies $Q = a \cdot G$. If it is impossible to find such a in probabilistic polynomial time, then the ECDL assumption holds.

3 System Model and Security Requirements

3.1 System Model

As shown in Fig. 1, an ACA system consists of three types of entities, namely, roadside units (RSU), on-board units (OBU), and trust authority (TA). TA is in charge of the system's key management and, when needed, may reveal the identities of malevolent cars. RSUs are communication devices that are placed on both sides of the street and are in charge of managing cross-domain authentication and transmitting traffic management data, and OBUs are mounted on the vehicle end, which can transmit vehicle status data.

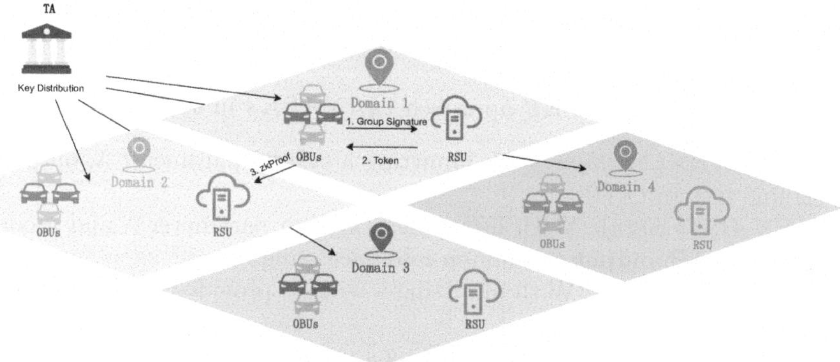

Fig. 1. System model

Initially, the vehicle provides TA with its actual identity registration when cross-domain authentication is needed. TA creates a pair of keys for each vehicle, records its details in the public information list, and associates the vehicle's identity with the trace list. After that, the vehicle sends a group signature with a timestamp to the current RSU using its private key. The current RSU verifies the group signature. If it is successful, it creates a temporary encrypted pass and transmits it to nearby vehicles. The vehicle creates and transmits a zero-knowledge proof to the new RSU after obtaining the pass. The proof is confirmed by the new RSU. The vehicle is permitted to pass if it passes; if not, the new RSU can decrypt the temporary encrypted pass to get the original group signature. Finally, the RSU might request TA to track if the vehicle exhibits unusual behavior, like forging a signature. Using the saved trace list, TA uses the group signature to recover the vehicle's true identification.

3.2 ACA Definition

An ACA scheme comprises three phases: Initialization, Authentication and Trace.

- **Initialization** According to the existence of three entities, there are two main stages: system parameter generation and vehicle registration. In the stage of system parameter generation, TA runs the system initialization algorithm and the group manager's key generation algorithm of the SM2 group signature; RSU runs the system initialization algorithm and the key generation algorithm of SM9 encryption algorithm and the system also runs *Setup* algorithm and *Compile* algorithm of zk-SNARKs. In the stage of vehicle registration, TA runs the group members' key generation algorithm and writes the corresponding data on blockchain.
- **Authentication** There are two main stages in authentication phases: mobile relay authentication and mobile authentication. In the first stage, the vehicle runs the *Sign* algorithm of the SM2 group signature, and OldRSU runs the encryption algorithm of the SM9 algorithm. In the stage of mobile authentication, OldRSU generates a zkProof and publishes it, and NewRSU verifies the zkProof and outputs 1 indicating the vehicle of the zkProof is valid; otherwise, it outputs 0.
- **Trace** TA can reveal the vehicle's real identity by running the *Trace* algorithm of SM2 group signature.

Definition 1. *(Correctness) If the following requirements are met, then the ACA scheme is correct:*

1. *The OBUs are able to perform cross-domain authentication after running the Sign algorithm of the SM2 group signature, which means the OldRSU is able to successfully verify the validity of the group signature.*
2. *TA can successfully trace the identity of the signer if the vehicle exhibits malicious behavior.*
3. *The NewRSU can successfully verify the zkProof to ensure the validity of vehicle's authentication.*

3.3 Security Model

Definition 2. *(Conditional Anonymity): Conditional anonymity means that, except from the group management, no one else can identify the signer.*

The anonymity of ACA scheme can be captured by the following game between a simulator $\mathcal{S}$ and an adversary $\mathcal{A}$:

Initialization: The simulator $\mathcal{S}$ runs the **Setup** algorithm of SM2 group signature, sends the group public key to $\mathcal{A}$ and keeps the group private key.

Queries: The adversary $\mathcal{A}$ can require three kinds of oracles: $\mathcal{JO}, \mathcal{SO}, \mathcal{TO}$.

$\mathcal{JO}$-**Query**: With input a new member with identity ID_i, output the corresponding private key SK_i of ID_i.

$\mathcal{SO}$-**Query**: With input a group member's identity ID_i and a message m, output a group signature signed by ID_i.

$\mathcal{CO}$-**Query**: With input a valid public information B_i, output the corresponding private key SK_i.

Challenge: The simulator $\mathcal{S}$ provides two group signatures $G_{s_b}, b \in \{0,1\}$. $\mathcal{A}$ guesses the identification of b'.

Advantage: $\mathcal{A}$ wins the game with the probability as follows:

$$\mathbf{Adv} = \mathbf{Pr}\left[b' = b\right]$$

Definition 3. *(Unforgeability): Unforgeability means that anyone cannot forge a valid group signature without valid keys.*

The unforgeability of ACA scheme can be captured by the following game between a simulator $\mathcal{S}$ and an adversary $\mathcal{A}$:

Initialization: The simulator $\mathcal{S}$ runs the **Setup** algorithm of SM2 group signature, sends the group public key to $\mathcal{A}$ and keeps the group private key.

Queries: The adversary $\mathcal{A}$ can require three kinds of oracles: $\mathcal{JO}, \mathcal{SO}, \mathcal{TO}$.

$\mathcal{JO}$-**Query**: With input a new member with identity ID_i, output the corresponding private key SK_i of ID_i.

$\mathcal{SO}$-**Query**: With input a group member's identity ID_i and a message m, output a group signature signed by ID_i.

$\mathcal{CO}$-**Query**: With input a valid public information B_i, output the corresponding private key SK_i.

Challenge: The adversary $\mathcal{A}$ outputs a forged group signature Σ.

Advantage: $\mathcal{A}$ wins the game with the probability as follows:

$$\mathbf{Adv} = \mathbf{Pr}\left[GS.Verify(params, \Sigma) = 1\right]$$

Definition 4. *(Traceability): Traceability refers to the group manager's ability to effectively track down every legitimate group signature produced by this group.*

The traceability of ACA scheme can be captured by the following game between a simulator $\mathcal{S}$ and an adversary $\mathcal{A}$:

Initialization: The simulator $\mathcal{S}$ runs the **Setup** algorithm of SM2 group signature, sends the group public key to $\mathcal{A}$ and keeps the group private key.

Queries: The adversary $\mathcal{A}$ can require three kinds of oracles: $\mathcal{JO}, \mathcal{SO}, \mathcal{TO}$.

$\mathcal{JO}$-**Query**: With input a new member with identity ID_i, output the corresponding private key SK_i of ID_i.

$\mathcal{SO}$-**Query**: With input a group member's identity ID_i and a message m, output a group signature signed by ID_i.

$\mathcal{TO}$-**Query**: With input a group signature, output the signer's identity.

Challenge: The adversary $\mathcal{A}$ outputs a forged group signature Σ.

Advantage: $\mathcal{A}$ wins the game with the probability as follows:

$$\mathbf{Adv} = \mathbf{Pr}\left[\begin{array}{c} GS.Verify(params, \Sigma) = 1 \\ GS.Trace(params, \Sigma, tsk) = 1 \end{array}\right]$$

4 Our ACA Construction

4.1 Initialization

System Parameters Generation.

- Trusted Authority Initialization
  a. Generate the parameters of SM2 group signature as follows:
  - With input a security parameter λ, output the SM2 group signature public parameters $\mathbb{PP}_1 = (\mathbb{G}, a, b, E(F_p), F_p, p, q, G_1, G_2, H_1, H_2)$, where $E(F_p)$ is the elliptic curve defined as $y^2 = x^3 + ax + b$, F_p is the field of $E(F_p)$, $\mathbb{G}$ is an additive cyclic group, G_1 and G_2 are the generators of $\mathbb{G}$, p is the number of elements in the finite field F_p, q is the order of $\mathbb{G}$, and $H_1 : \{0,1\}^* \to G_1$ and $H_2 : \{0,1\}^* \to \mathbb{Z}_q$ are secure hash functions.

  b. Generate the private key and public key of TA as follows:
  - TA randomly selects two big prime numbers $\alpha, \beta \in \mathbb{Z}_q^*$, and computes $N = \alpha\beta$.
  - TA randomly selects a number $x \in \mathbb{Z}_q^*$ as the trace private key and computes the trace public key as

$$tpk = x \cdot G_2. \tag{9}$$

  - TA publishes the group public key $PK_1 = (\mathbb{PP}_1, N, tpk)$.
- Road-Side Units Initialization
  a. TA generates the parameters of SM9 algorithm: $\mathbb{PP}_2 \leftarrow SM9.Setup$.
  b. RSU generates and publishes the public key of RSU_i as follows

$$PK_2 \leftarrow SM9.KeyGen(k_i, \mathbb{PP}_2)$$

  where $k_i \in \mathbb{Z}_q$ is randomly chosen by RSU_i.
- zk-SNARKs pre-computations
  a. TA deploys the verification contract to generate its constraint system QAP.

$$QAP \leftarrow zkSNARK.Compile(\lambda).$$

  b. TA generates the common reference string as follows

$$(crs) \leftarrow zkSNARK.Setup(\lambda, QAP).$$

  Publish the system public parameters $Params = (PK_1, PK_2, crs)$.

Vehicle Registration. The following are the details of the on-board units' key generation algorithm of SM2 group signature:

- OBU_i applies for joining the group and sends its real identity ID_i to TA.

- For every ID_i ($i \in \{0, n\}$), where n is the number of vehicles, TA computes the group members' private key:

$$ID_i \cdot sk_i \equiv 1 \mod \phi(N). \tag{10}$$

Then TA calculates the members' public information

$$B_i = sk_i \cdot G_2 \tag{11}$$

- TA computes $SK_{i,0}$ and $SK_{i,1}$ as follows:

$$SK_{i,0} = H_1(sk_i), \tag{12}$$

$$SK_{i,1} = x \cdot G_1 + N \cdot G_1 - H_1(sk_i) \tag{13}$$

and sends $SK_i = ((SK_{i,0}, SK_{i,1}), sk_i)$ to OBU_i, adds B_i into the public information list $NList$, and writes $\{ID_i, B_i\}$ on blockchain, where $NList$ is public.

4.2 Authentication

Mobile Relay Authentication Protocol.

- Token-request Phase
  The vehicle that wants to perform anonymous cross-domain authentication generates its request as follows:
  - OBU_i randomly selects two elements $d, l \in \mathbb{Z}_q$ and refreshes the private key as follows:

$$SK^*_{i,0} = SK_{i,0} + l \cdot G_1, \tag{14}$$

$$H_m = H_1(m). \tag{15}$$

$$\sigma_1 = SK^*_{i,0} + d \cdot H_m, \tag{16}$$

$$\sigma_2 = d \cdot G_1. \tag{17}$$

  - OBU_i selects two random elements $r, r^* \in \mathbb{Z}^*_q$, refreshes the private key $SK^*_{i,1}$, and computes intermediate parameters $(x_1, y_1), R, k, z, T, S, C$ as follows:

$$SK^*_{i,1} = SK_{i,1} - l \cdot G_1, \tag{18}$$

$$(x_1, y_1) = R = r^* \cdot G_2, \tag{19}$$

$$k = H_2(m||R), \tag{20}$$

$$z = (k + x_1) \mod n, \tag{21}$$

$$T = r \cdot G_1 + sk_i \cdot G_2, \tag{22}$$

$$S = r^* + rsk_i, \tag{23}$$

$$C = sk_i \cdot G_2 + r^* \cdot tpk. \tag{24}$$

- OBU_i outputs SM2 group signature and sends it to OldRSU:

$$\Sigma = (\sigma_1^*, \sigma_2^*, \sigma_3^*) = (SK_{i,1}^* + \sigma_1, \sigma_2, T||R||C||S||k||r||z). \tag{25}$$

- Token-generate Phase
The OldRSU verifies the group signature as follows:
  - The OldRSU computes B_i' as follows:

$$B_i' = T - r \cdot G_1. \tag{26}$$

  and checks whether it exists in $NList$. If it exists, continue the following steps; otherwise, output $\perp$ to cancel the verification.
  - The OldRSU computes (x_1', y_1') and k' as follows

$$(x_1', y_1') = R' = S \cdot G_2 - r \cdot B_i, \tag{27}$$

$$k' = H_2(m||R'). \tag{28}$$

  and compares k with k'. Continues if $k = k'$; otherwise, returns $\perp$.
  - The OldRSU calculates z' as following

$$z' = x_1' + k'. \tag{29}$$

  After calculation, the OldRSU compares z' with z, the signature is valid if all the equations (26) to (29) are right; otherwise, returns $\perp$ to indicate the signature is invalid.

Then, OldRSU generates a temporary authentication token using the NewRSU's public key pk_{NewRSU}, the SM2 group signature Σ, its own identification $OldRSU$, and a timestamp $Timestamp$ as follows:

$$Token = SM9.Encrypt(pk_{NewRSU}, \Sigma||OldRSU||Timestamp). \tag{30}$$

The OldRSU sends the token to neighboring vehicles.

The Mobile Authentication Protocol.

- After the vehicle OBU_i receives the token sent by OldRSU, it generates a zkProof π as follows, and sends $\pi, Token$ to NewRSU:

$$\pi \leftarrow zkSNARK.Prove(crs, OldRSU, NewRSU, Token, \Sigma, T_{stamp})$$

where T_{stamp} is a timestamp.
- NewRSU verifies the zkProof π generated by vehicle as $0/1 \leftarrow zkSNARK.Verify(crs, \pi)$ and allows OBU_i to enter if it is valid; otherwise, NewRSU decrypts the $Token$ using its private key as follows to get the SM2 group signature Σ using its private key sk_{NewRSU} and sends Σ to TA to trace the identification of the signer.

$$\Sigma = SM9.Decrypt(sk_{NewRSU}, Token)$$

4.3 Trace

- TA traces the identification according to Σ and reveals the vehicle's real identification as in $GS.Trace$ algorithm as follows:
  - The group manager (namely, TA) computes B_i' and matches corresponding B_i' in $NList$ to examine whether B_i is valid.

$$B_i' = C' - x \cdot R'. \tag{31}$$

  - The group manager traverses the information recorded on blockchain before and matches the signer's identification ID_i with B_i.

5 Correctness and Security Analysis

5.1 Correctness

Theorem 1. *(Correctness) The proposed ACA scheme is correct.*

The Correctness of Verification.

$$\begin{aligned} B_i' = T' - r' \cdot G_1 = sk_i \cdot G_2' = B' \\ (x_1', y_1') = R' = S \cdot G_2 + r \cdot B_i = R = (x_1, y_1) \\ k' = H_2(m||R') = k \\ z' = x_1' + k' \mod m = z \end{aligned}$$

The Correctness of Traceability.

$$\begin{aligned} B_i' &= C' - x \cdot R' \\ &= sk_i \cdot G_2 + r^* \cdot tpk - x \cdot r^* \cdot G_2 \\ &= sk_i \cdot G_2 \\ &= B_i \end{aligned}$$

After the group manager calculates the real public information of the signer, it would be able to traverse $TRList$ and match the signer's identification with B_i.

The Correctness of zkProof. According to the properties of ZKP, after a right calculation of $zkSNARK$, the following equality exists:

$$\pi \leftarrow zkSNARK(crs, OldRSU - pk, Newdomain, Token, ID_i, Timestamp)$$

Thus, if the corresponding parameters are input, the $zkSNARK$ will output 1, indicating the validity of π as follows:

$$0/1 \leftarrow zkSNARK.Verify(crs, \pi)$$

5.2 Security Analysis

Theorem 2. *(Conditional Anonymity) Assume ECDLP is hard, the proposed ACA scheme is anonymous.*

Proof. Assuming that an adversary $\mathcal{A}$ can break the anonymity of ACA with overwhelming probability, we build a simulator $\mathcal{S}$ to solve $ECDLP$.

Initialization: For given $ECDLP(G, Q)$, $\mathcal{S}$ randomly selects two big prime numbers $\alpha, \beta \in \mathbb{Z}_q^*$ and computes $N = \alpha\beta$. The trace public key of the group is

$$tpk = Q = x \cdot G. \tag{32}$$

Then, $\mathcal{S}$ publishes the group public key PK and generates the group members' key as above.

Queries: $\mathcal{A}$ can submit oracle queries to $\mathcal{S}$ as follows.

$\mathbf{H_1}$-Query. $\mathcal{S}$ maintains hash list L_{H_1}, records $(H_1(m), m)$, where $H_1(m)$ is a mapping of m under the additive cyclic group G_1. When $\mathcal{A}$ inquires a message m from H_1, $\mathcal{S}$ checks whether there is a record in L_{H_1} and returns $H_1(m)$ if exists; otherwise, generates a uniformly distributed string in G_1, records $(H_1(m), m)$ into L_{H_1} and sends $H_1(m)$ to $\mathcal{A}$.

$\mathbf{H_2}$-Query. $\mathcal{S}$ maintains hash list L_{H_2}, records $(H_2(m), m, R)$, where $H_2(m)$ is a mapping of m and R under the additive cyclic group G_2. When $\mathcal{A}$ inquires a tuple (m, R) from H_2, $\mathcal{S}$ checks whether there is a corresponding record in L_{H_2} and returns $H_2(m||R)$ if exists; otherwise, generates a string uniformly distributed in G_2, records $(H_2(m), m, R)$ into L_{H_2} and sends $H_1(m)$ to $\mathcal{A}$.

$\mathcal{JO}$-Query. $\mathcal{A}$ inquires a new member with identification $ID_i \in \mathbb{Z}_q^*$, $\mathcal{JO}$ computes as in $GS.KeyGen$ and returns ID_i's private key SK_i.

$\mathcal{SO}$-Query. $\mathcal{A}$ inquires a group signature with a group member's identity ID_i and a timestamp $Timestamp$, $\mathcal{SO}$ determines whether ID_i is valid and computes the private key of ID_i. Then $\mathcal{SO}$ uses $Timestamp$ as the message, computes the group signature as above and sends it to $\mathcal{A}$.

$\mathcal{CO}$-Query. $\mathcal{A}$ inquires about a valid public information B_i, which can be found in $NList$, $\mathcal{CO}$ returns its private key SK_i.

Challenge: $\mathcal{S}$ provides two group signatures $G_{s_b}, b \in \{0, 1\}$. $\mathcal{A}$ guesses the identification of the signer b'. According to the guess, $\mathcal{S}$ can calculate solution of $ECDLP$ as follows:

$$B_0 = T_0 - r_0 \cdot G_1, \tag{33}$$

$$B_1 = T_1 - r_1 \cdot G_1, \tag{34}$$

$$x = (C_0 + C_1 - B_0 - B_1)^{-1} 2(R_0 + R_1). \tag{35}$$

Thus, $\mathcal{S}$ can solve $ECDLP$.

However, due to the difficulty of $ECDLP$, the above assumption is not valid. That means, $\mathcal{A}$ can guess the right answer with only $\frac{1}{2}$ probability.

Theorem 3. *(Unforgeability) Assume ECDLP is hard, the proposed ACA scheme is unforgeable.*

Proof. Assume there is an adversary $\mathcal{A}$ that can break the unforgeability of ACA scheme with an undeniable probability; for an instance of problem (G, Q) on elliptic curve $E(F_q)$, we build a simulator $\mathcal{S}$ to solve $ECDLP$.

Initialization: For given $ECDLP(G, Q)$, $\mathcal{S}$ randomly selects two big prime numbers $\alpha, \beta \in \mathbb{Z}_q^*$ and computes $N = \alpha\beta$. The trace public key of the group is

$$tpk = Q = x \cdot G. \tag{36}$$

Then, $\mathcal{S}$ publishes the group public key PK and generates the group members' key as above.

Queries: $\mathcal{A}$ can submit oracle queries to $\mathcal{S}$ as follows.

$\mathbf{H_1}$-Query. $\mathcal{S}$ maintains hash list L_{H_1}, records $(H_1(m), m)$, where $H_1(m)$ is a mapping of m under the additive cyclic group G_1. When $\mathcal{A}$ inquires a message m from H_1, $\mathcal{S}$ researches whether there is a corresponding record in L_{H_1} and returns $H_1(m)$ if exists; otherwise, generates a string uniformly distributed in G_1, records $(H_1(m), m)$ into L_{H_1} and sends $H_1(m)$ to $\mathcal{A}$.

$\mathbf{H_2}$-Query. $\mathcal{S}$ maintains hash list L_{H_2}, records $(H_2(m), m, R)$, where $H_2(m)$ is a mapping of m and R under the additive cyclic group G_2. When $\mathcal{A}$ inquires a tuple (m, R) from H_2, $\mathcal{S}$ researches whether there is a corresponding record in L_{H_2} and returns $H_2(m||R)$ if exists; otherwise, generates a string uniformly distributed in G_2, records $(H_2(m), m, R)$ into L_{H_2} and sends $H_2(m)$ to $\mathcal{A}$.

$\mathcal{JO}$-Query. $\mathcal{A}$ inquires a new member with identification $ID_i \in \mathbb{Z}_q^*$, $\mathcal{JO}$ computes as in $GS.KeyGen$ and returns ID_i's private key SK_i.

$\mathcal{SO}$-Query. $\mathcal{A}$ inquires a group signature with a group member's identification ID_i and a timestamp $Timestamp$, $\mathcal{SO}$ determines whether ID_i is valid and computes the private key of ID_i. Then $\mathcal{SO}$ uses $Timestamp$ as the message, computes the group signature as above and sends it to $\mathcal{A}$.

$\mathcal{CO}$-Query. $\mathcal{A}$ inquires a valid public information B_i, which can be found in $NList$, $\mathcal{CO}$ returns its private key SK_i.

Challenge: $\mathcal{A}$ outputs an SM2 group signature $\Sigma = (\sigma_1^*, \sigma_2^*, \sigma_3^*) = (SK_{i,1}^* + \sigma_1, \sigma_2, T||C||S||k||r||z)$, which is not generated by $\mathcal{SO}$ and the signer's private key has also not been queried from $\mathcal{CO}$ and $\mathcal{JO}$. As signature is not generated from $\mathcal{SO}$, the group manager will believe the signature is legal and calculate the solution of ECDLP as follows:

$$B_i = T - r \cdot G_1, \tag{37}$$

$$x = (C - B_i)^{-1} R. \tag{38}$$

Thus, $\mathcal{S}$ can solve ECDLP as above.

As ECDLP is hard, the above assumption does not hold, and the ACA scheme satisfies unforgeability.

Theorem 4. *(Traceability) Assume ECDLP is hard, the proposed ACA scheme is traceable.*

Proof. Assume there is an adversary $\mathcal{A}$ that can break the traceability of ACA with an undeniable probability. Given a problem instance (G, Q) on elliptic curve $E(F_q)$, we build a simulator $\mathcal{S}$ to solve $ECDLP$.

Initialization: For given $ECDLP(G, Q)$, $\mathcal{S}$ randomly selects two big prime numbers $\alpha, \beta \in \mathbb{Z}_q^*$ and computes $N = \alpha\beta$. The trace public key of the group is

$$tpk = Q = x \cdot G. \tag{39}$$

Then, $\mathcal{S}$ publishes the group public key PK and generates the group members' key as above.

Queries: $\mathcal{A}$ can get oracle queries from $\mathcal{S}$ as $\mathcal{H}, \mathcal{JO}, \mathcal{SO}, \mathcal{TO}$.

H_1-Query. $\mathcal{S}$ maintains hash list L_{H_1}, records $(H_1(m), m)$, where $H_1(m)$ is a mapping of m under the additive cyclic group G_1. When $\mathcal{A}$ inquires a message m from H_1, $\mathcal{S}$ researches whether there is a corresponding record in L_{H_1} and returns $H_1(m)$ if exists; otherwise, generates a string uniformly distributed in G_1, records $(H_1(m), m)$ into L_{H_1} and returns $H_1(m)$ to $\mathcal{A}$.

H_2-Query. $\mathcal{S}$ maintains hash list L_{H_2}, records $(H_2(m), m, R)$, where $H_2(m)$ is a mapping of m and R under the additive cyclic group G_2. When $\mathcal{A}$ inquires a tuple (m, R) from H_2, $\mathcal{S}$ researches whether there is a corresponding record in L_{H_2} and returns $H_2(m||R)$ if exists; otherwise, generates a string uniformly distributed in G_2, records $(H_2(m), m, R)$ into L_{H_2} and returns $H_2(m)$ to $\mathcal{A}$.

$\mathcal{JO}$-Query. $\mathcal{A}$ inquires a new member with identification $ID_i \in \mathbb{Z}_q^*$, $\mathcal{JO}$ computes as in $GS.KeyGen$ and returns ID_i's corresponding private key SK_i.

$\mathcal{SO}$-Query. $\mathcal{A}$ inquires a group signature with a group member's identification ID_i and a timestamp $Timestamp$, $\mathcal{SO}$ determines whether ID_i is valid and computes the private key of ID_i. Then $\mathcal{SO}$ uses $Timestamp$ as a message, computes the group signature as above, and returns it to $\mathcal{A}$.

$\mathcal{TO}$-Query. $\mathcal{A}$ inquires about the signer's identification of a group signature Σ. In order to respond the queries correctly, $\mathcal{TO}$ computes the signer's public information B_i as in $GS.Verify$ algorithm and returns the corresponding identification to $\mathcal{A}$.

Challenge: $\mathcal{A}$ outputs an SM2 group signature $\Sigma = (\sigma_1^*, \sigma_2^*, \sigma_3^*) = (SK_{i,1}^* + \sigma_1, \sigma_2, T||C||S||k||r||z)$, which is generated by an identification that has not been queried from $\mathcal{JO}$, and the group signature is also not generated by $\mathcal{SO}$. As the identification of the signer is not queried from $\mathcal{JO}$, the group manager cannot trace the identification of the signer, which means that this breaks the traceability of the SM2 group signature.

According to the signature produced by $\mathcal{A}$, $\mathcal{S}$ can calculates

$$B_i = T - r \cdot G_1, \tag{40}$$

$$x = (C - B_i)^{-1} R. \tag{41}$$

Thus, $\mathcal{S}$ can solve ECDLP as above.

However, as ECDLP is hard, the above assumption does not hold, and the ACA scheme satisfies traceability.

6 Efficiency Analysis

In this section, we analyze the ACA scheme's computation cost and communication cost in theory, exactly the efficiency of the SM2 group signature, and we instantiate the scheme based on python 3.9 with library math, hashlib on a Macbook with Apple M2 chip, featuring an 8-core CPU, 8GB unified memory, and a 512GB solid-state drive, running macOS Sonoma14.5.

6.1 Computation Cost

Following the comparison methodology in [6], we summarize the time cost of the operations involved in the SM2 group signature in Table 1. Based on experiments conducted on an Apple M2 chip, the time for the addition of one point in the group $\mathbb{G}$ is approximately 0.02 ms, the multiplication of one point in $\mathbb{G}$ takes approximately 6.79 ms, a single hash function operation takes 0.02 ms, a hash-to-point operation takes around 6.86 ms, a bilinear pairing operation takes around 14.50ms, a exponentiation operation takes aound 40.00ms, and a bilinear pairing exponentiation operation takes around 7.25ms.

Table 1. Time cost of the operations

Operation	execution time (ms)
T_{G2a}	0.02
T_{G2m}	6.79
T_h	0.02
T_{ph}	6.86
T_{bpt}	14.50
T_{ep}	40.00
T_{ept}	7.25

Table 2 presents a performance comparison of various group signature schemes. Specifically, T_{ep} denotes an exponentiation in $\mathbb{G}_1$, T_{bpt} denotes a pairing operation, T_{ept} represents an exponentiation in $\mathbb{G}_t$, T_{G2m} and T_{G2a} represent point multiplication and point addition in $\mathbb{G}$, respectively, while T_h and T_{ph} denote a hash function and a hash-to-point function, respectively. G_t refers to the cyclic group used in [10,24]. According to the descriptions in [10,24], the computational complexity of both schemes is calculated and reported in Table 2.

Table 2. Comparison of computation complexity and communication cost

Scheme	Sign	Verify	Communication cost
[24]	$5T_{ep} + 3T_{ept} + 3T_{bpt} + T_{ph} + T_h$	$4T_{ep} + 4T_{ept} + 5T_{bpt} + T_{ph} + T_h$	356 bytes
[10]	$3T_{ep} + 13T_{ept} + 2T_{bpt}$	$13T_{ept} + 5T_{bpt}$	768 bytes
This scheme	$8T_{G2m} + 6T_{G2a} + T_h + T_{ph}$	$3T_{G2m} + 2T_{G2a} + T_h$	300 bytes

Table 2 further compares the SM2 group signature scheme with those in [10,24] in terms of computational complexity and communication overhead.

The scheme in [10] involves up to 13 T_{ept} and 5 T_{bpt}, resulting in substantial computational cost. The scheme in [24] also entails multiple exponentiations and pairing operations, which leads to a moderate computational burden. In contrast, the SM2 group signature scheme relies primarily on low-cost group operations in $\mathbb{G}$, such as point multiplication (T_{G2m}) and point addition (T_{G2a}), completely avoiding expensive pairing computations and thus significantly reducing overall computational complexity.

6.2 Communication Cost

In comparison of communication cost, we set $\mathbb{Z}_q = 20\ bytes, |\mathbb{G}_1| = 128\ bytes, |\mathbb{G}| = 40\ bytes$ as [6], and we can calculate the communication cost of the SM2 group signature is $40 * 6 + 20 * 3 = 300\ bytes$, the communication cost of [24] is $4 * 20 + 128 * 2 = 356\ bytes$, and the communication cost of [10] is 768 *bytes*. The SM2 group signature achieves a 14–38% advantage over contemporary schemes, which can reduce channel contention and accelerate cross-domain handovers and minimize storage overhead.

Therefore, our ACA scheme significantly reduces both computational complexity and communication overhead while ensuring security, making it more advantageous for practical deployment, especially in scenarios with stringent efficiency and resource constraints.

7 Conclusion

To promote low cross-domain trust transmission efficiency and address the risk of privacy leakage due to vehicle identity disclosure, this paper designed an anonymous cross-domain authentication mechanism based on SM2 group signatures for vehicle networks. Conditional anonymity of vehicle identity is achieved by building a group signature based on the SM2 algorithm. By combining the tracking function provided by blockchain with zk-SNARKs lightweight verification, the communication overhead of a single authentication is reduced to 300 bytes, and the latency is kept within 15 ms, while guaranteeing traceability and conditional anonymity. Our ACA offers a secure and effective authentication solution for the dynamic networking environment of IoVs, which may be expanded to road collaboration of 5G vehicles and future emergency rescue situations.

Acknowledgements. This article is supported in part by the open program of State Key Laboratory of Intelligent Vehicle Safety Technology (No. IVSTSKL-202442), the Key R&D Program of Zhejiang Province (No. 2025C01084), the Natural Science Foundation of China (No. 62303037), and the Zhejiang Provincial Natural Science Foundation (LQN25F020032).

References

1. Abbasinezhad-Mood, D., Ghaemi, H.: Dual-signature blockchain-based key sharing protocol for secure v2v communications in multi-domain IOV environments. IEEE Trans. Intell. Transp. Syst. **25**(10), 13407–13416 (2024). https://doi.org/10.1109/TITS.2024.3410114
2. Ateniese, G., Camenisch, J., Joye, M., Tsudik, G.: A practical and provably secure coalition-resistant group signature scheme. In: Bellare, M. (ed.) Advances in Cryptology — CRYPTO 2000, pp. 255–270. Springer, Berlin, Heidelberg (2000). https://doi.org/10.1007/3-540-44598-6_16
3. Aydin, Y., Kurt, G.K., Ozdemir, E., Yanikomeroglu, H.: A flexible and lightweight group authentication scheme. IEEE Internet Things J. **7**(10), 10277–10287 (2020). https://doi.org/10.1109/JIOT.2020.3004300
4. Boneh, D., Boyen, X., Shacham, H.: Short group signatures. In: Franklin, M. (ed.) Advances in Cryptology – CRYPTO 2004, pp. 41–55. Springer, Berlin, Heidelberg (2004). https://doi.org/10.1007/978-3-540-28628-8_3
5. Chaum, D., van Heyst, E.: Group signatures. In: Davies, D.W. (ed.) Advances in Cryptology — EUROCRYPT'91, pp. 257–265. Springer, Berlin, Heidelberg (1991). https://doi.org/10.1007/3-540-46416-6_22
6. Chen, B., Wang, Z., Xiang, T., Yang, J., He, D., Choo, K.K.R.: BCGS: blockchain-assisted privacy-preserving cross-domain authentication for vanets. Vehicular Commun. **41**, 100602 (2023). https://doi.org/10.1016/j.vehcom.2023.100602
7. Chen, J., Zhan, Z., He, K., Du, R., Wang, D., Liu, F.: Xauth: efficient privacy-preserving cross-domain authentication. IEEE Trans. Dependable Secure Comput. **19**(5), 3301–3311 (2022). https://doi.org/10.1109/TDSC.2021.3092375
8. Dureja, A., Sangwan, S.: A review: efficient transportation—future aspects of IOV. In: Singh, P.K., Noor, A., Kolekar, M.H., Tanwar, S., Bhatnagar, R.K., Khanna, S. (eds.) Evolving Technologies for Computing, Communication and Smart World, pp. 97–108. Springer Singapore, Singapore (2021). https://doi.org/10.1007/978-981-15-7804-5_8
9. Feng, X., Cui, K., Wang, L., Liu, Z., Ma, J.: PBAG: a privacy-preserving blockchain-based authentication protocol with global-updated commitment in IOVs. IEEE Trans. Intell. Transp. Syst. **25**(10), 13524–13545 (2024). https://doi.org/10.1109/TITS.2024.3399200
10. Feng, X., Shi, Q., Xie, Q., Wang, L.: P2ba: a privacy-preserving protocol with batch authentication against semi-trusted RSUS in vehicular ad hoc networks. IEEE Trans. Inf. Forensics Secur. **16**, 3888–3899 (2021). https://doi.org/10.1109/TIFS.2021.3098971
11. Gabay, D., Akkaya, K., Cebe, M.: Privacy-preserving authentication scheme for connected electric vehicles using blockchain and zero knowledge proofs **69**(6), 5760–5772. https://doi.org/10.1109/TVT.2020.2977361
12. Goldwasser, S., Micali, S., Rackoff, C.: The knowledge complexity of interactive proof-systems. In: Proceedings of the Seventeenth Annual ACM Symposium on Theory of Computing, pp. 291–304. STOC '85, Association for Computing Machinery, New York (1985). https://doi.org/10.1145/22145.22178
13. Huang, C., et al.: Blockchain-assisted transparent cross-domain authorization and authentication for smart city. IEEE Internet Things J. **9**(18), 17194–17209 (2022). https://doi.org/10.1109/JIOT.2022.3154632
14. Lin, H.T., Jhuang, W.L.: Blockchain-based lightweight certificateless authenticated key agreement protocol for v2v communications in IOV. IEEE Internet Things J. **11**(16), 27744–27759 (2024). https://doi.org/10.1109/JIOT.2024.3400320

15. Lin, X., Lu, R.: GSIS: Group Signature and ID-based Signature-Based Secure and Privacy-Preserving Protocol, pp. 21–49 (2015). https://doi.org/10.1002/9781119082163.ch2
16. Liu, Y., Wang, Y., Chang, G.: Efficient privacy-preserving dual authentication and key agreement scheme for secure v2v communications in an IOV paradigm. IEEE Trans. Intell. Transp. Syst. **18**(10), 2740–2749 (2017). https://doi.org/10.1109/TITS.2017.2657649
17. Liu, Y., et al.: Secure traffic data sharing in UAV-assisted vanet through certificateless proxy re-encryption and consortium blockchain. Peer-to-Peer Netw. Appl. **18**(3), 143 (2025). https://doi.org/10.1007/s12083-025-01920-1
18. Luo, C.: Distributed cross-domain anonymous authentication scheme in internet of things. IEEE Internet Things J. **12**(13), 24710–24721 (2025). https://doi.org/10.1109/JIOT.2025.3555770
19. Luo, M., Zhou, X., Qiu, M.: A revocable anonymous cross-domain communication scheme for smart grid based on ring signcryption. Peer-to-Peer Network. Appl. **17**(1), 125–138 (2024). https://doi.org/10.1007/s12083-023-01579-6
20. Mei, Q., Guo, W., Zhao, Y., Nie, L., Adhikari, D.: Blockchain-based privacy-preserving incentive scheme for internet of electric vehicle. Inf. Fusion **115**, 102732 (2025). https://doi.org/10.1016/j.inffus.2024.102732
21. Nakamoto, S.: Bitcoin: a peer-to-peer electronic cash system. Tech. rep. (2008). https://buybsv.com/uploads/2021/04/bitcoin-white-paper.pdf
22. Roychoudhury, P., Roychoudhury, B., Saikia, D.K.: A group-based authentication scheme for vehicular moving networks. In: 2016 International Conference on Accessibility to Digital World (ICADW), pp. 93–96. IEEE. https://doi.org/10.1109/ICADW.2016.7942519
23. Tian, J., Shen, Y., Wang, Y.: A provable privacy protection authentication protocol for vehicle-to-vehicle communication. IEEE Trans. Intell. Transp. Syst., 1–16 (2025). https://doi.org/10.1109/TITS.2025.3562303
24. Wang, Q., Gao, D., Foh, C.H., Leung, V.C.: An edge computing-enabled decentralized authentication scheme for vehicular networks. In: ICC 2020 - 2020 IEEE International Conference on Communications (ICC), pp. 1–7 (2020). https://doi.org/10.1109/ICC40277.2020.9149021
25. Wang, W., Hu, N., Liu, X.: BlockCAM: a blockchain-based cross-domain authentication model. In: 2018 IEEE Third International Conference on Data Science in Cyberspace (DSC), pp. 896–901. IEEE. https://doi.org/10.1109/DSC.2018.00143
26. Wang, Y., Ding, Y., Wu, Q., Wei, Y., Qin, B., Wang, H.: Privacy-preserving cloud-based road condition monitoring with source authentication in vanets. IEEE Trans. Inf. Forensics Secur. **14**(7), 1779–1790 (2019). https://doi.org/10.1109/TIFS.2018.2885277
27. Wen, B., Wang, Y., Ding, Y., Zheng, H., Qin, B., Yang, C.: Security and privacy protection technologies in securing blockchain applications. Inf. Sci. **645**, 119322 (2023). https://doi.org/10.1016/j.ins.2023.119322
28. Xiong, W., Wang, Y., Wei, Y.: NTRU-CLS: efficient quantum-resistant NTRU lattice-based certificateless signature scheme for vanets. Comput. Netw. **256**, 110885 (2025). https://doi.org/10.1016/j.comnet.2024.110885
29. Yue, X., Chen, B., Wang, X., Duan, Y., Gao, M., He, Y.: An efficient and secure anonymous authentication scheme for vanets based on the framework of group signatures. IEEE Access **6**, 62584–62600 (2018). https://doi.org/10.1109/ACCESS.2018.2876126

30. Yue, X., Xu, J., Chen, B., He, Y.: A practical group signatures for providing privacy-preserving authentication with revocation. In: Li, J., Liu, Z., Peng, H. (eds.) Security and Privacy in New Computing Environments, pp. 226–245. Springer International Publishing, Cham (2019). https://doi.org/10.1007/978-3-030-21373-2_18
31. Zeng, M., Cui, J., Zhang, Q., Zhong, H., He, D.: Efficient revocable cross-domain anonymous authentication scheme for iiot. IEEE Trans. Inf. Forensics Secur. **20**, 996–1010 (2025). https://doi.org/10.1109/TIFS.2024.3523198
32. Zhang, L., Li, J., Yang, Y.: Message linkable group signature with information binding and efficient revocation for privacy- preserving announcement in vanets. IEEE Trans. Dependable Secure Comput. **21**(6), 5667–5680 (2024). https://doi.org/10.1109/TDSC.2024.3381436
33. Zhang, L., Yang, X., Zheng, Y., Yu, T., Yang, A., Han, N.: EACAS: an efficient anonymous cross-domain authentication scheme in internet of vehicles. IEEE Internet Things J. **12**(7), 7749–7762 (2025). https://doi.org/10.1109/JIOT.2024.3505209

A Provably Secure and Fault-Tolerant Verifiable Encryption Scheme with Blockchain-Based Private Key Custody

Lin Zhong[1,4], Yujue Wang[2], Yang Zhang[3(✉)], Jun Du[1], Kevin He[4], Andrew Zhang[1], and Fanyin Meng[5]

[1] Sinohope Technology Holdings Limited, Hong Kong, China
[2] Hangzhou Innovation Institute of Beihang University, Hangzhou, China
[3] Information Science and Engineering, Lanzhou University, Lanzhou, China
zhyang@lzu.edu.cn
[4] Bitlayer Labs Ltd, Vistra Corporate Service Centre, Virgin Islands, UK
[5] Beijing Beike Rongzhi Cloud Computing Technology Co., Ltd, Beijing Academy of Science and Technology, Beijing, China

Abstract. In the domain of security, data protection ultimately hinges on secure storage of private keys. To this end, we propose a Provably Secure and fault-tolerant verifiable encryption scheme, in which private keys are encrypted and stored on the blockchain, allowing secure and decentralized key custody. It allows a user to manage only one key, reducing the complexity of key management. In addition, the proposed scheme features public verifiability, allowing anyone to verify whether the ciphertext corresponds to a valid private key without revealing the key itself. Furthermore, our scheme is fault-tolerant; even if the ciphertext stored on the blockchain undergoes some degree of tampering, it can still accurately retrieve the correct private key with probability 99%. Compared to existing verifiable decryption schemes, our scheme provides both public verifiability and fault tolerance. Experimental tests indicate that the encryption and verification times of our scheme are only about 53 milliseconds, while the decryption time is merely 1 millisecond, offering a good user experience and high security.

Keywords: Verifiable encryption · Private Key Custody · Fault-tolerant · Blockchain

1 Introduction

As the digitalization process continues to accelerate, the security of information systems has become a central issue in both global technological development and policy formulation. In particular, with the widespread adoption of emerging technologies such as cloud computing [27], blockchain [4], artificial intelligence

L. Zhang and K.-K. R. Choo (Eds.): MobiQuitous 2025, LNICST 684, pp. 309–325, 2026.
https://doi.org/10.1007/978-3-032-22503-0_17

[12,26], and the Internet of Things [2,20], ensuring the confidentiality, integrity, and availability of sensitive data has become an inescapable challenge. Cryptographic techniques, as the foundational tools for safeguarding data security, rely heavily on the secure management of private keys [1,24]. Whether in symmetric or asymmetric cryptographic systems, the compromise of a private key results in a fundamental breakdown of security: attackers may bypass authentication mechanisms, decrypt sensitive information, or even manipulate critical data. Therefore, secure storing and managing private keys under various threat models is a prerequisite for building a trustworthy computing environment.

However, in practical deployments, key management presents numerous challenges. Traditional key management systems typically depend on local storage by the user or delegation to a third-party custodian [23]. This not only imposes high security requirements on end users, but also introduces risks associated with centralized trust. In multikey systems, users must often manage multiple key copies, significantly increasing complexity and the likelihood of human error. Furthermore, with the growing prevalence of decentralized infrastructures, such as blockchains and trustless computation platforms, there is an urgent demand for security mechanisms that eliminate reliance on trusted third parties and support self-verification [13]. Although existing verifiable decryption techniques aim to enhance the trustworthiness of decryption operations by allowing users to validate whether a ciphertext has been correctly decrypted, they often overlook the verifiability of the encryption phase itself and lack resilience against ciphertext corruption during storage. The absence of fault tolerance implies that even minor disturbances may render the system inoperable, which is unacceptable in high availability contexts.

To address these challenges, we propose a Provably Secure and fault-tolerant verifiable encryption (PSFVE) scheme with blockchain-based private key custody. In PSFVE, a user's private key is encrypted and stored directly on the blockchain, simplifying key management, since the user only needs to maintain a single master key, while allowing public verification of the validity of ciphertext without disclosing the underlying private key. Moreover, the proposed PSFVE scheme is fault-tolerant; that is, even if the on-chain ciphertext suffers a certain degree of tampering or corruption, the correct private key can still be recovered with up to 99% probability, thus significantly improving robustness. In general, our PSFVE scheme strikes a careful balance between security, decentralization, user experience, and resilience, offering clear advantages over existing approaches.

Specifically, we make the following contributions.

- We propose a framework for the PSFVE system that allows users to encrypt and store private keys on the blockchain, allowing them to manage only one key, which reduces the complexity of key management.
- The PSFVE scheme is distinguished by its fault tolerance. Even if the ciphertext stored on the blockchain undergoes some degree of manipulation, it can still accurately retrieve the correct private key with probability 99%.

- The PSFVE scheme is constructed using an elliptic curve group, Key Derivation Function (KDF), hash functions, and symmetric encryption. The security of the PSFVE scheme can be reduced to the security of symmetric encryption, ensuring that the PSFVE scheme is both secure and efficient.
- Comparative analysis reveals that our PSFVE scheme offers both public verifiability and fault tolerance, features that are absent in other verifiable schemes. The experimental results confirm that the encryption, decryption, and verification processes of our PSFVE scheme are exceptionally fast, occurring at the millisecond level.

2 Related Works

In Verifiable Encryption (VE) research, many schemes focus on decryption verifiability and secure time control. Döttling et al. [7] proposed a VE scheme allowing time-locked decryption via signature-based witness encryption (SWE), where decryption is permitted once a threshold number of valid signatures is published. Miao et al. [19] designed an outsourced VE scheme that offloads encryption and decryption to the cloud, using key splitting and short signatures to ensure verifiable ciphertext transformation. Li et al. [15] introduced a verifiable and fair attribute-based proxy re-encryption scheme for cloud data sharing, guaranteeing re-encryption correctness and preventing malicious server accusations. Bois et al. [5] developed a modular verifiable computation scheme for encrypted data, supporting nondeterministic operations without revealing inputs. Atapoor et al. [3] constructed a verifiable fully homomorphic encryption (FHE) scheme for circuits of arbitrary depth, employing lattice-based SNARKs and double-CRT for efficient proof verification.

To enhance data security, researchers have extended verifiability to cryptographic systems, enabling flexible computation. Li et al. [16] proposed a verifiable fuzzy multikeyword-ranked search scheme using locality-sensitive hashing, Bloom filters, and homomorphic MACs for verification. Lin et al. [18] designed a lattice-based verifiable identity keyword search with delegated algorithms and identity-based encryption for secure sharing. Zhang et al. [29] developed a verifiable multikeyword search scheme resistant to offline guessing attacks, ensuring signature unforgeability. Tong et al. [25] introduced a verifiable encrypted image retrieval scheme using polynomial-based access policies and homomorphic MACs for the correctness search result. Chen et al. [6] presented a blockchain-based verifiable dynamic searchable encryption (SE) scheme with hash proof chains for public verification and parallel search efficiency.

Recent work also explores the integration of VE with symmetric encryption in SE systems, balancing efficiency with verifiability. Guo et al. [11] proposed a blockchain-based and forward private dynamic SE scheme with smart contracts for verification digests and a lightweight cloud-based structure. Yuan et al. [28] introduced a fault-tolerant and verifiable dynamic SE scheme, enhancing existing VE-SE schemes without sacrificing forward security. Guo et al. [10] further developed a verifiable search protocol for forward-private conjunctive queries, employing puncturable PRFs and inverted indexes. Peng et al. [21] designed a blockchain-based SE scheme with state chains to resist file injection attacks, ensuring forward privacy and supporting efficient search and access control.

3 Preliminaries

Before presenting the PSFVE scheme, we first review a few concepts related to discrete logarithms, symmetric encryption, hash functions, and key derivation functions.

Discrete Logarithm: Within a group defined by elliptic curves, $k \cdot G$ can be defined for all integers k, where the discrete logarithm $\log_G(H)$ is an integer k such that $H = k \cdot G$. However, currently there is no efficient algorithm to compute k given H and G.

Symmetric Cryptography: It utilizes the same cryptographic keys for both encrypting plaintext and decrypting ciphertext. In the encryption stage, it requires a key key and a plaintext msg as inputs and produces a ciphertext C

$$\mathsf{SymEnc}_{key}(msg) \rightarrow C.$$

In the decryption stage, it takes a key key and a ciphertext C as inputs and returns the original plaintext msg

$$\mathsf{SymDec}_{key}(C) \rightarrow msg.$$

Hash Function: A hash function takes an input of a random string of arbitrary length, denoted as $\{0,1\}^*$, and outputs a fixed-size random string of n bits, denoted as $\{0,1\}^n$

$$\mathsf{hash} : \{0,1\}^* \rightarrow \{0,1\}^n.$$

Key Derivation Function (KDF): A KDF takes an input of a random string of n bits, denoted $\{0,1\}^n$, and outputs a random string of any desired length, denoted as $\{0,1\}^*$,

$$\mathsf{KDF} : \{0,1\}^n \rightarrow \{0,1\}^*.$$

4 PSFVE Definitions

In this section, we introduce the PSFVE system model. Then we provide a formal definition of the model and define the key properties of the scheme: consistency, public verifiability, and security.

For a message msg, a user encrypts it using a public key X and stores the ciphertext in the cloud. This process requires strict secure storage of the corresponding private keys x. Therefore, a recovery key is used to encrypt the corresponding private keys x and store the ciphertext on the blockchain, facilitating efficient and secure storage of keys.

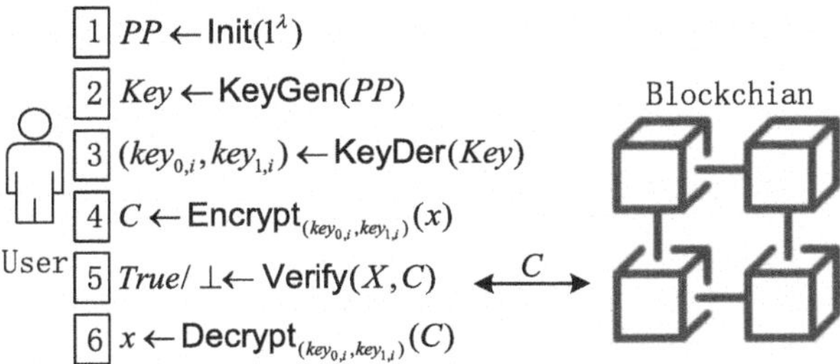

Fig. 1. The PSFVE system

As shown in Fig. 1, the PSFVE scheme includes the following six steps: Initialization (Init), Key Generation (KeyGen), Key Derivation (KeyDer), Encryption (Encrypt), Verification (Verify), and Decryption (Decrypt). The Init algorithm generates the public parameters of the system. The user invokes the algorithm KeyGen to produce the recovery key Key. The user invokes the algorithm KeyDer, takes as input the encryption-required key Key, and outputs n pairs of encryption-required key pairs $(key_{0,i}, key_{1,i})$, where $i = 0, \cdots, n-1$. The user employs the Encrypt algorithm, takes as input the encryption-required key pairs $(key_{0,i}, key_{1,i})$ and the private keys x, outputs ciphertexts, and broadcasts them on the blockchain. He can invoke the Verify algorithm, takes as input the ciphertext C and the corresponding public key X, and outputs the determination of the validity of the ciphertext. If valid, then accept and store it; otherwise, a symbol is outputted that signifies an error. The user retrieves the ciphertext from the blockchain and calls the Verify algorithm again. If invalid, then reject; otherwise, calls the algorithm Decrypt, takes as input the ciphertext C and the recovery key Key, and outputs the private key x. The user then decrypts the corresponding message msg by using the private key x.

A PSFVE scheme can be formally defined with the following six efficient algorithms:

Definition 1. *A PSFVE scheme can be formally defined with the following six efficient algorithms:*

- $PP \leftarrow \mathsf{Init}(1^\lambda)$: *This polynomial-time system initialization algorithm takes a security parameter λ as input and outputs the system's public parameters PP.*
- $Key \leftarrow \mathsf{KeyGen}(PP)$: *This polynomial-time key generation algorithm takes as input the public parameters PP and outputs the recovery key Key.*
- $(key_{0,i}, key_{1,i}) \leftarrow \mathsf{KeyDer}(Key)$: *This polynomial-time key derivation algorithm takes the recovery key Key as input and outputs n pairs of keys $(key_{0,i}, key_{1,i})$, where $i = 0, \cdots, n-1$.*
- $C \leftarrow \mathsf{Encrypt}_{(key_{0,i}, key_{1,i})}(x)$: *This polynomial-time encryption algorithm takes n pairs of encryption keys $(key_{0,i}, key_{1,i})$ and the private key x as inputs and outputs the ciphertext C.*

- *True/⊥* $\leftarrow$ $\mathsf{Verify}(X, C)$: *This polynomial-time verification algorithm takes the public key X and the ciphertext C as input and outputs a validity judgment. If valid, it is stored; otherwise, a symbol signifying error is outputted.*
- $x \leftarrow \mathsf{Decrypt}_{(key_{0,i},key_{1,i})}(C)$: *This polynomial-time decryption algorithm invokes the key derivation algorithm* KeyDer, *takes as input the recovery key* Key, *and obtains n pairs of keys* $(key_{0,i}, key_{1,i}), i = 0, \cdots, n-1$; *then, it takes as input the ciphertext C and n pairs of keys* $(key_{0,i}, key_{1,i}), i = 0, \cdots, n-1$ *and outputs the private key x. Therefore, the user can decrypt the corresponding message msg using the private key x.*

A PSFVE scheme is secure if it has the properties of consistency, public verifiability, fault tolerance, and security.

Definition 2 (Consistency). *For any* $(PP, Key, key_{0,i}, key_{1,i}, x, C)$, $i = 0, \cdots, n-1$, *if the ciphertext C is an encryption of the private key x, the decryption algorithm can output x with probability 1:*

$$\Pr\left[\begin{array}{c} PP \leftarrow \mathsf{Init}(1^\lambda), Key \leftarrow \mathsf{KeyGen}(PP), \\ (key_{0,i}, key_{1,i}) \leftarrow \mathsf{KeyDer}(Key), C \leftarrow \mathsf{Encrypt}_{(key_{0,i},key_{1,i})}(x) : \\ x \leftarrow \mathsf{Decrypt}_{(key_{0,i},key_{1,i})}(C) \end{array}\right] = 1.$$

Definition 3 (Public Verifiability). *For any* $(PP, Key, key_{0,i}, key_{1,i}, X, C), i = 0, \cdots, n-1$, *if the ciphertext C is an encryption of the private key x, the verification algorithm can output True with probability 1:*

$$\Pr\left[\begin{array}{c} PP \leftarrow \mathsf{Init}(1^\lambda), Key \leftarrow \mathsf{KeyGen}(PP), \\ (key_{0,i}, key_{1,i}) \leftarrow \mathsf{KeyDer}(Key), C \leftarrow \mathsf{Encrypt}_{(key_{0,i},key_{1,i})}(x) : \\ True \leftarrow \mathsf{Verify}(X, C) \end{array}\right] = 1.$$

Definition 4 (Fault Tolerance). *Assume that the ciphertext stored on the blockchain undergoes some degree of tampering, the user can obtain the tampered ciphertext and can get the correct private key x with probability 99%:*

$$\Pr\left[\begin{array}{c} PP \leftarrow \mathsf{Init}(1^\lambda), Key \leftarrow \mathsf{KeyGen}(PP), \\ (key_{0,i}, key_{1,i}) \leftarrow \mathsf{KeyDer}(Key), C \leftarrow \mathsf{Encrypt}_{(key_{0,i},key_{1,i})}(x), \\ C' \leftarrow \mathcal{A}(C), x' \leftarrow \mathsf{Decrypt}_{(key_{0,i},key_{1,i})}(C') : x = x' \end{array}\right] \geq 99\%.$$

Definition 5 (Security). *The challenger generates the recovery key Key, and the polynomial-time attacker chooses two private keys* x_0, x_1. *The challenger randomly selects one of these private keys* x_b *for encryption, where* $b \in \{0, 1\}$. *The advantage that the attacker correctly guesses is negligible* $negl(\cdot)$

$$\Pr\left[\begin{array}{c} PP \leftarrow \mathsf{Init}(1^\lambda), Key \leftarrow \mathsf{KeyGen}(PP), \\ (key_{0,i}, key_{1,i}) \leftarrow \mathsf{KeyDer}(Key), (x_0, x_1) \leftarrow A(PP), \\ C \leftarrow \mathsf{Encrypt}_{(key_{0,i},key_{1,i})}(x_b) : A(x_0, x_1, C) = b \end{array}\right] \leq \frac{1}{2} + negl(\lambda).$$

5 PSFVE Construction

In this section, we present a concrete construction of the PSFVE scheme based on hash functions, KDF, symmetric encryption, and elliptic curve groups.

- **Init**: Let G be a generator of the Elliptic Curve group $\mathbb{G}$ with order q. The hash function is $\mathsf{hash} : \{0,1\}^* \rightarrow \{0,1\}^{256}$, the KDF is $\mathsf{KDF} : \{0,1\}^{256} \rightarrow \{0,1\}^*$, and the symmetric encryption denotes as $\mathsf{SymEnc}, \mathsf{SymDec}$, for encryption and decryption, respectively.
- **KeyGen**: A user selects a random string of k bits, denoted as $\{0,1\}^k$, where $k \geq 110$, to serve as his recovery key Key.
- **KeyDer**: The user takes the recovery key Key as inputs, and uses the KDF to derive n pairs of subkeys as follows:

$$key_{0,i} := \mathsf{KDF}(Key, i), \quad key_{1,i} := \mathsf{KDF}(Key, n+i),$$

  where $i = 0, \cdots, n-1$.
- **Encrypt**: The message that needs to be encrypted by the user is the private key x, and the corresponding public key is X, where $X = x \cdot G$. It consists of five steps. Let $x = x_i$, where $i = 0, \cdots, n-1$.

  (1) He selects n random numbers $r_i \in [0, q-1]$, takes the elliptic curve generator G and n subkeys $\{key_{0,i}\}, i = 0, \cdots, n-1$ as inputs, and calculates as follows:

$$R_i := r_i \cdot G, \quad C_{0,i} := \mathsf{SymEnc}_{key_{0,i}}(r_i).$$

  (2) He takes the private key x_i and n random numbers r_i for $i = 0, \cdots, n-1$ as inputs, and calculates as follows:

$$y_i := (r_i + x_i) \bmod q.$$

  (3) He takes n subkeys $\{key_{1,i}\}$ and $\{y_i\}$ as inputs, and calculates as follows:

$$C_{1,i} := \mathsf{SymEnc}_{key_{1,i}}(y_i).$$

  (4) He takes the ciphertext $(R_i, C_{0,i}, C_{1,i})$ and the corresponding public key X as inputs, and calculates as follows:

$$\xi := \mathsf{hash}\left(X, R_0, \cdots, R_{n-1}, C_{0,0}, C_{1,0}, \cdots, C_{0,n-1}, C_{1,n-1}\right) \bmod 2^n,$$

  (5) Staggered disclosure: Given that ξ comprises n bits and there are n pairs of subkeys $(key_{0,i}, key_{1,i})$ and plaintexts (r_i, y_i), one set of subkeys and plaintexts will be disclosed based on each bit value of ξ. Specifically:
  - If the i-th bit of ξ is 0, then disclose $(key_{0,i}, r_i)$;
  - If the i-th bit of ξ is 1, then disclose $(key_{1,i}, y_i)$.

  Note that only one set from every pair is disclosed, referred to as "staggered disclosure", which does not compromise the private key x. The private key x would only be revealed if both sets $(key_{0,i}, r_i)$ and $(key_{1,i}, y_i)$ are disclosed. The revealing method is

$$x_i := y_i - r_i \bmod q.$$

Therefore, disclosing only one set of subkeys and plaintext in every pair will not compromise the private key x, thereby ensuring the scheme's security. Finally, the ciphertexts, public key, encryption keys, and plaintexts are summarized as follows:

$$C = \left(R_0, \cdots, R_{n-1}, C_{0,1}, C_{1,1}, \cdots, C_{0,n-1}, C_{1,n-1}, X, key_{0,i}, key_{1,i}, r_i, y_i\right).$$

- **Verify**: It consists of three steps.
(1) The user takes the ciphertexts C as inputs, and calculates a random number ξ'

$$\xi' := \mathsf{hash}\left(X, R_0, \cdots, R_{n-1}, C_{0,0}, C_{1,0}, \cdots, C_{0,n-1}, C_{1,n-1}\right) \bmod 2^n.$$

(2) If the i-th bit of ξ' is 0, then it takes the elliptic curve generator G, the sub-key and random number $(key_{0,i}, r_i)$, part of ciphertexts $(R_i, C_{0,i})$ as inputs, and checks whether the following equations hold

$$R_i = r_i \cdot G, \quad C_{0,i} = \mathsf{SymEnc}_{key_{0,i}}(r_i).$$

The first equation verifies that the disclosed random number r_i is correct, while the second equation confirms that the ciphertext $C_{0,i}$ corresponds to the r_i. If both equations hold, the verification is accepted; otherwise, a symbol signifying error is outputted.
(3) If the i-th bit of ξ' is 1, then it takes the elliptic curve generator G, the public key X, the sub-key and plaintext $(key_{1,i}, y_i)$, part of ciphertexts $(R_i, C_{1,i})$ as inputs, and checks whether the following equations hold

$$y_i \cdot G = R_i + X, \quad C_{1,i} = \mathsf{SymEnc}_{key_{1,i}}(y_i).$$

By using the public key X, the first equation verifies that y_i corresponds to a correct private key x; the second equation confirms that the ciphertext $C_{1,i}$ corresponds to the correct y_i. If both equations hold, the verification is accepted; otherwise, a symbol signifying error is outputted.
If all the above-mentioned equations hold, the ciphertexts C are stored on the blockchain; otherwise, a symbol signifying error is outputted.
Since n sets are verified, the probability of successful cheating by an adversary is $\frac{1}{2^n}$. If $n \geq 110$, the cheating probability is negligible. Typically, n is set at 110 or higher.
- **Decrypt**: It consists of three steps.
(1) The user takes the recovery key Key as inputs, performs the KeyDer to get n pairs of subkeys $(key_{0,i}, key_{1,i})$

$$key_{0,i} := \mathsf{KDF}(Key, i), \quad key_{1,i} := \mathsf{KDF}(Key, n+i),$$

(2) He retrieves C' from the blockchain, takes part of ciphertexts $(C'_{0,i}, C'_{1,i})$ and n pairs of subkeys $(key_{0,i}, key_{1,i})$ as inputs, and computes as follows:

$$r'_i := \mathsf{SymDec}_{key_{0,i}}(C'_{0,i}), \quad y'_i := \mathsf{SymDec}_{key_{1,i}}(C'_{1,i}).$$

(3) He takes (r'_i, y'_i) for $i = 0, \cdots, n-1$ as inputs, and calculates private keys x'_i as follows:

$$x'_i := y'_i - r'_i \bmod q.$$

(4) He takes x'_i for $i = 0, \cdots, n-1$ and the corresponding public key X as inputs, and checks these x'_i as follows:

$$x'_i \cdot G = X.$$

If one of the equations holds, x'_i is the correct private key, otherwise, a symbol signifying error is outputted.

6 Security Analysis

In this section, we demonstrate that our PSFVE construction satisfies the properties of consistency, public verifiability, fault tolerance, and security.

Theorem 1 (Consistency). *The private key x'_i decrypted by the user is equal to the private key x that was encrypted and broadcasted to the blockchain.*

Proof. Since the recovery key Key remains unchanged, the key derivation function KeyDer will derive the same n pairs of subkeys $(key_{0,i}, key_{1,i})$.

In the decryption phase, the user obtains n pairs of random numbers r'_i and responses y'_i that are identical to the original r_i and y_i:

$$r'_i = r_i, \quad y'_i = y_i.$$

Therefore, the private keys x'_i retrieved are equal to the original private key x:

$$x'_i = x.$$

Theorem 2 (Public Verifiability). *The user can verify the correctness of the private key x without knowing the private key itself.*

Proof. The user gets the ciphertexts C' that is equal to the C sent by the user, so:

$$\xi' = \xi.$$

Therefore, if the i-th bit of ξ' is 0, he can verify the following two equations:

$$R_i = r_i \cdot G, \quad C_{0,i} = \mathsf{SymEnc}_{key_{0,i}}(r_i).$$

If the i-th bit of ξ' is 1, he can verify the following two equations:

$$y_i \cdot G = R_i + X, \quad C_{1,i} = \mathsf{SymEnc}_{key_{1,i}}(y_i).$$

The Eq. (6) for the response is given by:

$$y_i \cdot G = (r_i + x_i) \cdot G = R_i + X.$$

The Eq. (6) ensures that y_i corresponds to the correct private key x_i. Thus, he can verify the correctness of the private key x without actually knowing the private key itself.

Theorem 3 (Fault Tolerance). *The proposed PSFVE scheme has 99% fault tolerance, which means that even if the ciphertext stored on the blockchain undergoes some degree of manipulation, the user can still retrieve a correct private key x with probability 99%.*

Proof. The user generates n pairs of subkeys $key_{0,i}, key_{1,i}$ using his recovery key Key. The tampered with ciphertext is denoted as C'. Consequently, he can decrypt to obtain n pairs of random numbers r'_i and responses y'_i, and compute n private keys x'_i, where $i = 0, \cdots, n-1$.

He takes x'_i for $i = 0, \cdots, n-1$ and the corresponding public key X as input, and verifies the following equation:

$$x'_i \cdot G = X.$$

If the equation holds for any x'_i, then x'_i is the correct private key; otherwise, a symbol signifying an error is outputted. As long as one of these n private keys satisfies the equation, it is the correct private key. Therefore, the proposed PSFVE scheme achieves a 99% level of fault tolerance.

Theorem 4 (Security). *Given an adversary $\mathcal{A}$ with an advantage ε in breaking the proposed PSFVE scheme in time τ with q_D decryption oracle queries and q_K random oracle queries, the upper bound for the advantage in breaking the symmetric encryption scheme* SymEnc *in time τ' is*

$$Success^{SymEnc}(\tau') \geq \frac{\varepsilon}{2} - \frac{2q_D}{2^k} - \frac{q_K}{2^n}.$$

Here, $\tau' \leq \tau + q_K \cdot T$, where T is the computation time of symmetric encryption.

Proof. We use variables with asterisks $(R_1^*, \cdots, R_n^*, C_{0,1}^*, C_{1,1}^*, \cdots, C_{0,n}^*, C_{1,n}^*)$ as challenge ciphertexts, and variables without asterisks $(R_1, \cdots, R_n, C_{0,1}, C_{1,1}, \cdots, C_{0,n}, C_{1,n})$ as ciphertexts queried by the adversary $\mathcal{A}$ to the decryption oracle $\mathcal{D}$.

Game 0: The adversary $\mathcal{A}$ sends two private keys (x_0, x_1) to the challenger $\mathcal{C}$. The challenger $\mathcal{C}$ flips a coin to generate a challenge $b \in \{0, 1\}$, takes the recovery key Key^* and n random numbers $r_i^*, i = 0, \cdots, n-1$ as inputs, runs KDF and SymEnc algorithm, and calculates as follows:

$$\begin{aligned} key_{0,i}^* &:= \mathsf{KDF}(Key^*, i), & key_{1,i}^* &:= \mathsf{KDF}(Key^*, n+i), \\ R_i^* &:= r_i^* \cdot G, & C_{0,i}^* &:= \mathsf{SymEnc}_{key_{0,i}^*}(r_i^*), \\ y_i^* &:= r_i^* + x_{b,i}, & C_{1,i}^* &:= \mathsf{SymEnc}_{key_{1,i}^*}(y_i^*). \end{aligned}$$

Let $x_b = x_{b,i}$, where $i = 0, \cdots, n-1$. The challenge ciphertext C^* is

$$C^* = \left(R_0^*, \cdots, R_{n-1}^*, C_{0,1}^*, C_{1,1}^*, \cdots, C_{0,n-1}^*, C_{1,n-1}^*, (key_{0,i}^*, r_i^*), (key_{1,i}^*, y_i^*).\right).$$

For C^*, the adversary $\mathcal{A}$ generates a guess b'. In this process, the adversary $\mathcal{A}$ can access the random oracle $\mathcal{K}$ and the decryption oracle $\mathcal{D}$. However, it cannot submit the challenge ciphertext C^* to the decryption oracle $\mathcal{D}$ for the decryption query, and it cannot query the random oracle $\mathcal{K}$ for the staggered opening values $(key^*_{0,i}, key^*_{1,i}), i \in \{0, \cdots, n-1\}$.

Let S_0 denote the event $b' = b$, and use S_i to denote the game i below. By definition, we have

$$\Pr[S_0] = \frac{1}{2} + \frac{\varepsilon}{2}.$$

Game 1: Now we simulate the random oracle and the decryption oracle. Perform q_K random queries on the oracle $\mathcal{K}$. Before the query, the storage list of the random oracle $\mathcal{K}$ is empty. For a new query value, select a new random value and return it; for an existing query, return the previously recorded result.

Perform q_D decryption oracle $\mathcal{D}$ queries. For a query,

$$C = \big(R_0, \cdots, R_{n-1}, C_{0,1}, C_{1,1}, \cdots, C_{0,n-1}, C_{1,n-1}, (key_{0,i}, r_i), (key_{1,i}, y_i)\big)$$

the decryption oracle calculates as follows:

$$\begin{aligned} key_{0,i} &:= \mathsf{KDF}(Key, i). & key_{1,i} &:= \mathsf{KDF}(Key, n+i). \\ r_i &:= \mathsf{SymDec}_{key_{0,i}}(C_{0,i}). & y_i &:= \mathsf{SymDec}_{key_{1,i}}(C_{1,i}). \\ x_{b,i} &:= y_j - r_i. \end{aligned}$$

Send the private key $x_{b,i}$ to the adversary $\mathcal{A}$. The q_K random oracle $\mathcal{K}$ queries and the q_D decryption oracle $\mathcal{D}$ queries will not compromise the challenge private key x_b.

Therefore, **Game 1** is indistinguishable from **Game 0**, we have

$$\Pr[S_1] = \Pr[S_0].$$

Game 2: The challenger chooses n pairs of random numbers $(key^+_{0,i}, key^+_{1,i}), i \in \{0, \cdots, n-1\}$ to replace the calculation results of the KDF; then calculates as follows:

$$\begin{aligned} R^*_i &:= r^*_i \cdot G, & C^*_{0,i} &:= \mathsf{SymEnc}_{key^+_{0,i}}(r^*_i), \\ y^*_i &:= r^*_i + x_{b,i}, & C^*_{1,i} &:= \mathsf{SymEnc}_{key^+_{1,i}}(y^*_i). \end{aligned}$$

He computes the hash value

$$\xi := \mathsf{hash}\left(R^*_0, \cdots, R^*_{n-1}, C^*_{0,0}, C^*_{1,0}, \cdots, C^*_{0,n-1}, C^*_{1,n-1}\right) \bmod n.$$

and uses it to disclose the corresponding set of $(key^+_{0,i}, r^*_i)$ or $(key^+_{1,i}, y^*_i)$.

If the adversary $\mathcal{A}$ does not query the random oracle $\mathcal{K}$ for Key^*, then **Game 1** and **Game 2** are perfectly indistinguishable. Let Ask_2 denote the event that the adversary queries Key^*, then

$$|\Pr[S_2] - \Pr[S_1]| \leq \Pr[Ask_2].$$

Game 3: Next, modify the simulation of the decryption oracle $\mathcal{D}$ to reject the case where the decryption oracle is queried while the corresponding random oracle is queried. Let Ask_3 denote the querying of the private key to the decryption oracle $\mathcal{D}$ without querying Key^* to the random oracle $\mathcal{K}$. If Key^* is guessed correctly, then the simulation of **Game 3** is different from **Game 2**

$$|\Pr[S_3] - \Pr[S_2]| \leq \frac{q_D}{2^k}, \quad |\Pr[Ask_3] - \Pr[Ask_2]| \leq \frac{q_D}{2^k}.$$

Game 4: On the basis of **Game 3**, the challenger chooses n random numbers $r_i^+, i = 0, \cdots, n-1$ to replace $r_i^*, i = 0, \cdots, n-1$, then calculates the ciphertext as follows:

$$R_i^* := r_i^+ \cdot G, \qquad C_{0,i}^* := \mathsf{SymEnc}_{key_{0,i}^+}(r_i^+),$$
$$y_i^* := r_i^+ + x_{b,i}, \quad C_{1,i}^* := \mathsf{SymEnc}_{key_{1,i}^+}(y_i^*).$$

If the adversary $\mathcal{A}$ does not query the decryption oracle $\mathcal{D}$ for $r_i^*, i = 0, \cdots, n-1$, then **Game 3** and **Game 4** are perfectly indistinguishable. Let Ask_4 denote querying the private key $r_i^*, i = 0, \cdots, n-1$ to the decryption oracle $\mathcal{D}$, then we have

$$\Pr[S_4] = \Pr[S_3], \quad \Pr[Ask_4] = \Pr[Ask_3].$$

In this case, x_b is randomized by the random numbers $r_i^+, i = 0, \cdots, n-1$, and $r_i^+, i = 0, \cdots, n-1$ have never appeared before. Therefore, the input of the adversary $\mathcal{A}$ is random and independent of b, then we have

$$\Pr[S_4] = \frac{1}{2}.$$

Game 5: On the basis of **Game 4**, the challenger chooses n random points $R_i^+, i = 0, \cdots, n-1$, and calculates the ciphertexts as follows:

$$R_i^* := R_i^+, \qquad C_{0,i}^* := \mathsf{SymEnc}_{key_{0,i}^+}(r_i^+),$$
$$y_i^* := r_i^+ + x_{b,i}, \quad C_{1,i}^* := \mathsf{SymEnc}_{key_{1,i}^+}(y_i^*).$$

Since the assumption of discrete logarithm computational complexity holds, the randomly selected points $R_i^+, i = 0, \cdots, n-1$ are indistinguishable from the calculated random points $r_i^+ \cdot G$. We have

$$\Pr[S_5] = \frac{1}{2}, \quad \Pr[Ask_5] = \Pr[Ask_4].$$

Game 6: On the basis of **Game 5**, the challenger chooses n sets of random numbers $(C_{0,i}^+, C_{1,i}^+)$, $i = 0, \cdots, n-1$, and calculates the ciphertexts as follows:

$$R_i^* := R_i^+, \quad C_{0,i}^* := C_{0,i}^+ y_i^* := r_i^+ + x_{b,i}, \quad C_{1,i}^* := C_{1,i}^+.$$

If the discrete logarithm assumption holds, the randomly selected points $R_i^+, i = 0, \cdots, n-1$ are indistinguishable from the random points $r_i^+ \cdot G$.

$$\Pr[S_6] = \frac{1}{2}, \quad \Pr[Ask_6] = \Pr[Ask_5].$$

Game 7: In the simulation of the decryption oracle $\mathcal{D}$, reject earlier if the corresponding recovery key Key does not query the random oracle $\mathcal{K}$. The receiver uses the symmetric decryption scheme

$$r_i := \mathsf{SymDec}_{key_{0,i}}(C_{0,i}). \quad y_j := \mathsf{SymDec}_{key_{1,i}}(C_{1,i}).$$

to get r_i, and y_i which are random. Therefore, $x_b = y_i - r_i$ is random.

Let Ask_6 denote the event that the adversary $\mathcal{A}$ queries the random oracle $\mathcal{K}$ for the decryption keys $(key_{0,i}, key_{1,i})$, resulting in querying the plaintext corresponding to the ciphertexts $(C^+_{0,i}, C^+_{1,i})$ in the symmetric encryption. Therefore,

$$|\Pr[Ask_7] - \Pr[Ask_6]| \leq \frac{q_K}{2^n}.$$

The advantage of the adversary $\mathcal{A}$ in breaking the SymEnc is

$$\Pr[Ask_7] \leq Success^{SymEnc}(\tau + q_K \cdot T_{SymEnc}).$$

Therefore, summing up all the above inequalities, the upper bound of the advantage is

$$Success^{SymEnc}(\tau') \geq \frac{\varepsilon}{2} - \frac{2q_D}{2^k} - \frac{q_K}{2^n}$$

This completes the proof.

7 Comparison

As shown in Table 1, the proposed PSFVE scheme is compared with the ones from [9,14,22] in terms of ciphertext length (Cipher-Length), encryption complexity (Encrypt), decryption complexity (Decrypt), verification complexity (Verify), and fault tolerance (FT). Compared to elliptic curve point multiplication ($E_{\mathbb{G}}$), the computational complexities of hash functions (hash) and symmetric encryption ($\mathsf{SymEnc}, \mathsf{SymDec}$) are negligible. Therefore, the focus is primarily on the complexities of elliptic curve point multiplication ($E_{\mathbb{G}}$) and bilinear mapping (P). The complexity of the schemes in [9,14,22] all depends on l, where l is typically set to 10, 20, 50, 80, or 100.

In terms of ciphertext length, the schemes from [9,14,22] are advantageous when l is 10, 20, or 50; however, the proposed PSFVE scheme becomes advantageous when l is 80 or 100. In terms of encryption complexity, regardless of the value of l, our scheme has the lowest encryption complexity, involving only 110 elliptic curve point multiplications, while the schemes from [9,14,22] all involve bilinear mapping. Compared to bilinear mapping, the complexity of elliptic curve point multiplication is negligible. Regarding decryption complexity, the solutions of [9,14,22] involve bilinear mapping, whereas our scheme only involves symmetric encryption and hash functions, making its decryption complexity negligible. In terms of verification complexity, Green, Hohenberger, and Waters' scheme [9] lacks a verification feature, while the schemes in [14,22] have verification complexities of $4E_{\mathbb{G}}$ and $E_{\mathbb{G}}$, respectively; our PSFVE scheme has a verification complexity of $110E_{\mathbb{G}}$. The verification process only involves elliptic curve point multiplication, which has a lower complexity. Finally, only our PSFVE scheme has FT capabilities, while the other three schemes do not support FT.

Table 1. Comparison

Scheme	Cipher-Length	Encrypt	Decrypt	Verify	FT
Green et al. [9]	$(1+2l)\|\mathbb{G}\|$	$\mathsf{P}+(2+3l)E_{\mathbb{G}}$	$(2+l)\mathsf{P}+2lE_{\mathbb{G}}$	–	–
Lai et al. [14]	$(3+4l)\|\mathbb{G}\|$	$2\mathsf{P}+(6+6l)E_{\mathbb{G}}$	$(4+2l)\mathsf{P}+(2+4l)E_{\mathbb{G}}$	$4E_{\mathbb{G}}$	–
Qin et al. [22]	$(1+2l)\|\mathbb{G}\|+160$	$\mathsf{P}+(2+3l)E_{\mathbb{G}}$	$(2+l)\mathsf{P}+(2l)E_{\mathbb{G}}$	$E_{\mathbb{G}}$	–
Our PSFVE	$110(3\|\mathbb{G}\|+256)$	$110E_{\mathbb{G}}$	Almost 0	$110E_{\mathbb{G}}$	√

8 Tests

We implemented all schemes using a 224-bit MNT elliptic curve from the Stanford Pairing-Based Crypto (PBC) library [17]. For a security parameter $\lambda = 80$ bits, we used a random 128-bit symmetric key. The KDF and hash function utilize SHA-3, while symmetric encryption employs AES. Experiments were conducted on an Intel Core i5-12500H processor with 16GB RAM, running the 64-bit Windows 11 operating system. All three implementations are slight modifications of the libfenc ABE library [8], which incorporates the Water's CP-ABE scheme. Encryption, decryption, and verification times were estimated by averaging results over 100 iterations. We present the performance results of the four schemes, where the numbers ($l = 10, 20, \cdots$) indicate the number of keys (or policies).

As shown in Fig. 2.1, when l is set to $10, 20, 50, 80, 100$, the ciphertext lengths of schemes from [9,14,22], compared to our scheme, are depicted. Our scheme maintains a constant ciphertext length of 57,480k bits. The ciphertext lengths in the schemes from [9,14,22] increase as l increases. When l is set to 10, 20, or 50, the ciphertexts of the schemes from [9,14,22] are shorter; however, when l is set to 80 or 100, the ciphertext of our scheme is shorter.

As shown in Fig. 2.2, when l is set to $10, 20, 50, 80, 100$, the encryption durations for schemes from [9,14,22], compared to our scheme, are depicted. The time units are in milliseconds. The schemes from [9,14,22] use bilinear mapping, which makes them relatively time-consuming. In contrast, our scheme only involves elliptic curve point multiplication, symmetric encryption, and hash functions, resulting in extremely fast speeds.

As shown in Fig. 2.3, when l is set to $10, 20, 50, 80, 100$, the decryption durations for schemes from [9,14,22], compared to our scheme, are depicted. The time units are in seconds. The schemes from [9,14,22] use bilinear mapping, which makes them relatively time-consuming. Meanwhile, our scheme only involves elliptic curve point multiplication, symmetric encryption, and hash functions, resulting in almost negligible time consumption.

Finally, as shown in Fig. 2.4, for l values of $10, 20, 50, 80$, and 100, the verification times for the schemes from [9,14,22], as well as our scheme, are relatively low.

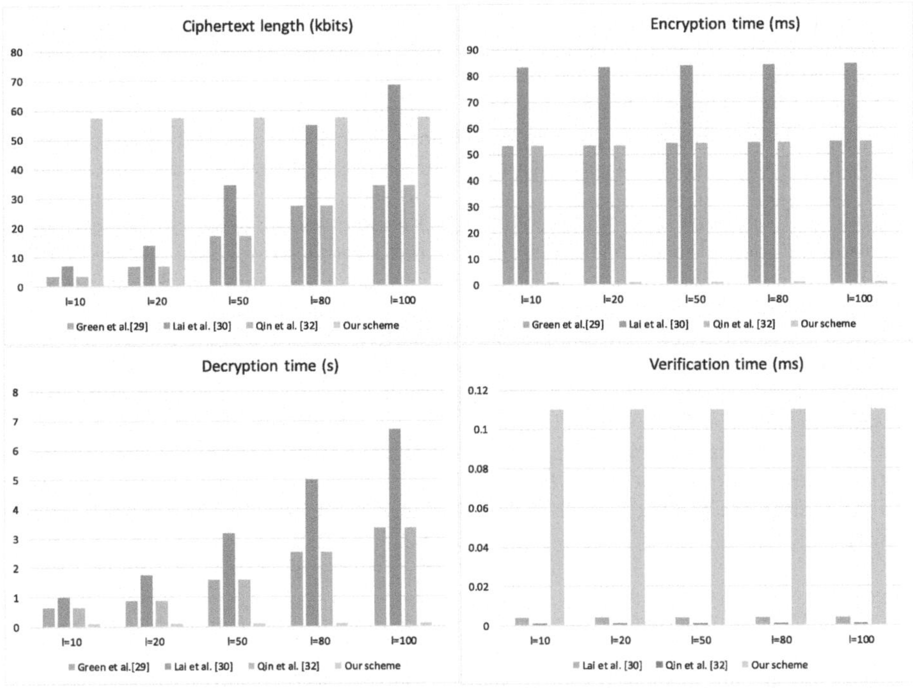

Fig. 2. Experimental Tests

9 Conclusion

We proposed a PSFVE scheme to address the issue of key security storage. This scheme incorporates hash functions, symmetric encryption, and elliptic curve multiplication but does not require bilinear mapping, making it more efficient. Security analysis indicated that the PSFVE scheme's security relies on symmetric encryption, thus ensuring a high level of security. Unlike existing verifiable decryption schemes, our scheme offers both public verifiability and 99% fault tolerance. Experimental tests demonstrated that the encryption and verification times of our scheme are approximately 53 milliseconds, and the decryption time is merely 1 millisecond, providing both a good user experience and high security.

References

1. Ahmad, S., Mehfuz, S., Urooj, S., Alsubaie, N.: Machine learning-based intelligent security framework for secure cloud key management. Clust. Comput. **27**(5), 5953–5979 (2024). https://doi.org/10.1007/s10586-024-04288-8
2. Aouedi, O., et al.: A survey on intelligent internet of things: applications, security, privacy, and future directions. IEEE Commun. Surv. Tutor. **27**(2), 1238–1292 (2025). https://doi.org/10.1109/COMST.2024.3430368

3. Atapoor, S., Baghery, K., Pereira, H.V.L., Spiessens, J.: Verifiable FHE via lattice-based SNARKs. IACR Commun. Cryptol. **1**(1) (2024). https://doi.org/10.62056/a6ksdkp10
4. Augusto, A., Belchior, R., Correia, M., Vasconcelos, A., Zhang, L., Hardjono, T.: Sok: security and privacy of blockchain interoperability. In: 2024 IEEE Symposium on Security and Privacy (SP), pp. 3840–3865 (2024). https://doi.org/10.1109/SP54263.2024.00255
5. Bois, A., Cascudo, I., Fiore, D., Kim, D.: Flexible and efficient verifiable computation on encrypted data. In: Garay, J.A. (ed.) Public-Key Cryptography – PKC 2021, pp. 528–558. Springer International Publishing, Cham (2021). https://doi.org/10.1007/978-3-030-75248-4_19
6. Chen, B., Xiang, T., He, D., Li, H., Choo, K.K.R.: BPVSE: publicly verifiable searchable encryption for cloud-assisted electronic health records. IEEE Trans. Inf. Forensics Secur. **18**, 3171–3184 (2023). https://doi.org/10.1109/TIFS.2023.3275750
7. Döttling, N., Hanzlik, L., Magri, B., Wohnig, S.: Mcfly: verifiable encryption to the future made practical. In: Baldimtsi, F., Cachin, C. (eds.) Financial Cryptography and Data Security, pp. 252–269. Springer Nature Switzerland, Cham (2024). https://doi.org/10.1007/978-3-031-47754-6_15
8. Green, M., Akinyele, J.A.: The functional encryption library (5). https://code.google.com/archive/p/libfenc/
9. Green, M., Hohenberger, S., Waters, B.: Outsourcing the decryption of ABE ciphertexts. In: 20th USENIX Security Symposium (USENIX Security 11). USENIX Association, San Francisco (2011). https://doi.org/10.5555/2028067.2028101
10. Guo, C., Li, W., Tang, X., Choo, K.K.R., Liu, Y.: Forward private verifiable dynamic searchable symmetric encryption with efficient conjunctive query. IEEE Trans. Dependable Secure Comput. **21**(2), 746–763 (2024). https://doi.org/10.1109/TDSC.2023.3262060
11. Guo, Y., Zhang, C., Wang, C., Jia, X.: Towards public verifiable and forward-privacy encrypted search by using blockchain. IEEE Trans. Dependable Secure Comput. **20**(3), 2111–2126 (2023). https://doi.org/10.1109/TDSC.2022.3173291
12. Kalota, F.: A primer on generative artificial intelligence. Educ. Sci. **14**(2) (2024). https://doi.org/10.3390/educsci14020172
13. Kotzer, A., Gandelman, D., Rottenstreich, O.: Sok: applications of sketches and rollups in blockchain networks. IEEE Trans. Netw. Serv. Manage. **21**(3), 3194–3208 (2024). https://doi.org/10.1109/TNSM.2024.3372604
14. Lai, J., Deng, R.H., Guan, C., Weng, J.: Attribute-based encryption with verifiable outsourced decryption. IEEE Trans. Inf. Forensics Secur. **8**(8), 1343–1354 (2013). https://doi.org/10.1109/TIFS.2013.2271848
15. Li, W., Susilo, W., Xia, C., Huang, L., Guo, F., Wang, T.: Secure data integrity check based on verified public key encryption with equality test for multi-cloud storage. IEEE Trans. Dependable Secur. Comput. **21**(6), 5359–5373 (2024). https://doi.org/10.1109/TDSC.2024.3375369
16. Li, X., et al.: VRFMS: verifiable ranked fuzzy multi-keyword search over encrypted data. IEEE Trans. Serv. Comput. **16**(1), 698–710 (2023). https://doi.org/10.1109/TSC.2021.3140092
17. Lynn, B.: The stanford pairing based crypto library (2014). https://crypto.stanford.edu/pbc/
18. Mei, L., Xu, C., Xu, L., Yu, X., Zuo, C.: Verifiable identity-based encryption with keyword search for Iot from lattice. Comput. Mater. Continua **68**(2), 2299–2314 (2021). https://doi.org/10.32604/cmc.2021.017216

19. Miao, Y., et al.: Verifiable outsourced attribute-based encryption scheme for cloud-assisted mobile e-health system. IEEE Trans. Dependable Secure Comput. **21**(4), 1845–1862 (2024). https://doi.org/10.1109/TDSC.2023.3292129
20. Mu, X., Antwi-Afari, M.F.: The applications of Internet of Things (IoT) in industrial management: a science mapping review. Int. J. Prod. Res. **62**(5), 1928–1952 (2024). https://doi.org/10.1080/00207543.2023.2290229
21. Peng, T., Gong, B., Zhang, J.: Towards privacy preserving in 6g networks: verifiable searchable symmetric encryption based on blockchain. Appl. Sci. **13**(18) (2023). https://doi.org/10.3390/app131810151
22. Qin, B., Deng, R.H., Liu, S., Ma, S.: Attribute-based encryption with efficient verifiable outsourced decryption. IEEE Trans. Inf. Forensics Secur. **10**(7), 1384–1393 (2015). https://doi.org/10.1109/TIFS.2015.2410137
23. Takei, Y., Shudo, K.: Pragmatic analysis of key management for cryptocurrency custodians. In: 2024 IEEE International Conference on Blockchain and Cryptocurrency (ICBC), pp. 747–765 (2024). https://doi.org/10.1109/ICBC59979.2024.10634356
24. Tang, X., Guo, C., Choo, K.K.R., Jiang, X., Liu, Y.: A secure and lightweight cloud data deduplication scheme with efficient access control and key management. Comput. Commun. **222**, 209–219 (2024). https://doi.org/10.1016/j.comcom.2024.05.003
25. Tong, Q., et al.: VFIRM: verifiable fine-grained encrypted image retrieval in multi-owner multi-user settings. IEEE Trans. Serv. Comput. **15**(6), 3606–3619 (2022). https://doi.org/10.1109/TSC.2021.3083512
26. Varghese, C., Harrison, E.M., O'Grady, G., Topol, E.J.: Artificial intelligence in surgery. Nat. Med. **30**(5), 1257–1268 (2024). https://doi.org/10.1038/s41591-024-02970-3
27. Yanamala, A.K.Y.: Emerging challenges in cloud computing security: a comprehensive review. Int. J. Adv. Eng. Technol. Innov. **1**(4), 448–479 (2024)
28. Yuan, D., Cui, S., Russello, G.: We can make mistakes: fault-tolerant forward private verifiable dynamic searchable symmetric encryption. In: 2022 IEEE 7th European Symposium on Security and Privacy (EuroS&P), pp. 587–605 (2022). https://doi.org/10.1109/EuroSP53844.2022.00043
29. Zhang, Y., Zhu, T., Guo, R., Xu, S., Cui, H., Cao, J.: Multi-keyword searchable and verifiable attribute-based encryption over cloud data. IEEE Trans. Cloud Comput. **11**(1), 971–983 (2023). https://doi.org/10.1109/TCC.2021.3119407

A Lightweight Multi-authority KP-ABE Scheme Supporting Large Attribute Universes

Miao Wang[1], Zhengjun Jing[1], Chunsheng Gu[1], Runmeng Du[2], and Yuanjian Zhou[1](✉)

[1] Jiangsu University of Technology, ChangZhou 213001, China
zhouyuanjian@jsut.edu.cn
[2] Xi'an Polytechnic University, Xi'an 710699, China

Abstract. Attribute-based encryption (ABE) has gained widespread recognition as an effective mechanism for fine-grained access control in distributed systems. Nevertheless, the efficiency of ABE deployments remains a critical challenge, as most existing constructions depend on the bilinear pairing–a cryptographic operation that introduces considerable computational overhead and becomes a performance bottleneck.

This paper presents a novel lightweight multi-authority key-policy ABE (KP-ABE) scheme supporting large attribute universes. Unlike existing approaches, our construction achieves this without relying on bilinear pairings, and its security is proven to rely solely on the decisional Diffie-Hellman (DDH) assumption in the standard model. To the best of our knowledge, this constitutes the first multi-authority KP-ABE scheme that simultaneously achieves large attribute universe support while eliminating the need for bilinear pairings. Comprehensive performance evaluations demonstrate that our proposed scheme offers substantial improvements in both functionality and efficiency compared to the existing related schemes.

Keywords: ABE · Multi-authority · Large attribute universe · DDH assumption

1 Introduction

The rapid proliferation of cloud computing and related network paradigms has exposed significant limitations in traditional data protection technologies. Traditional role-based access control systems, while widely deployed, suffer from some shortcomings, such as excessively coarse granularity, limited scalability and flexibility [1]. ABE emerges as a transformative solution to these challenges. This innovative public-key cryptographic primitive characterizes system participants through descriptive attributes, utilizing these attributes as public keys for encryption while precisely governing decryption capabilities. By enabling attribute-centric data protection, ABE offers superior expressiveness that facilitates truly fine-grained access control with enhanced flexibility and efficiency.

L. Zhang and K.-K. R. Choo (Eds.): MobiQuitous 2025, LNICST 684, pp. 326–343, 2026.
https://doi.org/10.1007/978-3-032-22503-0_18

This cryptographic advancement presents a viable approach to address the critical security requirements of modern cloud environments.

The first ABE scheme was proposed by Sahai and Waters [2]. In this scheme, the user is identified by a certain attribute set, and the sender encrypts messages by specifying an attribute set. As long as the number of intersection elements of the above two attribute sets is larger than the given threshold d, the user is able to decrypt the ciphertext. The excellent access control model has received widespread attention in the academic community for ABE. During the past 20 years, numerous studies have emerged on trade-offs among efficiency, access structures, underlying assumptions and security [3–9]. However, in these initial schemes, user attributes were managed by a single authority, and this deployment was not entirely feasible and was only applicable in cases where a trusted domain managed all the data. In fact, in many scenarios, the strategies involved are quite complex and require crossing multiple trusted domains, with different entities managing different user information. Although ABE with single authority achieved one-to-many access control, centralized management of user attributes was a limiting factor for its application. Therefore, multi-authority ABE emerged.

In 2007, Chase [10] introduced a natural extension that supports multiple authorities to manage various attributes and generate decryption key components for users who have attributes under their control. This construction sets up a trusted central authority (CA) to generate secret keys for all attribute authority, which does not need to manage any attributes but has the highest power to decrypt any ciphertext. Subsequently, a few works have involved the construction of multi-authority ABE. After some initial attempts [11–14] with different limitations, an ABE scheme without trusted CA supporting multiple authorities was proposed by Lewko and Waters [15] relying on some assumptions over bilinear groups. In this scheme, the attribute authorities operate independently and can join the system freely. They are able to spontaneously generate their own public/secret keys and issue the decryption key components for users reflecting their attributes. To further improve efficiency, Rouselakis and Waters [16] designed a scheme relied on a non-standard q-type assumption. Until now, there have been quite a few results for different security and properties [17–25].

All of the above works have driven the development of ABE, but their security was based on bilinear Diffie-Hellman problems or their variants, finding some constructions relied on different assumptions is natural. Firstly, conceptually, this is important because more constructions not only increase our confidence about a scheme's existence, but also require new techniques when using different assumptions, which in turn brings us a new understanding of the primitive. Secondly, it is important for the efficiency that the computation cost of these schemes relying on bilinear pairings is much higher. It makes the ABE system encounter a bottleneck in efficiency.

Within this general goal, we conduct an in-depth literature investigation. Currently, there are only two multi-authority ABE schemes without bilinear pairings. One is the scheme [26] proposed by Das and Namasudra, which works in the classical discrete logarithm. This scheme did not have the trusted CA set, and its claimed security depends on the DDH assumption. Recently, it was pointed out that the construction cannot resist user key forgery and the design of encryption algorithms is insecure by Wang et al. [27]. In addition, in the security model, it did not consider the presence of corrupted attribute authorities. The other is the scheme [27] proposed by Wang et al., which is a decentralized multi-authority ABE scheme and avoids using bilinear pairings as the underlying construction block. It did not involve any trusted CA and could support the access structures implemented by non-monotonic LSSS. In the standard model, the scheme had adaptive security under chosen plaintext attacks (CPA) and could resist any type of user collusion attacks in multi-authority scenarios.

While existing pairing-free ABE schemes represent important theoretical advances, they suffer from a critical practical limitation: their public parameters are proportional to the supported attribute universe size. This scaling behavior renders them unsuitable for large-scale deployments, as expanding attribute sets leads to prohibitively large system parameters. In dynamic environments like cloud storage and distributed systems, where new users and attributes (e.g., departmental affiliations or job roles) frequently emerge, such schemes require complete reconfiguration of authority keys for each attribute addition, severely compromising system scalability. Therefore, the actual application requirements have prompted researchers to continue exploring lightweight multi-authority ABE schemes that support large attribute universes.

Our Contribution. To overcome these limitations, we propose a pairing-free multi-authority KP-ABE scheme that supports large attribute universes, achieving the design goal of lightweight decryption and constant-size system public parameters. The detailed description is as follows:

i) The proposed scheme completes the elimination of bilinear pairings. By replacing bilinear pairings with exponentiation operations, it results in significantly lighter decryption overhead. The security of this pairing-free construction is formally proven to depend solely on the DDH assumption in the standard model.
ii) The proposed scheme supports large attribute universes, realizing constant-size public parameters of the system that remain fixed regardless of attribute space growth. This design eliminates the need for system reconfiguration when expanding attributes, significantly reducing management overhead while ensuring the scalability of system.
iii) The proposed scheme completes the elimination of the trusted CA requirement, removing this single point of failure. Except for global coordination between the attribute authorities, any party can independently serve as an attribute authority through simple key generation. And it can successfully prevent any user collusion attack.
iv) Finally, experimental comparisons confirm the efficiency advantages of our scheme, demonstrating substantially lower computational overhead (from pairing-free operations) and reduced storage needs (through constant-size

parameters) compared to conventional ABE systems. These improvements make it particularly suitable for practical deployments.

2 Related Work

The first multi-authority ABE scheme was introduced by Chase [10]. The scheme introduced the concept of global identifier (gid), assigning each user a unique gid that remains constant throughout the system's lifespan. Additionally, it assumed a trusted CA that did not monitor any attributes, but would distribute a unique key to each user and secret key to each attribute authority. The CA has the power to decrypt all ciphertext. In order to weaken the power of CA, Lin-Cao [14] presented a scheme with distributed CA based on some secret sharing protocols. The scheme realized m-resilience, in which the security is guaranteed for a maximum of m collusive users. Subsequently, Chase [13] provided a multi-authority ABE scheme that completely removed the trusted CA and protected users' privacy. In the initialization stage, the attribute authorities need to negotiate the seed key parameters and establish trust relationship. And it introduced an anonymous key issuing protocol to prevent hostile authorities from gathering information about some particular users. After initial limited attempts, in 2011, Lewko and Waters designed a decentralized CP-ABE scheme [15]. In this scheme, a party can freely become an attribute authority without global coordination in addition to creation in the initial trusted setup. The interruption of some authorities would not prevent the operation of others, which makes an important improvement not only in efficiency but also in security. To further enhance efficiency, Rouselakis and Waters [16] designed a scheme in the random oracle model. Additionally, Rahulamathavan and Veluru also provided a decentralized construction [17] to protect user privacy. Compared to the scheme [13], it reduced the complexity of the system, but also needed interactions between users and authorities. Similarly, there are other multi-authority ABE schemes [18,19,21,22]. They all used some anonymous secret key issuing protocols and required multiple interactions between users and attribute authorities. Recently, utilizing functional encryption as a modular, Ambrona and Gay provided a scheme [23] from asymmetric prime-order pairings supporting non-monotonic access structures. Datta et al. presented a scheme [24] that could support access structures defined by circuits NC^1 and was proven adaptively secure. Concurrently, they introduced another multi-authority ABE scheme [25] which was been proven to be fully adaptively secure. Later, Chen et al. put forth an enhanced scheme [28] characterized by shorter parameters and supported many-use of attributes. Furthermore, multi-authority ABE has found diverse applications in various scenarios, such as combining with blockchain to achieve secure and efficient data sharing [29–32], among others.

Towards the known attacks by quantum computers [33] on the construction based on groups, there are currently a handful of ABE schemes based on the LWE assumption, but only a few attempts at multi-authority ABE [34–37]. Both constructions [34,36] from LWE employ a trusted CA for the creation of public and secret key pairs for these authorities. Once the setup is completed, all the authorities will be permanently fixed. And both schemes can only guarantee security against a limited user collusion. In 2021, Datta et al. [35] presented a decentralized construction from LWE. It removed the trusted CA. Any entity has the potential to act as an attribute authority independently without the need for global coordination, with the exception of the creation in the initial trusted setup. It successfully resists user collusion attacks. In order to further improve security, Waters et al. [37] recently proposed a new technique to construct multi-authority ABE scheme, and proved its security without reliance on random oracles.

3 Preliminaries

3.1 Notations

In the paper, to make the expression more concise, we use PPT to represent probabilistic polynomial time. Let $[n] = \{1, \cdots, n\}, \sum_k = \sum_{k \in [n]}, n \in \mathbb{N}$. We use $x \leftarrow_R \mathbb{Z}_p$ to represent that x is randomly chosen from $\mathbb{Z}_p$. We make bold lowercase letters (or with an index) as vectors, such as $\boldsymbol{\nu}$, $\boldsymbol{\nu}_{k,gid}$. We make bold uppercase letters (or with an index) as matrices, such as M, M_k. In addition, we define the i-th row of matrix M as M_i, the i-th row of matrix M_k as $M_{k,i}$, and an element in the i-th row and the j-th column as $M(i,j)$ or $M_k(i,j)$. By default, we assume that all vectors are row vectors.

3.2 Complexity Assumption

Definition 1. (DDH assumption). *Let $\mathbb{G}$ represent a group with prime order p, and g represent a generator of $\mathbb{G}$. Choosing $a, b, z \leftarrow_R \mathbb{Z}_p$, the DDH assumption is that any PPT adversary can only distinguish the tuple (g^a, g^b, g^{ab}) from the tuple (g^a, g^b, g^z) with a negligible advantage at most.*

3.3 Linear Secret Sharing Scheme

Definition 2. (LSSS). *For the party set P, a secret sharing scheme π achieving access structure $\mathbb{A}$ is named linear (over $\mathbb{Z}_p$) if*

- *The shares held by the parties form a vector over $\mathbb{Z}_p$.*
- *For the scheme π, there is a share-generating matrix M with l rows and d columns, and a row-labeling injective function $\rho(x)$ which assigns to each row of M a party, i.e. the i-th row of M is assigned to a party named $\rho(i) \in P$. Considering the vector $\boldsymbol{\nu} = (s, r_2, \cdots, r_d)$, $s \in \mathbb{Z}_p$ is the shared secret, and $r_2, \cdots, r_d \in \mathbb{Z}_p$ are selected randomly, then $M\boldsymbol{\nu}^\top$ is the vector composed of l shares associated with the secret s. The share $(M\boldsymbol{\nu}^\top)_i$ (the i-th component of $M\boldsymbol{\nu}^\top$) is held by the party $\rho(i) \in P$. We use the pair (M, ρ) to denote the LSSS realizing access structure $\mathbb{A}$.*

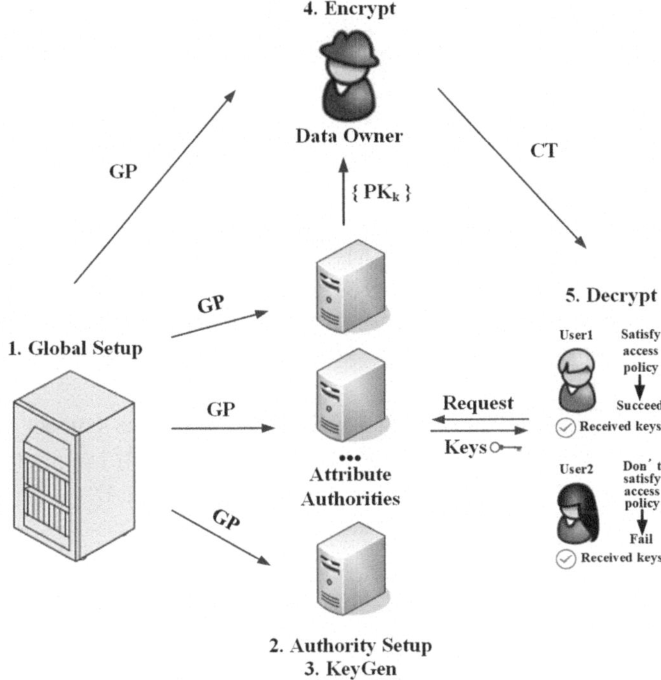

Fig. 1. The System Model of Multi-authority KP-ABE.

It is important to note that the above LSSS satisfies the property of linear reconstruction: For an access structure $\mathbb{A}$, assuming $S \in \mathbb{A}$ is an authorized set, and defining $I \subset \{1, 2, \cdots, l\}$ as $I = \{i : \rho(i) \in S\}$, then it has a linear combination of these rows of M indexed by I, which results in the vector $(1, 0, \cdots, 0) \in \mathbb{Z}_p^d$. And assuming that $\{\lambda_i\}_{i \in I}$ are valid shares of the secret s, it has constants $\{c_i \in \mathbb{Z}_p\}_{i \in I}$ that make $\sum_{i \in I} \lambda_i \cdot c_i = s$.

3.4 The Notion of Multi-authority KP-ABE for LSSSs

Suppose that there are N attribute authorities, a multi-authority KP-ABE scheme supporting LSSS-realizable access structures includes five algorithms (**Global Setup**, **Authority Setup**, **KeyGen**, **Encrypt**, **Decrypt**). The system model is shown in Fig. 1. Specifically, these algorithms are described below.

- **Global Setup** $(1^\lambda) \rightarrow (GP)$: It takes in the security parameter λ, and outputs the system public parameters GP.
- **Authority Setup** $(GP) \rightarrow (PK_k, SK_k)$: The algorithm is run by an attribute authority A_k, which inputs GP, and outputs the public and secret key pair (PK_k, SK_k) for A_k.
- **KeyGen** $(SK_k, gid, \widetilde{A}_k^u, (M_k, \rho)) \rightarrow (D_{k,u})$: The algorithm is also run by an attribute authority A_k. For a user u with the identifier gid, it inputs the

secret key SK_k, the LSSS access policy (M_k, ρ), the user's gid and his/her attribute set $\widetilde{A}_k^u$ related to the authority A_k. Then it outputs the decryption key $D_{k,u}$.

- **Encrypt** $(GP, \{PK_k\}_{k\in[N]}, \{\widetilde{A}_k^c\}_{k\in[N]}, m) \rightarrow (CT)$: The encryption algorithm takes as input the parameters GP, public key set $\{PK_k\}_{k\in[N]}$ and an encrypted message m for the attribute set $\{\widetilde{A}_k^c\}_{k\in[N]}$. Then output the ciphertext CT.
- **Decrypt** $(GP, gid, CT, \{D_{k,u}\}_{k\in[N]}) \rightarrow (m)$: The decryption algorithm takes as input GP, CT, a user u with the identifier gid and its decryption keys $\{D_{k,u}\}_{k\in[N]}$. For all $k \in [N]$, if the subset $\widetilde{A}_k^u \cap \widetilde{A}_k^c$ satisfies the access policy (M_k, ρ), it outputs the message m. Otherwise, the decryption fails.

Correctness. A multi-authority KP-ABE construction is correct if for every $\lambda \in \mathbb{N}$, every message m encrypted for an attribute set $\{\widetilde{A}_k^c\}_{k\in[N]}$, every user u with an attribute set $\{\widetilde{A}_k^u\}_{k\in[N]}$, where for each $k \in [N]$, $\widetilde{A}_k^u \cap \widetilde{A}_k^c$ satisfies the access policy (M_k, ρ), it holds that

$$Pr\left[m' = m \middle| \begin{array}{c} GP \leftarrow \textbf{Global Setup}(1^\lambda) \\ \forall k \in [N] : PK_k, SK_k \leftarrow \textbf{Authority Setup}(GP) \\ \forall k \in [N] : D_{k,u} \leftarrow \textbf{KeyGen}(SK_k, gid, \widetilde{A}_k^u, (M_k, \rho)) \\ CT \leftarrow \textbf{Encrypt}(GP, \{PK_k\}_{k\in[N]}, \{\widetilde{A}_k^c\}_{k\in[N]}, m) \\ m' \leftarrow \textbf{Decrypt}(GP, gid, CT, \{D_{k,u}\}_{k\in[N]}) \end{array} \right] = 1.$$

Security. The security against CPA for the N-authority KP-ABE system is defined in the selective-attribute model, where the attacker can choose the challenge attribute set and corrupted attribute authorities (up to $N-2$), but must provide them to the challenger before these public parameters of the attribute authorities are published. It is similar to the schemes [13,27]. The detailed description of the game can be referred to theirs.

Definition 3. *In the aforementioned designated game, a N-authority KP-ABE scheme is semantically secure, if for any PPT adversary, there is a negligible function $\varepsilon(\cdot)$ that makes for all $\lambda \in \mathbb{N}$, the adversary succeeds with a probability $\frac{1}{2} + \varepsilon(\lambda)$ at most.*

4 The Proposed Multi-authority KP-ABE Scheme Supporting Large Attribute Universes

The large attribute universe model was first proposed in [2], where the universe of attributes is exponentially large, but the size of public parameters is a fixed value which depends on the maximum length of the encrypted identity in such a setting. Suppose that the maximum length of the encrypted attribute set is n. We use the non-monotone LSSS (M, ρ) of Datta et al. [35] to realize the access structures, where ρ refers to an injective row-labeling function that links an attribute to a single row in M, and the values in the share-generating matrix M come from $\{-1, 0, 1\}$, the secret reconstruction can be achieved using small coecients c_i, i.e., drawn from $\{0,1\}$. The final Multi-authority KP-ABE scheme supporting large attribute universes is shown below:

Global Setup. For a specified security parameter λ, the algorithm creates a group $\mathbb{G}$ with the prime order p and the generator g. It also generates a hash function H: $\{0,1\}^* \to \mathbb{Z}_p$ with gid input. Finally, it outputs the system public parameters GP$= (\mathbb{G}, p, g, H)$.
Authority Setup.

- (Master Public/Secret Key) Attribute authority A_k chooses $\omega_k \leftarrow_R \mathbb{Z}_p$ as a secret key, then sets $Y_k = g^{\omega_k}$ as a public key.
- (Secret Aggregation) Authority A_k chooses $x_k^j \leftarrow_R \mathbb{Z}_p, j \in [N]$, and sets $x_k = \sum_{j\in[N]} x_k^j$. Then send x_k^j to the authority A_j, $j \in [N] \setminus \{k\}$. Finally, each A_k can compute $X_k = \sum_{j\in[N]} x_j^k$. Obviously, it has $\sum_k X_k = \sum_k x_k$.
- Authority A_k chooses $t_{k,1}, \cdots, t_{k,n+1} \leftarrow_R \mathbb{Z}_p$, and defines function $T_k(x) = x^n \prod_{i=1}^{n+1} t_{k,i} \cdot \Delta_{i,S}(x)$, where $S = \{1, \cdots, n+1\}$, $T_k(x)$ is publicly computable, which is used to replace the previous group element $T_{k,x}$ for attribute x.
- Authority A_k also picks an LSSS access policy $(\mathbf{M}_k \in {\mathbb{Z}_p}^{n_k \times l}, \rho)$ as before. In addition, pick $s_k, h_k \leftarrow_R \mathbb{Z}_p$, and set $S_k = g^{s_k}, H_k = g^{h_k}$.

Then for each authority A_k, $SK_k = \{\omega_k, s_k, h_k, x_k\}$, $PK_k = \{Y_k, X_k, S_k, H_k, (\mathbf{M}_k, \rho), t_{k,1}, \cdots, t_{k,n+1}\}$.

KeyGen. For a user u with gid and attribute subset $\widetilde{A}_k^u$, the attribute authority A_k computes $r_{k,u} = x_k H(gid)$ and $\zeta_{k,u} = \omega_k + r_{k,u}$, then chooses a random vector $\boldsymbol{\beta}_{k,u} \in {\mathbb{Z}_p}^l$ with $\zeta_{k,u}$ as its first entry and sets $\boldsymbol{s}_k = (s_k, 0, \cdots, 0)$. Finally, the decryption keys for the user u are generated as

$$D_{k,u} = \left\{ d_{k,i} = \mathbf{M}_{k,i}(\boldsymbol{\beta}_{k,u} - \boldsymbol{s}_k)^\top + T_k(i) \cdot h_k \right\}_{i\in\widetilde{A}_k^u}.$$

Encrypt. For the message m and the attribute set $\{\widetilde{A}_k^c\}_{k\in[N]}$, the algorithm chooses $s \leftarrow_R \mathbb{Z}_p$, then generates the ciphertext $CT = (C_0, C_1, C_2)$ as follows:

$$C_0 = m \cdot \prod_{k=1}^{N} g^{\omega_k \cdot s}, C_1 = g^s,$$

$$C_2 = \{\mathcal{S}_{k,i} = (S_k)^{\mathbf{M}_k(i,1)\cdot s}, \mathcal{H}_{k,i} = (H_k)^{T_k(i)\cdot s}\}_{k\in[N], i\in\widetilde{A}_k^c}.$$

Decrypt. For a user u, if there is an attribute subset I_k of $\widetilde{A}_k^u \cap \widetilde{A}_k^c$ for $k \in [N]$, which satisfies the access policy $(\mathbf{M}_k, \rho)$, compute

- For each attribute authority A_k, $k \in [N]$:
  - Find constants $c_i \in \mathbb{Z}_p$ such that $\sum_{i\in I_k} c_i \mathbf{M}_{k,i} = (1, 0, \cdots, 0)$.

- For each $i \in I_k$, compute

$$\frac{{C_1}^{d_{k,i}} \cdot \mathcal{S}_{k,i}}{\mathcal{H}_{k,i}} = g^{\mathbf{M}_{k,i}\boldsymbol{\beta}_{k,u}^{\top} \cdot s}.$$

Then multiply all the values $g^{(\mathbf{M}_{k,i}\boldsymbol{\beta}_{k,u}^{\top} \cdot s) \cdot c_i}$ to get $F_k = g^{\zeta_{k,u} \cdot s}$.

- Multiply all the values F_k to get

$$G = \prod_{k=1}^{N} F_k = g^{s \cdot (\sum \omega_k + \sum r_{k,u})},$$

and compute $r = H(gid) \sum X_k = \sum r_{k,u}$.

- Recover m by $\frac{C_0 \cdot (C_1)^r}{G}$.

4.1 Preventing User Collusion Attacks

To prevent user collusion attacks, it needs global coordination among attribute authorities. We introduce data aggregation technology and a homomorphic function $f(x) = xH(\cdot)$, where $H(\cdot)$ is a collision-resistant hash function. Every authority A_k has a secret key x_k, users can compute the sum of secrets $\sum x_k$ without knowing the secret key x_k. Specifically, each authority A_k picks $x_k^j \leftarrow_R \mathbb{Z}_p, j \in [N]$ satisfying $x_k = \sum_{j \in [N]} x_k^j$, and sends x_k^j to A_j. Then each A_k computes $X_k = \sum_{j \in [N]} x_j^k$ and exposes X_k as a public key. Obviously, it has $\sum X_k = \sum x_k$. When a user u with gid requests the decryption keys, authority A_k uses the output of the hash function H with gid as input as the randomness to tie multiple key components together. It sets $r_{k,u} = x_k H(gid)$, thereby generating a unique share $\zeta_{k,u} = \omega_k + r_{k,u}$ for the user, where ω_k is the master secret key of the authority A_k, and it implicitly sets the system master secret key $msk = \sum \omega_k$. Only the user with sufficient attributes from all authorities A_k can recover $g^{\sum_k \zeta_{k,u} \cdot s}$ from the ciphertext. Then using the homomorphic property $f(x+y) = f(x) + f(y)$, the user can compute $H(gid) \sum X_k = \sum r_{k,u}$ in the exponent space. Finally, $g^{msk \cdot s}$ can be obtained by combining some information in the ciphertext. Obviously, in this setting, user collusion attacks are ineffective.

4.2 Security Proof

Theorem 1. *The proposed scheme is adaptively secure against CPA if the DDH assumption holds.*

Proof of Theorem 1. Suppose that there is a PPT adversary $\mathcal{A}$ who can attack this scheme with non-negligible probability ε. The challenger can then build a simulator $\mathcal{B}$ to break the DDH assumption by $\mathcal{A}$ with an advantage $\varepsilon/2$. Flip a fair binary coin ζ outside of the view of $\mathcal{B}$.

If $\zeta = 0$, it sets $T = (A, B, Z) = (g^a, g^b, g^{ab})$.

If $\zeta = 1$, it sets $T = (A, B, Z) = (g^a, g^b, g^z), z \leftarrow_R \mathbb{Z}_p$.

After receiving the tuple $T = (A, B, Z)$ from the challenger, $\mathcal{B}$ judges whether it belongs to (g^a, g^b, g^{ab}) or (g^a, g^b, g^z).

As explained in the security game, let the set of attributes that the adversary $\mathcal{A}$ chooses to challenge be $\{\widetilde{A}_k^w\}_{k \in [N]}$. Denote the corrupted attribute authority set as C_A and the honest attribute authority set as H_A, where $| H_A | \geq 2$. Assume that one of the honest attribute authorities is named A_κ. Then the reduction begins:

Setup. For the corrupted authorities $A_k \in C_A$: $\mathcal{B}$ chooses $\upsilon_k, t_{k,1}, \cdots, t_{k,n+1}, s_k, h_k \leftarrow_R \mathbb{Z}_p$, an LSSS access policy $(\mathbf{M}_k \in \mathbb{Z}_p{}^{n_k \times l}, \rho)$ and sets $Y_k = g^{\upsilon_k}, S_k = g^{s_k}, H_k = g^{h_k}$. $\mathcal{B}$ also picks $x_k^j \leftarrow_R \mathbb{Z}_p, j \in [N]$ and sends x_k^j to A_j. Let $x_k = \sum_{j \in [N]} x_k^j, X_k = \sum_{j \in [N]} x_j^k$. Then the public parameters are $\{Y_k, (\mathbf{M}_k, \rho), S_k, H_k,$
$X_k, t_{k,1}, \cdots, t_{k,n+1}\}$, the secret keys are $\{\upsilon_k, s_k, h_k, x_k, x_j^k\}_{j \in [N]}$. $\mathcal{B}$ provides the public parameters and secret keys of these corrupted authorities to $\mathcal{A}$ and computes $T_k(x) = x^n \prod_{i=1}^{n+1} t_{k,i} \Delta_{i,S}(x)$.

For these honest authorities $A_k (k \neq \kappa)$: $\mathcal{B}$ generates $\upsilon_k, t_{k,1}, \cdots, t_{k,n+1}, s_k, h_k \leftarrow_R \mathbb{Z}_p$, an LSSS access policy $(\mathbf{M}_k \in \mathbb{Z}_p{}^{n_k \times l}, \rho)$ and sets $Y_k = g^{\upsilon_k}, S_k = g^{s_k}, H_k = g^{h_k}$. $\mathcal{B}$ also picks $x_k^j \leftarrow_R \mathbb{Z}_p, j \in [N]$ and sends x_k^j to A_j. Let $x_k = \sum_{j \in [N]} x_k^j, X_k = \sum_{j \in [N]} x_j^k$. Then the public parameters are $\{Y_k, (\mathbf{M}_k, \rho), S_k, H_k,$
$X_k, t_{k,1}, \cdots, t_{k,n+1}\}$, the secret keys are $\{\upsilon_k, s_k, h_k, x_k, x_j^k\}_{j \in [N]}$. $\mathcal{B}$ sends the public parameters to $\mathcal{A}$ and computes $T_k(x)$ as before.

For the honest attribute authority A_κ: $\mathcal{B}$ chooses $t_{\kappa,1}, \cdots, t_{\kappa,n+1}, h_\kappa, \alpha_\kappa \leftarrow_R \mathbb{Z}_p$, an LSSS access policy $(\mathbf{M}_\kappa \in \mathbb{Z}_p{}^{n_\kappa \times l}, \rho)$ and implicitly sets $s_\kappa = a + \alpha_\kappa$. Then let $S_\kappa = g^{a+\alpha_\kappa} = A \cdot g^{\alpha_\kappa}, H_\kappa = g^{h_\kappa}$, $Y_\kappa = g^a \prod_{k=1,k\neq\kappa}^{N} Y_k^{-1} = g^{a - \sum_{k, A_k \in H_A} \upsilon_k - \sum_{k, A_k \in C_A} \upsilon_k} = A \cdot g^{-\sum_{k, A_k \in H_A} \upsilon_k - \sum_{k, A_k \in C_A} \upsilon_k}$. $\mathcal{B}$ picks $x_\kappa^j \leftarrow_R \mathbb{Z}_p, j \in [N]$ and sends x_κ^j to authority A_j. Let $x_\kappa = \sum_{j \in [N]} x_\kappa^j, X_\kappa = \sum_{j \in [N]} x_j^\kappa$. Hence, the public parameters are $\{Y_\kappa, (\mathbf{M}_\kappa, \rho), H_\kappa, S_\kappa, X_\kappa, t_{\kappa,1}, \cdots, t_{\kappa,n+1}\}$, the secret keys are implicitly $\{a - \sum_{k, A_k \in H_A} \upsilon_k - \sum_{k, A_k \in C_A} \upsilon_k, s_\kappa, h_\kappa, x_\kappa, x_j^\kappa\}_{j \in [N]}$. Then $\mathcal{B}$ sends the public parameters to $\mathcal{A}$ and computes $T_\kappa(x)$ as before.

Secret key queries. Queries for a user u with a gid to the honest attribute authorities $A_k, k \neq \kappa$: Compute $r_{k,u} = x_k H(gid)$ and set $\zeta_{k,u} = \upsilon_k + r_{k,u}, \boldsymbol{s}_k = (s_k, 0, \cdots, 0)$, then choose a random vector $\boldsymbol{\beta}_{k,u}$ with $\zeta_{k,u}$ as its first entry. For $i \in \widetilde{A}_k^u$, it means $d_{k,i} = \mathbf{M}_{k,i} (\boldsymbol{\beta}_{k,u} - \boldsymbol{s}_k)^\top + T_k(i) \cdot h_k$.

Queries for the user u to the honest attribute authority A_κ: It should satisfy the fact that $\widetilde{A}_\kappa^u \cap \widetilde{A}_\kappa^w$ cannot meet the access policy $(\mathbf{M}_\kappa, \rho)$. Compute $r_{\kappa,u} = x_\kappa H(gid)$ and implicitly set $\zeta_{\kappa,u} = (a - \sum_{k, A_k \in C_A} \upsilon_k - \sum_{k, A_k \in H_A} \upsilon_k) + r_{\kappa,u}, s_\kappa = a + \alpha_\kappa$. Then choose a random vector $\boldsymbol{\beta}_{\kappa,u}$ with $\zeta_{\kappa,u}$ as its first entry and set $\boldsymbol{\beta}_{\kappa,u} = (\zeta_{\kappa,u}, \beta_{\kappa,2}, \cdots, \beta_{\kappa,l})$, $\boldsymbol{s}_\kappa = (s_\kappa, 0, \cdots, 0)$. For $i \in \widetilde{A}_\kappa^u$, it generates the decryption keys as follows:

$$
\begin{aligned}
d_{\kappa,i} =& (\mathbf{M}_{\kappa i}(\boldsymbol{\beta}_{\kappa,u} - \boldsymbol{s}_{\kappa})^{\top} + T_{\kappa}(i) \cdot h_{\kappa} \\
=& a \cdot \mathbf{M}_{\kappa}(i,1) - a \cdot \mathbf{M}_{\kappa}(i,1) - \alpha_{\kappa} \cdot \mathbf{M}_{\kappa}(i,1) + \sum_{j \in \{2,\cdots,l\}} \beta_{\kappa,j} \cdot \mathbf{M}_{\kappa}(i,j) \\
&+ T_{\kappa}(i) \cdot h_{\kappa} + \Big(- \sum_{k, A_k \in C_A} v_k - \sum_{k, A_k \in H_A} v_k + r_{\kappa,u} \Big) \cdot \mathbf{M}_{\kappa}(i,1) \\
=& \sum_{j \in \{2,\cdots,l\}} \beta_{\kappa,j} \cdot \mathbf{M}_{\kappa}(i,j) + T_{\kappa}(i) \cdot h_{\kappa} - \alpha_{\kappa} \cdot \mathbf{M}_{\kappa}(i,1) \\
&+ \Big(- \sum_{k, A_k \in C_A} v_k - \sum_{k, A_k \in H_A} v_k + r_{\kappa,u} \Big) \cdot \mathbf{M}_{\kappa}(i,1)
\end{aligned}
$$

Therefore, $\mathcal{B}$ can generate the decryption keys for the user u, and the distribution is identical to that of the proposed scheme.

Challenge. $\mathcal{B}$ will receive two challenge messages m_0, m_1 from $\mathcal{A}$. It picks a random $\beta \in \{0, 1\}$ and returns the ciphertext of m_β associated with the challenge attribute set $\{\widetilde{A}_k^w\}$ of the user w. The ciphertext is shown as the following:

$$C_0 = m_\beta \cdot Z, C_1 = B,$$

$$
\begin{aligned}
C_2 =& \{(\mathcal{H}_{k,i} = B^{T_k(i) \cdot h_k})_{k \in [N]}, (\mathcal{S}_{k,i} = B^{\mathbf{M}_k(i,1) \cdot s_k})_{k \in [N]/\{\kappa\}} \\
& \cup (\mathcal{S}_{\kappa,i} = Z^{\mathbf{M}_\kappa(i,1)} \cdot B^{\alpha_\kappa \cdot \mathbf{M}_k(i,1)})\}_{i \in \widetilde{A}_k^w}.
\end{aligned}
$$

If $\zeta = 0$, then $Z = g^{ab}$. Let $s = b$, then get $C_0 = m_\beta \cdot Z = m_\beta \cdot g^{ab} = m_\beta \cdot g^{as}$, $C_1 = B = g^s$. C_2 can be generated as follows, for $i \in \widetilde{A}_k^w$, if $k \in [N]/\{\kappa\}$, $\mathcal{S}_{k,i} = B^{\mathbf{M}_k(i,1) \cdot s_k} = g^{b\mathbf{M}_k(i,1) \cdot s_k} = S_k{}^{\mathbf{M}_k(i,1) \cdot s}$. If $k = \kappa$, $\mathcal{S}_{k,i} = Z^{\mathbf{M}_k(i,1)} \cdot B^{\alpha_k \cdot \mathbf{M}_k(i,1)} = g^{ab \cdot \mathbf{M}_k(i,1) + b\alpha_k \cdot \mathbf{M}_k(i,1)} = (S_k)^{\mathbf{M}_k(i,1) \cdot s}$. And $\mathcal{H}_{k,i} = B^{T_k(i) \cdot h_k} = g^{bT_k(i) \cdot h_k} = (H_k)^{T_k(i)s}$ for $k \in [N]$. It is the real ciphertext of m_β under the challenge attribute set $\{\widetilde{A}_k^w\}$.

If $\zeta = 1$, then $Z = g^z$. It has $C_0 = m_\beta \cdot Z = m_\beta \cdot g^z$. C_0 will be a random value because z is random, it contains no information about m_β from $\mathcal{A}$'s view.

More secret key queries. $\mathcal{A}$ then submits more key queries. $\mathcal{B}$ will respond to these queries exactly as long as they satisfy the requirement as before.

Guess. $\mathcal{B}$ will receive a guess β' from $\mathcal{A}$. If $\beta' = \beta$, $\mathcal{B}$ will output $\zeta' = 0$ and guess that it is given $Z = g^{ab}$. Otherwise, $\mathcal{B}$ will output $\zeta' = 1$, indicating that it is given $Z = g^z$ for a random z.

Obviously, the public parameters and private keys generated by $\mathcal{B}$ are identical to those of the actual scheme. Through the analysis, the advantage of $\mathcal{B}$ in breaking the DDH assumption is $\frac{1}{2}Pr[\zeta' = \zeta \mid \zeta = 0] - \frac{1}{2}Pr[\zeta' = \zeta \mid \zeta = 1] = \frac{\varepsilon}{2}$.

Hence, the proposed scheme is secure as long as the DDH assumption holds.

5 Performance Analysis

In this section, we conduct a performance analysis of the proposed scheme. The compared schemes are some recently published multi-authority ABE schemes, namely the schemes AG23 [23], DKW23 [25], DN23 [26] and WCD25 [27], where the schemes WCD25 [27] and DN23 [26] are the latest multi-authority ABE schemes without bilinear pairings, the schemes AG23 [23] and DKW23 [25] are the recently proposed schemes with bilinear pairings as the underlying building blocks, but all the compared schemes are decentralized. The following comparisons of them are made respectively from the aspects of functionality, parameter size and computation cost.

Table 1 summarizes the functions of the compared schemes, respectively, presenting the relied assumption, the access structures, security model, whether multiple authorities and large attribute universes are supported, whether bilinear pairings are based and whether user collusion attacks are resisted. As shown in Table 1, all the compared schemes support multiple authorities. The schemes DN23, WCD25 and ours do not use bilinear pairings, and the security is based on the DDH assumption. It is worth noting that only our scheme can support large attribute universes, which avoids the reconfiguration of the public keys and private keys of authorities and management overhead caused by adding new attributes, and enhances the scalability of the system. In terms of access structures, since the access policies are implemented using the non-monotonic LSSS technology, our scheme can support any access structure represented by the NC^1 circuit, achieving the same flexibility as AG23, DKW23 and WCD25, while the scheme DN23 supports DNF access structures. Additionally, our scheme is similar to WCD25, and their security proofs are completed in the standard model, while the security proofs of AG23 and DKW23 are completed in the random oracle model.

Table 1. Functional Comparison among Different Schemes

Scheme	AG23 [23]	DKW23 [25]	DN22 [26]	WCD25 [27]	Ours
Multi-authority	✓	✓	✓	✓	✓
Bilinear Pairing	✓	✓	×	×	×
Large Universe	×	×	×	×	✓
Access Structure	NC^1	NC^1	DNF	NC^1	NC^1
Assumption	SXDH	k-Lin	DDH	DDH	DDH
Security Model	random oracle	random oracle	\	standard	standard

Table 2 summarizes the parameter sizes of the compared schemes, respectively, the key size of the attribute authorities (AA), the user key size, and the ciphertext (CT) size. Suppose that there are N attribute authorities, and each of them is responsible for n_k attributes, each user has n_{u_k} attributes reflected in each authority, the total number of attributes of a user is n_u and the number of attributes reflected in the ciphertext is n_c. As shown in Table 2, in terms of User KeySize and CT Size, our scheme has almost the same advantages as WCD25 and DN23, which is superior to AG23 and DKW23. But the AA KeySize of our scheme is a constant value and is independent of the number of attributes managed by the attribute authorities. Here, n is the pre-set value. Therefore, in terms of parameter size, our scheme is the best.

Table 2. Parameter Sizes for Different Schemes

Scheme	AA KeySize	User KeySize	CT Size
AG23 [23]	$4 \mid \mathbb{G}_1 \mid +3 \mid \mathbb{G}_2 \mid$	$3n_u \mid \mathbb{G}_2 \mid$	$8n_c \mid \mathbb{G}_1 \mid$
DKW23 [25]	$2n_k \mid \mathbb{G}_1 \mid$	$2n_u \mid \mathbb{G}_1 \mid$	$4n_c \mid \mathbb{G}_1 \mid +1 \mid \mathbb{G}_T \mid$
DN22 [26]	$2n_k \mid \mathbb{G}_1 \mid$	$n_u \mid \mathbb{Z}_p \mid$	$(2n_c + 1) \mid \mathbb{G}_1 \mid$
WCD25 [27]	$(2n_k + 1) \mid \mathbb{G}_1 \mid +1 \mid \mathbb{Z}_p \mid$	$n_u \mid \mathbb{Z}_p \mid$	$(2n_c + 2) \mid \mathbb{G}_1 \mid$
Ours	$3 \mid \mathbb{G}_1 \mid +(n + 1) \mid \mathbb{Z}_p \mid$	$n_u \mid \mathbb{Z}_p \mid$	$(2n_c + 2) \mid \mathbb{G}_1 \mid$

Table 3. Computation Cost for Different KeyGen Algorithms

Scheme	KeyGen per AA
AG23 [23]	$12n_{u_k}T_{e_1} + 4n_{u_k}T_{pa} + 8n_{u_k}T_{mm} + 6n_{u_k}T_{ma}$
DKW23 [25]	$2n_{u_k}T_{e_1} + T_{pa}$
DN22 [26]	$n_{u_k}T_{ma} + n_{u_k}T_{mm}$
WCD25 [27]	$(l + 1)n_{u_k}T_{ma} + ln_{u_k}T_{mm}$
Ours	$(l + 1)n_{u_k}T_{ma} + ln_{u_k}T_{mm}$

Table 4. Computation Cost for Different Encrypt Algorithms

Scheme	Encrypt
AG23 [23]	$9n_cT_{e_1} + 3n_cT_{pa} + 2n_cT_{mm}$
DKW23 [25]	$6n_cT_{e_1} + 2n_cT_{pa} + 2n_c(L - 1)T_{ma} + T_{e_t}$
DN22 [26]	$(2n_c + 1)T_{e_1} + (2n_c + 1)T_{pa} + (2Ln_c - 2)T_{ma}$
WCD25 [27]	$(2n_c + 2)T_{e_1} + NT_{pa}$
Ours	$(2n_c + 2)T_{e_1} + 2n_cT_{mm} + NT_{pa}$

Tables 3, 4 and 5 show the computation cost on the compared schemes, regarding user key generation, encryption and decryption. Some results omit

Table 5. Computation Cost for Different Decrypt Algorithms

Scheme	Decrypt
AG23 [23]	$3n_dT_{bp} + n_dT_{e_1} + 2n_dT_{e_t} + 2n_dT_{pa}$
DKW23 [25]	$4n_dT_{bp} + 2n_dT_{e_1} + n_dT_{e_t} + (2n_d - 1)T_{pa}$
DN22 [26]	$3n_dT_{e_1} + 3n_dT_{pa}$
WCD25 [27]	$n_dT_{e_1} + (2n_d + 1)T_{pa} + T_{e_1} + T_{mm} + (N - 1)T_{ma}$
Ours	$2n_dT_{e_1} + (2n_d + 1)T_{pa} + T_{e_1} + T_{mm} + (N - 1)T_{ma}$

the computation cost of some less influential operations, which can be precalculated and remain valid until the entire system is reset, such as the calculation of hash functions, $T_k(x)$ and the solutions of linear equations in LSSS with respect to the vector $(1, 0, \cdots, 0)$. The relevant symbol descriptions are shown in Table 7. To present a more intuitive comparison in terms of efficiency, experimental tests are conducted. These tests utilize Type A pairing on the curve $y^2 = x^3 + x$ in the field $E(F_q)$, with parameters set to $rBits = 160$ and $qBits = 512$. The experiments are carried out on a laptop running Windows 10, equipped with an Intel Core i7-8565U CPU 1.80 GHz processor and 8 GB RAM. The system is implemented using the JPBC library [38]. The computation cost of some key operations is shown in Table 6.

Table 6. Runtime of Key Operations

T_{bp}	T_{e_1}	T_{e_t}	T_{pa}	T_{mm}	T_{ma}
5.652ms	7.553ms	0.700 ms	0.003 ms	0.00023 ms	0.00011 ms

Table 7. Notations for Performance Analysis

Notations	Descriptions
T_{bp}	The computation cost of a pairing in an elliptic curve group.
T_{e_1}	The computation cost of an exponentiation in $\mathbb{G}_1$ or $\mathbb{G}_2$.
T_{e_t}	The computation cost of an exponentiation in $\mathbb{G}_t$.
T_{pa}	The computation cost of an addition in an elliptic curve group.
T_{mm}	The computation cost of a modular multiplication in $\mathbb{Z}_p^*$.
T_{ma}	The computation cost of a modular addition in $\mathbb{Z}_p$.

Figure 2 presents the comparison of the computation cost for different algorithms. When considering that the number of attributes managed by each attribute authority is the same (assuming $l = n_k = 20$, where l is the column size of the access policy matrix related to the KeyGen algorithm in our scheme), Fig. 2 (a) indicates that, except for DN23, our key generation algorithm has the same significant advantage as WCD25, both are superior to other schemes. When considering that the system has the same number of attribute authorities (assuming $N = 5$, $L = lN = 100$, where L is the column size of the access policy matrix when encrypting in the schemes [32]), Fig. 2 (b) shows that the encryption algorithms of DN23, WCD25 and ours have almost the same computational cost, all are better than other schemes. Finally, Fig. 2 (c) indicates that as the number of attributes n_d increases, the computation cost of our decryption algorithm is only slightly higher than that of WCD25, but it is significantly better than other schemes.

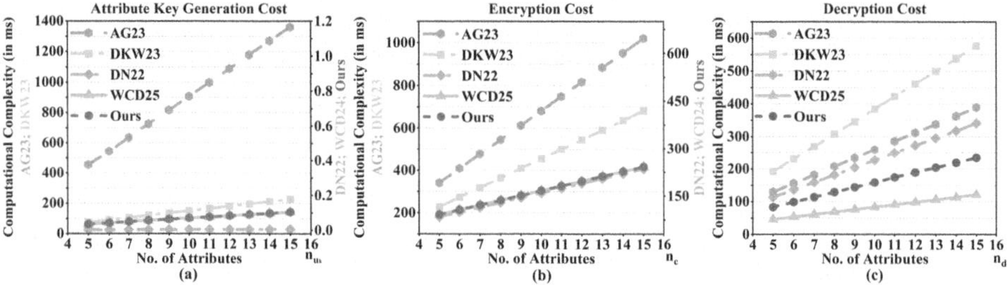

Fig. 2. Comparison of Computation Cost against Three Different Algorithms.

Regarding the computation cost of the key generation algorithms, it should be noted that although the KenGen algorithm of DN23 is superior to that of others, there is still some space that needs improvement in its construction, which has two security vulnerabilities. The relevant proof is provided in the literature [27]. Furthermore, although the decryption cost of our scheme is slightly higher than that of WCD25, our scheme is capable of supporting large attribute universes. When new attributes need to be added, there is no need to reset the system. The related authority can automatically issue keys about the new attributes to users, thus enhancing the scalability of the system and reducing management costs. Through a comprehensive comparison of computational efficiency and other performance, our scheme demonstrates clear advantages and practicality.

6 Conclusion

Most of the existing ABE schemes are constructed based on bilinear mapping technology, and the large number of bilinear pairing computations result in their low efficiency. To address the high computation cost caused by bilinear pairing, researchers have begun to study lightweight ABE. However, the public parameters of the related schemes currently proposed increase linearly with the size of the attribute set, making it impossible for them to be applied efficiently in scenarios with large attribute universes. To further improve the practicality and applicability of the ABE mechanism, the paper proposes a lightweight multi-authority KP-ABE scheme that supports large attribute universes. In the standard model, its security is proved based on the DDH assumption, and the comprehensive performance analysis indicates that it has better computational and storage efficiency.

References

1. Parast, F.K., Sindhav, C., Nikam, S., Yekta, H.I., Kent, K.B., Hakak, S.: Cloud computing security: a survey of service-based models. Comput. Secur. **114**, 102580 (2022)
2. Sahai, A., Waters, B.: Fuzzy identity-based encryption. In: Proceedings of the EUROCRYPT, 2005, pp. 457–473 (2005)
3. Bethencourt, J., Sahai, A., Waters, B.: Ciphertext-policy attribute-based encryption. In: IEEE Symposium on Security and Privacy, 2007, pp. 321–334 (2007)
4. Cheung, L., Newport, C.: Provably secure ciphertext policy ABE. In: Proceedings of the 14th ACM Conference on Computer and Communications Security, 2007, pp. 456–465 (2007)
5. Lewko, A., Okamoto, T., Sahai, A., Takashima, K., Waters, B.: Fully secure functional encryption: Attribute-based encryption and (hierarchical) inner product encryption. In: Proceedings of the EUROCRYPT, 2010, pp. 62–91 (2010)
6. Chen, J., Gay, R., Wee, H.: Improved dual system ABE in prime-order groups via predicate encodings. In: Proceedings of EUROCRYPT, 2015, pp. 595–624 (2015)
7. Gong, J., Wee, H.: Adaptively secure ABE for DFA from k-Lin and more. In: Proceedings of EUROCRYPT, 2020, pp. 278–308 (2020)
8. Kowalczyk, L., Wee, H.: Compact adaptively secure ABE for NC^1 from k-Lin. J. Cryptol. **33**(3), 954–1002 (2020)
9. Lin, H., Luo, J.: Compact Adaptively Secure ABE from k-Lin: Beyond NC^1 and and towards NL. In: Proceedings of EUROCRYPT, 2020, pp. 247–277 (2020)
10. Chase, M.: Multi-authority attribute based encryption. In: Theory of Cryptography: 4th Theory of Cryptography Conference, 2007, pp. 515–534 (2007)
11. Müller, S., Katzenbeisser, S., Eckert, C.: Distributed attribute-based encryption. In: Information Security and Cryptology–ICISC: 11th International Conference, 2008, pp. 20–36 (2008)
12. Müller, S., Katzenbeisser, S., Eckert, C.: On multi-authority ciphertext-policy attribute-based encryption. Bull. Korean Math. Society pp. 803–819 (2009)
13. Chase, M., Chow, S.S.M.: Improving privacy and security in multi-authority attribute-based encryption. In: Proceedings of the 16th ACM Conference on Computer and Communications Security, 2009, pp. 121–130 (2009)
14. Lin, H., Cao, Z., Liang, X., Shao, J.: Secure threshold multi authority attribute based encryption without a central authority. In: Progress in Cryptology-INDOCRYPT: 9th International Conference on Cryptology in India, 2008, pp. 426–436 (2008)
15. Lewko, A., Waters, D.: Decentralizing attribute-based encryption. In: Annual international Conference on the Theory and Applications of Cryptographic Techniques, 2011, pp. 568–588 (2011)

16. Rouselakis, Y., Waters, B.: Efficient statically-secure large-universe multi-authority attribute-based encryption. In: International Conference on Financial Cryptography and Data Security, 2015, pp. 315–332 (2015)
17. Rahulamathavan, Y., Veluru, S., Han, J., Li, F., Rajarajan, M., Lu, R.: User collusion avoidance scheme for privacy-preserving decentralized key-policy attribute-based encryption. IEEE Trans. Comput. **65**(9), 2939–2946 (2015)
18. Qian, H., Li, J., Zhang, Y.: Privacy-preserving decentralized ciphertext-policy attribute-based encryption with fully hidden access structurePrivacy-preserving decentralized ciphertext-policy attribute-based encryption with fully hidden access structure. In: Information and Communications Security: 15th International Conference, 2013, pp. 363–372 (2013)
19. Han, J., Susilo, W., Mu, Y., Zhou, J., Au, M.H.A.: Improving privacy and security in decentralized ciphertext-policy attribute-based encryption. IEEE Trans. Inform. Forensics Secur. **10**(3), 665–678 (2014)
20. Yuanjian, Z., Tianci, Z., Zhengjun, J., Quanyu, Z., Yongkang, Z.: A blockchain-based privacy-preserving data aggregation scheme with robustness in smart grids. J. Supercomput. **81**(5), 675–701 (2025)
21. Ge, A., Zhang, J., Zhang, R., Ma, C., Zhang, Z.: Security analysis of a privacy-preserving decentralized key-policy attribute-based encryption scheme. IEEE Trans. Parallel Distrib. Syst. **24**(11), 2319–2321 (2012)
22. Han, J., Susilo, W., Mu, Y., Yan, J.: Privacy-preserving decentralized key-policy attribute-based encryption. IEEE Trans. Parallel Distrib. Syst. **23**(11), 2150–2162 (2012)
23. Ambrona, M., Gay, R.: Multi-Authority ABE for non-monotonic access structures. In: IACR International Conference on Public-Key Cryptography, 2023, pp. 306–335 (2023)
24. Datta, P., Ilan, K., Waters, B.: Decentralized multi-authority ABE for NC^1 from BDH. J. Cryptol. 1–31 (2023)
25. Datta, P., Komargodski, I., Waters, B.: Fully adaptive decentralized multi-authority ABE. In: Proceedings EUROCRYPT, 2023, pp. 447–478 (2023)
26. Das, S., Namasudra, S.: MACPABE: multi-Authority-based CP-ABE with efficient attribute revocation for IoT-enabled healthcare infrastructure. Int. J. Netw. Manage **33**(3), 1–20 (2023)
27. Wang, M., Cao, Z., Dong, X., Du, R., Chen, J.: Decentralized multi-authority KP-ABE scheme without bilinear pairings. IEEE Internet Things J. **12**(1), 726–738 (2025)
28. Chen, J., Chu, Q., Gao, Y., Ning, J., Wang, L.: Improved fully adaptive decentralized MA-ABE for NC1 from MDDH. In: International Conference on the Theory and Application of Cryptology and Information Security, 2023, pp. 3–32 (2023)
29. Banerjee, S., Bera, B., Das, A.K., Chattopadhyay, S., Khan, M.K., Rodrigues, J.J.P.C.: Private blockchain-envisioned multi-authority CP-ABE-based user access control scheme in IIoT. Comput. Commun. **169**, 99–113 (2021)
30. Tu, S., Waqas, M., Huang, F., Abbas, G., Abbas, Z.H.: A revocable and outsourced multi-authority attribute-based encryption scheme in fog computing. Comput. Netw. 108196–108204 (2021)
31. Zhao, C., Xu, L., Li, J., Fang, H., Zhang, Y.: Toward secure and privacy-preserving cloud data sharing: Online/offline multiauthority CP-ABE with hidden policy. IEEE Syst. J. **16**(3), 4804–4815 (2022)
32. Yu, J., Liu, S., Xu, M., Guo, H., Zhong, F., Cheng, W.: An efficient revocable and searchable MA-ABE scheme with blockchain assistance for C-IoT. IEEE Internet Things J. **10**(3), 2754–2766 (2022)

33. Shor, P.W.: Algorithms for quantum computation: discrete logarithms and factoring. In: IEEE Proceedings 35th Annual Symposium on Foundations of Computer Science, 1994 pp. 124–134 (1994)
34. Kim, S.: Multi-authority attribute-based encryption from LWE in the OT model. Cryptology ePrint Archive (2019)
35. Datta, P., Komargodski, I., Waters, B.: Decentralized multi-authority ABE for DNFs from LWE. In: Proceeidngs of the EUROCRYPT, 2021, pp. 177–209 (2021)
36. Zhedong, W., Xiong, F., Feng-Hao, L.: FE for inner products and its application to decentralized ABE. In: IACR International Workshop on Public Key Cryptography, 2019, pp. 97–127 (2019)
37. Waters, B., Wee, H., Wu, D.J.: Multi-authority ABE from lattices without random oracles. In: Theory of Cryptography Conference, 2022, pp. 651–679 (2022)
38. Angelo, D., Iovino, V.: jPBC: Java pairing based cryptography. In: IEEE Symposium on Computers and Communications, 2011, pp. 850–855 (2011)

A Hierarchical Key-Based Dynamic Cross-Domain Authentication Scheme for VANETs

Shuai Jian[1] and Gang Shen[1,2,3](✉)

[1] School of Computer Science and Artificial Intelligence, Hubei University of Technology, Wuhan 430068, China
jianshuai@hbut.edu.cn
[2] Hubei Provincial Key Laboratory of Green Intelligent Computing Power Network, Wuhan 430068, China
shengang@hbut.edu.cn
[3] Hubei Provincial Engineering Research Center for Digital & Intelligent Manufacturing Technologies and Applications, Wuhan, China

Abstract. The increasing adoption of vehicular ad hoc networks (VANETs) introduces significant challenges to cross-domain authentication mechanisms in multi-domain environments, particularly regarding the balance between efficiency and security. Current schemes suffer from issues such as complex certificate management, key escrow and poor real-time performance, and are unable to meet the dynamic cross-domain communication requirements of vehicles. Consequently, this paper proposes a cross-domain identity authentication scheme based on hierarchical key architecture. First, the hierarchical key architecture is designed. trusted Authority (TA), area agent Nodes (ATA) and vehicles collaborate to generate vehicle keys, achieving decentralised key management. Secondly, the dynamic accumulator is combined with the Ceph distributed storage system to create a privacy-enhanced, cross-domain verification architecture. Ultimately, security analysis and experimental results verify that our scheme is resilient against common attacks and satisfies essential security requirements. Compared with existing schemes, cross-domain batch authentication incurs at least 40% less computational overhead and 30% less communication overhead, significantly improving authentication performance in dynamic multi-domain environments.

Keywords: Vehicular ad hoc networks (VANETs) · Cross-domain authentication · Hierarchical key architecture · Dynamic accumulator

1 Introduction

The rapid advancement of vehicular ad hoc networks (VANETs) enables seamless connectivity among vehicles, infrastructure, and user devices to the internet. This enables the efficient exchange and sharing of vehicle information and drives the development of intelligent transportation systems [1,2]. In a typical

L. Zhang and K.-K. R. Choo (Eds.): MobiQuitous 2025, LNICST 684, pp. 344–368, 2026.
https://doi.org/10.1007/978-3-032-22503-0_19

VANETs environment, the framework comprises a trusted authority (TA), multiple roadside units (RSUs), and a large number of vehicles equipped with on-board units (OBUs). It supports three communication modes: vehicle-to-infrastructure (V2I), vehicle-to-vehicle (V2V) and vehicle-to-roadside unit (V2R). TA serves as an authoritative third party responsible for initialising the system environment and managing vehicles [3]. RSUs serve as wireless intermediaries between TA and vehicles, disseminating critical information and instructions to in-range vehicles. [4]. Vehicles function as essential network nodes that collect and relay emergency messages [5]. However, VANETs' operation as open wireless networks exposes them to security threats like data interception, tampering, and malicious exploitation by attackers. These security vulnerabilities severely threaten user privacy by leaking vehicle location information and tracking driving behaviour. They may also lead to direct threats to traffic safety, such as forging emergency messages and disseminating false road conditions [6]. Therefore, ensuring communication security in VANETs application scenarios hinges on implementing a reliable identity authentication mechanism to prevent unauthorised access and data tampering.

Researchers have proposed several authentication schemes, including public key infrastructure-based (PKI-based), identity-based (ID-based), and certificateless authentication schemes [7–12]. Al-Riyami and Paterson proposed the Certificateless Signature(CLS) scheme [13], which combines the technical advantages of the previous two approaches by generating part of the private key through a Key Generation Centre (KGC) and combining it with user generated secret values to form the complete private key. The approach eliminates PKI-based certificate burdens and mitigates key custody challenges of ID-based systems. However, vehicles may traverse different domains, such as different cities, during operation. Nevertheless, most current verification schemes remain limited to single-domain authentication [14–17]. Cross-domain authentication is critical, yet existing schemes are inefficient and rely on domain management centres or blockchain. They also involve cumbersome processes, incur high costs and introduce new attack risks and privacy issues. The growing demand for cross-domain vehicle interactions has exposed three technical bottlenecks in multi-domain collaborative authentication: compatibility issues caused by differences in authentication standards between domains; latency constraints caused by centralised trust mechanisms; and privacy protection dilemmas brought about by distributed architectures. In scenarios with stringent real-time requirements, building an authentication framework that balances cross-domain authentication and privacy protection while ensuring real-time performance has become a core challenge that is hindering the development of VANETs.

1.1 Our Motivation

In VANETs environment, with the widespread popularity of vehicles and the continuous development of intelligent transportation systems, cross-domain authentication schemes have become a key technology to ensure secure communication and information interaction among vehicles. Empirical evidence confirms that conventional single-domain authentication fails to satisfy the efficiency demands of cross-domain scenarios [18]. The motivation underpinning this study is outlined as follows.

1. *Security Flaws in Existing schemes:* Despite the evident advantages of existing schemes, there are significant shortcomings. Essentially, PKI-based schemes carry a single-point failure risk due to their centralized certificate management. The utilisation of ID-based schemes, despite the elimination of certificate transmission, gives rise to key escrow risks. This is attributable to the fact that KGC exerts complete control. In an effort to enhance key management, certificateless schemes have been developed. However, these schemes can result in elevated computational overheads due to their reliance on complex cryptographic constructs.
2. *Multi-Domain Collaborative Authentication Requirements:* In a multi-domain VANETs environment, vehicles frequently have to communicate and authenticate across different domains. Authentication standards and trust relationships can vary among domains, thus preventing vehicles from directly authenticating when crossing domains. Some cross-domain authentication schemes are dependent on technologies such as central servers or blockchain. However, these schemes encounter performance bottlenecks and scalability issues in practical applications [4,9,15,18].

Therefore, we propose a scheme employing hierarchical key architecture and privacy-preserving verification algorithms. This scheme achieves high-speed responses while rigorously analysing and proving the security of the scheme. It provides an authentication scheme that balances efficiency and security for dynamic VANETs environments.

1.2 Our Contribution

1. Our scheme proposes a hierarchical key architecture, constructed by TA, regional agent nodes (ATA), and vehicle. Concurrently, a cross-domain key dynamic update mechanism has been proposed. Upon entering a new domain, a vehicle is required to generate a temporary key and bind a time-effectiveness label. The old key becomes invalid when the domain is switched, thus enabling the dynamic update of cross-domain keys.
2. Our scheme deeply integrates the dynamic accumulator with the Ceph distributed file system to build a cross-domain verification privacy protection architecture. Our scheme employs the accumulator to ensure the protection of identity privacy. Additionally, it utilises the Ceph's Controlled Replication Under Scalable Hashing (CRUSH) algorithm for the purpose of storing data in a distributed manner. Our scheme combines pairing-free signatures and aggregate verification, reducing computational and communication overheads and enabling real-time mutual authentication among a large number of vehicles.

3. Under the Random Oracle Model (ROM), our scheme resists adaptive chosen-message attacks. Experimental results indicate that in comparison with existing schemes, the computational overhead is reduced by at least approximately 40% and the communication overhead is decreased by at least approximately 30%. This achieves a balance between security and efficiency.

1.3 Organization

Section 2 surveys related work. Section 3 introduces core technologies and theoretical foundations. Section 4 details the system and threat models. Section 5 elaborates the scheme's design and implementation. Section 6 formally verifies security. Section 7 evaluates performance experimentally. Section 8 concludes the work.

2 Related Work

To ensure VANET security, researchers have developed diverse privacy-preserving authentication schemes. In conventional PKI-based schemes, a Certificate Authority (CA) issues digital certificates to vehicles, and identity authentication is accomplished via certificate verification. Asghar et al. [19] proposed a PKI-based authentication scheme for VANETs, in which CA is responsible for issuing certificates to legitimate users. Nevertheless, with the continuous growth in the number of users and certificates, this scheme faces increasingly complex certificate management issues. Chen et al. [20] proposed an anonymous authentication scheme for cross-domain authentication. Notwithstanding the fact that this scheme compresses the certificate verification path through a multi-level Merkle hash tree, it depends on CA. Ma et al. [21] proposed a cross-domain authentication model with multiple intermediaries under PKI. These improvements are achieved by implementing a distribution of user private keys and utilising a cross-domain authentication server proxy. However, its revocation mechanism relies on a centralized coordination node, which may introduce security vulnerabilities in distributed collaboration.

To address the inherent certificate management challenges in PKI-based schemes, Ali et al. [22] proposed an identity-based signature and conditional privacy-preserving authentication scheme (IBS-CPPA) that does not involve bilinear pairing. However, as the generation of private keys is dependent on TA, the key escrow problem is present. A broadcast proxy re-encryption scheme based on identity has been proposed to enable flexible and efficient data sharing in VANETs [23]. Notwithstanding, the efficacy of this scheme is contingent upon the credibility of proxy nodes and the anti-collusion assumption. Furthermore, the full anonymity mechanism may impede the process of tracing malicious vehicles and determining liability.

To overcome the certificate management bottleneck of PKI-based schemes and the key escrow issue of ID-based schemes, CLS schemes have emerged as a scheme. Tomar A and Tripathi S [9] proposed a blockchain-based certificateless authentication scheme that mitigates the centralisation risk through a distributed architecture. Nevertheless, in areas characterised by dense vehicular traffic, the efficacy of this scheme is compromised by on-chain transaction congestion, reducing the timeliness of key management. A certificateless aggregate signature (CLAS)-based authentication scheme has been proposed for VANETs [24], aiming to enhance authentication efficiency. However, due to the absence of dynamic binding verification, the public key management mechanism is vulnerable to substitution attacks. A mechanism integrating certificateless message authentication with blockchain technology and incorporating a threshold multi-signature mechanism was proposed by Zhang et al. [25]. However, in scenarios with high network concurrency such as high-density traffic flow, the multi-signature consensus process in this scheme can cause fluctuations in authentication delay. Zhong et al. [18] proposed a cross-domain batch authentication scheme based on blockchain and accumulators. However, the static consensus mechanism of this scheme has difficulty adapting to the dynamic network topology changes caused by the high-speed movement of vehicles, resulting in a substantial increase in authentication delay. Compared with the blockchain-based scheme in [18], our scheme uses the Ceph distributed file system, which has the advantages of real-time performance relying on the CRUSH algorithm and nearby replica scheduling, scalability of linear node expansion, and adaptability of dynamically adjusting storage strategies. It is suitable for scenarios with stringent requirements for real-time performance and scalability, such as real-time cross-domain verification in high-density urban traffic, high-speed emergency vehicle authentication, and dynamic data sharing in vehicle-road cooperation.

In summary, our analysis indicates that traditional PKI-based schemes suffer from certificate management complexity and centralization risks [19]– [21]. ID-based schemes have the key escrow problem [22,23]. Although certificateless and blockchain-based schemes alleviate the burden of certificate and key management through a distributed architecture, they still face performance bottlenecks. These include on-chain delays in high-concurrency scenarios and failure to adapt to drastic topological changes induced by vehicles' high-speed movement, and poor performance against common network attacks [9,18,24,25]. Therefore, designing an efficient and secure cross-domain identity authentication scheme remains challenging.

3 Preliminaries

This section presents the core technologies and theoretical foundations employed in the proposed scheme.

3.1 Ceph Distributed File System

Ceph is a high-performance and scalable distributed storage system that has gained significant popularity in the field of cloud computing and large-scale data storage scenarios. The core components of Ceph include Ceph Monitor (MON), Ceph Object Storage Daemon (OSD), and Ceph Manager (MGR). The MON is responsible for cluster management and consistency maintenance, the OSD for data storage and replication, and the MGR mainly addresses issues related to cluster monitoring, management, and scalability. Ceph utilises the CRUSH algorithm for the purpose of data distribution. This algorithm, based on hashing and hierarchical mapping strategies, enables uniform data distribution across the cluster and avoids the performance bottleneck of traditional centralized directory services. Furthermore, the Ceph system is engineered to guarantee elevated data availability and reliability by employing multi-replica storage methodologies and erasure coding techniques. In the event of the failure of some storage nodes, the integrity of data and continuous access can still be guaranteed.

The technical design of the Ceph distributed file system highly aligns with the core goals of cross-domain authentication, namely "efficiency, security, reliability, and scalability". Its advantages are reflected in the deep synergy between the storage architecture and the authentication scenario: In terms of reducing cross - domain authentication latency, the decentralized positioning of the CRUSH algorithm directly calculates the data storage location. Combined with dynamic nearby replica scheduling, high-frequency authentication data is pre-synchronized to the edge nodes of the current domain. This significantly shortens the latency compared to traditional centralized and simple distributed storage, meeting the real-time requirements of scenarios such as VANETs.

3.2 Certificateless Signature

Certificateless signature technology seamlessly merges strengths of PKI-based and ID-based schemes. It resolves inherent limitations in traditional mechanisms, achieving superior security-efficiency equilibrium for large-scale networks and resource-constrained environments.

4 System Model and Adversary Model

This section presents a detailed description of the system model and adversary model.

4.1 System Model

As shown in Fig. 1, the system comprises four key components: 1) TA; 2) ATAs; 3) RSUs; and 4) vehicles. Each entity's responsibilities are detailed subsequently.

1. As the trusted entity with substantial computational resources, TA generates the system's master key pair and public parameters. It issues partial private keys to ATAs and RSUs, assigns pseudonyms and partial keys to vehicles, identifies malicious vehicles' real identities, and revokes them.

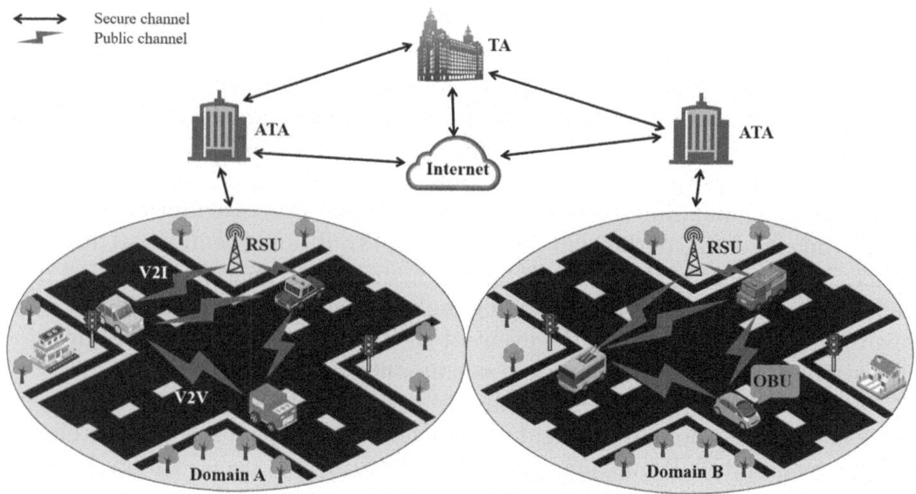

Fig. 1. System model of VANETs.

2. ATA, as the agent of TA in a designated area, assumes responsibility for the coordination and management of vehicle authentication and information interaction within that area. ATA generates partial private keys for local vehicles, and generates temporary partial private keys for each vehicle entering the area. Furthermore, it is responsible for the processing of cross-domain authentication requests and is capable of identifying the real identities of local malicious vehicles.
3. RSU is a roadside wireless communication device whose primary function is to facilitate data exchange with nearby vehicles through wireless communication, enabling the collection of real-time information.
4. Vehicles are capable of conducting identity authentication with local vehicles in order to verify each other's legitimacy. Simultaneously, they are capable of facilitating cross-domain communication and key negotiation with vehicles from other domains.

The Ceph distributed file system is collaboratively maintained by TA and ATA. The architecture has been designed to take full advantage of the high scalability and distributed features of Ceph, with the result that the storage requirements for large quantities of vehicle data and the demands for real-time queries can be met in an effective manner. Specifically, TA is responsible for global metadata management, and Ceph dynamically allocates data blocks via the CRUSH algorithm. Each ATA node is responsible for maintaining a local OSD cluster, the purpose of which is to store the dynamic accumulator states and pseudonym verification information of vehicles within its administrative region. Employing hierarchical storage mitigates inherent single-point-of-failure threats in centralized infrastructures. Furthermore, the data replication strategy employed ensures the high availability of cross-domain data. The Ceph system utilises a two-tier storage architecture. The storage of hot data, which is defined as cross-domain vehicle information that is frequently verified, is localised at ATA. Conversely, cold data is stored in the Ceph cluster in a persistent manner. This design significantly reduces the latency of cross-domain authentication.

The cost differences between Ceph and traditional storage solutions are primarily manifested in the total life-cycle investment. Traditional storage depends on specialized hardware, entailing high initial procurement costs. For expansion, it needs vertical upgrades, that is, replacing with equipment of higher configurations, which causes a notable growth in costs. Additionally, its operation and maintenance rely on professional support, resulting in high labor expenses. Conversely, Ceph is constructed based on general-purpose hardware, featuring a lower initial investment. It adopts horizontal expansion for capacity increase, merely by adding ordinary nodes, and its cost grows linearly with the scale. Meanwhile, by relying on automated tools, Ceph can achieve failure self-healing and load balancing, significantly reducing manual operation and maintenance costs. It also has lower long-term energy consumption. Especially in large-scale deployment scenarios, the cost advantage of Ceph is even more pronounced.

4.2 Adversary Model

In our scheme, we categorize adversaries into two types—external adversaries and internal adversaries—based on variations in their capabilities.

1. *External Adversary:* The first type of attacker $\mathcal{A}_1$, is not able to obtain the system master key and the secret value corresponding to the original public key of a user. However, $\mathcal{A}_I$ has the capability to initiate a multitude of associated attacks through unauthorised public-key replacement operations.
2. *Internal Adversary:* The second category of attacker $\mathcal{A}_2$, is an ATA entity with semi-trusted attributes. It can obtain the master key, but without the cooperation of the user, it cannot replace the user's public key.

Adversary $\mathcal{A}$ ($\mathcal{A}_1$ or $\mathcal{A}_2$) and simulator $\mathcal{S}$ ($\mathcal{S}_1$ or $\mathcal{S}_2$) conduct simulations through games (*Game 1* or *Game 2*). The following section will outline the specific processes of *Game 1* and *Game 2*.

Game 1: This game is played in the presence of adversary $\mathcal{A}_1$ and simulator $\mathcal{S}_1$.

Initialization Phase: $\mathcal{S}_1$ generates the master key tsk and system parameters $params$. Then it secretly stores tsk and sends $params$ to $\mathcal{A}_1$.

Query Phase: In this phase, $\mathcal{A}_1$ is capable of adaptively initiating a series of queries to $\mathcal{S}_1$ and obtaining responses from $\mathcal{S}_1$.

1. *Partial Private Key Query:* $\mathcal{A}_1$ requests to obtain the partial private key of PID_i. Subsequently, $\mathcal{S}_1$ generates the corresponding partial private keys psk_{1i} and psk_{2i} and sends them to $\mathcal{A}_1$.
2. *Secret Value Query:* $\mathcal{A}_1$ makes a request to obtain the secret value of PID_i. $\mathcal{S}_1$ generates the corresponding secret value c_i and transmits it to $\mathcal{A}_1$.

3. *Private Key Query:* $\mathcal{A}_1$ requests to obtain the private key of PID_i. $\mathcal{S}_1$ generates the corresponding private key vsk_i, and transmits it to $\mathcal{A}_1$.
4. *Public Key Query:* $\mathcal{A}_1$ requests to obtain the public key of PID_i. $\mathcal{S}_1$ generates the corresponding public key VPK_i and transmits it to $\mathcal{A}_1$.
5. *Public Key Replacement:* $\mathcal{A}_1$ submits the public key VPK_i' for replacing that of PID_i. Subsequently, $\mathcal{S}_1$ replaces the public key of PID_i with VPK_i'.
6. *Signature Query:* $\mathcal{A}_1$ requests to obtain the signature of PID_i on message m_i. Subsequently, $\mathcal{S}_1$ generates the corresponding valid signature σ_i and transmits it to $\mathcal{A}_1$.

Forgery Phase: Finally, $\mathcal{A}_1$ forges a signature σ_i^* on the message m_i^* for the challenged identity PID_i^*. The adversary, designated $\mathcal{A}_1$, is considered to have won the game if the subsequent two conditions are met. $\mathcal{A}_1$ has not issued any partial private key queries or private key queries for PID_i and the signature σ_i is valid while $\mathcal{A}_1$ has never queried for the signature regarding $\{PID_i^*, m_i^*\}$.

Game 2: This game is played in the presence of adversary $\mathcal{A}_2$ and simulator $\mathcal{S}_2$.

Initialization Phase: $\mathcal{S}_2$ generates the master key tsk and system parameters $params$. Then it sends tsk and $params$ to $\mathcal{A}_2$.

Query Phase: In this phase, $\mathcal{A}_2$ can adaptively initiate partial private key queries, secret value queries, private key queries, public key queries, and signature queries to $\mathcal{S}_2$. Compared with *Game 1*, $\mathcal{A}_2$ cannot perform public key replacement queries, while the specific content of other queries is similar to that in *Game 1*.

Forgery Phase: Finally, $\mathcal{A}_2$ forges a signature σ_i^* on the message m_i^* for the challenged identity PID_i^*. The adversary, designated $\mathcal{A}_2$, is considered to have won the game if the subsequent two conditions are met. $\mathcal{A}_2$ has not issued any partial private key queries or private key queries for PID_i and the signature σ_i is valid while $\mathcal{A}_2$ has never queried for the signature regarding $\{PID_i^*, m_i^*\}$.

4.3 Security Requirements

1. *Identity Authentication and Integrity:* Message legitimacy is verifiable by recipients, guaranteeing authenticity, non-alteration, and freshness to counter spoofing and manipulation.
2. *Traceability and Revocation:* In the event of malevolent conduct, such as the dissemination of erroneous traffic conditions, TA and ATA are capable of ascertaining the genuine identity of vehicle. Furthermore, TA and ATA will add the malicious vehicle to the revocation list.
3. *Unlinkability:* It is impossible for any adversary to verify that two messages have been transmitted by the same vehicle.
4. *Security of Session Key:* The employment of a secure session key is pivotal in ensuring that only authorised participants are able to access it. This prevents message decryption by unauthorised parties due to key leakage and maintains the confidentiality of communication content.

5. *Forward and Backward Security:* In the event of key leakage, all session keys established previously or communication contents based on this key remain secure, being impervious to decryption or forgery by attackers. Following the updating of the key of an entity, the utilisation of the previous key is rendered impossible for the purposes of decrypting or engaging in the communication contents of new sessions.
6. *Resistance to Various Common Attacks:* Cross-domain authentication schemes in VANETs must be resilient against various threats.

5 Our Proposed Scheme

This section offers a detailed exposition of our cross-domain authentication scheme, which comprises the following six phases. To improve understanding of the scheme's logic, Table 1 lists the core symbols and their semantic explanations.

5.1 System Initialization Phase

The system initialization phase is executed by TA. It generates global parameters by inputting the security parameter κ and performs the following operations.

1. TA selects an additive cyclic group G of order q, where the order q is a large prime number, and P is a generator of the group G. TA randomly selects $tsk \in \mathbb{Z}_q^*$ as the private key of the system and computes $TPK = tskP$ as the public key of TA. Moreover, a set of secure hash functions $H_i : \{0,1\}^* \to \mathbb{Z}_q^*$ is chosen, where $i = 1, \ldots, 5$.
2. TA selects two large prime numbers p and q, and computes $n = pq$. TA initialises the accumulator value Acc as n and initialises the hash table S, setting all values to $False$. The size of the hash table is m. Finally, TA publishes the system parameter params $= \{q, P, G, TPK, H_i\}$ and secretly stores tsk.

5.2 Registration Phase

1. *Registration of ATAs and RSUs:*
   (a) ATA_A transmits the identity information ID_{ATA}, in conjunction with the registration request, to TA. Following the reception of ID_{ATA} and the registration request from ATA_A, TA randomly selects $x_A \in \mathbb{Z}_q^*$, and subsequently calculates $X_A = x_AP$, $h_{1A} = H_1(X_A, ID_{ATA})$ and $psk_A = x_A + tskh_A$, where psk_A is the partial private key of ATA_A. Then TA sends $\{X_A, psk_A, h_{1A}\}$ to ATA_A.
   (b) When ATA_A receives $\{X_A, psk_A, h_{1A}\}$, it randomly selects $r_A \in \mathbb{Z}_q^*$ and computes $R_A = r_AP$. Then ATA_A generates its private key $atsk_A = r_A + psk_A$ and public key $ATPK_A = atsk_AP$ and clandestinely stores $atsk_A$.

The registration process for RSU_i is analogous to that for ATA_A, as previously outlined.

2. *Registration of Vehicles:* Take vehicle V_i in domain A managed by ATA_A as an example.
   (a) Vehicle V_i transmits both the request for registration and ID_{V_i} to TA. Following the reception of the registration request and the ID_{V_i} from V_i, TA randomly selects $pid_{1i} \in \mathbb{Z}_q^*$, subsequently calculates $PID_{1i} = pid_{1i}P$, $pid_{2i} = tsk\, H_2(PID_{1i}, ID_{V_i}, T_e)$ and $PID_{2i} = pid_{2i}P$, and generates the pseudonym $PID_i = (PID_{1i}, PID_{2i}, T_e)$ of vehicle V_i, where T_e represents the validity timestamp of the pseudonym of vehicle V_i.
   (b) TA transmits the pseudonym PID_i of vehicle V_i and the message for generating the partial private key of vehicle V_i to ATA_A of the domain in which vehicle V_i is located. ATA_A then randomly selects $b_i \in \mathbb{Z}_q^*$ and computes $B_i = b_iP$ and $psk_{2i} = atskB_i$. Finally, ATA_A sends psk_{2i} and B_i to vehicle V_i through a secure channel.
   (c) TA selects $d_i \in \mathbb{Z}_q^*$ at random and calculates $D_i = d_iP$, $h_{1i} = H_1(D_i, ID_{V_i})$ and $psk_{1i} = tskh_{1i}$, Where psk_{1i} is part of the private key of vehicle V_i. Subsequently, TA will dispatch $\{PID_i, D_i, psk_{1i}, T_e\}$ to vehicle V_i.
   (d) Upon receipt of the pseudonym and the partial private key, V_i randomly selects $c_i \in \mathbb{Z}_q^*$ and computes $C_i = c_iP$. Thereafter, V_i generates its private key $vsk_i = c_i + psk_{1i} + psk_{2i}$ and public key $VPK_i = vsk_iP$, and keeps vsk_i confidential. Ultimately, V_i uploads its pseudonym PID_i, public key VPK_i and pertinent parameters to the system.

Table 1. Main symbols and descriptions

Symbol	Description
κ	Security parameter
tsk	Master key of TA
TPK	The system public key
$atsk$	Master key of ATA
$ATPK$	The public key of ATA
vsk_i	Master key of vehicle
VPK_i	The public key of vehicle
ID_{V_i}	The real identity of vehicle
PID_i	The pseudonym of vehicle
$H_i(i = 1, \cdots, 5)$	Secure one-way hash functions
T_1, T_2, T_3, T_e, T_p	Timestamp
m_i	Message
σ	Signature

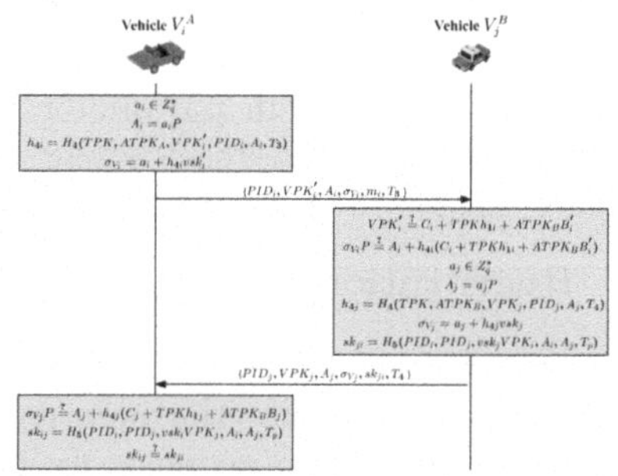

Fig. 2. Cross-domain authentication.

5.3 Cross-Domain Pre-Certification Phase

Assume that vehicle V_i^A intends to communicate across domains with vehicle V_j^B in domain B. The detailed steps of cross-domain pre-authentication are as follows.

1. Vehicle V_i^A transmits the $\{PID_i, VPK_i, ID_{V_i}, T_e, T_1\}$ and cross-domain request to ATA_A, where T_1 denotes the current timestamp.
2. Upon receipt of the message from vehicle V_i^A, ATA_A performs a preliminary verification of the timestamps T_e and T_1 to ascertain the freshness of the message and the validity of vehicle V_i^A pseudonym. Subsequently, ATA_A calculates $a_{3i} = H_3(PID_i, VPK_i, ID_{V_i}, T_e)$, subsequently adding a_{3i} to the dynamic accumulator using Algorithm 1, and generating a current accumulator value $Acc_{current}$, and a old accumulator value Acc_{old} for the purpose of subsequent authentication. ATA_A sends $\{PID_i, VPK_i, a_{3i}, Acc_{current}, Acc_{old}\}$ and a request for generating the temporary partial private key of vehicle V_i^A for cross-domain communication to ATA_B.

Algorithm 1. Add Identity Information to Accumulator

```
1: Input: Accumulator element a_{3i}.
2: Output: Accumulator value Acc_{current}, Acc_{old}.
3: a_i = hashToPrime(a_{3i});
4: S[a_i] = True;
5: Acc_{old} = Acc_{current};
6: Acc_{current} = Acc_{current}^{a_i} mod n;
7: return Acc_{current}, Acc_{old};
```

3. Upon receipt of the message from ATA_A, ATA_B queries whether a_{3i} is in the accumulator through Algorithm 2. In the event that this is not the case, cross-domain authentication is terminated. Otherwise, the verification of identity authenticity and legitimacy is successful. Then, ATA_B randomly selects $b_i' \in \mathbb{Z}_q^*$ and calculates $B_i' = b_i'P$ and $psk_{2i}' = atsk_B B_i'$. ATA_B then transmits $\{psk_{2i}', B_i', T_p\}$ to vehicle V_i^A, where T_p denotes the timestamp of the validity period of vehicle V_i^A temporary private key.
4. Upon receipt of the message from ATA_B, vehicle V_i^A generates a temporary private key $vsk_i' = c_i + psk_{1i} + psk_{2i}'$ and a temporary public key $VPK_i' = vsk_i'P$. The temporary public key functions as the credential for cross-domain communication with the domain in which V_j^B is located.

5.4 Cross-Domain Authentication Phase

After completing the pre-authentication phase, vehicles V_i^A and V_j^B engage in cross-domain communication and negotiate a session key. The specific steps involved are outlined below. The process of vehicle cross-domain authentication is shown in Fig. 2.

Algorithm 2. Query Identity Information in Accumulator

1: **Input:** Identity information a_{3i}, accumulator value $Acc_{current}, Acc_{old}$.
2: **Output:** `True` or `False`.
3: $a_i = hashToPrime(a_{3i})$;
4: **if** $S[a_i]! =$ `True` **then**
5:     **return** `False`;
6: **end if**
7: $temp = Acc_{current}^{-a_i} \mod n$;
8: **if** $Acc_{old} == temp$ **then**
9:     $S[a_i] =$ `False`;
10:     $Acc_{current} = temp$;
11:     **return** `True`;
12: **else**
13:     **return** `False`;
14: **end if**

1. Vehicle V_i^A randomly selects $a_i \in \mathbb{Z}_q^*$ and calculates $A_i = a_i P$ and $h_{4i} = H_4(ATPK_A, VPK_i', PID_i, A_i, T_2)$. Then, V_i^A generates a signature $\sigma_{V_i} = a_i + h_{4i} vsk_i'$ using its temporary private key vsk_i', where T_2 denotes the current timestamp. The temporary public key VPK_i', obtained during the pre-authentication phase, serves as the communication credential. Finally, vehicle V_i^A transmits $\{PID_i, VPK_i', A_i, \sigma_{V_i}, m_i, T_2\}$ to vehicle V_j^B via the public channel, where m_i represents the real-time traffic information of vehicle V_i^A.
2. Upon receipt of the message from vehicle V_i^A, vehicle V_j^B first ascertains the freshness of the timestamp T_2. Thereafter, it verifies the public key VPK_i' of vehicle V_i^A. If $VPK_i' = C_i + TPKh_{1i} + ATPK_B B_i'$ holds, vehicle V_j^B completes the verification of the validity, integrity, and cross-domain legality of the public key VPK_i' of vehicle V_i^A. Subsequently, if equation $\sigma_{V_i} P = A_i + h_{4i}(C_i + TPKh_{1i} + ATPK_B B_i')$ holds, the verification of vehicle V_i^A passes and the process continues to the next step. Otherwise, vehicle V_j^B rejects the request and terminates the session.
3. Vehicle V_j^B randomly selects $a_j \in \mathbb{Z}_q^*$ and calculates $A_j = a_j P$. Subsequently, vehicle V_j^B generates signatures $\sigma_{V_j} = a_j + h_{4j} vsk_j$, where $h_{4j} = H_4(ATPK_B, VPK_j, PID_j, A_j, T_3)$ and T_3 denotes the current timestamp. Vehicle V_j^B generates a session key $sk_{ji} = H_5(PID_i, PID_j, vsk_j VPK_i, A_i, A_j, T_p)$ and saves sk_{ji} locally. In conclusion, vehicle V_j^B transmits $\{PID_j, VPK_j, A_j, \sigma_{V_j}, m_j, T_3\}$ to vehicle V_i^A via the public channel.
4. Upon receipt of the message from vehicle V_j^B, vehicle V_i^A first ascertains the freshness of the timestamp T_3. Subsequently, if equation $\sigma_{V_j} P = A_j + h_{4j}(C_j + TPKh_{1j} + ATPK_B B_j)$ holds, the verification of vehicle V_i^B passes and the process continues to the next step. Otherwise, vehicle V_j^A rejects the request and terminates the session.

5. Vehicle V_j^A calculates $sk_{ij} = H_5(PID_i, PID_j, vsk_i VPK_j, A_i, A_j, T_p)$. Then it verifies whether $sk_{ij} = sk_{ji}$ holds. In the event that this is not the case, the message is discarded and the session is terminated. Vehicle V_j^A establishes sk_{ij} as the session key for cross-domain communication with vehicle V_i^B and saves it locally.

5.5 Batch Authentication Phase

Taking ATA_B in Domain B as an example, when it receives requests from one vehicle in the same domain, or multiple vehicles in the same domain, or multiple vehicles from multiple regions to conduct cross-domain communication with vehicles in Domain B, ATA_B can perform batch verification to reduce the overhead of single-time verification.

$$\begin{aligned}\sum_{i=1}^{n}\sigma_{V_i}P &= \sum_{i=1}^{n}a_iP + \sum_{i=1}^{n}(h_{4i}vsk_i')P = \sum_{i=1}^{n}A_i + \sum_{i=1}^{n}h_{4i}(C_i + TPKh_{i1} + ATPK_BB_i') \\ &= \sum_{i=1}^{n}A_i + \sum_{i=1}^{n}h_{4i}C_i + TPK\sum_{i=1}^{n}h_{4i}h_{i1} + ATPK_B\sum_{i=1}^{n}h_{4i}B_i'.\end{aligned} \tag{1}$$

ATA_B verifies whether Eq. 1 holds. If it does not hold, the authentication fails. Otherwise, the authentication is successful.

6 Safety Certification and Safety Analysis

This section will formally prove and analyze the corresponding security properties of the proposed scheme.

6.1 Security Proof

Theorem 1. *In the ROM, it is assumed that there is an adversary $\mathcal{A}_1$, capable of forging a valid signature with a non-negligible probability ε, within the framework of Probabilistic Polynomial Time (PPT). In the course of the signature-forging process, the aforementioned adversary instigates q_1 H_1 queries, q_s private key queries, q_p partial private-key queries, and q_v secret-value queries. It follows that a challenger B must exist who can solve the Discrete Logarithm (DL) problem with a non-negligible advantage $\frac{(e-1)\varepsilon}{e^2 q_1(q_n+1)}$, where e is the base of the natural logarithm and $q_n = q_s + q_p + q_v$.*

Proof: In the context of the challenge tuple (P, aP), where $a \in \mathbb{Z}_q^*$, the objective of the challenger B is to solve for the value of a. S_1 simulates a real-world environment, and its interaction process with the adversary $\mathcal{A}_1$ is as follows.

Initialization Phase: S_1 initializes the system and generates system parameters $params = \{q, P, G, TPK, H_i\}$. In the course of this process, S_1 sets $TPK = tskP$ and treats H_1 and H_4 as hash oracles. Consequently, S_1 transmits *params* to the adversary $\mathcal{A}_1$. Moreover, S_1 is responsible for maintaining the lists, namely L_{pk}, L_1 and L_4. These lists record the queries about public keys made by $\mathcal{A}_1$, as well as the subsequent queries to H_1 and H_4 hash oracles.

Query Phase: S_1 selects PID_i^* as the challenged identity.

1. *Public Key Query:* When $\mathcal{A}_1$ queries the public key of PID_i, S_1 first verifies the existence of $(\mathrm{PID}_i, VPK_i, C_i, c_i, B_i, b_i, psk_{1i}, psk_{2i}, h_{1i})$ in the list L_{pk}. In the event of its existence, S_1 directly returns VPK_i to $\mathcal{A}_1$. Otherwise, S_1 performs the following operations.
   (a) If $\mathrm{PID}_i \neq \mathrm{PID}_i^*$, S_1 randomly selects $c_i, psk_{1i}, psk_{2i}, h_{1i} \in \mathbb{Z}_q^*$, and calculate $B_i = \frac{psk_{2i}P}{ATPK}$ and $C_i = c_iP$. Subsequently, S_1 calculates $VPK_i = C_i + h_{1i}TPK + B_iATPK$ and inserts $(\mathrm{PID}_i, VPK_i, C_i, c_i, B_i, \perp, psk_{1i}, psk_{2i}, h_{1i})$ into the list L_{pk}.
   (b) If $\mathrm{PID}_i = \mathrm{PID}_i^*$, S_1 randomly selects $c_i, b_i, h_{1i} \in \mathbb{Z}_q^*$, and calculate $B_i = b_iP$ and $C_i = c_iP$. Subsequently, S_1 calculates $VPK_i = C_i + h_{1i}TPK + B_iATPK$ and inserts $(\mathrm{PID}_i, VPK_i, C_i, c_i, B_i, b_i, \perp, \perp, h_{1i})$ into the list L_{pk}.

   Subsequently, S_1 modifies the h_{1i} value in the relevant (D_i, ID_{V_i}, h_{1i}) within L_1 and finally returns VPK_i to $\mathcal{A}_1$.
2. H_1 *Oracle Query:* In the event of adversary $\mathcal{A}_1$ makes a query to the hash oracle H_1 for the tuple (D_i, ID_{V_i}), S_1 is required to undertake the following operations: If there is already a record of (D_i, ID_{V_i}, h_{1i}) in the list L_1, S_1 will directly return the corresponding h_{1i} to $\mathcal{A}_1$. In the event that this is not the case, S_1 randomly selects $h_{1i} \in \mathbb{Z}_q^*$. Subsequently, S_1 incorporates the newly generated tuple (D_i, ID_{V_i}, h_{1i}) into the list L_1 and responds to $\mathcal{A}_1$ with h_{1i} as the result of the query.
3. H_4 *Oracle Query:* In the event of adversary $\mathcal{A}_1$ makes a query to the hash oracle H_4 for the tuple $(ATPK, VPK_i, PID_i, A_i, T_3)$, S_1 is required to undertake the following operations: If there is already a record of $(ATPK, VPK_i, PID_i, A_i, T_3, h_{4i})$, S_1 in the list L_4, S_1 will directly return the corresponding h_{4i} to $\mathcal{A}_1$. In the event that this is not the case, S_1 randomly selects $h_{4i} \in \mathbb{Z}_q^*$. Subsequently, S_1 incorporates the newly generated tuple $(ATPK, VPK_i, PID_i, A_i, T_3, h_{4i})$ into the list L_4 and responds to $\mathcal{A}_1$ with h_{4i} as the result of the query.
4. *Partial Private Key Query:* In the event of $\mathcal{A}_1$ initiating a partial private-key query for PID_i, and if $\mathrm{PID}_i = \mathrm{PID}_i^*$, S_1 will terminate and output $\perp$. In the absence of such a file, S_1 will check whether $(\mathrm{PID}_i, VPK_i, C_i, c_i, B_i, b_i, psk_{1i}, psk_{2i}, h_{1i})$ in the list L_{pk} exists in the list L_{pk}. In the event of its existence, S_1 extracts the corresponding (psk_{1i}, psk_{2i}). If not, S_1 instigates a public-key query for PID_i with the objective of obtaining (psk_{1i}, psk_{2i}). Subsequently, S_1 returns (psk_{1i}, psk_{2i}) to $\mathcal{A}_1$.
5. *Secret Value Query:* When $\mathcal{A}_1$ queries S_1 for the secret value of PID_i, S_1 checks whether $(\mathrm{PID}_i, VPK_i, C_i, c_i, B_i, b_i, psk_{1i}, psk_{2i}, h_{1i})$ in the list L_{pk} exists in the list L_{pk}. In the event of such a scenario, S_1 will directly return the corresponding c_i to $\mathcal{A}_1$. If not, S_1 instigates a public-key query for PID_i, subsequently returning c_i to $\mathcal{A}_1$.

6. *Private Key Query:* In the event of $\mathcal{A}_1$ querying for the private key of PID_i, if $\mathrm{PID}_i = \mathrm{PID}_i^*$, S_1 will terminate and output $\perp$. If not, S_1 will check whether $(\mathrm{PID}_i, VPK_i, C_i, c_i, B_i, b_i, psk_{1i}, psk_{2i}, h_{1i})$ exists in the list L_{pk}. If it exists, S_1 extracts the corresponding $(c_i, psk_{1i}, psk_{2i})$. If not, S_1 initiates a public-key query to obtain these three values. Finally, S_1 calculates $vsk_i = c_i + psk_{1i} + psk_{2i}$ and returns vsk_i to $\mathcal{A}_1$.
7. *Public Key Replacement:* Upon receipt of a (PID_i, VPK_i') from $\mathcal{A}_1$ for a public-key replacement, S_1 updates the tuple corresponding to PID_i in the list L_{pk} to $(\mathrm{PID}_i, VPK_i', \perp, \perp, B_i', \perp, \perp, \perp, \perp)$.
8. *Signature Query:* Upon submission of (PID_i, m_i) for signature query by $\mathcal{A}_1$, S_1 performs a preliminary check to ascertain the presence of a tuple corresponding to PID_i in L_{pk}. If not, S_1 instigates a public-key query for PID_i. Subsequently, S_1 randomly selects $\sigma_i, h_{4i} \in \mathbb{Z}_q^*$ and calculates $A_i = \sigma_i P - h_{4i} VPK_i$, where VPK_i is extracted from the list L_{pk}. Finally, S_1 inserts $(ATPK, VPK_i, PID_i, A_i, T_3, h_{4i})$ into the list L_4 and returns σ_i as the signature to $\mathcal{A}_1$.

Forgery Phase: The adversary $\mathcal{A}_1$ forges the signature σ_i^* of (PID_i^*, m_i^*) and the tuple $(PID_i^*, VPK_i^*, A_i^*, \sigma_i^*, m_i^*)$, and then transmits the tuple $(PID_i^*, VPK_i^*, A_i^*, \sigma_i^*, m_i^*)$ to S_1. The adversary $\mathcal{A}_1$ is considered to have won the game if the following two conditions are met. $\mathcal{A}_1$ has not issued any partial private key queries or private key queries for PID_i and the signature σ_i is valid while $\mathcal{A}_1$ has never queried for the signature regarding $\{PID_i^*, m_i^*\}$.

If $\mathrm{PID}_i \neq \mathrm{PID}_i^*$, then S_1 aborts and outputs $\perp$. Otherwise, and based on the Forking Lemma [26], after $\mathcal{A}_1$ replays with the same random values D_i, S_1 can change the output of the oracle H_1 to give a different $h_{1i}^{*'}$. Specifically, although the query responses for the parameters related to PID_i remain consistent, the challenger B can obtain two different tuples, namely $(\mathrm{PID}_i^*, VPK_i^*, \sigma_i^*, m_i^*, A_i^*, a_i^*, B_i^*, b_i^*, C_i^*, c_i^*, h_{1i}^*, h_{4i}^*)$ and $(\mathrm{PID}_i^*, VPK_i^*, \sigma_i^{*'}, m_i^*, A_i^*, a_i^*, B_i^*, b_i^*, C_i^*, c_i^*, h_{1i}^{*'}, h_{4i}^*)$. Therefore, the following two equations can be satisfied.

$$\begin{cases} \sigma_i^* P = A_i^* + h_{4i}^* \left(C_i^* + TPKh_{1i}^* + ATPKB_i^* \right) \\ \sigma_i^{*'} P = A_i^* + h_{4i}^* \left(C_i^* + TPKh_{1i}^{*'} + ATPKB_i^* \right). \end{cases}$$

Subsequently, the challenger B combines these two equations to perform the following calculations:

$$\begin{aligned} (\sigma_i^{*'} - \sigma_i^*)P &= \left[A_i^* + h_{4i}^* \left(C_i^* + TPKh_{1i}^{*'} + ATPKB_i^* \right) \right] - \left[A_i^* + h_{4i}^* \left(C_i^* + TPKh_{1i}^* + ATPKB_i^* \right) \right] \\ &= h_{4i}^* \left(TPKh_{1i}^{*'} - TPKh_{1i}^* \right) = h_{4i}^* \left(h_{1i}^{*'} - h_{1i}^* \right) TPK = h_{4i}^* \left(h_{1i}^{*'} - h_{1i}^* \right) tskP. \end{aligned}$$

Ultimately, the challenger B outputs $a = tsk = \frac{\sigma_i^{*'} - \sigma_i^*}{h_{4i}^*(h_{1i}^{*'} - h_{1i}^*)}$ as the scheme to the DL problem.

Probability Analysis: Should Challenger B succeed in resolving the DL issue, it is imperative that the subsequent three conditions are met. Let C_1 denote that the game does not terminate during the query phase. Let C_2 denote that the game does not terminate during the forgery phase. Let C_3 denote that the adversary $\mathcal{A}_1$ is capable of forging a valid signatures.

The probability that the game does not abort during the query phase for $\mathcal{A}_1$ is $\Pr[C_1] = \left[1 - \frac{1}{q_1}\right]^{q_n}$. The probability that the game does not abort during the forgery phase for $\mathcal{A}_1$ is $\Pr[C_2] = \frac{1}{q_n+1}$. The probability that $\mathcal{A}_1$ can forge a valid signature is $\Pr[C_3] \geq \left(1 - \frac{1}{e}\right)\left(\frac{\varepsilon}{q_1}\right)$. After that, we can obtain the advantage of S_1 as

$$\varepsilon' = \Pr[C_1 \wedge C_2 \wedge C_3] \geq \left(1 - \frac{1}{q_1}\right)^{q_n}\left(\frac{1}{q_n+1}\right)\left(1 - \frac{1}{e}\right)\frac{\varepsilon}{q_1} \geq \frac{(e-1)\varepsilon}{e^2 q_1 (q_n+1)}.$$

Theorem 2. *In the ROM, it is assumed that there is an adversary $\mathcal{A}_2$, capable of forging a valid signature with a non-negligible probability ε, within the framework of PPT. In the course of the signature-forging process, the aforementioned adversary instigates q_1 H_1 queries, q_s private key queries, and q_v secret-value queries. It follows that a challenger B must exist who can solve the DL problem with a non-negligible advantage $\frac{(e-1)\varepsilon}{e^2 q_1 (1+q_s+q_v)}$, where e is the base of the natural logarithm.*

Proof: In the context of the challenge tuple (P, aP), where $a \in \mathbb{Z}_q^*$, the objective of the challenger B is to solve for the value of a. S_2 simulates a real-world environment, and its interaction process with the adversary $\mathcal{A}_2$ is as follows.

Initialization Phase: S_2 is responsible for the system's initialisation.S_2 randomly selects $tsk \in \mathbb{Z}_q^*$ and calculates $TPK = tskP$. Subsequently, it generates the system parameters $params = \{q, P, G, TPK, H_i\}$, regarding H_1 and H_4 as hash oracles.Consequently, S_2 transmits $params$ to the adversary $\mathcal{A}_2$. Moreover, S_2 is responsible for maintaining the lists, namely L_{pk}, L_1 and L_4. These lists record the queries about public keys made by $\mathcal{A}_2$, as well as the subsequent queries to H_1 and H_4 hash oracles.

Query Phase: S_2 selects PID_i^* as the challenged identity.

1. *Public Key Query:* When $\mathcal{A}_2$ queries the public key of PID_i, S_2 first verifies the existence of $(\mathrm{PID}_i, VPK_i, C_i, c_i, B_i, b_i, psk_{1i}, psk_{2i}, h_{1i})$ in the list L_{pk}. In the event of its existence, S_2 directly returns VPK_i to $\mathcal{A}_2$. Otherwise, S_2 randomly selects $b_i, h_{1i} \in \mathbb{Z}_q^*$, computes $B_i = b_i P$, $psk_{1i} = tskh_{1i}$ and $psk_{2i} = atskB_i$, and subsequently performs the following calculations.
   (a) If $\mathrm{PID}_i \neq \mathrm{PID}_i^*$, S_2 randomly selects $c_i \in \mathbb{Z}_q^*$, and calculate $C_i = c_i P$. Subsequently, S_2 calculates $VPK_i = C_i + h_{1i} TPK + B_i ATPK$ and inserts $(\mathrm{PID}_i, VPK_i, C_i, c_i, B_i, b_i, psk_{1i}, psk_{2i}, h_{1i})$ into the list L_{pk}.
   (b) If $\mathrm{PID}_i = \mathrm{PID}_i^*$, S_2 sets $C_i = cP$. Subsequently, S_2 calculates $VPK_i = C_i + h_{1i} TPK + B_i ATPK$ and inserts $(\mathrm{PID}_i, VPK_i, C_i, \perp, B_i, b_i, psk_{1i}, psk_{1i}, h_{1i})$ into the list L_{pk}.
   Subsequently, S_2 modifies the h_{1i} value in the relevant (D_i, ID_{V_i}, h_{1i}) within L_1 and finally returns VPK_i to $\mathcal{A}_2$.

2. *Secret Value Query:* When $\mathcal{A}_2$ queries S_2 for the secret value of PID_i, if $\mathrm{PID}_i = \mathrm{PID}_i^*$, S_2 will terminate and output $\perp$.If not,S_2 checks whether $(\mathrm{PID}_i, VPK_i, C_i, c_i, B_i, b_i, psk_{1i}, psk_{2i}, h_{1i})$ exists in the list L_{pk}. In the event of such a scenario, S_2 will directly return the corresponding c_i to $\mathcal{A}_2$. If not, S_2 instigates a public-key query for PID_i, subsequently returning c_i to $\mathcal{A}_2$.
3. *H_1 Oracle Query, H_4 Oracle Query, Partial Private Key Query, Private Key Query, and Signature Query:* The logic of these queries is similar to that of the corresponding queries in Theorem 1. Due to space constraints, details will not be elaborated here.

Forgery Phase: The adversary $\mathcal{A}_2$ forges the signature σ_i^* of (PID_i^*, m_i^*) and the tuple $(PID_i^*, VPK_i^*, A_i^*, \sigma_i^*, m_i^*)$, and then transmits the tuple $(PID_i^*, VPK_i^*, A_i^*, \sigma_i^*, m_i^*)$ to S_2. The adversary $\mathcal{A}_2$ is considered to have won the game if the following two conditions are met. $\mathcal{A}_2$ has not issued any partial private key queries or private key queries for PID_i and the signature σ_i is valid while $\mathcal{A}_2$ has never queried for the signature regarding $\{PID_i^*, m_i^*\}$.

If $\mathrm{PID}_i \neq \mathrm{PID}_i^*$, then S_2 aborts and outputs $\perp$. Otherwise, and based on the Forking Lemma [26], after $\mathcal{A}_2$ replays with the same random values D_i, S_2 can change the output of the oracle H_1 to give a different $h_{1i}^{*'}$. Specifically, although the query responses for the parameters related to PID_i remain consistent, the challenger B can obtain two different tuples, namely $(\mathrm{PID}_i^*, VPK_i^*, \sigma_i^*, m_i^*, A_i^*, a_i^*, B_i^*, b_i^*, C_i^*, c_i^*, h_{1i}^*, h_{4i}^*)$ and $(\mathrm{PID}_i^*, VPK_i^*, \sigma_i^{*'}, m_i^*, A_i^*, a_i^*, B_i^*, b_i^*, C_i^*, c_i^*, h_{1i}^{*'}, h_{4i}^*)$. Therefore, the following two equations can be satisfied.

$$\begin{cases} \sigma_i^* P = A_i^* + h_{4i}^* \left(C_i^* + TPKh_{1i}^* + ATPKB_i^*\right) \\ \sigma_i^{*'} P = A_i^* + h_{4i}^* \left(C_i^* + TPKh_{1i}^{*'} + ATPKB_i^*\right). \end{cases}$$

Subsequently, the challenger B combines these two equations to perform the following calculations:

$$\begin{aligned} (\sigma_i^{*'} - \sigma_i^*)P &= \left[A_i^* + h_{4i}^* \left(C_i^* + TPKh_{1i}^{*'} + ATPKB_i^*\right)\right] - \left[A_i^* + h_{4i}^* \left(C_i^* + TPKh_{1i}^* + ATPKB_i^*\right)\right] \\ &= h_{4i}^* \left(TPKh_{1i}^{*'} - TPKh_{1i}^*\right) = h_{4i}^* \left(h_{1i}^{*'} - h_{1i}^*\right) TPK = h_{4i}^* \left(h_{1i}^{*'} - h_{1i}^*\right) tskP. \end{aligned}$$

Ultimately, the challenger B outputs $a = tsk = \frac{\sigma_i^{*'} - \sigma_i^*}{h_{4i}^*(h_{1i}^{*'} - h_{1i}^*)}$ as the scheme to the DL problem.

Probability Analysis: Should Challenger B succeed in resolving the DL issue, it is imperative that the subsequent three conditions are met. Let C_1 denote that the game does not terminate during the query phase. Let C_2 denote that the game does not terminate during the forgery phase. Let C_3 denote that the adversary $\mathcal{A}_2$ is capable of forging a valid signatures.

The probability that the game does not abort during the query phase for $\mathcal{A}_2$ is $\Pr[C_1] = \left[1 - \frac{1}{q_1}\right]^{(q_s+q_v)}$. The probability that the game does not abort during the forgery phase for $\mathcal{A}_2$ is $\Pr[C_2] = \frac{1}{q_s+q_v+1}$. The probability that $\mathcal{A}_2$

can forge a valid signature is $\Pr[C_3] \geq (1-\frac{1}{e})\left(\frac{\varepsilon}{q_1}\right)$. After that, we can obtain the advantage of S_2 as

$$\varepsilon' = \Pr[C_1 \wedge C_2 \wedge C_3] \geq \left(1-\frac{1}{q_1}\right)^{(q_s+q_v)}\left(\frac{1}{q_s+q_v+1}\right)\left(1-\frac{1}{e}\right)\frac{\varepsilon}{q_1} \geq \frac{(e-1)\varepsilon}{e^2 q_1(q_s+q_v+1)}.$$

In summary, if a PPT adversary $\mathcal{A}$ ($\mathcal{A}_1$ or $\mathcal{A}_2$) can win the above game with a non-negligible advantage ε', then a challenger B can solve the DL problem with an advantage ε'. However, the Discrete Logarithm problem is difficult for any PPT adversary, which contradicts the above assumption. Consequently, our scheme is resistant to adaptive chosen-message attacks.

6.2 Security Analysis

1. *Identity Authentication and Integrity:* Our scheme uses a certificateless signature algorithm and a two-stage authentication process. A vehicle's private key is generated from the partial private keys distributed by TA and ATA, as well as the local secret value. Using public parameters and the sender's public key, the receiver authenticates the signature. This checks the signature's validity.
2. *Traceability and Revocation:* Our scheme enables the tracing of malicious behaviour while protecting privacy. During registration, TA records the mapping between the pseudonym PID_i and the real identity ID_{V_i} when allocating PID_i to a vehicle. When malicious behaviour is detected, TA or ATA determines vehicle's domain through its long-term public key VPK_i. Then, by combining the registration information, the real identity can be resolved. The identity of the malicious vehicle is added to the revocation list and its privileges are revoked and broadcast.
3. *Unlinkability:* Our scheme adopts dynamic temporary keys and timestamps. New keys are generated when vehicles cross domains, and these keys become invalid after domain switching. Moreover, the temporary keys used in different sessions are uncorrelated. Meanwhile, the real identity is concealed by a pseudonym, making it impossible for an adversary to link different behaviors of the same vehicle or infer its identity through message analysis.
4. *Security of Session Key:* Session keys derive from a vehicle's private key and the target's public key. Attackers cannot compute private keys, and timestamp-bound session keys ensure security through automatic expiration.
5. *Forward and Backward Security:* In our scheme, we secure the authentication messages and session keys by incorporating random numbers and timestamps. This design ensures that if a random number is leaked in a single phase, it only affects the current session. This prevents the derivation of other messages or session keys and ensures the security of historical session keys remains uncompromised, thereby achieving secure isolation between sessions.
6. *Resistance to Various Common Attacks:* Our scheme employs timestamped messages to resist replay attacks. To defend against man-in-the-middle attacks, vehicles sign messages with their private keys, and the receiving party

verifies the message signatures through public keys to ensure the authenticity of the messages. Regarding collusion attacks, a hierarchical key architecture is adopted. Vehicles generate complete private keys by combining partial keys and local secret values. Even if TA and ATAs collude, it is difficult for them to steal vehicle privacy information. In addition, a dynamic accumulator combined with Ceph distributed storage is used to protect vehicle identities. Even if multiple ATAs collude, it is difficult for them to steal vehicle privacy information through such collusion, thus ensuring the security of the system.

7 Performance Analysis

This section conducts a systematic comparison between the proposed scheme and state-of-the-art alternatives across three critical dimensions. To reduce experimental biases, our scheme and the comparative schemes utilize the same elliptic curve and cryptographic library. Moreover, we reproduced the comparative schemes.

7.1 Comparison of Security Features

Table 2 presents the comparison results of security features. Here, "✓" indicates that the scheme satisfies the corresponding security feature, while "×" indicates that it does not. As illustrated in Table 2, the proposed scheme in [27] does not satisfy the security requirement for cross-domain batch authentication. Similarly, the scheme in [28] does not fulfil the security requirement for anonymity. Additionally, the schemes in [18,27,28] do not meet the security requirements for collusion attack resistance and cross-domain key dynamic update. In contrast to prior approaches, our scheme satisfies the complete set of security requirements.

Table 2. Comparison of security features

Security Features	[18]	[27]	[28]	Our
Anonymity	✓	✓	×	✓
Authentication	✓	✓	✓	✓
Unlinkability	✓	✓	✓	✓
Traceability	✓	✓	✓	✓
Cross-domain Batch Authentication	✓	×	✓	✓
Resistance to Replay Attacks	✓	✓	✓	✓
Resistance to Man-in-the-Middle Attacks	✓	✓	✓	✓
Forward and Backward Security	✓	✓	✓	✓
Resistance to Collusion Attacks	×	×	×	✓
Dynamic Update of Cross-Domain Keys	×	×	×	✓

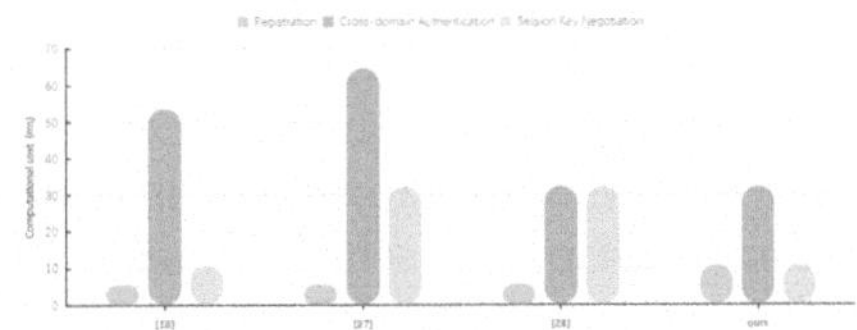

Fig. 3. Comparison of computational costs for each stage.

7.2 Comparison of Computational Cost

To ensure a fair comparison of computational overheads, our experiments were conducted under a unified standard. The hardware environment comprised a 2.50 GHz Intel Core i5-12400F processor, 32 GB of memory and the Windows 11 operating system. The experiments were implemented in the IntelliJ IDEA 2024.3.4.1 environment using the Java programming language in combination with the JPBC cryptographic library. We constructed a cryptographic group structure based on a non-singular elliptic curve $E : y^2 = x^3 + 5x + b \pmod p$ and used it to generate an elliptic curve additive group G with prime order q and a generator P. This achieved a security level of 80 bits. In this case, both p and q are 160 bit prime numbers and $e : G_1 \times G_1 = G_2$ is a bilinear group.

Table 3. Symbol, description and operation time

Symbol	Description	Time (ms)
T_{ECA}	ECC point addition $P + W$	0.0263
T_{ECM}	ECC scalar multiplication $x \cdot P$	5.3462

Table 4. Communication efficiency comparison

Scheme	1 Message	n Messages
[18]	$4\|G_1\| + 3\|Z_q^*\| + 1\|T\| = 576$	$576n$
[27]	$4\|G_1\| + 1\|Z_q^*\| + 1\|T\| = 536$	$536n$
[28]	$3\|G_1\| + 3\|Z_q^*\| + 1\|T\| = 448$	$448n$
Our	$2\|G_1\| + 3\|Z_q^*\| + 1\|T\| = 320$	$320n$

In the evaluation of computational costs, we focus on the core time-consuming operations within our scheme and the comparison schemes. Based on these standards, we ran 2,000 rounds of operations through the JPBC cryptographic library. The data from the first 500 rounds was excluded as warm-up data. The simulation time of the remaining rounds was recorded, and the average value was calculated. The results were listed in Table 3. Table 5 presents the theoretical analysis results of the computational costs at each stage. Subsequently, based on the results in Table 5, we plotted the comparison charts of the computational costs at each stage, as shown in Fig. 3, and the chart of the computational costs for cross-domain batch authentication, as shown in Fig. 4. As demonstrated in Fig. 3, when evaluated in comparison to alternative schemes [18,27,28], the computational cost of our scheme during the registration stage is marginally higher than that of other schemes. Nevertheless, it is evident that, in the cross-domain authentication and session key negotiation stages, the computational cost of the proposed scheme is considerably lower than that of alternative schemes. It can be seen from Fig. 4 that when our scheme conducts batch authentication with all comparison schemes, the computational cost increases with the increase in the number of vehicles. However, compared with other schemes, the computational cost of our scheme is consistently the lowest. Our scheme demonstrates remarkable advantages in computational efficiency, and the computational cost of cross-domain batch authentication in our scheme is at least 40% lower than that of the comparison schemes.

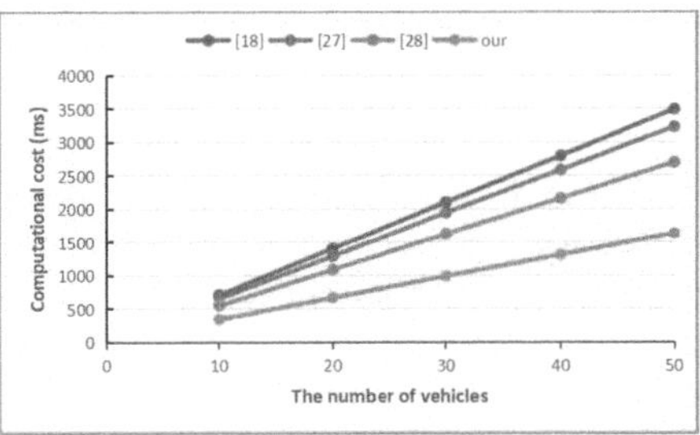

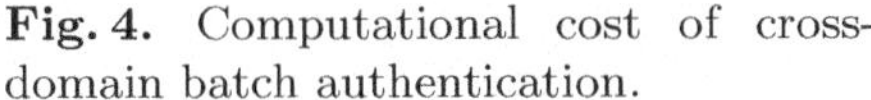
Fig. 4. Computational cost of cross-domain batch authentication.

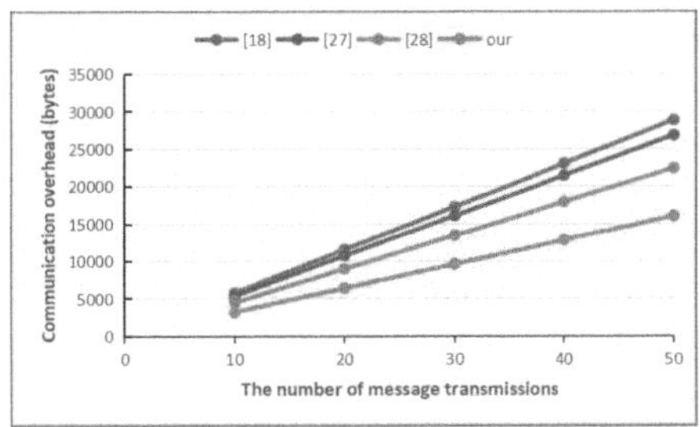

Fig. 5. Communication overhead for n message transmissions.

Table 5. Computational efficiency comparison

Scheme	Registration	Cross-domain Authentication	Session Key Negotiation	Batch Verification (n)
[18]	$1T_{ECM} + 1T_{ECA}$	$10T_{ECM} + 2T_{ECA}$	$2T_{ECM}$	$(13n + 2)T_{ECM} + (4n - 1)T_{ECA}$
[27]	$1T_{ECM} + 1T_{ECA}$	$12T_{ECM} + 7T_{ECA}$	$6T_{ECM} + 4T_{ECA}$	$(12n + 2)T_{ECM} + (8n - 1)T_{ECA}$
[28]	$1T_{ECM} + 2T_{ECA}$	$6T_{ECM} + 5T_{ECA}$	$6T_{ECM} + 4T_{ECA}$	$(10n + 2)T_{ECM} + (10n - 1)T_{ECA}$
Our	$2T_{ECM} + 2T_{ECA}$	$6T_{ECM} + 3T_{ECA}$	$2T_{ECM}$	$(6n + 4)T_{ECM} + (4n - 1)T_{ECA}$

7.3 Comparison of Communication Overhead

In this section, we analyze and compare the communication overheads of our scheme and the comparison schemes. We mainly consider the size of authentication messages in the cross-domain authentication phase. The length of group G_1 is 128 bytes, the length of finite field $\mathbb{Z}_q^*$ is 20 bytes, and the length of timestamp T is 4 bytes. Here, n represents the number of transmitted messages. We use the same method to calculate the communication overheads for our scheme and the schemes with which we are making comparisons, and list the results in Table 4. To more clearly observe the differences, we plot the communication overheads when vehicles transmit n authentication messages based on the results in Table 4, as shown in Fig. 5. Figure 5 clearly shows that cross-domain communication overhead increases with the number of authentication messages and that our scheme has the lowest communication overhead.

Based on the aforementioned analysis, which involved a comprehensive comparison of security, computational and communication overheads, our scheme guarantees the security and effectiveness of authentication and shows better performance in terms of computational cost and communication overhead than existing schemes [18,27,28]. The computational cost of cross-domain batch authentication is reduced by at least 40%, and communication overhead is decreased by at least 30%. Therefore, our scheme is better suited to communication scenarios in the Internet of Vehicles with limited resources.

8 Conclusion

In response to the risks of single-point failures, key escrow, and real-time bottlenecks in cross-domain authentication within VANETs, this paper presents a dynamic multi-domain cross-domain authentication scheme based on a hierarchical key architecture. A hierarchical key architecture consisting of TA, ATA, and vehicles is constructed, and a cross-domain key dynamic update mechanism is proposed. By integrating dynamic accumulators and Ceph distributed storage, the privacy protection of vehicle identities is ensured, and the cross-domain query efficiency and system scalability are enhanced. This scheme can reduce the computational overhead by at least 40% and the communication overhead by at least 30%. The scheme can withstand common attacks. Furthermore, its unforgeability against adaptive chosen-message attacks within the ROM has been validated through formal proof. Our scheme is highly suitable for large-scale VANETs and delivers efficient, secure authentication support for cross-domain communication in VANETs with dynamic multi-domain attributes. Future research will focus on exploring the trade-off between storage and bandwidth in the integration of Ceph in resource-constrained vehicular networks, as well as the scalability issue in dense urban environments.

Acknowledgments. This work was supported in part by the Guiding Program of Scientific Research Plan of Hubei Province under Grant B2023033.

References

1. Cui, J., Wei, L., Zhong, H., Zhang, J., Xu, Y., Liu, L.: Edge computing in VANETs-an efficient and privacy-preserving cooperative downloading scheme. IEEE J. Sel. Areas Commun. **38**(6), 1191–1204 (2020)
2. Qureshi, K.N., Din, S., Jeon, G., Piccialli, F.: Internet of vehicles: key technologies, network model, solutions and challenges with future aspects. IEEE Trans. Intell. Transp. Syst. **22**(3), 1777–1786 (2021)
3. Khelifi, H., et al.: Named data networking in vehicular ad hoc networks: state-of-the-art and challenges. IEEE Commun. Surv. Tutor. **22**(1), 320–351 (2020)
4. Guo, X., Lu, X., Jiang, Y., Fang, J., Zhang, D.: DBCPCA: double-layer blockchain-assisted conditional privacy-preserving cross-domain authentication for VANETs. Ad Hoc Netw. **163**, 103600 (2024)
5. Lai, C., Lu, R., Zheng, D., Shen, X.: Security and privacy challenges in 5G-enabled vehicular networks. IEEE Netw. **34**(2), 37–45 (2020)
6. Verma, G.K., et al.: Escrow-free and efficient dynamic anonymous privacy-preserving batch verifiable authentication scheme for VANETs. Ad Hoc Netw. **166**, 103670 (2025)
7. Pandey, P.K., Kansal, V., Swaroop, A.: PKI-SMR: PKI based secure multipath routing for unmanned military vehicles (UMV) in VANETs. Wirel. Netw. **30**(2), 595–615 (2024)
8. Zhu, F., et al.: Certificate-based anonymous authentication with efficient aggregation for wireless medical sensor networks. IEEE Internet Things J. **9**(14), 12209–12218 (2022)

9. Tomar, A., Tripathi, S.: BCAV: blockchain-based certificateless authentication system for vehicular network. Peer-to-Peer Netw. Appl. **15**(3), 1733–1756 (2022)
10. Qi, J., Gao, T., Deng, X., Zhao, C.: A pseudonym-based certificateless privacy-preserving authentication scheme for VANETs. Vehicular Commun. **38**, 100535 (2022)
11. Zhou, X., Luo, M., Vijayakumar, P., Peng, C., He, D.: Efficient certificateless conditional privacy-preserving authentication for VANETs. IEEE Trans. Veh. Technol. **71**(7), 7863–7875 (2022)
12. Genc, Y., Aytas, N., Akkoc, A., Afacan, E., Yazgan, E.: ELCPAS: a new efficient lightweight certificateless conditional privacy preserving authentication scheme for IoV. Veh. Commun. **39**, 100549 (2023)
13. Al-Riyami, S.S., Paterson, K.G.: Certificateless public key cryptography. In: Proceedings of the International Conference on the Theory and Application of Cryptology and Information Security, pp. 452–473 (2003)
14. Xie, D., Yang, J., Bian, W., Chen, F., Wang, T.: An improved identity-based anonymous authentication scheme resistant to semi-trusted server attacks. IEEE Internet Things J. **10**(1), 734–746 (2023)
15. Anilkumar, S., Rafeek, J.: Soteria: A blockchain assisted lightweight and efficient certificateless handover authentication mechanism for VANET. In: Proceedings of the 2023 3rd International Conference on Advances in Computing, Communication, Embedded and Secure Systems (ACCESS), Kalady, Ernakulam, India, pp. 226–232 (2023)
16. Wang, L., Xu, J., Qin, B., Wen, M., Chen, K.: An efficient fuzzy certificateless signature-based authentication scheme using anonymous biometric identities for VANETs. IEEE Trans. Dependable Secure Comput. **22**(1), 292–307 (2025)
17. Qiao, Z., et al.: An anonymous and efficient certificate-based identity authentication protocol for VANET. IEEE Internet Things J. **11**(7), 11232–11245 (2024)
18. Zhong, Q., Zhao, X., Xia, Y., Liu, X.: CD-BASA: an efficient cross-domain batch authentication scheme based on blockchain with accumulator for VANETs. IEEE Trans. Intell. Transp. Syst. **25**(10), 14560–14571 (2024)
19. Asghar, M., Doss, R.R.M., Pan, L.: A scalable and efficient PKI based authentication protocol for VANETs. In: Proceedings of the 2018 28th International Telecommunication Networks and Applications Conference (ITNAC), Sydney, NSW, Australia, pp. 1–3 (2018)
20. Chen, J., Zhan, Z., He, K., Du, R., Wang, D., Liu, F.: XAuth: efficient privacy-preserving cross-domain authentication. IEEE Trans. Dependable Secure Comput. **19**(5), 3301–3311 (2022)
21. Ma, M., Wang, S., Li, Y.: A model based on multiple intermediate entity for cross-domain authentication in public key infrastructure and blockchain system. In: Proceedings of the 2022 3rd International Conference on Electronics, Communications and Information Technology (CECIT), Sanya, China, pp. 446–453 (2022)
22. Ali, I., Lawrence, T., Li, F.: An efficient identity-based signature scheme without bilinear pairing for vehicle-to-vehicle communication in VANETs. J. Syst. Archit. **103**, 101692 (2020)
23. Zhang, J., Su, S., Zhong, H., Cui, J., He, D.: Identity-based broadcast proxy re-encryption for flexible data sharing in VANETs. IEEE Trans. Inf. Forensics Security. **18**, 4830–4842 (2023)
24. Zhu, F., Yi, X., Abuadbba, A., Khalil, I., Huang, X., Xu, F.: A security-enhanced certificateless conditional privacy-preserving authentication scheme for vehicular ad hoc networks. IEEE Trans. Intell. Transp. Syst. **24**(10), 10456–10466 (2023)

25. Zhang, L., Xu, J.: Blockchain-based anonymous authentication for traffic reporting in VANETs. Connection Sci. **34**(1), 1038–1065 (2022)
26. Pointcheval, D., Stern, J.: Security arguments for digital signatures and blind signatures. J. Cryptol. **13**, 361–396 (2000)
27. Zhu, Y., Zhou, Y., Wang, J., Yang, B., Zhang, M.: A lightweight cross-domain direct identity authentication protocol for VANETs. IEEE Internet Things J. **11**(23), 37741–37757 (2024)
28. Dong, J., Xu, G., Ma, C., Liu, J., Cliff, U.G.O.: Blockchain-based certificate-free cross-domain authentication mechanism for industrial internet. IEEE Internet Things J. **11**(2), 3316–3330 (2024)

Secure and Flexible HD Wallets: Enabling Mnemonic Updates and Threshold-Controlled Key Derivation

Decun Luo[1], Wei Huang[2], Haibin Zheng[3], Yujue Wang[3], Qianhong Wu[1(✉)], Bo Qin[2], and Hai Liang[4]

[1] School of Cyber Science and Technology, Beihang University, Beijing, China
[2] School of Information, Renmin University of China, Beijing, China
[3] Hangzhou Innovation Institute of Beihang University, Hangzhou, China
[4] Guilin University of Electronic Technology, Guilin, Guangxi, China

Abstract. Cryptographic wallets are fundamental for secure key management and asset protection in blockchain systems. While deterministic wallets, such as those formalized in BIP32, have become the de facto standard for hierarchical key derivation, their limited flexibility constrains practical usability. In particular, traditional deterministic wallets suffer from insufficient mnemonic recoverability and lack mechanisms for collaborative multi-party control, which undermines both resilience and user experience. To address these limitations, we introduce a novel framework for mnemonic-updatable hierarchical deterministic (HD) wallets. Our design leverages Chameleon hash functions as the core of the key derivation process, enabling controlled seed updates through trapdoor-based collision finding. Furthermore, we observe that chain codes obtained from hardened key derivation naturally function as threshold shares. Building on this, we propose a threshold-controlled subkey derivation scheme, allowing any subtree of the wallet to support secure, multiparty computation of child keys and recovery of parent chain codes. Both theoretical analysis and experimental results demonstrate that our scheme achieves low overhead and practical applicability in real-world scenarios.

Keywords: Cryptographic wallets · Mnemonic Update · Threshold Derivation · Hierarchical Deterministic

1 Introduction

With the widespread adoption of decentralized blockchain technologies such as Bitcoin [22] and Ethereum [5], the security of blockchain key management has become a focal point of research. *Cryptocurrency wallets* are specialized solutions for blockchain key management and are also foundational components for protecting user assets. These wallets are tasked with securely storing and using private keys. Private keys are the cryptographic credentials required to authorize transactions and manage digital assets [19]. Hence, wallets play a dual role. They

L. Zhang and K.-K. R. Choo (Eds.): MobiQuitous 2025, LNICST 684, pp. 369–388, 2026.
https://doi.org/10.1007/978-3-032-22503-0_20

serve both as usability tools and as security-critical modules that uphold the end-user's autonomy and asset sovereignty [4]. A compromise in wallet key management can result in catastrophic and irreversible loss. Such risks may arise from seed leakage, flawed recovery procedures, or insecure key derivation [17,27,30]. A breach in wallet key management can result in catastrophic and irreversible losses, such as theft of funds and privacy breaches. Such incidents may arise from mnemonic leakage, flaws in the recovery process, or insecure key derivation mechanisms. As a result, both academia and industry have explored secure wallet management schemes, such as *hierarchical deterministic* (HD) wallets, and have provided formal security proofs [9].

The HD wallet [26] has become the mainstream solution in cryptocurrency wallet practice, enabling scalable and consistent key derivation. This scheme is standardized through a set of Bitcoin Improvement Proposals (BIPs), including BIP-32, BIP-39, and BIP-44 [23,25,26]. For details, the BIP32 defines the deterministic derivation of keys from a master node using structured paths. BIP-39 specifies the generation and encoding of mnemonic seed phrases. BIP-44 establishes conventions for multi-account and multi-asset hierarchy structures. In an HD wallet, a single master seed, which is typically encoded as a human-readable 12 or 24-word mnemonic, is sufficient to deterministically derive an entire hierarchy of key pairs. This approach offers several compelling advantages: improved organizational control through path-based structure, streamlined backup and recovery using a single mnemonic, and enhanced privacy through frequent address rotation [9]. Moreover, because key derivation is stateless and deterministic, HD wallets are highly scalable and reproducible across devices and platforms.

However, compared to digital wallets in mature traditional payment systems, cryptocurrency wallets still have substantial room for improvement in complex application scenarios. Here, we summarize the key technical challenges (TCs) for enhancing the security of cryptocurrency wallets in complex usage scenarios.

TC-I: Static Seed Binding. All derived keys are irreversibly bound to the original mnemonic. Therefore, if the user forgets or needs to replace the mnemonic, all assets in the old wallet must be transferred to a newly constructed wallet. Clearly, this process is costly and inflexible [14].

TC-II: Monolithic Control Derivation. The wallet owner possesses the exclusive authority to derive the entire key tree. In scenarios where multiple sub-entities require self-management, this characteristic hinders the fine-grained delegation or partitioning of wallet keys, making it challenging to allocate ownership of subtrees or to enforce organizational separation of duties [29].

TC-III: Insufficient Collaborative Capability. Hardened derivation results in the lack of correlation among child keys under the same parent node. This characteristic makes it difficult for entities holding sibling child keys to collaborate with each other in multi-party scenarios.

Problem Statements. In summary, these challenges constrain and hinder both individual and institutional users' experiences with cryptocurrencies. Specifically, enterprises require isolated key control to enable collaborative governance while maintaining security, whereas end users demand robust wallet recoverability. This motivates our central research question:

Can we design a flexible wallet that supports seed updating, self-derivable management, and partial collaboration, without compromising security?

Security Requirements. For the aforementioned flexible wallet, we defined a set of security requirements as follows.

- *Collision Non-Malleability:* Without knowledge of the trapdoor, it is computationally infeasible to generate a new seed and corresponding randomness that collides under the Chameleon hash.
- *Forward Security:* The leakage of the derived master key (chain code and private key) does not compromise the original trapdoor or the original seed, assuming the hardness of the CDHP.
- *Correctness and Determinism:* The Lagrange interpolation over any t valid shares always yields the correct parent chain code cc_i. Furthermore, the computation of g^{cc_i} via distributed exponentiation is deterministic and unambiguous in the prime-order group G.
- *Threshold Privacy:* Any coalition of fewer than t participants learns no information about the parent chain code cc_i or its exponentiated form g^{cc_i}, beyond their own shares. This property holds unconditionally due to the information-theoretic security of Shamir's secret sharing.
- *Threshold Recoverability:* Given any t valid child chain code shares with distinct indices, the parent chain code cc_i and its exponentiated value g^{cc_i} can be uniquely and correctly reconstructed by Lagrange interpolation and distributed exponentiation, ensuring the availability and liveness of derivation.

1.1 Our Contributions

We propose a flexible hierarchical deterministic wallet (FHD) that addresses the core limitations of conventional seed-based architectures. Our design introduces three complementary innovations:

- **Chameleon Hash-Based Mnemonic Updatable**. To support seamless seed rotation without disrupting the existing key hierarchy, we leverage Chameleon hash functions [18] as the cryptographic anchor for master seed binding. By exploiting the trapdoor collision property, a new seed can be constructed that yields the same hash digest as the original one, thereby preserving all previously derived public keys. This mechanism enables verifiable and non-destructive seed updates, while preventing rollback or forgery without access to the trapdoor.
- **Threshold-Controlled Key Derivation**. To enable local autonomy and collaboration within key subtrees, we have integrated Shamir's Secret Sharing (SSS) [24], splitting the parent node's chain code of a subtree into multiple shares and distributing them among the chain codes of several child nodes.

Only when t out of n child node chain codes participate in threshold-secure multiparty computation can a valid share of the parent node's chain code be reconstructed, thereby unlocking derivation capability at that level. This approach not only enhances the fault tolerance and robustness of the key tree but also enables local collaboration among child key nodes.
- **Flexibly Collaborative HD Wallet.** Based on the two mechanisms described above, we design a hierarchical deterministic wallet instance compatible with BIP32. This instance is constructed with 256-bit security. Users only need to memorize a single mnemonic; at any time, the wallet mnemonic can be updated via a Chameleon hash trapdoor, even if the original mnemonic has been forgotten. Furthermore, our wallet scheme supports threshold autonomy over the chain code of any level; that is, child node users can restore the parent node's chain code through secure multiparty computation, thereby achieving self-controlled derivation.

1.2 Related Work

HD Wallet. HD wallets, introduced by BIP-32 [26], enable scalable key generation via tree-based derivation from a single seed. Das *et al.* [8,9] provided formal models to assess BIP-32's security, particularly regarding hardened and non-hardened derivation. Building on these foundations, several schemes have proposed enhanced functionalities. Arcula [10] integrates identity-based encryption for secure key recovery. While this approach offers a novel solution for key recovery, it introduces additional dependencies on identity-based cryptographic techniques, which may have their own security considerations. On the other hand, HDWSA^2 [28] incorporates stealth addresses into the derivation path, improving transaction privacy. This enhancement addresses the critical issue of privacy in blockchain transactions, demonstrating a significant advancement in user anonymity protection. Eleshin *et al.* [12] further highlighted user misunderstanding around mnemonic seed phrases, revealing practical risks in wallet usability and recovery. Their findings underscore the importance of user education and intuitive wallet design to mitigate these usability challenges.

Threshold Key Management. Threshold cryptography enhances resilience by enabling private keys to be jointly generated or used by multiple parties, avoiding single points of failure. Foundational work on threshold ECDSA [13,20] and its efficient variants [11] has led to practical signing protocols for decentralized settings. Recent advances, such as traceable secret sharing [3], further introduce accountability and auditability in collaborative key usage, reflecting an increasing demand for flexible key lifecycle management. However, traditional hierarchical key derivation lacks native support for such features, and existing attempts to bridge threshold schemes with deterministic wallets [7,29] remain constrained by static derivation and limited update capability. These challenges motivate new approaches that support secure, fine-grained key updates within threshold settings—particularly via cryptographic primitives like Chameleon hash functions, which offer controlled collision generation and verifiable update semantics in multi-party environments.

Enhanced Wallet Designs. Recent efforts have explored hybrid architectures that combine HD wallet derivation with threshold cryptographic controls. Das *et al.* [7] proposed a BIP-32–compatible threshold scheme using pseudorandom functions, though it lacks support for hardened derivation. Zhong *et al.* [29] introduced a distributed key derivation protocol for institutional settings, focusing on scalability and custody. These designs enhance robustness but introduce integration complexity, especially across heterogeneous blockchain platforms. Concurrently, usability and lifecycle management have gained attention. Mangipudi *et al.* [21] identified mismatches between user expectations and the security guarantees of multi-device wallets. Guthoff *et al.* [15] revealed operational concerns among finance professionals, while Hanzlik *et al.* [16] addressed revocability and privacy challenges in FIDO2-compatible authentication, which share similarities with wallet recovery mechanisms.

Although previous research has made both theoretical and practical advances in the design of HD wallets, threshold control, and usability, there remains a lack of innovation in flexibility for client-side tools. This motivates continued exploration of secure and flexible wallet infrastructures to improve user experience.

2 Preliminaries

Notation. Let G denote a cyclic group of prime order q, with generator g. Let $H : \{0,1\}^* \rightarrow G^*$ be a cryptographic hash function with output length n. Let $sd \in \mathbb{Z}_q^*$ denote a random seed, and $r \in \mathbb{Z}_q^*$ denote a random scalar. For any $x \in \mathbb{N}$, $[x] := \{1, 2, \ldots, x\}$. Let h denote a hash output, with $h[0 : n/2]$ and $h[n/2 : n]$ denoting its first and second halves, respectively. Let cc_i denote a chain code at level i, and sk_i the corresponding private key. Let $\mathcal{F}(x)$ denote a degree-$(t-1)$ polynomial over $\mathbb{F}_q$, with constant term a_0. We write $x \xleftarrow{\$} \mathcal{X}$ to denote that x is sampled uniformly at random from the finite set $\mathcal{X}$.

2.1 Gap Diffie-Hellman Groups

Consider a cyclic group G of prime order q, where g is a generator and both group operations and inversion can be performed efficiently. Within this setting, several fundamental computational challenges are defined as follows:

- *Discrete Logarithm (DLP).* The task is, given $g \in G$ and $h \in G$, to identify $a \in \mathbb{Z}_q^*$ such that $h = g^a$, whenever such an a exists.
- *Decisional Diffie-Hellman (DDHP).* Given a quadruple (g, g^a, g^b, g^c) with $a, b, c \in \mathbb{Z}_q^*$, the challenge is to determine whether $c \equiv ab \pmod q$.
- *Computational Diffie-Hellman (CDHP).* The objective is, for given elements (g, g^a, g^b), to compute g^{ab}.

We refer to the tuple (g, g^a, g^b, g^c) as a Diffie-Hellman tuple, which is said to be valid if $c \equiv ab \pmod q$. A *gap Diffie-Hellman group* is characterized by the property that there exists an efficient algorithm to solve DDHP, yet CDHP remains computationally intractable with non-negligible probability. Such groups frequently arise in the context of cryptographic constructions based on supersingular elliptic curves or hyperelliptic curves over finite fields.

2.2 Chameleon Hash Functions

A Chameleon hash function [2,6] is a cryptographic hash with the additional property that, given a trapdoor, one can efficiently find collisions. In the absence of the trapdoor, the function remains collision-resistant. This dual property is foundational in constructing primitives such as redactable signatures, key-homomorphic commitments, and secure seed update mechanisms.

Let G be a GDH group with generator g, and let $x \in \mathbb{Z}_q$ be the trapdoor. Define the public hash key as $\mathsf{chpk} = (g, h \leftarrow g^x)$.

- *Hash Evaluation.* Given a message $m \in \mathbb{Z}_q$ and randomness $r \in \mathbb{Z}_q$, the Chameleon hash is computed as:

$$\mathsf{CH}(\mathsf{chpk}, m, r) = g^m h^r = g^{m+xr}.$$

- *Trapdoor Collision.* Given an initial pair (m, r) and a new message m', the trapdoor holder can compute:

$$r' = \frac{m - m'}{x} + r \mod q,$$

such that:

$$\mathsf{CH}(\mathsf{chpk}, m, r) = \mathsf{CH}(\mathsf{chpk}, m', r').$$

A Chameleon hash function is considered secure if it upholds the following essential requirements:

- *Semantic security:* Given any two messages m and m', the outputs $\mathsf{CH}(m, r)$ and $\mathsf{CH}(m', r)$, when r is chosen at random, are computationally indistinguishable from each other by any efficient adversary.
- *Collision Resistance:* In the absence of the trapdoor x, no probabilistic polynomial-time algorithm can find (m', r') such that $\mathsf{CH}(m', r') = \mathsf{CH}(m, r)$ for a given message m and random value r with non-negligible probability.

2.3 Shamir's Secret Sharing

Shamir's threshold secret sharing scheme [24] enables a secret $s \in \mathbb{Z}_q$ to be distributed among n parties such that any subset of t shares can reconstruct s, while any fewer reveal no information.

- *Sharing Phase.* The dealer selects a random degree-$(t-1)$ polynomial:

$$f(x) = s + a_1 x + a_2 x^2 + \cdots + a_{t-1} x^{t-1}, \quad a_i \xleftarrow{\$} \mathbb{Z}_q.$$

  Each participant P_i receives the share $s_i := f(i)$.
- *Reconstruction Phase.* Given any t shares $\{(i, s_i)\}_{i \in \mathcal{T}}$, one interpolates the secret as:

$$s = f(0) = \sum_{i \in \mathcal{T}} s_i \cdot \lambda_i^{(0)} \mod q,$$

  where the Lagrange coefficients are defined as:

$$\lambda_i^{(0)} = \prod_{\substack{j \in \mathcal{T} \\ j \neq i}} \frac{-j}{i-j} \mod q.$$

Shamir's threshold secret sharing scheme possesses the following core security features:

- *Threshold privacy:* Any collection of fewer than t shares reveals no information about the underlying secret; for every set of at most $(t-1)$ shares, the secret s is uniformly distributed over $\mathbb{Z}_q$, even conditioned on those shares.
- *Robust recoverability:* Provided any subset of t or more valid shares, the secret can be efficiently and uniquely reconstructed through polynomial interpolation, regardless of which participants contribute the shares.

2.4 Hierarchical Deterministic Wallets

A hierarchical deterministic wallet, as specified by BIP32 and extended in BIP44 [23,26], organizes key material into a tree structure, where each node deterministically derives its descendants from its own state and an associated index.

Each node in the derivation tree is represented as a tuple (sk, pk, cc), where $sk \in \mathbb{Z}_q$ is the private key, $pk = g^{sk}$ is the corresponding public key, and $cc \in \{0,1\}^{256}$ denotes the chain code that acts as key material for the PRF-based derivation mechanism.

Depending on the type of index i used for derivation, two distinct key derivation mechanisms are defined:

- *Hardened Derivation ($i \geq 2^{31}$):* Requires the parent private key sk for child key generation:

$$I = \mathsf{HMAC}_{\mathsf{SHA512}}(cc, \mathtt{0x00} \| sk \| i), \quad I = I_L \| I_R,$$

$$sk' = \mathtt{parse256}(I_L) + sk \mod q, \qquad cc' = I_R.$$

- *Non-Hardened Derivation ($i < 2^{31}$):* Allows child key computation from the parent public key:

$$I = \mathsf{HMAC}_{\mathsf{SHA512}}(cc, pk \| i), \quad I = I_L \| I_R,$$

$$sk' = \mathtt{parse256}(I_L) + sk \mod q, \qquad pk' = pk \cdot g^{\mathtt{parse256}(I_L)}, \qquad cc' = I_R.$$

The security of HD wallets is characterized by the following formal properties [9] (Fig. 1):

- *Forward Secrecy:* In hardened derivation, compromise of any child key material (sk', cc') does not enable efficient recovery of the parent private key sk, assuming the intractability of the discrete logarithm and the PRF inversion.

$$\Pr[\text{Recover } sk \mid sk', cc'] \leq 2^{-\kappa}$$

- *Hierarchical Security:* The security model is robust under recursive derivations, supporting scalable key management without loss of security guarantees at any hierarchy level.
- *Public Key Transparency:* For non-hardened derivations, any party possessing the parent public key and chain code can independently derive all descendant public keys, facilitating watch-only wallet functionality.

$$pk' = pk \cdot g^{\texttt{parse256}(I_L)}$$

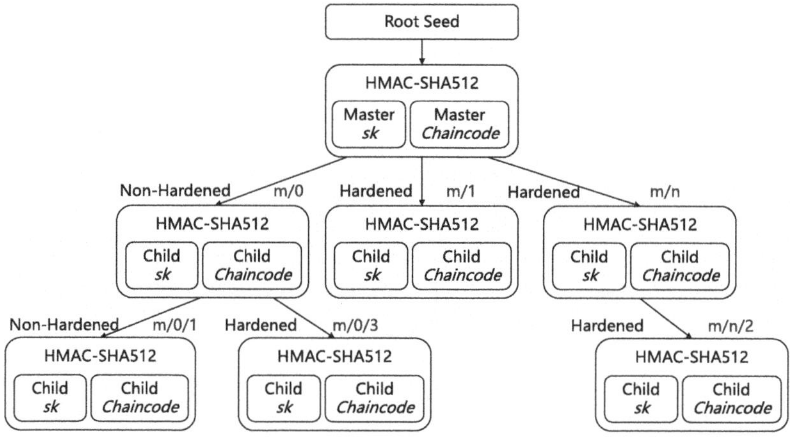

Fig. 1. Structure of an HD Wallet.

3 Our Secure FHD Wallet Solution

We describe our FHD wallet scheme in two parts. First, we propose a mnemonic updatable hierarchical deterministic wallet scheme, which enables updating the master random seed and mnemonic using a Chameleon hash function. Then, we further enhance the flexibility of the FHD wallet by allowing subkeys under a given key tree level to be self-derived via threshold mechanisms, even if the mnemonic has been forgotten.

3.1 Mnemonic Updatable

In this section, we introduce the concept of an HD wallet with an updatable mnemonic. Specifically, we enhance the flexibility of the master key derivation layer using a CDHP-based Chameleon hash function, which enables users to find hash collisions that produce the same output for a given random seed. This allows different mnemonic inputs to derive the same key tree.

Basic Construction. A mnemonic-updatable HD wallet scheme consists of the following algorithms:

- **Parameters Generation** ($\mathcal{PG}$): First, define a secure cryptographic hash function $H : \{0,1\}^* \rightarrow G^*$ with output length n. Let g be a generator of a Gap Diffie-Hellman group G of prime order q. Thus, the system parameters are $pp = \{G, q, g, H, n\}$.
- **Key Generation** ($\mathcal{KG}$): The user randomly selects a random seed sd and a secret key sk, where $sk \in \mathbb{Z}_q^*$ and $sd \in \mathbb{Z}_q^*$, then computes the public key $pk = g^{sk}$ and publishes it.
- **Master Key Derivation** ($\mathcal{MKD}$): Given the user's private key sk, public key pk, and random seed sd, randomly select an integer $r \in \mathbb{Z}_q^*$, and then computes $\mathcal{R} \leftarrow g^r, \mathcal{Y} \leftarrow pk^r$. We define the derived hash function as

$$\mathcal{CH} : h \leftarrow H(sd, \mathcal{R}, \mathcal{Y}) = g^{sd} \cdot \mathcal{Y} = g^{sd} \cdot pk^r \tag{1}$$

  where h is the hash output. Let $h[0 : n/2]$ and $h[n/2 : n]$ denote the first and second halves of h, respectively. Specifically, $h[0 : n/2]$ is used as the master chain code, and $h[n/2 : n]$ is used as the master private key.
- **Child Key Derivation** ($\mathcal{CKD}$): Given the parent chain code (or previous subchain code) cc_{i-1}, the parent private key (or previous subprivate key) sk_{i-1}, and an index value i, compute the hash value $h_{c,i} \leftarrow H(cc_{i-1} \parallel sk_{i-1} \parallel i)$.
  Here, $h_{c,i}[0 : n/2]$ is the subchain code cc_i, and $h_{c,i}[n/2 : n]$ is the subprivate key sk_i.

- **Seed Update** ($\mathcal{SU}$): For any valid hash value h, this algorithm can use trapdoor x to compute a hash collision:

$$\mathcal{SU}\,(x, sd, \mathcal{R}, \mathcal{Y}, sd') = (\mathcal{R}', \mathcal{Y}') \tag{2}$$

  where $\mathcal{R}' = \mathcal{R} \cdot g^{sk^{-1}(sd-sd')} = g^r \cdot g^{sk^{-1}(sd-sd')}$ and $\mathcal{Y}' = \mathcal{Y} \cdot g^{sd-sd'} = y^r \cdot g^{sd-sd'}$. A valid sd' satisfies $CH(sd', \mathcal{R}', \mathcal{Y}') = \mathcal{CH}(sd, \mathcal{R}, \mathcal{Y})$. Therefore, sd' is a valid random seed that produces the same hash value as sd.

Security Analysis. We analyze the security of the mnemonic-updatable HD wallet scheme from the following two theorems:

Theorem 1 (Collision Non-Malleability). *Let* $\mathcal{CH}(sd, \mathcal{R}, \mathcal{Y}) = g^{sd} \cdot pk^r$, *where* $(\mathcal{R}, \mathcal{Y}) = (g^r, pk^r)$ *and* $pk = g^{sk}$. *Then, under the Computational Diffie-Hellman (CDH) assumption, no probabilistic polynomial-time (PPT) adversary can generate* $(sd' \neq sd, \mathcal{R}', \mathcal{Y}')$ *such that*

$$\mathcal{CH}(sd', \mathcal{R}', \mathcal{Y}') = \mathcal{CH}(sd, \mathcal{R}, \mathcal{Y})$$

without knowing the trapdoor sk.

Proof. Suppose an adversary outputs $(sd', \mathcal{R}', \mathcal{Y}')$ such that:

$$g^{sd'} \cdot \mathcal{Y}' = g^{sd} \cdot pk^r \quad \Rightarrow \quad \mathcal{Y}' = g^{sd-sd'} \cdot pk^r$$

Assuming $\mathcal{R}' = g^{r'}$, we expect:

$$\mathcal{Y}' = pk^{r'} = g^{sk \cdot r'} \quad \Rightarrow \quad g^{sk \cdot r'} = g^{sd-sd'} \cdot g^{sk \cdot r} \Rightarrow g^{sk \cdot (r'-r)} = g^{sd-sd'}$$

Taking discrete logs:

$$sk \equiv \frac{sd - sd'}{r' - r} \pmod q$$

This contradicts the assumption that computing sk is infeasible. Hence, producing such a collision implies solving CDHP, which is hard in the assumed GDH group.

Theorem 2 (Forward Security). *Let the adversary learn* $h = \mathcal{CH}(sd, \mathcal{R}, \mathcal{Y}) = g^{sd} \cdot pk^r$ *and the derived master key (e.g., chain code and private key). Then, under the CDH assumption, the seed sd and trapdoor sk remain computationally hidden.*

Proof. From the adversary's view:

$$h = g^{sd} \cdot pk^r = g^{sd} \cdot g^{sk \cdot r} = g^{sd + sk \cdot r}$$

Without knowing sk or r, recovering sd from h reduces to solving:

$$\log_g(h \cdot \mathcal{Y}^{-1}) = sd$$

which is a discrete logarithm problem in G, assumed to be hard. Similarly, extracting sk from $pk = g^{sk}$ is also DLog-hard, and computing $g^{sk \cdot r}$ from (g, g^{sk}, g^r) is a CDHP instance. Thus, the adversary gains negligible advantages in learning sd or sk.

Proof. **Correctness.** By construction:

$$\mathcal{R}' = \mathcal{R} \cdot g^{sk^{-1}(sd-sd')}, \quad \mathcal{Y}' = \mathcal{Y} \cdot g^{sd-sd'}$$

Then:

$$\mathcal{CH}(sd', \mathcal{R}', \mathcal{Y}') = g^{sd'} \cdot \mathcal{Y}' = g^{sd'} \cdot g^{sd-sd'} \cdot \mathcal{Y} = g^{sd} \cdot \mathcal{Y} = h$$

Soundness. Suppose an adversary generates a valid $(sd^*, \mathcal{R}^*, \mathcal{Y}^*)$ such that:

$$\mathcal{CH}(sd^*, \mathcal{R}^*, \mathcal{Y}^*) = h = g^{sd} \cdot pk^r \Rightarrow \mathcal{Y}^* = g^{sd-sd^*} \cdot pk^r$$

Assuming $\mathcal{Y}^* = pk^{r^*} = g^{sk \cdot r^*}$, then:

$$g^{sk \cdot r^*} = g^{sd-sd^*} \cdot g^{sk \cdot r} \Rightarrow g^{sk(r^*-r)} = g^{sd-sd^*} \Rightarrow sk = \frac{sd - sd^*}{r^* - r} \mod q$$

Thus, forging such a valid tuple implies solving CDHP in G, contradicting the security assumption.

3.2 Threshold-Controlled Key Derivation

Next, we introduce a threshold-controlled key derivation scheme. Specifically, by employing Shamir's secret sharing, we allow any (t, n) deterministically derived subkeys to reconstruct the parent key tree's chain code collaboratively. Once the chain code of the key tree is obtained, the master key of that subtree gains self-governance. In other words, the subtree's master key can independently derive all keys within the subtree without relying on the root seed.

Basic Construction. A threshold-controlled key derivation scheme consists of the following algorithms:

- **Parameters Setup** ($\mathcal{PS}$): Define a threshold t and a total number of participants n. Let q be a sufficiently large prime and $\mathbb{F}_q$ the corresponding finite field such that $q > n$. The above serve as the public parameters pp.
- **Polynomial Generation** ($\mathcal{PLG}$): Given an index value i, a secret value s, and a random number θ, where $a \in \mathbb{F}_q$, a random polynomial $\mathcal{F}(x)$ is generated according to Eq. (3).

$$\mathcal{F}(x) = a + a_1 x + a_2 x^2 + ... + a_{t-1} x^{t-1} \tag{3}$$

where $a_0 = s$, $a_k = H(a_{k-1} \,\|\, i)$, and $k \in \{1, 2, \ldots, t-1\}$.
- **Threshold Child Key Derivation** ($\mathcal{TCKD}$): Given a key index j, parent private key sk_i, parent chain code cc_i, and polynomial $\mathcal{F}_i(x)$ with $\mathcal{F}_i(0) = cc_i$, the child private key $sk_{i+1,j}$ and child chain code $cc_{i+1,j}$ are derived according to Eq. (4)

$$\begin{aligned} h_{i+1,j} &= H(sk_i \,||\, g^{cc_i}) \\ cc_{i+1,j} &= \mathcal{F}_i(j) \\ sk_{i+1,j} &= h_{i+1,j}[n/2{:}n] \end{aligned} \tag{4}$$

- **Parent Chain Code Recovery** ($\mathcal{PCCR}$): For a key tree KT at level i, given at least t pairs of child private keys and chain codes $\{sk_{i+1,j}, cc_{i+1,j}\}_{j=0}^{j<t}$, compute g^{cc_i}, the encrypted chain code value of the key tree KT, through the following steps.

  First, each party computes its own Lagrange coefficient by Eq. (5).

$$\lambda_k = \prod_{\substack{1 \le m \le t \\ m \ne k}} \frac{-x_m}{x_k - x_m} \tag{5}$$

  Then, each party computes its recovery share as $share_k = g^{cc_{i+1,j}^k}$. All t parties send their respective share_j to the aggregator, who multiplies these results together by Eq. (6).

$$g^{cc_i} = \prod_{k=1}^{t} \left(g^{cc_{i+1,j}^k \cdot \lambda_k} \right) \tag{6}$$

  Thus, the encrypted chain code g^{cc_i} of the key tree KT can be recovered. According to Eq. (4), other child keys at this level can be derived without revealing each party's chain code.

Security Analysis. We analyze the security of the threshold-controlled wallet scheme from the following three theorems:

Theorem 3 (Correctness and Determinism). *Let $\mathcal{F}_i(x)$ be a degree-$t-1$ polynomial over $\mathbb{F}_q$ with constant term cc_i. Given any t valid evaluation points $\{x_j, cc_{i+1,j}\}_{j=1}^{t}$ where $cc_{i+1,j} = \mathcal{F}_i(x_j)$, the Lagrange interpolation over these points correctly reconstructs cc_i. Furthermore, the reconstruction of g^{cc_i} via Eq. (6) is deterministic and unambiguous.*

Proof. This is a direct consequence of the correctness of Shamir's secret sharing scheme.

Let $\mathcal{F}_i(x) = cc_i + a_1 x + \cdots + a_{t-1} x^{t-1}$, and let $\{(x_j, y_j)\}_{j=1}^{t}$ be t distinct evaluations with $y_j = \mathcal{F}_i(x_j)$. Lagrange interpolation guarantees that:

$$\mathcal{F}_i(0) = \sum_{j=1}^{t} \lambda_j \cdot y_j = cc_i$$

where λ_j are the standard Lagrange coefficients.

Now, consider the exponentiated shares $g^{y_j} = g^{cc_{i+1,j}}$ and the aggregated result:

$$g^{cc_i} = \prod_{j=1}^{t} (g^{cc_{i+1,j}})^{\lambda_j} = g^{\sum_{j=1}^{t} \lambda_j \cdot cc_{i+1,j}} = g^{cc_i}$$

Since exponentiation is injective in the group G and all operations are over a prime-order field $\mathbb{F}_q$, the result is deterministic and unique. Thus, the parent chain code can be uniquely and correctly recovered from any t valid child codes.

Theorem 4 (Threshold Privacy). *In the proposed threshold-controlled wallet construction, any coalition of fewer than t participants cannot gain any information about the parent chain code* cc_i *or its exponentiated value* g^{cc_i}*, except for what is already known from their own shares.*

Proof. According to Shamir's secret sharing scheme, the $t-1$ or fewer shares $\{cc_{i+1,j}\}$ are evaluations of a randomly constructed degree-$(t-1)$ polynomial $\mathcal{F}_i(x)$, whose constant term is cc_i.

For any $t-1$ shares, the set of possible cc_i values is uniform over $\mathbb{F}_q$, and thus the adversary learns nothing about cc_i beyond their own share.

Since exponentiation is a deterministic and injective mapping in the cyclic group G, the same property holds for g^{cc_i}, which remains information-theoretically hidden from any coalition of fewer than t participants.

Theorem 5 (Threshold Recoverability). *In the proposed scheme, given any* t *valid child chain code shares* $\{cc_{i+1,j}\}_{j=1}^{t}$ *corresponding to distinct indices, the parent chain code* cc_i *and its exponentiated form* g^{cc_i} *can be uniquely and correctly reconstructed by Lagrange interpolation and distributed exponentiation.*

Proof. By the correctness of Shamir's scheme, Lagrange interpolation with any t valid points $\{x_j, cc_{i+1,j}\}_{j=1}^{t}$ yields the unique polynomial $\mathcal{F}_i(x)$, whose constant term is $cc_i = \mathcal{F}_i(0)$.

By applying the same Lagrange coefficients in the exponent, we have:

$$g^{cc_i} = \prod_{j=1}^{t} (g^{cc_{i+1,j}})^{\lambda_j} = g^{\sum_{j=1}^{t} \lambda_j \cdot cc_{i+1,j}} = g^{cc_i}$$

Therefore, the parent chain code and its exponentiation are always uniquely and correctly recoverable by any set of t valid shares, as claimed.

3.3 Constructing FHD Wallet

In this section, we provide an overview of how our mnemonic updatable wallet scheme and threshold-controlled child key derivation (CKD) can be used to construct a hierarchical deterministic wallet instance. Our FHD wallet architecture is illustrated in Fig. 2. Next, we will construct and utilize our FHD wallet through the following steps.

Initialization. To set up the wallet, the user executes $\mathcal{PG}$ and $\mathcal{PS}$ to generate and publish the system parameters. The lengths of the hash function and finite field q are determined according to the NIST security level [1]. In general, we choose SHA512 as the PRF to ensure a 256-bit security level for output keys, and set the length of the finite field q to 512 bits. The user then samples a 256-bit random seed as the mnemonic using the $\mathcal{KG}$ method. Subsequently, the root node deterministically derives the hardened node using $\mathcal{MKD}$, resulting in the master key and master chain code. All non-root nodes are derived from the root node using the standard SHA512-based hardened derivation method. For each

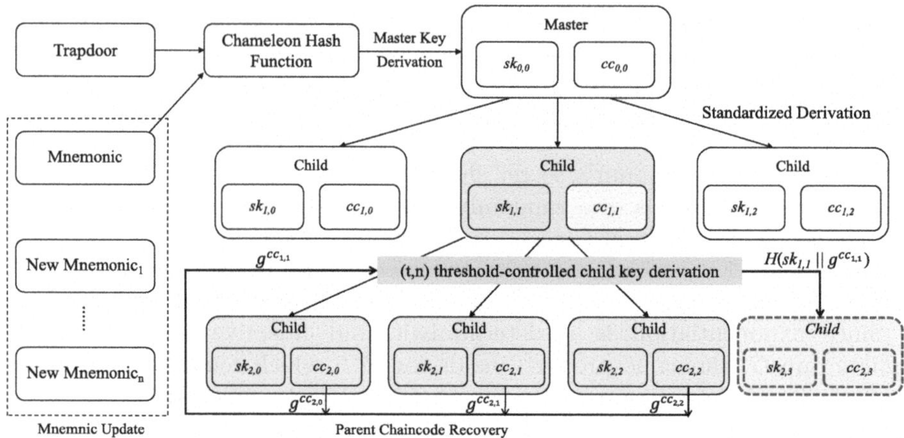

Fig. 2. The structure of our FHD wallet.

output hash, the upper 256 bits are used as the chain code and the lower 256 bits as the hardened private key.

Threshold Child Key Derivation. The user selects a threshold parameter t to recover the chain code, depending on the specific use case and security requirements. For example, for a multi-device personal wallet, using $t = 2$ and $n = 5$ may be sufficient, while enterprise wallets may require more devices, such as $t = 31$ and $n = 64$. In the next section, we demonstrate that our solution remains practically efficient even for such large parameters.

Subsequently, in an enterprise scenario, a department administrator designates the key tree rooted at the i-th node as an autonomously derivable subtree. During the derivation process, the algorithm executes $\mathcal{PLG}$ to generate a random polynomial $\mathcal{F}$. The administrator then runs the $\mathcal{TCKD}$ algorithm, inputting the private key and chain code cc_m, to generate a subkey and sub-chain code (sk_i, cc_i) for each department manager in the key tree. That is, each sub-chain code is a share of the polynomial $\mathcal{F}$. In the absence of the upper administrator, at least t department managers can jointly compute to reconstruct the administrator's chain code cc_m using their own chain code shares. Therefore, the derivation of keys for the subtree can be performed as long as at least t users collaborate.

Mnemonic Update. When initializing the wallet, the user generates a trapdoor x for the seed update algorithm using the $\mathcal{KG}$ algorithm. Subsequently, the user can derive and store keys using the $\mathcal{MKD}$ and $\mathcal{CKD}$ algorithms. When it is necessary to replace the mnemonic, the user executes the $\mathcal{SU}$ algorithm, randomly sampling a new seed and inputting the update trapdoor x, the old seed, and the public parameters $\mathcal{R}, \mathcal{Y}$ to generate new parameters $\mathcal{R}', \mathcal{Y}'$. At this point, the user inputs the new mnemonic and the derivation path into $\mathcal{MKD}$ to produce a key tree identical to the original one.

4 Evaluation

In this section, following the construction outlined above, we evaluate the properties and performance of the FHD wallet for hardened node derivation under a threshold setting. Specifically, we theoretically compare the FHD wallet based on Chameleon hash functions with BIP32 hardened node derivation and the BCTW-based [7] threshold derivation scheme. BIP32 is the canonical blockchain key derivation method, while the BTCW scheme is a BIP32-compatible distributed derivation protocol. Table 1 shows the theoretical comparison results.

Table 1. Comparison of HD wallets.

Scheme	Threshold Derivation	Mnemonic Updatable	Flexibility	Computation Overhead†
BIP32 [26]	No	No	No	$O(n)$
BCTW [7]	Yes	No	Yes	$O(t \cdot n)$
Ours	Yes	Yes	Yes	$O(t \cdot n)$

† denotes the overhead of deriving n parties' key.

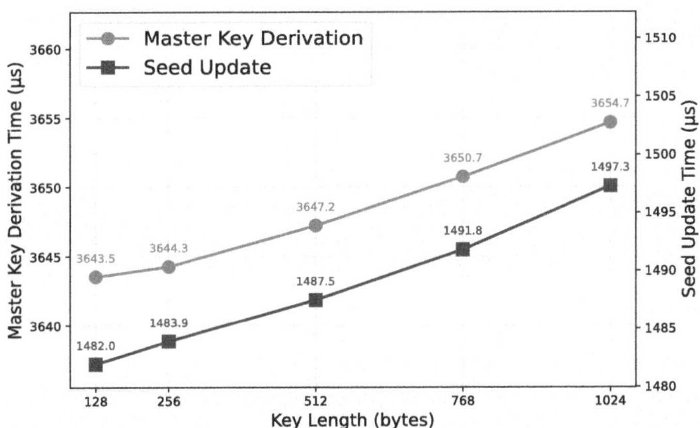

Fig. 3. The execution overhead of $\mathcal{MKD}$ and $\mathcal{SU}$ under different key lengths.

In addition, we implemented a proof of concept for our FHD wallet using Go 1.23 and evaluated the practical performance of wallet key derivation. The evaluation was conducted at the 256-bit security level, using SHA-512 as the standard hash function and the P-512 elliptic curve for the Chameleon hash implementation. All experiments were performed on a single machine equipped with an Intel(R) Xeon(R) Gold 6230 CPU at 2.10 GHz. We evaluated the scheme in terms of runtime cost for different parameters t and n, assuming the worst-case corruption of $t = n/2 - 1$. Each test was repeated 10,000 times, and the average was taken.

Table 2. Performance comparison of the CKD algorithms in FHD and BCTW.

(t, n)	Our $\mathcal{TCKD}$	TVRF [7]
(2, 5)	93	33584
(4, 10)	204	64652
(7, 16)	411	106987
(15, 32)	989	232976
(31, 64)	2893	510765

As shown in Fig. 3, the overhead of our FHD wallet master key derivation and mnemonic update increases slightly with the seed length, reaching approximately 3654 μs and 1497 μs, respectively. In Table 2, the cost of our child key derivation $\mathcal{TCKD}$ increases with the number of derivations, but even for enterprise wallet users with $n = 64$, the overhead is only 2893 μs. Compared to BCTW's TVRF-based derivation, our $\mathcal{TCKD}$ method reduces computational overhead by more than 99% across all parameter settings, with the reduction ratio ranging from 99.43% to 99.72%. This consistent efficiency advantage underscores the scalability and practicality of $\mathcal{TCKD}$.

5 Discussion

Our FHD wallet provides a unified framework for addressing two persistent challenges in wallet design: mnemonic updatable and collaborative child key derivation. By integrating chameleon hash-based mnemonic updates with threshold-controlled derivation, the scheme extends beyond the limitations of conventional seed-based wallets, enabling deployment in diverse practical settings where robustness and usability are both essential. The proposed threshold key derivation mechanism enables several high-impact applications:

- **Collaborative Asset Management.** In institutional custody and DAO treasuries, threshold derivation embeds governance rules directly into the key hierarchy. High-value operations, such as withdrawals or treasury allocations, require a quorum of designated participants, achieving stronger auditability and reducing reliance on external multisignature scripts.
- **Hierarchical Delegation and Recovery.** For enterprises and consortium chains, threshold-controlled subtrees enable local autonomy without exposing global secrets. The same mechanism ensures fault-tolerant recovery: as long as a quorum of child nodes remains intact, higher-level derivation can be securely restored.
- **Cross-Domain Interoperability.** In multi-chain environments, threshold derivation offers a unified cryptographic enforcement layer across heterogeneous ledgers, mitigating fragmented trust in cross-chain custodial services and ensuring consistent policy enforcement.

Collectively, these scenarios demonstrate how threshold-controlled derivation elevates hierarchical wallets into collaborative, governance-aware infrastructures, delivering stronger guarantees of compliance, resilience, and interoperability.

In deploying the threshold key-derivation mechanism, careful consideration must be given to the trade-offs between security, availability, and user experience. For a given subtree with n participants and threshold t, higher t values increase resistance to collusion but reduce the probability that enough participants are available when a key derivation is needed, while lower t values improve availability but may increase security risk.

Additionally, usability is affected by the operational complexity of mnemonic updates and threshold recovery. Practical deployment requires balancing the cognitive and procedural cost for users against the system's resilience to compromise, ensuring that both individual participants and organizations can manage keys effectively without excessive burden.

Performance and scalability also play a role in multi-party or cross-institutional scenarios: as the number of participants grows, communication and computation overhead increase, which must be accounted for when choosing threshold parameters and deployment architectures.

6 Conclusion

In this paper, we addressed the flexibility limitations inherent in deterministic wallets by proposing a novel concept of mnemonic updatability, leveraging Chameleon hash functions as the core of key derivation. This enables efficient seed updates via trapdoor-generated hash collisions. Building on this foundation, we further demonstrated that the hardened child key chain codes in deterministic wallets can be naturally utilized as threshold shares. Accordingly, we designed a threshold-autonomous derivation method applicable to any deterministic key tree, empowering subkeys to collaboratively recover parent chain code through secure multiparty computation, thereby enabling autonomous derivation at each layer. We analyzed that, under the CDH assumption, both the trapdoor for mnemonic updating and the parent chain code will never be compromised. Our theoretical analysis and experimental evaluation confirm that the proposed solution is both practical and effective, significantly enhancing the flexibility and security of deterministic wallets for real-world blockchain applications.

Acknowledgments. This paper is supported by the National Key R&D Program of China through project 2022YFB2702900, the Natural Science Foundation of China through projects U21A20467, U24B20144 and 62272464, the Zhejiang Provincial Natural Science Foundation LQN25F020032, and the Zhejiang Provincial Science and Technology Program Project 2025C01084.

References

1. Barker, E., Burr, W., Branstad, D., Smid, S.: Recommendation for key management – part 1: general. NIST Special Publication 800-57 Part 1 Revision 5, National Institute of Standards and Technology (2020). https://doi.org/10.6028/NIST.SP.800-57p1r2007
2. Bellare, M., Ristov, T.: A characterization of chameleon hash functions and new, efficient designs. J. Cryptol. **27**(4), 799–823 (2014). https://doi.org/10.1007/s00145-013-9155-8
3. Boneh, D., Partap, A., Rotem, L.: Traceable secret sharing: Strong security and efficient constructions. In: Annual International Cryptology Conference, pp. 221–256. Springer (2024). https://doi.org/10.1007/978-3-031-68388-6_9
4. Bonneau, J., Miller, A., Clark, J., Narayanan, A., Kroll, J.A., Felten, E.W.: SoK: research perspectives and challenges for bitcoin and cryptocurrencies. In: 2015 IEEE Symposium on Security and Privacy, pp. 104–121. IEEE (2015). https://doi.org/10.1109/SP.2015.14
5. Buterin, V.: Ethereum white paper: a next-generation smart contract and decentralized application platform (2013). https://ethereum.org/en/whitepaper
6. Chen, X., Zhang, F., Kim, K.: Chameleon hashing without key exposure. In: International Conference on Information Security, pp. 87–98. Springer (2004). https://doi.org/10.1007/978-3-540-30144-8_8
7. Das, P., et al.: Bip32-compatible threshold wallets. In: Proceedings of the 20th ACM Asia Conference on Computer and Communications Security, pp. 856–872 (2025). https://doi.org/10.1145/3708821.3710830
8. Das, P., Erwig, A., Faust, S., Loss, J., Riahi, S.: The exact security of BIP32 wallets. In: Proceedings of the 2021 ACM SIGSAC Conference on Computer and Communications Security, pp. 1020–1042 (2021). https://doi.org/10.1145/3460120.3484807
9. Das, P., Faust, S., Loss, J.: A formal treatment of deterministic wallets. In: Proceedings of the 2019 ACM SIGSAC Conference on Computer and Communications Security, pp. 651–668 (2019). https://doi.org/10.1145/3319535.3354236
10. Di Luzio, A., Francati, D., Ateniese, G.: Arcula: a secure hierarchical deterministic wallet for multi-asset blockchains. In: Cryptology and Network Security (CANS 2020), vol. 12579, pp. 323–343. Springer (2020). https://doi.org/10.1007/978-3-030-65411-5_16
11. Doerner, J., Kondi, Y., Lee, E., Shelat, A.: Threshold ECDSA in three rounds. In: 2024 IEEE Symposium on Security and Privacy (SP), pp. 3053–3071. IEEE (2024). https://doi.org/10.1109/SP54263.2024.00178
12. Eleshin, F., Sun, Q., Ye, M., Das, S., Hong, J.I.: Of secrets and seedphrases: conceptual misunderstandings and security challenges for seed phrase management among cryptocurrency users. In: Proceedings of the 2025 CHI Conference on Human Factors in Computing Systems, pp. 1–19 (2025). https://doi.org/10.1145/3706598.3713209
13. Gennaro, R., Goldfeder, S.: Fast multiparty threshold ECDSA with fast trustless setup. In: Proceedings of the 2018 ACM SIGSAC Conference on Computer and Communications Security, pp. 1179–1194 (2018). https://doi.org/10.1145/3243734.3243859
14. Groth, J., Shoup, V.: On the security of ECDSA with additive key derivation and presignatures. In: Annual International Conference on the Theory and Applications of Cryptographic Techniques, pp. 365–396. Springer (2022). https://doi.org/10.1007/978-3-031-06944-4_13

15. Guthoff, C., Anell, S., Hainzinger, J., Dabrowski, A., Krombholz, K.: Perceptions of distributed ledger technology key management-an interview study with finance professionals. In: 2023 IEEE Symposium on Security and Privacy (SP), pp. 588–605. IEEE (2023). https://doi.org/10.1109/SP46215.2023.10335652
16. Hanzlik, L., Loss, J., Wagner, B.: Token meets wallet: formalizing privacy and revocation for fido2. In: 2023 IEEE Symposium on Security and Privacy (SP), pp. 1491–1508. IEEE (2023). https://doi.org/10.1109/SP46215.2023.10179373
17. Houy, S., Schmid, P., Bartel, A.: Security aspects of cryptocurrency wallets–a systematic literature review. ACM Comput. Surv. **56**(1), 1–31 (2023). https://doi.org/10.1145/3596906
18. Krawczyk, H., Rabin, T.: Chameleon signatures. In: Proceedings of the Network and Distributed System Security Symposium (NDSS) 2000, pp. 143–154. Internet Society (2000). https://www.ndss-symposium.org/ndss2000/chameleon-signatures
19. Li, M., et al.: Tockowl: asynchronous consensus with fault and network adaptability. In: Proceedings of the 34th USENIX Conference on Security Symposium, pp. 4167–4186. USENIX Security 2025, USENIX Association, USA (2025). https://www.usenix.org/conference/usenixsecurity25/presentation/li-minghang
20. Lindell, Y., Nof, A.: Fast secure multiparty ECDSA with practical distributed key generation and applications to cryptocurrency custody. In: Proceedings of the 2018 ACM SIGSAC Conference on Computer and Communications Security, pp. 1837–1854 (2018). https://doi.org/10.1145/3243734.3243788
21. Mangipudi, E.V., Desai, U., Minaei, M., Mondal, M., Kate, A.: Uncovering impact of mental models towards adoption of multi-device crypto-wallets. In: Proceedings of the 2023 ACM SIGSAC Conference on Computer and Communications Security, pp. 3153–3167 (2023). https://doi.org/10.1145/3576915.3623218
22. Nakamoto, S.: Bitcoin: a peer-to-peer electronic cash system (2008). https://bitcoin.org/bitcoin.pdf
23. Palatinus, M., et al.: BIP-44: Multi-Account Hierarchy for Deterministic Wallets (2014). https://github.com/bitcoin/bips/blob/master/bip-0044.mediawiki
24. Shamir, A.: How to share a secret. Commun. ACM **22**(11), 612–613 (1979). https://doi.org/10.1145/359168.359176
25. Slush, et al.: BIP-39: mnemonic code for generating deterministic keys (2013). https://github.com/bitcoin/bips/blob/master/bip-0039.mediawiki
26. Wuille, P., et al.: BIP-32: hierarchical deterministic wallets (2012). https://github.com/bitcoin/bips/blob/master/bip-0032.mediawiki
27. Yi, X., Wu, D., Jiang, L., Fang, Y., Zhang, K., Zhang, W.: An empirical study of blockchain system vulnerabilities: modules, types, and patterns. In: Proceedings of the 30th ACM Joint European Software Engineering Conference and Symposium on the Foundations of Software Engineering, pp. 709–721. ESEC/FSE 2022, Association for Computing Machinery, New York, NY, USA (2022). https://doi.org/10.1145/3540250.3549105

28. Yin, X., Liu, Z., Yang, G., Chen, G., Zhu, H.: HDWSA^{2}2: a secure hierarchical deterministic wallet supporting stealth address and signature aggregation. IEEE Trans. Dependable Secure Comput. **22**(3), 2624–2641 (2025). https://doi.org/10.1109/TDSC.2024.3520828
29. Zhong, L., Wang, Y., Ding, Y., Du, J., He, K., Zhang, A.: Distributed key derivation for multi-party management of blockchain digital assets. In: 2023 IEEE 29th International Conference on Parallel and Distributed Systems (ICPADS), pp. 715–720. IEEE (2023). https://doi.org/10.1109/ICPADS60453.2023.00109
30. Zhou, L., et al.: SoK: decentralized finance (defi) attacks. In: 2023 IEEE Symposium on Security and Privacy (SP), pp. 2444–2461. IEEE (2023). https://doi.org/10.1109/SP46215.2023.10179435

One More Bit, Much More Security? Differential Fault Analysis on 5-Bit S-Box AEAD in Mobile and Ubiquitous Computing Devices

Yang Gao[1,2], Qingjun Yuan[1,2,3](✉), Xiangyu Wang[1,2], Wenqi He[1,2], Haojin Zhang[1,2], Haopeng Fan[1,2], and Yongjuan Wang[1,2](✉)

[1] Henan Key Laboratory of Network Cryptography Technology, University of Information Engineering, Zhengzhou, Henan, China
gcxyuan@outlook.com

[2] Key Laboratory of Cyberspace Security, Ministry of Education, Zhengzhou, Henan, China
pingkwyj@163.com

[3] MoE Key Lab for Intelligent Networks and Network Security, Xi'an Jiaotong University, Xi'an, Shaanxi, China

Abstract. The rapid growth of resource-constrained devices in mobile and ubiquitous computing demands cryptographic solutions that balance efficiency and security. Lightweight cryptography (LWC), such as the standardized cipher Ascon, is central to this goal, yet prior work has mainly examined 4-bit S-box ciphers while little is known about 5-bit designs. This study presents the first systematic differential fault analysis (DFA) of ciphers based on 5-bit S-boxes, including Ascon, SHAMASH, ISAP, and Sycon. Specifically, we demonstrate that the main key can be recovered using 64 stuck-at faults and approximately 264 random-nibble fault injections for Ascon. Similar attack complexity enables recovery of the session key in ISAP and the final-round state in Sycon, while roughly 257 5-bit faults suffice for SHAMASH. Our findings reveal that 5-bit S-box-based ciphers offer increased resistance to DFA, but remain vulnerable under targeted fault models. We further analyze the impact of nonce configurations, showing that nonce-respect scenarios require only 2.5 additional tag queries per S-box to emulate nonce-misuse attacks. Finally, we assess the practicality of our methods and propose countermeasures, offering actionable insights for hardening LWC deployments in realistic, ubiquitous computing environments. Codes and data are available at: https://github.com/VGD-AcE/EAI-MobiQuitous-2025.

Keywords: Ubiquitous computing · Internet of Things (IoT) · Lightweight cryptography (LWC) · Authenticated encryption with associated data (AEAD) · Differential fault analysis (DFA) · 5-bit S-box

L. Zhang and K.-K. R. Choo (Eds.): MobiQuitous 2025, LNICST 684, pp. 389–409, 2026.
https://doi.org/10.1007/978-3-032-22503-0_21

1 Introduction

The rapid proliferation of mobile and ubiquitous computing—spanning the Internet of Things (IoT), wireless sensor networks, wearable health monitors, and cyber-physical control systems—is transforming how users interact with technology and how devices collaborate in interconnected ecosystems. These environments often involve resource-constrained devices operating under tight limitations in computation, memory, and energy [1,2]. Such devices frequently handle sensitive data while engaging in real-time, multi-device interactions. To facilitate secure yet efficient communications for resource-limited systems, lightweight cryptography (LWC) has developed into a robust research frontier [3,4]. Recognizing its critical role, the National Institute of Standards and Technology (NIST) launched a standardization initiative, culminating in the 2023 selection of the Ascon authenticated encryption with associated data (AEAD) family as the new LWC standard [5]. A notable characteristic of Ascon—and of several other candidates such as ISAP [6], SHAMASH [7], and Sycon [8]—is the adoption of 5-bit S-boxes, replacing the traditional 4-bit designs seen in LWCs like PRESENT [9]. This shift reflects a carefully engineered trade-off: the aim is to achieve stronger cryptographic resistance while preserving implementability on severely resource-constrained platforms common in ubiquitous, mobile, and user-interactive ecosystems [10].

Given the increased complexity of these ciphers, understanding their theoretical and physical attack surface has become a pressing challenge. Many researchers have conducted security assessments on LWCs [11,12]. Among these, fault analysis is an effective technique for compromising cryptosystems by introducing hardware or software faults that disrupt or interfere with the system's operation [13]. However, most existing fault attack research focuses on relatively simple, smaller 4-bit S-boxes that are commonly used in traditional LWCs. In contrast, except for the current-standard Ascon algorithm, other AEAD algorithms that utilize 5-bit S-boxes remain largely unexplored in the context of fault attacks, leaving a critical gap in the literature. Specifically, the 5-bit S-box introduces a larger state space, making it significantly harder to analyze compared to the 4-bit S-boxes used in traditional lightweight ciphers. This added complexity leads to a higher number of possible fault injections and more intricate fault propagation trails, which in turn complicate fault attack strategies.

To address this gap, this study conducts a comprehensive differential fault analysis (DFA) on 5-bit S-box AEAD algorithms from the NIST LWC competition—including Ascon, SHAMASH, ISAP, and Sycon. Initially, we inject multiple random-xor faults into the 5-bit S-box. If the unique input value cannot be isolated, one of the bits of the S-box is fixed using stuck-at fault injection, while the remaining four bits are extracted and treated as a 4-bit S-box. This reduced representation is then analyzed within the context of traditional LWC. Subsequently, the complete intermediate state of all S-boxes is restored through the classic random-nibble fault injection. Critically, our methodology addresses both nonce-respect and nonce-misuse scenarios—reflecting deployment realities in mobile and human-interactive systems. By investigating fault injection techniques tailored to these ciphers, we aim to identify potential vulnerabilities and provide enhanced security analysis of AEAD systems for ubiquitous computing deployments. The specific contributions are as follows:

1. We provide a detailed introduction to a class of AEAD cryptographic primitives with 5-bit S-boxes that emerged in the LWC competition. For the Ascon, SHAMASH, ISAP, and Sycon algorithms, we propose a novel DFA method to restore the intermediate state of the S-box during the final permutation, enabling the recovery of either the main or session key.
2. We distinguish between and provide detailed explanations for the analysis methods applied to the two special cases of nonce-respect and nonce-misuse in AEAD algorithms. Our results show that the two cases are equivalent, requiring only a limited additional complexity step to guess the faulty tag.
3. We identify the optimal "stuck-at" positions for each algorithm and conduct simulated DFA experiments based on these positions. Experimental results indicate that ciphers with 5-bit S-boxes demand a greater number of fault injections to successfully recover the key than those with 4-bit S-boxes under similar fault models. This observation suggests that the 5-bit S-box exhibits enhanced DFA resistance compared to the 4-bit S-box.
4. We evaluate the practical feasibility of the proposed fault attack and discuss several countermeasures to mitigate the attack, including the use of alternative S-box designs that could replace those in the analyzed algorithms.

The remainder of this paper is organized as follows. Section 2 introduces the AEAD mode and the target cipher specifications. Section 3 discusses the impact of 4- and 5-bit S-box structures on DFA, with a focus on nonce configuration scenarios. Section 4 evaluates the effectiveness of DFA on four LWC competition candidates. Section 5 presents our simulation results. Section 6 reviews related work and discusses both the applicability of the proposed fault attack and possible countermeasures. Finally, Sect. 7 concludes the paper.

2 Background

2.1 AEAD Algorithm

AEAD schemes are essential for securing communication in mobile and ubiquitous systems, especially in resource-constrained IoT devices [14,15]. They combine symmetric encryption with authentication, while associated data (AD) are only authenticated, enabling protocols where headers must be verified but not encrypted [16]. If authentication fails, a failure tag is returned; otherwise, the plaintext is released, preventing chosen ciphertext attacks. The encryption and decryption functions are defined as follows:

$$\mathcal{E} : \{0,1\}^k \times \{0,1\}^v \times \{0,1\}^* \times \{0,1\}^* \rightarrow \{0,1\}^* \times \{0,1\}^t$$
$$\mathcal{D} : \{0,1\}^k \times \{0,1\}^v \times \{0,1\}^* \times \{0,1\}^* \times \{0,1\}^t \rightarrow \{0,1\}^* \cup \perp .$$

We set $k, v, t \geq 1$ and let $K \in \{0,1\}^k$, $N \in \{0,1\}^v$, $A \in \{0,1\}^*$, $P \in \{0,1\}^*$, $T \in \{0,1\}^t$, and $C \in \{0,1\}^*$ denote the key, nonce, AD, plaintext, verification tag, and ciphertext, respectively. The AEAD algorithm is a triplet $\Pi = (\mathcal{K}, \mathcal{E}, \mathcal{D})$, with a key generation algorithm $\mathcal{K}$ that returns a random K, encryption algorithm $\mathcal{E}_K(N, A, P)$, and decryption algorithm $\mathcal{D}_K(N, A, C, T)$. Here, $\mathcal{E}$ outputs a (C, T) pair and $\mathcal{D}$ outputs plaintext P or an invalid symbol $\perp$ (if the tag fails verification).

2.2 Ascon-128

The Ascon cipher is an AEAD algorithm based on a sponge duplex [17] structure. In Ascon, state S is 320 bits, with a rate $r = 64$ bits and capacity $c = 256$ bits. In encryption, the 320-bit sponge state is divided into five 64-bit words: X_0, X_1, X_2, X_3, and X_4, and $S = S_r||S_c = X_0||X_1||X_2||X_3||X_4$.

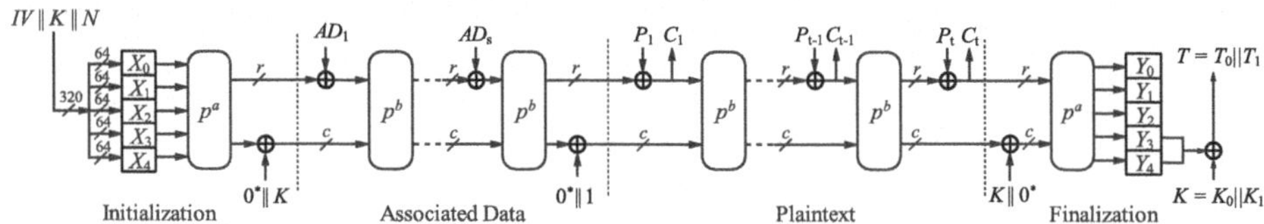

Fig. 1. Ascon structure.

As depicted in Fig. 1, the permutation p is the core Ascon element and has three sub-transformations: p_C, p_S, and p_L; i.e., $p = p_L \circ p_S \circ p_C$. p_S is a non-linear operation representing a substitution layer consisting of 64 5-bit S-boxes. Therefore, the input 5 bits of any $\mathrm{S}(x)$ are obtained from five 64-bit words X_0, X_1, X_2, X_3, X_4; that is, one bit is extracted from each word, where one bit from X_0 and one bit from X_4 act as the least significant bit (LSB) and the most significant bit (MSB), respectively, for the S-box input. The Ascon S-box is an affine equivalent of the Keccak S-box [18]. Table 1 lists the S-box values.

Table 1. 5-bit S-box in Ascon

x	0	1	2	3	4	5	6	7	8	9	10	11	12	13	14	15
$\mathrm{S}(x)$	4	11	31	20	26	21	9	2	27	5	8	18	29	3	6	28
x	16	17	18	19	20	21	22	23	24	25	26	27	28	29	30	31
$\mathrm{S}(x)$	30	19	7	14	0	13	17	24	16	12	1	25	22	10	15	23

For a detailed introduction to sub-transformations p_C and p_L, please refer to [19]. Finally, during the Finalization process, tags are generated by whitening the key:

$$T_0 = K_0 \oplus Y_3, T_1 = K_1 \oplus Y_4, T = T_0||T_1$$

2.3 SHAMASH

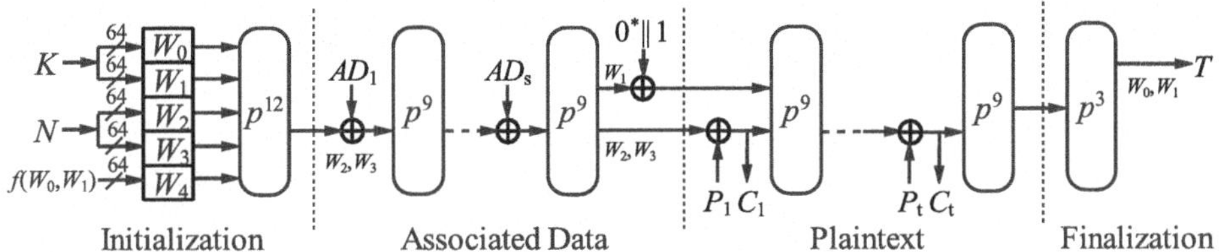

Fig. 2. SHAMASH structure.

As illustrated in Fig. 2, SHAMASH is another AEAD algorithm based on a sponge duplex structure. The internal state of the algorithm is 320 bits, which is described as consisting of five 64-bit words W_0, W_1, W_2, W_3, W_4. The 128-bit key K and the 128-bit nonce N are used as the input of the encryption initialization. The round function p consists of three parts, among which the S-box layer is defined as in Table 2.

Table 2. 5-bit S-box in SHAMASH

x	0	1	2	3	4	5	6	7	8	9	10	11	12	13	14	15
S(x)	16	14	13	2	11	17	21	30	7	24	18	28	26	1	12	6
x	16	17	18	19	20	21	22	23	24	25	26	27	28	29	30	31
S(x)	31	25	0	23	20	22	8	27	4	3	19	5	9	10	29	15

For a detailed introduction to the constant addition layer and diffusion layer, please refer to [7]. After the ciphertext is generated, W_0 and W_1 are output as tags in the finalization phase (without whitening key). Since K is only used in the Initialization process and is directly used as an intermediate state word in the calculation, state-recovery is equivalent to key-recovery.

2.4 ISAP-A-128A

Isap-A-128A is a sponge-based authentication encryption scheme with a key K of 128 bits, nonce N of 320 bits, and a rate r_H of 64 bits. It uses the same round function p as the Ascon algorithm. The following Fig. 3 is a flowchart for verifying the generated tag.

For details regarding the round function, refer to the description of Ascon above. Specifically, in the finalization phase of the ISAP algorithm, the tag T is generated by the upper 128 bits of the 320-bit intermediate state of the last round, which is completely different from Ascon using the lower 128 bits to

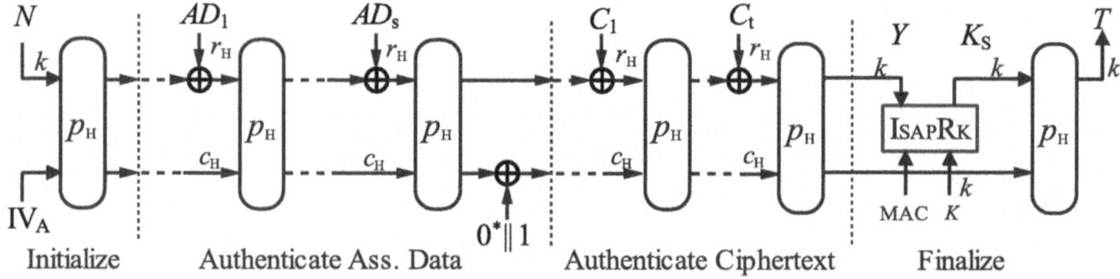

Fig. 3. ISAP structure.

generate T. In addition, it is also important to note that the re-keying component $\text{I}_{\text{SAP}}\text{R}_{\text{K}}$ is introduced in the finalization phase. This component is irreversible in algorithm design, resulting in the inability to recover the main key K if the attacker manages to obtain the session key K_S.

2.5 Sycon-AEAD-64

The Sycon algorithm uses the MonkeyDuplex sponge mode [20] to implement the authentication encryption function. It consists of a 128-bit key K, a 128-bit nonce N, and a 64-bit IV cascade to form a 320-bit initial state and a 64-bit rate word. The encryption and tag generation process is shown in Fig. 4.

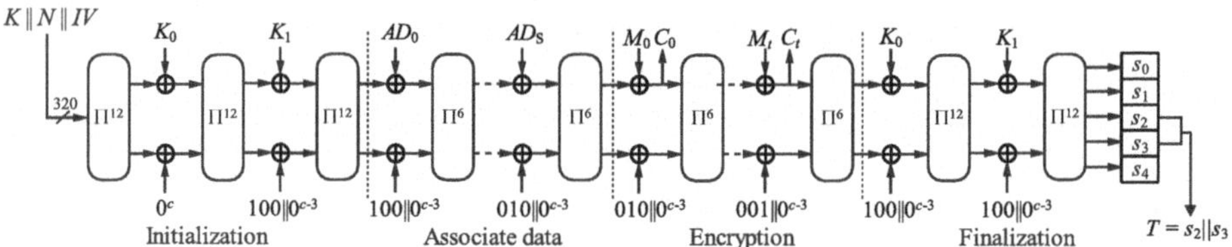

Fig. 4. Sycon structure.

The round function R of the Sycon permutation consists of three different transformation sequences: S-Box (SB), SubBlockDiffusion (SD), and AddRoundConst (RC), which is $R = RC \circ SD \circ SB$. The ρ-round permutation, denoted as Π^ρ, is constructed as:

$$\Pi^\rho = \underbrace{R \circ \cdots \circ R}_{\rho \text{ times}}$$

SB is as follows in Table 3:

For a detailed introduction to SD and RC, please refer to [8]. After the encryption or decryption algorithm is completed, it enters the finalization phase and outputs a 128-bit tag. In this phase, the key is reabsorbed into the state through two permutation calls, utilizing the rate. Given a state

Table 3. 5-bit S-box in Sycon

x	0	1	2	3	4	5	6	7	8	9	10	11	12	13	14	15
S(x)	8	19	30	7	6	25	16	13	11	15	3	24	17	12	4	27
x	16	17	18	19	20	21	22	23	24	25	26	27	28	29	30	31
S(x)	11	0	29	20	1	14	23	26	28	21	9	2	31	18	10	5

$s = s_4||s_3||s_2||s_1||s_0$, the tag extraction function (denoted as ExtTag(s)) extracts the tag from the state by concatenating the contents of s_2 and s_3, that is, ExtTag(s)$= s_2||s_3$.

3 Changes in DFA in the New Computing Landscape

DFA [21] is a powerful cryptanalytic technique that has been widely used to evaluate traditional lightweight ciphers such as LBlock [22], PRESENT [23], and MIBS [24]. By inducing faults during the execution of a cipher and analyzing the differences between correct and faulty outputs, DFA enables attackers to recover internal states and ultimately extract secret keys.

In resource-constrained and highly interconnected environments—such as IoT deployments, edge networks, and mobile platforms—DFA must adapt to new structural and practical realities. One major development arises from the structural evolution of LWCs. To improve security margins without compromising efficiency, many modern AEAD schemes now adopt 5-bit S-boxes in place of the 4-bit variants traditionally used in earlier lightweight designs. This transition reflects an ongoing effort to strengthen resistance to fault attacks while maintaining implementability on constrained hardware, especially in environments where cryptographic operations are tightly coupled with real-time responsiveness and limited power budgets.

Simultaneously, the proliferation of human-machine interfaces and the decentralization of system architectures have introduced new avenues for attack, particularly in relation to nonce management. In practice, nonce misuse—arising from software misconfigurations or user-side errors—has become increasingly common [25]. Such misuse weakens the security guarantees of AEAD schemes and introduces additional opportunities for DFA in scenarios that deviate from idealized cryptographic models.

The shifts in algorithm design and real-world deployment together reshape the landscape of fault analysis. In the following sections, we analyze how these trends influence both the feasibility and methodology of DFA, and we propose new strategies for attacking and evaluating AEAD ciphers that employ 5-bit S-boxes in modern ubiquitous computing environments.

3.1 4-Bit vs. 5-Bit S-Boxes

DFA has long been an effective cryptanalytic technique for evaluating lightweight ciphers. Traditional LWC designs such as PRESENT, LBlock, and TWINE commonly employ 4-bit S-boxes to balance efficiency with minimal resource consumption. These small S-boxes, while hardware-friendly, are often less robust in terms of differential uniformity and nonlinearity—properties that directly influence the cipher's resistance to fault-based attacks. As a result, DFA strategies for 4-bit S-box ciphers are well understood and highly effective.

A typical DFA method on a 4-bit S-box cipher proceeds by injecting a random nibble fault into the input of the last one to three rounds of the cipher. Because the S-box structure is small and its differential distribution table is limited in scope, the attacker can often solve a set of simple equations of the form $\mathrm{S}(m) \oplus \mathrm{S}(m \oplus \alpha) = \beta$ to deduce the actual S-box input m. By repeating this process across multiple faulty ciphertexts, the attacker can recover sufficient internal state information to infer the main key K.

However, this approach becomes significantly more complex with the emergence of new-generation LWCs such as Ascon, SHAMASH, and Sycon, which adopt 5-bit S-boxes as a core design element. These larger S-boxes substantially expand the input space (from 16 to 32 values), increase the nonlinearity, and disrupt the statistical predictability of differential propagation. Consequently, fault injection into a 5-bit S-box rarely yields differential equations with unique or even manageable solutions. This impairs the attacker's ability to identify exact S-box inputs based on output differences, even when multiple faults are injected.

Additionally, the output observable to the attacker is often limited to a truncated intermediate state used to compute the authentication tag, further constraining the effectiveness of fault analysis. Unlike 4-bit designs where intermediate rounds or full ciphertext may be directly useful, the 5-bit S-box-based AEAD schemes often expose only partial internal values at the finalization step—reducing the amount of exploitable information available to the attacker.

In summary, while the shift to 5-bit S-boxes enhances cryptographic robustness and reflects a necessary evolution for deployment in increasingly constrained environments, it also introduces new challenges for DFA—particularly in terms of analytical complexity, state observability, and the uniqueness of fault propagation patterns.

3.2 Nonce-Misuse vs. Nonce-Respect Scenarios

In theory, AEAD schemes are designed to operate under a nonce-respect scenario, where each encryption invocation uses a unique, non-repeating nonce to ensure cryptographic correctness and security. However, this assumption is frequently violated in ubiquitous computing environments. Due to interface misconfigurations, incomplete protocol integration, firmware limitations, or user-induced errors, nonces may be inadvertently reused, creating nonce-misuse scenarios. Such misuse introduces new and powerful attack vectors, particularly for fault-based cryptanalysis such as DFA [26].

Nonce-Misuse: In this scenario, the attacker is able to obtain both the ciphertext and tag for the same plaintext, key, nonce, and AD. Specifically, in the finalization phase, prior to generating the tag, the internal state of the cipher will be identical during two executions with the same inputs. As a result, the attacker can inject faults into the repeated encryption operation and gather multiple faulty tag values.

Nonce-Respect: In this scenario, the attacker cannot observe the correct and incorrect outputs of the same input. However, the AEAD algorithm requires that the nonce be the same during the decryption process as it was during the corresponding encryption. If the nonce differs, tag verification will fail. Thus, encryption and decryption pairs can be viewed as natural replays with a fixed nonce. Consequently, we focus on injecting faults during the decryption phase, which can be repeated. Specifically, injecting faults in the finalization stage of decryption will change the tag, which is recorded as T^*. When T^* is inconsistent with the tag T obtained when there is no fault injection during the encryption process, it will cause the verification to fail. Our goal is to change the input during decryption to $K \times N \times AD \times C \times T^*$ to pass the verification and obtain the output difference $\beta = T \oplus T^*$.

Based on the preceding analysis, once the correct faulty tag T^* is guessed, the corresponding differential equation can be derived. From that point onward, the attack process in the nonce-respect scenario becomes identical to that in the nonce-misuse scenario. Moreover, since $\beta = T \oplus T^*$ and the correct tag T is known, guessing T^* is effectively equivalent to guessing β. As introduced in Sect. 2, all target AEAD ciphers generate the final 128-bit tag T by concatenating two 64-bit intermediate state words during the finalization phase. Therefore, considering the case of a single S-box injecting a nibble fault, there are four possible output differences, namely $\beta' = \{00, 01, 10, 11\}$. According to statistical analysis under the "*sampling without replacement*" model, when the probabilities of the four possible outcomes are equal, the expected number of T^* guesses needed to recover the correct β' for a single S-box is

$$E_{Guess} = 1 \cdot \frac{1}{4} + 2 \cdot \frac{3}{4} \cdot \frac{1}{3} + 3 \cdot \frac{3}{4} \cdot \frac{2}{3} \cdot \frac{1}{2} + 4 \cdot \frac{3}{4} \cdot \frac{2}{3} \cdot \frac{1}{2} \cdot 1 = 2.5.$$

Therefore, for a single S-box, tag verification can be passed with an additional 2.5 guesses of faulty tags during decryption. This means that the restriction that nonce cannot be reused in the nonce-respect scenario is lifted, aligning it with the nonce-misuse scenario in the proposed fault model. For convenience, we will proceed with the nonce-misuse assumption in the following discussion.

4 DFA of Candidates with 5-Bit S-Boxes in LWC Competition

Our primary objective is to recover the key K of the target algorithm through a limited number of (as few as possible) fault injections. The key K is typically incorporated into different stages and structures across various algorithms. For example, in the Ascon algorithm, the whitening key operation is introduced during the finalization phase, while SHAMASH integrates K in the Initialization stage, and ISAP introduces K in the special component $\mathrm{I_{SAP}R_K}$ function. However, since K cannot be recovered directly regardless of its placement in the algorithm, attackers must instead target intermediate states—making these points critical for successful key recovery. Given that the S-box is the sole nonlinear component in this class of AEAD algorithm, fault injections can be strategically applied to the inputs of the S-boxes. By analyzing the resulting output tag, it is possible to deduce the input to the S-box and, subsequently, to reconstruct the intermediate state before it passes through the S-box layer. The attack conditions and specific assumptions in our analysis are summarized as follows:

- In the nonce-misuse scenario, an attacker can repeatedly restart the cryptographic device and encrypt the same plaintext with the same parameters (AD, nonce).
- In the nonce-respect scenario, an attacker can repeatedly restart the cryptographic device but cannot encrypt the same plaintext with the same parameters (AD, nonce). However, the attacker can decrypt the corresponding ciphertext using the same parameters (AD, nonce) as in an encryption request and verify its tag.
- In both scenarios, an attacker can repeatedly inject stuck-at and 5(4)-bit random-XOR faults at any position in the final round of permutation during the finalization stage, with the random fault values following a uniform distribution.

4.1 Key Recovery Attack on Ascon

Based on the previous analysis, we consider injecting faults into the S-box input of the last round of p permutation in the finalization phase. As the last nonlinear transformation of the entire Ascon algorithm, this will produce unknown differences in the output of the S-box. From the differential diffusion criterion of cryptographic algorithms, nonlinear components alter difference values, whereas linear components primarily propagate and replicate difference values [27]. Consequently, these differences maintain linearity following p_L and XOR operations with the key, manifesting as differences in the output tag T of the entire Ascon algorithm. In the DFA implementation, a correct tag and several faulty tags are generated the discrepancies between these tags can be mapped to S-box output differences using inverse linear transformation. Assuming correct Ascon encryption execution, the resulting tag is given by:

$$T = (K_0 \oplus Y_3)||(K_1 \oplus Y_4) = (K_0 \oplus \Sigma_3(X_3))||(K_1 \oplus \Sigma_4(X_4)).$$

After fault injection at the S-box input in the final round of p during Finalization, the tag becomes:

$$T^* = (K_0 \oplus Y_3^*)||(K_1 \oplus Y_4^*) = (K_0 \oplus \Sigma_3(X_3^*))||(K_1 \oplus \Sigma_4(X_4^*)).$$

Note that $X_3(X_3^*)$ and $X_4(X_4^*)$ correspond to the second-lowest and lowest 64-bit correct(faulty) words in the intermediate state, respectively. More specifically, the LSB and second LSB of the 5-bit XOR values of the correct and faulty outputs of each of the 64 S-boxes before and after fault injection are discernable. This information, combined with an appropriate fault model, enables deduction of the S-box layer input and subsequent acquisition of X_3 and X_4.

A natural analysis of the 5-bit S-box differential distribution table reveals certain properties; however, these properties are insufficient for recovering the 128-bit key. Therefore, we explore strategic manipulation to transform the 5-bit S-box into a 4-bit S*-box, as such a transformation could potentially expose differential distribution properties similar to those observed for other classic LWCs. According to the characteristics of the Ascon algorithm, after the attacker injects a fault into a single S-box in the last round of finalization, only β', the last two bits of the output difference, can be obtained after fault injections during the final S-box layer of finalization. Consequently, it is necessary to transform the classical differential equation $\mathrm{S}^*(m) \oplus \mathrm{S}^*(m \oplus \alpha) = \beta$ to $\mathrm{S}^*(m) \oplus \mathrm{S}^*(m \oplus \alpha) = \beta'$, where $\beta' = \beta \bmod 4$. That is, only four possibilities exist for β': $\{00, 01, 10, 11\}$.

Next, we examine how to process the 5-bit S-box to achieve the most effective analysis. Our objective is to determine the input value with as few fault injections as possible. In other words, we hope that the best case is to obtain the unique S-box input value m after two fault injections. Here, we introduce the following definition.

Let $\alpha_1 \rightarrow \alpha_2 \rightarrow \cdots \rightarrow \alpha_n$ represent the fault injection sequence, where the first injection is α_1, the second is α_2, etc., until α_n. The set $\langle \alpha_1 \rightarrow \alpha_2 \rightarrow \cdots \rightarrow \alpha_n \rangle$ denotes the possible input values of S*-box under this condition. We define $|\langle \alpha_1 \rightarrow \alpha_2 \rightarrow \cdots \rightarrow \alpha_n \rangle|$ as the cardinality of this set, i.e., the number of possible S-box input values under the given fault injection sequence. When a unique input value m is obtained, we have $|\langle \alpha_1 \rightarrow \alpha_2 \rightarrow \cdots \rightarrow \alpha_n \rangle| = 1$. As discussed earlier, for the original 5-bit S-box there exists $\min\{|\langle \alpha_i \rightarrow \alpha_j \rangle|\} = 2, 0 \leq \alpha_i, \alpha_j \leq 31$, implying that a unique S-box input cannot be derived using only two fault injections. To address this limitation, we turn our attention to the transformed 4-bit S*-boxes. Since each of the 5 bits can be forced to 0 or 1, there are $2 \times 5 = 10$ possible stuck-at configurations to consider in the reduced setting.

Table 4 demonstrates significant variance in the importance of the five-bit positions within the Ascon S-box for a successful differential analysis. Here, the classification is based on $\min\{|\langle \alpha_i \rightarrow \alpha_j \rangle|\}$.

$$\min\{|\langle \alpha_i \rightarrow \alpha_j \rangle|\} = \begin{cases} 4, & \textsf{bad position} \\ 2, & \textsf{moderate position} \\ 1, & \textsf{good position} \end{cases}$$

From the perspective of the attacker, the most significant bit (MSB) x_0 and the second MSB x_1 are bad positions. In contrast, the least significant bit (LSB) x_4 and second LSB x_3 are moderate positions. Only one possible good position can be determined, i.e., the S-box middle (3rd) bit, x_2. Here, $\min\{|\langle \alpha_i \rightarrow \alpha_j \rangle|\} = 1$,

Table 4. 10 possible S*-boxes under different stuck-at faults in Ascon.

Stuck-at fault	The corresponding output when the remaining 4-bit input of the S-box is 0 to 15	$\min\{\lvert\langle\alpha_i \to \alpha_j\rangle\rvert\}$
x_4 stuck-at-0	4,31,26,9,27,8,29,6,30,7,0,17,16,1,22,15	2
x_4 stuck-at-1	11,20,21,2,5,18,3,28,19,14,13,24,12,25,10,23	2
x_3 stuck-at-0	4,11,26,21,27,5,29,3,30,19,0,13,16,12,22,10	2
x_3 stuck-at-1	31,20,9,2,8,18,6,28,7,14,17,24,1,25,15,23	2
x_2 stuck-at-0	4,11,31,20,27,5,8,18,30,19,7,14,16,12,1,25	1
x_2 stuck-at-1	26,21,9,2,29,3,6,28,0,13,17,24,22,10,15,23	1
x_1 stuck-at-0	4,11,31,20,26,21,9,2,30,19,7,14,0,13,17,24	4
x_1 stuck-at-1	27,5,8,18,29,3,6,28,16,12,1,25,22,10,15,23	4
x_0 stuck-at-0	4,11,31,20,26,21,9,2,27,5,8,18,29,3,6,28	4
x_0 stuck-at-1	30,19,7,14,0,13,17,24,16,12,1,25,22,10,15,23	4

suggesting that the S*-box input can be conclusively determined by at least two fault injections. Furthermore, $\min\{\lvert\langle\alpha_i \to \alpha_j\rangle\rvert\} = 1$ in both stuck-at-0 and stuck-at-1 faults. The program confirms that the differential distribution tables for both fault models are identical, as shown in Table 5.

The above analysis demonstrates that after performing the stuck-at operation on the middle bit of the original S-box of the Ascon algorithm, at least two random-nibble fault injections are sufficient to recover the S-box input value. Once the 5-bit S-box input value is obtained, the algorithm proceeds to derive the two 64-bit words X_3 and X_4 output by the 64 S-boxes, followed by the finalization results of the two 64-bit words Y_3 and Y_4. Subsequently, Y_3 and Y_4 are XORed with the two tag words T_0 and T_1, respectively, to recover the two 64-bit keywords.

$$T = T_0 || T_1, K_0 = Y_3 \oplus T_0, K_1 = Y_4 \oplus T_1$$

4.2 Key Recovery Attack on SHAMASH

The analysis of the S-box of the SHAMASH algorithm is relatively straightforward. For a full 5-bit S-box, although there is $\min\{\lvert\langle\alpha_i \to \alpha_j\rangle\rvert\} = 2, 0 \leq \alpha_i, \alpha_j \leq 31$, that is, it is impossible to recover the unique S-box input value with just two fault injections. However, there exists $\min\{\lvert\langle\alpha_i \to \alpha_j \to \alpha_k\rangle\rvert\} = 1, 0 \leq \alpha_i, \alpha_j, \alpha_k \leq 31$, which means that at least three fault injections are required to find the unique input value. Furthermore, according to the program results, regardless of the specific 5-bit S-box input value, the number of fault injection sequences $\alpha_i \to \alpha_j \to \alpha_k$ that successfully recover the unique input value after three injections is always 14816. This implies that the probability of a single S-box recovering the input value after three fault injections is $14816/32^3 = 45.21\%$.

Table 5. Differential distribution table of S^* after stuck-at fault injection in x_2.

α	$\beta' = 00$	$\beta' = 01$	$\beta' = 10$	$\beta' = 11$
0	0,1,2,3,4,5, 6,7,8,9,10,11, 12,13,14,15	-	-	-
1	12,13,14,15	8,9,10,11	4,5,6,7	0,1,2,3
2	-	8,9,10,11, 12,13,14,15	-	0,1,2,3, 4,5,6,7
3	0,1,2,3, 8,9,10,11	4,5,6,7, 12,13,14,15	-	-
4	-	-	1,3,5,7, 8,10,12,14	0,2,4,6, 9,11,13,15
5	1,3,4,6	0,2,5,7	8,10,13,15	9,11,12,14
6	0,2,4,6	1,3,5,7	9,11,13,15	8,10,12,14
7	-	-	0,2,5,7, 9,11,12,14	1,3,4,6, 8,10,13,15
8	1,2,9,10	5,6,13,14	0,3,8,11	4,7,12,15
9	-	1,2,5,6, 8,11,12,15	-	0,3,4,7, 9,10,13,14
10	5,6,12,15	1,2,8,11	4,7,13,14	0,3,9,10
11	1,2,5,6, 9,10,13,14	-	0,3,4,7, 8,11,12,15	-
12	0,7,11,12	3,4,8,15	2,5,9,14	1,6,10,13
13	0,4,9,13	3,7,10,14	2,6,11,15	1,5,8,12
14	3,4,10,13	0,7,9,14	1,6,8,15	2,5,11,12
15	3,7,8,12	0,4,11,15	1,5,10,14	2,6,9,13

According to the algorithm introduction in the previous section, K is only used in the Initialization process, and K is directly used as an intermediate state word in the calculation. Therefore, after recovering the S-box input value, the encryption process of the reverse algorithm can be applied to directly recover the 128-bit K.

4.3 Session Key Recovery Attack on ISAP

The 5-bit S-box of ISAP is identical to that of Ascon, meaning that regardless of how many times a 5-bit fault is injected, the differential equation $S(m) \oplus S(m \oplus \alpha) = \beta$ cannot obtain a unique input value m. The difference between the two lies in the process of generating tags. For the ISAP algorithm, the final tag is the result of cascading the high (rather than low) two-bit output by 64 S-boxes after linear transformation. That is, for the differential equation $S^*(m) \oplus S^*(m \oplus \alpha) = \beta$, at this time $\beta' = \beta \gg 3 \ mod \ 4$, so the differential distribution table of the 4-bit S-box obtained after applying a stuck-at fault at different positions has also changed completely, and we have Table 6:

Table 6. The number of possible S*-box input values obtained after two fault injections under different stuck-at models in ISAP.

Stuck-at fault (St)	St-x_4	St-x_3	St-x_2	St-x_1	St-x_0
$\min\{\lvert\langle\alpha_i \to \alpha_j\rangle\rvert\}$	1	2	2	4	1

This table shows that there are two good positions, specifically the LSB and the MSB. After injecting stuck-at faults at these positions, the S-box input value can be recovered by injecting random-nibble faults into the remaining four bits. After recovering the 64 S-box input values of the last round, because there is no whitening key operation in the finalization phase, the output K_S of the $\mathrm{I_{SAP}R_K}$ component can only be obtained by reversing the round function p_H. As per the algorithm description, the design of the $\mathrm{I_{SAP}R_K}$ component makes it difficult to reverse the $\mathrm{I_{SAP}R_K}$ input $K||IV$ from the session key K_S. Therefore, this attack can only recover the session key K_S by obtaining the intermediate state from the cipher's final round. Additional auxiliary means are required to recover the main key K from the session key K_S, such as the leakage of $Y_i \sim Y_w$ in the Re-keying phase of the $\mathrm{I_{SAP}R_K}$ component.

4.4 Intermediate State Recovery Attack on Sycon

In the Sycon cipher, similar to previous cases, no matter how many times 5-bit faults are injected, the differential equation $\mathrm{S}(m) \oplus \mathrm{S}(m \oplus \alpha) = \beta$ cannot obtain a unique input value m. According to the algorithm details introduced above, Sycon takes the 64-bit words X_2 and X_3 output by finalization as tags, so for the differential equation $\mathrm{S}^*(m) \oplus \mathrm{S}^*(m \oplus \alpha) = \beta'$, there is $\beta' = \beta \gg 1 \; mod \; 4$ at this time. Therefore, by fixing one bit, the 5-bit S-box can be transformed into a 4-bit S*-box, resulting in the following cases.

Table 7. The number of possible S*-box input values obtained after two fault injections under different stuck-at models in Sycon.

Stuck-at fault (St)	St-x_4	St-x_3	St-x_2	St-x_1	St-x_0
$\min\{\lvert\langle\alpha_i \to \alpha_j\rangle\rvert\}$	1	1	4	1	1

Table 7 shows that, except for the middle bit x_2, the other four positions are all good positions. After injecting stuck-at faults at these positions, injecting random-nibble faults at the remaining 4 bits can restore the S-box input value. Because the finalization process requires the unknown 64-bit subkeys K_0 and K_1

as input, this attack can only recover the 320-bit intermediate state after K_1 is involved in the operation, but it cannot restore the key K. However, recovering the full intermediate state still poses a significant security threat, as it may enable key inference, ciphertext forgery, or facilitate other advanced attacks.

5 Experiment

To evaluate the proposed 5-bit S-box AEAD ciphers, experiments were conducted on a workstation equipped with an Intel Core i7-1260P processor (2.1GHz), 16GB RAM, and a 64-bit operating system. Software development was performed using Microsoft Visual Studio 2022 with Visual C++, and Wolfram Mathematica version 12.1 was utilized for auxiliary computations. All source codes and experimental data are publicly available at: https://github.com/VGD-AcE/EAI-MobiQuitous-2025.

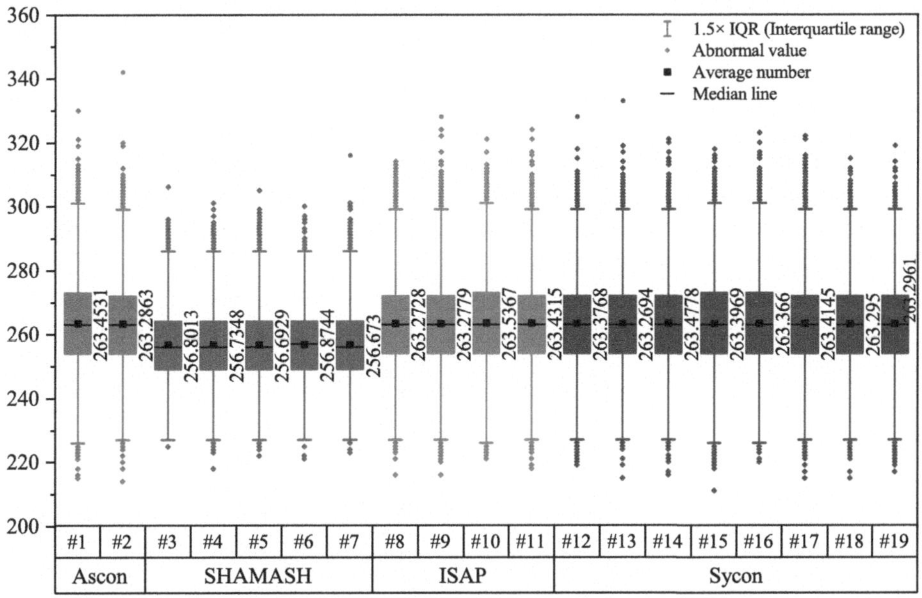

Fig. 5. Fault injection number of recovering 64 S-boxes in 19 groups of experiments.

For Ascon (experiments #1 ∼ #2), ISAP (experiments #8 ∼ #11), and Sycon (experiments #12 ∼ #19), we employed a similar fault injection approach. Specifically, we respectively introduced "stuck-at-0" and "stuck-at-1" faults at multiple good positions within the algorithm. These good positions refer to carefully selected points in the internal state of the algorithm, chosen to help filter unique S-box input values, as shown in Sect. 4. After injecting these stuck-at faults, we further simulated fault conditions by injecting random-nibble faults at the remaining 4-bit positions.

For SHAMASH (experiments #3 $\sim$ #7), there was no need to pre-set stuck-at faults at specific positions. Instead, we conducted five independent sets of experiments, each involving the direct injection of a 5-bit random-xor fault model into the algorithm.

For each fault injection model, we set up an independent experimental set, ensuring that we could observe how each cipher responds to different types of fault conditions. Each experimental set contained 10,000 attack trials. The results of these experiments, including the detailed statistical characteristics of the different algorithms under various fault conditions, are depicted in Fig. 5.

6 Discussion

6.1 Comparison of Ciphers with 4-Bit and 5-Bit S-Boxes on DFA

Table 8 summarizes DFA results for AEAD algorithms compared with traditional LWCs. As shown in this table, both the theoretical and practical numbers of fault injection for the 4-bit S-box ciphers are in the dozens (no more than 100), while the theoretical numbers of fault injection for the 5-bit S-box ciphers are 192, with the practical fault injection number exceeding 200. Additionally, only Ascon and SHAMASH can fully recover the main key K, whereas ISAP can only recover the session key, and Sycon can only recover the intermediate state. This clearly indicates that the DFA resistance of the 5-bit S-box AEAD algorithm is stronger than that of the 4-bit S-box LWCs.

Table 8. Comparison of ciphers with 4-bit and 5-bit S-boxes on DFA

S-box type	Ciphers	Theoretical numbers of fault injection	Practical numbers of fault injection	Computational complexity
4-bit S-box	TWINE [28]	**48** 4-bit random fault	**72.08** on average	$\sim$
	LBlock [28]	**48** 4-bit random fault	**67.36** on average	$\sim$
	MIBS [24]	**12** 4-bit random fault	**15.48** on average	2^2
	PRESENT [29]	**32** 4-bit random fault	**>32**	$2^{10.94}$
	GIFT [29]	**64** 4-bit random fault	**87**	$2^{11.91}$
5-bit S-box	Ascon (Proposed attack)	**64** stuck-at + **128** 4-bit random fault	**264**	$\sim$
	SHAMASH (Proposed attack)	**192** 5-bit random fault	**257**	$\sim$
	ISAP (Proposed attack)	**64** stuck-at + **128** 4-bit random fault	**264**	Session key recovery only
	Sycon (Proposed attack)	**64** stuck-at + **128** 4-bit random fault	**264**	Intermediate state recovery only

For most traditional LWCs with 4-bit S-boxes (e.g., PRESENT), the differential equations generally yield a unique solution after at least two fault injections. Consequently, the number of fault injections required to recover the key is relatively low. However, compared to the 4-bit S-box, a 5-bit S-box offers a significantly larger state space and higher nonlinearity. These characteristics make it much harder to derive a unique solution to the differential equations, thereby providing a higher level of resistance against DFA. As a result, algorithms employing 5-bit S-boxes typically require more fault injections (e.g., SHAMASH) or the integration of additional fault injection techniques (e.g., Ascon) to execute successful DFA. This explains why AEAD algorithms with 5-bit S-boxes exhibit significantly higher security against DFA compared to traditional LWCs with 4-bit S-boxes.

6.2 Fault Model Feasibility and Practicality

This subsection examines key considerations related to the adopted fault models, emphasizing their feasibility and associated implementation challenges.

The stuck-at fault injection model assumes that attackers can force the value of a single bit or a 64-bit word to be 0 or 1. Practical experiments conducted by Roscian et al. [30] on the random access memory (RAM) of a microcontroller demonstrated successful induction of stuck-at faults using a laser beam. Piscitelli et al. [31] observed a higher occurrence rate stuck-at fault compared to that of bit-flip faults. Although costly equipment is required for laser-induced malfunctions, Skorobogatov [32] demonstrated that stuck-at faults can be precisely injected in terms of both location and timing [33].

The random-nibble fault injection model assumes that faults can be injected at nibble granularity. Agoyan et al. [34] confirmed that random faults of nibble granularity are practically achievable using traditional fault injection techniques such as clock glitches. Kumar et al. [35] and Breier et al. [36] reported that nibble fault injection is notably easier than single-bit fault injection for laser-induced faults because of the laser beam diameter and spot size. In other words, the latter process demands greater control and precision. Additionally, Kumar et al. [37] proposed that hardware Trojans can be used to inject random-nibble faults into the application-specific integrated circuit (ASIC) implementation of the PRINCE cipher. Patranabis et al. [38] combined random-nibble fault injection with side-channel analysis and conducted practical experiments on the PRESENT and GIFT algorithms.

In contrast, for the practical implementation of the attack, the random-nibble fault can be regarded as four bit-flips injected simultaneously. Therefore, the feasibility of simultaneously injecting multiple faults must be explored. Colombier et al. [39] presented a new four-spot laser fault injection setup to inject four simultaneous, non-contiguous faults. Nishiyama et al. [40] demonstrated that when using intentional electromagnetic interference fault injection of continuous sinusoidal waves, the occurrence rate of one(multi)-bit fault can be adjusted by controlling the frequency, phase, and amplitude of the injected sinusoidal wave.

6.3 Countermeasures

In mobile and ubiquitous computing environments, devices are not only resource-constrained but also physically accessible and widely distributed. These characteristics significantly increase the practicality and feasibility of fault injection attacks, underscoring the need for robust countermeasures that remain lightweight yet effective in real-world deployments.

Error randomization involves introducing supplementary operations on the cipher to randomize fault-injection-induced errors, thereby preventing the leakage of valuable information about the data-dependent fault distribution to potential attackers. The AES infection countermeasure, proposed in [41] and evaluated in [42], serves as an illustrative example. For the 5-bit S-box, the faulty tag randomization approach can be employed directly through fault space transformation.

Another countermeasure is algorithm enhancement. Specifically, the 5-bit S-box can be redesigned so that no matter which bit is targeted with a stuck-at fault, no fault injection sequence can filter the unique S-box input. This can be achieved while preserving all essential cryptographic properties of the original S-box, including algebraic degree, differential uniformity, nonlinearity, and the number of linear and differential branches. For example, in the case of the Ascon algorithm, the modified 5-bit S-box [43] is shown in Table 9.

Table 9. Improved 5-bit S-box with DFA resistance in Ascon.

x	0	1	2	3	4	5	6	7	8	9	10	11	12	13	14	15
S(x)	4	25	31	6	26	7	9	16	27	5	8	18	15	17	20	14
x	16	17	18	19	20	21	22	23	24	25	26	27	28	29	30	31
S(x)	30	19	21	28	0	13	3	10	2	12	1	11	22	24	29	23

7 Conclusion

The proliferation of mobile and ubiquitous computing platforms—ranging from IoT devices to edge systems and wearables—has made AEAD a foundational security primitive in these resource-constrained environments. Motivated by this need, and by the LWC competition which explicitly emphasizes resistance to "side-channel and fault attacks" [44], this study presents the first comprehensive DFA method of AEAD candidates employing 5-bit S-boxes—a structural evolution from traditional 4-bit designs intended to enhance lightweight security.

Our analysis demonstrates that using specific fault injection strategies, the main key of Ascon can be recovered with approximately 64 stuck-at faults and 264 random-nibble faults. Similar strategies allow the session key of ISAP to be retrieved and the final-round intermediate state of Sycon to be exposed. In contrast, SHAMASH requires only around 257 5-bit faults for full key recovery, without stuck-at fault injection. Importantly, our attack model remains applicable across both nonce-respect and nonce-misuse settings, with the latter particularly relevant in ubiquitous environments where interface misconfigurations and user errors are common.

Furthermore, we show that LWCs employing 5-bit S-boxes exhibit significantly stronger resistance to DFA compared to traditional 4-bit designs, thereby offering enhanced security for IoT devices operating in constrained environments. To further improve DFA resilience in real-world implementations, we also propose practical countermeasures, including error randomization and S-box redesign.

Looking forward, we aim to generalize our analysis to broader classes of AEAD algorithms, including those not built on 5-bit S-boxes, and evaluate their performance under realistic deployment scenarios involving physical access and imperfect configurations. These efforts support the development of security solutions that are both lightweight and robust for future ubiquitous computing environments.

References

1. Liu, F., et al.: Gearing resource-poor mobile devices with powerful clouds: architectures, challenges, and applications. IEEE Wireless Commun. **20**(3), 14–22 (2013)
2. Li, X., Feng, G., Sun, Y., Qin, Y., Yang, R.: A unified framework for joint sensing and communication in resource constrained mobile edge networks. IEEE Trans. Mob. Comput. **22**(10), 5643–5656 (2022)
3. Mohd, B.J., Hayajneh, T., Vasilakos, A.V.: A survey on lightweight block ciphers for low-resource devices: comparative study and open issues. J. Netw. Comput. Appl. **58**, 73–93 (2015)
4. Pandey, S., Bhushan, B.: Recent lightweight cryptography (LWC) based security advances for resource-constrained IoT networks. Wirel. Netw. **30**(4), 2987–3026 (2024)
5. NIST: Lightweight Cryptography Standardization Process: NIST Selects Ascon. https://csrc.nist.gov/News/2023/lightweight-cryptography-nist-selectsascon. Accessed 2023
6. Dobraunig, C., Eichlseder, M., Mangard, S., Mendel, F., Unterluggauer, T.: ISAP–towards side-channel secure authenticated encryption. IACR Trans. Symmetric Cryptol. 80–105 (2017)
7. NIST: Shamash (and shamashash) (version 1). https://csrc.nist.gov/CSRC/media/Projects/LightweightCryptography/documents/round-1/specdoc/ShamashAndShamashash-spec.pdf. Accessed 2019
8. Mandal, K., Saha, D., Sarkar, S., Todo, Y.: Sycon: a new milestone in designing ASCON-like permutations. J. Cryptogr. Eng. **12**(3), 305–327 (2022)
9. Bogdanov, A., et al.: PRESENT: an ultra-lightweight block cipher. In: CHES 2007. LNCS, vol. 4727, pp. 450–466. Springer, Vienna (2007)
10. Radhakrishnan, I., Jadon, S., Honnavalli, P.B.: Efficiency and security evaluation of lightweight cryptographic algorithms for resource-constrained IoT devices. Sensors **24**(12), 4008 (2024)

11. Zhang, F., Guo, S., Zhao, X., Li, C., Wang, Y.: A framework for the analysis and evaluation of algebraic fault attacks on lightweight block ciphers. IEEE Trans. Inf. Forensics Secur. **11**(5), 1039–1054 (2016)
12. Hatzivasilis, G., Fysarakis, K., Papaefstathiou, I., Manifavas, C.: A review of lightweight block ciphers. J. Cryptogr. Eng. **8**, 141–184 (2018)
13. Giraud, C., Thiebeauld, H.: A survey on fault attacks. In: CARDIS 2004, IFIP, pp. 159–176. Springer, Toulouse (2004)
14. Tu, S., Badshah, A., Alasmary, H., Alotaibi, E., Gumaei, A.: EAKE-WC: efficient and anonymous authenticated key exchange scheme for wearable computing. IEEE Trans. Mob. Comput. **23**(5), 4752–4763 (2023)
15. Athanasiou, G.S., Boufeas, D., Konstantopoulou, E.: A robust ASCON cryptographic coprocessor for secure IoT applications. In: 2024 Panhellenic Conference on Electronics & Telecommunications (PACET), pp. 1–6. IEEE (2024)
16. Rogaway, P.: Authenticated-encryption with associated-data. In: Proceedings of the 9th ACM Conference on Computer and Communications Security, pp. 98–107 (2002)
17. Bertoni, G., Daemen, J., Peeters, M., Van Assche, G.: Cryptographic sponge functions. Technical Report, Citeseer (2011)
18. Kermani, M.M., Jalali, A., Azarderakhsh, R., Xie, J., Choo, K.-K.R.: Reliable inversion in GF(2^8) with redundant arithmetic for secure error detection of cryptographic architectures. IEEE Trans. Comput.-Aided Des. Integr. Circ. Syst. **37**(3), 696–704 (2017)
19. Dobraunig, C., Eichlseder, M., Mendel, F., Schläffer, M.: Ascon v1.2: lightweight authenticated encryption and hashing. J. Cryptol. **34**(3), 33 (2021)
20. Bertoni, G., Daemen, J., Peeters, M., Van Assche, G.: Permutation-based encryption, authentication and authenticated encryption. Directions in Authenticated Ciphers, pp. 159–170 (2012)
21. Biham, E., Shamir, A.: Differential fault analysis of secret key cryptosystems. In: CRYPTO'97, LNCS, vol. 1294, pp. 513–525. Springer, Heidelberg (1997)
22. Zhao, L., Nishide, T., Sakurai, K.: Differential fault analysis of full LBlock. In: International Workshop on Constructive Side-Channel Analysis and Secure Design (COSADE), LNCS, vol. 7275, pp. 135–150. Springer, Heidelberg (2012)
23. Bagheri, N., Ebrahimpour, R., Ghaedi, N.: New differential fault analysis on PRESENT. EURASIP J. Adv. Signal Process. **2013**, 1–10 (2013)
24. Gao, Y., Wang, Y., Yuan, Q., Wang, T., Wang, X.: Probabilistic analysis of differential fault attack on MIBS. IEICE Trans. Inf. Syst. **102-D**(2), 299–306 (2019)
25. Adomnicăi, A., Minematsu, K., Shikata, J.: Lightweight yet nonce-misuse secure authenticated encryption for very short inputs. IEEE Internet Things J. (2024)
26. Khairallah, M., Bhasin, S., Chattopadhyay, A.: On misuse of nonce-misuse resistance: Adapting differential fault attacks on (few) CAESAR winners. In: 2019 IEEE 8th International Workshop on Advances in Sensors and Interfaces (IWASI), pp. 189–193. IEEE (2019)
27. Heys, H.M.: A tutorial on linear and differential cryptanalysis. Cryptologia **26**(3), 189–221 (2002)
28. Gao, Y., Wang, Y., Yuan, Q., Wang, T., Wang, X.: Improvement of differential fault attack based on lightweight ciphers with GFN structure. In: Sun, X., Pan, Z., Bertino, E. (eds.) ICAIS 2019, LNCS, vol. 11633, pp. 549–560. Springer, New York (2019)
29. Luo, H., Chen, W., Ming, X., Wu, Y.: General differential fault attack on PRESENT and GIFT cipher with nibble. IEEE Access **9**, 37697–37706 (2021)

30. Roscian, C., Sarafianos, A., Dutertre, J.-M., Tria, A.: Fault model analysis of laser-induced faults in SRAM memory cells. In: 2013 Workshop on Fault Diagnosis and Tolerance in Cryptography (FDTC), pp. 89–98. IEEE (2013)
31. Piscitelli, R., Bhasin, S., Regazzoni, F.: Fault Attacks, Injection Techniques and Tools for Simulation. Springer, Cham (2017)
32. Skorobogatov, S.: Optical fault masking attacks. In: 2010 Workshop on Fault Diagnosis and Tolerance in Cryptography (FDTC), pp. 23–29. IEEE (2010)
33. Barenghi, A., Breveglieri, L., Koren, I., Naccache, D.: Fault injection attacks on cryptographic devices: theory, practice, and countermeasures. Proc. IEEE **100**(11), 3056–3076 (2012)
34. Agoyan, M., Dutertre, J.-M., Naccache, D., Robisson, B., Tria, A.: When clocks fail: on critical paths and clock faults. In: International Conference on Smart Card Research and Advanced Applications, pp. 182–193. Springer (2010)
35. Kumar, R., Jovanovic, P., Polian, I.: Precise fault-injections using voltage and temperature manipulation for differential cryptanalysis. In: 2014 IEEE 20th International On-Line Testing Symposium (IOLTS), pp. 43–48. IEEE (2014)
36. Breier, J., He, W., Jap, D., Bhasin, S., Chattopadhyay, A.: Attacks in reality: the limits of concurrent error detection codes against laser fault injection. J. Hardware Syst. Secur. **1**, 298–310 (2017)
37. Kumar, R., Jovanovic, P., Burleson, W., Polian, I.: Parametric Trojans for fault-injection attacks on cryptographic hardware. In: 2014 Workshop on Fault Diagnosis and Tolerance in Cryptography (FDTC), pp. 18–28. IEEE (2014)
38. Patranabis, S., Datta, N., Jap, D., Breier, J., Bhasin, S., Mukhopadhyay, D.: SCADFA: combined SCA+ DFA attacks on block ciphers with practical validations. IEEE Trans. Comput. **68**(10), 1498–1510 (2019)
39. Colombier, B., et al.: Multi-spot laser fault injection setup: new possibilities for fault injection attacks. In: International Conference on Smart Card Research and Advanced Applications, pp. 151–166. Springer (2021)
40. Nishiyama, H., Fujimoto, D., Kim, Y., Sone, H., Hayashi, Y.-I.: IEMI fault injection method using continuous sinusoidal wave with controlled frequency, amplitude, and phase. In: 13th International Workshop on Electromagnetic Compatibility of Integrated Circuits (EMC Compo), pp. 97–101. IEEE (2022)
41. Tupsamudre, H., Bisht, S., Mukhopadhyay, D.: Destroying fault invariant with randomization: a countermeasure for AES against differential fault attacks. In: CHES 2014, LNCS, vol. 8731, pp. 93–111. Springer, Busan (2014)
42. Patranabis, S., Chakraborty, A., Mukhopadhyay, D.: Fault tolerant infective countermeasure for AES. J. Hardware Syst. Secur. **1**, 3–17 (2017)
43. Joshi, P., Mazumdar, B.: SSFA: subset fault analysis of ASCON-128 authenticated cipher. Microelectron. Reliab. **123**, 114155 (2021)
44. McKay, K., Bassham, L., Sönmez Turan, M., Mouha, N.: Report on lightweight cryptography (NISTIR 8114, Draft). National Institute of Standards and Technology (2016)

A Blockchain-Assisted Outsourced Signcryption Scheme for Fine-Grained VSN Data Sharing System

Siyuan Chen(✉) and Yi Rong

School of Computer Science and Technology, Shanghai University of Electric Power, Shanghai, China
siyuanchen1900@shiep.edu.cn, ashsmoke@mail.shiep.edu.cn

Abstract. Vehicular Social Network (VSN), as an extension of the Internetof Vehicles, enhance communication and user experience. However, the deployment of VSN introduces critical security vulnerabilities, including data privacy leakage and forgery attacks. To address these risks, attribute-based signcryption emerges as a widely recognized solution. Nevertheless, prior work imposes high computational overhead and lacks verifiable lightweight performance. This paper presents a new secure and efficient data-sharing system for VSN, leveraging blockchain-assisted Attribute-Based Signcryption. Our scheme attains dual optimization: computation lightness by outsourcing intensive operations, and communication compactness through constant-size ciphertexts of only 5 group elements, overcoming critical efficiency limitations in VSN data sharing. To eliminate single points of failure, our scheme utilizes consortium blockchain to achieve decentralized key distribution with multi-authority in VSN. Security analysis demonstrates that our scheme satisfies IND-CCA2 and EUF-CMA security requirements. Experimental results demonstrate the efficiency advantagment: requiring only 8 exponentiations for signcryption and 1 for decryption locally, and reducing ciphertext size by approximately 60–80% compared to attribute-linear schemes, achieving signcryption times of 15 ms and decryption times of 3 ms for 100 attributes.

Keywords: Vehicular Social Networks · Signcryption Scheme · Consortium Blockchain · Attribute-based Encryption

1 Introduction

Vehicular Social Networks (VSNs), which integrate Internet of Vehicles technologies with social networking concepts, offer a foundation for real-time communication between vehicles and infrastructure, thus improving traffic efficiency and user experience [7]. Figure 1 illustrates a typical VSN scenario, showing the communication between different entities. With the growing adoption of electric vehicles and in-vehicle intelligence, the proliferation of multimedia devices,

L. Zhang and K.-K. R. Choo (Eds.): MobiQuitous 2025, LNICST 684, pp. 410–425, 2026.
https://doi.org/10.1007/978-3-032-22503-0_22

expandable interfaces, and integrated sensor technologies has brought data sharing and privacy protection in VSN to the forefront. With the increasing demand for intelligent vehicular services, the contradiction between service richness and data privacy has become more pronounced. In VSN, data exchange involves not only vehicle status but also sensitive user information, raising serious privacy and security concerns. To address this, various cryptographic techniques have been explored. Due to its fine-grained access policies, ABE is particularly effective for ensuring secure data sharing in dynamic VSN scenarios. However, many ABE-based schemes lack proper identity authentication for data providers, hindering data integrity and authenticity verification. Consequently, signcryption schemes combining ABE with digital signatures have been widely adopted to meet both access control and authentication requirements. Zhang et al. [16] improved a framework based on attributes by integrating a group signature while preserving their anonymity. Although such designs satisfy security demands in VSN, the limited storage and computational resources of the On-Board Unit (OBU) necessitate more lightweight and efficient solutions. Therefore, a practical vehicular social network should aim to meet the following design objectives.

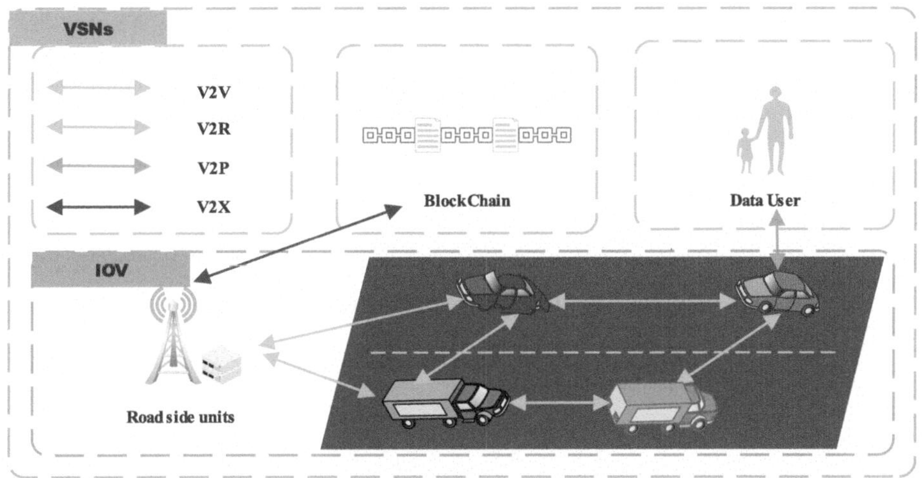

Fig. 1. Application scenarios

An attribute based data sharing solution should adopt a distributed architecture, avoiding reliance on a single authority that may become a performance bottleneck or point of failure under high demand. Decentralization enhances fault tolerance, security, and flexibility by distributing control and reducing the risk of misuse or data leakage. Meanwhile, a lightweight design is essential in vehicular social networks to meet real time communication needs. By offloading computation and storage to the cloud, resource constrained devices can reduce local overhead, lower latency, and improve efficiency. Simplified protocols further enhance adaptability to dynamic environments while conserving bandwidth and ensuring security.

In response to the aforementioned limitations, we propose a blockchain-enhanced data-sharing framework for vehicular social networks, built upon KP-ABSC. The core advantages of our approach are outlined below.

1. **Lightweight Computation:** In our scheme, some computations are outsourced to nearby RSU, reducing the burden on resource-constrained devices. Data owners only need to perform eight exponentiation operations for signcryption, while data users require just one exponentiation operation for decryption.
2. **Constant Ciphertext Size:** The ciphertext length remains constant regardless of the number of attributes, containing only five group elements, which helps reduce communication overhead.
3. **Distributed key distribution:** We combine a consortium blockchain with multiple authorities for the distribution of attribute key, where multiple consortium nodes replace a single authority. This reduces the difficulty of key management and avoids system bottlenecks.

The remainder of this paper is organized as follows. Section 2 and Sect. 3 review related work and preliminaries, respectively. Section 4 presents the system and security models. Section 5 describes the proposed data-sharing scheme. Section 6 analyzes its performance, and Sect. 7 concludes the paper.

2 Related Work

Table 1. Functionality Comparison of Attribute-Based Schemes

Scheme	Access Structure	Outsource	Constant-size Ciphertext	Multi-Authority	Blockchain
[1]	And-Gate	✓	×	×	×
[3]	LSSS/Access Tree	✓	×	×	×
[8]	LSSS	✓	×	×	×
[16]	LSSS	✓	×	✓	✓
[12]	LSSS	✓	×	✓	✓
Ours	LSSS	✓	✓	✓	✓

A variety of schemes have been introduced to address vehicle privacy leakage in data sharing scenarios, as discussed in [1,16,17], and [3]. Attribute-based encryption can prevent privacy leakage of vehicle users and provide access control. However,a single ABE [4] cannot provide authentication for data. The authenticity of data can be ensured using attribute-based signatures, which validate whether the associated attributes fulfill the defined access structure. Combining ABE and ABS logically to achieve attribute-based signcryption offers better computational efficiency compared to directly combining ABE and ABS (Table 1).

In order to reduce communication costs, Rao et al. [9] proposed a constant-size ciphertext data sharing scheme. Subsequently, [5,10,11,14,17], made improvements based on the ideas of this scheme. The related research work on lightweight, no system bottlenecks in VSN data sharing schemes is summarized below. As a commonly adopted approach, outsourced computation reduces local computational overhead and enhances efficiency by delegating intensive tasks to external servers [15]. Huo et al. [6] introduced a blockchain-based outsourcing scheme featuring fairness, security, verifiability, and scalability. Their design partitions tasks into multiple subtasks and supports batch verification, with results recorded on-chain. To overcome the drawback that most outsourced ABE schemes merely check the correctness of the cloud's decryption without deterring false accusations from mobile devices. Chen et al. [2] developed a revocable and verifiable outsourced decryption framework based on smart contracts. In attribute-based data sharing schemes for Vehicular Social Networks, all existing solutions adopt outsourced computation to reduce local load. However, their schemes do not take into account the ciphertext length, resulting in a considerable communication cost. Zhang et al. [16] presented a key distribution scheme based on consortium blockchain to replace the multi-authority approach, but it cannot provide verification of ciphertexts.

3 Preliminaries

3.1 Bilinear Maps

Let $\mathbb{G}$ and $\mathbb{G}_T$ be two multiplicative cyclic groups of prime order p, and g is the generator of $\mathbb{G}$. A bilinear pairing is a function $e : \mathbb{G} \times \mathbb{G} \rightarrow \mathbb{G}_T$ that satisfies:

1. Bilinearity: $\forall g_1, g_2 \in \mathbb{G}$, $a, b \in \mathbb{Z}_p$, it holds that $e(g_1^a, g_2^b) = e(g_1, g_2)^{ab}$.
2. Non-degeneracy: $\exists g_1, g_2 \in \mathbb{G}$ such that $e(g_1, g_2) \neq 1$.
3. Computability: The value $e(g_1, g_2)$ is computable.

3.2 Linear Secret Sharing Scheme

A secret sharing scheme Γ defined over a set of parties $\mathcal{P}$ is said to be linear:

1. Each share is represented as a vector over the finite field $\mathbb{Z}_p$.
2. Exists a matrix $\mathbb{M}$ of dimension $l \times n$, where each row x is associated with a party through a function $\rho : \{1, \ldots, l\} \rightarrow \mathcal{P}$.
3. To share a secret $s \in \mathbb{Z}_p$, the dealer chooses a random vector $v = (s, r_2, \ldots, r_n)^T$ and computes the share vector $\mathbb{M}v$. The x-th component of this vector corresponds to the share given to party $\rho(x)$.

3.3 D-Cover-Free Family

A d-cover-free family (denoted as d-CFF) $\mathcal{F} = (S, \mathcal{B})$ consists of an element set S of size m and a collection $\mathcal{B}$ of n subsets of S, where $d < m < n$. The family satisfies the property that, for any d distinct subsets $B_{i_1}, \ldots, B_{i_d} \in \mathcal{B}$ and any other subset $B \in \mathcal{B} \setminus \{B_{i_1}, \ldots, B_{i_d}\}$, the following condition holds:

$$\left| B \setminus \bigcup_{k=1}^{d} B_{i_k} \right| \geq 1.$$

This implies that no subset in $\mathcal{B}$ can be completely covered by the union of at most d other subsets. To facilitate analysis and simplify operations, a d-CFF can be equivalently represented in matrix form.

Let $\mathcal{F} = (S, \mathcal{B})$ be a d-CFF where $S = \{s_1, \ldots, s_m\}$ and $\mathcal{B} = \{B_1, \ldots, B_n\}$ are ordered sets. The incidence matrix $\mathcal{M}$ of $\mathcal{F}$ is defined as:

$$\mathcal{M}[i, j] = \begin{cases} 1, & \text{if } s_i \in B_j, \\ 0, & \text{otherwise.} \end{cases}$$

Here, each row $\mathcal{M}_i \in \{0,1\}^n$ corresponds to an element $s_i \in S$, and each column represents a subset $B_j \in \mathcal{B}$. Consequently, the matrix $\mathcal{M}$ has m rows and n columns, providing a convenient structural representation of the d-CFF.

4 System Framework

4.1 System Model

The proposed vehicular social network is designed as a decentralized architecture that integrates roadside units into a consortium blockchain framework. RSUs operate as fog computing nodes and simultaneously act as blockchain nodes, which are categorized into four functional roles: *outsourced computing nodes*, *batch-processing nodes*, *leader nodes*, and *storage nodes*.

System Registration. In conventional VSNs, vehicles are required to communicate with multiple entities and perform extensive cryptographic operations, resulting in heavy computational and communication overhead. In contrast, the proposed system exploits the edge computing capability of RSUs and their wired communication advantage. Except during the registration phase, vehicles communicate only with nearby RSUs, significantly reducing communication cost. Roadside RSUs function as outsourced computing nodes, executing outsourced signcryption and decryption. Batch-processing nodes are selected according to their geographic location and computational capacity; they aggregate data within a region over a given time interval, perform fault-tolerant batch verification, and generate attribute keys. A leader node is elected via the Raft algorithm to manage system parameters, collect attribute keys, handle vehicle registration, and package verified data into blocks. To further alleviate system burdens, storage nodes with strong storage and communication capacity maintain blockchain data persistently.

Entity Registration. Upon joining the system, each vehicle receives a pair of signcryption and decryption keys generated by the leader node based on its attributes. Both key types consist of two components: a local key and an outsourced key. During decryption, only a single duplex interaction between the vehicle and its nearby RSU is required.

Data Upload. A vehicle data owner (VDO) transmits an outsourced encryption key and partial parameters to its nearby RSU, which returns a partial ciphertext. The VDO then completes local encryption and submits the ciphertext to the RSU. The RSU verifies the timestamp before forwarding the ciphertext to a batch-processing node. Invalid ciphertexts are revoked, while valid ones are aggregated and fault-tolerantly verified. The verified ciphertexts are packaged into a block and broadcast across the blockchain network. Edge RSUs maintain only local ledgers to reduce storage cost and improve retrieval efficiency, whereas storage nodes retain the global ledger for backup.

- *Signcrypt:* The VDO sends its outsourced encryption key and partial parameters to the nearby RSU, which performs outsourced signcryption and returns a partial ciphertext. The VDO completes the local encryption and submits the resulting ciphertext back to the RSU.
- *Fault-tolerant Batch Verification:* The RSU verifies the timestamp of each received ciphertext and filters out invalid ones. Valid ciphertexts are aggregated by a batch-processing node and verified using a fault-tolerant batch verification mechanism.
- *Block Packaging and Broadcasting:* The verified ciphertexts are packaged into a block and broadcast to the blockchain network. Edge RSUs maintain local ledgers to reduce storage cost and improve retrieval efficiency, while storage nodes maintain the global ledger for backup.

Data Access. When requesting data, a vehicle data user (VDU) sends its outsourced decryption key and query to the nearby RSU. The RSU searches its local ledger for the requested data. If unavailable locally, the RSU retrieves it from a storage node. Otherwise, the RSU performs partial decryption and returns the intermediate result, enabling the VDU to complete the final decryption. This design requires only a single duplex communication with the RSU, thereby greatly improving communication efficiency (Fig. 2).

4.2 Security Model

This section outlines the security guarantees of our attribute-based signcryption scheme, focusing on two core properties: message confidentiality and ciphertext unforgeability.

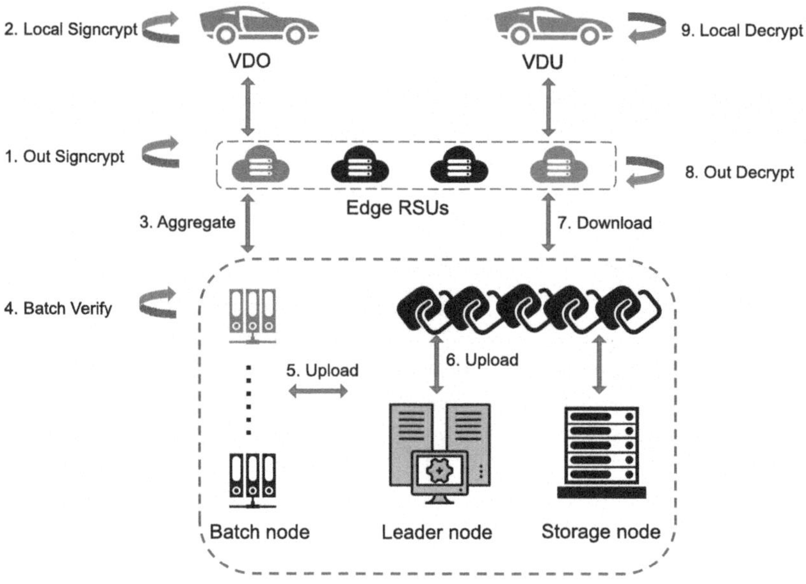

Fig. 2. System framework

Message Confidentiality: Message confidentiality is characterized by indistinguishability under adaptive chosen ciphertext attacks under a selectively chosen attribute set (IND-CCA2), this is represented as a game between challenger $\mathcal{C}$ and adversary $\mathcal{A}$.

Guess: After interacting with the challenger, the adversary outputs a bit b' as a guess for the challenge bit b. The adversary wins if $b' = b$, and the advantage is measured by:

$$\mathsf{Adv}_{\mathcal{A}}^{\text{IND-CCA2}} = \left| \Pr[b' = b] - \frac{1}{2} \right|$$

Definition 1: The scheme is considered to be IND-CCA2 secure if no adversary $\mathcal{A}$ running in time $\mathcal{T}$ and making no more than q_{SK} key generation queries for signing, q_{DK} for decryption, q_{SC} signcryption queries, and q_{US} un-signcryption queries, the advantage is less than a negligible value ϵ.

Ciphertext Unforgeability: This property is characterized by existential unforgeability under adaptive chosen message attacks in a selective attribute setting (EUF-CMA). It is modeled as a game between $\mathcal{C}$ and $\mathcal{A}$.

$$\mathsf{Adv}_{\mathcal{A}}^{\text{EUF-CMA-sAtt}} = \Pr[\mathcal{A} \text{ wins}]$$

Definition 2: A scheme achieves EUF-CMA security if any efficient adversary within time $\mathcal{T}$ and making at most q_{SK} *SignKeyGen* queries, q_{DK} *DecKeyGen* queries, q_{SC} *Signcrypt* queries, and q_{US} *Un-Signcrypt* queries has success probability at most ϵ.

5 Construction

5.1 System Initialization

The leader node defines the message domain as $\mathcal{M} = \{0,1\}^{l_m}$. If a message exceeds the length limit l_m, it is partitioned into segments. Let $U_s = \{att_{s,i,j}\}$ denote the set of signature-related attributes, and $U_e = \{att_{e,i,j}\}$ denote the encryption attribute set, where i indexes the node and j represents the attribute's unique identifier. Each node independently manages its own local attributes, satisfying $U_{s,i} \subseteq U_s$ and $U_{e,i} \subseteq U_e$, with the union across all nodes reconstructing the global sets U_s and U_e. Given a security parameter κ, the leader node executes the global setup algorithm and publishes the global parameters GP. Additionally, the following hash functions are defined:

$$H_1 : \{0,1\}^* \to \mathbb{Z}_p, \quad H_2 : \mathbb{G}_T \times \mathbb{G} \times \mathbb{Z}_p \to \{0,1\}^{l_m}, \quad H_3 : \{0,1\}^* \to \{0,1\}^l,$$

The leader node first selects a bilinear group $\mathbb{G}$ of prime order p with generator g and a pairing $e : \mathbb{G} \times \mathbb{G} \to \mathbb{G}_T$. It then randomly samples the following elements from $\mathbb{G}$: $X_0, Y_0, \eta_1, \eta_2, \mu_0, \mu_1, \ldots, \mu_l \in_R \mathbb{G}$, where $\in_R$ denotes uniform random selection over $\mathbb{G}$.

The leader publishes the global system parameters as

$$GP = \left(\mathbb{G}, \mathbb{G}_T, p, g, e, X_0, Y_0, \eta_1, \eta_2, \mu_0, \mu_1, \ldots, \mu_l, \mathcal{M}, \mathcal{U}_s, \mathcal{U}_e\right),$$

For key generation, the leader node assigns each blockchain node a distinct value $\alpha_i \in \mathbb{Z}_p^*$ and computes the corresponding partial public key $Z_i = e(g,g)^{\alpha_i}$. For each $att_{s,i,j} \in att_{s,i}$ and $att_{e,i,j} \in att_{e,i}$, the leader node randomly selects corresponding elements $X_{i,j}, Y_{i,j} \in \mathbb{G}$. The node's master secret key is set as $MSK_i = \alpha_i$, and the public key is defined as:

$$PK_i = \left(Z_i, \{X_{i,j}\}_{att_{s,i,j} \in att_{s,i}}, \{Y_{i,j}\}_{att_{e,i,j} \in att_{e,i}}\right).$$

5.2 Entity Registration

Step 1: Vehicle Detection and Key Issuance. Smart contracts detect vehicles joining the VSN system. Once a new vehicle is detected, the leader node generates the vehicle's public/private key pair and notifies batch processing nodes to generate attribute keys. The batch nodes generate the keys, and the leader aggregates them and securely transmits them to the vehicle.

- Pick random $\alpha_{i,s} \in \mathbb{Z}_p$, where $\alpha_{i,s} < MSK_i$, compute $S_{i,0} = g^{\alpha_i - \alpha_{i,s}}$.
- Construct LSSS vector $\boldsymbol{v}_{i,s} = (\alpha_{i,s}, v_{i,s,2}, \ldots, v_{i,s,c_{s,j}})$ with random values.
- For each row in $\mathbf{S}_i$, pick $r_{i,j} \in \mathbb{Z}_p$ and compute $\lambda_{\rho_i}(j) = \mathbf{S}_{i,j}\boldsymbol{v}_{i,s}$,

$$S_{i,j} = g^{\lambda_{\rho_i(j)}}(X_0 X_{i,\rho_i(j)})^{r_{i,j}}, \quad S'_{i,j} = g^{r_{i,j}}, \quad S''_{i,j} = \{X_{i,k}^{r_{i,j}}\}_{att_{s,i,k} \in \mathcal{U}_{s,i} \setminus \{\rho_i(j)\}}$$

Set the local signature key $SSK_i = ((\mathbb{S}_i, \rho_i), S_{i,0})$ and the outsourced signature key $OSK_i = \{S_{i,j}, S'_{i,j}, S''_{i,j} : j \in [l_{s,i}]\}$.

The decryption key generation (DSK_i, ODK_i) follows the same procedure, except that the base element is computed as $D_{i,0} = UPK^{\alpha_i - \alpha_{i,e}}$, with $\alpha_{i,e} \in \mathbb{Z}_p$. The final local and outsourced decryption keys differ from the signature keys accordingly. The leader node also selects a unique $\theta \in \mathbb{Z}_p^*$, sets $USK = 1/\theta$ as the vehicle's secret key, and computes the corresponding public key $UPK = g^\theta$.

5.3 Data Upload

When a Vehicle Data Owner (VDO) wants to share data, it first selects a signcryption attribute set U_s corresponding to the LSSS structure $(\mathbb{S}_i, \rho_i)_{i\in[N]}$ and an encryption attribute set U_d for access control. For each $(\mathbb{S}_i, \rho_i)$, the VDO computes constants $\{w_{i,j} \in \mathbb{Z}_p\}_{j\in J_{s,i}}$ satisfying $\sum_{j\in J_{s,i}} w_{i,j}\mathbf{S}_{i,j} = (1, 0, \ldots, 0)_{c_{s,i}}$, which are then transmitted to the nearest RSU. By interacting only with nearby RSUs, the VDO reduces communication latency and leverages the RSU's edge computing capability.

The RSU executes the partial signcrypt algorithm, choose random $\xi \in \mathbb{Z}_p$. Compute:

$$\sigma'_1 = g^\xi \prod\nolimits_{j\in J_{s,i},\, i\in[N]} (S'_{i,j})^{w_{i,j}},$$
$$\sigma'_2 = (X_0 \prod\nolimits_{\rho_i(j)\in U_s,\, i\in[N]} X_{i,j})^\xi \prod\nolimits_{j\in J_{s,i},\, i\in[N]} (S_{i,j} \prod_{\substack{k\in U_s \\ k\neq\rho_i(j)}} S''_{i,j,k})^{w_{i,j}}$$

and returns the intermediate result to the VDO, which then performs the local signcrypt computation to generate the final ciphertext CT. Generate timestamp τ and threshold τ_{end}. The detailed process is as follows, choose $\beta, \gamma \in \mathbb{Z}_p$.

$$C_1 = g^\beta, \quad C_2 = (Y_0 \prod_{\phi_i(j)\in U_d,\, i\in[N]} Y_{i,j})^\beta, \quad C_3 = H_2(\Theta, \sigma_1, \chi) \oplus M,$$
$$\sigma_1 = g^{\beta\gamma}, \sigma_2 = \sigma'_1, \quad \Theta = (\prod_{i\in[N]} Z_i)^\beta, \quad \chi = H_1(\sigma_2), \quad \mu = H_1(C_1),$$
$$(m_1, \ldots, m_l) = H_3(\sigma_2 \| U_s \| U_d \| \tau \| \tau_{\text{end}}), \zeta = H_4(\sigma_1 \| \sigma_2 \| C_1 \| C_2 \| C_3 \| U_s \| U_d),$$
$$\sigma_3 = ((\eta_1^\mu \eta_2)^{\gamma\theta} \cdot \mu_0 \prod_{k\in[l]} \mu_k^{m_k})^\beta \cdot \sigma'_2 \cdot \prod_{i\in[N]} S_{i,0}$$

Then generate $CT = (U_s, U_e, C_1, C_2, C_3, \sigma_1, \sigma_2, \sigma_3, \tau_{\text{end}})$

Once the VDO initiates an upload request, the nearby RSU first verifies the timestamp and forwards valid ciphertexts to the regional batch processing node. The batch node aggregates ciphertexts over a time window and performs fault-tolerant batch verification. Successfully verified ciphertexts are packaged into a new block and broadcast to the network. Failed ciphertexts are discarded, and the corresponding VDO is notified. By keeping ledger data at regional RSUs, communication overhead and storage pressure are significantly reduced. The process of batch verification algorithm is as follows:

Compute for each record $t = 1, \ldots, L$:

$$\mathbf{m} = H_3(\sigma_2 \| U_s \| U_d \| \tau \| \tau_{end}), \quad \theta = H_4(\sigma_1 \| \sigma_2 \| C_1 \| C_2 \| C_3 \| U_s \| U_d),$$

$$\mu = H_1(C_1), \quad A_1 = \mu_0 \prod_{k=1}^{l} \mu_k^{m_k}, \quad A_2 = K_0 \prod_{\rho_i(j) \in U_s} K_{i,j},$$

$$A_3 = (\eta_1^{\mu} \eta_2)^{\theta}, \quad B_3 = \sigma_1 \prod_i Z_i.$$

Pick small random values $\mathbf{r} = (r_1, \ldots, r_L)$ and compute

$$V_1^{\text{batch}} = \prod_{t=1}^{L} \left[e(A_1, C_{1,t}) \cdot e(A_2, \sigma_{2,t}) \cdot e(A_3, B_3) \right]^{r_t},$$

$$V_2^{\text{batch}} = e\left(\prod_{t=1}^{L} \sigma_{3,t}^{-r_t}, g \right).$$

If $V_1^{\text{batch}} \cdot V_2^{\text{batch}} = 1$, return 1; otherwise return $\perp$.

Fault-Tolerant Batch Verification

Input: 125 signatures with associated data:

$$\{(M_t, \sigma_{1,t}, \sigma_{2,t}, \sigma_{3,t}, C_{1,t}, U_{s,t}, U_{d,t}, \tau_t, \tau_{end,t}, C_{2,t}, C_{3,t})\}_{t=1}^{125}$$

Step 1: Construct 2-Cover-Free Family Grouping

- Divide the 125 signatures into 25 groups $G_1, \ldots, G_{25}$ according to a 2-cover-free incidence matrix $\mathcal{M}$.
- Each group contains exactly 5 signatures, ensuring any invalid signature appears in at most 2 groups.

Step 2: Group Verification

$$\text{GroupResult}[i] \leftarrow \text{BatchVerify}(G_i), \quad i = 1, \ldots, 25$$

Step 3: Identify Valid Signatures

- A signature σ_t is valid if it passes verification in all groups containing it.
- The 2-cover-free property ensures up to 2 invalid signatures can be tolerated in a batch of 125.

Output: Set of valid signatures $\{\sigma_t : \sigma_t \text{ is valid}\}$.

5.4 Vehicle Data Access

The VDU sends its outsourced decryption key ODK_i along with the access request to a nearby RSU. The RSU first checks its local ledger for the requested data. If the data is not present locally, the RSU fetches it from the storage nodes; otherwise, it proceeds directly with partial decryption.

The VDU selects constants $\{w_{i,j} \in \mathbb{Z}_p\}_{j \in J_{d,i}}$ satisfying $\sum_{j \in J_{d,i}} w_{i,j}\mathbf{D}_{i,j} = (1, 0, \ldots, 0)_{c_{d,i}}$ and chooses $\zeta \in \mathbb{Z}_p$, then computes $D_0 = \prod_{i \in [N]} D_{i,0}^{\zeta}$ The VDU sends $(C_1, C_2, D_0, \{ODK_i, \{w_{i,j}\}_{j \in J_{d,i}}\}_{i \in [N]})$ to the RSU for partial decryption. The RSU computes

$$E_1' = \prod_{j \in J_{d,i}, i \in [N]} (D_{i,j} \prod_{k \in U_d, k \neq \phi_i(j)} D''_{i,j,k})^{w_{i,j}}, \quad E_1'' = \prod_{j \in J_{d,i}, i \in [N]} (D'_{i,j})^{w_{i,j}}$$

$$E_1 = \frac{e(C_1, E_1')}{e(C_2, E_1'')}, \quad E_2 = e(C_1, D_0)$$

and returns (E_1, E_2) to the VDU in a single response. Finally, the VDU recovers the message:

$$\chi = H_1(\sigma_2), \quad \Theta = E_1 E_2^{\zeta}, \quad M = C_3 \oplus H_2(\Theta, \sigma_1, \chi)$$

In our scheme, the VDU only interacts with the RSU once in a duplex communication, significantly improving communication efficiency.

6 Performance Evaluation

This section presents a comparative evaluation of our scheme against existing approaches, focusing on security properties, communication and storage overhead, as well as computational efficiency.

Table 2. Communication and Storage Costs

Scheme	Signcrypt Key		Decrypt Key		Ciphertext
	SSK	OSK	DSK	ODK	
[17]	$(2n_s + 2)\vert\mathbb{G}\vert$	-	$(2n_e + 2)\vert\mathbb{G}\vert$	-	$5\vert\mathbb{G}\vert + \vert\tau\vert + msg$
[13]	$(n_s + N)\vert\mathbb{G}\vert$	$(2n_s + 2n_e + N + 1)\vert\mathbb{G}\vert$	$(n_e + N)\vert\mathbb{G}\vert$	$(n_e + N)\vert\mathbb{G}\vert$	$(n_s + 2n_e + 3)\vert\mathbb{G}\vert + \vert\mathbb{G}_T\vert + 2n_e\vert\mathbb{Z}_p\vert + \vert\tau\vert$
[14]	$2\vert\mathbb{G}\vert$	$(n_s u_s + n_s)\vert\mathbb{G}\vert$	$(n_e + 2)\vert\mathbb{G}\vert$	$(n_e + 2)\vert\mathbb{G}\vert$	$(n_e + 6)\vert\mathbb{G}\vert + \vert\tau\vert + msg$
[5]	$N\vert\mathbb{G}\vert$	$(n_s u_s + n_s)\vert\mathbb{G}\vert$	$N\vert\mathbb{G}\vert$	$(n_e u_e + n_e)\vert\mathbb{G}\vert$	$5\vert\mathbb{G}\vert + 2\vert\tau\vert + msg$
Ours	$N\vert\mathbb{G}\vert$	$(n_s u_s + n_s)\vert\mathbb{G}\vert$	$\vert\mathbb{Z}_p\vert$	$(n_e u_e + n_e + N)\vert\mathbb{G}\vert$	$5\vert\mathbb{G}\vert + \vert\tau\vert + msg$

Table 3. Computation Costs

Scheme	Local Signcryption	Outsource Signcryption	Local Verify	Local Un-signcryption	Outsource Un-signcryption
[17]	$(3n_s + 3n_e + 4)E$	–	$2E + 4P$	$2n_eE + 6P$	–
[13]	$(n_s + 5)E + E_T$	$(u_s + 5n_s + 3n_e + 2)E$	$(n_s + 2)E + (n_s + 3)P$	E_T	$3n_eE + n_eE_T + (2n_e + N)P$
[14]	$(2n_e + 10)E + SE_{enc}$	$(2n_s + 2)E$	$6E + E_T$	$E_T + SE_{dec}$	$(2n_e + 2)E + 7P$
[5]	$7E + E_T$	$(2n_s + 2)E$	$E + E_T$	P	$(2n_e + 2)E + 6P$
Ours	$7E + E_T$	$(2n_s + 2)E$	H	E_T	$(2n_e + 2)E + 7P$

6.1 Theoretical Analysis

Communication and Storage Cost: We compare the communication and storage overhead of our scheme with several signcryption schemes. As summarized in Table 2, many existing schemes incur key and ciphertext sizes that grow linearly with the number of attributes, which limits their scalability in large-scale settings. Our scheme minimizes overhead by outsourcing most computations to RSU. The signcryption key includes $N|\mathbb{G}|$ for SSK and $(n_s u_s + n_s)|\mathbb{G}|$ for OSK, while the decryption key comprises only $|\mathbb{Z}_p|$ for DSK and $(n_e u_e + n_e + N)|\mathbb{G}|$ for ODK. Notably, our ciphertext size is constant: $5|\mathbb{G}| + |\tau| + msg$, regardless of the number of attributes, which is especially advantageous in bandwidth-limited environments like VSN. In summary, our scheme achieves low storage cost, constant-size ciphertext, and scalable key management, making it well-suited for vehicular social networks.

Computation Cost: We evaluate the computation costs of our scheme across five key stages: local signcryption, outsourced signcryption, local verification, local un-signcryption, and outsourced un-signcryption. Exponentiations in $\mathbb{G}$ and $\mathbb{G}_T$ are denoted as E and E_T, pairings as P, and hash operations as H.

Traditional schemes perform most operations locally and scale poorly with the number of attributes, leading to high costs on constrained devices. Some partially outsource computations but still rely heavily on pairing operations and per-attribute processing. Our scheme, by contrast, fully offloads expensive computations to RSU. Local signcryption requires only $7E + E_T$, regardless of the number of attributes. Outsourced signcryption incurs $(2n_s + 2)E$, and verification is reduced to a single hash operation (H), eliminating any pairing or exponentiation on the user side. Local un-signcryption only needs E_T, and outsourced un-signcryption requires $(2n_e + 2)E + 7P$, while maintaining policy expressiveness. In summary, our scheme achieves constant local computation, avoids pairing operations at the user side, and efficiently delegates attribute related workloads.

6.2 Processing Performance

We assess the computational efficiency of our scheme against LH-ABSC [14] and OMDAC [13]. Experiments were conducted on Ubuntu 18.04 with a 5.60 GHz Intel i7-14700K CPU, using Python 3.8.6 and Charm-Crypto 0.50. The implementation adopts a Type A elliptic curve, and standard hash functions (SHA-1,

SHA-512) from the Charm-Crypto library. Symmetric encryption in LH-ABSC is implemented via the toolbox library.

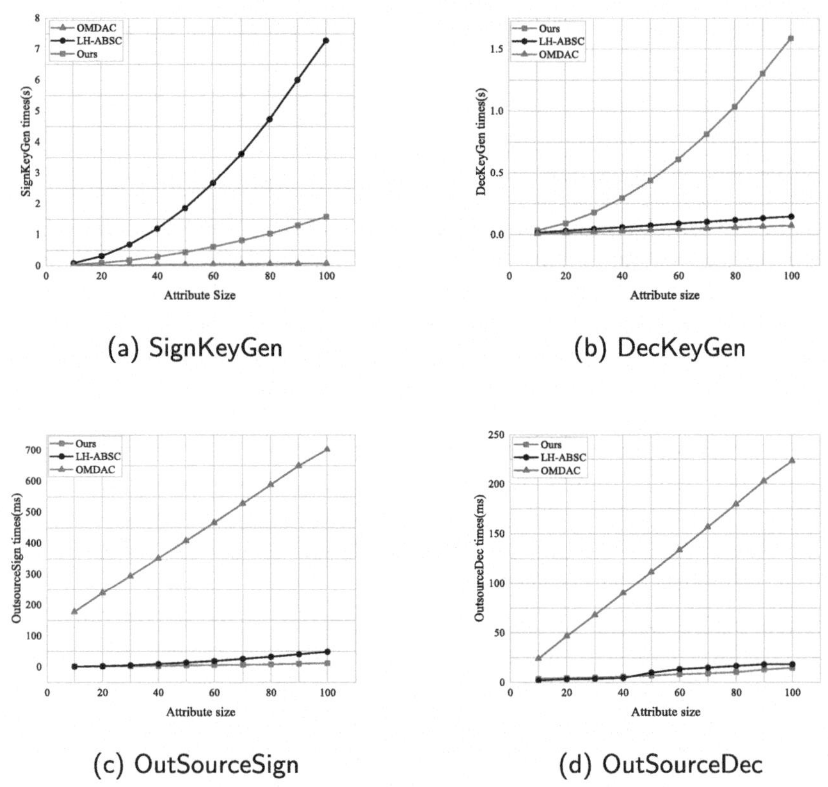

Fig. 3. Computation cost key generation and outsoucing operations

As shown in Fig. 3, the computation cost of SignKeyGen in LH-ABSC increases rapidly with the number of attributes due to complex operations, while OMDAC maintains a consistently low overhead. Our scheme exhibits a moderate and linear growth trend, primarily because the outsourced key generation requires one exponentiation per attribute. The DecKeyGen phase of our scheme introduces marginally greater overhead than the other two compared approaches. However, since both SignKeyGen and DecKeyGen are executed with the assistance of a consortium blockchain, these operations do not become a bottleneck in the overall cryptographic system.

As illustrated in Fig. 3, the computation costs of both OutSourceSign and OutSourceDec in our scheme increase gradually with the number of attributes due to attribute-wise exponentiation. However, compared to LH-ABSC and OMDAC, our scheme maintains lower overhead in outsourced operations. Since

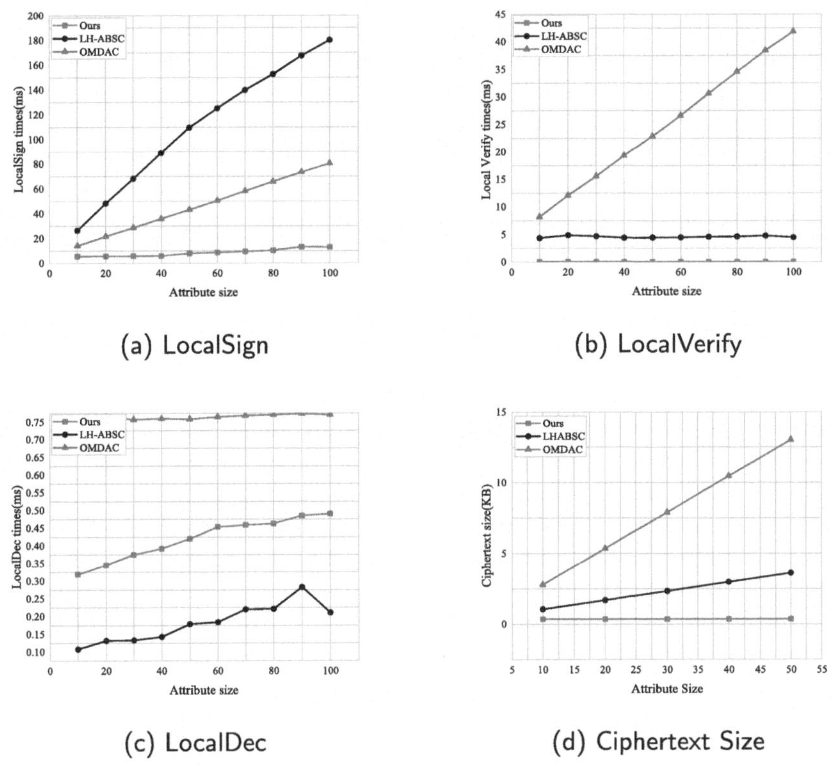

Fig. 4. Computation cost of local operations.

the outsourcing tasks are handled by RSU with strong computational capabilities, the local devices are relieved from intensive computation, resulting in a more efficient and lightweight client-side performance.

Figure 3 further illustrates the local computational costs and ciphertext size of different schemes with increasing attribute sizes. In Fig. 3(a), our scheme maintains a nearly constant local signcryption time, unrelated to the quantity of attributes, as most of the heavy computation is delegated to RSU. In contrast, both LH-ABSC and OMDAC incur significantly higher local costs, which increase rapidly due to attribute-related exponentiations, consistent with the signcryption complexity shown in Table 3. In Fig. 4(b), the verification time of our scheme remains minimal and does not grow with attribute size. This is because our verification algorithm only involves a single hash operation, whereas other schemes such as OMDAC require attribute-wise pairing operations, leading to steep growth in verification cost. Figure 4(c) presents the local decryption time. While our scheme performs one exponentiation operation, similar to LH-ABSC, the absolute time is slightly higher due to fixed computation overhead. However, it remains significantly more efficient than OMDAC, whose local decryption time is nearly twice as large due to more pairing operations.

Figure 4(d) demonstrates the impact of attribute size on the resulting ciphertext length. Our scheme achieves the smallest and most stable ciphertext overhead, as it does not embed attribute-related data directly into the ciphertext. In comparison, both LH-ABSC and OMDAC show a linear increase in ciphertext size, consistent with their linear attribute-dependency in encryption structure. Overall, our scheme achieves significant efficiency in local computation and communication overhead by offloading expensive operations to RSU and minimizing attribute-related growth in local operations.

7 Conclusion

This work introduces a secure data-sharing mechanism tailored for Vehicular Social Networks, which integrates consortium blockchain technology with attribute-based signcryption. By outsourcing computations to nearby Road Side Units and keeping ciphertext size constant regardless of attributes, the scheme reduces computational and communication overhead. The multi-authority blockchain design eliminates single points of failure and ensures secure, decentralized data storage and verification. Our approach offers an efficient and practical solution for secure data sharing in VSN. Future work will focus on improving scalability and enhancing security against emerging threats.

References

1. Bao, Y., Qiu, W., Cheng, X., Sun, J.: Fine-grained data sharing with enhanced privacy protection and dynamic users group service for the IoV. IEEE Trans. Intell. Transp. Syst. **24**(11), 13035–13049 (2023). https://doi.org/10.1109/TITS.2022.3187980
2. Chen, L., Xu, S., Zhang, H., Weng, J.: Fair-and-exculpable-attribute-based searchable encryption with revocation and verifiable outsourced decryption using smart contract. IEEE Internet Things J. **12**(4), 4302–4317 (2025). https://doi.org/10.1109/JIOT.2024.3484227
3. Feng, C., Yu, K., Aloqaily, M., Alazab, M., Lv, Z., Mumtaz, S.: Attribute-based encryption with parallel outsourced decryption for edge intelligent IoV. IEEE Trans. Veh. Technol. **69**(11), 13784–13795 (2020). https://doi.org/10.1109/TVT.2020.3027568
4. Ge, C., Liu, Z., Susilo, W., Fang, L., Wang, H.: Attribute-based encryption with reliable outsourced decryption in cloud computing using smart contract. IEEE Trans. Dependable Secure Comput. **21**(2), 937–948 (2024). https://doi.org/10.1109/TDSC.2023.3265932
5. Gong, B., et al.: Slim: a secure and lightweight multi-authority attribute-based signcryption scheme for IoT. IEEE Trans. Inf. Forensics Secur. **19**, 1299–1312 (2024). https://doi.org/10.1109/TIFS.2023.3331566
6. Huo, L., Wu, L., Zhang, Z., Li, C., He, D., Wang, J.: Libras: a fair, secure, verifiable, and scalable outsourcing computation scheme based on blockchain. IEEE Trans. Inf. Forensics Secur. **19**, 5725–5737 (2024). https://doi.org/10.1109/TIFS.2024.3403489

7. Li, J., He, Y., Zhang, K., Yuan, P., Yu, J.: Fuzzy multi-keyword search for multi-owner scenario in IoV. IEEE Trans. Veh. Technol. **74**(4), 5698–5712 (2025). https://doi.org/10.1109/TVT.2024.3521019
8. Pengshou Xie, Yang, H., Feng, T., Yan, Y.: Implementing efficient attribute encryption in IoV under cloud environments. Comput. Netw. **218**, 109363 (2022). https://doi.org/10.1016/j.comnet.2022.109363
9. Rao, Y.S., Dutta, R.: Expressive attribute based signcryption with constant-size ciphertext. In: Progress in Cryptology – AFRICACRYPT 2014, pp. 398–419. Cham (2014). https://doi.org/10.1007/978-3-319-06734-6_24
10. Rao, Y.S., Dutta, R.: Expressive bandwidth-efficient attribute based signature and signcryption in standard model. In: Information Security and Privacy, pp. 209–225. Cham (2014). https://doi.org/10.1007/978-3-319-08344-5_14
11. Rao, Y.S., Dutta, R.: Efficient attribute-based signature and signcryption realizing expressive access structures. Int. J. Inf. Secur. **15**, 81–109 (2016). https://doi.org/10.1007/s10207-015-0289-6
12. Ren, Y., Chen, C., Hu, M., Feng, G., Zhang, X.: BFDAC: a blockchain-based and fog-computing-assisted data access control scheme in vehicular social networks. IEEE Internet Things J. **11**(2), 3510–3523 (2024). https://doi.org/10.1109/JIOT.2023.3296906
13. Xu, Q., Tan, C., Fan, Z., Zhu, W., Xiao, Y., Cheng, F.: Secure data access control for fog computing based on multi-authority attribute-based signcryption with computation outsourcing and attribute revocation. Sensors **18**(5) (2018). https://doi.org/10.3390/s18051609
14. Yu, J., Liu, S., Wang, S., Xiao, Y., Yan, B.: LH-ABSC: a lightweight hybrid attribute-based signcryption scheme for cloud-fog-assisted IoT. IEEE Internet Things J. **7**(9), 7949–7966 (2020). https://doi.org/10.1109/JIOT.2020.2992288
15. Zhang, K., Hu, X., Zhao, J., Wei, L., Ning, J.: Blockchain-based revocable key-aggregate searchable encryption for group data sharing in cloud-assisted industrial IoT. IEEE Internet Things J. **12**(11), 16899–16911 (2025). https://doi.org/10.1109/JIOT.2025.3534837
16. Zhang, L., Zhang, Y., Wu, Q., Mu, Y., Rezaeibagha, F.: A secure and efficient decentralized access control scheme based on blockchain for vehicular social networks. IEEE Internet Things J. **9**(18), 17938–17952 (2022). https://doi.org/10.1109/JIOT.2022.3161047
17. Zhao, Y., Ruan, A., Dan, G., Huang, J., Ding, Y.: Efficient multi-authority attribute-based signcryption with constant-size ciphertext. In: 2021 IEEE Conference on Dependable and Secure Computing (DSC), pp. 1–8 (2021). https://doi.org/10.1109/DSC49826.2021.9346249

Heavy Hitter Identification in Large Domains with Personalized Local Differential Privacy

Yuying He[1], Lele Yu[1,2], Pengfei Zhang[3], Peiyong Sun[4], Weizhi Meng[5], and Yining Liu[6](✉)

[1] School of Computer Science and Information Security, Guilin University of Electronic Technology, Guilin 541004, Guangxi, China
[2] Key Lab of Education Blockchain and Intelligent Technology, Ministry of Education, Guangxi Normal University, Guilin 541004, China
[3] School of Computer Science and Engineering, Anhui University of Science and Technology, Huainan 232001, China
[4] Hebi Institute of Engineering and Technology, Henan Polytechnic University, Hebi 458030, China
[5] School of Computing and Communications, Lancaster University, Lancaster, UK
[6] School of Data Science and Artificial Intelligence, Wenzhou University of Technology, Wenzhou 325035, Zhejiang, China
20240035@wzut.edu.cn

Abstract. Local Differential Privacy (LDP) is a well-established framework for protecting user data during collection. Nonetheless, most existing solutions impose identical privacy levels on all users, overlooking diverse individual privacy needs and thus degrading the accuracy of frequency estimation. This limitation becomes more pronounced when user privacy sensitivities vary widely, as a fixed privacy budget may overprotect some users while underprotecting others. Meanwhile, in large-domain settings such as user activity logs and web browsing histories, identifying heavy hitters through exhaustive frequency estimation becomes computationally impossible due to the exponential growth of possible values. To tackle these issues, we propose PPEM, a large-scale heavy hitter identification scheme that supports personalized privacy protection. PPEM first partitions users based on privacy levels and further groups users within each privacy level. Each group adopts a prefix-based perturbation mechanism, where users only report a prefix of their item, significantly reducing communication and computational overhead. In addition, we introduce the POLH mechanism to enhance frequency estimation under personalized LDP constraints and develop a weighted combination method to effectively aggregate data from multiple privacy groups. Extensive experiments on real-world URL and synthetic datasets demonstrate the efficacy of PPEM in balancing privacy and utility.

This research was supported by the Innovation Project of Guangxi Graduate Education under Grant YCBZ2024166, and in part by Research Fund of Key Lab of Education Blockchain and Intelligent Technology, Ministry of Education (No. EBME24-F-M-03).

L. Zhang and K.-K. R. Choo (Eds.): MobiQuitous 2025, LNICST 684, pp. 426–444, 2026.
https://doi.org/10.1007/978-3-032-22503-0_23

Keywords: Local Differential Privacy · Data Collection · Heavy Hitter

1 Introduction

With the rapid development of the Internet and big data technologies, mobile applications are increasingly applied in various domains of human activity. The large volume of user data generated by smart devices has become a valuable asset for organizations. This data is widely used in data mining tasks such as anomaly detection and frequent itemset mining. However, since it often contains sensitive personal information, direct analysis may lead to privacy breaches. Differential Privacy (DP) [1] provides a mathematically rigorous framework for protecting user privacy. By adding random noise to data or query results, DP ensures that the output is insensitive to the inclusion or exclusion of any single individual, regardless of the attacker's background knowledge.

Local Differential Privacy (LDP) [2] strengthens this protection by applying the perturbation directly on the user's local side, eliminating the need for a trusted aggregator. Owing to its strong privacy guarantees and practical utility, LDP has been widely used in tasks such as frequency estimation and heavy hitter identification. To identify heavy hitters (i.e., the top-k most frequent items), most existing methods estimate the frequency of every item in the domain, which requires querying all possible values. However, this becomes computationally infeasible when $|D|$ is large. To address this challenge, approaches such as Optimized Local Hashing (OLH) allow users to respond with simple binary answers to server-generated queries, reducing client-side complexity. Wang et al. [3] introduced an innovative method for encoding data into binary vectors. In this approach, each user group is only required to perturb and report a limited length prefix of the data. Consequently, the server conducts its search within this reduced prefix space, rather than across the entire domain.

However, a major limitation of these approaches is the assumption that all users have identical privacy requirements. In real-world scenarios, users often have diverse and personalized privacy preferences for the same type of data, influenced by their background, occupation, or personal sensitivity. For instance, consumption records are highly sensitive for online store owners, as they may reveal critical commercial information such as purchasing channels and cost structures, which could be maliciously analyzed and exploited by competitors. However, for ordinary consumers, shared shopping records consist primarily of experiences or reviews. Even if viewed by others, they merely serve as consumption references without involving risks of commercial confidentiality. Uniform privacy budgets may result in underprotection of sensitive data or overprotection of nonsensitive data, thereby compromising both security and utility. Therefore, it is imperative to dynamically customize the intensity of local differential privacy according to individual privacy requirements, so as to strike a balance between precise protection and data utility.

While some work, such as that by Song et al. [4], has introduced adaptive data collection mechanisms that support flexible switching between RAPPOR and KRR mechanisms, there is still limited work addressing personalized privacy protection under large data domains. Unlike existing approaches, this study provides a dedicated solution for large-scale domain data mining with user-specific privacy budgets in the LDP model. To tackle this challenge, we propose PPEM for personalized privacy protection based on prefix extension, which achieves personalized privacy protection according to the different privacy preferences of local individuals. Our method specifically addresses this gap by effectively balancing personalized privacy protection and data utility, making it particularly well-suited for frequent item identification in large-scale data environments.

The main contributions of this paper are summarized as follows:

- We propose a heavy hitter identification algorithm, named PPEM, within the framework of the personalized local differential privacy (PLDP) model. It is capable of identifying heavy hitters and estimating their frequencies in large-scale data domains.
- The PPEM algorithm employs an efficient prefix extension mechanism and an optimized candidate generation strategy, which significantly reduce the communication and computation costs on the user side. Meanwhile, it uses a weighted combination-based estimation merging method to effectively aggregate data from multiple privacy groups.
- The privacy guarantees and accuracy of PPEM are formally analyzed, and its effectiveness is validated through extensive experiments. Comprehensive experiments on both real-world and synthetic datasets demonstrate that PPEM achieves high accuracy and efficiency in identifying heavy hitters under the same privacy constraints across large data domains.

The remainder of this paper is organized as follows. Section 2 reviews related work. Section 3 presents the background and concepts related to PLDP and heavy hitter identification. Section 4 presents the proposed algorithm in detail and offers privacy analysis. Section 5 reports experimental results. Section 6 concludes the paper.

2 Related Work

2.1 Local Differential Privacy

The concept of differential privacy was first proposed by Dwork [1] as a means of addressing the issue of personal privacy leakage that may occur during the process of statistical data analysis. Differential Privacy (DP) has been extensively applied across diverse domains, including geographic location information protection [5] and data publication [6]. Local differential privacy (LDP) is designed to address the issue of untrusted data collectors [2]. In this scenario, users do not send raw data to collectors but instead send data that has been processed through a randomized algorithm. By moving the noise addition process to the client side, LDP reduces the privacy leakage risks associated with untrusted data collectors, thus providing stronger privacy protection. This approach is well-suited to the current internet environment, where distributed users tend to distrust service providers. In 2016, Apple [7] became the first company to adopt Local Differential Privacy technology in its iOS and macOS systems, thereby protecting user privacy and popularising the concept of differential privacy. This subsequently attracted the attention of a greater number of researchers. The field of study surrounding LDP has grown considerably in recent times, with the technology being applied in a multitude of real-world scenarios, including recommendation algorithms [8].

2.2 Personalized Local Differential Privacy

However, the traditional LDP has not considered the personalized privacy needs of users in the data collection process, proposed by Warner [9], which may lead to insufficient protection of highly sensitive information or excessive perturbation of less sensitive information. In response to this shortcoming, research on Personalized Local Differential Privacy (PLDP) has emerged. Nie et al. [10] first proposed an optimization framework for histogram estimation utility based on RAPPOR, allowing users to dynamically allocate perturbation intensity according to their privacy needs; Shen et al. [11] further extended it to joint distribution estimation of multidimensional data, where users allocate personalized privacy budgets locally, and the server uses LASSO regression to reconstruct the joint distribution; Song et al. [4] proposed an adaptive data collection scheme, which determines adaptive boundaries based on the minimum mean square error, allowing users to flexibly switch between RAPPOR and KRR perturbation mechanisms for efficient and customized privacy protection.

2.3 Heavy Hitter Identification

Heavy hitter identification, also known as frequent item mining or top-k item mining, aims to discover data items that appear more frequently than a given threshold, such as identifying items with a frequency greater than 20%.

Erlingsson et al. [3] proposed a basic version of the RAPPOR algorithm, which is capable of identifying heavy hitter areas and reconstructing the overall data distribution. Bassily and Smith [12] developed Binary Local Hashing (BLH) technology, which allows users to randomly select a hash function from a set of predefined hash functions to hash their data items into a single bit, and then use random responses to perturb that bit. Qin et al. [13] devised the LDPMiner protocol, which employs "padding sampling" techniques and a strategy of allocating privacy budgets. This protocol is divided into two stages: firstly, frequent candidate itemsets are identified, and secondly, a frequency analysis is conducted on these candidates. To address the high computational complexity caused by large attribute domains, Wang et al. [14] proposed a prefix extension mechanism (PEM), which groups users and requires each group to report a prefix of a certain length. Following a number of iterations, the data collector is able to identify items that occur with a high frequency. Wang et al. [15] introduced the PrivSet framework, which does not require the partitioning of the privacy budget, as the entire dataset is randomized into a subset, but this increases communication costs. Currently, there are few algorithms that take into account the varying privacy needs of users, especially in the context of big data domains. Therefore, we propose a method for mining top-k frequent items in big data domains that caters to the different privacy requirements of individual users.

3 Preliminaries

3.1 Personalized Local Differential Privacy

Local differential privacy (LDP) allows for the collection of user data without the involvement of a trusted third party. The users introduce a certain level of noise into their data and then send the results to a third party. The LDP mechanism guarantees that for any given input value, the probability of its transmission to the server is similar to the probability of sending any other value. We introduce the definition of ε-LDP below.

Definition 1 (ε-Local Differential Privacy). *Given a randomized algorithm $\mathcal{M}$ satisfies ε-local differential privacy (ε-LDP), if and only if for any input $x, x' \subseteq D$, and any output $y \in \text{Range}(\mathcal{M})$, the following condition must be satisfied:*

$$\Pr(\mathcal{M}(x) = y) \leq e^{\varepsilon} \cdot \Pr(\mathcal{M}(x') = y) \tag{1}$$

where $\text{Range}(\mathcal{M})$ *denotes the set of all possible outputs of the algorithm $\mathcal{M}$.The parameter ε is called the privacy budget. A smaller ε indicates a stronger privacy guarantee, more perturbation noise, and lower data utility.*

A significant benefit of Local Differential Privacy (LDP) is its sequential composition and parallel composition, which guarantee that the overall privacy protection is maintained when multiple mechanisms adhering to LDP are combined.

Theorem 1 (Sequential composition [17]**).** *Given a sequence of computations $\mathcal{M} = \{\mathcal{M}_1, \mathcal{M}_2, \ldots, \mathcal{M}_m\}$, if each computation $\mathcal{M}_i$ $(1 \leq i \leq m)$ satisfies ε_i-differential privacy, then $\mathcal{M}$ satisfies sum(ε_i)-differential privacy.*

Theorem 2 (Parallel composition [17]**).** *Split the dataset D into k disjoint parts $\{D_1, D_2, ..., D_k\}$ such that $D = D_1 \cup D_2 \cup ... \cup D_k$, if $\mathcal{M}(x)$ satisfies ε-differential privacy, then $\mathcal{M}(D_1), \mathcal{M}(D_2), \ldots, \mathcal{M}(D_k)$ all satisfy ε-differential privacy.*

Theorem 3 (Post-processing Theorem [17]**).** *For any method ψ which works on the output of a ε -differentially private mechanism $\mathcal{M}$ without accessing the raw data, the integrated procedure $\psi \circ \mathcal{M}$ remains ε -differentially private.*

Sequential composition allows the total privacy budget to be divided among multiple sub-tasks, with each sub-task receiving a share of the budget. In contrast, parallel composition enables the data set to be partitioned into several non-overlapping subsets, on which differential privacy algorithms can be applied independently. The post-processing theorem guarantees that any operations performed on already privatized data will not compromise its original privacy protection.

Definition 2 (ε-PLDP). *A randomized algorithm M satisfies ε-PLDP if and only if for any input x, x' and user u , and for any possible output y, the following condition holds:*

$$\frac{\Pr[M(x) = y]}{\Pr[M(x') = y]} \leq e^{\varepsilon_u} \tag{2}$$

In the traditional Local Differential Privacy (LDP) framework, the privacy budget parameter is typically set as a global constant shared by all users. In contrast, the Personalized Local Differential Privacy (PLDP) model introduces a novel approach by allowing the privacy budget to be configured locally, thereby granting users effective control over their own privacy levels.

3.2 LDP Frequency Estimation Protocols

Generalized Randomized Response. Generalized randomized response (GRR) [9] mechanism is designed to address multi-class classification problems involving d possible values. In this method, each user reports their value with probability p, while one of the remaining $d-1$ values is reported with the residual probability. The standard Randomized Response (RR) is a particular case of GRR that applies exclusively to binary inputs. The perturbation function is formally defined as:

$$\forall y \in D, \Pr[\Psi_{\mathrm{GRR}(\varepsilon)}(v) = y] = \begin{cases} p = \frac{e^{\varepsilon}}{e^{\varepsilon}+d-1}, & \text{if } y = v \\ q = \frac{1}{e^{\varepsilon}+d-1}, & \text{if } y \neq v \end{cases} \tag{3}$$

where each user reports their true value with probability p, and a randomly chosen incorrect value with probability $q = \frac{1}{e^{\varepsilon}+d-1}$. The mechanism satisfies ε-LDP as the privacy ratio $\frac{p}{q} = e^{\varepsilon}$. The frequency of $x \in D$ is estimated according to the following equation:

$$\Phi_{\mathrm{GRR}(\varepsilon)}(x) := \frac{C(x) - nq}{p - q} \tag{4}$$

Where $C(x)$ is the number of times the value x is reported by all users, and n is the total number of users. This estimation is an unbiased estimation of the real counts of user data [18], and its variance is:

$$\mathrm{Var}[\Phi_{\mathrm{GRR}(\varepsilon)}(x)] = \frac{d - 2 + e^{\varepsilon}}{(e^{\varepsilon} - 1)^2} \cdot n \tag{5}$$

Optimized Local Hashing. Optimized Local Hashing (OLH) [18] is a protocol designed to handle large domain sizes d. It first uses a hash function to map an input value into a smaller domain of size g (typically $g \ll d$), and then applies randomized response to the hashed value in the smaller domain. Both the hashing step and the randomization step result in information loss. The choice of the parameter g is a tradeoff between losing information during the hashing step and losing information during the randomization step. As found in [18], the optimal (minimal variance) choice of g is $\lceil e^{\varepsilon} + 1 \rceil$.

In OLH, the reporting protocol is defined as:

$$\Psi_{\mathrm{OLH}(\varepsilon)}(x) := (H, \Psi_{\mathrm{GRR}(\varepsilon)}(H(x))) \tag{6}$$

where H is chosen randomly from a family of hash functions. H maps the input domain D into the domain $[1, \dots, g]$, i.e., $H : D \to [1, \dots, g]$, and then runs GRR on the domain $[1, \dots, g]$.

For each value $x \in D$, the data collector computes the number of reported values $C(x) = |\{u \mid H(x) = y\}|$. The perturbation probabilities are:

$$p = \frac{e^{\varepsilon}}{e^{\varepsilon} + g - 1}, \quad q = \frac{1}{e^{\varepsilon} + g - 1} \tag{7}$$

The data collector can then obtain an unbiased estimate of item frequency by using the following equation:

$$\Phi_{\mathrm{OLH}(\varepsilon)}(x) := \frac{C(x) - n \cdot q}{p - q} \tag{8}$$

The variance of estimation is:

$$\mathrm{Var}[\Phi_{\mathrm{OLH}(\varepsilon)}(x)] = n \cdot \frac{4e^{\varepsilon}}{(e^{\varepsilon} - 1)^2} \tag{9}$$

3.3 Problem Definition

Problem Statement. This paper addresses the problem of identifying heavy hitters under personalized local differential privacy (PLDP) in large-scale data domains. We consider a system consisting of N users and an untrusted data aggregator. Each user possesses a value $x \in D$, where D denotes a large-scale data domain, and has personalized privacy requirements categorized into m distinct levels. The data aggregator's objective is to identify the top-k most frequent values while preserving each user's personalized privacy. The heavy hitter identification problem is defined as the identification of the top-k items or the recognition of items that occur with a frequency exceeding a specific threshold. This study explores the definition of heavy hitters using the top-k approach. Specifically, we say that a value $x \in D$ is among the top-k most frequent if $\left|\{y \in D : f(y) > f(x)\}\right| < k$. The objective of this paper is to design a personalized local differential privacy mechanism that accurately identifies the top-k most frequent values in the data domain while protecting user privacy.

Threat Model. The framework discussed in this paper comprises two primary components: the client side and the server side. Specifically, users generate and store data on their local terminal devices, which subsequently transmit the perturbed data to the server. The server is responsible for aggregating the raw data and conducting heavy hitter identification. However, this architecture is susceptible to several security threats, as highlighted by Zhao et al. [19].

As depicted in Fig. 1, three primary threats have been identified. First, adversaries may intercept the raw data during transmission. Secondly, attackers may target the server directly in order to steal the collected data. Thirdly, malicious server administrators may exploit their access to steal the raw data. Collectively, these threats undermine the trustworthiness of the server, necessitating robust security measures to safeguard user data.

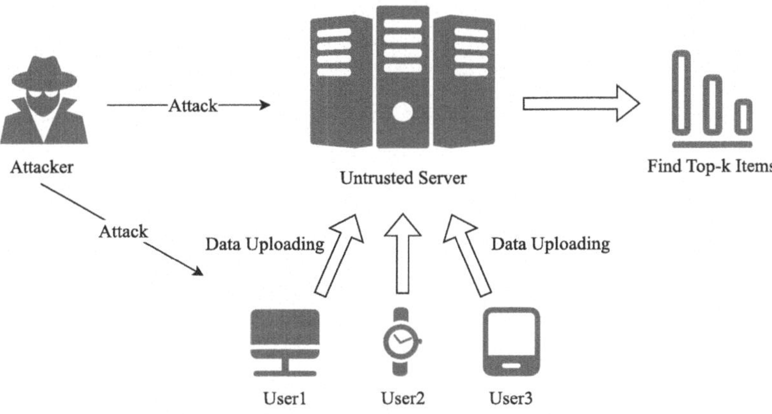

Fig. 1. Threat model considered in this paper.

4 Proposed Method

4.1 Overview

This paper addresses the problem of identifying heavy hitters under personalized local differential privacy (PLDP) in large-scale data domains. As shown in Fig. 2, the process consists of the following steps: first, users are divided into m groups, denoted as $G_1, \cdots, G_m$, based on their individual privacy protection levels (i.e., their privacy budgets ε). Subsequently, each of the m groups is subdivided into n subgroups through nested grouping, allowing for finer granularity in user partitioning. These subgroups are represented as $G_{i1}, \cdots, G_{in}$ for $i = 1, 2, ..., m$. Within each subgroup sharing identical privacy levels, binary-encoded user values undergo prefix partitioning. The POLH (personalized-optimized local hashing) mechanism is then applied to these prefixes, perturbing them based on their lengths and resulting in a set of top-k items under each privacy level. The users send their perturbed data to the aggregator. The aggregator initially performs bias correction, followed by a weighted combination method to integrate corrected results across privacy levels. This approach effectively addresses the need for personalized privacy protection while improving the accuracy of identifying heavy hitters and the overall efficiency of the system. It is particularly well-suited to privacy-preserving heavy hitter identification in large-scale data scenarios. Algorithm 1 shows the pseudocode for heavy hitter identification.

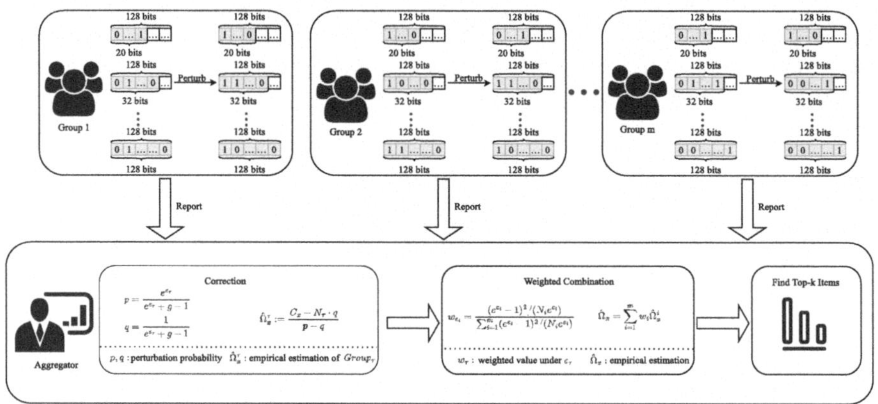

Fig. 2. The overview of PPEM.

4.2 Multi-level User Grouping

Under the Personalized Local Differential Privacy (PLDP) setting, we assume that users are divided into m levels of privacy budget, denoted $\varepsilon_1 < \varepsilon_2 < \cdots < \varepsilon_m$, where m is a parameter greater than 2, and ε_i is the privacy budget for group G_i $(i = 1, 2, ..., m)$. A larger ε results in less noise, weaker privacy protection, and higher data utility.

We first divide users into m groups $G_1, G_2, ..., G_m$ according to their individual privacy requirements (privacy budgets), where each group shares the same privacy level and different groups apply different privacy budgets.

To reduce communication and computation costs in the large domain setting, we adopt a prefix-extension-based approach to extract heavy hitters. Specifically, we perform grouping again within each group $G_1, G_2, ..., G_m$ obtained in the first step.

Following the prefix partitioning within groups as described in the following Section, each group G_i is randomly split into n subgroups, denoted as $G_{i1}, ..., G_{in}$. These second-level groups can be constructed using hash functions or by having each user randomly select a subgroup for participation. Through this two-level grouping, we finally obtain $m \times n$ groups, denoted as G_{ij}, where $i = 1, ..., m$ and $j = 1, ..., n$.

As described in Algorithm 1, we first partition users into m groups, denoted as $G_1, G_2, \ldots, G_m$, according to their privacy level in line 1. Then, we randomly split each group G_i into n subgroups, denoted as $G_{i1}, \ldots, G_{in}$ in lines 3–4.

4.3 Prefix Partitioning Within Groups

This paper addresses the challenge of identifying heavy hitters in a large domain within the framework of Personalized Local Differential Privacy (PLDP). For simplicity, we assume that each value is represented as a binary string of length l. In the context of the same privacy level, to identify the top-k heavy hitters, users in group G_i (where $i = 1, 2, \ldots, m$) apply the FO protocol to randomly report a prefix of their value, with the length of the prefix being s_{ij}.

$$s_{ij} = \lceil \log_2 k \rceil + \left\lceil \frac{l - \lceil \log_2 k \rceil}{n} \cdot j \right\rceil \tag{10}$$

Assuming $D_{i1} = \{0,1\}^{s_{i1}}$, the aggregator begins by utilizing the reports from the first group of users G_{i1} to identify the set of frequent prefixes within the domain D_{i1}. The discovered set of candidates is denoted as C_{i1}. In the next step, the aggregator extends these candidates to form the domain for the second group, defined as $D_{i2} = C_{i1} \times \{0,1\}^{s_{i2}-s_{i1}}$, and collects reports from the second user group G_{i2} to identify a new set of frequent prefixes, denoted by C_{i2}.

This iterative process continues across successive user groups. In each step j, the domain D_{ij} is constructed based on the candidate set from the previous step, and the aggregator identifies frequent prefixes C_{ij} within this refined domain. The iteration proceeds until the final group D_{in}, from which the top-k heavy hitters are ultimately extracted, denoted by C_{in}.

As demonstrated in Algorithm 1, the users in each group sanitize their s_{ij}-bit prefixes and report noisy data to the aggregator in lines 5–10. The aggregator initially constructs D_{ij} in line 16, receives the reported data from the users, and record N_{ij} in line 17, and then corrects the frequency of the values in D_{ij} in line 18. Finally, the aggregator obtains the collection of heavy hitters of group G_i in line 19–21.

4.4 Personalized Perturbation Protocol

The proposed POLH is a direct method based on OLH in personalized local differential privacy scenarios. Due to the different privacy protection requirements of each user, users are divided into different groups according to different privacy budgets, namely $G_1, \ldots, G_m$. Among them, the privacy budget for ε_τ corresponds to user group G_τ, which is used to perturb a value in this group with OLH.

Specifically, users in group G_τ first select a specific permutation function H from a permutation family to permute item x to $H(x)$, with its output size g equal to $\lceil e^{\varepsilon_\tau} + 1 \rceil$. Each hash value $H(x)$ is perturbed by the following formula:

$$\Pr(y \mid H(x)) = \begin{cases} \dfrac{e^{\varepsilon_\tau}}{e^{\varepsilon_\tau}+g-1}, \text{ if } y = H(x); \\ \dfrac{1}{e^{\varepsilon_\tau}+g-1}, \text{ if } y \neq H(x). \end{cases} \tag{11}$$

Let p and q denote the probability that the perturbed output y equals or does not equal $H(x)$, respectively:

$$p = \frac{e^{\varepsilon_\tau}}{e^{\varepsilon_\tau}+g-1}, \quad q = \frac{1}{e^{\varepsilon_\tau}+g-1}. \tag{12}$$

After perturbation, users in group G_τ report $\langle H, y\rangle$ to the aggregator. The aggregator estimates the frequency for each value using the following corrected equation:

$$\hat{\Omega}_x^\tau = \frac{C_x - N_\tau \cdot q}{p-q} \tag{13}$$

where C_x is the number of reports observed to "support" input x, and N_τ is the number of users in group G_τ. We note that the variance of OLH as $n \cdot \frac{4e^\varepsilon}{(e^\varepsilon-1)^2}$. Since POLH independently performs OLH within each group, according to the parallel composition theorem, the variance of POLH can be formulated as follows.

$$\text{Var}_x^\tau = N_\tau \cdot \frac{4e^{\varepsilon_\tau}}{(e^{\varepsilon_\tau}-1)^2} \tag{14}$$

4.5 Weighted Combination

Since the direct estimation merging method may result in a relatively higher estimation error, especially when the data distribution of each group is uneven, we propose the weighted combination (WC) method for effective data aggregation. This method combines group-specific estimates $\hat{\Omega}_x^{\varepsilon_i}$ using variance-minimizing weights. For each item x, the combined estimate is computed as:

$$\hat{\Omega}_x = \sum_{i=1}^{m} w_{\varepsilon_i} \hat{\Omega}_x^{\varepsilon_i} \tag{15}$$

where the weight for group i is given by:

$$w_{\varepsilon_i} = \frac{(e^{\varepsilon_i}-1)^2/(N_i e^{\varepsilon_i})}{\sum_{i=1}^{m}(e^{\varepsilon_i}-1)^2/(N_i e^{\varepsilon_i})} \tag{16}$$

Here, N_i denotes the number of users in group G_i with privacy budget ε_i, and $\hat{\Omega}_x^{\varepsilon_i}$ is the frequency estimate for item x within group G_i.

The final frequency distribution is obtained as $\hat{\Omega} = [\hat{\Omega}_1, \hat{\Omega}_2, \ldots, \hat{\Omega}_d]$ where d is the domain size.

As shown in Algorithm 1, the aggregator initially collects C_{in} in line 23–24, and then combines them by weighted combination in line 26. Finally, the aggregator obtains heavy hitters W_{mn} of all groups in line 27.

Algorithm 1. *Mining heavy hitters under PLDP*

Require: Privacy levels $\varepsilon_1, \varepsilon_2, \ldots, \varepsilon_m$, number of users N, number of privacy levels m, number of prefix extensions n, number of heavy hitters k, data domain D, domain length l.

Ensure: Heavy hitters W_{mn} under PLDP.

1: Partition users into m groups $G_1, G_2, \ldots, G_m$ according to their privacy level ε_i
2: Initialize $C_{00} = \emptyset$
3: **for** $i = 1$ to m **do**
4: Partition users in group G_i into n subgroups $G_{i1}, \ldots, G_{in}$
5: Initialize $s_{i0} = \lceil \log_2 k \rceil$, $C_{i0} = \{0,1\}^{s_{i0}}$
6: **for** $j = 1$ to n **do**
7: $s_{ij} = \lceil \log_2 k \rceil + \left\lceil \frac{l - \lceil \log_2 k \rceil}{n} \cdot j \right\rceil$
8: Each user in G_{ij} creates s_{ij}-bit prefixes from their value x
9: Perturb prefix x to y using the following probability mechanism:

$$\Pr(y \mid H(x)) = \begin{cases} \frac{e^{\varepsilon_i}}{e^{\varepsilon_i}+g-1}, & \text{if } y = H(x) \\ \frac{1}{e^{\varepsilon_i}+g-1}, & \text{if } y \neq H(x) \end{cases}$$

10: Report $\langle i, j, H, y \rangle$ to the aggregator
11: **end for**
12: **end for**
13: **for** $i = 1$ to m **do**
14: **for** $j = 1$ to n **do**
15: $s_{ij} = \lceil \log_2 k \rceil + \left\lceil \frac{l - \lceil \log_2 k \rceil}{n} \cdot j \right\rceil$
16: Construct domain $D_{ij} = C_{i(j-1)} \times \{0,1\}^{s_{ij} - s_{i(j-1)}}$
17: Receive reports from users in G_{ij} and record $N_{ij} = |G_{ij}|$
18: Correct prefix frequencies using:

$$\hat{\Omega}_x^i = \frac{C_x - N_{ij} \cdot q}{p - q}, \quad p = \frac{e^{\varepsilon_i}}{e^{\varepsilon_i} + g - 1}, \quad q = \frac{1}{e^{\varepsilon_i} + g - 1} \quad \text{(Correction)}$$

19: Construct top-k estimated prefixes C_{ij}
20: **end for**
21: Save the final subgroup result of group i: $C_{in} = C_{i,n}$
22: **end for**
23: **for** $i = 1$ to m **do**
24: Collect C_{in} (final subgroup result of group i)
25: **end for**
26: Combine C_{in} (for $i = 1, 2, \ldots, m$) using weighted combination:

$$w_{\varepsilon_i} = \frac{(e^{\varepsilon_i} - 1)^2 / (N_i e^{\varepsilon_i})}{\sum_{i=1}^{m} (e^{\varepsilon_i} - 1)^2 / (N_i e^{\varepsilon_i})}, \quad \hat{\Omega}_x = \sum_{i=1}^{m} w_{\varepsilon_i} \cdot \hat{\Omega}_x^{\varepsilon_i} \quad \text{(Weighted Combination)}$$

27: Obtain top-k items W_{mn} from combined estimates

4.6 Privacy Guarantee

In this section, we first prove the privacy guarantees of the proposed PPEM algorithm, followed by an analysis of the privacy properties of the employed perturbation method, POLH.

Theorem 4 (Privacy of PPEM). *The proposed PPEM mechanism can ensure a rigorous PLDP guarantee if the perturbation mechanism M satisfies ε-PLDP.*

Proof. For any two inputs $x, x' \in D$ and any output $\langle i, y\rangle \in \text{Range(PPEM)}$,

$$\frac{\Pr[\text{PPEM}(x) = \langle i, y\rangle]}{\Pr[\text{PPEM}(x') = \langle i, y\rangle]} = \frac{\Pr[\mathcal{M}(x[0:s_i]) = y] \cdot \Pr[i]}{\Pr[\mathcal{M}(x'[0:s_i]) = y] \cdot \Pr[i]},$$

where $\mathcal{M}$ is the POLH perturbation mechanism with domain size 2^s for a prefix length s_i. Given that $\mathcal{M}$ is ε-PLDP, we have

$$\frac{\Pr[\mathcal{M}(x[0:s_i]) = y]}{\Pr[\mathcal{M}(x'[0:s_i]) = y]} \leq e^{\varepsilon},$$

and therefore,

$$\frac{\Pr[\text{PPEM}(x) = \langle i, y\rangle]}{\Pr[\text{PPEM}(x') = \langle i, y\rangle]} \leq e^{\varepsilon}$$

Therefore, we can conclude that PPEM is ε-PLDP.

Theorem 5 (Privacy of POLH). *POLH satisfies ε-PLDP.*

Proof. Let $\mathcal{M}$ denote the POLH perturbation mechanism. For any two users' prefix $v[0:s_i], v'[0:s_i]$ and any output $\langle y, H\rangle \in \text{Range}(\mathcal{M})$,

$$\frac{\Pr[\text{POLH}(x[0:s_i]) = \langle y, H\rangle]}{\Pr[\text{POLH}(x'[0:s_i]) = \langle y, H\rangle]} = \frac{\Pr[\mathcal{M}(v[0:s_i]) = y] \cdot \Pr[H]}{\Pr[\mathcal{M}(v'[0:s_i]) = y] \cdot \Pr[H]},$$

where y is a set of noisy values.

According to Eq. (11), we have

$$\frac{\Pr[\mathcal{M}(H(x[0:s_i]) = y]}{\Pr[\mathcal{M}(H(x'[0:s_i]) = y]} = \frac{\frac{e^{\varepsilon_\tau}}{e^{\varepsilon_\tau}+g-1}}{\frac{1}{e^{\varepsilon_\tau}+g-1}} = e^{\varepsilon_\tau},$$

Thus, POLH satisfies ε-PLDP.

5 Experiment

This section presents the results of an experimental evaluation of the proposed scheme for heavy hitter identification on a large scale.

5.1 Setup of Experiments

Datasets. The datasets for our experiments are outlined below.

- **Synthetic Dataset.** We constructed a dataset containing 100,000 records based on the geometric distribution $GE(0.05)$, with a domain size of 2^{64}, where each user owns one record. Each record has one item.
- **URL Dataset.**
We created a dataset containing 500,000 records based on the popular websites across the globe[1] First, each URL was padded or truncated to a uniform length of 16 characters, then each character was converted to its corresponding ASCII code, resulting in each value being represented by 128 bits (16×8).

Utility Measure. In our experiments, we used two common metrics to measure the performance of PPEM: the F1-score, nDCG.

- **F-score (F1).** The F1 score [16] is employed to evaluate the comprehensive accuracy of classification models, taking into account two principal metrics: precision and recall. Precision refers to the proportion of items identified in D' that truly belong to D, while recall measures how many items in D are correctly included in D'. The F1 score is calculated as the harmonic mean of precision and recall, with a higher value indicating superior algorithm performance under the premise of privacy protection, and thus greater usability. The formula for calculating the F1 score is as follows.

$$\text{precision} = \frac{|D \cap D'|}{|D'|} \quad \text{ecall} = \frac{|D \cap D'|}{|D|} \tag{17}$$

where D and D' be the sets of actual and published heavy hitters, $precision = \frac{|D \cap D'|}{D'}$, and $recall = \frac{|D \cap D'|}{D}$.
- **Normalized Discounted Cumulative Gain (nDCG).** Normalized Discounted Cumulative Gain (nDCG) is a widely used evaluation metric in top-k recommendation systems. It evaluates the quality of a ranked list by considering both the relevance of the retrieved items and their positions in the ranking. Given the true top-k item set T and an estimated ranked list E of length k, we define the binary relevance score rel_i for each item i at position r in E as:

$$rel_i = \begin{cases} 1, & i \in T \\ 0, & \text{otherwise} \end{cases} \tag{18}$$

The Discounted Cumulative Gain (DCG) of the estimated list E is then computed as:

[1] Popular Websites Across the Globe. Kaggle (2017). https://www.kaggle.com/datasets/bpali26/popular-websites-across-the-globe/. Last accessed 14 Jun 2025.

$$DCG_k = \sum_{r=1}^{k} \frac{rel_r}{\log_2(r+1)} \tag{19}$$

The Ideal DCG (IDCG) assumes all k relevant items are ranked in the top k positions, and is defined as:

$$IDCG_k = \sum_{r=1}^{k} \frac{1}{\log_2(r+1)} \tag{20}$$

The normalized DCG is computed as the ratio:

$$NDCG_k = \frac{DCG_k}{IDCG_k} \tag{21}$$

where $NDCG_k = 0$ when $IDCG_k = 0$. Specifically, our proposed method and baselines are independently executed 30 times, and the average nDCG scores are reported to evaluate and compare the ranking performance.

Experimental Design. To explore the practical utility of the weighted combination strategy in PPEM, we designed five sets of controlled experiments. First, four different privacy levels were set, and the dataset was randomly partitioned into these groups with uniform distribution, corresponding to Group 1 ($\varepsilon = 2$), Group 2 ($\varepsilon = 3$), Group 3 ($\varepsilon = 4$), and Group 4 ($\varepsilon = 5$). By integrating the results of the four groups, a comprehensive output of the weighted combination was finally formed. Additionally, the experiment systematically investigated the impact mechanisms of key variables such as the number of heavy hitters k and the bits of prefix extension $Step - length$ on the algorithm's performance.

5.2 Effect of Different Parameters

Effect of k. As shown in Fig. 3, the performance of PPEM displays a non-monotonic trend (initial improvement followed by degradation) with increasing k on the synthetic dataset. This behavior stems from inherent characteristics of the synthetic dataset: closely spaced frequencies among high-frequency items make their ranking vulnerable to noise interference, leading to inaccurate identification of heavy hitters at small k. At the same time, the significant frequency gap between frequent and infrequent items causes performance to first increase, then decrease as k grows. In contrast, the weighted combination maintains consistently strong performance through effective integration of subgroup information, demonstrating optimal noise resistance at higher k.

As shown in Fig. 4, PPEM performance shows a decreasing trend with increasing k on the URL dataset. This occurs because a higher k requires identifying more heavy hitters, which may include some infrequent items. Low-frequency values are especially vulnerable to noise interference, and their recognition errors lead to overall performance degradation. By contrast, the weighted combination

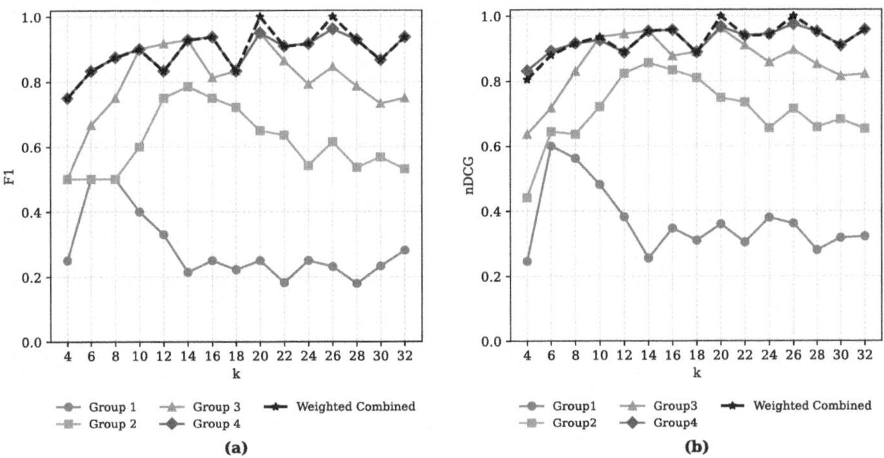

Fig. 3. Evaluation on the synthetic dataset, varying k while $Step - length = 10$.

maintains stronger performance by effectively combining subgroup advantages. This approach reduces performance decline, resulting in improved model stability and robustness.

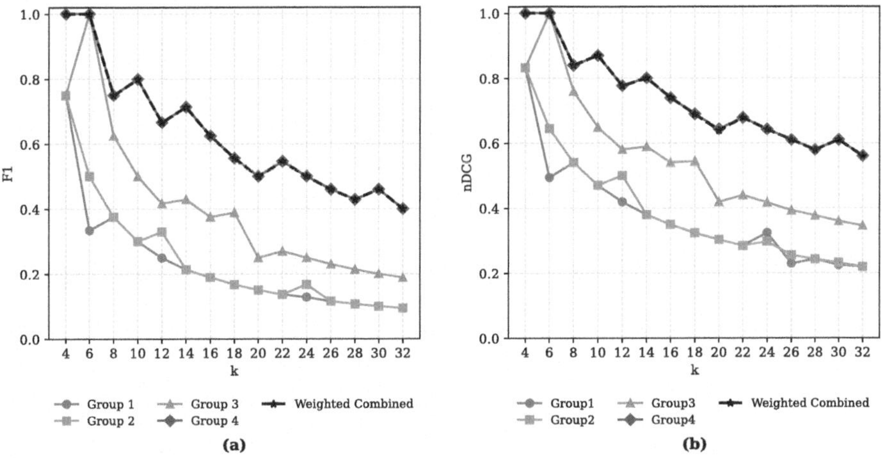

Fig. 4. Evaluation on the URL dataset, varying k while $Step - length = 10$.

Effect of $\boldsymbol{Step - length}$. As illustrated in Fig. 5, the performance of the PPEM algorithm improves with increasing $Step - length$ on the synthetic dataset. Specifically, the weighted combination consistently maintains a high level of performance by effectively leveraging the advantages of each subgroup. Since the estimation for the current subgroup relies on the results from the preceding subgroup, estimation errors would accumulate, and the cumulative error increases with the number of subgroups. Consequently, increasing the $Step - length$ reduces the required number of subgroups, thereby effectively mitigating error accumulation and ultimately enhancing the overall algorithmic performance.

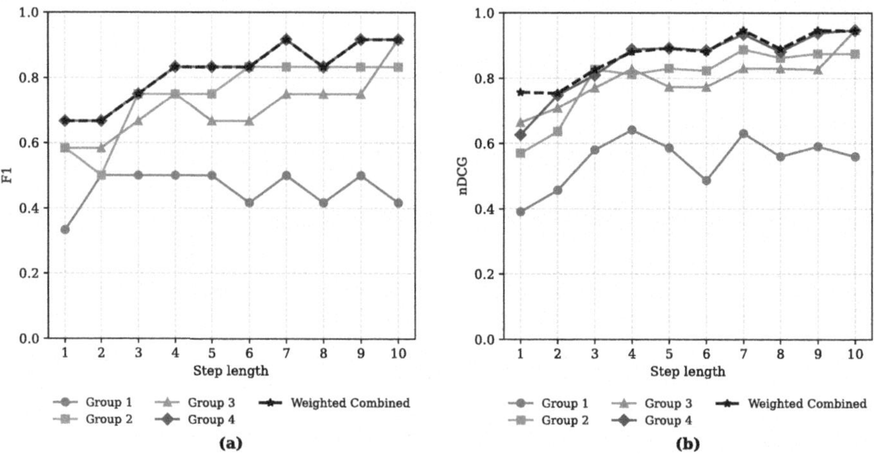

Fig. 5. Evaluation on the synthetic dataset, varying $Step - length$ while fixing $k = 12$.

As shown in the Fig. 6, on the URL dataset, as the $Step - length$ increases, the overall performance of PPEM shows an upward trend. Specifically, the result after the weighted combination continues to rise and stabilizes at a relatively high level. In general, we can observe that a larger $Step - length$ can provide better

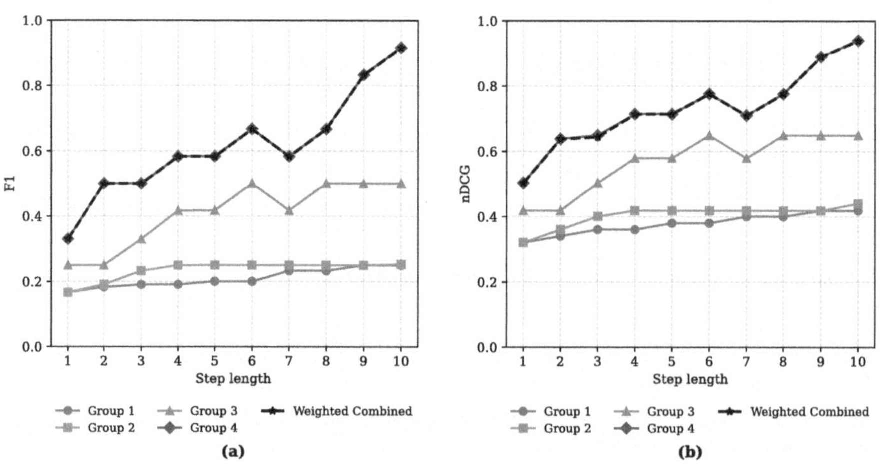

Fig. 6. Evaluation on the URL dataset, varying $Step - length$ while fixing $k = 12$.

utility. This is because a larger $Step - length$ can reduce the number of groups, mitigating the accumulation of statistical noise caused by excessive subdivision.

6 Conclusion

We have proposed a method called PPEM for identifying the heavy hitters within large domain data within the context of personalized local differential privacy. In this method, users only perturb and report the prefixes of their items, which significantly reduces the computational and communication overhead. Additionally, the POLH mechanism has been introduced to address the data frequency estimation issue under personalized local differential privacy. We employ a weighted combination method (WC) to effectively integrate data from each statistical group. Finally, experiments conducted on both synthetic and URL datasets have validated the effectiveness of the PPEM method.

A major limitation of PPEM lies in its grouping strategy, which requires the data collector to know each participant's privacy budget in advance to form groups. However, these privacy budgets themselves constitute sensitive information that requires protection, an issue that current methods do not adequately address. In future work, we aim to develop mechanisms that protect both users' private data and their privacy preferences in order to better meet the needs of real-life applications.

Funding Information. Wenzhou Science and Technology Plan under Grant ZG2023028.

References

1. Dwork, C.: Differential privacy: a survey of results. In: International Conference on Theory and Applications of Models of Computation 2008, pp. 1–19. Springer (2008). https://doi.org/10.1007/978-3-540-79228-4_1
2. Duchi, J. C., Jordan, M. I., Wainwright, M. J.: Local privacy and statistical minimax rates. In: IEEE 54th Annual Symposium on Foundations of Computer Science 2013, pp. 429–438. IEEE, Berkeley, CA, USA (2013). https://doi.org/10.1109/FOCS.2013.53
3. Erlingsson, U., Pihur, V., Korolova, A.: Rappor: randomized aggregatable privacy-preserving ordinal response. In: Proceedings of the 2014 ACM SIGSAC Conference on Computer and Communications Security, pp. 1054–1067. ACM, Scottsdale, AZ, USA (2014). https://doi.org/10.1145/2660267.2660348
4. Song, H., Shen, H., Zhao, N., et al.: Adaptive personalized privacy-preserving data collection scheme with local differential privacy. J. King Saud Univ.-Comput. Inf. Sci. **36**(4), 102042 (2024). https://doi.org/10.1016/j.jksuci.2024.102042
5. Zhang, P., Cheng, X., Zhang, Z., Zhu, Y., Zhang, J.: Maximizing area coverage in privacy-preserving worker recruitment: a prior knowledge-enhanced geo-indistinguishable approach. IEEE Trans. Inf. Forensics Secur. **20**, 5138–5151 (2025). https://doi.org/10.1109/TIFS.2025.3568163

6. Zhang, P., Fang, X., Zhang, Z., Fang, X., Liu, Y., Zhang, J.: Horizontal multi-party data publishing via discriminator regularization and adaptive noise under differential privacy. Inf. Fusion **120**, 103046 (2025). https://doi.org/10.1016/j.inffus.2025.103046
7. Thakurta, A.G., et al.: Emoji frequency detection and deep link frequency. US Patent 9,705,908 (2017)
8. Zhang, P., Sun, H., Zhang, Z., Cheng, X., Zhu, Y., Zhang, J.: Privacy-preserving recommendations with mixture model-based matrix factorization under local differential privacy. IEEE Trans. Ind. Inf. 1–9 (2025). https://doi.org/10.1109/TII.2025.3555993
9. Warner, S.L.: Randomized response: a survey technique for eliminating evasive answer bias. J. Amer. Stat. Assoc. **60**(309), 63–69 (1965). https://doi.org/10.1080/01621459.1965.10480775
10. Nie, Y.W., Yang, W., Huang, L., et al.: A utility-optimized framework for personalized private histogram estimation. IEEE Trans. Knowl. Data Eng. **31**(4), 655–669 (2018). https://doi.org/10.1109/TKDE.2018.2841360
11. Shen, Z., Xia, Z., Yu, P.: PLDP: personalized local differential privacy for multidimensional data aggregation. Secur. Commun. Netw. **2021**(1), 6684179 (2021). https://doi.org/10.1155/2021/6684179
12. Bassily, R., Smith, A.: Local, private, efficient protocols for succinct histograms. In: Proceedings of the Forty-Seventh Annual ACM Symposium on Theory of Computing 2015, pp. 127–135. ACM, USA (2015). https://doi.org/10.1145/2746539.2746632
13. Qin, Z., Yang, Y., Yu, T., Khalil, I., Xiao, X., Ren, K.: Heavy hitter estimation over set-valued data with local differential privacy. In: Proceedings of the ACM SIGSAC Conference on Computer and Communications Security 2016, pp. 192–203. ACM, Vienna, Austria (2016). https://doi.org/10.1145/2976749.2978409
14. Wang, T., Li, N., Jha, S.: Locally differentially private heavy hitter identification. IEEE Trans. Dependable Secure Comput. **18**(2), 982–993 (2019). https://doi.org/10.1109/TDSC.2019.2927695
15. Wang, S., Huang, L., Nie, Y., et al.: Privset: set-valued data analyses with local differential privacy. In: IEEE INFOCOM 2018 - IEEE Conference on Computer Communications, pp. 1088–1096. IEEE, Honolulu, Hawaii, USA (2018). https://doi.org/10.1109/INFOCOM.2018.8486234
16. Manning, C.D., Raghavan, P., Schütze, H.: Introduction to Information Retrieval, 1st edn. Cambridge University Press, Cambridge (2008)
17. McSherry, F.D.: Privacy integrated queries: an extensible platform for privacy-preserving data analysis. In: Proceedings of the ACM SIGMOD International Conference on Management of Data 2009, pp. 19–30. ACM (2009). https://doi.org/10.1145/1559845.1559850
18. Wang, T., Blocki, J., Li, N., Jha, S.: Locally differentially private protocols for frequency estimation. In: 26th USENIX Security Symposium 2017, pp. 729–745. USENIX Association, Vancouver, BC, Canada (2017)
19. Zhao, D., Zhao, S., Chen, H.: Efficient protocols for heavy hitter identification with local differential privacy. Front. Comp. Sci. **16**(5), 165303 (2022). https://doi.org/10.1007/s11704-021-0412-y

A Dynamic Load Balancing Scheme with Differential Privacy for Traffic Analysis in Security Crowdsourcing Platforms

Tengyuan Liu[1], Zhenyu Li[1], Chunhai Li[1,2], and Zhaoyu Su[2](✉)

[1] School of Computer Science and Information Security, Guilin University of Electronic Technology, Guilin 541004, China

[2] Guangxi Engineering Research Center of Industrial Internet Security and Blockchain, Guilin University of Electronic Technology, Guilin 541004, China

szyguet@guet.edu.cn, yfx@mails.guet.edu.cn

Abstract. With the rapid growth of applications like 5G, ICS, and mobile crowdsensing, high-throughput network traffic poses increasing challenges for efficient packet processing and privacy protection. To address this, we propose DP-DMAPSA(Differential Privacy-based Dynamic Multi-dimensional Adaptive Packet Scheduling Algorithm), a dynamic, adaptive scheduling framework based on DPDK(Data Plane Development Kit) that integrates differential privacy into load balancing. DP-DMAPSA features a multi-dimensional, load-aware scheduling algorithm that considers queue depth, CPU usage, and processing latency. To safeguard sensitive load data, it applies Laplace and Gaussian noise to these metrics before making scheduling decisions. The final core selection is based on a weighted combination of hash values and noise-protected load indicators. Additionally, the framework adapts scheduling granularity in real time to improve resource utilization. Experiments show that DP-DMAPSA improves system throughput by 30%, outperforming traditional methods in both performance and privacy.

Keywords: High-Throughput Network · DPDK · Differential Privacy · Adaptive Scheduling · Privacy-preserving Networking

1 Introduction

Security crowdsourcing has established itself as a critical cybersecurity paradigm, harnessing the collective intelligence of a distributed "crowd" of users and devices for collaborative tasks like malware analysis, threat intelligence sharing, and network attack detection. While powerful, this model presents a formidable challenge: the aggregation of diverse security data including suspicious files, URL samples, and traffic logs from global nodes generates high velocity data streams. This influx imposes immense strain on a system's real-time packet processing capabilities, necessitating that modern network infrastructure be engineered to

L. Zhang and K.-K. R. Choo (Eds.): MobiQuitous 2025, LNICST 684, pp. 445–458, 2026.
https://doi.org/10.1007/978-3-032-22503-0_24

handle millions of packets per second (Mpps) while maintaining low latency and ensuring robustness against dynamic traffic patterns. Consequently, achieving efficient packet processing in multi-core processor environments has emerged as a critical challenge in constructing contemporary communication infrastructures [1]. This approach leverages parallel computation to distribute packet processing tasks across multiple cores.

However, attaining optimal load balancing in these systems remains a formidable hurdle. Traditional scheduling algorithms often struggle to adapt to dynamic traffic fluctuations [2] and face potential privacy threats from traffic analysis attacks [3]. Furthermore, they frequently fail to concurrently optimize for multiple performance metrics, such as queue depth, CPU utilization, and processing latency. The enforcement of stringent data privacy regulations like GDPR has also made the protection of sensitive information within network traffic statistics a critical concern, adding another layer of complexity to system design. Modern data centers face unprecedented demands for processing high-concurrency traffic. The Data Plane Development Kit (DPDK) [4] facilitates high-performance packet handling by bypassing kernel overhead through user-space packet processing, zero-copy mechanisms, and polling-mode drivers. However, its effectiveness is heavily dependent on efficient load balancing strategies across processing cores. In parallel, programmable data plane approaches have emerged, offering line-rate processing capabilities [2].

Traditional scheduling algorithms like Round-Robin [5] and Highest Random Weight (HRW) [6] ensure flow consistency but exhibit poor performance under dynamic traffic conditions. Round-Robin overlooks core utilization, leading to potential core overload, while HRW fails to adapt to real-time load variations. Furthermore, these methods do not address privacy, leaving load data vulnerable to inference attacks. Although some privacy-aware solutions have been proposed [3], their integration into real-time systems remains underexplored. For instance, homomorphic encryption can provide privacy but at the cost of significantly reduced throughput. Differential privacy offers a promising alternative. For example, NetDPSyn achieves (ε, δ)-differential privacy for flow-level traffic statistics [7], yet it does not address dynamic scheduling. While recent studies have explored its application in real-time systems [8], integrating privacy protection into high-performance load balancing without compromising throughput remains an open challenge. Therefore, the core problem addressed in this paper is how to design a load balancing framework that not only maintains high throughput under dynamic traffic but also ensures that sensitive load statistics are protected from inference attacks. To tackle these issues, this paper introduces a novel load balancing framework named DP-DMAPSA, which builds upon DPDK and incorporates both differential privacy mechanisms and adaptive sub-flow scheduling techniques. DP-DMAPSA introduces the following key innovations:

- A multi-dimensional load-aware scheduling mechanism that dynamically selects target cores based on queue depth, CPU utilization, and processing latency;

- Integration of differential privacy mechanisms (including Laplace, Gaussian, and Exponential mechanisms) to protect load statistics while maintaining scheduling accuracy;
- An adaptive flow scheduling strategy that adjusts scheduling granularity according to traffic volume, optimizing both throughput and resource utilization.

These features enable DP-DMAPSA to achieve a significant throughput improvement of up to 30% and reduce the packet loss rate to nearly 0%. This ensures a high-performance, balanced load distribution while simultaneously guaranteeing privacy protection.

The remainder of this paper is organized as follows: Sect. 2 reviews related work. Section 3 details the packet scheduling algorithms. Section 4 evaluates the performance of the proposed method. Finally, Sect. 5 concludes the paper and outlines future research directions.

2 Related Works

2.1 Load Balancing Techniques in Multi-Core Environments

Load balancing in multi-core environments persists as a significant challenge in network system design. Traditional static approaches, such as Equal-Cost Multi-Path (ECMP) routing, distribute flows using hash functions but are susceptible to "hash polarization," which can lead to uneven load distribution [9]. Classical scheduling algorithms, including Round-Robin (RR) [10] and HRW [11], have demonstrated limitations in managing dynamic traffic fluctuations. While RR treats packets as the basic scheduling unit and achieves relatively effective load balancing, it disrupts flow consistency by assigning packets from the same flow to different cores, thereby degrading data locality.

In recent years, load balancing technologies have advanced considerably. Barbette et al. [12] introduced RSS++, a load and state-aware receive-side scaling mechanism. RSS++ dynamically adjusts its hashing function based on the real-time load of CPU cores to facilitate adaptive flow distribution. Experimental results show that RSS++ maintains flow consistency while keeping the inter-core load imbalance within 5%, significantly outperforming traditional static hashing methods. Despite these improvements, challenges remain, particularly in real-time node state monitoring, the overhead associated with adjustment decisions, and the complete elimination of load discrepancies among cores, especially when handling highly dynamic or complex traffic patterns.

2.2 Applications of Differential Privacy in Network Systems

Differential privacy is increasingly adopted in modern network systems, particularly in domains like federated learning and payment systems. In the context of federated learning for wireless networks, Tavangaran et al. [13] proposed a differential privacy-enhanced scheme for multi-base-station environments. They analyzed the convergence properties of the learning process and introduced an optimized resource block scheduling method, combined with artificial noise injection, to mitigate privacy leakage risks. Simulation results indicate that their proposed scheduler improves prediction accuracy by over 6% compared to random scheduling while significantly reducing privacy leakage.

Furthermore, the growing demand for privacy protection continues to drive innovation in differential privacy solutions. Wei et al. [14] introduced a verifiable differential privacy framework that leverages zero-knowledge proofs. This approach verifies the correctness of noise generation under differential privacy without revealing the actual noise values, thereby striking a balance between data privacy and system transparency.

Overall, the application of differential privacy in network systems effectively reduces the risk of sensitive information leakage while maintaining system performance and data utility.

2.3 Adaptive Scheduling Techniques

Adaptive scheduling techniques have become a key area of research, particularly for managing dynamic traffic patterns. For instance, Brock et al. [15] compared Remote Direct Memory Access (RDMA) and Remote Procedure Call (RPC) for implementing distributed data structures. Their findings indicate that each technique offers distinct advantages depending on the specific workload and network conditions, underscoring the importance of selecting communication mechanisms tailored to the application scenario. In a different approach, Xu et al. [16] explored machine learning-based traffic prediction algorithms for dynamic traffic management in intelligent transportation systems. By leveraging deep learning to capture the spatial-temporal distribution characteristics of traffic flows, their method achieves significantly higher prediction accuracy and efficiency than traditional statistical approaches. This study demonstrates that learning-based prediction models can more effectively adapt to complex and variable traffic patterns, thereby providing robust decision support for adaptive scheduling strategies.

3 The Full DP-DMAPSA Design

3.1 System Architecture

The DP-DMAPSA algorithm integrates differential privacy with multi-dimensional adaptive load balancing. It injects Laplace noise into core load metrics to protect privacy while calculating load imbalance. Scheduling decisions are determined by four weighted factors: a hash value, core load, processing latency, and queue depth. To further enhance privacy, Gaussian noise is added to the latency metric and Laplace noise to the queue depth. The final core selection is then performed using an exponential mechanism. Additionally, an overload protection strategy is implemented to prevent core saturation. This holistic approach achieves a balance between high performance and robust data confidentiality in network systems.

The system is built upon a master-worker architecture. The master core receives high-speed network packets and distributes them to worker cores according to the scheduling algorithm. Each worker core processes its assigned packets and subsequently releases the associated resources. This architecture fully leverages the high-performance features of the DPDK, including user-space processing, zero-copy mechanisms, and polling-mode drivers, which collectively enable low-latency, high-throughput packet handling. The system architecture is illustrated in Fig. 1.

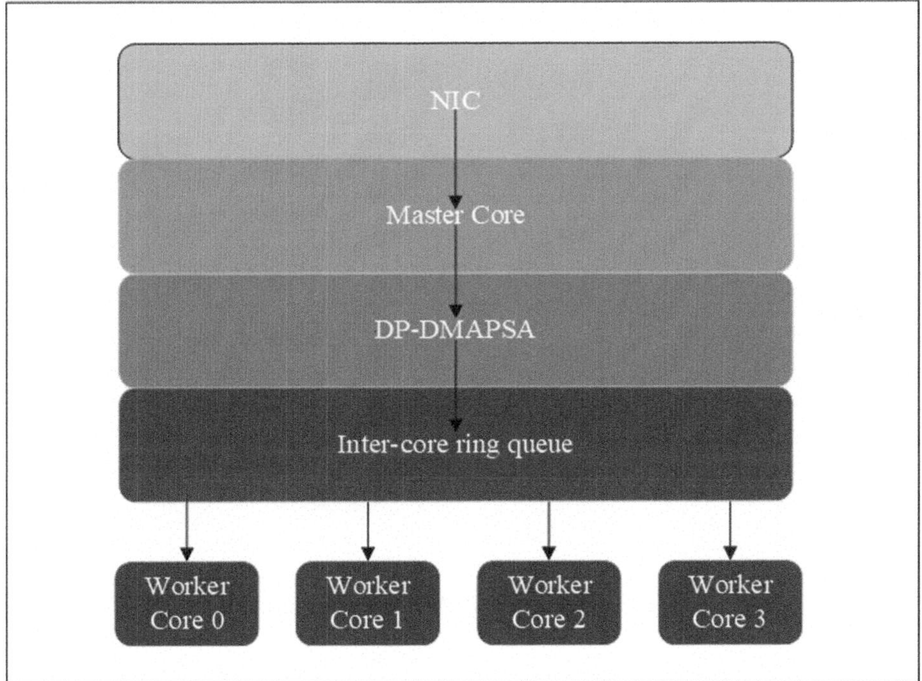

Fig. 1. DP-DMAPSA system architecture

The core of this work is the DP-DMAPSA algorithm, which combines differential privacy techniques with multi-dimensional load-aware scheduling. This design aims to address the challenge that traditional load balancing algorithms cannot simultaneously satisfy the requirements for high performance and privacy preservation. For instance, RR lacks flow consistency , Consistent Hashing does not account for real-time load variations , and existing load-aware algorithms may inadvertently expose sensitive system load data. Therefore, the design philosophy of DP-DMAPSA is to achieve the dual goals of protecting sensitive load information and ensuring efficient packet dispatching. The design philosophy of

DP-DMAPSA centers on the following principles and the principle of the DP-DMAPSA algorithm as displayed in Fig. 2:

- Leveraging differential privacy to protect load metrics and prevent inference of core load states through scheduling decisions.
- Utilizing multi-dimensional load indicators, including queue depth, CPU utilization, and packet processing latency.
- Dynamically adjusting scheduling policies to balance load distribution and flow consistency.
- Implementing adaptive flow granularity control to maximize overall system throughput.

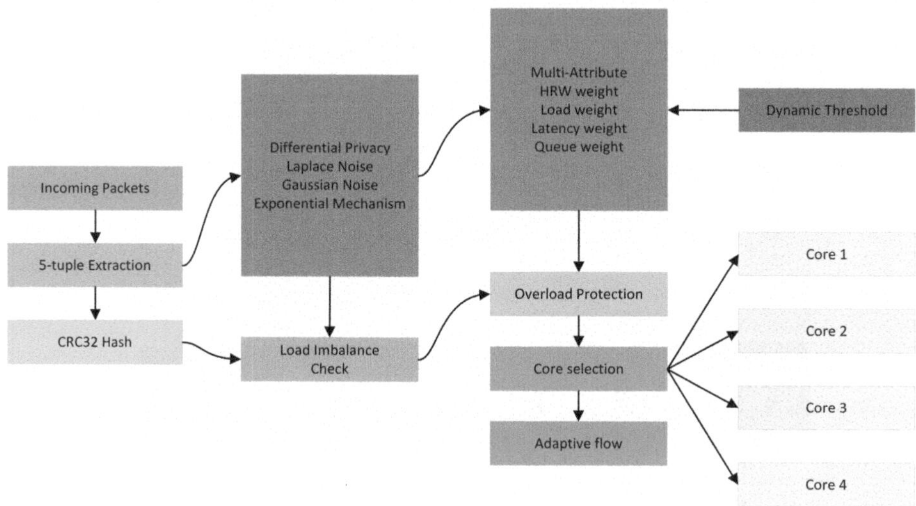

Fig. 2. DP-DMAPSA Algorithm Diagram

The implementation logic of the algorithm is closely aligned with the conceptual model depicted in Fig. 2. The complete scheduling workflow is detailed in Algorithm 1, which translates the entire process–from data extraction and hashing, through privacy-preserving processing, to multi-dimensional weighted decision-making–into executable pseudocode.

Line 1 initializes the target core array, clearing previous scheduling records to ensure a clean slate for handling new burst packets. Line 2 computes the flow ID using hash and module operations, mapping packets to subflows to maintain flow affinity and reduce packet reordering. Line 3 retrieves the cached target core assigned to the subflow. Line 4 checks whether the subflow requires reassignment to a new core. Line 6 invokes the DP_DMAPSA() function, which integrates differential privacy with the Highest Random Weight strategy to achieve a privacy-preserving yet performance-aware core selection, Line 7 updates the

Algorithm 1. DP-DMAPSA

Input: Incoming packet stream
Output: Packets assigned to appropriate cores
1: target[bsz_rd] ← {-1}
2: **for** each packet **do**
3: flow_id ← hash(5-tuple) mod current_bsz
4: core_id ← target[subflow_id]
5: **if** core_id == -1 **then**
6: core_id ← DP_DMAPSA(packet, C)
7: target[subflow_id] ← core_id
8: **end if**
9: Update_Threshold(core_id)
10: Enqueue_Packet(packet, core_id)
11: **end for**

cache with the newly selected core to accelerate future lookups. Line 8 updates the dynamic load threshold of the selected core to maintain adaptability under varying traffic conditions. Line 9 enqueues the packet into the corresponding queue of the assigned core to initiate processing. Line 10 concludes the scheduling loop, completing the dispatch process for the current burst batch.

In our proposed method, a hash-based design approach is employed. The DPDK's built-in CRC32 function is used to generate a unique identifier for each flow, ensuring flow affinity by consistently mapping the same flow to the same processing core. Moreover, the framework incorporates and extends the concept of the HRW algorithm. Unlike the traditional HRW–typically based on 5-tuple hashing for static request-server mapping in distributed systems, our implementation enhances it with differential privacy perturbations and multi-dimensional load awareness, significantly improving robustness and privacy guarantees under dynamic network conditions. To further enhance scheduling accuracy, the system incorporates an elastic subflow scheduling mechanism.

For each core, the overall scheduling weight is computed as follows:

$$DP\text{-}DMAPSA(c_i, f) = w_{\text{hash}}(c_i, f) \cdot w_{\text{load}}(c_i) \cdot w_{\text{delay}}(c_i) \cdot w_{\text{queue}}(c_i) \cdot B_i(1) \quad (1)$$

Assume that the system contains N worker cores, and define the following symbols: $C = c_1, c_2, ..., c_N$: the set of worker cores;f: a network flow uniquely identified by the 5-tuple $(src\_ip, dst\_ip, src\_port, dst\_port, proto)$; L_i: the load status of core c_i, which includes:the number of processed packets P_i, the queue depth Q_i, the average processing latency D_i. Upon receiving a burst of packets, the DP-DMAPSA algorithm evaluates multiple dimensions of system load, including queue depth, CPU utilization, and packet processing latency. These metrics are aggregated through a weighted combination to derive a composite scheduling score, which is then used to select the most appropriate target core. The first component, the Hash Weight, is calculated as follows:

$$w_{\text{hash}}(c_i, f) = \frac{H(f) \cdot (i + 1)}{2^{32} - 1} \quad (2)$$

Here, $\tilde{P}_i$ represents the number of packets processed by core i after applying differential privacy noise, while $\bar{P}$ denotes the average number of packets processed across all cores. The relative load is quantified by the ratio $\frac{\tilde{P}_i}{\bar{P}}$. Based on this, the delay weight is subsequently computed as follows:

$$w_{\text{load}}(c_i) = \frac{1}{1 + \frac{\tilde{P}_i}{\bar{P}+1}} \tag{3}$$

while $\tilde{P}_i$ represents the number of packets processed by the core after adding differential privacy noise. $\bar{P}$ denotes the average number of packets processed by all cores. The relative load is measured by the ratio $\frac{\tilde{P}_i}{\bar{P}}$. Subsequently, the delay weight is calculated by:

$$w_{\text{delay}}(c_i) = \frac{1}{1 + \frac{\tilde{D}_i}{\min_j \tilde{D}_j + 1}} \tag{4}$$

while $\tilde{D}_i$ represents the average processing delay of core i after adding differential privacy noise, and $\min_j \tilde{D}_j$ denotes the minimum processing delay among all cores (also after noise addition). The relative delay is measured by the ratio $\frac{\min_j \tilde{D}_j}{\tilde{D}_i}$, which helps identify and avoid assigning tasks to cores that may become performance bottlenecks. Finally, the queue depth weight is calculated as follows:

$$w_{\text{queue}}(c_i) = 1 - \frac{\tilde{Q}_i}{Q_{\max}} \tag{5}$$

while $\tilde{Q}_i$ represents the queue depth of core i after adding differential privacy noise, and $Q_{\max}$ denotes the maximum queue capacity. This weight directly affects the queuing delay of packets and helps prevent queue overflow and packet loss. The term $B_i(1)$ in the overall weight calculation can serve as a parameter to accelerate the load balancing process, especially during system startup, where it facilitates smoother operation.

To achieve a fine-grained and intelligent balance between consistency and load balancing, DP-DMAPSA introduces a sophisticated adaptive subflow scheduling mechanism. Unlike traditional methods that only consider incoming traffic volume, our approach dynamically adjusts the subflow granularity by taking into account both the current packet arrival rate and the real-time load of the worker cores. This dual-factor adaptation ensures the system responds more robustly to varying network conditions. First, we define a load factor, L_{factor}, which quantifies the current system pressure based on the average queue depth of all worker cores:

$$L_{\text{factor}} = 1 + \beta \cdot \left(\frac{\bar{Q}}{Q_{\max}}\right)^2 \tag{6}$$

Here, $Q_{\max}$ is the maximum queue capacity of a core, and β is a configurable hyperparameter that controls the sensitivity to system load. The quadratic term ensures that the load factor grows non-linearly, exerting a stronger influence as the system approaches its capacity.

This load factor is then integrated into our exponential mapping function to determine the scheduling granularity:

$$G(N, \bar{Q}) = G_{\min} + (G_{\max} - G_{\min}) \cdot \left(1 - e^{-\alpha \cdot L_{\text{factor}} \cdot \frac{N}{G_{\text{default}}}}\right) \quad (7)$$

In this enhanced formula, N is the number of packets in the current batch. The term L_{factor} acts as an accelerator for the granularity adjustment. Under low-load conditions ($\bar{Q} \approx 0$), $L_{\text{factor}} \approx 1$, and the granularity adapts primarily based on the incoming traffic N. However, as the system load increases, L_{factor} becomes greater than 1, causing the granularity G to increase more rapidly toward $G_{\max}$. This proactive adjustment helps to quickly reduce scheduling overhead when the system is under pressure, effectively preventing queue overflow and improving stability. This smooth, continuous function avoids the abrupt changes typical of piecewise adjustment methods, making the system more stable and responsive, particularly in bursty traffic scenarios. The parameters α and β can be flexibly configured to meet specific system requirements.

3.2 Security Model and Goals

This section defines the threat model that guides our privacy-preserving mechanisms.

Our primary goal is to protect sensitive system state information from being inferred by an attacker. This sensitive information includes real-time load metrics such as queue depth, CPU utilization, and packet processing latency, as well as sensitive traffic patterns that could be revealed through statistical analysis of scheduling decisions.

Assume a knowledgeable attacker who understands the entirety of the DP-DMAPSA algorithm, including the hashing methods and the multi-dimensional weight calculation. The attacker is capable of observing the final output of the scheduler–that is, which packets are assigned to which worker cores–but does not know the specific random noise values injected during the decision-making process. The attacker's objective is to analyze these observable scheduling decisions to reconstruct the true, non-privatized load status of the cores, thereby compromising the system's confidentiality. The integration of differential privacy is intended to formally mitigate this risk, providing a quantifiable measure of privacy protection against such inference attacks.

3.3 Formal Privacy Analysis

To ensure differential privacy, we first analyze the sensitivity of our load metrics. The L1 sensitivity of a function f is defined as $\Delta f = \max_{D,D'} ||f(D) - f(D')||_1$ for any two adjacent databases D and D' that differ by a single element. In our context, an adjacent database corresponds to a system state change caused by a single packet.

- For the processed packet count P_i and queue depth Q_i, adding or removing one packet changes the count by exactly 1. Therefore, their L1 sensitivity is $\Delta P = \Delta Q = 1$. This makes them suitable for the Laplace mechanism.
- For the average processing latency D_i, we assume the maximum possible latency for a single packet is bounded by $D_{\max}$. The L2 sensitivity can then be bounded, making it suitable for the Gaussian mechanism.

The DP-DMAPSA algorithm queries multiple sensitive metrics (P_i, D_i, Q_i) to compute the final scheduling weight. According to the composition theorem of differential privacy, the total privacy loss is the sum of the privacy losses from each query. We apply the basic composition theorem. If we allocate a privacy budget of ϵ_{load}, ϵ_{delay}, and ϵ_{queue} to the packet count, delay, and queue depth metrics respectively, the overall scheduling decision for a single packet will satisfy $(\epsilon_{\text{total}}, \delta_{\text{total}})$-differential privacy.

Therefore, the DP-DMAPSA algorithm provides $(\sum_j \epsilon_j, \sum_j \delta_j)$-differential privacy, where the summation is over all noised queries used in a scheduling decision. This formally guarantees that an adversary, as defined in our threat model, cannot reliably infer the precise load state of any individual core by observing the scheduler's output.

4 Results

In this section, we compare and evaluate our proposed method with the original HRW and CRC32. Our test server is an Intel server running on Ubuntu 22.04.5. We use pktgen-DPDK as the packet generator, and traffic is sent to the test server through a 10 Gbps link via a port. The version of DPDK used is 24.03.

4.1 Packet Loss Rate

The packet loss rate is a critical metric for evaluating the performance of load balancing algorithms, defined as the ratio of discarded packets to the total number of received packets. In this study, packet loss occurs when a core's input queue becomes full, causing incoming packets to be dropped. This mechanism effectively reflects the system's limitations under high-load conditions. To evaluate this, we collected three key statistics: the total number of received packets, the per-core packet distribution, and the number of packets discarded due to queue overflows. The packet loss rate, as the primary indicator of system performance under varying traffic loads, was computed based on these measurements. To assess the effectiveness of DP-DMAPSA in handling packet loss, we gradually increased the input traffic rate from 100 Mbps to 1000 Mbps, recording the packet loss rates for each scheduling algorithm. This was followed by long-term stability tests to evaluate their sustained performance over time. A comparative analysis of the packet loss rates for the three algorithms under different transmission rates is illustrated in Fig. 3.

Under low-load conditions, all algorithms maintain a packet loss rate below 10%. However, as the sending rate increases to 500Mbps, the packet loss rates

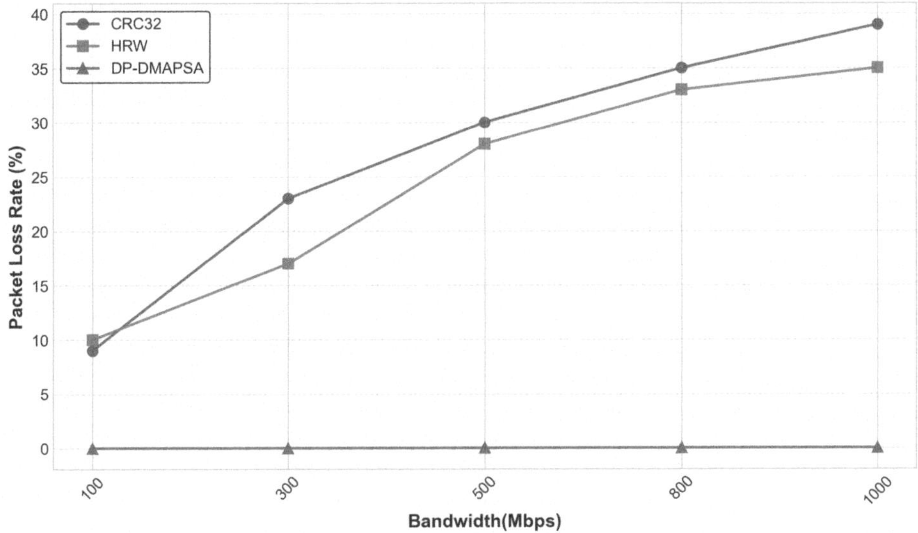

Fig. 3. Comparison of Packet Loss Rates for Different Scheduling Algorithms

for the CRC32 and HRW algorithms rise significantly to 30% and 27%, respectively. In sharp contrast, DP-DMAPSA maintains a zero packet loss rate. Even under heavier loads of 800–1000 Mbps, DP-DMAPSA sustains a negligible loss rate of just 0.01%. These results demonstrate that DP-DMAPSA consistently outperforms both HRW and CRC32 in packet loss performance across all tested traffic rates.

This superior performance is attributed to DP-DMAPSA's dynamic adaptive flow granularity mechanism. This feature effectively distributes packets to appropriate cores, which prevents queue overflow and enhances overall system throughput. Conversely, the other scheduling algorithms suffer from packet drops caused by core overload, leading to degraded performance.

A further performance evaluation was conducted using four typical packet sizes–64B, 256B, 512B, and 1500B–to represent small, medium, and large packet flows. These tests were run at a constant sending rate of 500Mbps. Each test was conducted for 60 s and repeated five times, with the results averaged to ensure accuracy. Figure 4 illustrates the resulting throughput performance for the three algorithms across these different packet sizes.

The impact of packet size on system throughput as shown in Fig. 4. As packet size increases from 64B to 1500B, all algorithms demonstrate improved throughput, attributable to more efficient network bandwidth utilization and reduced relative overhead from packet headers. Specifically, the throughput of DP-DMAPSA increases approximately sevenfold as packet size grows from 64B to 1500B.

Across all test scenarios, DP-DMAPSA consistently achieves the highest throughput. In small-packet scenarios (e.g., 64 B), it reaches approximately

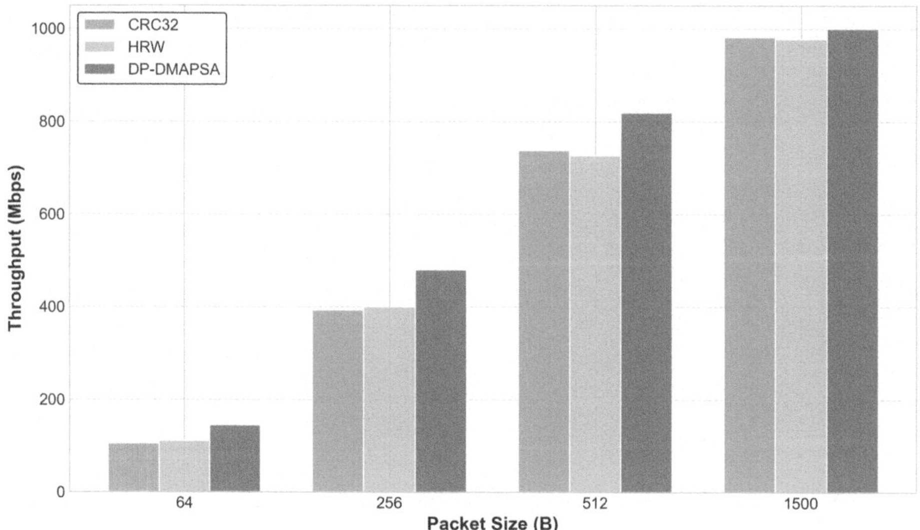

Fig. 4. Throughput Comparison of Scheduling Algorithms Across Different Packet Sizes

150 Mbps, outperforming CRC32 by about 30% and HRW by 27%. This performance advantage is also pronounced for medium-sized packets, where DP-DMAPSA surpasses both CRC32 and HRW by approximately 25–30%.

For 1500B packets, the performance gap between the three algorithms narrows. Yet, DP-DMAPSA still maintains the lead, achieving around 1000 Mbps, which is roughly 5% and 8% higher than CRC32 and HRW, respectively. These results indicate that while the impact of scheduling differences diminishes under near-line-rate conditions, DP-DMAPSA continues to deliver stable performance benefits.

5 Conclusions

Experimental results confirm that the DP-DMAPSA algorithm significantly outperforms traditional methods in both throughput and packet loss rate. Despite the computational overhead of its differential privacy mechanisms, the algorithm maintains exceptional performance, effectively leveraging computing resources to demonstrate its practicality and robustness in high-performance networking environments.

Despite its strong performance, the algorithm's reliance on a fixed privacy budget is a key limitation. Future work will focus on three areas: developing an adaptive privacy budget strategy, extending the framework to distributed environments, and incorporating machine learning to optimize scheduling decisions and system parameters.

For platforms like security crowdsourcing that depend on data contribution and analysis, our work offers a dual benefit: maintaining high performance while effectively safeguarding participant data privacy. Such a guarantee is essential for bolstering the platform's credibility and fostering wider user engagement. It lays a solid foundation for designing the next generation of secure and efficient network architectures.

Acknowledgments. This article is supported in part by the National Key R&D Program of China under project 2023YFB3107301.

References

1. Zhou, Z., He, M., Kellerer, W., Blenk, A., Foerster, K.T.: P4update: fast and locally verifiable consistent network updates in the p4 data plane. In: Proceedings of the 17th International Conference on emerging Networking EXperiments and Technologies, pp. 175–190 (2021)
2. Lee, J., Ko, H., Lee, H., Pack, S.: Flow-aware service function embedding algorithm in programmable data plane. IEEE Access **9**, 6113–6121 (2020)
3. Yan, J., Zhou, Y., Laifeng, L.: A node differential privacy-based method to preserve directed graphs in wireless mobile networks. Appl. Sci. **13**(14), 8089 (2023)
4. Belkhiri, A., Pepin, M., Bly, M., Dagenais, M.: Performance analysis of dpdk-based applications through tracing. J. Parallel Distrib. Comput. **173**, 1–19 (2023)
5. Hu, J., He, Y., Wang, J., Luo, W., Huang, J.: Rlb: reordering-robust load balancing in lossless datacenter networks. In: Proceedings of the 52nd International Conference on Parallel Processing, pp. 576–584 (2023)
6. Wei, Y., et al.: Heterogeneous graph neural network with semantic-aware differential privacy guarantees. Knowl. Inf. Syst. **65**(10), 4085–4110 (2023)
7. Sun, D., Chen, J.Q., Gong, C., Wang, T., Li, Z.: Netdpsyn: synthesizing network traces under differential privacy. In: Proceedings of the 2024 ACM on Internet Measurement Conference, pp. 545–554 (2024)
8. Owusu-Agyemeng, K., Qin, Z., Xiong, H., Liu, Y., Zhuang, T., Qin, Z.: Msdp: multi-scheme privacy-preserving deep learning via differential privacy. Pers. Ubiq. Comput. 1–13 (2023)
9. Gutiérrez, S.A., Botero, J.F., Branch-Bedoya, J.W.: An adaptable and agnostic flow scheduling approach for data center networks. J. Netw. Syst. Manag. **31**(1), 12 (2023)
10. Praditha, V.S., Hidayat, T.S., Akbar, M.A., Fajri, H., Lubis, M., Lubis, F.S., Safitra, M.F.: A systematical review on round robin as task scheduling algorithms in cloud computing. In: 2023 6th International Conference on Information and Communications Technology (ICOIACT), pp. 516–521. IEEE (2023)
11. Adewojo, A.A., Bass, J.M.: A novel weight-assignment load balancing algorithm for cloud applications. SN Comput. Sci. **4**(3), 270 (2023)
12. Barbette, T., Katsikas, G.P., Maguire Jr, G.Q., Kostić, D.: Rss++ load and state-aware receive side scaling. In: Proceedings of the 15th International Conference on Emerging Networking Experiments and Technologies, pp. 318–333 (2019)
13. Tavangaran, N., Chen, M., Yang, Z., Da Silva Jr, J.M.B., Poor, H.V.: On differential privacy for federated learning in wireless systems with multiple base stations. IET Commun. **18**(20), 1853–1867 (2024)

14. Wei, J., Chen, Y., Yang, X., Luo, Y., Pei, X.: A verifiable scheme for differential privacy based on zero-knowledge proofs. J. King Saud Univ. Comput. Inf. Sci. **37**(3), 1–15 (2025)
15. Brock, B.A., Chen, Y., Yan, J., Owens, J., Buluç, A., Yelick, K.: Rdma vs. rpc for implementing distributed data structures. In: 2019 IEEE/ACM 9th Workshop on Irregular Applications: Architectures and Algorithms (IA3), pp. 17–22. IEEE (2019)
16. Zheng, X., Yuan, J., Liqiang, Yu., Wang, G., Zhu, M.: Machine learning-based traffic flow prediction and intelligent traffic management. Int. J. Comput. Sci. Inf. Technol. **2**(1), 18–27 (2024)

Posters and Demos

Investigating the Effect of Professional Attire in Cartoon-Styled Embodied Agents on Health Learning Outcomes

Xinzhi Chen[1], Chanyuan Li[2], and Xueyang Wang[3](✉)

[1] Gold Mantis School of Architecture, Soochow University, Jiangsu, Suzhou, China
[2] The School of Design, East China Normal University, Shanghai, China
[3] Tongji College of Design and Innovation (Tongji D&I), Tongji University, Shanghai, China
2210910@tongji.edu.cn

Abstract. Embodied Conversational Agents (ECAs) are widely used in digital health education, but professional attire's impact on cartoon-styled ECAs is under-explored. Guided by social role signaling theory, a within-subject experiment (N = 32/group) compared cartoon ECAs (professional: white coat + stethoscope; casual) delivering nutrition advice. No significant knowledge difference (professional: $M = 10.75$, $SD = 4.02$; casual: $M = 9.84$, $SD = 4.02$; $p > 0.05$), but professional attire improved perceived professionalism ($\Delta M = +0.59$, $p = 0.021$), trust ($\Delta M = +0.38$, $p = 0.005$), visual-audio matching ($\Delta M = +0.75$, $p = 0.019$), and overall impression ($\Delta M = +0.25$, $p = 0.039$). Findings extend social agency models and guide balancing approachability/authority in health ECAs.

Keywords: ECAs · Cartoon Stylization · Professional Attire · Digital Health Education

1 Introduction

ECAs—virtual entities interacting via language, gestures, expressions—support digital health education (scalability/engagement [1]). Prior research focused on ECA realism, but professional attire's impact on cartoon-styled ECAs (avoids "uncanny valley" [2]) is untested.

Guided by CASA paradigm [3] and social role signaling theory [4] (attire triggers expertise judgments), we asked: (1) Does professional attire boost cartoon ECA-related health knowledge? (2) Does it influence user attitudes?

64 college students (20–27 years, 32/group) tested cartoon ECAs differing only in attire. Data showed equivalent knowledge retention but better subjective experience for professional attire.

L. Zhang and K.-K. R. Choo (Eds.): MobiQuitous 2025, LNICST 684, pp. 461–465, 2026.
https://doi.org/10.1007/978-3-032-22503-0_25

2 Related Work

ECAs enhance virtual nursing engagement [1]; high-fidelity ECAs risk "uncanny valley" [2], while cartoons boost approachability but may lower authority. Professional attire improves high-fidelity ECA credibility [5], but its cartoon efficacy is untested.

We adapted Godspeed Questionnaire Series (GQS) [6] for anthropomorphism/trust, adding health items to develop the 12-item ECA-UXE scale.

3 Method

Within-subject design manipulated Agent Attire (Professional vs. Casual); other ECA attributes (features, gestures, script) identical.

Participants: 64 college students (20–26 years; 36 females) with limited ECA familiarity, dietary health interest.

Two cartoon ECA versions (Blender + Live Link Face) delivered identical 2-min nutrition advice (professional: white coat + stethoscope; casual: light blue T-shirt/skirt (see Fig. 1).

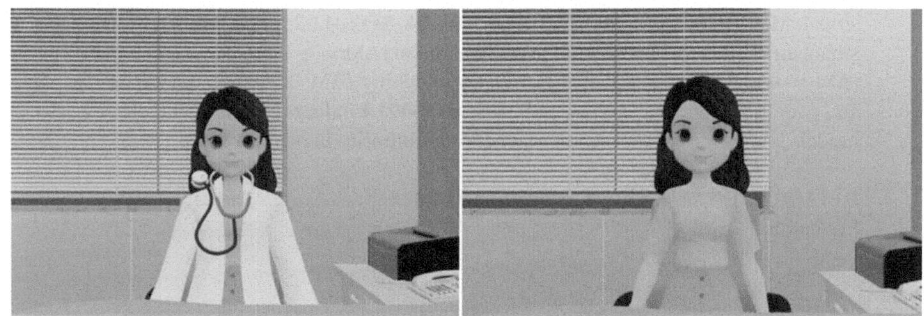

Fig. 1. Cartoon ECA wearing professional attire (left) and casual attire (right).

Procedure: Watch ECA video → 5-item knowledge test (15 points; multiple-choice/true-false) → ECA-UXE questionnaire; sessions: 10–12 min.

Measures: Knowledge test (content retention, e.g., fruit/vegetable intake); 12-item ECA-UXE scale (5-point Likert: professionalism, trust, compliance, visual-audio matching, overall impression); manipulation check (perceived professionalism, 5-point Likert).

4 Results

Nonparametric analyses (Shapiro-Wilk, $p < 0.05$).

Knowledge: No significant difference (professional: $M = 10.75$, $SD = 4.02$; casual: $M = 9.84$, $SD = 4.02$; $p > 0.05$. (see Fig. 2).

ECA-UXE outcomes (see Table 1 and Fig. 3): Professional attire improved Appearance Professionalism ($M = 3.25$ vs. 2.66, $p = 0.021$), Trust ($M = 3.75$ vs. 3.38, $p =$

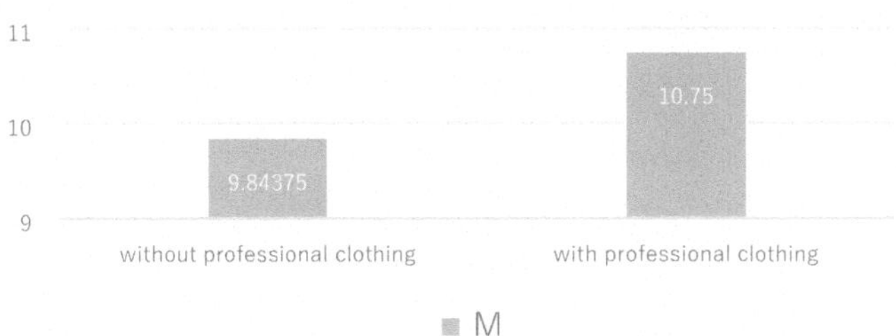

Fig. 2. Knowledge test core average.

0.005), Visual-Audio Matching (M = 3.63 vs. 2.88, p = 0.019), Overall Impression (M = 3.66 vs. 3.41, p = 0.039). Casual attire had higher Compliance (M = 3.69 vs. 3.66, p = 0.010); no differences in liking/usability (p > 0.05).

Table 1. User Experience Scale Data.

	Group	N	M ± SD	P
Appearance Professionalism	without professional clothing	32	2.6563 ± 0.8273	0.021
	with professional clothing	32	3.25 ± 1.0473	
Trust	without professional clothing	32	3.375 ± 0.7931	0.005
	with professional clothing	32	3.75 ± 0.9504	
Compliance	without professional clothing	32	3.6875 ± 0.6927	0.010
	with professional clothing	32	3.6563 ± 1.1531	
Visual-Audio Matching	without professional clothing	32	2.875 ± 0.8328	0.019
	with professional clothing	32	3.625 ± 0.9419	
Overall Impression	without professional clothing	32	3.4063 ± 0.8747	0.039
	with professional clothing	32	3.6563 ± 1.0957	

Qualitative feedback: Casual ECA lacked “doctor-like features”; professional ECA aligned with medical stereotypes but was “overly schematic.” Both needed better gestures/expressions.

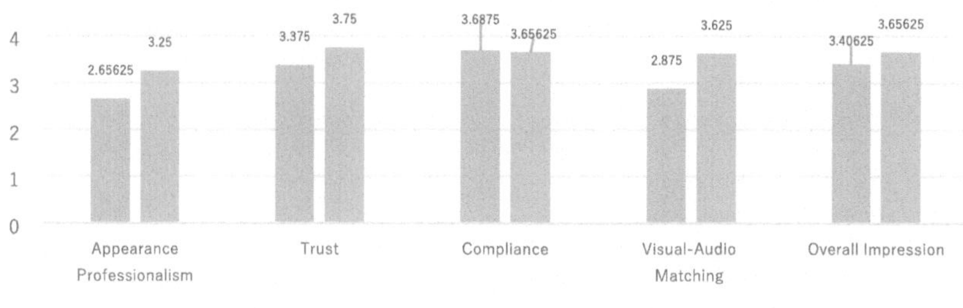

Fig. 3. The average values of the five items with significant differences

5 Discussion

Professional attire boosted cartoon ECA professionalism and trust (consistent with [5]), confirming occupational symbols work in stylized ECAs.

No knowledge effect is explained by cognitive load theory [7]: Extraneous (visual: ECA attire) and intrinsic (content: nutrition) loads were identical, so knowledge depended on content logic, not attire.

Limitations: Sample limited to Chinese college students; short interactions limit generalization (e.g., older adults with chronic conditions). Future work will expand groups.

6 Conclusion

Professional attire in cartoon ECAs improves user experience (professionalism, trust) without impacting knowledge retention. For designers, combine professional attire (white coat/stethoscope) with enhanced multimodal behavior (gestures, expressions) to balance authority and approachability.

Future research will validate findings in diverse populations to strengthen digital health relevance.

References

1. Bickmore, T.W., Pfeifer, L.M., Jack, B.W.: Taking the time to care: empowering low health literacy hospital patients with virtual nurse agents. In: Proceedings of the SIGCHI Conference on Human Factors in Computing Systems, pp. 1265–1274. ACM (2009). https://doi.org/10.1145/1518701.1518891
2. Mori, M., MacDorman, K.F., Kageki, N.: The uncanny valley [from the field]. IEEE Robot. Autom. Mag. **19**(2), 98–100 (2012). https://doi.org/10.1109/MRA.2012.2192811
3. Nass, C., Moon, Y.: Machines and mindlessness: social responses to computers. J. Soc. Issues **56**(1), 81–103 (2000). https://doi.org/10.1111/0022-4537.00153
4. Goffman, E.: The Presentation of Self in Everyday Life. Doubleday (1959). https://www.amazon.com/Presentation-Self-Everyday-Life/dp/0385094027

5. Parmar, D., Olafsson, S., Utami, D., Bickmore, T.: Looking the part: the effect of attire and setting on perceptions of a virtual health counselor. In: Proceedings of the International Conference on Intelligent Virtual Agents (IVA '18) (2018). https://doi.org/10.1145/3267851.3267915
6. Bartneck, C., Kulić, D., Croft, E., Zoghbi, S.: Measurement instruments for the anthropomorphism, animacy, likeability, perceived intelligence, and perceived safety of robots. Int. J. Soc. Robot. **1**(1), 71–81 (2009). https://doi.org/10.1007/s12369-008-0001-3
7. Sweller, J., van Merriënboer, J.J.G., Paas, F.G.W.C.: Cognitive architecture and instructional design. Educ. Psychol. Rev. **10**(3), 251–296 (1998). https://doi.org/10.1007/s10648-021-09624-7

Author Index

L. Zhang and K.-K. R. Choo (Eds.): MobiQuitous 2025, LNICST 684, pp. 467–468, 2026.
https://doi.org/10.1007/978-3-032-22503-0

The manufacturer's authorised representative in the EU is Springer Nature Customer Service Centre GmbH, Europaplatz 3, 69115 Heidelberg, Germany. If you have any concerns regarding our products, please contact ProductSafety@springernature.com

Printed and bound by CPI Group (UK) Ltd, Croydon, CR0 4YY
07/07/2026
02160917-0016